Plays, Poems, and Miscellanies

Charles Dickens

WILDSIDE PRESS

www.wildsidepress.com

PLAYS, POEMS, AND MISCELLANIES

CONTENTS

CONTENTS

CONTENTS

ILLUSTRATIONS

I

II

PLAYS, POEMS, AND MISCELLANIES

PLAYS

THE STRANGE GENTLEMAN

ACT I

SCENE I. — *A Room at the St. James's Arms; Door in Centre, with a Bolt on it. A Table with Cover, and two Chairs.*

Enter MRS. NOAKES.

MRS. NOAKES. Bless us, what a coachful! Four inside — twelve out; and the guard blowing the key-bugle in the fore-boot, for fear the informers should see that they have got one over the number. Post-chaise and a gig besides. — We shall be filled to the very attics. Now, look alive, there — bustle about.

Enter FIRST WAITER, *running.*

Now, John.

FIRST WAITER. Single lady, inside the stage, wants a private room, ma'am.

MRS. NOAKES. Much luggage?

FIRST WAITER. Four trunks, two bonnet-boxes, six brown-paper parcels, and a basket.

MRS. NOAKES. Give her a private room, directly. No. 1, on the first floor.

FIRST WAITER. Yes, ma'am.

[*Exit* FIRST WAITER, *running.*

Enter SECOND WAITER, *running.*

MRS. NOAKES. Now, Tom.

SECOND WAITER. Two young ladies and one gentleman, in a post-chaise, want a private sitting-room d'rectly, ma'am.

MRS. NOAKES. Brother and sisters, Tom?

SECOND WAITER. Ladies are something alike, ma'am. Gentleman like neither of 'em.

MRS. NOAKES. Husband and wife and wife's sister, perhaps. Eh, Tom?

SECOND WAITER. Can't be husband and wife, ma'am, because I saw the gentleman kiss one of the ladies.

MRS. NOAKES. Kissing one of the ladies! Put them in the small sitting-room behind the bar, Tom, that I may have an eye on them through the little window, and see that nothing improper goes forward.

SECOND WAITER. Yes, ma'am. (*Going.*)

MRS. NOAKES. And, Tom!

SECOND WAITER. Yes, ma'am.

MRS. NOAKES. Tell Cook to put together all the bones and pieces that were left on the plates at the great dinner yesterday, and make some nice soup to feed the stage-coach passengers with.

SECOND WAITER. Very well, ma'am.

[*Exit* SECOND WAITER.

Enter THIRD WAITER, *running.*

MRS. NOAKES. Now, Will.

THIRD WAITER. A strange gentleman in a gig, ma'am, wants a private sitting-room.

MRS. NOAKES. Much luggage, Will?

THIRD WAITER. One portmanteau, and a great-coat.

MRS. NOAKES. Oh! nonsense! — Tell him to go into the commercial room.

THIRD WAITER. I told him so, ma'am, but the Strange Gentleman says he *will* have a private apartment, and that it 's as much as his life is worth to sit in a public room.

MRS. NOAKES. As much as his life is worth?

THIRD WAITER. Yes, ma'am. — Gentleman says he does n't care if it 's a dark closet; but a private room of some kind he must and will have.

MRS. NOAKES. Very odd. — Did you ever see him before, Will?

THIRD WAITER. No, ma'am; he 's quite a stranger here. He 's a wonderful man to talk, ma'am — keeps on like a steam engine. Here he is, ma'am.

STRANGE GENTLEMAN (*without*). Now don't tell me, be

cause that 's all gammon and nonsense; and gammoned I never was, and never will be, by any waiter that ever drew the breath of life, or a cork. — And just have the goodness to leave my portmanteau alone, because I can carry it very well myself; and show me a private room without further delay; for a private room I must and will have. — Damme, do you think I 'm going to be murdered! —

Enter the three Waiters, — the STRANGE GENTLEMAN *following, carrying his portmanteau and great-coat.*

There — this room will do capitally well. Quite the thing, — just the fit. — How are you, ma'am? I suppose you are the landlady of this place? Just order those very attentive young fellows out, will you, and I 'll order dinner.

MRS. NOAKES (*to Waiters*). You may leave the room.

STRANGE GENTLEMAN. Hear that? — You may leave the room. Make yourselves scarce. Evaporate — disappear — come. [*Exeunt Waiters.*
That 's right. And now, madam, while we 're talking over this important matter of dinner, I 'll just secure us effectually against further intrusion. (*Bolts the door.*)

MRS. NOAKES. Lor, sir! Bolting the door, and *me* in the room!

STRANGE GENTLEMAN. Don't be afraid — I won't hurt you. I have no designs against you, my dear ma'am; but *I must be private*. (*Sits on the portmanteau.*)

MRS. NOAKES. Well, sir, — I have no objection to break through our rules for once; but it is not our way, when we 're full, to give private rooms to solitary gentlemen, who come in a gig, and bring only one portmanteau. You 're quite a stranger *here*, sir. If I 'm not mistaken, it 's your first appearance in this house.

STRANGE GENTLEMAN. You 're right, ma'am. It *is* my first, my very first — but not my last, I can tell you.

MRS. NOAKES. No?

STRANGE GENTLEMAN. No (*looking round him*). I like the look of this place. Snug and comfortable — neat and lively. You 'll very often find me at the St. James's Arms, I can tell you, ma'am.

MRS. NOAKES (*aside*). A civil gentleman. Are you a stranger in this town, sir?

STRANGE GENTLEMAN. Stranger! Bless you, no. I have been here for many years past, in the season.

MRS. NOAKES. Indeed!

STRANGE GENTLEMAN. Oh, yes. Put up at the Royal Hotel regularly for a long time; but I was obliged to leave it at last.

MRS. NOAKES. I have heard a good many complaints of it.

STRANGE GENTLEMAN. Oh! terrible! such a noisy house.

MRS. NOAKES. Ah!

STRANGE GENTLEMAN. Shocking! Din, din, din, — drum, drum, drum, all night. Nothing but noise, glare, and nonsense. I bore it a long time for old acquaintance sake; but what do you think they did at last, ma'am?

MRS. NOAKES. I can't guess.

STRANGE GENTLEMAN. Turned the fine Old Assembly Room into a stable, and took to keeping horses. I tried that, too, but I found I could n't stand it; so I came away, ma'am, and — and — here I am. (*Rises.*)

MRS. NOAKES. And I 'll be bound to say, sir, that you will have no cause to complain of the exchange.

STRANGE GENTLEMAN. I 'm sure not, ma'am; I know it, — I feel it, already.

MRS. NOAKES. About dinner, sir; what would you like to take?

STRANGE GENTLEMAN. Let me see; will you be good enough to suggest something, ma'am?

MRS. NOAKES. Why, a broiled fowl and mushrooms is a very nice dish.

STRANGE GENTLEMAN. You are right, ma'am; a broiled fowl and mushrooms form a very delightful and harmless amusement, either for one or two persons. Broiled fowl and mushrooms let it be, ma'am.

MRS. NOAKES. In about an hour, I suppose, sir?

STRANGE GENTLEMAN. For the second time, ma'am, you have anticipated my feelings.

MRS. NOAKES. You 'll want a bed to-night, I suppose, sir; perhaps you 'd like to see it? Step this way, sir, and — (*Going.*)

STRANGE GENTLEMAN. No, no, never mind. (*Aside.*) This is a plot to get me out of the room. She 's bribed by some-body who wants to identify me. I must be careful; I am exposed to nothing but artifice and stratagem. Never mind, ma'am, never mind.

MRS. NOAKES. If you 'll give me your portmanteau, sir, the Boots will carry it into the next room for you.

STRANGE GENTLEMAN (*aside*). Here 's diabolical ingenuity; she thinks it 's got the name upon it. (*To her.*) I 'm very much obliged to the Boots for his disinterested attention, ma'am, but with your kind permission this portmanteau will remain just exactly where it is ; consequently, ma'am (*with great warmth*), if the aforesaid Boots wishes to succeed in removing this portmanteau, he must previously remove *me*, ma'am, *me ;* and it will take a *pair* of very stout Boots to do that, ma'am, I promise you.

MRS. NOAKES. Dear me, sir, you need n't fear for your portmanteau in this house ; I dare say nobody wants it.

STRANGE GENTLEMAN. I hope not, ma'am, because in that case nobody will be disappointed. (*Aside.*) How she fixes her old eyes on me!

MRS. NOAKES (*aside*). I never saw such an extraordinary person in all my life. What can he be ? (*Looks at him very hard.*)   [*Exit* MRS. NOAKES.

STRANGE GENTLEMAN. She 's gone at last! Now let me commune with my own dreadful thoughts, and reflect on the best means of escaping from my horrible position. (*Takes a letter from his pocket.*) Here 's an illegal death-warrant; a pressing invitation .to be slaughtered ; a polite request just to step out and be killed, thrust into my hand by some disguised assassin in a dirty black calico jacket, the very instant I got out of the gig at the door. I know the hand ; there 's a ferocious recklessness in the cross to this " t," and a baleful malignity in the dot of that " i," which warns me that it comes from my desperate rival. (*Opens it, and reads.*) " Mr. Horatio Tinkles " — that 's him — " presents his compliments to his enemy " — that 's me — " and requests the pleasure of his company to-morrow morning, under the clump of trees, on Corpse Common," — Corpse Common ! — " to which any of the town's people will direct him, and where he hopes to have the satisfaction of giving him his gruel." — Giving him his gruel ! Ironical cut-throat ! — " His punctuality will be esteemed a personal favour, as it will save Mr. Tinkles the trouble and inconvenience of calling with a horsewhip in his pocket. Mr. Tinkles has ordered

breakfast at the Royal for *one*. It is paid for. The individual
who returns alive can eat it. Pistols — half-past five — precisely." — Bloodthirsty miscreant! *The* individual who returns
alive! I have seen him hit the painted man at the shooting-
gallery regularly every time in his centre shirt plait, except
when he varied the entertainments by lodging the ball playfully
in his left eye. Breakfast! I shall want nothing beyond the
gruel. What's to be done? Escape! I can't escape; concealment's of no use, he knows I am here. He has dodged
me all the way from London, and will dodge me all the way to
the residence of Miss Emily Brown, whom my respected but
swine-headed parents have picked out for my future wife. A
pretty figure I should cut before the old people, whom I have
never beheld more than once in my life, and Miss Emily Brown,
whom I have never seen at all, if I went down there, pursued
by this Salamander, who, I suppose, is her accepted lover!
What is to be done? I can't go back again; father would be
furious. What can be done? nothing! (*Sinks into a chair.*)
I must undergo this fiery ordeal, and submit to be packed up,
and carried back to my weeping parents, like an unfortunate
buck, with a flat piece of lead in my head, and a brief epitaph
on my breast, " Killed on Wednesday morning." No, I won't
(*starting up, and walking about*). I won't submit to it; I'll
accept the challenge, but first I'll write an anonymous letter to
the local authorities, giving them information of this intended
duel, and desiring them to place me under immediate restraint.
That's feasible; on further consideration, it's capital. My
character will be saved — I shall be bound over — he'll be
bound over — I shall resume my journey — reach the house —
marry the girl — pocket the fortune, and laugh at him. No
time to be lost; it shall be done forthwith. (*Goes to table,
and writes.*) There; the challenge accepted, with a bold defiance that'll look very brave when it comes to be printed.
Now for the other. (*Writes.*) " To the Mayor — Sir — A
Strange Gentleman at the St. James's Arms, whose name is
unknown to the writer of this communication, is bent upon
committing a rash and sanguinary act, at an early hour to-morrow morning. As you value human life, secure the amiable
youth, without delay. Think, I implore you, sir, think what
would be the feelings of those to whom he is nearest and dearest, if any mischance befall the interesting young man. Do not

neglect this solemn warning; the number of his room is seventeen." There (*folding it up*). Now if I can find any one who will deliver it secretly —

Tom Sparks, *with a pair of boots in his hand, peeps in.*

Tom. Are these here your 'n ?

Strange Gentleman. No.

Tom. Oh! (*Going back.*)

Strange Gentleman. Hallo! stop! are you the Boots ?

Tom (*still at the door*). I'm the head o' that branch o' the establishment. There's another man under me, as brushes the dirt off, and puts the blacking on. The fancy work's my department; I do the polishing, nothing else.

Strange Gentleman. You are the upper Boots, then ?

Tom. Yes, I'm the reg'lar; t' other one's only the deputy; top boots and half boots, I calls us.

Strange Gentleman. You're a sharp fellow.

Tom. Ah! I'd better cut, then. (*Going.*)

Strange Gentleman. Don't hurry, Boots — don't hurry; I want you. (*Rises and comes forward.*)

Tom. Well!

Strange Gentleman. Can — can — you be secret, Boots?

Tom. That depends entirely on accompanying circumstances; — see the point ?

Strange Gentleman. I think I comprehend your meaning, Boots. You insinuate that you could be secret (*putting his hand in his pocket*) if you had — five shillings, for instance, — is n't that it, Boots ?

Tom. That's the line o' argument I should take up; but that ain't exactly my meaning.

Strange Gentleman. No !

Tom. No. A secret's a thing as is always a rising to one's lips. It requires an astonishing weight to keep one on 'em down.

Strange Gentleman. Ah !

Tom. Yes; I don't think I could keep one snug — reg'lar snug, you know —

Strange Gentleman. Yes, regularly snug, of course.

Tom. If it had a less weight atop on it than ten shillin's.

Strange Gentleman. You don't think three half-crowns would do it ?

Tom. It might, I won't say it would n't, but I could n't warrant it.

Strange Gentleman. You could the other!

Tom. Yes.

Strange Gentleman. Then there it is. (*Gives him four half-crowns.*) You see these letters?

Tom. Yes, I can manage that without my spectacles.

Strange Gentleman. Well; that's to be left at the Royal Hotel. This, *this*, is an anonymous one; and I want it to be delivered at the Mayor's house, without his knowing from whom it came, or seeing who delivered it.

Tom (*taking the letters*). I say, you're a rum 'un, you are.

Strange Gentleman. Think so! Ha, ha! so are you.

Tom. Ay, but you're a rummer one than me.

Strange Gentleman. No, no, that's your modesty.

Tom. No, it ain't. I say, how vell you did them last haystacks. How do you contrive that 'ere now, if it's a fair question. Is it done with a pipe, or do you use them Lucifer boxes?

Strange Gentleman. Pipe, Lucifer boxes, haystacks! Why, what do you mean?

Tom (*looking cautiously round*). I know your name, old 'un.

Strange Gentleman. You know my name! (*Aside.*) Now, how the devil has he got hold of that, I wonder!

Tom. Yes, I know it. It begins with a "S."

Strange Gentleman. Begins with an S!

Tom. And ends with a "G" (*winking*). We've all heard talk of *Swing* down here.

Strange Gentleman. Heard talk of Swing! Here's a situation! Damme, d'ye think I'm a walking carbois of vitriol, and burn everything I touch? — Will you go upon the errand you're paid for?

Tom. Oh, I'm going, I'm going. It's nothing to me, you know; I don't care. I'll only just give these boots to the deputy, to take them to whoever they belong to, and then I'll pitch this here letter in at the Mayor's office window, in no time.

Strange Gentleman. Will you be off?

Tom. Oh, I'm going, I'm going. Close, you knows, close!

[*Exit* Tom.

STRANGE GENTLEMAN. In five minutes more the letter will be delivered; in another half hour, if the Mayor does his duty, I shall be in custody, and secure from the vengeance of this infuriated monster. I wonder whether they'll take me away? Egad! I may as well be provided with a clean shirt and a nightcap in case. Let's see, she said the next room was my bedroom, and, as I have accepted the challenge, I may venture so far now. (*Shouldering the portmanteau.*) What a capital notion it is; there'll be all the correspondence in large letters, in the county paper, and my name figuring away in roman capitals, with a long story, how I was such a desperate dragon, and so bent upon fighting, that it took four constables to carry me to the Mayor, and one boy to carry my hat. It's a capital plan — must be done — the only way I have of escaping unpursued from this place, unless I could put myself in the General Post, and direct myself to a friend in town. And then it's a chance whether they'd take me in, being so much over weight.

[*Exit* STRANGE GENTLEMAN *with portmanteau.*

MRS. NOAKES (*peeping in, then entering*).

MRS. NOAKES. This is the room, ladies, but the gentleman has stepped out somewhere, he won't be long, I dare say. Pray come in, miss.

Enter MARY *and* FANNY WILSON.

MARY. This is the Strange Gentleman's apartment, is it?

MRS. NOAKES. Yes, miss; shall I see if I can find him, ladies, and tell him you are here?

MARY. No; we should prefer waiting till he returns, if you please.

MRS. NOAKES. Very well, ma'am. He'll be back directly, I dare say; for it's very near his dinner time.

[*Exit* MRS. NOAKES.

MARY. Come, Fanny dear; don't give way to these feelings of depression. Take pattern by me — I feel the absurdity of our situation acutely; but you see that I keep up, nevertheless.

FANNY. It is easy for you to do so. *Your* situation is neither so embarrassing nor so painful a one as mine.

MARY. Well, my dear, it *may* not be, certainly; but the

circumstances which render it less so are, I own, somewhat incomprehensible to me. My harebrained, madcap swain, John
Johnson, implores me to leave my guardian's house, and accompany him on an expedition to Gretna Green. I with immense
reluctance, and after considerable pressing —

FANNY. Yield a very willing consent.

MARY. Well, we won't quarrel about terms ; at all events,
I *do* consent. He bears me off, and, when we get exactly half-
way, discovers that his money is all gone, and that we must
stop at this Inn until he can procure a remittance from London, by post. I think, my dear, you 'll own that *this* is rather
an embarrassing position.

FANNY. Compare it with mine. Taking advantage of your
flight, I send express to *my* admirer, Charles Tomkins, to say
that I have accompanied you ; first, because I should have been
miserable if left behind with a peevish old man alone ; secondly,
because I thought it proper that your sister should accompany
you —

MARY. And, thirdly, because you knew that he would immediately comply with this indirect assent to his entreaties of
three months' duration, and follow you without delay, on the
same errand. Eh, my dear ?

FANNY. It by no means follows that such was my intention, or that I knew he would pursue such a course, but supposing he *has* done so ; supposing this Strange Gentleman
should be himself —

MARY. *Supposing !* — Why, you know it is. You told
him not to disclose his name, on any account ; and the *Strange
Gentleman* is not a very common travelling name, I should
imagine ; besides, the hasty note, in which he said he should
join you here.

FANNY. Well, granted that it is he. In what a situation
am I placed. You tell me, for the first time, that *my* violent
intended must on no account be beheld by *your* violent intended, just now, because of some old quarrel between them, of
long standing, which has never been adjusted to this day. What
an appearance this will have ! How am I to explain it, or
relate your present situation ? I should sink into the earth with
shame and confusion.

MARY. Leave it to me. It arises from my heedlessness.
I will take it all upon myself, and see him alone. But tell

me, my dear — as you got up this love affair with so much secrecy and expedition during the four months you spent at Aunt Martha's, I have never yet seen Mr. Tomkins, you know. Is he so very handsome ?

FANNY. See him, and judge for yourself.

MARY. Well, I will; and you may retire till I have paved the way for your appearance. But just assist me first, dear, in making a little noise to attract his attention, if he really be in the next room, or I may wait here all day.

DUET, *at end of which*

[*Exit* FANNY. MARY *retires up.*

Enter STRANGE GENTLEMAN.

STRANGE GENTLEMAN. There; now with a clean shirt in one pocket, and a nightcap in the other, I 'm ready to be carried magnanimously to my dungeon in the cause of love.

MARY (*aside*). He says he 's ready to be carried magnanimously to a dungeon in the cause of love. I thought it was Mr. Tomkins ! Hem ! (*Coming down.*)

STRANGE GENTLEMAN (*seeing her*). Hallo ! Who 's this ! Not a disguised peace officer in petticoats. Beg your pardon, ma'am. (*Advancing towards her.*) What — did — you —

MARY. Oh, sir ; I feel the delicacy of my situation.

STRANGE GENTLEMAN (*aside*). Feels the delicacy of her situation ; Lord bless us, what 's the matter ! Permit me to offer you a seat, ma'am, if you 're in a delicate situation. (*He places chairs ; they sit.*)

MARY. You are very good, sir. You are surprised to see me here, sir ?

STRANGE GENTLEMAN. No, no, at least not .very ; rather, perhaps — rather. (*Aside.*) Never was more.astonished in all my life !

MARY (*aside*). His politeness, and the extraordinary tale I have to tell him, overpower me. I must summon up courage. Hem !

STRANGE GENTLEMAN. Hem !

MARY. Sir ! .

STRANGE GENTLEMAN. Ma'am !

MARY. You have arrived at this house in pursuit of a young lady, if I mistake not ?

STRANGE GENTLEMAN. You are quite right, ma'am. (*Aside.*) Mysterious female!

MARY. If you *are* the gentleman I'm in search of, you wrote a hasty note a short time since, stating that you would be found here this afternoon.

STRANGE GENTLEMAN (*drawing back his chair*). I — I — wrote a note, ma'am!

MARY. You need keep nothing secret from me, sir. I know all.

STRANGE GENTLEMAN (*aside*). That villain, Boots, has betrayed me! Know all, ma'am?

MARY. Everything.

STRANGE GENTLEMAN (*aside*). It must be so. She's a constable's wife.

MARY. You *are* the writer of that letter, sir? I think I am not mistaken.

STRANGE GENTLEMAN. You are not, ma'am; I confess I did write it. What was I to do, ma'am? Consider the situation in which I was placed.

MARY. In your situation, you had, as it appears to me, only one course to pursue.

STRANGE GENTLEMAN. You mean the course I adopted?

MARY. Undoubtedly.

STRANGE GENTLEMAN. I am very happy to hear you say so, though of course I should like it to be kept a secret.

MARY. Oh, of course.

STRANGE GENTLEMAN (*drawing his chair close to her, and speaking very softly*). Will you allow me to ask you, whether the constables are down stairs?

MARY (*surprised*). The constables!

STRANGE GENTLEMAN. Because if I am to be apprehended, I should like to have it over. I am quite ready, if it must be done.

MARY. No legal interference has been attempted. There is nothing to prevent your continuing your journey to-night.

STRANGE GENTLEMAN. But will not the other party follow?

MARY (*looking down*). The other party, I am compelled to inform you, is detained here by — by want of funds.

STRANGE GENTLEMAN (*starting up*). Detained here by want of funds! Hurrah! Hurrah! I have caged him at last.

I 'm revenged for all his blustering and bullying. This is a glorious triumph, ha, ha, ha! I have nailed him — nailed him to the spot!

MARY (*rising indignantly*). This exulting over a fallen foe, Sir, is mean and pitiful. In my presence, too, it is an additional insult.

STRANGE GENTLEMAN. Insult! I would n't insult you for the world, after the joyful intelligence you have brought me — I could hug you in my arms! — One kiss, my little constable's deputy. (*Seizing her.*)

MARY (*struggling with him*). Help! Help!

Enter JOHN JOHNSON.

JOHN. What the devil do I see! (*Seizes* STRANGE GENTLEMAN *by the collar.*)

MARY. John, and Mr. Tomkins, met together! They 'll kill each other. — Here, help! help!

[*Exit* MARY, *running.*

JOHN (*shaking him*). What do you mean by that, scoundrel?

STRANGE GENTLEMAN. Come, none of your nonsense — there 's no harm done.

JOHN. No harm done. — How dare you offer to salute that lady?

STRANGE GENTLEMAN. What did you send her here for?

JOHN. *I* send her here!

STRANGE GENTLEMAN. Yes, *you;* you gave her instructions, I suppose. (*Aside.*) Her husband, the constable, evidently.

JOHN. That lady, sir, is attached to me.

STRANGE GENTLEMAN. Well, I know she is; and a very useful little person she must be, to be attached to anybody, — it 's a pity she can't be legally sworn in.

JOHN. *Legally* sworn in! Sir, that is an insolent reflection upon the temporary embarrassment which prevents our taking the marriage vows. How dare you insinuate —

STRANGE GENTLEMAN. Pooh! pooh! — don't talk about daring to insinuate; it does n't become a man in your station of life —

JOHN. My station of life!

STRANGE GENTLEMAN. But as you have managed this

matter very quietly, and say you 're in temporary embarrassment
— here — here 's five shillings for you. (*Offers it.*)
JOHN. Five shillings! (*Raises his cane.*)
STRANGE GENTLEMAN (*flourishing a chair*). Keep off, sir!

Enter MARY, TOM SPARKS, *and Two Waiters.*

MARY. Separate them, or there 'll be murder!

(TOM *clasps* STRANGE GENTLEMAN *round the waist* — *the
Waiters seize* JOHN JOHNSON.)

TOM. Come, none o' that 'ere, Mr. S. We don't let private rooms for such games as these. — If you want to try it on
wery partickler, we don't mind making a ring for you in the
yard, but you must n't do it here.

JOHN. Let me get at him. Let me go; waiters — Mary,
don't hold me. I insist on your letting me go.

STRANGE GENTLEMAN. Hold him fast. — Call yourself a
peace officer, you prize-fighter!

JOHN (*struggling*). Let me go, I say!

STRANGE GENTLEMAN. Hold him fast! Hold him fast!

(TOM *takes* STRANGE GENTLEMAN *off. Waiters take* JOHN
off, MARY *following.*)

SCENE II. — *Another Room in the Inn.*

Enter JULIA DOBBS *and* OVERTON.

JULIA. You seem surprised, Overton.

OVERTON. Surprised, Miss Dobbs! Well I may be, when,
after seeing nothing of you for three years and more, you come
down here without any previous notice, for the express purpose
of running away — positively running away with a young man.
I am astonished, Miss Dobbs!

JULIA. You would have had better reason to be astonished
if I had come down here with any notion of positively running
away with an old one, Overton.

OVERTON. Old or young, it would matter little to me, if
you had not conceived the preposterous idea of entangling me
— *me*, an attorney, and mayor of the town, in so ridiculous a

scheme. — Miss Dobbs, I can't do it. — I really cannot consent to mix myself up with such an affair.

JULIA. Very well, Overton, very well. You recollect that in the lifetime of that poor old dear, Mr. Woolley, who —

OVERTON. Who would have married you, if he had n't died, and who, as it was, left you his property, free from all incumbrances, the incumbrance of himself, as a husband, not being among the least.

JULIA. Well, you may recollect that, in the poor old dear's lifetime, sundry advances of money were made to you, at my persuasion, which still remain unpaid. Oblige me by forwarding them to my agent in the course of the week, and I free you from any interference in this little matter. (*Is going.*)

OVERTON. Stay, Miss Dobbs, stay. As you say, we *are* old acquaintances, and there certainly *were* some small sums of money, which — which —

JULIA. Which certainly *are* still outstanding.

OVERTON. Just so, just so ; and which, perhaps, you would be likely to forget, if you had a husband — eh, Miss Dobbs, eh ?

JULIA. I have little doubt that I should. If I gained one through your assistance, indeed, — I can safely say I should forget all about them.

OVERTON. My dear Miss Dobbs, we perfectly understand each other. — Pray, proceed.

JULIA. Well — dear Lord Peter —

OVERTON. That 's the young man you 're going to run away with, I presume ?

JULIA. That 's the young *nobleman* who 's going to run away with me, Mr. Overton.

OVERTON. Yes, just so. — I beg your pardon — pray go on.

JULIA. Dear Lord Peter is young and wild, and the fact is his friends do not consider him very sagacious or strongminded. To prevent their interference, our marriage is to be a secret one. In fact, he is stopping now at a friend's hunting seat in the neighbourhood ; he is to join me here ; and we are to be married at Gretna.

OVERTON. Just so. — A matter, as it seems to me, which you can conclude without my interference.

JULIA. Wait an instant. To avoid suspicion, and prevent our being recognised and followed, I settled with him that you

should give out in this house that he was a lunatic, and that I
— his aunt — was going to convey him in a chaise, to-night, to
a private asylum at Berwick. I have ordered the chaise at
half-past one in the morning. You can see him, and make our
final arrangements. It will avert all suspicion if I have no
communication with him till we start. You can say to the
people of the house that the sight of me makes him furious.

OVERTON. Where shall I find him ? — Is he here ?

JULIA. You know best.

OVERTON. I !

JULIA. I desired him, immediately on his arrival, to write
you some mysterious nonsense, acquainting you with the number of his room.

OVERTON (*producing a letter*). Dear me ! he has arrived,
Miss Dobbs.

JULIA. No !

OVERTON. Yes — see here — a most mysterious and extraordinary composition, which was thrown in at my office window
this morning, and which I could make neither head nor tail of.
Is that his handwriting ? (*Giving her the letter.*)

JULIA (*taking letter*). I never saw it more than once, but
I know he writes very large and straggling. — (*Looks at
letter.*) Ha, ha, ha ! This is capital, is n't it ?

OVERTON. Excellent ! — Ha, ha, ha ! — So mysterious !

JULIA. Ha, ha, ha ! — So very good. — "Rash act."

OVERTON. Yes. Ha, ha !

JULIA. "Interesting young man."

OVERTON. Yes. — Very good.

JULIA. "Amiable youth !"

OVERTON. Capital !

JULIA. "Solemn warning !"

OVERTON. Yes. — That 's best of all. (*They both laugh.*)

JULIA. Number seventeen, he says. See him at once,
that 's a good creature. (*Returning the letter.*)

OVERTON (*taking letter*). I will. (*He rings a bell.*)

Enter WAITER.

Who is there in number seventeen, waiter ?

WAITER. Number seventeen, sir ? — Oh ! the Strange Gentleman, sir.

OVERTON. Show me the room.   [*Exit* WAITER.

(*Looking at* JULIA, *and pointing to the letter*.) "The Strange Gentleman." — Ha, ha, ha! Very good, — very good, indeed. — Excellent notion! (*They both laugh*.)

[*Exeunt severally.*

SCENE III. — *Same as the first.* — *A small table, with wine, dessert, and lights on it; two chairs.*

STRANGE GENTLEMAN *discovered seated at table.*

STRANGE GENTLEMAN. "The other party is detained here, by want of funds." Ha, ha, ha! I can finish my wine at my leisure, order my gig when I please, and drive on to Brown's in perfect security. I'll drink the other party's good health, and long may he be detained here. (*Fills a glass.*) Ha, ha, ha! The other party; and long may he — (*A knock.*) Hallo! I hope *this* is n't the other party. Talk of the — (*A knock.*) Well — (*setting down his glass*) — this is the most extraordinary private room that was ever invented. I am continually disturbed by unaccountable knockings. (*A gentle tap.*) There's another; that was a gentle rap — a persuasive tap — like a friend's forefinger on one's coat-sleeve. It *can't* be Tinkles with the gruel. — Come in.

OVERTON (*peeping in*).

OVERTON. Are you alone, my Lord?
STRANGE GENTLEMAN (*amazed*). Eh!
OVERTON. Are you alone, my Lord?
STRANGE GENTLEMAN. My Lord!
OVERTON (*stepping in, and closing the door*). You are right, sir, we cannot be too cautious, for we do not know who may be within hearing. You are very right, sir.
STRANGE GENTLEMAN (*rising from table, and coming forward*). It strikes me, sir, that you are very wrong.
OVERTON. Very good, very good; I like this caution; it shows me you are wide awake.
STRANGE GENTLEMAN. Wide awake! — damme, I begin to think I am fast asleep, and have been for the last two hours.
OVERTON (*whispering*). I — am — the mayor.
STRANGE GENTLEMAN (*in the same tone*). Oh!
OVERTON. This is your letter? (*Shows it;* STRANGE GENTLEMAN *nods assent solemnly.*) It will be necessary for

you to leave here to-night, at half-past one o'clock, in a post chaise and four; and the higher you bribe the postboys to drive at their utmost speed, the better.

STRANGE GENTLEMAN. You don't say so!

OVERTON. I do, indeed. You are not safe from pursuit here.

STRANGE GENTLEMAN. Bless my soul, can such dreadful things happen in a civilised community, Mr. Mayor?

OVERTON. It certainly does at first sight appear rather a hard case that people cannot marry whom they please, without being hunted down in this way.

STRANGE GENTLEMAN. To be sure. To be hunted down, and killed as if one was game, you know.

OVERTON. Certainly; and you *ain't* game, you know.

STRANGE GENTLEMAN. Of course not. But can't you prevent it? Can't you save me by the interposition of your power?

OVERTON. My power can do nothing in such a case.

STRANGE GENTLEMAN. Can't it, though?

OVERTON. Nothing whatever.

STRANGE GENTLEMAN. I never heard of such dreadful revenge, never! Mr. Mayor, I am a victim, I am the unhappy victim of parental obstinacy.

OVERTON. Oh, no; don't say that. You may escape yet.

STRANGE GENTLEMAN (*grasping his hand*). Do you think I may? Do you think I may, Mr. Mayor?

OVERTON. Certainly! certainly! I have little doubt of it, if you manage properly.

STRANGE GENTLEMAN. I thought I *was* managing properly. I understood the other party was detained here by want of funds.

OVERTON. Want of funds! — There's no want of funds in that quarter, I can tell you.

STRANGE GENTLEMAN. Ain't there, though?

OVERTON. Bless you, no. Three thousand a year! — But who told you there was a want of funds?

STRANGE GENTLEMAN. Why, she did.

OVERTON. *She!* You *have* seen her, then? She told me you had not.

STRANGE GENTLEMAN. Nonsense; don't believe her. She was in this very room half an hour ago.

OVERTON. Then I must have misunderstood her, and you must have misunderstood her, too. — But to return to business. Don't you think it would keep up appearances if I had you put under some restraint ?

STRANGE GENTLEMAN. I think it would. I am very much obliged to you. (*Aside.*) This regard for my character in an utter stranger, and in a mayor, too, is quite affecting.

OVERTON. I 'll send somebody up, to mount guard over you.

STRANGE GENTLEMAN. Thankee, my dear friend, thankee.

OVERTON. And if you make a little resistance, when we take you up stairs to your bedroom, or away in the chaise, it will be keeping up the character, you know.

STRANGE GENTLEMAN. To be sure. — So it will. — I 'll do it.

OVERTON. Very well, then. I shall see your Lordship again by and by. — For the present, my Lord, good evening. (*Going.*)

STRANGE GENTLEMAN. Lord ! — Lordship ! — Mr. Mayor.

OVERTON. Eh ? — Oh ! — I see. (*Comes forward.*) Practising the lunatic, my Lord. Ah, very good — very vacant look, indeed. — Admirable, my Lord, admirable ! — I say, my Lord, — (*pointing to letter*) — "*Admirable youth !*" — "Interesting young man." — "Strange Gentleman." — Eh ? Ha, ha, ha ! Knowing trick, indeed, my Lord, very !   [*Exit* OVERTON.

STRANGE GENTLEMAN. That mayor is either in the very last stage of mystified intoxication, or in the most hopeless state of incurable insanity. — I have no doubt of it. A little touched here (*tapping his forehead*). Never mind, he is sufficiently sane to understand my business at all events. (*Goes to table and takes a glass.*) Poor fellow ! — I 'll drink his health and speedy recovery. (*A knock.*) It is a most extraordinary thing, now, that every time I propose a toast to myself some confounded fellow raps at that door as if he were receiving it with the utmost enthusiasm. Private room ! — I might as well be sitting behind the little shutter of a twopenny Post Office, where all the letters put in were to be postpaid. (*A knock.*) Perhaps it 's the guard ! I shall feel a great deal safer if it is. Come in.

(*He has brought a chair forward, and sits.*)

Enter TOM SPARKS, *very slowly, with an enormous stick.
He closes the door, and, after looking at the* STRANGE
GENTLEMAN *very steadily, brings a chair, and sits
opposite him.*

STRANGE GENTLEMAN. Are you sent by the mayor of this
place to mount guard over me?

TOM. Yes, yes. — It 's all right.

STRANGE GENTLEMAN (*aside*). It 's all right — I 'm safe.
(*To* TOM, *with affected indignation.*) Now mind, I have been
insulted by receiving this challenge, and I want to fight the
man who gave it me. I protest against being kept here. I
denounce this treatment as an outrage.

TOM. Ay, ay. Anything you please, poor creature; don't put
yourself in a passion. It 'll only make you worse. (*Whistles.*)

STRANGE GENTLEMAN. This is most extraordinary behaviour. — I don't understand it. — What d' ye mean by behaving
in this manner? (*Rising.*)

TOM (*aside*). He 's a getting wiolent. I must frighten him
with a steady look. — I say, young fellow, do you see this here
eye? (*Staring at him, and pointing at his own eye.*)

STRANGE GENTLEMAN (*aside*). Do I see his eye! — What
can he mean by glaring upon me, with that large round optic!
— Ha! a terrible light flashes upon me. — He thought I was
"Swing" this morning. It was an insane delusion. — That
eye is an insane eye. — He 's a madman!

TOM. Madman! Damme, I think he is a madman with a
wengeance.

STRANGE GENTLEMAN. He acknowledges it. He is sensible of his misfortune! — Go away — leave the room instantly,
— and tell them to send somebody else. — Go away!

TOM. Oh, you unhappy lunatic!

STRANGE GENTLEMAN. What a dreadful situation! — I
shall be attacked, strangled, smothered, and mangled, by a madman! Where 's the bell?

TOM (*advancing and brandishing his stick*). Leave that
'ere bell alone — leave that 'ere bell alone — and come here!

STRANGE GENTLEMAN. Certainly, Mr. Boots, certainly. —
He 's going to strangle me. (*Going towards table.*) Let me
pour you out a glass of wine, Mr. Boots — pray do! (*Aside.*)
If he said "Yes," I 'd throw the decanter at his temple.

Tom. None o' your nonsense. — Sit down there. (*Forces him into a chair.*) I 'll sit here. (*Opposite him.*) Look me full in the face, and I won't hurt you. Move hand, foot, or eye, and you 'll never want to move either of 'em again.

Strange Gentleman. I 'm paralysed with terror.

Tom. Ha! (*Raising his stick in a threatening attitude.*)

Strange Gentleman. I 'm dumb, Mr. Boots — dumb, sir.

(*They sit gazing intently on each other ; Tom with the stick raised, as the Act Drop slowly descends.*)

ACT II

Scene I. — *The same as* Scene III., Act I.

Tom Sparks *discovered in the same attitude watching the* Strange Gentleman, *who has fallen asleep with his head over the back of his chair.*

Tom. He 's asleep ; poor unhappy wretch! How very mad he looks with his mouth wide open and his eyes shut! (Strange Gentleman *snores.*) Ah! there 's a wacant snore ; no meaning in it at all. I could ha' told he was out of his senses from the very tone of it. (*He snores again.*) That 's a wery insane snore. I should say he was melancholly mad, from the sound of it.

Enter Overton, Mrs. Noakes, *a Chambermaid, and Two Waiters ;* Mrs. Noakes *with a warming-pan, the Maid with a light.* Strange Gentleman *starts up, greatly exhausted.*

Tom (*starting up*). Hallo! — Hallo! Keep quiet, young fellow. Keep quiet!

Strange Gentleman. Out of the way, you savage maniac. Mr. Mayor (*crossing to him*), the person you sent to keep guard over me is a madman, sir. What do you mean by shutting me up with a madman? — What do you mean, sir, I ask?

Overton (*aside to* Strange Gentleman). Bravo! bravo! very good, indeed, — excellent!

STRANGE GENTLEMAN. Excellent, sir! — It's horrible! — The bare recollection of what I have endured makes me shudder, down to my very toe-nails.

MRS. NOAKES. Poor dear! — Mad people always think other people mad.

STRANGE GENTLEMAN. Poor dear! Ma'am! What the devil do you mean by " Poor dear " ? How dare you have a madman here, ma'am, to assault and terrify the visitors to your establishment ?

MRS. NOAKES. Ah! terrify, indeed! I'll never have another, to please anybody, you may depend upon that, Mr. Overton. (*To* STRANGE GENTLEMAN.) There, there. — Don't exert yourself, there's a dear.

STRANGE GENTLEMAN. Exert myself! — Damme! it's a mercy I have any life left to exert myself with. It's a special miracle, ma'am, that my existence has not long ago fallen a sacrifice to that sanguinary monster in the leather smalls.

OVERTON (*aside to* STRANGE GENTLEMAN). I never saw any passion more real in my life. Keep it up, it's an admirable joke.

STRANGE GENTLEMAN. Joke! — joke! — Peril a precious life, and call it a joke, — you, a man with a sleek head and a broad-brimmed hat, who ought to know better, calling it a joke ! — Are you mad, too, sir, — are you mad ? (*Confronting* OVERTON.)

TOM (*very loud*). Keep your hands off. Would you murder the wery mayor, himself, you mis-rable being ?

STRANGE GENTLEMAN. Mr. Mayor, I call upon you to issue your warrant for the instant confinement of that one-eyed Orson in some place of security.

OVERTON (*aside, advancing a little*). He reminds me that he had better be removed to his bedroom. He is right. — Waiters, carry the gentleman up stairs. — Boots, you will continue to watch him in his bedroom.

STRANGE GENTLEMAN. *He* continue! — What, am I to be boxed up again with this infuriated animal, and killed off, when he has done playing with me ? — I won't go — I won't go — help, there! help !

(*The Waiters cross to behind him.*)

Enter JOHN JOHNSON *hastily.*

JOHN (*coming forward*). What on earth is the meaning of this dreadful outcry, which disturbs the whole house?

MRS. NOAKES. Don't be alarmed, sir, I beg. — They're only going to carry an unfortunate gentleman, as is out of his senses, to his bedroom.

STRANGE GENTLEMAN (*to* JOHN). Constable — constable — do your duty — apprehend these persons — every one of them. Do you hear, officer, do you hear? — (*The Waiters seize him by the arms.*) — Here — here — you see this. You 've seen the assault committed. Take them into custody — off with them.

MRS. NOAKES. Poor creature! — He thinks you are a constable, sir.

JOHN. Unfortunate man! It is the second time to-day that he has been the victim of this strange delusion.

STRANGE GENTLEMAN (*breaking from Waiters and going to* JOHN). Unfortunate man! — What! do *you* think I am mad?

JOHN. Poor fellow! His hopeless condition is pitiable, indeed. (*Goes up.*)

STRANGE GENTLEMAN (*returning*). They 're all mad! — Every one of 'em!

MRS. NOAKES. Come now, come to bed — there 's a dear young man, do.

STRANGE GENTLEMAN. Who are you, you shameless old ghost, standing there before company, with a large warming-pan, and asking me to come to bed? — Are *you* mad?

MRS. NOAKES. Oh! he 's getting shocking now. Take him away. — Take him away.

OVERTON. Ah, you had better remove him to his bedroom at once.

(*The Waiters take him up by the feet and shoulders.*)

STRANGE GENTLEMAN. Mind, if I survive this, I 'll bring an action of false imprisonment against every one of you. Mark my words — especially against that villainous old mayor. — Mind, I 'll do it!

(*They bear him off, struggling and talking — the others crowding round, and assisting.*)

OVERTON (*following*). How well he does it. [*Exeunt.*

Enter a Waiter, showing in CHARLES TOMKINS *in a travelling coat.*

WAITER. This room is disengaged now, sir. There *was* a gentleman in it, but he has just left it.

CHARLES. Very well, this will do. I may want a bed here to-night, perhaps, waiter.

WAITER. Yes, sir. — Shall I take your card to the bar, sir?

CHARLES. My card! — No, never mind.

WAITER. No name, sir?

CHARLES. No — it does n't matter.

WAITER (*aside, as going out*). Another Strange Gentleman. [*Exit* WAITER.

CHARLES. Ah! — (*Takes off coat.*) — The sun and dust on this long ride have been almost suffocating. I wonder whether Fanny has arrived? If she has — the sooner we start forward on our journey further North the better. Let me see; she would be accompanied by her sister, she said in her note — and they would both be on the lookout for me. Then the best thing I can do is to ask no questions, for the present at all events, and to be on the lookout for them. Why, here she comes, walking slowly down the long passage, straight towards this room — she can't have seen me yet. — Poor girl, how melancholy she looks! I'll keep in the background for an instant, and give her a joyful surprise.

Enter FANNY.

FANNY. Was ever unhappy girl placed in so dreadful a situation! — Friendless, and almost alone, in a strange place — my dear, dear Charles a victim to an attack of mental derangement, and I unable to avow my interest in him, or express my anxious sympathy and solicitude for his sufferings! I cannot bear this dreadful torture of agonising suspense. I must and will see him, let the cost be what it may. (*She is going.*)

CHARLES (*coming forward*). Hist! Fanny!

FANNY (*starting, and repressing a scream*). Ch—Charles — here in this room!

CHARLES. Bodily present, my dear, in this very room. My darling Fanny, let me strain you to my bosom. (*Advancing.*)

FANNY (*shrinking back*). N—n—no, dearest Charles, no, not now. — (*Aside.*) — How flushed he is!

CHARLES. No ! — Fanny, this cold reception is a very different one to what I looked forward to meeting with, from you.

FANNY (*advancing, and offering the tip of her finger*). N—n—no — not cold, Charles; not cold. I do not mean it to be so, indeed. — How is your head, now, dear ?

CHARLES. How is my head ! After days and weeks of suspense and anxiety, when half our dangerous journey is gained, and I meet you here, to bear you whither you can be made mine for life, you greet me with the tip of your longest finger, and inquire after my head. — Fanny, what can you mean ?

FANNY. You — you have startled me rather, Charles. — I thought you had gone to bed.

CHARLES. Gone to bed ! — Why, I have but this moment arrived.

FANNY (*aside*). Poor, poor Charles !

CHARLES. Miss Wilson, what am I to —

FANNY. No, no; pray, pray, do not suffer yourself to be excited —

CHARLES. Suffer myself to be excited ! — Can I pc͡͡ʼibly avoid it ? Can I do aught but wonder at this extraordinai͡ nd sudden change in your whole demeanour ? — Excited ! But five minutes since, I arrived here, brimful of the hope and expectation which had buoyed up my spirits during my long journey. I find you cold, reserved, and embarrassed, — everything but what I expected to find you, — and then you tell me not to be excited.

FANNY (*aside*). He is wandering again. The fever is evidently upon him.

CHARLES. This altered manner and ill-disguised confusion all convince me of what you would fain conceal. Miss Wilson, you repent of your former determination, and love another !

FANNY. Poor fellow !

CHARLES. Poor fellow ! — What, am I pitied ?

FANNY. Oh, Charles, do not give way to this. Consider how much depends upon your being composed.

CHARLES. I see how much depends upon my being composed, ma'am — well, very well. — A husband depends upon it, ma'am. Your new lover is in this house, and if he overhears my reproaches he will become suspicious of the woman who has jilted *another*, and may jilt *him*. That's it, madam — a great deal depends, as you say, upon my being composed. — A great deal, ma'am.

FANNY. Alas! these are, indeed, the ravings of frenzy!

CHARLES. Upon my word, ma'am, you must form a very modest estimate of your own power, if you imagine that disappointment has impaired my senses. Ha, ha, ha! — I am delighted. I am delighted to have escaped you, ma'am. I am glad, ma'am — damn'd glad! (*Kicks a chair over.*)

FANNY (*aside*). I must call for assistance. He grows more incoherent and furious every instant.

CHARLES. I leave you, ma'am. — I am unwilling to interrupt the tender *tête-à-tête* with the other gentleman, to which you are, no doubt, anxiously looking forward. — To you I have no more to say. To *him* I must beg to offer a few rather unexpected congratulations on his approaching marriage.

[*Exit* CHARLES *hastily.*

FANNY. Alas! it is but too true. His senses have entirely left him. [*Exit.*

SCENE II., AND LAST. — *A Gallery in the Inn, leading to the Bedrooms. Four Doors in the Flat, and one at each of the upper Entrances, numbered from 20 to 25. A pair of boots at the door of 23.*

Enter CHAMBERMAID, *with two lights ; and* CHARLES TOMKINS.

MAID. This is your room, sir, No. 21. (*Opening the door.*)

CHARLES. Very well. Call me at seven in the morning.

MAID. Yes, sir. (*Gives him a light and*

[*Exit* CHAMBERMAID.

CHARLES. And at nine, if I can previously obtain a few words of explanation with this unknown rival, I will just return to the place from whence I came, in the same coach that brought me down here. I wonder who he is and where he sleeps. (*Looking round.*) I have a lurking suspicion of those boots (*pointing to No. 23*). They are an ill-looking, underhanded sort of pair, and an undefinable instinct tells me that they have clothed the feet of the rascal I am in search of. Besides myself, the owner of those ugly articles is the only per-

son who has yet come up to bed.   I will keep my eyes open
for half an hour or so ; and my ears, too.

[*Exit* CHARLES *into No. 21.*

Enter MRS. NOAKES, *with two lights, followed by* MARY *and*
FANNY.

MRS. NOAKES. Take care of the last step, ladies.   This
way, ma'am, if you please.   No. 20 is your room, ladies : nice
large double-bedded room, with coals and a rushlight.

FANNY (*aside to* MARY).   I must ask which is his room.
I cannot rest unless I know he has at length sunk into the
slumber he so much needs. (*Crosses to* MRS. NOAKES.) Which
is the room in which the Strange Gentleman sleeps ?

MRS. NOAKES. No. 23, ma'am.   There's his boots outside
the door. Don't be frightened of him, ladies. He's very quiet
now, and our Boots is a watching him.

FANNY. Oh, no — we are not afraid of him. (*Aside.*)
Poor Charles !

MRS. NOAKES (*going to door No. 20*). This way, if you
please ; you'll find everything very comfortable, and there's a
bell-rope at the head of the bed, if you want anything in the
morning.   Good night, ladies.

As MARY *and* FANNY *pass* MRS. NOAKES, FANNY *takes a*
light.

[*Exeunt* FANNY *and* MARY *into No. 20.*

MRS. NOAKES (*tapping at No. 23*). Tom — Tom —

Enter TOM *from No. 23.*

TOM. Is that you, missis ?

MRS. NOAKES. Yes. — How's the Strange Gentleman,
Tom ?

TOM. He was wery boisterous half an hour ago, but I
punched his head a little, and now he's uncommon comfortable.
He's fallen asleep, but his snores is still wery incoherent.

MRS NOAKES. Mind you take care of him, Tom.   They'll
take him away in half an hour's time.   It's very nearly one
o'clock now.

TOM. I'll pay ev'ry possible attention to him.   If he offers
to call out, I shall whop him again.   [*Exit* TOM *into No. 23.*

MRS. NOAKES (*looking off*). This way, ma'am, if you please. Up these stairs.

Enter JULIA DOBBS, *with a light.*

JULIA. Which did you say was the room in which I could arrange my dress for travelling?

MRS. NOAKES. No. 22, ma'am; the next room to your nephew's. Poor dear — he's fallen asleep, ma'am, and I dare say you'll be able to take him away very quietly by and by.

JULIA (*aside*). Not so quietly as you imagine, if he plays his part half as well as Overton reports he does. (*To* MRS. NOAKES.) Thank you. — For the present, good night.
[*Exit* JULIA.

MRS. NOAKES. Wish you good night, ma'am. There. — Now I think I may go down stairs again, and see if Mr. Overton wants any more negus. Why, who's this? Oh, I forgot — No. 24 ain't abed yet. — It's him.

Enter JOHN JOHNSON, *with a light.*

MRS. NOAKES. No. 24, sir, if you please.

JOHN. Yes, yes, I know. The same room I slept in last night.

MRS. NOAKES. Yes, sir. — Wish you good night, sir.
[*Exit* MRS. NOAKES.

JOHN. Good night, ma'am. The same room I slept in last night, indeed, and the same room I may sleep in to-morrow night, and the next night, and the night after that, and just as many more nights as I can get credit here, unless this remittance arrives. I could raise the money to prosecute my journey without difficulty were I on the spot; but my confounded thoughtless liberality to the post-boys has left me absolutely penniless. Well, we shall see what to-morrow brings forth.

(*He goes into No. 24, but immediately returns and places his boots outside his room door, leaving it ajar.*)
[*Exit* JOHN *into No. 24.*

CHARLES *peeping from No. 21, and putting out his boots.*

CHARLES. There's another pair of boots. Now I wonder which of these two fellows is the man. I can't help thinking it's No. 23. — Hallo! (*He goes in and closes his door.*)

The door of No. 20 opens ; FANNY comes out with a light in
a night shade. No. 23 opens. She retires into No. 20.

Enter TOM SPARKS, with a stable lantern, from No. 23.

TOM (*closing the door gently*). Fast asleep still. I may
as vell go my rounds, and glean for the deputy. (*Pulls out
a piece of chalk from his pocket, and takes up boots from
No. 23.*) Twenty-three. It 's difficult to tell what a fellow
is ven he hain't got his senses, but I think this here twenty-
three 's a timorious, faint-hearted genus. (*Examines the boots.*)
You want new soleing, No. 23. (*Goes to No. 24, takes up
boots, and looks at them.*) Hallo ! here 's a *bust ;* and there 's
been a piece put on in the corner. — I must let my missis know.
The bill 's always doubtful ven there 's any mending. (*Goes
to No. 21, takes up boots.*) French calf Vellingtons. — All 's
right here. These here French calves always comes it strong
— light vines, and all that 'ere. (*Looking round.*) Wery
happy to see there ain't no high-lows — they never drinks nothing but gin and vater. Them and the cloth boots is the vurst
customers an inn has. — The cloth boots is always obstemious,
only drinks sherry vine and vater, and never eats no suppers.
(*He chalks the number of the room on each pair of boots as
he takes them up.*) Lucky for you, my French calves, that you
ain't done with the patent polish, or you 'd ha' been witrioled
in no time. I don't like to put oil o' witriol on a well-made
pair of boots ; but ven they 're rubbed vith that 'ere polish, it
must be done, or the profession 's ruined.

[*Exit* TOM *with boots.*

Enter FANNY from No. 20, with light as before.

FANNY. I tremble at the idea of going into his room, but
surely at a moment like this, when he is left to be attended by
rude and uninterested strangers, the strict rules of propriety
which regulate our ordinary proceedings may be dispensed with.
I will but satisfy myself that he sleeps, and has those comforts
which his melancholy situation demands, and return immediately. (*Goes to No. 23, and knocks.*)

CHARLES TOMKINS *peeping from No. 21.*

CHARLES. I 'll swear I heard a knock. — A woman ! Fanny
Wilson — and at that door at this hour of the night !

(FANNY *comes forward.*)

Why what an ass I must have been ever to have loved that girl. — It *is* No 23, though. — I 'll throttle him presently. The next room door open — I 'll watch there. (*He crosses to No. 24, and goes in.*)

FANNY *returns to No. 23, and knocks — the door opens and the* STRANGE GENTLEMAN *appears, night-cap on his head and a light in his hand.* — FANNY *screams, and runs back into No. 20.*

STRANGE GENTLEMAN (*coming forward.*) Well, of all the wonderful and extraordinary houses that ever did exist, this particular tenement is the most extraordinary. I 've got rid of the madman at last — and it 's almost time for that vile old mayor to remove me. But where ? — I 'm lost, bewildered, confused, and actually begin to think I am mad. Half these things I 've seen to-day must be visions of fancy — they never could have really happened. No, no; I 'm clearly mad ! — I 've not the least doubt of it now. I 've caught it from that horrid Boots. He has inoculated the whole establishment. We 're all mad together. — (*Looking off.*) Lights coming up stairs ! — Some more lunatics.

[*Exit* STRANGE GENTLEMAN *in No. 23.*

Enter OVERTON *with a cloak,* MRS. NOAKES, TOM SPARKS *with lantern, and Three Waiters with lights. The Waiters range up.* TOM *is in corner, and* MRS. NOAKES *next to him.*

OVERTON. Remain there till I call for your assistance. (*Goes up to No. 23 and knocks.*)

Enter STRANGE GENTLEMAN *from No. 23.*

Now, the chaise is ready. — Muffle yourself up in this cloak. (*Puts it on the* STRANGE GENTLEMAN. — *They come forward.*)

STRANGE GENTLEMAN. Yes.

OVERTON. Make a little noise when we take you away, you know.

STRANGE GENTLEMAN. Yes — yes. — I say, what a queer room this is of mine. Somebody has been tapping at the wall for the last half hour, like a whole forest of woodpeckers.

OVERTON. Don't you know who that was?

STRANGE GENTLEMAN. No.

OVERTON. The other party.

STRANGE GENTLEMAN (*alarmed*). The other party!

OVERTON. To be sure. — The other party is going with you.

STRANGE GENTLEMAN. Going with me! — In the same chaise!

OVERTON. Of course. — Hush! (*Goes to No. 22. Knocks.*)

Enter JULIA DOBBS *from No. 22, wrapped up in a large cloak.*

Look here! (*Bringing her forward.* JULIA *is next to* MRS. NOAKES.)

STRANGE GENTLEMAN (*starting into corner*). I won't go — I won't go. This is a plot — a conspiracy. I won't go, I tell you. I shall be assassinated. — I shall be murdered!

FANNY *and* MARY *appear at No. 20,* JOHNSON *and* TOM-KINS *at 24.*

JOHN (*at the door*). I told you he was mad.

CHARLES (*at the door*). I see — I see — poor fellow!

JULIA (*crossing to* STRANGE GENTLEMAN *and taking his arm*). Come, dear, come.

MRS. NOAKES. Yes, do go, there's a good soul. Go with your affectionate aunt.

STRANGE GENTLEMAN (*breaking from her*). My affection-ate aunt!

JULIA returns to her former position.

TOM. He don't deserve no affection. I niver see such an un-fectionate fellow to his relations.

STRANGE GENTLEMAN. Take that wretch away, and smother him between two feather beds. Take him away, and make a sandwich of him directly.

JULIA (*to* OVERTON). What voice was that? — It was not Lord Peter's. (*Throwing off her cloak.*)

OVERTON. Nonsense — nonsense. — Look at him. (*Pulls cloak off* STRANGE GENTLEMAN.)

STRANGE GENTLEMAN (*turning round*). A woman!

JULIA. A stranger!

OVERTON. A stranger! What, ain't he your husband that is to — your mad nephew, I mean?

JULIA. No!

ALL. No!

STRANGE GENTLEMAN. No! — no, I'll be damned if I am. I ain't anybody's nephew. — My aunt's dead, and I never had an uncle.

MRS. NOAKES. And ain't he mad, ma'am?

JULIA. No.

STRANGE GENTLEMAN. Oh, I'm *not* mad. — I was mistaken just now.

OVERTON. And isn't he going away with you?

JULIA. No.

MARY (*coming forward next to* MRS. NOAKES). And isn't his name Tomkins?

STRANGE GENTLEMAN (*very loud*). No!

(*All these questions and answers should be very rapid.* JOHNSON *and* TOMKINS *advance to the ladies, and they all retire up.*)

MRS. NOAKES. What *is* his name? (*Producing a letter.*) It ain't Mr. Walker Trott, is it? (*She advances a little towards him.*)

STRANGE GENTLEMAN. Something so remarkably like it, ma'am, that, with your permission, I'll open that epistle. (*Taking letter.*)

All go up, but JULIA *and* STRANGE GENTLEMAN.

(*Opening letter.*) Tinkle's hand. (*Reads.*) " The challenge was a *ruse.* By this time I shall have been united at Gretna Green to the charming Emily Brown." — Then, through a horror of duels, I have lost a wife!

JULIA (*with her handkerchief to her eyes*). And through Lord Peter's negligence, I have lost a husband!

STRANGE GENTLEMAN. Eh! (*Regards her a moment, then beckons* OVERTON, *who comes forward.*) I say, didn't you say something about three thousand a year this morning?

OVERTON. I did.

STRANGE GENTLEMAN. You alluded to that party? (*Nodding towards* JULIA.)

OVERTON. I did.

STRANGE GENTLEMAN. Hem! (*Puts* OVERTON *back.*)

Permit me, ma'am (*going to her*), to sympathise most respectfully with your deep distress.

JULIA. Oh, sir! your kindness penetrates to my very heart.

STRANGE GENTLEMAN (*aside*). Penetrates to her heart! —
It's taking the right direction. — If I understand your sorrowing murmur, ma'am, you contemplated taking a destined husband away with you, in the chaise at the door?

JULIA. Oh! sir, spare my feelings — I did. — The horses
were ordered and paid for; and everything was ready. (*Weeps.*)

STRANGE GENTLEMAN (*aside*). She weeps. — Expensive
thing, posting, ma'am.

JULIA. Very, sir.

STRANGE GENTLEMAN. Eighteenpence a mile, ma'am, not
including the boys.

JULIA. Yes, sir.

STRANGE GENTLEMAN. *You* 've lost a husband, ma'am —
I have lost a wife. — Marriages are made above — I 'm quite
certain ours is booked. — Pity to have all this expense for
nothing — let 's go together.

JULIA (*drying her eyes*). The suddenness of this proposal,
sir —

STRANGE GENTLEMAN. Requires a sudden answer, ma'am.
— You don't say no — you mean yes. Permit me to — (*kisses
her*). — All right! Old one (*to* OVERTON), I 've done it. —
Mrs. Noakes, don't countermand the chaise. — We 're off directly.

CHARLES (*who with* FANNY *comes down*). So are we.

JOHN (*who with* MARY *comes down*). So are we, thanks
to a negotiated loan, and an explanation as hasty as the quarrel
that gave rise to it.

STRANGE GENTLEMAN. Three post-chaises and four, on to
Gretna, directly.   [*Exeunt* WAITERS.

I say — we 'll stop here as we come back?

JOHN *and* CHARLES. Certainly.

STRANGE GENTLEMAN. But before I go, as I fear I have
given a great deal of trouble here to-night — permit me to inquire whether you will view my mistakes and perils with an
indulgent eye, and consent to receive " *The Strange Gentleman* " again to-morrow.

CURTAIN.

THE VILLAGE COQUETTES

ACT I

SCENE I. — *A rick-yard, with a cart laden with corn-sheaves.* JOHN MADDOX, *and labourers, unloading it. Implements of husbandry, etc., lie scattered about. A gate on one side.* JOHN MADDOX *is in the cart, and dismounts at the conclusion of the Chorus.*

ROUND.

HAIL to the merry Autumn days, when yellow corn-fields shine,
Far brighter than the costly cup that holds the monarch's
  wine!
Hail to the merry harvest time, the gayest of the year,
The time of rich and bounteous crops, rejoicing, and good
  cheer!
'T is pleasant on a fine Spring morn to see the buds expand,
'T is pleasant in the Summer time to view the teeming land;
'T is pleasant on a Winter's night to crouch around the blaze, —
But what are joys like these, my boys, to Autumn's merry
  days!
Then hail to merry Autumn days, when yellow corn-fields shine,
Far brighter than the costly cup that holds the monarch's
  wine!
And hail to merry harvest time, the gayest of the year,
The time of rich and bounteous crops, rejoicing, and good
  cheer!

JOHN. Well done, my lads; a good day's work, and a warm one. Here, Tom (*to* VILLAGER), run into the house, and ask Miss Rose to send out some beer for the men, and a jug for Master Maddox; and d' ye hear, Tom, tell Miss Rose it 's a fine evening, and that if she 'll step out herself it 'll do her good, and do me good into the bargain. (*Exit* VILLAGER.) That 's right,

my lads, stow these sheaves away, before the sun goes down.
Let's begin fresh in the morning, without any leavings of to-
day. By this time to-morrow the last load will have been
carried, and then for our Harvest Home!

VILLAGERS. Hurrah! Hurrah!

(*First four lines of Round repeated.*)

Enter MARTIN STOKES.

MARTIN. Very good! Very good, indeed! — Always sing
while you work — capital custom! I always do when I work,
and I never work at all when I can help it; — another capital
custom. John, old fellow, how are you? — Give us your hand,
— hearty squeeze, — good shake, — capital custom number
three. Fine dry weather for the harvest, John. Talking of
that, I'm dry too; you always give away plenty of beer, here;
— capital custom number four. Trouble you for the loan of
that can, John.

JOHN (*taking it from the cart*). Here's the can, but as to
there being anything good in it, it's as dry as the weather, and
as empty as you. Hoo, hoo! (*Laughing boisterously, is suddenly checked by a look from* MARTIN.)

MARTIN. Hallo, John, hallo! I have often told you before,
Mr. Maddox, that I don't consider you in a situation of life
which entitles you to make jokes, far less to laugh at 'em. If
you must make a joke, do it solemnly and respectfully. If *I*
laugh, that's quite enough, and it must be far more gratifying to
your feelings than any contortions of that enormous mouth of
yours.

JOHN. Well, perhaps, as you say, I ought n't to make jokes
till I arrive, like you, at the dignity of a small piece of ground
and a cottage; but I must laugh at a joke, sometimes.

MARTIN. Must, must you! — Rather presuming fellow, this
Maddox. (*Aside.*)

JOHN. Why, when you make one of them rum jokes of
yours, — 'cod, I must laugh, then!

MARTIN. Oh! ah! you may laugh then, John; always
laugh at my jokes, — capital custom number five; no harm in
that, because you can't help it, you know. — Knowing fellow,
though. (*Aside.*)

JOHN. Remember that joke about the old cow, as you made

five years ago ? — 'cod, that was a joke! Hoo, hoo, hoo! —
I never shall forget that joke. I never see a cow, to this day,
without laughing.

MARTIN. Ha, ha, ha! very good, very good! — Devilish
clever fellow, this! (*Aside.*) Well, Jack, you behave yourself
well, all the evening, and perhaps I may make that joke again
before the day's out

JOHN. Thankee, that's very kind.

MARTIN Don't mention it, don't mention it; but I say,
John, I called to speak to you about more important matters.
— Something wrong here, ain't there? (*Mysteriously.*)

JOHN. Wrong! you're always fancying something wrong.

MARTIN. Fancying, — come, I like that. I say, why don't
you keep your harvest home at home, to-morrow night? Why
are we all to go up to the Squire's, as if we could n't be merry
in Benson's barn? And why is the Squire always coming down
here, looking after some people, and cutting out other people?
— ain't that wrong? Where's George Edmunds — old Benson's so fond of, and that Lucy *was* fond of, too, once upon a
time, — eh? Ain't that wrong? Where's your sweetheart,
Rose? — Ain't her walkings, and gigglings, and whisperings,
and simperings, with the Squire's friend, Mr. Sparkins Flam,
the talk of the whole place? Nothing wrong there, — eh?
(*Maddox goes up.*) Had him there; I knew there was something wrong. I'll keep a sharp eye upon these doings, for I
don't like these new-fangled customs. It was all very well in
the old time, to see the Squire's father come riding among the
people on his bay cob, nodding to the common folks, shaking
hands with me, and all that sort of thing; but when you
change the old country gentleman into a dashing fop from London, and the steady old steward into Mr. Sparkins Flam, the
case is very different. We shall see, — but if I might tell
Miss Lucy Benson a bit of my mind, I should say, "Stick to
an independent young fellow, like George Edmunds, and depend
upon it you will be happier than you would with all the show
and glitter of a squire's lady." And I should say to Rose, very
solemn, " Rose — "

(*Rose enters unperceived, with beer.*)

" Rose — "

ROSE (*starting*). Lord bless us! — What a hollow voice!

— Why, it 's Mr. Stokes! — What on earth is the matter with him?

MARTIN (*not seeing her*). "— Rose, — if you would be happy and contented, if you would escape destruction, shield yourself from dangerous peril, and save yourself from horrid ruin! —

ROSE. What dreadful words! —

MARTIN. "— you will at once, and without delay, bestow your hand on John Maddox; or if you would aspire to a higher rank in life, and a loftier station in society, you will cultivate the affections of Mr. Stokes, — Mr. Martin Stokes, — a young gentleman of great mental attractions, and very considerable personal charms; — leaving the false and fatal Flam to the ignominious fate which —"

ROSE. Why, Mr. Stokes! —

MARTIN. "— ignominious fate which —"

ROSE. Dear, he must be in a fit! Mr. Stokes!

MARTIN. Eh? — Ah! Miss Rose. — It 's you, is it?

ROSE. Me! Yes, and here have I been waiting all this time, while you were talking nonsense to yourself. Here, I have brought you some beer.

MARTIN. Oh! Miss Rose, if you go on in this way, you 'll bring us to our bier, instead of bringing our beer to us. (*Looking round.*) You may laugh, if you want to, very much, John.

JOHN. Hoo, hoo, hoo!

ROSE. Be quiet, oaf! And pray, sir (*to* MARTIN), to what may your most humorous observation refer?

MARTIN. Why, my dear Miss Rose, you know my way, — always friendly, — always thinking of the welfare of those I like best, and very seldom receiving any gratitude in return.

ROSE. I know you very seldom deserve any.

MARTIN. Ah! that 's exactly my meaning; that 's the way, you see. The moment I begin to throw out a hint to one of my dear friends, out comes some unkind and rude remark. But I bear it all for their sakes. I won't allow you to raise my ill nature, — you shan't stop me. I was going to say, — don't you think — now *don't* you think — that you — don't be angry — make rather — don't colour up, — *rather* too free with Mr. Sparkins Flam?

ROSE. *I* make free with Mr. Sparkins Flam! Why you odious, insolent creature!

MARTIN. Ah, of course — always the way — I told you so — I knew you 'd say that.

ROSE. And you, John, you mean-spirited scarecrow ; will you stand there, and see me insulted by an officious, impertinent —

MARTIN. Go on, go on! (*A gun fired.*) Hallo! (*Looking off.*) Here they are, the Squire and Mr. Sparkins Flam.

ROSE (*hastily adjusting her dress*). My goodness! Mr. Spar — run, John, run, there 's a dear !

JOHN (*not moving*). Very dear, I dare say.

ROSE. Run, and tell my uncle and Lucy that Mr. Spar — I mean that the Squire 's coming.

JOHN. I would n't ha' gone anyhow ; but nobody need go now, for here they are. Now, I 'm extinguished for the rest of the day.

Enter through the gate SQUIRE NORTON and MR. SPARKINS FLAM, dressed for sporting, with guns, etc., and two gamekeepers. On the other side, old BENSON and LUCY. MARTIN, during the whole scene, thrusts himself in the SQUIRE's way, to be taken notice of.

SQUIRE (*to gamekeeper, and putting down his gun*). Take the birds into the house. Benson, we have had a good day's sport, but a tiring one ; and as the load is heavy for my fellows, you 'll let our game remain where it is. I could not offer it to a better friend.

BENSON. Your honour 's very good, but —

SQUIRE. Nay, you make a merit of receiving the smallest favour.

BENSON. Not a merit of receiving, nor a boast of refusing it ; but a man in humble station should be cautious how he receives favours from those above him, which he never asks, and can never return. I have had too many such favours forced upon me by your honour, lately, and would rather not increase the number.

SQUIRE. But such a trifle —

BENSON. A trifle from an equal, but a condescension from a superior. Let your men carry your birds up to the Hall, sir, or, if they are tired, mine shall do it for them, and welcome. (*Retires up.*)

FLAM (*aside*). Swine and independence ! Leather breeches and liberty !

SQUIRE. At least I may be permitted to leave a few brace, as a present to the ladies. Lucy, I hope, will not object. (*Crosses to her.*)

LUCY. I feel much flattered by your honour's politeness — and — and — and —

ROSE. My cousin means to say, sir, that we 're very much obliged to your honour and Mr. Flam for your politeness, and that we are very willing to accept of anything, your honour.

FLAM (*aside*). Condescending little savage!

SQUIRE. You have spoken well, both for yourself and your cousin. Flam, this is Rose — the pretty little Rose, you know.

FLAM. Know! can I ever forget the charming Rose — the beautiful — the — the (*aside*) — the Cabbage Rose!

SQUIRE (*aside*). Keep that girl engaged, while I talk to the other one.

ROSE. Oh, Mr. Flam!

FLAM. Oh, Miss Rose! (*He salutes her.*)

BENSON. Your honour will not object to taste our ale, after your day's sport. The afternoon is fresh and cool, and 't will be pleasant here in the air. Here, Ben, Thomas, bring mugs here — quick — quick — and a seat for his honour.

[*Exeunt* BENSON, MADDOX, *etc.*

SQUIRE. It will be delightful — won't it, Flam?

FLAM. Inexpressibly charming! (*Aside.*) An amateur tea-garden. (*He retires a little up with* ROSE — *she coquetting.*)

SQUIRE (*to* LUCY). And in such society, how much the pleasure will be enhanced!

LUCY. Your honour knows I ought not to listen to you — George Edmunds would —

SQUIRE. Edmunds! a rustic! — you cannot love that Ed. munds, Lucy. Forget him — remember your own worth.

LUCY. I wish I could, sir. My heart will tell me, though, weak and silly as I am, that I cannot better show the consciousness of my own worth than by remaining true to my first and early love. Your honour rouses my foolish pride; but real, true love is not to be forgotten easily.

Song. — LUCY.

Love is not a feeling to pass away,
Like the balmy breath of a summer day;

It is not — it cannot be — laid aside ;
It is not a thing to forget or hide.
It clings to the heart, ah, woe is me !
As the ivy clings to the old oak-tree.

Love is not a passion of earthly mould,
As a thirst for honour, or fame, or gold :
For when all these wishes have died away,
The deep strong love of a brighter day,
Though nourish'd in secret, consumes the more,
As the slow rust eats to the iron's core.

Reënter OLD BENSON, JOHN MADDOX, *and* VILLAGERS, *with
jugs, seats, etc. ;* SQUIRE NORTON *seats himself next*
LUCY, *and* ROSE *contrives to sit next* MR. SPARKINS
FLAM, *which* MARTIN *and* MADDOX *in vain endeavour
to prevent.*

SQUIRE. Flam, you know these honest people ? all tenants
of my own.
FLAM. Oh, yes, I know 'em — pleasant fellows ! This —
this is — what 's his name ?
BENSON. Martin, sir, — Martin Stokes.
MARTIN (*starting forward*). A — a — Mr. Stokes, at your
service, sir, — how do you do, sir ? (*Shaking* FLAM *by the
hand, while speaking.*) I hope you are quite well, sir ; I am
delighted to see you looking so well, sir. I hope your majestic
father, and your fashionable mother, are in the enjoyment of
good health, sir. I should have spoken to you before, sir, only
you have been so very much engaged that I could n't succeed
in catching your honourable eye ; — very happy to see you, sir.
FLAM. Ah. Pleasant fellow, this Martin ! — agreeable manners, — no reserve about him.
MARTIN. Sir, you do me a great deal of honour. Mr. Norton, sir, I have the honour of drinking your remarkably good
health, — I admire you, sir.
SQUIRE (*laughing*). Sir, I feel highly gratified, I 'm sure.
MARTIN (*aside*). He 's gratified ! — I flatter myself I have
produced a slight impression here. (*Drinks.*)
FLAM (*turns round, sees* MADDOX). Ah, Ox !
JOHN. Ox ! Who do you call Ox ? Maddox is my name.

FLAM. Oh, mad Ox! true; I forgot the lunacy; — your health, mad Ox.

SQUIRE (*rising, and coming forward*). Come, Flam, another glass. Here, friends, is success to our Harvest Home!

MARTIN. Hear, hear! a most appropriate toast, most eloquently given, — a charming sentiment, delightfully expressed. Gentlemen (*to* VILLAGERS), allow me to have the pleasure of proposing Mr. Norton, if you please. Take your time from me. (*He gives the time, and they all cheer.*) Mr. Norton, sir, I beg to call upon you for a song.

Song. — SQUIRE NORTON.

That very wise head, old Æsop, said,
    The bow should be sometimes loose;
Keep it tight for ever, the string you sever : —
    Let 's turn his old moral to use.
The world forget, and let us yet,
    The glass our spirits buoying,
Revel to-night in those moments bright
    Which make life worth enjoying.
The cares of the day, old moralists say,
    Are quite enough to perplex one ;
Then drive to-day's sorrow away till to-morrow,
    And then put it off till the next one.
        Chorus. — The cares of the day, etc.

Some plodding old crones, the heartless drones!
    Appeal to my cool reflection,
And ask me whether such nights can ever
    Charm sober recollection.
Yes, yes! I cry, I 'll grieve and die,
    When those I love forsake me ;
But while friends so dear surround me here,
    Let Care, if he can, o'ertake me.
        Chorus. — The cares of the day, etc.

(*During the Chorus,* SQUIRE NORTON *and* FLAM *resume their guns, and go up the stage, followed by the various characters. The Chorus concludes as the Scene closes.*)

SCENE II. — *An open spot near the village, with stile and pathway leading to the church, which is seen in the distance.* GEORGE EDMUNDS *enters, with a stick in his hand.*

EDMUNDS. How thickly the fallen leaves lie scattered at the feet of that old row of elm-trees! When I first met Lucy on this spot, it was a fine spring day, and those same leaves were trembling in the sunshine, as green and bright as if their beauty would last for ever. What a contrast they present now, and how true an emblem of my own lost happiness!

Song. — GEORGE EDMUNDS.

Autumn leaves, autumn leaves, lie strewn around me here;
Autumn leaves, autumn leaves, how sad, how cold, how drear!
How like the hopes of childhood's day,
Thick clustering on the bough!
How like those hopes is their decay, —
How faded are they now!
Autumn leaves, autumn leaves, lie strewn around me here;
Autumn leaves, autumn leaves, how sad, how cold, how drear!

Wither'd leaves, wither'd leaves, that fly before the gale;
Wither'd leaves, wither'd leaves, ye tell a mournful tale,
Of love once true, and friends once kind,
And happy moments fled:
Dispersed by every breath of wind,
Forgotten, changed, or dead!
Autumn leaves, autumn leaves, lie strewn around me here;
Autumn leaves, autumn leaves, how sad, how cold, how drear!

An hour past the old time, and still no Lucy! 'T is useless lingering here: I 'll wait no longer. A female crossing the meadow! — 'T is Rose, the bearer of a letter or a message perhaps.

Enter ROSE. (*She avoids him.*)

EDMUNDS. No! Then I will see Lucy at once, without a moment's delay. (*Going.*)

ROSE. No, no, you can't. (*Aside.*) There 'll certainly be

bloodshed! I am quite certain Mr. Flam will kill him. He offered me, with the most insinuating speeches, to cut John's throat at a moment's notice; and when the Squire complimented him on being a good shot, he said he should like to "bag" the whole male population of the village. (*To him.*) You can't see her.

EDMUNDS. Not see her, and she at home! Were you instructed to say this, Rose?

ROSE. I say it, because I know you can't see her. She is not well; and — and —

EDMUNDS. And Mr. Norton is there, you would say.

ROSE. Mr. Norton!

EDMUNDS. Yes, Mr. Norton. Was he not there last evening? Was he not there the evening before? Is he not there at this moment?

Enter JOHN MADDOX.

JOHN. There at this moment? — Of course he is.

ROSE (*aside*). John here!

JOHN. Of course he is; of course he was there last night; and of course he was there the evening before. He 's always there, and so is his bosom friend and confidential demon, Mr. Sparkins Flam. Oh, George! we 're injured men, both of us.

EDMUNDS. Heartless girl! (*Retires up.*)

JOHN (*to* ROSE). Faithless person!

ROSE. Don't call me a person.

JOHN. You *are* a person, perjured, treacherous, and deceiving! Oh, George! if you had seen what I have seen to-day. Soft whisperings and loving smiles, gentle looks and encouraging sighs, — such looks and sighs as used once upon a time to be bestowed on us, George! If you had seen the Squire making up to Lucy, and Rose making up to Flam : — but I am very glad you did not see it, George, very. It would have broken your heart, as it has broken mine! Oh, Rose! could you break my heart?

ROSE. I could break your head with the greatest pleasure, you mischief-making booby; and if you don't make haste to wherever you 're going, somebody that I know of will certainly do so, very quickly.

JOHN. Will he, will he? — your friend, Mr. Flam, I suppose! Let him — that 's all : let him! (*Retires up.*)

Rose. Oh! I'll let him; you need n't be afraid of my interfering. Dear, dear, I wish Mr. Flam would come, for I will own, notwithstanding what graver people may say, that I enjoy a little flirtation as much as any one.

Song. — Rose.

Some folks who have grown old and sour
Say love does nothing but annoy.
The fact is, they have had their hour,
So envy what they can't enjoy.
I like the glance — I like the sigh —
That does of ardent passion tell!
If some folks were as young as I,
I'm sure they'd like it quite as well.

Old maiden aunts so hate the men,
So well know how wives are harried,
It makes them sad — not jealous — when
They see their poor dear nieces married.
All men are fair and false, they know,
And with deep sighs they assail 'em;
It's so long since they tried men, though,
I rather think their memories fail 'em.

— Here comes Mr. Flam. You'd better go, John. I know you'll be murdered.

John. Here I shall stop; let him touch me, and he shall feel the weight of my indignation.

Enter Flam.

Flam. Ah, my charmer! Punctual to my time, you see, my sweet little Damask Rose!

John (*coming down*). A great deal more like a monthly one, — constantly changing, and gone the moment you wear it.

Rose. Impertinent creature!

Flam. Who is this poetical cauliflower?

John. Don't pretend not to know me. You know who I am, well enough.

Flam. As I live, it's the Ox! — Retire, Ox, to your pasture, and don't rudely disturb the cooing of the doves Go and graze, Ox!

JOHN. Suppose I choose to remain here, what then?

FLAM. Why then you must be driven off, mad Ox. (*To Rose.*) Who is that other grasshopper?

ROSE. Hush, hush! for Heaven's sake, don't let him hear you! It's young Edmunds.

FLAM. Young Edmunds? And who the devil is young Edmunds? For beyond the natural inference that young Edmunds is the son of old Edmunds, curse me if the fame of young Edmunds has ever reached my ears.

ROSE (*in a low tone*). It's Lucy's former lover, whom she has given up for the Squire.

FLAM. The rejected cultivator?

ROSE. The same.

FLAM. Ah! I guessed as much from his earthy appearance. But, my darling Rose, I must speak with you, — I must — (*Putting his arm round her waist, sees* JOHN.) Good-bye, Ox!

JOHN. Good-bye!

FLAM. Pleasant walk to you, Ox!

JOHN (*not moving*). Thankee; — same to you!

FLAM. That other clodpole must not stay here either.

ROSE. Yes, yes! he neither sees nor hears us. Pray let him remain.

FLAM (*to* JOHN). You understand, Ox, that it is my wish that you forthwith retire and graze, — or, in other words, that you at once, and without delay, betake yourself to the farm, or the devil, or any other place where you are in your element, and won't be in the way.

JOHN. Oh, yes, I understand that.

FLAM. Very well; then the sooner you create a scarcity of such animals in this market, the better. Now, my dear Rose. (*Puts his arm round her waist again*). Are you gone, Ox?

JOHN. No.

FLAM. Are you going?

JOHN. By no means.

FLAM. This insolence is not to be borne.

ROSE. Oh, pray don't hurt him, — pray don't. Go away, you stupid creature, if you don't want to be ruined.

JOHN. That's just the very advice I would give you, Rose; do *you* go away, if you don't want to be ruined. As for me, this is a public place, and here I 'll remain just as long as I think proper.

FLAM (*quitting* ROSE, *and advancing towards him*). You will ?

JOHN. I will.

ROSE. Oh, dear, dear! I knew he 'd be murdered all along. I was quite certain of it.

JOHN. Don't frown and scowl at me, — it won't do, — it only makes me smile; and when you talk of insolence and put my blood up, I tell you at once that I am not to be bullied.

FLAM. Bullied ?

JOHN. Ay, bullied was the word, — bullied by a coward, if you like that better.

FLAM. Coward! (*Seizes his gun by the barrel, and aims a blow at him, with the butt-end;* EDMUNDS *rushes forward and strikes it up with his stick.*)

EDMUNDS. Hold your hand, sir, — hold your hand, or I 'll tell you to the ground. Maddox, leave this place directly; take the opposite path, and I 'll follow you. (*Exit* MADDOX.) As for you, sir, who, by the way of vindicating yourself from the charge of cowardice, raise your gun against an unarmed man, tell your protector, the Squire, from me, that he and his companions might content themselves with turning the heads of our farmers' daughters, and endeavouring to corrupt their hearts, without wantonly insulting the men they have most injured. Let this be a lesson to you, sir, — although you were armed you would have had the worst of a scuffle, and you may not have the benefit of a third person's interference at so critical a moment, another time; — remember this warning, sir, and benefit by it. [*Exit.*

FLAM (*aside*). If Norton does not take a dear revenge for this insult, I have lost my influence with him. Bully! coward! They shall rue it.

ROSE (*with her apron to her eyes*). Oh, Mr. Flam! I can't bear to think that you should have suffered all this, on my account.

FLAM (*aside*). On her account! — a little vanity! (*To her.*) Suffered! Why, my dear, it was the drollest and most humorous affair that ever happened. Here stand I, — the Honourable Sparkins Flam, — on this second day of September, one thousand seven hundred and twenty-nine; and positively and solemnly declare that all the coffee-houses, play-houses, faro-tables, brag-tables, assemblies, drums, and routs of a whole season put together could not furnish such a splendid piece of exquisite drollery. The idea is admirable. My affecting to quarrel with a ploughman, and submitting to be lectured by another caterpillar, whom I suffer to burst into a butterfly importance!

ROSE. Then you were not really quarrelling?

FLAM. Bless you, no! I was only acting.

ROSE. Lor'! how well you do act, to be sure.

FLAM. Come, let us retire into the house, or after this joke we shall be the gaze of all the animated potatoes that are planted in this hole of a village. Why do you hesitate, Damask?

ROSE. Why, I have just been thinking that if you go to all these coffee-houses, and play-houses, and fairs, and brags, and keep playing drums, and routing people about, you 'll forget me, when you go back to London.

FLAM (*aside*). More than probable. (*To her.*) Never fear; you will be generally known as Rose the lovely, and I shall be universally denominated Flam the constant.

Duet. — ROSE *and* SPARKINS FLAM.

FLAM.

'T is true I 'm caress'd by the witty,
   The envy of all the fine beaux,
The pet of the court and the city,
   But still I 'm the lover of Rose.

ROSE.

Country sweethearts, oh, how I despise!
   And oh! how delighted I am
To think that I shine in the eyes
   Of the elegant — sweet — Mr. Flam.

FLAM.

Allow me. (*Offers to kiss her.*)

ROSE.

Pray don't be so bold, sir. (*Kisses her.*)

FLAM.

What sweets on that honey'd lip hang!

ROSE.

Your presumption, I know, I should scold, sir,
But I really *can't* scold Mr. Flam.

Both.

Then let us be happy together,
Content with the world as it goes,
An unchangeable couple for ever,
Mr. Flam and his beautiful Rose.   [*Exeunt.*

SCENE III. — *The Farmer's Kitchen. A table and chairs.*

Enter OLD BENSON *and* MARTIN.

BENSON. Well, Stokes. Now you have the opportunity you have desired, and we are alone, I am ready to listen to the information which you wished to communicate to my private ear.

MARTIN. Exactly; — you said information, I think?

BENSON. *You* said information, or I have forgotten.

MARTIN. Just so, exactly; I said information. I *did* say information, why should I deny it?

BENSON. I see no necessity for your doing so, certainly. Pray go on.

MARTIN. Why, you see, my dear Mr. Benson, the fact is — won't you be seated? Pray sit down. (*Brings forward two chairs; — they sit.*) There, now, — let me see, — where was I?

BENSON. You were going to begin, I think.

MARTIN. Oh, — ah! — so I was; — I had n't begun, had I?

BENSON. No, no! Pray begin again, if you had.

MARTIN. Well, then, what I have got to say is not so much information as a kind of advice, or suggestion, or hint, or something of that kind; and it relates to — eh? — (*looking very mysterious*).

BENSON. What?

MARTIN. Yes (*nodding*). Don't you think there 's something wrong there?

BENSON. Where?

MARTIN. In that quarter.

BENSON. In what quarter? Speak more plainly, sir.

MARTIN. You know what a friendly feeling I entertain to your family. You know what a very particular friend of mine you are. You know how anxious I always am to prevent anything going wrong.

BENSON. Well! (*Abruptly.*)

MARTIN. Yes, I see you 're very sensible of it, but I 'll take it for granted : you need n't bounce and fizz about in that way, because it makes one nervous. Don't you think, now, *don't* you think, that ill-natured people may say — don't be angry, you know, because if I was n't a very particular friend of the family, I would n't mention the subject on any account; — don't you think that ill-natured people may say there 's something wrong in the frequency of the Squire's visits here ?

BENSON (*starting up furiously*). What!

MARTIN (*aside*). Here he goes again !

BENSON. Who dares suspect my child ?

MARTIN. Ah, to be sure, that 's exactly what I say. Who dares ? Damme, I should like to see 'em !

BENSON. Is it you ?

MARTIN. I ! Bless you, no, not for the world ! I ! — Come, that 's a good one. I only say what other people say, you know ; that 's all.

BENSON. And what are these tales, that idle, busy fools prate of with delight, among themselves, caring not whose ears they reach, so long as they are kept from the old man, whose blindness — the blindness of a fond and doting father — is subject for their rude and brutal jeering. What are they ?

MARTIN. Dear me, Mr. Benson, you keep me in a state of perpetual excitement.

BENSON. Tell me, without equivocation, what do they say ?

MARTIN. Why, they say they think it — not exactly wrong, perhaps; don't fly out, now — but among those remarkable coincidences which do occur sometimes that, whenever you go out of your house, the Squire and his friend should come into it; that Miss Lucy and Miss Rose, in the long walks they take every day, should be met and walked home with by the same gentlemen ; that long after you have gone to bed at night, the Squire and Mr. Sparkins Flam should still be seen hovering about the lane and meadow ; and that one of the lattice windows should be always open, at that hour.

BENSON. This is all ?

MARTIN. Ye—yes, — yes, that's all.

BENSON. Nothing beside ?

MARTIN. Eh ?

BENSON. Nothing beside ?

MARTIN. Why, there *is* something else, but I know you'll begin to bounce about again, if I tell it you.

BENSON. No, no ! let me hear it all.

MARTIN. Why, then, they do say that the Squire has been heard to boast that he had practised on Lucy's mind — that when he bid her, she would leave her father and her home, and follow him over the world.

BENSON. They lie ! Her breast is pure and innocent ! Her soul is free from guilt ; her mind from blemish. They lie ! I'll not believe it. Are they mad ? Do they think that I stand tamely by, and look upon my child's disgrace ? Heaven ! do they know of what a father's heart is made ?

MARTIN. My dear Mr. Benson, if you —

BENSON. This coarse and brutal boast shall be disowned. (*Going ;* MARTIN *stops him.*)

MARTIN. My dear Mr. Benson, you know it may not have been made after all, — my dear sir, —

BENSON (*struggling*). Unhand me, Martin ! Made or not made, it has gone abroad, fixing an infamous notoriety on me and mine. I'll hear its truth or falsehood from himself. (*Breaks from him, and exit.*)

MARTIN, *solus.* There'll be something decidedly wrong here presently. Hallo ! here's another very particular friend in a fume.

Enter YOUNG BENSON *hastily.*

MARTIN. Ah ! my dear fellow, how —

YOUNG BENSON. Where is Lucy ?

MARTIN. I don't know, unless she has walked out with the Squire.

YOUNG BENSON. The Squire !

MARTIN. To be sure ; she very often walks out with the Squire. Very pleasant recreation walking out with the Squire ; — capital custom, ain't it ?

YOUNG BENSON. Where's my father ?

MARTIN. Why, upon my word, I am unable to satisfy your

curiosity in that particular either. All I know of him is that he whisked out of this room in a rather boisterous and turbulent manner for an individual at his time of life, some few seconds before you whisked in. But what's the matter? — you seem excited. Nothing wrong, is there?

YOUNG BENSON (*aside*). This treatment of Edmunds, and Lucy's altered behaviour to him, confirm my worst fears. Where is Mr. Norton?

MARTIN (*calling off*). Ah! to be sure, — where is Mr. Norton?

Enter SQUIRE.

SQUIRE. Mr. Norton is here. Who wishes to see him?

MARTIN. To be sure, sir. Mr. Norton is here: who wishes to see him?

YOUNG BENSON. I do.

MARTIN. I don't. Old fellow, good-bye! Mr. Norton, good evening! (*Aside.*) There 'll be something wrong here, in a minute. [*Exit.*

SQUIRE. Well, young man?

YOUNG BENSON. If you contemplate treachery here, Mr. Norton, look to yourself. My father is an old man; the chief prop of his declining years is his child, — my sister. For your actions here, sir, you shall render a dear account to me.

SQUIRE. To *you*, peasant!

YOUNG BENSON. To me, sir. One other scene like that enacted by your creature, at your command, to-night, may terminate more seriously to him. For your behaviour here you are responsible to me.

SQUIRE. Indeed! Anything more, sir?

YOUNG BENSON. Simply this: — after injuring the old man beyond reparation, and embittering the last moments of his life, you may possibly attempt to shield yourself under the paltry excuse that, as a gentleman, you cannot descend to take the consequences from my hand. You *shall* take them from me, sir, if I strike you to the earth first. [*Exit.*

SQUIRE. Fiery and valorous, indeed! As the suspicions of the family are aroused, no time is to be lost: the girl must be carried off to-night, if possible. With Flam's assistance and management, she may be speedily removed from within the reach of these rustic sparks. In my cooler moments, the reflec tion of the misery I may inflict upon the old man makes my conduct appear base and dishonourable, even to myself. Pshaw! hundreds have done the same thing before me, who have been lauded and blazoned forth as men of honour. Honour in such cases, — an idle tale! — a by-word! Honour! There is much to be gleaned from old tales; and the legend of the child and the old man speaks but too truly.

Song. — Squire Norton.

The child and the old man sat alone
  In the quiet, peaceful shade
Of the old green boughs, that had richly grown
  In the deep, thick, forest glade.
It was a soft and pleasant sound,
  That rustling of the oak;
And the gentle breeze play'd lightly round,
  As thus the fair boy spoke: —

" Dear father, what can honour be,
  Of which I hear men rave?
Field, cell and cloister, land and sea,
  The tempest and the grave: —
It lives in all, 't is sought in each,
  'T is never heard or seen:
Now tell me, father, I beseech,
  What can this honour mean? "

" It is a name, — a name, my child, —
  It lived in other days,
When men were rude, their passions wild,
  Their sport, thick battle-frays.
When in armour bright the warrior bold
  Knelt to his lady's eyes:
Beneath the abbey-pavement old
  That warrior's dust now lies.

" The iron hearts of that old day
  Have moulder'd in the grave;
And chivalry has pass'd away,
  With knights so true and brave.

> The honour, which to them was life,
> Throbs in no bosom now ;
> It only gilds the gambler's strife,
> Or decks the worthless vow."

Enter LUCY.

SQUIRE. Lucy, dear Lucy.

LUCY. Let me entreat you not to stay here, sir! you will be exposed to nothing but insult and attack. Edmunds and my brother have both returned, irritated at something that has passed with my cousin Rose : — for my sake, — for my sake, Mr. Norton, spare me the pain of witnessing what will ensue, if they find you here. You little know what I have borne already.

SQUIRE. For your sake, Lucy, I would do much ; but why should I leave you to encounter the passion and ill-will, from which you would have me fly ?

LUCY. Oh, I can bear it, sir ; I deserve it but too well.

SQUIRE. Deserve it ! — you do yourself an injustice, Lucy. No ; rather let me remove you from a house where you will suffer nothing but persecution, and confer upon you a title which .the proudest lady in the land might wear. Here — here, on my knees. (*He bends on his knee, and seizes her hand.*)

Enter FLAM.

SQUIRE (*rising*). Flam here !

FLAM (*aside*). Upon my word ! — I thought we had been getting on pretty well in the open air, but they 're beating us hollow here, under cover.

SQUIRE. Lucy, but one word, and I understand your decision.

LUCY. I — I cannot subdue the feelings of uneasiness and distrust which the great difference between your honour's rank and mine awakens in my mind.

SQUIRE. Difference ! Hundreds of such cases happen every day.

LUCY. Indeed !

SQUIRE. Oh, 't is a matter of general notoriety, — is n't it, Flam ?

FLAM. No doubt of it. (*Aside.*) Don't exactly know yet what they are talking about, though.

SQUIRE. A relation of my own, a man of exalted rank, courted a girl far his inferior in station, but only beneath him in that respect. In all others she was on a footing of equality with himself, if not far above him.

LUCY. And were they married?

FLAM (*aside*). Rather an important circumstance in the case. I *do* remember that.

SQUIRE. They were, — after a time, when the resentment of his friends, occasioned by his forming such an attachment, had subsided, and he was able to acknowledge her, without involving the ruin of both.

LUCY. They were married privately at first, then?

FLAM (*aside*). I must put in a word here. Oh, yes, it was all comfortably arranged to everybody's satisfaction, — was n't it, Norton?

SQUIRE. Certainly. And a happy couple they were, were n't they, Flam?

FLAM. Happiest of the happy. As happy as (*aside*) — a separation could make them.

SQUIRE. Hundreds of great people have formed similar attachments, — have n't they, Flam?

FLAM. Undoubtedly. There was the Right Honourable Augustus Frederick Charles Thomson Camharado, and the German Baron Hyfenstyfenlooberhausen, and they were both married — (*aside*) to somebody else, first. Not to mention Damask and I, who are models of constancy. By the bye, I have lost sight of her, and I am interrupting you. (*Aside to* SQUIRE, *as he goes out.*) I came to tell you that she is ripe for an elopement, if you urge her strongly. Edmunds has been reproaching her to my knowledge. She 'll consent while her passion lasts.
[*Exit.*

SQUIRE. Lucy, I wait your answer. One word from you, and a few hours will place you far beyond the reach of those who would fetter your choice and control your inclinations. You hesitate. Come, decide. The Squire's lady, or the wife of Edmunds!

Duet. — LUCY *and* SQUIRE NORTON.

SQUIRE.

In rich and lofty station shine,
Before his jealous eyes:

In golden splendour, lady mine,
This peasant youth despise.

LUCY (*apart ; the* SQUIRE *regarding her attentively*).

Oh ! It would be revenge, indeed,
With scorn his glance to meet.
I, I, his humble pleading heed !
I 'd spurn him from my feet.

SQUIRE.

With love and rage her bosom 's torn,
And rash the choice will be ;

LUCY.

With love and rage my bosom 's torn,
And rash the choice will be.

SQUIRE.

From hence she quickly must be borne,
Her home, her home, she 'll flee.

LUCY.

Oh ! long shall I have cause to mourn
My home, my home, for thee !

Enter OLD BENSON.

BENSON. What do I see ! The Squire and Lucy.

SQUIRE. Listen. A chaise and four fleet horses, under the
direction of a trusty friend of mine, will be in waiting on the
highroad, at the corner of the Elm-Tree avenue, to-night, at
ten o'clock. They shall bear you whither we can be safe, and
in secret, by the first light of morning.

LUCY. His cruel harshness ; — it would be revenge, indeed.
But my father — my poor old father !

SQUIRE. Your father is prejudiced in Edmunds' favour ; and
so long as he thinks there is any chance of your being his, he
will oppose your holding communication with me. Situated as
you are now, you only stand in the way of his wealth and
advancement. Once fly with me, and in four-and-twenty hours
you will be his pride, his boast, his support.

OLD BENSON *coming forward.*

BENSON. It is a lie, a base lie! — (LUCY *shrieks, and throws herself at his feet*). My pride! my boast! She would be my disgrace, my shame; an outcast from her father's roof, and from the world. Support! — support *me* with the gold coined in her infamy and guilt! Heaven help me! Have I cherished her for this!

LUCY (*clinging to him*). Father! — dear, dear father!

SQUIRE. Hear me speak, Benson. Be calm.

BENSON. Calm! — Do you know that from infancy I have almost worshipped her, fancying that I saw in her young mind the virtues of a mother, to whom the anguish of this one hour would have been worse than death! Calm! — Do you know that I have a heart and soul within me; or do you believe that because I am of lower station I am a being of a different order from yourself, and that Nature has denied me thought and feeling! Calm! Man, do you know that I am this girl's father?

SQUIRE. Benson, if you will not hear me, at least do not, by hastily exposing this matter, deprive me of the inclination of making you some reparation.

BENSON. Reparation! You need be thankful, sir, for the grasp she has upon my arm. Money! If she were dying for want, and the smallest coin from you could restore her to life and health, sooner than she should take it from your hand, I would cast her from a sick bed to perish on the roadside.

SQUIRE. Benson, a word.

BENSON. Do not, I caution you; do not talk to me, sir. I am an old man, but I do not know what passion may make me do.

SQUIRE. These are high words, Benson. A farmer!

BENSON. Yes, sir; a farmer, — one of the men on whom you, and such as you, depend for the money they squander in profligacy and idleness. A farmer, sir! I care not for your long pedigree of ancestors, — my forefathers made them all. Here, neighbours, friends! (ROSE, MADDOX, STOKES, VILLAGERS, *etc., crowd on the stage.*) Hear this, hear this! your landlord, a high-born gentleman, entering the houses of your humble farmers, and tempting their daughters to destruction!

Enter YOUNG BENSON *and* GEORGE EDMUNDS.

YOUNG BENSON. What 's that I hear? (*Rushing towards the* SQUIRE, STOKES *interposes.*)

MARTIN. Hallo, hallo! Take hold of the other one, John. (MADDOX *and he remove them to opposite sides of the stage.*) Hold him tight, John, hold him tight. Stand still, there 's a good fellow. Keep back, Squire. Knew there 'd be something wrong, — ready to come in at the nick of time, — capital custom.

FLAM *enters and stands next the* SQUIRE.

SQUIRE. Exposed, baited! Benson, are you mad? Within the last few hours my friend here has been attacked and insulted on the very land you hold, by a person in your employ and young Edmunds there. I, too, have been threatened and insulted in the presence of my tenantry and workmen. Take care you do not drive me to extremities. Remember — the lease of this farm for seventy years, which your father took of mine, expires to-morrow; and that I have the power to refuse its renewal. Again I ask you, are you mad?

BENSON. Quit my house, villain!

SQUIRE. Villain! quit *my* house, then. This farm is mine, and you and yours shall depart from under its roof before the sun has set to-morrow. (BENSON *sinks into a chair in centre, and covers his face with his hands.*)

Sextette and Chorus.

LUCY — ROSE — EDMUNDS — SQUIRE NORTON — FLAM — YOUNG BENSON — *and Chorus.*

YOUNG BENSON.

Turn him from the farm! From his home will you cast
  The old man who has till'd it for years?
Every tree, every flower, is link'd with the past,
  And a friend of his childhood appears.

Turn *him* from the farm! O'er its grassy hillside,
  A gay boy he once loved to range;
His boyhood has fled, and its dear friends are dead,
  But these meadows have never known change.

EDMUNDS.

Oppressor, hear me.

LUCY.

On my knees I implore.

SQUIRE.

I command it, and you will obey.

ROSE.

Rise, dear Lucy, rise ; you shall not kneel before
The tyrant who drives us away.

SQUIRE.

Your sorrows are useless, your prayers are in vain;
I command it, and you will begone.
I 'll hear no more.

EDMUNDS.

No, they shall not beg again,
Of a man whom I view with deep scorn.

FLAM.

Do not yield.

YOUNG BENSON — SQUIRE — LUCY — ROSE.

Leave the farm !

EDMUNDS.

Your power I despise.

SQUIRE.

And your threats, boy, I disregard, too.

FLAM.

Do not yield.

YOUNG BENSON — SQUIRE — LUCY — ROSE.

Leave the farm !

ROSE.

If he leaves it, he dies.

EDMUNDS.

This base act, proud man, you shall rue.

YOUNG BENSON.

Turn him from the farm! From his home will you cast
The old man who has till'd it for years?
Every tree, every flower, is link'd with the past,
And a friend of his childhood appears!

SQUIRE.

Yes, yes, leave the farm! From his home I will cast
The old man who has till'd it for years;
Though each tree and flower is link'd with the past,
And a friend of his childhood appears.

Chorus.

He has turn'd from his farm, from his home he has cast,
The old man who has till'd it for years;
Though each tree and flower is link'd with the past,
And a friend of his childhood appears.

ACT II

SCENE I. — *An apartment in the Hall. A breakfast-table,
with urn and tea-service. A Livery Servant arranging
it. FLAM, in a morning gown and slippers, reclining on
the sofa.*

FLAM. Is the Squire out of bed yet?
SERVANT. Yes, sir, he will be down directly.
FLAM. Any letters from London?
SERVANT. One for your honour, that the man brought over
from the market-town, this morning.
FLAM. Give it me, blockhead! (*Servant gives it, and exit.*)
Never like the look of a great official-folded letter, with a large
seal; it's always an unpleasant one. Talk of discovering a
man's character from his handwriting! — I 'll back myself
against any odds to form a very close guess at the contents of a
letter from the form into which it is folded. This, now, I

should say, is a decidedly hostile fold. Let us see — " King's
Bench Walk — September 1st, 1729. Sir, I am instructed by
my client, Mr. Edward Montague, to apply to you — (the old
story — for the immediate payment, I suppose — what's this ?)
to apply to you for the instant restitution of the sum of two
hundred and fifty pounds, his son lost to you at play ; and to
acquaint you that unless it is immediately forwarded to my
office, as above, the circumstances of the transaction will be
made known ; and the unfair and fraudulent means by which
you deprived the young man of his money, publicly advertised.
— I am, sir, your obedient servant, John Ellis." The devil !
Who would believe, now, that such a trifling circumstance as
the mere insinuation of a small piece of gold into the corner of
two dice would influence a man's destiny ! What's to be done ?
If, by some dexterous stroke, I could manage to curry favour
with Norton, and procure some handsome present in return for
services rendered, — for " work and labour done and performed," as my obedient servant, John Ellis, would say, I
might keep my head above water yet. I have it ! He shall
have a joyful surprise. I'll carry this girl off for him,
and he shall know nothing of the enterprise until it is completed, or at least till she is fairly off. I have been well
rewarded for similar services before, and may securely calculate
on his gratitude in the present instance. He is here. (*Puts
up the letter.*)

Enter Squire Norton.

Squire (*seating himself at table*). Has any application for
permission to remain on the farm been made from Benson, this
morning, Flam ?

Flam. None.

Squire. I am very sorry for it, although I admire the old
man's independent spirit. I am very sorry for it. Wrong as
I know I have been, I would rather that the first concession
came from him.

Flam. Concession !

Squire. The more I reflect upon the occurrences of yesterday, Flam, the more I regret that, under the influence of
momentary passion and excitement, I should have used so
uncalled for a threat against my father's oldest tenant. It is
an act of baseness to which I look back with abhorrence.

FLAM (*aside*). What weathercock morality is this!

SQUIRE. It was unnecessary violence.

FLAM. Unnecessary! Oh, certainly; no doubt you could have attained your object without it, and can still. There is no occasion to punish the old man.

SQUIRE. Nor will I. He shall not leave the farm, if I myself implore and beg him to remain.

Enter SERVANT.

SERVANT. Two young women to speak with your honour.

Enter LUCY *and* ROSE.

SQUIRE. Lucy!

FLAM (*aside*). She must be carried off to-night, or she certainly will save me the trouble, and I shall lose the money.

LUCY. Your honour may be well surprised to see me here, after the events of yesterday. It has cost me no trifling struggle to take this step, but I hope my better feelings have at length prevailed, and conquered my pride and weakness. I wish to speak to your honour with nobody by.

FLAM (*aside*). Nobody by! I rather suspect I'm not particularly wanted here. (*To them.*) Pray allow us to retire for a few moments. Rose, my dear.

ROSE. Well!

FLAM. Come along.

LUCY. Rose will remain here. I brought her for that purpose.

FLAM. Bless me! that's very odd. As you please, of course, but I really think you'll find her very much in the way. (*Aside.*) Acting propriety! So much the better for my purpose; a little coyness will enhance the value of the prize.

[*Exit* FLAM.

LUCY. Mr. Norton, I come here to throw myself upon your honourable feelings as a man and as a gentleman. Oh, sir! now that my eyes are opened to the misery into which I have plunged myself, by my own ingratitude and treachery, do not — do not add to it the reflection that I have driven my father in his old age from the house where he was born, and in which he hoped to have died.

SQUIRE. Be calm, Lucy; your father shall continue to hold the farm; the lease shall be renewed.

LUCY. I have more to say to your honour still, and what I
have to add may even induce your honour to retract the promise you have just now made me.

SQUIRE. Lucy! what can you mean?

LUCY. Oh, sir! call me coquette, faithless, treacherous,
deceitful, what you will; I deserve it all; — but believe me, I
speak the truth when I make the humiliating avowal. A weak,
despicable vanity induced me to listen with a ready ear to your
honour's addresses, and to cast away the best and noblest
heart that ever woman won.

SQUIRE. Lucy, 't was but last night you told me that your
love for Edmunds had vanished into air; that you hated and
despised him.

LUCY. I know it, sir, too well. He laid bare my own guilt,
and showed me the ruin which impended over me. He spoke
the truth. Your honour more than confirmed him.

SQUIRE (*after a pause*). Even the avowal you have just
made, unexpected as it is, shall not disturb my resolution.
Your father shall not leave the farm.

Quartette.

LUCY — ROSE — SQUIRE NORTON — *and afterwards* YOUNG
BENSON.

SQUIRE.

Hear me, when I swear that the farm is your own
Through all changes Fortune may make;
The base charge of falsehood I never have known;
This promise I never will break.

ROSE *and* LUCY.

Hear him, when he swears that the farm is our own
Through all changes Fortune may make;
The base charge of falsehood he never has known;
This promise he never will break.

Enter YOUNG BENSON.

YOUNG BENSON.

My sister here! Lucy! begone, I command.

SQUIRE.

To your home I restore you again.

YOUNG BENSON.

No boon I 'll accept from that treacherous hand
As the price of my sister's fair fame.

SQUIRE.

To your home —

YOUNG BENSON (*to* LUCY).

Hence, away!

LUCY.

Brother, dear, I obey.

SQUIRE.

I restore.

YOUNG BENSON.

Hence, away!

YOUNG BENSON, ROSE, *and* LUCY.

Let us leave.

LUCY.

He swears it, dear brother.

SQUIRE.

I swear it.

YOUNG BENSON.

Away!

SQUIRE.

I swear it.

YOUNG BENSON.

You swear to deceive.

SQUIRE.

Hear me, when I swear that the farm is your own
Through all changes Fortune may make.

LUCY *and* ROSE.

Hear him, when he swears that the farm is our own
Through all changes Fortune may make.

YOUNG BENSON.

Hear him swear, hear him swear, that the farm is our own
Through all changes Fortune may make.

SQUIRE.

The base charge of falsehood I never have known,
This promise I never will break.

LUCY *and* ROSE.

The base charge of falsehood he never has known,
This promise he never will break.

YOUNG BENSON.

The base charge of falsehood he often has known,
This promise he surely will break.

[*Exeunt omnes.*

Reënter FLAM, *in a walking-dress.*

FLAM. The coast is clear at last. What on earth the conversation can have been, at which Rose *was* wanted, and I was not, I confess my inability to comprehend; but away with speculation, and now to business. (*Rings.*)

Enter SERVANT.

Pen and ink.

SERVANT. Yes, sir. [*Exit* SERVANT.

FLAM (*solus*). Nearly all the tenantry will be assembled here at the ball to-night; and if the father of this rustic dulcinea is reinstated in his farm, he and his people will no doubt be among the number. It will be easy enough to entice the girl into the garden, through the window opening on the lawn; a chaise can be waiting in the quiet lane at the side, and some trusty fellow can slip a hasty note into Norton's hands informing him of the flight, and naming the place at which he can join us. (*Reënter* SERVANT *with pen, ink, taper, and two sheets of note-paper; he places them on the table, and exit.*) I may as well reply to my friend Mr. John Ellis's obliging favour now, too, by promising that the money shall be forwarded in the course of three days' post. (*Takes the letter from his pocket, and lays it on the table.*) Lie you there. First, for Norton's note. — "Dear Norton, — Knowing your wishes — seized the girl — no blame attach to you. Join us as soon as people have dispersed in search of her in all directions but the right one, — fifteen miles off." (*Folds it ready for an envelope and lays it by the side of the other letter.*) Now for John Ellis. Why, what does the rascal mean by bringing but two sheets of paper? No matter: that affair will keep cool till to-morrow, when I have less business on my hands, and more money in my pockets, I hope. (*Crumples the letter he has just written, hastily up, thrusts it into his pocket, and folds the wrong one in the envelope. As he is sealing it,*

Enter MARTIN, *very cautiously.*

MARTIN (*peeping*). There he is, hatching some mysterious and diabolical plot. If I can only get to the bottom of these dreadful designs, I shall immortalise myself. What a lucky dog I am to be such a successful gleaner of news, and such a confidential person into the bargain, as to be the first to hear that he wanted some trustworthy person. All comes of talking to everybody I meet, and drawing out everything they hear. Capital custom! He don't see me. Hem! (*Coughs very loud, and, when* FLAM *looks round, nods familiarly.*) How are you again?

FLAM. How am I again? Who the devil are you? — and what do you want here?

MARTIN. Hush!

FLAM. Eh?

MARTIN. Hush! I'm the man.

FLAM. *The* man!

MARTIN. Yes, the man that you asked the ostler at the George to recommend you; the trustworthy man that knows all the bye-roads well, and can keep a secret; the man that you wanted to lend you a hand in a job that —

FLAM. Hush, hush!

MARTIN. Oh! you're beginning to hush now, are you?

FLAM. Have n't I seen your face before?

MARTIN. To be sure you have. You recollect admiring my manners at Benson's yesterday. You must remember Mr. Martin Stokes. You *can't* have forgotten him — not possible!

FLAM (*aside*). A friend of Benson! — a dangerous rencontre. Another moment, and our conversation might have taken an awkward turn. (*To him.*) So you are Stokes, eh? Benson's friend Stokes?

MARTIN. To be sure. Ha, ha! I knew you could n't have forgotten me. Pleasant Stokes, they call me, clever Stokes, sometimes; — but that 's flattery.

FLAM. No, surely.

MARTIN. Yes, 'pon my life! it is. Can't bear flattery, — don't like it at all.

FLAM. Well, Mr. Stokes —

MARTIN (*aside*). Now for the secret.

FLAM. I am very sorry you have had the trouble of coming up here, Mr. Stokes, because I have changed my plan, and shall not require your valuable services. (*Goes up to the table.*)

MARTIN (*aside*). Something wrong here: try him again. You 're sure you don't want me?

FLAM. Quite.

MARTIN. That 's unlucky, because, as I have quarrelled with Benson —

FLAM. Quarrelled with Benson!

MARTIN. What! did n't you know that?

FLAM. Never heard of it. Now I think of it, Mr. Stokes, I *shall* want your assistance. Pray sit down, Mr. Stokes.

MARTIN. With pleasure. (*They sit.*) I say, I *thought* you wanted me.

FLAM. Ah! you 're a sharp fellow.

MARTIN. You don't mean that?

FLAM. I do, indeed.

MARTIN (*aside*). You would if you knew all.

FLAM (*aside*). Conceited hound!

MARTIN (*aside*). Poor devil!

FLAM. Mr. Stokes, I need n't impress upon a gentleman of your intelligence the necessity of secrecy in this matter.

MARTIN. Of course not: see all — say nothing. Capital custom: — (*aside*) not mine, though. Go on.

FLAM. You would n't mind playing Benson a trick, — just a harmless trick ?

MARTIN. Certainly not. Go on.

FLAM. I 'll trust you.

MARTIN. So you may. Go on.

FLAM. A chaise and four will be waiting to-night, at ten o'clock precisely, at the little gate that opens from the garden into the lane.

MARTIN. No ; will it, though ? Go on.

FLAM. Don't interrupt me, Stokes. Into that chaise you must assist me in forcing as quickly as possible and without noise —

MARTIN. Yes. Go on.

FLAM. Whom do you think ?

MARTIN. Don't know.

FLAM. Can't you guess whom ?

MARTIN. No.

FLAM. Try.

MARTIN. Eh ! what ! — Miss —

FLAM. Hush, hush ! You understand me, I see. Not another word ; not another syllable.

MARTIN. But do you really mean to run away with —

FLAM (stopping his mouth). You understand me ; — that 's quite sufficient.

MARTIN (aside). He 's going to run away with Rose. Why, if I had n't found this out, John Maddox — one of my most particular friends — would have gone stark, staring, raving mad with grief. (To him.) But what will become of Miss Lucy, when she has lost Rose ?

FLAM. No matter. We cannot take them both, without the certainty of an immediate discovery. Meet me at the corner of the avenue, before the ball commences, and I will communicate any further instructions I may have to give you. Meanwhile take this (gives him money) as an earnest of what you shall receive when the girl is secured. Remember, silence and secrecy.

MARTIN. Silence and secrecy (exit FLAM), — confidence and two guineas. I am perfectly bewildered with this tremendous secret. What shall I do ? Where shall I go ? — To my particular friend, old Benson, or young Benson, or George Edmunds ? or — no ; I 'll go and paralyse my particular friend, John Maddox. Not a moment is to be lost. I am all in a flutter. Run away with Rose! I suppose he 'll run away with Lucy next. *I* should n't wonder. Run away with Rose! I never did — *[Exit hastily.*

SCENE II. — *An open spot in the Village.*

Enter SQUIRE NORTON.

SQUIRE. My mind is made up. This girl has opened her whole heart to me; and it would be worse than villainy to pursue her further. I will seek out Benson and Edmunds, and endeavour to repair the mischief my folly has occasioned. I have sought happiness in the dissipation, of crowded cities, in vain. A country life offers health and cheerfulness; and a country life shall henceforth be mine, in all seasons.

Song. — SQUIRE NORTON.

There 's a charm in Spring, when everything
　　Is bursting from the ground;
When pleasant showers bring forth the flowers,
　　And all is life around.

In summer day, the fragrant hay
　　Most sweetly scents the breeze;
And all is still, save murmuring rill,
　　Or sound of humming bees.

Old Autumn come, with trusty gun
　　In quest of birds we roam:
Unerring aim, we mark the game,
　　And proudly bear it home.

A winter's night has its delight,
　　Well warm'd to bed we go;
A winter's day, we 're blithe and gay,
　　Snipe-shooting in the snow.

A country life, without the strife
　　And noisy din of town,
Is all I need, I take no heed
　　Of splendour or renown.

And when I die, oh, let me lie
Where trees above me wave ;
Let wild plants bloom around my tomb,
My quiet country grave !   [*Exit.*

SCENE III. — *The Rick-yard.*   *Same as Act I., Scene I.*

EDMUNDS *and* MADDOX *meeting.*

JOHN. Ah, George ! Why this is kind to come down to
the old farm to-day, and take one peep at us before we leave it
for ever. I suppose it's fancy, now, George, but to my thinking I never saw the hedges look so fresh, the fields so rich, or
the old house so pretty and comfortable, as they do this morning. It's fancy, that, George, — ain't it ?

EDMUNDS. It's a place you may well be fond of, and
attached to, for it's the prettiest spot in all the country round.

JOHN. Ah ! you always enter into my feelings ; and speaking of that, I want to ask your advice about Rose. I meant to
come up to you to-day, on purpose. Do you think she is fond
of me, George ?

EDMUNDS (*smiling*). What do *you* think ? She has not
shown any desperate warmth of affection of late, has she ?

JOHN. No — no, she certainly has not, but she used to
once, and the girl has got a good heart after all ; and she came
crying to me, this morning, in the little paddock, and somehow
or other my heart melted towards her ; and — and — there's
something very pleasant about her manner, — is n't there,
George ?

EDMUNDS. No doubt of it, as other people besides ourselves
would appear to think.

JOHN. You mean Mr. Flam ? (*Edmunds nods assent.*)
Ah ! it's a bad business, altogether ; but still there are some
excuses to be made for a young country girl, who has never
seen a town gentleman before, and can't be expected to know
as well as you and I, George, what the real worth of one is.
However that may be, Rose came into the little paddock this
morning, as I was standing there, looking at the young colts,
and thinking of all our misfortunes ; and first of all she walked
by me, and then she stopped at a little distance, and then she
walked back, and stopped again ; and I heard her sobbing as if

her heart would burst; and then she came a little nearer, and at last she laid her hand upon my arm, and looked up in my face; and the tears started into my eyes, George, and I could n't bear it any longer, for I thought of the many pleasant days we had been happy together, and it hurt me to think that she should ever have done anything to make her afraid of me, or me unkind to her.

EDMUNDS. You're a good fellow, John, an excellent fellow. Take her; I believe her to have an excellent disposition, though it is a little disguised by girlish levity sometimes; — you may safely take her, — if she had far less good feeling than she actually possesses, she could never abuse your kind and affectionate nature.

JOHN. Is that your advice? Give me your hand, George (*they shake hands*), I will take her. You shall dance at our wedding, and I don't quite despair yet of dancing at yours, at the same time.

EDMUNDS. At mine! Where is the old man? I came here to offer him the little cottage in the village, which belongs to me. There is no tenant in it now : it has a pretty garden, of which I know he is fond, and it may serve his turn till he has had time to look about him.

JOHN. He is somewhere about the farm; walk with me across the yard, and perhaps we may meet him — this way.

[*Exeunt.*

Enter YOUNG BENSON.

YOUNG BENSON. The worst portion of the old man's hard trial is past. I have lingered with him in every field on the land, and wandered through every room in the old house. I can neither blame his grief, nor console him in his affliction, for the farm has been the happy scene of my birth and boyhood; and I feel, in looking on it for the last time, as if I were leaving the dearest friends of my youth, for ever.

Song. — YOUNG BENSON.

My fair home is no longer mine;
  From its roof-tree I'm driven away,
Alas! who will tend the old vine,
  Which I planted in infancy's day!

The garden, the beautiful flowers,
  The oak with its branches on high,
Dear friends of my happiest hours,
  Among ye, I long hoped to die.
The briar, the moss, and the bramble,
  Along the green paths will run wild:
The paths where I once used to ramble,
  An innocent, light-hearted child.

At the conclusion of the song enter to the symphony OLD
  BENSON, *with* LUCY *and* ROSE.

YOUNG BENSON (*advancing to meet him*). Come, father,
come!

OLD BENSON. I am ready, boy. We have but to walk a few
steps, and the pang of leaving is over. Come, Rose, bring on
that unhappy girl; come!

As they are going, enter the SQUIRE, *who meets them.*

SQUIRE. I am in time.

BENSON (*to* YOUNG BENSON, *who is advancing*). Harry,
stand back. Mr. Norton, if by this visit you intend to mock
the misery you have inflicted here, it is a heartless insult that
might have been spared.

SQUIRE. You do me an injustice, Benson. I come here not
to insult your grief, but to entreat, implore you, to remain. The
lease of this farm shall be renewed; I beseech you to remain here.

BENSON. It is not the quitting even the home of my infancy,
which most men love, that bows my spirit down to-day. Here,
in this old house, for near two hundred years, my ancestors
have lived and died, and left their names behind them free from
spot or blemish. I am the first to cross its threshold with the
brand of infamy upon me. Would to God I had been borne from
its porch a senseless corpse many weary years ago, so that I had
been spared this hard calamity! You have moved an old man's
weakness, but not with your revenge, sir. You implore me to
remain here. I spurn your offer. *Here!* A father yielding
to the destroyer of his child's good name and honour! Say no
more, sir. Let me pass.

Enter, behind, STOKES *and* EDMUNDS.

SQUIRE. Benson, you are guilty of the foulest injustice, not

to me, but to your daughter.　After her fearless confession to
me this morning of her love for Edmunds, and her abhorrence of
my professions, I honour her too much to injure her or you.

LUCY.　Dear father, it is true, indeed.　The noble behaviour
of his honour to me, this morning, I can never forget, or be too
grateful for.

BENSON.　Thank God! thank God!　I can look upon her
once again.　My child! my own child!　(*He embraces her with
great emotion.*)　I have done your honour wrong, and I hope
you 'll forgive me.　(*They shake hands.*)

MARTIN (*running forward*).　So have I! so have I!　I
have done his honour wrong, and I hope he 'll forgive me, too.
You don't leave the farm, then?　Hurrah!　(*A man carrying
a pail, some harness, etc., crosses the stage.*)　Hallo, young fellow! go back, go back! don't take another thing away, and
bring back all you have carried off; they are going to stop in
the farm.　Hallo! you fellows!　(*Calling off.*)　Leave the barn
alone, and put everything in its place.　They are going to stop
in the farm.　　　　　　　　　　　　　　　　[*Exit bawling.*

BENSON (*seeing* EDMUNDS).　What! George here, and turning away from his old friend, too, without a look of congratula-
tion or a shake of the hand, just at the time when, of all others,
he had the best right to expect it!　For shame, George, for
shame!

EDMUNDS.　My errand here is rendered useless.　By accident,
and not intentionally, I partly overheard just now the nature of
the avowal made by your daughter to Mr. Norton this morning.

BENSON.　You believe it, George.　You cannot doubt its
truth.

EDMUNDS.　I *do* believe it.　But I have been hurt, slighted,
set aside for another.　My honest love has been despised ; my
affection has been remembered, only to be tried almost beyond
endurance.　Lucy, all this from *you*, I freely forgive.　Be what
you have been once, and what you may so well become again.
Be the high-souled woman ; not the light and thoughtless
trifler that disgraces the name.　Let me see you this, and you
are mine again.　Let me see you what you have been of late,
and I never can be yours!

BENSON.　Lead her in, Rose.　Come, dear, come!　(*The
BENSONS and* ROSE *lead her slowly away.*)

EDMUNDS.　Mr. Norton, if this altered conduct be sincere, it

aeserves a much better return than my poor thanks can ever be
to you. If it be feigned, to save some purposes of your own,
the consequences will be upon your head.

SQUIRE. And I shall be prepared to meet them.

Duet. — SQUIRE NORTON *and* EDMUNDS.

SQUIRE.

Listen, though I do not fear you,
Listen to me, ere we part.

EDMUNDS.

List to *you !* Yes, I will hear you.

SQUIRE.

Yours alone is Lucy's heart,
I swear it, by that Heaven above me.

EDMUNDS.

What ! can I believe my ears !
Could I hope that she still loves me !

SQUIRE.

Banish all these doubts and fears :
If a love were e'er worth gaining,
 If love were ever fond and true,
No disguise or passion feigning,
 Such is her young love for you.
Listen, though I do not fear you,
 Listen to me ere we part.

EDMUNDS.

List to you ! yes, I will hear you,
Mine alone is her young heart.

[*Exeunt severally.*

SCENE IV. — *The avenue leading to the Hall, by moonlight.
The house in the distance, gaily illuminated.*

Enter FLAM *and* MARTIN.

FLAM. You have got the letter I gave you for the Squire ?

MARTIN. All right. Here it is.

FLAM. The moment you see me leave the room, slip it into the Squire's hand; you can easily do so, without being recognised, in the confusion of the dance, and then follow me. You perfectly understand your instructions?

MARTIN. Oh, yes; — I understand them well enough.

FLAM. There's nothing more, then, that you want to know?

MARTIN. No, nothing, — oh, yes, there is. I want to know whether — whether —

FLAM. Well, go on.

MARTIN. Whether you could conveniently manage to let me have another couple of guineas, before you go away in the chaise. Payment beforehand, — capital custom. And if you don't, perhaps I may not get them at all, you know : (*aside*) seeing that I don't intend to go at all, I think it's very likely.

FLAM. You're a remarkably pleasant fellow, Stokes, in general conversation, — very, — but when you descend into particularities, you become excessively prosy. On some points, — money matters, for instance, — you have a very grasping imagination, and seem disposed to dilate upon them at too great a length. You must cure yourself of this habit, — you must, indeed. Good-bye, Stokes; you shall have the two guineas doubled when the journey is completed. Remember, — ten o'clock. [*Exit* FLAM.

MARTIN. I shan't forget ten o'clock, depend upon it. Now to burst upon my particular friend, Mr. John Maddox, with the awful disclosure. He must pass this way on his road to the Hall. Here they come, — don't see him, though. (*Groups of male and female villagers in cloaks, etc., cross the stage on their way to the Hall.*)

MARTIN. How are you, Tom? How do, Will?

VILLAGERS. How do, Mas'r Stokes?

MARTIN (*shaking hands with them*). How do, Susan? Mind, Cary, you're my first partner. Always kiss your first partner, — capital custom. (*Kisses her.*) Good-bye! See you up at the Hall.

VILLAGERS. Ay, ay, Mas'r Stokes. [*Exeunt Villagers.*

MARTIN. Not among them. (*More villagers cross.*) Nor them. Here he comes : — Rose with him, too, — innocent little victim, little thinking of the atrocious designs that are going on against her!

Enter MADDOX *and* ROSE, *arm in arm.*

JOHN. Ha, ha, ha! that was a good 'un, — was n't it? Ah! Martin, I wish I'd seen you a minute ago. I made such a joke! How you would ha' laughed!

MARTIN (*mysteriously beckoning* MADDOX *away from* ROSE, *and whispering*). I want to speak to you.

JOHN (*whispering*). What about?

ROSE. Lor'! don't stand whispering there, John. If you have anything to say, Mr. Stokes, say it before me.

JOHN (*taking her arm*). Ah! say it before her! Don't mind her, Martin ; she's to be my wife, you know, and we're to be on the mutual-confidence principle; ain't we, — Rose?

ROSE. To be sure. Why don't you speak, Mr. Stokes? I suppose it's the old story, — something wrong.

MARTIN. Something wrong! I rather think there is; and you little know what it is, or you would n't look so merry. What I have got to say — don't be frightened, Miss Rose — relates to — don't alarm yourself, Master Maddox.

JOHN. I ain't alarming myself; you're alarming me. Go on!

ROSE. Go on! — can't you?

MARTIN. Relates to Mr. Flam.

JOHN (*dropping* ROSE'S *arm*). Mr. Flam!

MARTIN. Hush! — and Miss Rose.

ROSE. Me! Me and Mr. Flam!

MARTIN. Mr. Flam intends at ten o'clock, this very night, — don't be frightened, Miss, — by force, in secret, and in a chaise and four, too, — to carry off, against her will, and elope with, Miss Rose.

ROSE. Me! Oh! (*Screams, and falls into the arms of* MADDOX.)

JOHN. Rub her hands, Martin, she's going off in a fit.

MARTIN. Never mind; she'd better go off in a fit than a chaise.

ROSE (*recovering*). Oh, John! don't let me go.

JOHN. Let you go! — not if I set the whole Hall on fire.

ROSE. Hold me fast, John.

JOHN. I'll hold you fast enough, depend upon it.

ROSE. Come on the other side of me, Mr. Stokes; take my arm; hold me tight, Mr. Stokes.

MARTIN. Don't be frightened, I'll take care of you. (*Takes her arm.*)

ROSE. Oh! Mr. Stokes.

MARTIN. Oh, indeed! Nothing wrong, — eh?

ROSE. Oh! Mr. Stokes — pray forgive my having doubted that there was — Oh! what a dreadful thing! What is to be done with me?

MARTIN. Upon my word, I don't know. I think we had better shut her up in some place under ground — had n't we, John? — or, stay, — suppose we borrow the keys of the family vault, and lock her up there, for an hour or two.

JOHN. Capital!

ROSE. Lor'! surely you may find out some more agreeable place than that, John.

MARTIN. I have it. — I'm to carry her off.

BOTH. You!

MARTIN. Me, — don't be afraid of me: — all my management. You dance with her all the evening, and I'll keep close to you. If anybody tries to get her away, you knock him down, — and I'll help you.

JOHN. That's the plan; — come along.

ROSE. Oh, I am so frightened! Hold me fast, Mr. Stokes, — Don't let me go, John! [*Exeunt, talking.*

Enter LUCY.

LUCY. Light-hearted revellers! how I envy them! How painful is my situation, — obliged with a sad heart to attend a festivity, from which the only person I would care to meet will, I know, be absent. But I will not complain. He shall see that I can become worthy of him, once again. I have lingered here so long, watching the soft shades of evening as they closed around me, that I cannot bear the thought of exchanging this beautiful scene for the noise and glare of a crowded room.

Song. — LUCY.

How beautiful at even-tide
　　To see the twilight shadows pale,
Steal o'er the landscape, far and wide,
　　O'er stream and meadow, mound and dale.

How soft is Nature's calm repose
When evening skies their cool dews weep:
The gentlest wind more gently blows,
As if to soothe her in her sleep!

The gay morn breaks,
Mists roll away,
All Nature awakes
To glorious day.
In my breast alone
Dark shadows remain;
The peace it has known
It can never regain.

SCENE THE LAST. — *A spacious ball-room, brilliantly illuminated. A window at the end, through which is seen a
moonlit landscape. A large concourse of country people,
discovered. — The* SQUIRE *—* FLAM *— the* BENSONS *—*
LUCY *—* ROSE *—* MARTIN, *and* MADDOX.

SQUIRE. Welcome, friends, welcome all! Come, choose
your partners, and begin the dance.
FLAM (*to Lucy*). Your hand for the dance?
LUCY. Pray excuse me, sir; I am not well. My head is
oppressed and giddy. I would rather sit by the window which
looks into the garden, and feel the cool evening air. (*She goes
up. He follows her.*)
JOHN (*aside*). Stand by me, Martin. He's gone to order
the chaise, perhaps.
ROSE. Oh! pray don't let me be taken away, Mr. Stokes.
MARTIN. Don't be frightened, — don't be frightened. Mr.
Flam is gone. I'll give the Squire the note in a minute.
SQUIRE. Now, — begin the dance.

A Country Dance.

(MARTIN *and* MADDOX, *in their endeavours to keep close to*
ROSE, *occasion great confusion. As the* SQUIRE *is looking at some particular couple in the dance,* MARTIN
*steals behind him, thrusts the letter in his hands, and
resumes his place. The* SQUIRE *looks round as if to*

*discover the person who has delivered it; but being
unsuccessful, puts it up, and retires among the crowd of
dancers. Suddenly a violent scream is heard, and the
dance abruptly ceases. Great confusion.* MARTIN *and*
MADDOX *hold* ROSE *firmly.*)

SQUIRE. What has happened? Whence did that scream
proceed?

SEVERAL VOICES. From the garden! — from the garden!

EDMUNDS (*without*). Raise him, and bring him here. Lucy,
— dear Lucy!

BENSON. Lucy! My child! (*Runs up the stage, and
exit into garden.*)

MARTIN. *His* child! Damme! they can't get this one, so
they 're going to run away with the other. Here 's some mistake here. Let me go, Rose. Come along, John. Make
way there, — make way!

(*As they run towards the window,* EDMUNDS *appears at it,
without a hat, and his dress disordered, with* LUCY *in
his arms. He delivers her to her father and* ROSE.)

ROSE. Lucy, — dear Lucy, — look up!

BENSON. Is she hurt, George? — is the poor child injured?

EDMUNDS. No, it is nothing but terror; she will be better
instantly. See! she is recovering now. (*Lucy gradually re-
covers, as* FLAM, *his clothes torn, and face disfigured, is led
in by* MADDOX *and* MARTIN.)

BENSON. Mr. Norton, this is an act of perjury and baseness,
of which another instant would have witnessed the completion.

SQUIRE (*to* FLAM). Rascal! this is your deed.

FLAM (*aside to* NORTON). That 's right, Norton, keep it up.

SQUIRE. Do not address me with your odious familiarity,
scoundrel!

FLAM. You don't really mean to give me up?

SQUIRE. I renounce you from this instant.

FLAM. You do? — then take the consequences.

SQUIRE. Benson, — Edmunds, — friends, — I declare to you
most solemnly that I had neither hand nor part in this disgraceful outrage. It has been perpetrated without my knowledge, wholly by that scoundrel.

FLAM. 'T is false; it was done with his consent. He has

In his pocket, at this moment, a letter from me, acquainting him with my intention.

ALL. A letter!

SQUIRE. A letter *was* put into my hands five minutes since; but it acquainted me, not with this fellow's intention, but with his real dishonourable and disgraceful character, to which I had hitherto been a stranger. (*To* FLAM.) Do you know that handwriting, sir? (*Showing him the letter.*)

FLAM. Ellis's letter! (*Searching his pockets, and producing the other.*) I must, — ass that I was! — I did — inclose the wrong one.

SQUIRE. You will quit my house this instant; its roof shall not shelter you another night. Take that with you, sir, and begone. (*Throws him a purse.*)

FLAM (*taking it up*). Ah! I suppose you think this munificent, now — eh? I could have made twice as much of you in London, Norton, I could, indeed, to say nothing of my exhibiting myself for a whole week to these clods of earth, which would have been cheap, dirt-cheap, at double the money. Bye-bye, Norton! Farewell, grubs! [*Exit.*

SQUIRE. Edmunds, you have rescued your future wife from brutal violence; you will not leave her exposed to similar attempts in future?

EDMUNDS. Even if I would, I feel, now that I have preserved her, that I could not.

SQUIRE. Then take her, and with her the old farm, which from henceforth is your own. *You* will not turn the old man out, I suppose?

EDMUNDS (*shaking* BENSON *by the hand*). I don't think we are very likely to quarrel on that score; and most gratefully do we acknowledge your honour's kindness. Maddox!

JOHN. Hallo!

EDMUNDS. I shall not want that cottage and garden we were speaking of, this morning, now. Let me imitate a good example, and bestow it on *your* wife, as *her* marriage portion.

ROSE. Oh, delightful! Say certainly, John, — can't you?

JOHN. Thankee, George, thankee! I say, Martin, I have arrived at the dignity of a cottage and a piece of ground, at last.

MARTIN. Yes, you may henceforth consider yourself on a level with me.

SQUIRE. Resume the dance.

MARTIN. I beg your pardon. One word. (*Whispers the* SQUIRE.)

SQUIRE. I hope not. Recollect, you have been mistaken before, to-day. You had better inquire.

MARTIN. I will. (*To the audience.*) My very particular friend, if he will allow me to call him so, —

SQUIRE. Oh, certainly.

MARTIN. My very particular friend, Mr. Norton, wishes me to ask my other particular friends here, whether there's — anything wrong? We are delighted to hear your approving opinion in the old way. You *can't* do better. It's a capital custom.

Dance and Finale. — Chorus.

Join the dance, with step as light
As every heart should be to-night;
Music, shake the lofty dome,
In honour of our Harvest Home.

Join the dance, and banish care,
All are young, and gay, and fair;
Even age has youthful grown,
In honour of our Harvest Home.

Join the dance, bright faces beam,
Sweet lips smile, and dark eyes gleam;
All these charms have hither come,
In honour of our Harvest Home.

Join the dance, with step as light,
As every heart should be to-night;
Music, shake the lofty dome,
In honour of our Harvest Home.

Quintet.

LUCY — ROSE — EDMUNDS — THE SQUIRE — YOUNG BENSON.

No light bound
Of stag or timid hare,

O'er the ground
Where startled herds repair,
Do we prize
So high, or hold so dear,
As the eyes
That light our pleasures here.
No cool breeze
That gently plays by night,
O'er calm seas,
Whose waters glisten bright;
No soft moan
That sighs across the lea,
Harvest Home,
Is half so sweet as thee!

Chorus.

Hail to the merry autumn days, when yellow cornfields shine,
Far brighter than the costly cup that holds the monarch's
    wine !
Hail to the merry harvest-time, the gayest of the year,
The time of rich and bounteous crops, rejoicing, and good cheer
                  Hail! Hail! Hail!

IS SHE HIS WIFE?

OR, SOMETHING SINGULAR!

SCENE I. — *A Room opening into a Garden. A Table laid for Breakfast ; Chairs, etc.* MR. *and* MRS. LOVETOWN, *discovered at Breakfast. The former in a dressing-gown and slippers, reading a newspaper. A Screen on one side.*

LOVETOWN (*yawning*). Another cup of tea, my dear, — O Lord !

MRS. LOVETOWN. I wish, Alfred, you would endeavour to assume a more cheerful appearance in your wife's society. If you are perpetually yawning and complaining of *ennui* a few months after marriage, what am I to suppose you 'll become in a few years ? It really is very odd of you.

LOVETOWN. Not at all odd, my dear, not the least in the world ; it would be a great deal more odd if I were not. The fact is, my love, I 'm tired of the country ; green fields, and blooming hedges, and feathered songsters are fine things to talk about and read about and write about ; but I candidly confess that I prefer paved streets, area railings, and dustman's bells, after all.

MRS. LOVETOWN. How often have you told me that, blessed with my love, you could live contented and happy in a desert.

LOVETOWN (*reading*). " Artful impostor ! "

MRS. LOVETOWN. Have you not over and over again said that fortune and personal attractions were secondary considerations with you ? That you loved me for those virtues which, while they gave additional lustre to public life, would adorn and sweeten retirement ?

LOVETOWN (*reading*). " Soothing syrup ! "

MRS. LOVETOWN. You complain of the tedious sameness of a country life. Was it not you yourself who first proposed our residing permanently in the country ? Did you not say that I should then have an ample sphere in which to exercise those charitable feelings which I have so often evinced, by selling at those benevolent fancy fairs ?

LOVETOWN (*reading.*) " Humane man-traps ! "

MRS. LOVETOWN. He pays no attention to me, — Alfred dear, —

LOVETOWN (*stamping his foot*). Yes, my life.

MRS. LOVETOWN. Have you heard what I have just been saying, dear ?

LOVETOWN. Yes, love.

MRS. LOVETOWN. And what can you say in reply ?

LOVETOWN. Why, really, my dear, you 've said it so often before in the course of the last six weeks that I think it quite unnecessary to say anything more about it. (*Reads.*) " The learned judge delivered a brief but impressive summary of the unhappy man's trial."

MRS. LOVETOWN (*aside*). I could bear anything but this neglect. He evidently does not care for me.

LOVETOWN (*aside*). I could put up with anything rather than these constant altercations and little petty quarrels. I repeat, my dear, that I am very dull in this out of the way villa, — confoundedly dull, — horridly dull.

MRS. LOVETOWN. And *I* repeat that if you took any pleasure in your wife's society, or felt for her as you once professed to feel, you would have no cause to make such a complaint.

LOVETOWN. If I did not know you to be one of the sweetest creatures in existence, my dear, I should be strongly disposed to say that you were a very close imitation of an aggravating female.

MRS. LOVETOWN. That 's very curious, my dear, for I declare that, if I had n't known *you* to be such an exquisite, good-tempered, attentive husband, I should have mistaken you for a very great brute.

LOVETOWN. My dear, you 're offensive.

MRS. LOVETOWN. My love, you 're intolerable. (*They turn their chairs back to back.*)

MR. FELIX TAPKINS *sings without.*

The wife around her husband throws
    Her arms to make him stay ;

"My dear, it rains, it hails, it blows,
　　And you cannot hunt to-day."
　　But a hunting we will go,
　　And a hunting we will go, — wo — wo — wo !
　　And a hunting we will go.

MRS. LOVETOWN. There 's that dear, good-natured creature,
Mr. Tapkins, — do you ever hear *him* complain of the tedious-
ness of a country life ?　Light-hearted creature, — his lively
disposition and rich flow of spirits are wonderful, even to me.
(*Rising.*)

LOVETOWN. They need not be a matter of astonishment to
anybody, my dear, — he 's a bachelor.

MR. FELIX TAPKINS *appears at window.*

TAPKINS. Ha, ha !　How are you both ? — Here 's a morning !　Bless my heart alive, *what* a morning !　I 've been
gardening ever since five o'clock, and the flowers have been
actually growing before my very eyes.　The London Pride is
sweeping everything before it, and the stalks are half as high
again as they were yesterday.　They 're all run up like so
many tailors' bills, after that heavy dew of last night broke
down half my rosebuds with the weight of its own moisture, —
something like a dew, that ! — reg'lar *doo,* eh ? — come, that 's
not so bad for a before-dinner one.

LOVETOWN. Ah, you happy dog, Felix !

TAPKINS. Happy !　of course I am, — Felix by name, Felix
by nature, — what the deuce should I be unhappy for, or anybody be unhappy for ?　What 's the use of it, that 's the point.

MRS. LOVETOWN. Have you finished your improvements
yet, Mr. Tapkins ?

TAPKINS. At Rustic Lodge ?　(*She nods assent.*)　Bless
your heart and soul !　you never saw such a place, — cardboard
chimneys, Grecian balconies, — Gothic parapets, thatched roof.

MRS. LOVETOWN. Indeed !

TAPKINS. Lord bless you, yes, — green verandah, with ivy
twining round the pillars.

MRS. LOVETOWN. How very rural !

TAPKINS. Rural, my dear Mrs. Lovetown !　delightful !　The
French windows, too !　Such an improvement !

MRS. LOVETOWN. I should think they were !

TAPKINS. Yes, *I* should think they were. Why, on a fine summer's evening the frogs hop off the grass-plot into the very sitting-room.

MRS. LOVETOWN. Dear me!

TAPKINS. Bless you, yes! Something like the country, — quite a little Eden. Why, when I'm smoking under the verandah, after a shower of rain, the black beetles fall into my brandy and water.

MR. *and* MRS. LOVETOWN. No! Ha, ha, ha!

TAPKINS. Yes. And I take 'em out again with the teaspoon, and lay bets with myself which of them will run away the quickest. Ha, ha, ha! (*They all laugh.*) Then the stable, too. Why, in Rustic Lodge the stables are close to the dining-room window.

LOVETOWN. No!

TAPKINS. Yes. The horse can't cough but I hear him. There's compactness. Nothing like the cottage style of architecture for comfort, my boy. By the bye, I have left the new horse at your garden gate this moment.

MRS. LOVETOWN. The new horse!

TAPKINS. The new horse! Splendid fellow, — such action! Puts out its feet like a rocking-horse, and carries its tail like a hat-peg. Come and see him.

LOVETOWN (*laughing*). I can't deny you anything.

TAPKINS. No, that's what they all say, especially the — eh? (*Nodding and winking.*)

LOVETOWN. Ha, ha, ha!

MRS. LOVETOWN. Ha, ha, ha! I'm afraid you're a very bad man, Mr. Tapkins; I'm afraid you're a shocking man, Mr. Tapkins.

TAPKINS. Think so? No, I don't know, — not worse than other people similarly situated. Bachelors, my dear Mrs. Lovetown, bachelors — eh! old fellow? (*Winking to* LOVETOWN.)

LOVETOWN. Certainly, certainly.

TAPKINS. *We* know — eh? (*They all laugh.*) By the bye, talking of bachelors puts me in mind of Rustic Lodge, and talking of Rustic Lodge puts me in mind of what I came here for. You must come and see me this afternoon. Little Peter Limbury and his wife are coming.

MRS. LOVETOWN. I detest that man.

LOVETOWN. The wife is supportable, my dear.

TAPKINS. To be sure, so she is. You 'll come, and that 's enough. Now come and see the horse.

LOVETOWN. Give me three minutes to put on my coat and boots, and I 'll join you. I won't be three minutes.

[*Exit* LOVETOWN.

TAPKINS. Look sharp, look sharp! — Mrs. Lovetown, will you excuse me one moment? Jim, — these fellows never know how to manage horses, — walk him gently up and down, — throw the stirrups over the saddle to show the people that his master 's coming, and if anybody asks what that fine animal's pedigree is, and who he belongs to, say he 's the property of Mr. Felix Tapkins of Rustic Lodge, near Reading, and that he 's the celebrated horse who ought to have won the New-market Cup last year, only he did n't. [*Exit* TAPKINS.

MRS. LOVETOWN. My mind is made up, — I can bear Alfred's coldness and insensibility no longer, and come what may I will endeavour to remove it. From the knowledge I have of his disposition I am convinced that the only mode of doing so will be by rousing his jealousy and wounding his vanity. This thoughtless creature will be a very good instrument for my scheme. He plumes himself on his gallantry, has no very small share of vanity, and is easily led. I see him crossing the garden. (*She brings a chair hastily forward.*)

Enter FELIX TAPKINS.

TAPKINS (*singing*).

" My dear, it rains, it hails, it blows, — "

MRS. LOVETOWN (*tragically*). Would that I had never beheld him!

TAPKINS (*aside*). Hallo! She 's talking about her husband. I knew by their manner there had been a quarrel, when I came in this morning.

MRS. LOVETOWN. So fascinating, and yet so insensible to the tenderest of passions as not to see how devotedly I love him.

TAPKINS (*aside*). I thought so.

MRS. LOVETOWN. That he should still remain unmarried is to me extraordinary.

TAPKINS. Um!

MRS. LOVETOWN. He ought to have married long since.

TAPKINS (*aside*). Eh! Why, they are n't married! — "ought to have married long since." — I rather think he ought.

MRS. LOVETOWN. And though I am the wife of another, —

TAPKINS (*aside*). Wife of another!

MRS. LOVETOWN. Still, 1 grieve to say that I cannot be blind to his extraordinary merits.

TAPKINS. Why, he 's run away with somebody else's wife! The villain! — I must let her know I 'm in the room, or there 's no telling what I may hear next. (*Coughs.*)

MRS. LOVETOWN (*starting up in affected confusion*). Mr. Tapkins! (*They sit.*) Bring your chair nearer. I fear, Mr. Tapkins, that I have been unconsciously giving utterance to what was passing in my mind. I trust you have not overheard my confession of the weakness of my heart.

TAPKINS. No — no — not more than a word or two.

MRS. LOVETOWN. That agitated manner convinces me that you have heard more than you are willing to confess. Then why — why should I seek to conceal from you — that, though I esteem my husband, I — I — love — another?

TAPKINS. I heard you mention that little circumstance.

MRS. LOVETOWN. Oh! (*Sighs.*)

TAPKINS (*aside*). What the deuce is she Oh-ing at? She looks at me as if I were Lovetown himself.

MRS. LOVETOWN (*putting her hand on his shoulder with a languishing air*). Does my selection meet with your approbation?

TAPKINS (*slowly*). It does n't.

MRS. LOVETOWN. No!

TAPKINS. Decidedly not. (*Aside.*) I 'll cut that Lovetown out, and offer myself. Hem! Mrs. Lovetown.

MRS. LOVETOWN. Yes, Mr. Tapkins.

TAPKINS. I know an individual —

MRS. LOVETOWN. Ah! an individual!

TAPKINS. An individual, — I may, perhaps, venture to say an estimable individual, — who for the last three months has been constantly in your society, who never yet had courage to disclose his passion, but who burns to throw himself at your feet. Oh! (*Aside.*) I 'll try an Oh or two now, — Oh! (*Sighs.*) That 's a capital Oh!

MRS. LOVETOWN (*aside*). He must have misunderstood me

before, for he is evidently speaking of himself. Is the gentle‑
man you speak of handsome, Mr. Tapkins?

TAPKINS. He is generally considered remarkably so.

MRS. LOVETOWN. Is he tall?

TAPKINS. About the height of the Apollo Belvidere.

MRS. LOVETOWN. Is he stout?

TAPKINS. Of nearly the same dimensions as the gentleman
I have just named.

MRS. LOVETOWN. His figure is —

TAPKINS. Quite a model.

MRS. LOVETOWN. And he is —

TAPKINS. Myself. (*Throws himself on his knees and
seizes her hand.*)

Enter LOVETOWN.

(TAPKINS *immediately pretends to be diligently looking for
something on the floor.*)

MRS. LOVETOWN. Pray don't trouble yourself. I'll find it.
Dear me! how could I lose it?

LOVETOWN. What have you lost, love? I should almost
imagine that you had lost yourself, and that our friend Mr.
Tapkins here had just found you.

TAPKINS (*aside*) Ah! you always will have your joke, —
funny dog! funny dog! Bless my heart and soul, there's that
immortal horse standing outside all this time! He'll catch his
death of cold! Come and see him at once, — come — come.

LOVETOWN. No. I can't see him to-day. I had forgotten.
I've letters to write, — business to transact, — I'm engaged.

TAPKINS (*to* MRS. LOVETOWN). Oh! if he's engaged, you
know, we'd better not interrupt him.

MRS. LOVETOWN. Oh! certainly! Not by any means.

TAPKINS (*taking her arm*). Good-bye, old fellow.

LOVETOWN (*seating himself at table*). Oh! — good-bye.

TAPKINS (*going*). Take care of yourself. I'll take care of
Mrs. L. [*Exeunt* TAPKINS *and* MRS. LOVETOWN.

LOVETOWN. What the deuce does that fellow mean by lay‑
ing such emphasis on Mrs. L.? What's my wife to him, or
he to my wife? Very extraordinary! I can hardly believe
that, even if he had the treachery to make any advances, she
would encourage such a preposterous intrigue. (*Walks to and
fro.*) She spoke in his praise at breakfast-time, though, — and

they have gone away together to see that confounded horse. But stop, I must keep a sharp eye upon them this afternoon, without appearing to do so. I would not appear unnecessarily suspicious for the world. Dissembling in such a case, though, is difficult — very difficult.

Enter a SERVANT.

SERVANT. Mr. and Mrs. Peter Limbury.

LOVETOWN. Desire them to walk in. [*Exit* SERVANT. A lucky visit! it furnishes me with a hint. This Mrs. Limbury is a vain, conceited woman, ready to receive the attentions of anybody who feigns admiration for her, partly to gratify herself, and partly to annoy the jealous little husband whom she keeps under such strict control. If I pay particular attention to *her*, I shall lull my wife and that scoundrel Tapkins into a false security, and have better opportunities of observation. They are here.

Enter MR. *and* MRS. LIMBURY.

LOVETOWN. My dear Mrs. Limbury.

LIMBURY. Eh ?

LOVETOWN (*not regarding him*). How charming — how delightful — how divine you look to-day.

LIMBURY (*aside*). Dear Mrs. Limbury, — charming, — divine and beautiful look to-day ! They are smiling at each other, — he squeezes her hand. I see how it is. I always thought he paid her too much attention.

LOVETOWN. Sit down, — sit down.

(LOVETOWN *places the chairs so as to sit between them, which* LIMBURY *in vain endeavours to prevent.*)

MRS. LIMBURY. Peter and I called, as we passed in our little pony-chaise, to inquire whether we should have the pleasure of seeing you at Tapkins's this afternoon.

LOVETOWN. Is it possible you can ask such a question ? Do you think I could stay away ?

MRS. LIMBURY. Dear Mr. Lovetown ! (*Aside.*) How polite, — he 's quite struck with me.

LIMBURY (*aside*). Wretched miscreant ! a regular assignation before my very face.

LOVETOWN (*to* MRS. LIMBURY). Do you know I entertained

some apprehensions — some dreadful fears — that you might not be there.

LIMBURY. Fears that we might n't be there? Of course we shall be there.

MRS. LIMBURY. Now don't talk, Peter.

LOVETOWN. I thought it just possible, you know, that you might not be agreeable —

MRS. LIMBURY. Oh, Peter is always agreeable to anything that is agreeable to me. Are n't you, Peter?

LIMBURY. Yes, dearest. (*Aside.*) Agreeable to anything that 's agreeable to her! O Lor'!

MRS. LIMBURY. By the bye, Mr. Lovetown, how do you like this bonnet?

LOVETOWN. Oh, beautiful!

LIMBURY (*aside*). I must change the subject. Do you know, Mr. Lovetown, I have often thought, and it has frequently occurred to me — when —

MRS. LIMBURY. Now don't talk, Peter. (*To* LOVETOWN.) The colour is so bright, is it not?

LOVETOWN. It might appear so elsewhere, but the brightness of those eyes casts it quite into shade.

MRS. LIMBURY. I know you are a connoisseur in ladies' dresses; how do you like those shoes?

LIMBURY (*aside*). Her shoes! What will she ask his opinion of next?

LOVETOWN. Oh, like the bonnet, you deprive them of their fair chance of admiration. That small and elegant foot engrosses all the attention which the shoes might otherwise attract. That taper ankle, too —

LIMBURY (*aside*). Her taper ankle! My bosom swells with the rage of an ogre. Mr. Lovetown, — I —

MRS. LIMBURY. Now, pray do not talk so, Limbury. You 've put Mr. Lovetown out as it is.

LIMBURY (*aside*). Put him out! I wish I could put him out, Mrs. Limbury. I must.

Enter SERVANT, *hastily.*

SERVANT. I beg your pardon, sir, but the bay pony has got his hind leg over the traces, and he 's kicking the chaise to pieces!

LIMBURY. Kicking the *new* chaise to pieces!

LOVETOWN. Kicking the new chaise to pieces! The bay pony! Limbury, my dear fellow, fly to the spot! (*Pushing him out.*)

LIMBURY. But, Mr. Lovetown, I —

MRS. LIMBURY. Oh! he'll kick, somebody's brains out, if Peter don't go to him.

LIMBURY. But perhaps he'll kick my brains out if I do go to him.

LOVETOWN. Never mind, don't lose an instant, — not a moment. (*Pushes him out, both talking together.*)

[*Exit* LIMBURY.

(*Aside.*) Now for it, — here's my wife. Dearest Mrs. Limbury — (*Kneels by her chair, and seizes her hand.*)

Enter MRS. LOVETOWN.

MRS. LOVETOWN (*aside*). Can I believe my eyes? (*Retires behind the screen.*)

MRS. LIMBURY. Mr. Lovetown!

LOVETOWN. Nay. Allow me in one hurried interview, which I have sought for in vain for weeks, — for months, — to say how devotedly, how ardently I love you. Suffer me to retain this hand in mine. Give me one ray of hope.

MRS. LIMBURY. Rise, I entreat you, — we shall be discovered.

LOVETOWN. Nay, I will not rise till you promise me that you will take an opportunity of detaching yourself from the rest of the company and meeting me alone in Tapkins's grounds this evening. I shall have no eyes, no ears for any one but yourself.

MRS. LIMBURY. Well, — well, — I will — I do —

LOVETOWN. Then I am blest, indeed!

MRS. LIMBURY. I am so agitated. If Peter or Mrs. Lovetown — were to find me thus — I should betray all. I'll teach my husband to be jealous! Let us walk round the garden.

LOVETOWN. With pleasure, — take my arm. Divine creature! (*Aside.*) I'm sure she is behind the screen. I saw her peeping. Come. [*Exit* LOVETOWN *and* MRS. LIMBURY.

MRS. LOVETOWN (*coming forward*). Faithless man! His coldness and neglect are now too well explained. O Alfred! Alfred! how little did I think when I married you, six short months since, that I should be exposed to so much wretched-ness! I begin to tremble at my own imprudence, and the situation in which it may place me ; but it is now too late to recede. I must be firm. This day will either bring my project to the explanation I so much desire, or convince me of what I too much fear, — my husband's aversion. Can this woman's husband suspect their intimacy ? If so, he may be able to prevent this assignation taking place. I will seek him instantly. If I can but meet him at once, he may prevent her going at all. [*Exit* MRS. LOVETOWN.

Enter TAPKINS.

TAPKINS. This, certainly, is a most extraordinary affair. Not her partiality for me, — that's natural enough, — but the confession I overheard about her marriage to another. I have been thinking that, after such a discovery, it would be highly improper to allow Limbury and his wife to meet her without warning him of the fact. The best way will be to make him acquainted with the real state of the case. Then he must see the propriety of not bringing his wife to my house to-night. Ah ! here he is. I'll make the awful disclosure at once, and petrify him.

Enter LIMBURY.

LIMBURY. That damned little bay pony is as bad as my wife. There's no curbing either of them ; and as soon as I have got the traces of the one all right, I lose all traces of the other.

TAPKINS. Peter !

LIMBURY. Ah ! Tapkins !

TAPKINS. Hush ! Hush ! (*Looking cautiously round.*) If you have a moment to spare, I've got something of great importance to communicate.

LIMBURY. Something of great importance, Mr. Tapkins! (*Aside.*) What can he mean ? Can it relate to Mrs. Limbury ? The thought is dreadful. You horrify me !

TAPKINS. You'll be more horrified presently. What I am about to tell you concerns yourself and your honour very materially ; and I beg you to understand that I communicate it — in the strictest confidence.

LIMBURY. Myself and my honour ! I shall dissolve into nothing with horrible anticipations !

TAPKINS (*in a low tone*). Have you ever observed anything remarkable about Lovetown's manner ?

LIMBURY. Anything remarkable?

TAPKINS. Ay, — anything very odd, and rather unpleasant?

LIMBURY. Decidedly! No longer than half an hour ago, — in this very room, I observed something in his manner particularly odd and exceedingly unpleasant.

TAPKINS. To your feelings as a husband?

LIMBURY. Yes, my friend, yes, yes; — you know it all, I see!

TAPKINS. What! Do *you* know it?

LIMBURY. I 'm afraid I do; but go on — go on.

TAPKINS (*aside*). How the deuce can he know anything about it? Well, this oddness arises from the peculiar nature of his connection with — You look very pale.

LIMBURY. No, no, — go on, — " connection with — "

TAPKINS. A certain lady, — you know whom I mean.

LIMBURY. I do, I do! (*Aside.*) Disgrace and confusion! I 'll kill her with a look! I 'll wither her with scornful indignation! Mrs. Limbury! — viper!

TAPKINS (*whispering with caution.*) They — are n't — married.

LIMBURY. *They* are n't married! *Who* are n't?

TAPKINS. Those two, to be sure!

LIMBURY. *Those* two! *What* two?

TAPKINS. Why, them. And the worst of it is she 's — she 's married to somebody else.

LIMBURY. Well, of course I know that.

TAPKINS. You know it?

LIMBURY. Of course I do. Why, how you talk! Is n't she my wife?

TAPKINS. *Your* wife! Wretched bigamist! Mrs. Lovetown your wife?

LIMBURY. Mrs. Lovetown! What! Have you been talking of Mrs. Lovetown all this time? My dear friend! (*Embraces him.*) The revulsion of feeling is almost insupportable. I thought you were talking about Mrs. Limbury.

TAPKINS. No!

LIMBURY. Yes. Ha, ha! But I say, what a dreadful fellow this is — another man's wife! Gad, I think he wants to run away with every man's wife he sees. And Mrs. Lovetown, too, — horrid!

TAPKINS. Shocking!

LIMBURY. I say, I ought n't to allow Mrs. Limbury to associate with her, ought I?

TAPKINS. Precisely my idea. You had better induce your wife to stay away from my house to-night.

LIMBURY. I 'm afraid I can't do that.

TAPKINS. What, has she any particular objection to staying away?

LIMBURY. She has a very strange inclination to go, and 't is much the same; however, I 'll make the best arrangement I can!

TAPKINS. Well, so be it. Of course I shall see *you?*

LIMBURY. Of course.

TAPKINS. Mind the secret, — close — close — you know, as a Cabinet minister answering a question.

LIMBURY. You may rely upon me.

[*Exit* LIMBURY *and* TAPKINS.

SCENE II. — *A Conservatory on one side. A Summer-House on the other.*

Enter LOVETOWN.

LOVETOWN. So far, so good. My wife has not dropped the slightest hint of having overheard the conversation between me and Mrs. Limbury; but she cannot conceal the impression it has made upon her mind, or the jealousy it has evidently excited in her breast. This is just as I wished. I made Mr. Peter Limbury's amiable helpmate promise to meet me here. I know that refuge for destitute reptiles (*pointing to summer-house*) is Tapkins's favourite haunt, and if he has any assignation with my wife, I have no doubt he will lead her to this place. A woman 's coming down the walk. Mrs. Limbury, I suppose, — no, my wife, by all that 's actionable. I must conceal myself here, even at the risk of a shower of black beetles, or a marching regiment of frogs. (*Goes into conservatory.*)

Enter MRS. LOVETOWN.

MRS. LOVETOWN. I cannot have been mistaken. I am certain I saw Alfred here; he must have secreted himself somewhere to avoid me. Can his assignation with Mrs. Limbury have been discovered? Mr. Limbury's behaviour to me just now was strange in the extreme ; and after a variety of incoherent expressions he begged me to meet him here, on a subject, as he said, of great delicacy and importance to myself. Alas! I fear that my husband's neglect and unkindness are but too well known. The injured little man approaches. I summon all my fortitude to bear the disclosure.

Enter Mr. Limbury.

Limbury (*aside*). Now as I could not prevail on Mrs. Limbury to stay away, the only distressing alternative I have is to inform Mrs. Lovetown that I know her history, and to put it to her good feeling whether she had n't better go.

Lovetown (*peeping*). Limbury! what the deuce can that little wretch want here ?

Limbury. I took the liberty, Mrs. Lovetown, of begging you to meet me in this retired spot, because the esteem I still entertain for you, and my regard for your feelings, induce me to prefer a private to a public disclosure.

Lovetown (*peeping*). "Public disclosure!" what on earth is he talking about ? I wish he 'd speak a little louder.

Mrs. Lovetown. I am sensible of your kindness, Mr. Limbury, and, believe me, most grateful for it. I am fully prepared to hear what you have to say.

Limbury. It is hardly necessary for me, I presume, to say, Mrs. Lovetown, that I have accidentally discovered the whole secret.

Mrs. Lovetown. The whole secret, sir ?

Lovetown (*peeping*). Whole secret! What secret ?

Limbury. The whole secret, ma'am, of this disgraceful — I must call it disgraceful — and most abominable intrigue.

Mrs. Lovetown (*aside*). My worst fears are realized, — my husband's neglect is occasioned by his love for another.

Lovetown (*peeping*). Abominable intrigue! My first suspicions are too well founded. He reproaches my wife with her infidelity, and she cannot deny it, — that villain Tapkins !

Mrs. Lovetown (*weeping*). Cruel — cruel — Alfred !

Limbury. You may well call him cruel, unfortunate woman. His usage of you is indefensible, unmanly, scandalous.

Mrs. Lovetown. It is. It is, indeed.

LIMBURY. It's very painful for me to express myself in such plain terms, Mrs. Lovetown; but allow me to say, as delicately as possible, that you should not endeavour to appear in society under such unusual and distressing circumstances.

MRS. LOVETOWN. Not appear in society! Why should I quit it?

LOVETOWN (*peeping*). Shameful woman!

LIMBURY. Is it possible you can ask such a question?

MRS. LOVETOWN. What should I do? Where can I go?

LIMBURY. Gain permission to return once again to your husband's roof.

MRS. LOVETOWN. My husband's roof?

LIMBURY. Yes, the roof of your husband, your wretched, unfortunate husband!

MRS. LOVETOWN. Never!

LIMBURY (*aside*). She's thoroughly hardened, steeped in vice beyond redemption. Mrs. Lovetown, as you reject my well-intentioned advice in this extraordinary manner, I am reduced to the painful necessity of expressing my hope that you will, — now pray don't think me unkind, — that you will never attempt to meet Mrs. Limbury more.

MRS. LOVETOWN. What! Can you suppose I am so utterly dead to every sense of feeling and propriety as to meet that person, — the destroyer of my peace and happiness, — the wretch who has ruined my hopes and blighted my prospects for ever? Ask your own heart, sir, — appeal to your own feelings. *You* are naturally indignant at her conduct. *You* would hold no further communication with her. Can you suppose, then, *I* would deign to do so? The mere supposition is an insult!   [*Exit* MRS. LOVETOWN *hastily.*

LIMBURY. What can all this mean? I am lost in a maze of astonishment, petrified at the boldness with which she braves it out. Eh! it's breaking upon me by degrees. I see it. What did she say? "Destroyer of peace and happiness, — person — ruined hopes and blighted prospects — *her.*" I see it all. That atrocious Lovetown, that Don Juan multiplied by twenty, that unprecedented libertine, has seduced Mrs. Limbury from her allegiance to her lawful lord and master. He first of all runs away with the wife of another man, and he is no sooner tired of her than he runs away with another wife of another man. I thirst for his destruction. I — (LOVETOWN *rushes from the conservatory and embraces* LIMBURY, *who disengages himself.*) Murderer of domestic happiness, behold your victim!

LOVETOWN. Alas! you speak but too truly. (*Covering his face with his hands.*) I am the victim.

LIMBURY. I speak but too truly! — He avows his own criminality. I shall throttle him. I know I shall. I feel it.

Enter MRS. LIMBURY.

MRS. LIMBURY (*aside*). My husband here! (*Goes into conservatory.*)

Enter TAPKINS.

TAPKINS (*aside*). Not here, and her husband with Limbury. I 'll reconnoitre. (*Goes into summer-house.*)

LIMBURY. Lovetown, have you the boldness to look an honest man in the face?

LOVETOWN. Oh, spare me! I feel the situation in which I am placed acutely, deeply. Feel for me when I say that from that conservatory I overheard the greater part of what passed between you and Mrs. Lovetown.

LIMBURY. You did?

LOVETOWN. Need I say how highly I approve both of the language you used, and the advice you gave her?

LIMBURY. What! you want to get rid of her, do you?

LOVETOWN. Can you doubt it?

TAPKINS (*peeping*). Hallo! he wants to get rid of her. Queer!

LOVETOWN. Situated as I am, you know, I have no other resource, after what has passed. I must part from her.

MRS. LIMBURY (*peeping*). What can he mean?

LIMBURY (*aside*). I should certainly throttle him, were it not that the coolness with which he refers to the dreadful event paralyses me. Mr. Lovetown, look at me! Sir, consider the feelings of an indignant husband, sir!

LOVETOWN. Oh, I thank you for those words. Those strong expressions prove the unaffected interest you take in the matter.

LIMBURY. Unaffected interest! I shall go raving mad with passion and fury! Villain! Monster! To embrace the opportunity afforded him of being on a footing of friendship.

LOVETOWN. To take a mean advantage of his being a single man.

LIMBURY. To tamper with the sacred engagements of a married woman.

LOVETOWN. To place a married man in a disgraceful and humiliating situation.

LIMBURY. Scoundrel! Do you mock me to my face?

LOVETOWN. Mock *you!* What d' ye mean? Who the devil are you talking about?

LIMBURY. Talking about — *you!*

LOVETOWN. Me!

LIMBURY. Designing miscreant! Of whom do *you* speak?

LOVETOWN. Of whom should I speak but that scoundrel Tapkins?

TAPKINS. Me! What the devil do you mean by that?

LOVETOWN. Ha! (*Rushing at him, is held back by* LIMBURY.)

LIMBURY (*to* TAPKINS). Avoid him. Get out of his sight. He 's raving mad with conscious villainy.

TAPKINS. What are you all playing at *I spy I* over my two acres of infant hay for?

LOVETOWN (*to* TAPKINS). How dare you tamper with the affections of Mrs. Lovetown?

TAPKINS. Oh, is that all? Ha, ha!

LOVETOWN. All!

TAPKINS. Come, come, none of your nonsense.

LOVETOWN. Nonsense! Designate the best feelings of our nature nonsense!

TAPKINS. Pooh! pooh! Here, I know all about it.

LOVETOWN (*angrily*). And so do I, sir! And so do I.

TAPKINS. Of course you do. And you 've managed very well to keep it quiet so long. But you 're a deep fellow, by Jove! you 're a deep fellow!

LOVETOWN. Now, mind! I restrain myself sufficiently to ask you once again, before I knock you down, by what right dare you tamper with the affections of Mrs. Lovetown?

TAPKINS. Right! Oh, if you come to strict right, you know, nobody has a right but her husband.

LOVETOWN. And who is her husband? Who is her husband?

TAPKINS. Ah! to be sure, that 's the question. Nobody that I know. I hope — poor fellow —

LOVETOWN. I 'll bear these insults no longer! (*Rushes*

towards TAPKINS. LIMBURY *interposes. A scream is heard from the conservatory — a pause.*)

TAPKINS. Something singular among the plants! (*He goes into the conservatory and returns with* MRS. LIMBURY.) A flower that would n't come out of its own accord. I was obliged to force it. Tolerably full blown now, at all events.

LIMBURY. My wife! Traitress! Fly from my presence! Quit my sight! Return to the conservatory with that demon in a frock-coat!

Enter MRS. LOVETOWN.

TAPKINS. Hallo! Somebody else!

LOVETOWN (*aside*). My wife here!

MRS. LOVETOWN (*to* LIMBURY). I owe you some return for the commiseration you expressed just now for my wretched situation. The best, the only one I can make you is to entreat you to refrain from committing any rash act, however excited you may be, and to control the feelings of an injured husband.

TAPKINS. Injured husband! Decidedly singular!

LOVETOWN. The allusion of that lady I confess my utter inability to understand. Mr. Limbury, to you an explanation is due, and I make it more cheerfully, as my abstaining from doing so might involve the character of your wife. Stung by the attentions which I found Mrs. Lovetown had received from a scoundrel present —

TAPKINS (*aside*). That's me.

LOVETOWN. I, partly to obtain opportunities of watching her closely, under an assumed mask of levity and carelessness, and partly in the hope of awaking once again any dormant feelings of affection that might still slumber in her breast, affected a passion for your wife which I never felt, and to which she never really responded. The second part of my project, I regret to say, has failed. The first has succeeded but too well.

LIMBURY. Can I believe my ears? But how came Mrs. Peter Limbury to receive those attentions?

MRS. LIMBURY. Why, not because I liked them, of course, but to assist Mr. Lovetown in his project, and to teach you the misery of those jealous fears. Come here, you stupid, little, jealous, insinuating darling.

TAPKINS (*aside*). It strikes me very forcibly that I have

made a slight mistake here, which is something particularly singular.

MRS. LOVETOWN. Alfred, hear me! I am as innocent as yourself. Your fancied neglect and coldness hurt my weak vanity, and roused some foolish feelings of angry pride. In a moment of irritation I resorted to some such retaliation as you have yourself described. That I did so from motives as guiltless as your own, I call Heaven to witness. That I repent my fault, I solemnly assure you.

LOVETOWN. Is this possible?

TAPKINS. Very possible, indeed! Believe your wife's assurance and my corroboration. Here, give and take is all fair, you know. Give me your hand and take your wife's. Here, Mr. and Mrs. L. (*To* LIMBURY.) Double L, — I call them. (*To* LOVETOWN.) Small italic and Roman capital. (*To* MR. *and* MRS. LIMBURY, *who come forward.*) Here, it's all arranged. The key to the whole matter is that I've been mistaken, which is something singular. If I have made another mistake in calculating on *your* kind and lenient reception of our last half-hour's misunderstanding (*to the audience*), I shall have done something more singular still. Do you forbid me committing any more mistakes, or may I announce my intention of doing something singular again?

POEMS

THE FINE OLD ENGLISH GENTLEMAN

NEW VERSION

(To be said or sung at all Conservative Dinners)

I 'LL sing you a new ballad, and I 'll warrant it first-rate,
Of the days of that old gentleman who had that old estate;
When they spent the public money at a bountiful old rate
On every mistress, pimp, and scamp, at every noble gate,
  In the fine old English Tory times;
  Soon may they come again !

The good old laws were garnished well with gibbets, whips, and
  chains,
With fine old English penalties, and fine old English pains,
With rebel heads, and seas of blood once hot in rebel veins;
For all these things were requisite to guard the rich old gains
  Of the fine old English Tory times;
  Soon may they come again !

This brave old code, like Argus, had a hundred watchful eyes,
And every English peasant had his good old English spies,
To tempt his starving discontent with fine old English lies,
Then call the good old Yeomanry to stop his peevish cries,
  In the fine old English Tory times;
  Soon may they come again !

The good old times for cutting throats that cried out in their
  need,
The good old times for hunting men who held their fathers'
  creed,

The good old times when William Pitt, as all good men agreed,
Came down direct from Paradise at more than railroad
    speed. . . .
        Oh the fine old English Tory times;
        When will they come again !

In those rare days the Press was seldom known to snarl or
    bark,
But sweetly sang of men in power, like any tuneful lark ;
Grave judges, too, to all their evil deeds were in the dark ;
And not a man in twenty score knew how to make his mark.
        Oh the fine old English Tory times ;
        Soon may they come again !

Those were the days for taxes, and for war's infernal din ;
For scarcity of bread, that fine old dowagers might win ;
For shutting men of letters up, through iron bars to grin,
Because they did n't think the Prince was altogether thin,
        In the fine old English Tory times ;
        Soon may they come again !

But Tolerance, though slow in flight, is strong-winged in the
    main,
That night must come on these fine days, in course of time, was
    plain ;
The pure old spirit struggled, but its struggles were in vain ;
A nation's grip was on it, and it died in choking pain,
        With the fine old English Tory days,
        All of the olden time.

The bright old day now dawns again ; the cry runs through the
    land,
In England there shall be dear bread, — in Ireland, sword and
    brand ;
And poverty and ignorance shall swell the rich and grand.
So, rally round the rulers with the gentle iron hand,
        Of the fine old English Tory days ;
        Hail to the coming time !

THE QUACK DOCTOR'S PROCLAMATION

TUNE — "*A Cobbler there was.*"

An astonishing Doctor has just come to town,
Who will do all the faculty perfectly brown :
He knows all diseases, their causes, and ends ;
And he " begs to appeal to his medical friends."
> Tol de rol :
> Diddle doll :
> Tol de rol, de dol,
> Diddle doll,
> Tol de rol doll.

He 's a magnetic Doctor, and knows how to keep
The whole of a Government snoring asleep
To popular clamours ; till popular pins
Are stuck in their midriffs — and then he begins.
> Tol de rol.

He 's a clairvoyant subject, and readily reads
His countrymen's wishes, condition, and needs,
With many more fine things I can't tell in rhyme
— And he keeps both his eyes shut, the whole of the time.
> Tol de rol.

You must n't expect him to talk ; but you 'll take
Most particular notice the Doctor 's awake,
Though for aught from his words or his looks that you reap, he
Might just as well be most confoundedly sleepy.
> Tol de rol.

Homœopathy, too, he has practised for ages
(You 'll find his prescriptions in Luke Hansard's pages) ;
Just giving his patient, when maddened by pain,
Of Reform the ten thousandeth part of a grain.
> Tol de rol.

He 's a medicine for Ireland, in portable papers ;
The infallible cure for political vapours ;

A neat label round it his 'prentices tie —
" Put your trust in the Lord, and keep this powder dry ! "
Tol de rol.

He 's a corn-doctor also, of wonderful skill,
— No cutting, no rooting-up, purging, or pill, —
You 're merely to take, 'stead of walking or riding,
The sweet schoolboy exercise — innocent sliding.
Tol de rol.

There 's no advice gratis.   If high ladies send
His legitimate fee, he 's their soft-spoken friend.
At the great public counter, with one hand behind him
And one in his waistcoat, they 're certain to find him.
Tol de rol.

He has only to add he 's the real Doctor Flam,
All others being purely fictitious and sham ;
The house is a large one, tall, slated, and white,
With a lobby, and lights in the passage at night.
Tol de rol :
Diddle doll :
Tol de rol, de doll,
Diddle doll,
Tol de rol doll.

SUBJECTS FOR PAINTERS

(AFTER PETER PINDAR)

To you, Sir Martin, and your co-R. A.'s,
I dedicate, in meek, suggestive lays,
   Some subjects for your academic palettes ;
Hoping, by dint of these my scanty jobs,
To fill with novel thoughts your teeming nobs,
   As though I beat them in with wooden mallets.

To you, MACLISE, who Eve's fair daughters paint
With Nature's hand, and want the maudlin taint
   Of the sweet Chalon school of silk and ermine ;

To you, E. LANDSEER, who from year to year
Delight in beasts and birds, and dogs and deer,
  And seldom give us any human vermin: —

To all who practise art, or make believe,
I offer subjects they may take or leave.

Great Sibthorp and his butler, in debate
(*Arcades ambo*) on affairs of state,
  Not altogether " gone," but rather funny;
Cursing the Whigs for leaving in the lurch
Our d—d good, pleasant, gentlemanly Church,
  Would make a picture — cheap at any money.

Or Sibthorp as the Tory Sec.-at-War,
Encouraging his mates with loud " Yhor! Yhor!"
  From Treasury benches' most conspicuous end;
Or Sib's mustachios curling with a smile,
As an expectant Premier, without guile,
  Calls him his honourable and gallant friend.

Or Sibthorp travelling in foreign parts,
Through that rich portion of our Eastern charts
  Where lies the land of popular tradition;
And fairly worshipp'd by the true devout
In all his comings-in and goings-out,
  Because of the old Turkish superstition.

Fame with her trumpet blowing very hard,
And making earth rich with celestial lard,
  In puffing deeds done through Lord Chamberlain Howe;
While some few thousand persons of small gains,
Who give their charities without such pains,
  Look up, much wondering what may be the row.

Behind them Joseph Hume, who turns his pate
To where great Marlborough House in princely state
  Shelters a host of lacqueys, lords, and pages,
And says he knows of dowagers a crowd,
Who, without trumpeting so very loud,
  Would do as much, and more, for half the wages.

Limn, Sirs, the highest Lady in the land,
When Joseph Surface, fawning, cap in hand,
  Delivers in his list of patriot-mortals;
Those gentlemen of honour, faith, and truth,
Who, foul-mouth'd, spat upon her maiden youth,
  And dog-like did defile her palace portals.

Paint me the Tories, full of grief and woe,
Weeping (to voters) over Frost and Co.,
  Their suffering, erring, much-enduring brothers;
And in the background don't forget to pack,
Each grinning ghastly from its bloody sack,
  The heads of Thistlewood, Despard, and others.

Paint, squandering the Club's election gold,
Fierce lovers of our Constitution old,
  Lords who 're that sacred lady's greatest debtors;
And let the law, forbidding any voice
Or act of Peer to influence the choice
  Of English people, flourish in bright letters.

Paint that same dear old lady, ill at ease,
Weak in her second childhood, hard to please,
  Unknowing what she ails or what she wishes;
With all her Carlton nephews at the door,
Deafening both aunt and nurses with their roar,
  — Fighting already for the loaves and fishes.

Leaving these hints for you to dwell upon,
I shall presume to offer more, anon.

PROLOGUE

TO MR. WESTLAND MARSTON'S PLAY OF

"THE PATRICIAN'S DAUGHTER"

SPOKEN BY MR. MACREADY

No tale of streaming plumes and harness bright
Dwells on the poet's maiden theme to-night;

No trumpet's clangour and no battle's fire
Breathe in the trembling accents of his lyre.
Enough for him if, in his lowly strain,
He wake one household echo not in vain;
Enough for him if, in his boldest word,
The beating heart of man be faintly stirr'd.
That mournful music, that, like chords which sigh
Through charmed gardens, all who hear it die,
That solemn music he does not pursue
To distant ages out of human view;
Nor listen to its wild and mournful chime
In the dark caverns on the shore of Time;
But musing, with a calm and steady gaze,
Before the crackling flame of living days,
He hears it whisper, through the busy roar,
Of what shall be, and what has been before.

Awake the Present! Shall no scene display
The tragic passion of the passing day?
Is it with man as with some meaner things,
That out of death his solemn purpose springs?
Can this eventful life no moral teach,
Unless he be for aye beyond its reach?
Obscurely shall he suffer, rot, and fade,
Made noble only by the sexton's spade?

Awake the Present! though the steel-clad age
Find life alone within the storied page,
Iron is worn at heart by many still;
The tyrant Custom binds the serf-like will;
If the sharp rack and chain and screw be gone,
These latter days have tortures of their own.
The guiltless writhe, while guilt is stretch'd in sleep,
And Virtue lies, too often, dungeon deep.

Awake the Present! What the Past has sown
Is in its harvest garner'd, reap'd, and grown.
How pride engenders pride, and wrong breeds wrong,
And Truth and Falsehood, hand in hand, along
High places walk in monster-like embrace, —
The modern Janus with the double face; —

How social usage hath the power to change
Good thought to evil in its highest range,
To cramp the noble soul, and turn to ruth
The kindling impulse of our glowing youth,
Crushing the spirit in its house of clay, —
Learn from the lesson of the present day.
Not light its import, and not poor its mien,
Yourselves the actors, and your home the scene.

A WORD IN SEASON

THEY have a superstition in the East,
    That ALLAH, written on a piece of paper,
Is better unction than can come of priest,
    Of rolling incense, and of lighted taper:
Holding that any scrap which bears that name,
    In any characters, its front imprest on,
Shall help the finder through the purging flame,
    And give his toasted feet a place to rest on.

Accordingly, they make a mighty fuss
    With every wretched tract and fierce oration,
And hoard the leaves — for they are not, like us,
    A highly civilised and thinking nation:
And, always stooping in the miry ways,
    To look for matter of this earthy leaven,
They seldom, in their dust-exploring days,
    Have any leisure to look up to Heaven.

So have I known a country on the earth,
    Where darkness sat upon the living waters,
And brutal ignorance, and toil, and dearth,
    Were the hard portion of its sons and daughters;
And yet where they who should have op'd the door
    Of charity and light, for all men's finding,
Squabbled for words upon the altar-floor,
    And rent the Book, in struggles for the binding.

The gentlest man among these pious Turks
God's living image ruthlessly defaces;

Their best high-churchman, with no faith in works,
  Bowstrings the Virtues in the market-places:
The Christian Pariah, whom both sects curse,
  (They curse all other men, and curse each other,)
Walks thro' the world, not very much the worse —
  Does all the good he can, and loves his brother.

THE BRITISH LION

A NEW SONG, BUT AN OLD STORY

TUNE — *The Great Sea-Snake*

OH, p'raps you may have heard, and if not, I 'll sing
  Of the British Lion free,
That was constantly a going for to make a spring
  Upon his en-e-me;
But who, being rather groggy at the knees,
  Broke down, always, before;
And generally gave a feeble wheeze
  Instead of a loud roar.

      Right toor rol, loor rol, fee faw fum,
        The British Lion bold!
      That was always a going for to do great things,
        And was always being " sold " !

He was carried about, in a carawan,
  And was show'd in country parts,
And they said, " Walk up! Be in time! He can
  Eat Corn-Law Leagues like tarts ! "
And his showmen, shouting there and then,
  To puff him did n't fail;
And they said, as they peep'd into his den,
  " Oh, don't he wag his tail ! "

Now, the principal keeper of this poor old beast,
  WAN HUMBUG was his name,
Would once every day stir him up — at least —
  And was n't that a game !

For he had n't a tooth, and he had n't a claw,
   In that " struggle " so " sublime ; "
And, however sharp they touch'd him on the raw,
   He could n't come up to time.

And this, you will observe, was the reason why
   WAN HUMBUG, on weak grounds,
Was forced to make believe that he heard his cry
   In all unlikely sounds.
So, there was n't a bleat from an Essex Calf,
   Or a Duke, or a Lordling slim ;
But he said, with a wery triumphant laugh,
   " I 'm blest if that ain't him."

At length, wery bald in his mane and tail,
   This British Lion grow'd :
He pined and declined, and he satisfied
   The last debt which he owed.
And when they came to examine the skin
   It was a wonder sore,
To find that the an-i-mal within
   Was nothing but a BOAR !

    Right toor rol, loor rol, fee faw fum,
     The British Lion bold !
    That was always a going for to do great things,
     And was always being " sold "!
                   CATNACH.

THE HYMN OF THE WILTSHIRE LABOURERS

O GOD, who by thy Prophet's hand
   Didst smite the rocky brake,
Whence water came, at thy command,
   Thy people's thirst to slake ;
Strike, now, upon this granite wall,
   Stern, obdurate, and high ;
And let some drops of pity fall
   For us who starve and die !

The God, who took a little child,
    And set him in the midst,
And promised him His mercy mild,
    As, by Thy Son, Thou didst :
Look down upon our children dear,
    So gaunt, so cold, so spare,
And let their images appear,
    Where Lords and Gentry are !

O God, teach them to feel how we,
    When our poor infants droop,
Are weaken'd in our trust in Thee,
    And how our spirits stoop ;
For, in Thy rest, so bright and fair,
    All tears and sorrows sleep :
And their young looks, so full of care,
    Would make Thine Angels weep !

The God, who with His finger drew
    The Judgment coming on,
Write, for these men, what must ensue,
    Ere many years be gone !
O God whose bow is in the sky,
    Let them not brave and dare,
Until they look (too late) on high,
    And see an Arrow there !

O God, remind them ! In the bread
    They break upon the knee,
Those sacred words may yet be read,
    " In memory of Me ! "
O God, remind them of His sweet
    Compassion for the poor,
And how He gave them Bread to eat,
    And went from door to door !

PROLOGUE TO "THE LIGHTHOUSE"

BY WILKIE COLLINS

Slow music all the time; unseen speaker; curtain down.

A STORY of those rocks where doom'd ships come
To cast them wreck'd upon the steps of home,
Where solitary men, the long year through —
The wind their music and the brine their view —
Warn mariners to shun the beacon-light;
A story of those rocks is here to-night.
Eddystone Lighthouse!

> *[Exterior view discovered.*

              In its ancient form,
Ere he who built it wish'd for the great storm
That shiver'd it to nothing,[1] once again
Behold outgleaming on the angry main!
Within it are three men; to these repair
In our frail bark of Fancy, swift as air!
They are but shadows, as the rower grim
Took none but shadows in his boat with him.
So be *ye* shades, and, for a little space,
The real world a dream without a trace.
Return is easy. It will have ye back
Too soon to the old beaten dusty track;
For but one hour forget it. Billows, rise,
Blow, winds; fall, rain; be black, ye midnight skies;
And you who watch the light, arise! arise!

> *[Exterior view rises and discovers the scene.*

[1] "When Winstanley had brought his work to completion, he is said to have expressed himself so satisfied as to its strength that he only wished he might be there in the fiercest storm that ever blew. In this wish he was not disappointed, although the result was entirely the reverse of the builder's anticipations. In November, 1703, Winstanley went off to the lighthouse to superintend some repairs which had become necessary. On the night of the 26th, a storm of unparalleled fury burst along the coast, in which the lighthouse and its builder were swept completely away." — Smiles's *Lives of the Engineers.*

THE SONG OF THE WRECK

I

THE wind blew high, the waters raved,
  A ship drove on the land,
A hundred human creatures saved
  Kneel'd down upon the sand.
Three-score were drov/n'd, three-score were thrown
  Upon the black rocks wild,
And thus among them, 'eft alone,
  They found one helpiess child.

II

A seaman rough, to shipwreck bred,
  Stood out from all the rest,
And gently laid the lonely head
  Upon his honest breast.
And travelling o'er the desert wide
  It was a solemn joy,
To see them, ever side by side,
  The sailor and the boy.

III

In famine, sickness, hunger, thirst,
  The two were still but one,
Until the strong man droop'd the first,
  And felt his labours done.
Then to a trusty friend he spake,
  " Across the desert wide,
O take this poor boy for my sake ! "
  And kiss'd the child, and died.

IV

Toiling along in weary plight
  Through heavy jungle, mire,
These two came later every night
  To warm them at the fire.

Until the captain said one day,
"O seaman good and kind,
To save thyself now come away,
And leave the boy behind!"

v

The child was slumbering near the blaze;
"O captain, let him rest
Until it sinks, when God's own ways
Shall teach us what is best!"
They watch'd the whiten'd ashy heap,
They touch'd the child in vain;
They did not leave him there asleep,
He never woke again.

CHILD'S HYMN

FROM THE WRECK OF THE GOLDEN MARY

HEAR my prayer, O! Heavenly Father,
Ere I lay me down to sleep;
Bid thy Angels, pure and holy,
Round my bed their vigil keep.

My sins are heavy, but thy mercy
Far outweighs them every one;
Down before thy Cross I cast them,
Trusting in thy help alone.

Keep me through this night of peril
Underneath its boundless shade;
Take me to thy rest, I pray thee,
When my pilgrimage is made.

None shall measure out thy patience
By the span of human thought;
None shall bound the tender mercies
Which thy holy Son has bought.

Pardon all my past transgressions,
  Give me strength for days to come;
Guide and guard me with thy blessing
  Till thy Angels bid me home.

PROLOGUE TO "THE FROZEN DEEP"

BY WILKIE COLLINS

Curtain rises ; Mists and darkness ; Soft music throughout.

ONE savage footprint on the lonely shore
Where one man listen'd to the surge's roar,
Not all the winds that stir the mighty sea
Can ever ruffle in the memory.
If such its interest and thrall, O then
Pause on the footprints of heroic men,
Making a garden of the desert wide
Where PARRY conquer'd death and FRANKLIN died.

To that white region where the LOST lie low,
Wrapt in their mantles of eternal snow, —
Unvisited by change, nothing to mock
Those statues sculptured in the icy rock,
We pray your company ; that hearts as true
(Though nothings of the air) may live for you ;

Nor only yet that on our little glass
A faint reflection of those wilds may pass,
But that the secrets of the vast Profound
Within us, an exploring hand may sound,
Testing the region of the ice-bound soul,
Seeking the passage at its northern pole,
Softening the horrors of its wintry sleep,
Melting the surface of that " Frozen Deep."

Vanish, ye mists ! But ere this gloom departs,
And to the union of three sister arts

We give a winter evening, good to know
That in the charms of such another show,
That in the fiction of a friendly play,
The Arctic sailors, too, put gloom away,
Forgot their long night, saw no starry dome,
Hail'd the warm sun, and were again at Home.

Vanish, ye mists! Not yet do we repair
To the still country of the piercing air;
But seek, before we cross the troubled seas,
An English hearth and Devon's waving trees.

THE BLACKSMITH

OLD ENGLAND, she has great warriors,
  Great princes and poets great;
But the Blacksmith is not to be quite forgot
  In the history of the State.

He is rich in the best of all metals,
  Yet silver he lacks, and gold;
And he payeth his due, and his heart is true,
  Though he bloweth both hot and cold.

The boldest is he of incendiaries
  That ever the wide wo l saw,
And a forger as rank as e'er robb'd the Bank,
  Though he never doth break the law.

He hath shoes that are worn by strangers,
  Yet he laugheth and maketh more;
And a share (conceal'd) in the poor man's field,
  Yet it adds to the poor man's store.

Then, hurrah for the iron Blacksmith!
  And hurrah for his iron crew!
And whenever we go where his forges glow,
  We 'll sing what A MAN can do.

MISCELLANIES

SUNDAY UNDER THREE HEADS

DEDICATION

To the Right Reverend The Bishop of London.

MY LORD, — You were among the first, some years ago, to expatiate on the vicious addiction of the lower classes of society to Sunday excursions; and were thus instrumental in calling forth occasional demonstrations of those extreme opinions on the subject, which are very generally received with derision, if not with contempt.

Your elevated station, my Lord, affords you countless opportunities of increasing the comforts and pleasures of the humbler classes of society — not by the expenditure of the smallest portion of your princely income, but by merely sanctioning with the influence of your example their harmless pastimes and innocent recreations.

That your Lordship would ever have contemplated Sunday recreations with so much horror, if you had been at all acquainted with the wants and necessities of the people who indulged in them, I cannot imagine possible. That a Prelate of your elevated rank has the faintest conception of the extent of those wants, and the nature of those necessities, I do not believe.

For these reasons, I venture to address this little pamphlet to your Lordship's consideration. I am quite conscious that the outlines I have drawn afford but a very imperfect description of the feelings they are intended to illustrate; but I claim for them one merit — their truth, and freedom from exaggeration. I may have fallen short of the mark, but I have never overshot it; and while I have pointed out what appears to me to be injustice on the part of others, I hope I have carefully abstained from committing it myself. I am, my Lord,

Your Lordship's most obedient, humble servant,

TIMOTHY SPARKS.

June, 1836.

SUNDAY UNDER THREE HEADS

I

AS IT IS

THERE are few things from which I derive greater pleasure
than walking through some of the principal streets of London
on a fine Sunday, in summer, and watching the cheerful faces,
of the lively groups with which they are thronged. There is
something, to my eyes at least, exceedingly pleasing in the
general desire evinced by the humbler classes of society to
appear neat and clean on this their only holiday. There are
many grave old persons, I know, who shake their heads with
an air of profound wisdom, and tell you that poor people dress
too well nowadays; that when they were children, folks knew
their stations in life better; that you may depend upon it, no
good will come of this sort of thing in the end, — and so forth;
but I fancy I can discern in the fine bonnet of the working-
man's wife, or the feather-bedizened hat of his child, no inconsiderable evidence of good feeling on the part of the man
himself, and an affectionate desire to expend the few shillings
he can spare from his week's wages in improving the appearance
and adding to the happiness of those who are nearest and
dearest to him. This may be a very heinous and unbecoming
degree of vanity, perhaps, and the money might possibly be
applied to better uses; it must not be forgotten, however, that
it might very easily be devoted to worse; and if two or three
faces can be rendered happy and contented by a trifling improvement of outward appearance, I cannot help thinking that
the object is very cheaply purchased, even at the expense of
a smart gown, or a gaudy riband. There is a great deal of very
unnecessary cant about the over-dressing of the common people.
There is not a manufacturer or tradesman in existence who
would not employ a man who takes a reasonable degree of pride
in the appearance of himself and those about him, in preference

to a sullen, slovenly fellow who works doggedly on, regardless of his own clothing and that of his wife and children, and seeming to take pleasure or pride in nothing.

The pampered aristocrat, whose life is one continued round of licentious pleasures and sensual gratifications; or the gloomy enthusiast, who detests the cheerful amusements he can never, enjoy, and envies the healthy feelings he can never know, and who would put down the one and suppress the other, until he made the minds of his fellow-beings as besotted and distorted as his own; — neither of these men can by possibility form an adequate notion of what Sunday really is to those whose lives are spent in sedentary or laborious occupations, and who are accustomed to look forward to it through their whole existence, as their only day of rest from toil, and innocent enjoyment.

The sun that rises over the quiet streets of London on a bright Sunday morning shines, till his setting, on gay and happy faces. Here and there, so early as six o'clock, a young man and woman in their best attire may be seen hurrying along on their way to the house of some acquaintance, who is included in their scheme of pleasure for the day; from whence, after stopping to take " a bit of breakfast," they sally forth, accompanied by several old people, and a whole crowd of young ones, bearing large hand-baskets full of provisions, and Belcher handkerchiefs done up in bundles, with the neck of a bottle sticking out at the top, and closely packed apples bulging out at the sides, — and away they hurry along the streets leading to the steam-packet wharfs, which are already plentifully sprinkled with parties bound for the same destination. Their good-humour and delight know no bounds — for it is a delightful morning, all blue overhead, and nothing like a cloud in the whole sky; and even the air of the river at London Bridge is something to them, shut up as they have been, all the week, in close streets and heated rooms. There are dozens of steamers to all sorts of places, — Gravesend, Greenwich, and Richmond; and such numbers of people that, when you have once sat down on the deck, it is all but a moral impossibility to get up again, — to say nothing of walking about, which is entirely out of the question. Away they go, joking and laughing, and eating and drinking, and admiring everything they see, and pleased with everything they hear, to climb Windmill Hill, and catch a glimpse of the rich cornfields and beautiful orchards of Kent; or to stroll among the fine old trees of Greenwich Park, and survey the wonders of Shooter's Hill, and Lady James's Folly; or to glide past the beautiful meadows of Twickenham and Richmond, and to gaze with a delight which only people like them can know on every lovely object in the fair prospect around. Boat follows boat, and coach succeeds coach, for the next three hours; but all are filled, and all with the same kind of people — neat and clean, cheerful and contented.

They reach their places of destination, and the taverns are crowded; but there is no drunkenness or brawling, for the class of men who commit the enormity of making Sunday excursions take their families with them; and this in itself would be a check upon them, even if they were inclined to dissipation, which they really are not. Boisterous their mirth may be, for they have all the excitement of feeling that fresh air and green fields can impart to the dwellers in crowded cities, but it is innocent and harmless. The glass is circulated, and the joke goes round; but the one is free from excess, and the other from offence; and nothing but good-humour and hilarity prevail.

In streets like Holborn and Tottenham Court Road, which form the central market of a large neighbourhood, inhabited by a vast number of mechanics and poor people, a few shops are open at an early hour of the morning; and a very poor man, with a thin and sickly woman by his side, may be seen with their little basket in hand, purchasing the scanty quantity of necessaries they can afford, which the time at which the man received his wages, or his having a good deal of work to do, or the woman's having been out charing till a late hour, prevented their procuring overnight. The coffee-shops, too, at which clerks and young men employed in counting-houses can procure their breakfasts, are also open. This class comprises, in a place like London, an enormous number of people, whose limited means prevent their engaging for their lodgings any other apartment than a bedroom, and who have consequently no alternative but to take their breakfasts at a coffee-shop, or go without it altogether. All these places, however, are quickly closed; and by the time the church-bells begin to ring, all appearance of traffic has ceased. And then, what are the signs of immorality that meet the eye? Churches are well filled, and Dissenters' chapels are crowded to suffocation. There is no preaching to empty benches while the drunken and dissolute populace run riot in the streets.

Here is a fashionable church, where the service commences at a late hour, for the accommodation of such members of the congregation — and they are not a few — as may happen to have lingered at the Opera far into the morning of the Sabbath; an excellent contrivance for poising the balance between God and Mammon, and illustrating the ease with which a man's duties to both may be accommodated and adjusted. How the carriages rattle up, and deposit their richly-dressed burdens beneath the lofty portico! The powdered footmen glide along the aisle, place the richly-bound prayer-books on the pew-desks, slam the doors, and hurry away, leaving the fashionable members of the congregation to inspect each other through their glasses, and to dazzle and glitter in the eyes of the few shabby people in the free seats. The organ peals forth, the hired singers commence a short hymn, and the congregation condescendingly rise, stare about them, and converse in whispers. The clergyman enters the reading-desk, — a young man of noble family and elegant demeanour, notorious at Cambridge for his knowledge of horse-flesh and dancers, and celebrated at Eton for his hopeless stupidity. The service commences. Mark the soft voice in which he reads, and the impressive manner in which he applies his white hand, studded with brilliants, to his perfumed hair. Observe the graceful emphasis with which he offers up the prayers for the King, the Royal Family, and all the Nobility; and the nonchalance with which he hurries over the more uncomfortable portions of the service, the seventh commandment, for instance, with a studied regard for the taste and feeling of his auditors, only to be equalled by that displayed by the sleek divine who succeeds him, who murmurs, in a voice kept down by rich feeding, most comfortable doctrines for exactly twelve minutes, and then arrives at the anxiously expected "Now to God," which is the signal for the dismissal of the congregation. The organ is again heard; those who have been asleep wake up, and those who have kept awake smile and seem greatly relieved; bows and congratulations are exchanged, the livery servants are all bustle and commotion, bang go the steps, up jump the footmen, and off rattle the carriages: the inmates discoursing on the dresses of the congregation, and congratulating themselves on having set so excellent an example to the community in general, and Sunday pleasurers in particular.

Enter a less orthodox place of religious worship, and observe
the contrast. A small close chapel with a whitewashed wall,
and plain deal pews and pulpit, contains a closely-packed congregation, as different in dress, as they are opposed in manner, to that
we have just quitted. The hymn is sung — not by paid singers,
but by the whole assembly at the loudest pitch of their voices,
unaccompanied by any musical instrument, the words being
given out, two lines at a time, by the clerk. There is something in the sonorous quavering of the harsh voices, in the lank
and hollow faces of the men, and the sour solemnity of the
women, which bespeaks this a stronghold of intolerant zeal and
ignorant enthusiasm. The preacher enters the pulpit. He is
a coarse, hard-faced man of forbidding aspect, clad in rusty black,
and bearing in his hand a small plain Bible from which he
selects some passage for his text, while the hymn is concluding.
The congregation fall upon their knees, and are hushed into
profound stillness as he delivers an extempore prayer, in which
he calls upon the Sacred Founder of the Christian faith to bless
his ministry, in terms of disgusting and impious familiarity not
to be described. He begins his oration in a drawling tone, and
his hearers listen with silent attention. He grows warmer as
he proceeds with his subject, and his gesticulation becomes pro-
portionately violent. He clenches his fists, beats the book
upon the desk before him, and swings his arms wildly about his
head. The congregation murmur their acquiescence in his doctrines; and a short groan occasionally bears testimony to the
moving nature of his eloquence. Encouraged by these symptoms of approval, and working himself up to a pitch of
enthusiasm amounting almost to frenzy, he denounces Sabbath-
breakers with the direst vengeance of offended Heaven. He
stretches his body half out of the pulpit, thrusts forth his arms
with frantic gestures, and blasphemously calls upon the Deity
to visit with eternal torments those who turn aside from the
Word, as interpreted and preached by — himself. A low moan-
ing is heard, the women rock their bodies to and fro, and wring
their hands; the preacher's fervour increases, the perspiration
starts upon his brow, his face is flushed, and he clenches his
hands convulsively, as he draws a hideous and appalling picture
of the horrors preparing for the wicked in a future state. A
great excitement is visible among his hearers, a scream is heard,
and some young girl falls senseless on the floor. There is a

momentary rustle, but it is only for a moment — all eyes are turned towards the preacher. He pauses, passes his handkerchief across his face, and looks complacently round. His voice resumes its natural tone, as with mock humility he offers up a thanksgiving for having been successful in his efforts, and having been permitted to rescue one sinner from the path of evil. He sinks back into his seat, exhausted with the violence of his ravings ; the girl is removed, a hymn is sung; a petition for some measure for securing the better observance of the Sabbath, which has been prepared by the good man, is read ; and his worshipping admirers struggle who shall be the first to sign it.

But the morning service has concluded, and the streets are again crowded with people. Long rows of cleanly-dressed charity children, preceded by a portly beadle and a withered schoolmaster, are returning to their welcome dinner ; and it is evident from the number of men with beer-trays, who are running from house to house, that no inconsiderable portion of the population are about to take theirs at this early hour. The bakers' shops, in the humbler suburbs especially, are filled with men, women, and children, each anxiously waiting for the Sunday dinner. Look at the group of children who surround that working-man who has just emerged from the baker's shop at the corner of the street, with the reeking dish, in which a diminutive joint of mutton simmers above a vast heap of half-browned potatoes. How the young rogues clap their hands, and dance round their father, for very joy at the prospect of the feast ; and how anxiously the youngest and chubbiest of the lot lingers on tiptoe by his side, trying to get a peep into the interior of the dish. They turn up the street, and the chubby-faced boy trots on as fast as his little legs will carry him, to herald the approach of the dinner to " mother," who is standing with a baby in her arms on the door-step, and who seems almost as pleased with the whole scene as the children themselves ; whereupon " baby," not precisely understanding the importance of the business in hand, but clearly perceiving that it is something unusually lively, kicks and crows most lustily, to the unspeakable delight of all the children and both the parents ; and the dinner is borne into the house amidst a shouting of small voices, and jumping of fat legs, which would fill Sir Andrew Agnew with astonishment ; as well it might, seeing that baronets, generally speaking, eat pretty comfortable

dinners all the week through, and cannot be expected to understand what people feel who only have a meat dinner on one
day out of every seven.

The bakings being all duly consigned to their respective
owners, and the beerman having gone his rounds, the church
bells ring for afternoon service, the shops are again closed, and
the streets are more than ever thronged with people : some who
have not been to church in the morning, going to it now;
others who have been to church, going out for a walk ; and
others — let us admit the full measure of their guilt — going
for a walk, who have not been to church at all. I am afraid
the smart servant of all work, who has been loitering at the
corner of the square for the last ten minutes, is one of the
latter class. She is evidently waiting for somebody, and though
she may have made up her mind to go to church with him one
of these mornings, I don't think they have any such intention
on this particular afternoon. Here he is, at last. The white
trousers, blue coat, and yellow waistcoat — and more especially
that cock of the hat — indicate, as surely as inanimate objects
can, that Chalk Farm, and not the parish church, is their
destination. The girl colours up, and puts out her hand with
a very awkward affectation of indifference. He gives it a gallant squeeze, and away they walk, arm in arm, the girl just
looking back towards her " place " with an air of conscious self-
importance, and nodding to her fellow-servant who has gone up
to the two-pair-of-stairs window to take a full view of " Mary's
young man," which being communicated to William, he takes
off his hat to the fellow-servant : a proceeding which affords
unmitigated satisfaction to all parties, and impels the fellow-
servant to inform Miss Emily confidentially, in the course of
the evening, that " the young man as Mary keeps company with
is one of the most genteelest young men as ever she see."

The two young people who have just crossed the road, and
are following this happy couple down the street, are a fair specimen of another class of Sunday pleasurers. There is a dapper
smartness, struggling through very limited means, about the
young man, which induces one to set him down at once as a
junior clerk to a tradesman or attorney. The girl no one could
possibly mistake. You may tell a young woman in the employment of a large dressmaker at any time, by a certain neatness
of cheap finery, and humble following of fashion, which pervade

her whole attire ; but unfortunately there are other tokens not
to be misunderstood — the pale face with its hectic bloom, the
slight distortion of form which no artifice of dress can wholly
conceal, the unhealthy stoop, and the short cough — the effects
of hard work and close application to a sedentary employment,
upon a tender frame. They turn towards the fields. The
girl's countenance brightens, and an unwonted glow rises in her
face. They are going to Hampstead or Highgate, to spend their
holiday afternoon in some place where they can see the sky,
the fields, and trees, and breathe for an hour or two the pure
air, which so seldom plays upon that poor girl's form, or exhil-
arates her spirits.

I would to God that the iron-hearted man who would deprive
such people as these of their only pleasures could feel the sinking of heart and soul, the wasting exhaustion of mind and body,
the utter prostration of present strength and future hope, attendant upon that incessant toil which lasts from day to day, and
from month to month ; that toil which is too often protracted
until the silence of midnight, and resumed with the first stir of
morning.   How marvellously would his ardent zeal for other
men's souls diminish after a short probation, and how enlightened and comprehensive would his views of the real object and
meaning of the institution of the Sabbath become !

The afternoon is far advanced — the parks and public drives
are crowded.   Carriages, gigs, phaetons, stanhopes, and vehicles
of every description, glide smoothly on.   The promenades are
filled with loungers on foot, and the road is thronged with
loungers on horseback.   Persons of every class are crowded together, here, in one dense mass.   The plebeian, who takes his
pleasure on no day but Sunday, jostles the patrician, who takes
his from year's end to year's end.   You look in vain for any
outward signs of profligacy or debauchery.   You see nothing
before you but a vast number of people, the denizens of a large
and crowded city, in the needful and rational enjoyment of air
and exercise.

It grows dusk.   The roads leading from the different places
of suburban resort are crowded with people on their return
home, and the sound of merry voices rings through the gradually
darkening fields.   The evening is hot and sultry.   The rich
man throws open the sashes of his spacious dining-room, and
quaffs his iced wine in splendid luxury.   The poor man, who

has no room to take his meals in, but the close apartment to which he and his family have been confined throughout the week, sits in the tea-garden of some famous tavern, and drinks his beer in content and comfort. The fields and roads are gradually deserted, the crowd once more pour into the streets, and disperse to their several homes; and by midnight all is silent and quiet, save where a few stragglers linger beneath the window of some great man's house, to listen to the strains of music from within, or stop to gaze upon the splendid carriages which are waiting to convey the guests from the dinner party of an Earl.

There is a darker side to this picture, on which, so far from its being any part of my purpose to conceal it, I wish to lay particular stress. In some parts of London, and in many of the manufacturing towns of England, drunkenness and profligacy, in their most disgusting forms, exhibit in the open streets, on Sunday, a sad and a degrading spectacle. We need go no farther than St. Giles's, or Drury Lane, for sights and scenes of a most repulsive nature. Women with scarcely the articles of apparel which common decency requires, with forms bloated by disease, and faces rendered hideous by habitual drunkenness — men reeling and staggering along — children in rags and filth — whole streets of squalid and miserable appearance, whose inhabitants are lounging in the public road, fighting, screaming, and swearing — these are the common objects which present themselves in, these are the well-known characteristics of, that portion of London to which I have just referred.

And why is it that all well-disposed persons are shocked, and public decency scandalised, by such exhibitions?

These people are poor — that is notorious. It may be said that they spend in liquor money with which they might purchase necessaries, and there is no denying the fact; but let it be remembered that even if they applied every farthing of their earnings in the best possible way, they would still be very — very poor. Their dwellings are necessarily uncomfortable, and to a certain degree unhealthy. Cleanliness might do much, but they are too crowded together, the streets are too narrow, and the rooms too small, to admit of their ever being rendered desirable habitations. They work very hard all the week. We know that the effect of prolonged and arduous labour is to produce, when a period of rest does arrive, a sensation of lassitude

which it requires the application of some stimulus to overcome.
What stimulus have they? Sunday comes, and with it a ces-
sation of labour. How are they to employ the day, or what
inducement have they to employ it, in recruiting their stock of
health? They see little parties, on pleasure excursions, passing through the streets; but they cannot imitate their example,
for they have not the means. They may walk, to be sure, but
it is exactly the inducement to walk that they require. If
every one of these men knew that by taking the trouble to walk
two or three miles he would be enabled to share in a good
game of cricket, or some athletic sport, I very much question
whether any of them would remain at home.

But you hold out no inducement, you offer no relief from
listlessness, you provide nothing to amuse his mind, you afford
him no means of exercising his body. Unwashed and unshaven,
he saunters moodily about, weary and dejected. In lieu of the
wholesome stimulus he might derive from nature, you drive
him to the pernicious excitement to be gained from art. He
flies to the gin-shop as his only resource; and when, reduced
to a worse level than the lowest brute in the scale of creation,
he lies wallowing in the kennel, your saintly lawgivers lift up
their hands to heaven, and exclaim for a law which shall convert
the day intended for rest and cheerfulness, into one of universal
gloom, bigotry, and persecution.

II

AS SABBATH BILLS WOULD MAKE IT

THE provisions of the bill introduced into the House of Commons by Sir Andrew Agnew, and thrown out by that House on
the motion for the second reading, on the 18th of May in the
present year, by a majority of thirty-two, may very fairly be taken
as a test of the length to which the fanatics, of which the honourable Baronet is the distinguished leader, are prepared to go.
No test can be fairer; because while on the one hand this
measure may be supposed to exhibit all that improvement which
mature reflection and long deliberation may have suggested, so
on the other it may very reasonably be inferred that if it be
quite as severe in its provisions, and to the full as partial in its

operation, as those which have preceded it, and experienced a similar fate, the disease under which the honourable Baronet and his friends labour is perfectly hopeless, and beyond the reach of cure.

The proposed enactments of the bill are briefly these : All work is prohibited on the Lord's Day, under heavy penalties, increasing with every repetition of the offence.   There are penalties for keeping shops open — penalties for drunkenness — penalties for keeping open houses of entertainment — penalties for being present at any public meeting or assembly — penalties for letting carriages, and penalties for hiring them — penalties for travelling in steamboats, and penalties for taking passengers — penalties on vessels commencing their voyage on Sunday — penalties on the owners of cattle who suffer them to be driven on the Lord's Day — penalties on constables who refuse to act, and penalties for resisting them when they do.   In addition to these trifles, the constables are invested with arbitrary, vexatious, and most extensive powers ; and all this in a bill which sets out with a hypocritical and canting declaration that " nothing is more acceptable to God than the *true and sincere* worship of Him according to His holy will, and that it is the bounden duty of Parliament to promote the observance of the Lord's Day, by protecting every class of society against being required to sacrifice their comfort, health, religious privileges, and conscience, for the convenience, enjoyment, or supposed advantage of any other class on the Lord's Day " !   The idea of making a man truly moral through the ministry of constables, and sincerely religious under the influence of penalties, is worthy of the mind which could form such a mass of monstrous absurdity as this bill is composed of.

The House of Commons threw the measure out certainly, and by so doing retrieved the disgrace — so far as it could be retrieved — of placing among the printed papers of Parliament such an egregious specimen of legislative folly ; but there was a degree of delicacy and forbearance about the debate that took place which I cannot help thinking as unnecessary and uncalled for, as it is unusual in parliamentary discussions.   If it had been the first time of Sir Andrew Agnew's attempting to palm such a measure upon the country, we might well understand, and duly appreciate, the delicate and compassionate feeling due to the supposed weakness and imbecility of the man, which prevented his proposition being exposed in its true colours, and induced this Hon. Member to bear testimony to his excellent motives, and that Noble Lord to regret that he could not — although he had tried to do so — adopt any portion of the bill. But when these attempts have been repeated, again and again; when Sir Andrew Agnew has renewed them session after session, and when it has become palpably evident to the whole House that —

> His impudence of proof in every trial
> Kens no polite, and heeds no plain denial,

it really becomes high time to speak of him and his legislation, as they appear to deserve, without that gloss of politeness, which is all very well in an ordinary case, but rather out of place when the liberties and comforts of a whole people are at stake.

In the first place, it is by no means the worst characteristic of this bill, that it is a bill of blunders : it is, from beginning to end, a piece of deliberate cruelty and crafty injustice. If the rich composed the whole population of this country, not a single comfort of one single man would be affected by it. It is directed exclusively, and without the exception of a solitary instance, against the amusements and recreations of the poor. This was the bait held out by the Hon. Baronet to a body of men who cannot be supposed to have any very strong sympathies in common with the poor, because they cannot understand their sufferings or their struggles. This is the bait which will in time prevail, unless public attention is awakened, and public feeling exerted, to prevent it.

Take the very first clause, the provision that no man shall be allowed to work on Sunday — "That no person, upon the Lord's Day, shall do, or hire or employ any person to do, any manner of labour, or any work of his or her ordinary calling." What class of persons does this affect ? The rich man ? No. Menial servants, both male and female, are specially exempted from the operation of the bill. " Menial servants " are among the poor people. The bill has no regard for them. The Baronet's dinner must be cooked on Sunday, the Bishop's horses must be groomed, and the Peer's carriage must be driven. So the menial servants are put utterly beyond the pale of grace ; — unless, indeed, they are to go to heaven through the sanctity of their masters, and possibly they might think even that rather an uncertain passport.

There is a penalty for keeping open houses of entertainment. Now, suppose the bill had passed, and that half a
dozen adventurous licensed victuallers, relying upon the excitement of public feeling on the subject, and the consequent
difficulty of conviction (this is by no means an improbable
supposition), had determined to keep their houses and gardens
open, through the whole Sunday afternoon, in defiance of the
law. Every act of hiring or working, every act of buying or
selling, or delivering, or causing anything to be bought or sold,
is specifically made a separate offence — mark the effect. A
party, a man and his wife and children, enter a tea-garden, and
the informer stations himself in the next box, from whence he
can see and hear everything that passes. " Waiter ! " says the
father. " Yes, sir." " Pint of the best ale ! " " Yes, sir."
Away runs the waiter to the bar, and gets the ale from the
landlord. Out comes the informer's note-book — penalty on
the father for hiring, on the waiter for delivering, and on the
landlord for selling, on the Lord's Day. But it does not stop
here. The waiter delivers the ale, and darts off, little suspecting
the penalties in store for him. " Hollo," cries the father,
" waiter ! " " Yes, sir." " Just get this little boy a biscuit,
will you ? " " Yes, sir." Off runs the waiter again, and down
goes another case of hiring, another case of delivering, and
another case of selling ; and so it would go on ad infinitum,
the sum and substance of the matter being, that every time a
man or woman cried " Waiter ! " on Sunday, he or she would
be fined not less than forty shillings, nor more than a hundred ;
and every time a waiter replied, " Yes, sir," he and his master
would be fined in the same amount : with the addition of a
new sort of window duty on the landlord, to wit, a tax of
twenty shillings an hour for every hour beyond the first one,
during which he should have his shutters down on the Sabbath.

With one exception, there are, perhaps, no clauses in the
whole bill so strongly illustrative of its partial operation, and
the intention of its framer, as those which relate to travelling
on Sunday. Penalties of ten, twenty, and thirty pounds, are
mercilessly imposed upon coach proprietors who shall run their
coaches on the Sabbath ; one, two, and ten pounds upon those
who hire, or let to hire, horses and carriages upon the Lord's
Day, but not one syllable about those who have no necessity to
hire, because they have carriages and horses of their own ; not

one word of a penalty on liveried coachmen and footmen. The whole of the saintly venom is directed against the hired cabriolet, the humble fly, or the rumbling hackney-coach, which enables a man of the poorer class to escape for a few hours from the smoke and dirt, in the midst of which he has been confined throughout the week : while the escutcheoned carriage and the dashing cab may whirl their wealthy owners to Sunday feasts and private oratorios, setting constables, informers, and penalties at defiance. Again, in the description of the places of public resort which it is rendered criminal to attend on Sunday, there are no words comprising a very fashionable promenade. Public discussions, public debates, public lectures and speeches, are cautiously guarded against ; for it is by their means that the people become enlightened enough to deride the last efforts of bigotry and superstition. There is a stringent provision for punishing the poor man who spends an hour in a news-room, but there is nothing to prevent the rich one from lounging away the day in the Zoölogical Gardens.

There is, in four words, a mock proviso, which affects to forbid travelling " with any animal " on the Lord's Day. This, however, is revoked, as relates to the rich man, by a subsequent provision. We have, then, a penalty of not less than fifty nor more than one hundred pounds, upon any person participating in the control, or having the command, of any vessel which shall commence her voyage on the Lord's Day, should the wind prove favourable. The next time this bill is brought forward (which will no doubt be at an early period of the next session of Parliament), perhaps it will be better to amend this clause by declaring, that from and after the passing of the Act, it shall be deemed unlawful for the wind to blow at all upon the Sabbath. It would remove a great deal of temptation from the owners and captains of vessels.

The reader is now in possession of the principal enacting clauses of Sir Andrew Agnew's bill, with the exception of one, for preventing the killing or taking of "*fish, or other wild animals*," and the ordinary provisions which are inserted for form's sake in all Acts of Parliament. I now beg his attention to the clauses of exemption.

They are two in number. The first exempts menial servants from any rest, and all poor men from any recreation : outlaws a milkman after nine o'clock in the morning, and makes eating houses lawful for only two hours in the afternoon; permits a medical man to use his carriage on Sunday, and declares that a clergyman may either use his own, or hire one.

The second is artful, cunning, and designing; shielding the rich man from the possibility of being entrapped, and affecting at the same time to have a tender and scrupulous regard for the interests of the whole community. It declares, " that nothing in this Act contained shall extend to works of piety, charity, or necessity."

What is meant by the word " necessity " in this clause? Simply this — that the rich man shall be at liberty to make use of all the splendid luxuries he has collected around him, on any day in the week, because habit and custom have rendered them " necessary " to his easy existence; but that the poor man, who saves his money to provide some little pleasure for himself and family at lengthened intervals, shall not be permitted to enjoy it. It is not " necessary " to him, — Heaven knows, he very often goes long enough without it. This is the plain English of the clause. The carriage and pair of horses, the coachman, the footman, the helper, and the groom, are " necessary " on Sundays, as on other days, to the bishop and the nobleman; but the hackney-coach, the hired gig, or the taxed cart, cannot possibly be " necessary " to the working-man on Sundays, for he has it not at other times. The sumptuous dinner and the rich wines are " necessaries " to a great man in his own mansion; but the pint of beer and the plate of meat degrade the national character in an eating-house.

Such is the bill for promoting the true and sincere worship of God according to his Holy Will, and for protecting every class of society against being required to sacrifice their health and comfort on the Sabbath. Instances in which its operation would be as unjust as it would be absurd might be multiplied to an endless amount; but it is sufficient to place its leading provisions before the reader. In doing so I have purposely abstained from drawing upon the imagination for possible cases; the provisions to which I have referred stand in so many words upon the bill as printed by order of the House of Commons; and they can neither be disowned nor explained away.

Let us suppose such a bill as this to have actually passed both branches of the legislature; to have received the royal assent; and to have come into operation. Imagine its effect in a great city like London.

Sunday comes, and brings with it a day of general gloom and
austerity. The man who has been toiling hard all the week
has been looking towards the Sabbath, not as to a day of rest
from labour, and healthy recreation, but as one of grievous
tyranny and grinding oppression. The day which his Maker
intended as a blessing, man has converted into a curse. Instead
of being hailed by him as his period of relaxation, he finds it
remarkable only as depriving him of every comfort and enjoyment. He has many children about him, all sent into the
world at an early age, to struggle for a livelihood ; one is kept
in a warehouse all day, with an interval of rest too short to
enable him to reach home, another walks four or five miles to
his employment at the docks, a third earns a few shillings
weekly, as an errand boy, or office messenger; and the employment of the man himself detains him at some distance from his
home from morning till night. Sunday is the only day on
which they could all meet together, and enjoy a homely meal
in social comfort; and now they sit down to a cold and cheer-
less dinner : the pious guardians of the man's salvation having,
in their regard for the welfare of his precious soul, shut up the
bakers' shops. The fire blazes high in the kitchen chimney of
these well-fed hypocrites, and the rich steams of the savoury
dinner scent the air. What care they to be told that this class
of men have neither a place to cook in — nor means to bear the
expense, if they had ?

Look into your churches — diminished congregations, and
scanty attendance. People have grown sullen and obstinate,
and are becoming disgusted with the faith which condemns them
to such a day as this, once in every seven. And as you cannot make people religious by Act of Parliament, or force them
to church by constables, they display their feeling by staying
away.

Turn into the streets, and mark the rigid gloom that reigns
over everything around. The roads are empty, the fields are
deserted, the houses of entertainment are closed. Groups of
filthy and discontented-looking men are idling about at the street
corners, or sleeping in the sun ; but there are no decently
dressed people of the poorer class, passing to and fro. Where
should they walk to ? It would take them an hour, at least, to
get into the fields, and when they reached them, they could
procure neither bit nor sup, without the informer and the

penalty. Now and then, a carriage rolls smoothly on, or a well-mounted horseman, followed by a liveried attendant, canters by ; but with these exceptions, all is as melancholy and quiet as if a pestilence had fallen on the city.

Bend your steps through the narrow and thickly inhabited streets, and observe the sallow faces of the men and women, who are lounging at the doors, or lolling from the windows. Regard well the closeness of these crowded rooms, and the noisome exhalations that rise from the drains and kennels ; and then laud the triumph of religion and morality which condemns people to drag their lives out in such stews as these, and makes it criminal for them to eat or drink in the fresh air, or under the clear sky. Here and there, from some half-opened window, the loud shout of drunken revelry strikes upon the ear, and the noise of oaths and quarrelling — the effect of the close and heated atmosphere — is heard on all sides. See how the men all rush to join the crowd that are making their way down the street, and how loud the execrations of the mob become as they draw nearer. They have assembled round a little knot of constables, who have seized the stock in trade, heinously exposed on Sunday, of some miserable walking-stick seller, who follows clamouring for his property. The dispute grows warmer and fiercer, until at last some of the more furious among the crowd rush forward to restore the goods to their owner. A general conflict takes place ; the sticks of the constables are exercised in all directions ; fresh assistance is procured ; and half a dozen of the assailants are conveyed to the station-house, struggling, bleeding, and cursing. The case is taken to the police-office on the following morning ; and after a frightful amount of perjury on both sides, the men are sent to prison for resisting the officers, their families to the work-house to keep them from starving : and there they both remain for a month afterwards, glorious trophies of the sanctified enforcement of the Christian Sabbath. Add to such scenes as these the profligacy, idleness, drunkenness, and vice, that will be committed to an extent which no man can foresee, on Monday, as an atonement for the restraint of the preceding day, and you have a very faint and imperfect picture of the religious effects of this Sunday legislation, supposing it could ever be forced upon the people.

But let those who advocate the cause of fanaticism reflect well upon the probable issue of their endeavours. They may, by perseverance, succeed with Parliament. Let them ponder on the probability of succeeding with the people. You may deny the concession of a political question for a time, and a nation will bear it patiently. Strike home to the comforts of every man's fireside — tamper with every man's freedom and liberty — and one month, one week, may rouse a feeling abroad which a king would gladly yield his crown to quell, and a peer would resign his coronet to allay.

It is the custom to affect a deference for the motives of those who advocate these measures, and a respect for the feelings by which they are actuated. They do not deserve it. If they legislate in ignorance, they are criminal and dishonest; if they do so with their eyes open, they commit wilful injustice; in either case, they bring religion into contempt. But they do NOT legislate in ignorance. Public prints, and public men, have pointed out to them, again and again, the consequences of their proceedings. If they persist in thrusting themselves forward, let those consequences rest upon their own heads, and let them be content to stand upon their own merits.

It may be asked, What motives can actuate a man who has so little regard for the comfort of his fellow-beings, so little respect for their wants and necessities, and so distorted a notion of the beneficence of his Creator ? I reply, An envious, heartless, ill-conditioned dislike to seeing those whom fortune has placed below him cheerful and happy — an intolerant confidence in his own high worthiness before God, and a lofty impression of the demerits of others — pride, selfish pride, as inconsistent with the spirit of Christianity itself, as opposed to the example of its Founder upon earth.

To these may be added another class of men — the stern and gloomy enthusiasts, who would make earth a hell, and religion a torment ; men who, having wasted the earlier part of their lives in dissipation and depravity, find themselves, when scarcely past its meridian, steeped to the neck in vice, and shunned like a loathsome disease. Abandoned by the world, having nothing to fall back upon, nothing to remember but time misspent, and energies misdirected, they turn their eyes and not their thoughts to Heaven, and delude themselves into the impious belief that, in denouncing the lightness of heart of which they cannot partake, and the rational pleasures from which they never derived enjoyment, they are more than remedy

ing the sins of their old career, and — like the founders of
monasteries and builders of churches, in ruder days — establishing a good set claim upon their Maker.

III

AS IT MIGHT BE MADE

THE supporters of Sabbath Bills, and more especially the
extreme class of Dissenters, lay great stress upon the declarations occasionally made by criminals from the condemned cell
or the scaffold, that to Sabbath-breaking they attribute their
first deviation from the path of rectitude ; and they point to
these statements as an incontestable proof of the evil consequences which await a departure from that strict and rigid
observance of the Sabbath which they uphold. I cannot help
thinking that in this, as in almost every other respect connected
with the subject, there is a considerable degree of cant, and a
very great deal of wilful blindness. If a man be viciously disposed — and, with very few exceptions, not a man dies by the
executioner's hands who has not been in one way or other a
most abandoned and profligate character for many years — if a
man be viciously disposed, there is no doubt that he will turn
his Sunday to bad account, that he will take advantage of it to
dissipate with other bad characters as vile as himself ; and that
in this way he may trace his first yielding to temptation, possibly his first commission of crime, to an infringement of the Sabbath.   But this would be an argument against any holiday at
all.   If his holiday had been Wednesday instead of Sunday,
and he had devoted it to the same improper uses, it would
have been productive of the same results.   It is too much to
judge of the character of a whole people by the confessions of
the very worst members of society.   It is not fair to cry down
things which are harmless in themselves, because evil-disposed
men may turn them to bad account.   Who ever thought of deprecating the teaching poor people to write, because some porter
in a warehouse had committed forgery ?   Or into what man's
head did it ever enter to prevent the crowding of churches,
because it afforded a temptation for the picking of pockets ?
When the Book of Sports, for allowing the peasantry of Eng-

land to divert themselves with certain games in the open air, on Sundays, after evening service, was published by Charles the First, it is needless to say the English people were comparatively rude and uncivilised. And yet it is extraordinary to how few excesses it gave rise, even in that day, when men's minds were not enlightened, or their passions moderated, by the influence of education and refinement. That some excesses were committed through its means, in the remoter parts of the country, and that it was discontinued in those places, in consequence, cannot be denied ; but generally speaking, there is no proof whatever on record of its having had any tendency to increase crime, or to lower the character of the people.

The Puritans of that time were as much opposed to harmless recreations and healthful amusements as those of the present day, and it is amusing to observe that each in their generation advance precisely the same description of arguments. In the British Museum there is a curious pamphlet, got up by the Agnews of Charles's time, entitled, " A Divine Tragedie lately acted, or a Collection of sundry memorable examples of Gods judgements upon Sabbath-breakers, and other like Libertines, in their unlawfull Sports, happening within the Realme of England, in the compass only of two yeares last past, since the Booke [of Sports] was published, worthy to be knowne and considered of all men, especially such who are guilty of the sinne or Arch-patrons thereof." This amusing document contains some fifty or sixty veritable accounts of balls of fire that fell into churchyards and upset the sporters, and sporters that quarrelled and upset one another, and so forth ; and among them is one anecdote containing an example of a rather different kind, which I cannot resist the temptation of quoting, as strongly illustrative of the fact that this blinking of the question has not even the recommendation of novelty.

" A woman about Northampton, the same day that shee heard the booke for sports read, went immediately, and having 3. pence in her purse, hired a fellow to goe to the next Towne to fetch a Minstrell, who comming, shee with others fell a dauncing, which continued within night ; at which time shee was got with child, which at the birth shee murthering, was detected and apprehended, and being convented before the justice, shee confessed it, and withall told the occasion of it, saying it was her falling to sport on the Sabbath, upon the reading of the booke, so as for this treble sinful act, her presumtuous profaning of the Sabbath, which brought her adultery & that murther, shee was according to the Law, both of God and man, put to death. Much sinne and misery followeth upon Sabbath-breaking."

It is needless to say, that if the young lady near Northampton had "fallen to sport" of such a dangerous description, on any other day but Sunday, the first result would probably have been the same: it never having been distinctly shown that Sunday is more favourable to the propagation of the human race than any other day in the week. The second result — the murder of the child — does not speak very highly for the amiability of her natural disposition ; and the whole story, supposing it to have had any foundation at all, is about as much chargeable upon the Book of Sports as upon the Book of Kings. Such "sports" have taken place in Dissenting Chapels before now, but religion has never been blamed in consequence ; nor has it been proposed to shut up the chapels on that account.

The question, then, very fairly arises, whether we have any reason to suppose that allowing games in the open air on Sundays, or even providing the means of amusement for the humbler classes of society on that day, would be hurtful and injurious to the character and morals of the people.

I was travelling in the west of England a summer or two back, and was induced by the beauty of the scenery, and the seclusion of the spot, to remain for the night in a small village, distant about seventy miles from London. The next morning was Sunday ; and I walked out, towards the church. Groups of people — the whole population of the little hamlet apparently — were hastening in the same direction. Cheerful and good-humoured congratulations were heard on all sides, as neighbours overtook each other, and walked on in company. Occasionally I passed an aged couple, whose married daughter and her husband were loitering by the side of the old people, accommodating their rate of walking to their feeble pace, while a little knot of children hurried on before ; stout young labourers in clean round frocks, and buxom girls with healthy, laughing faces, were plentifully sprinkled about in couples, and the whole scene was one of quiet and tranquil contentment, irresistibly captivating. The morning was bright and pleasant, the hedges were green and blooming, and a thousand delicious scents were wafted on the air from the wild flowers which blossomed on either side of the footpath. The little church was one of those venerable simple buildings which abound in the English counties; half overgrown with moss and ivy, and standing in the centre of a little plot of ground, which, but for the green mounds with which it was studded, might have passed for a lovely meadow. I fancied that the old clanking bell, which was now summoning the congregation together, would seem less terrible when it rung out the knell of a departed soul than I had ever deemed possible before — that the sound would tell only of a welcome to calmness and rest, amidst the most peaceful and tranquil scene in nature.

I followed into the church — a low-roofed building with small arched windows, through which the sun's rays streamed upon a plain tablet on the opposite wall, which had once recorded names, now as undistinguishable on its worn surface as were the bones beneath, from the dust into which they had resolved. The impressive service of the Church of England was spoken — not merely *read* — by a grey-headed minister, and the responses delivered by his auditors, with an air of sincere devotion as far removed from affectation or display as from coldness or indifference. The psalms were accompanied by a few instrumental performers, who were stationed in a small gallery extending across the church at the lower end, over the door; and the voices were led by the clerk, who, it was evident, derived no slight pride and gratification from this portion of the service. The discourse was plain, unpretending, and well adapted to the comprehension of the hearers. At the conclusion of the service, the villagers waited in the churchyard to salute the clergyman as he passed; and two or three, I observed, stepped aside, as if communicating some little difficulty, and asking his advice. This, to guess from the homely bows, and other rustic expressions of gratitude, the old gentleman readily conceded. He seemed intimately acquainted with the circumstances of all his parishioners; for I heard him inquire after one man's youngest child, another man's wife, and so forth; and that he was fond of his joke I discovered from overhearing him ask a stout, fresh-coloured young fellow, with a very pretty bashful-looking girl on his arm, "When those banns were to be put up?" — an inquiry which made the young fellow more fresh-coloured, and the girl more bashful, and

which, strange to say, caused a great many other girls who
were standing round, to colour up also, and look anywhere but
in the faces of their male companions.

As I approached this spot in the evening, about half an hour
before sunset, I was surprised to hear the hum of voices, and
occasionally a shout of merriment from the meadow beyond the
churchyard; which I found, when I reached the stile, to be
occasioned by a very animated game of cricket, in which the
boys and young men of the place were engaged, while the
females and old people were scattered about, some seated on the
grass watching the progress of the game, and others sauntering
about in groups of two or three, gathering little nosegays of
wild roses and hedge flowers. I could not but take notice of
one old man in particular, with a bright-eyed granddaughter by
his side, who was giving a sun-burnt young fellow some instructions in the game, which he received with an air of profound
deference, but with an occasional glance at the girl, which induced me to think that his attention was rather distracted from
the old gentleman's narration of the fruits of his experience.
When it was his turn at the wicket, too, there was a glance
towards the pair every now and then, which the old grandfather
very complacently considered as an appeal to his judgment of
a particular hit, but which a certain blush in the girl's face,
and a downcast look of the bright eye, led me to believe was
intended for somebody else than the old man, — and understood
by somebody else, too, or I am much mistaken.

I was in the very height of the pleasure which the contemplation of this scene afforded me, when I saw the old clergyman
making his way towards us. I trembled for an angry interruption to the sport, and was almost on the point of crying out,
to warn the cricketers of his approach; he was so close upon
me, however, that I could do nothing but remain still, and
anticipate the reproof that was preparing. What was my agreeable surprise to see the old gentleman standing at the stile, with
his hands in his pockets, surveying the whole scene with evident
satisfaction! And how dull I must have been not to have
known, till my friend the grandfather (who, by the bye, said he
had been a wonderful cricketer in his time) told me, that it was
the clergyman himself who had established the whole thing;
that it was his field they played in; and that it was he who
had purchased stumps, bats, ball, and all!

It is such scenes as this I would see near London, on a Sunday evening. It is such men as this who would do more in one year to make people properly religious, cheerful, and contented, than all the legislation of a century could ever accomplish.

It will be said — it has been very often — that it would be matter of perfect impossibility to make amusements and exercises succeed in large towns, which may be very well adapted to a country population. Here, again, we are called upon to yield to bare assertions on matters of belief and opinion, as if they were established and undoubted facts. That there is a wide difference between the two cases, no one will be prepared to dispute ; that the difference is such as to prevent the application of the same principle to both, no reasonable man, I think, will be disposed to maintain. The great majority of the people who make holiday on Sunday now are industrious, orderly, and well-behaved persons. It is not unreasonable to suppose that they would be no more inclined to an abuse of pleasures provided for them, than they are to an abuse of the pleasures they provide for themselves ; and if any people, for want of something better to do, resort to criminal practices on the Sabbath as at present observed, no better remedy for the evil can be imagined than giving them the opportunity of doing something which will amuse them, and hurt nobody else.

The propriety of opening the British Museum to respectable people on Sunday has lately been the subject of some discussion. I think it would puzzle the most austere of the Sunday legislators to assign any valid reason for opposing so sensible a proposition. The Museum contains rich specimens from all the vast museums and repositories of Nature, and rare and curious fragments of the mighty works of art, in bygone ages : all calculated to awaken contemplation and inquiry, and to tend to the enlightenment and improvement of the people. But attendants would be necessary, and a few men would be employed upon the Sabbath. They certainly would ; but how many ? Why if the British Museum, and the National Gallery, and the Gallery of Practical Science, and every other exhibition in London, from which knowledge is to be derived and information gained, were to be thrown open on a Sunday afternoon, not fifty people would be required to preside over the whole : and it would take treble the number to enforce a Sabbath bill in any three populous parishes.

I should like to see some large field, or open piece of ground, in every outskirt of London, exhibiting each Sunday evening, on a larger scale, the scene of the little country meadow. I should like to see the time arrive, when a man's attendance to his religious duties might be left to that religious feeling which most men possess in a greater or less degree, but which was never forced into the breast of any man by menace or restraint. I should like to see the time when Sunday might be looked forward to, as a recognised day of relaxation and enjoyment, and when every man might feel, what few men do now, that religion is not incompatible with rational pleasure and needful recreation.

How different a picture would the streets and public places then present! The museums, and repositories of scientific and useful inventions, would be crowded with ingenious mechanics and industrious artisans, all anxious for information, and all unable to procure it at any other time. The spacious saloons would be swarming with practical men : humble in appearance, but destined, perhaps, to become the greatest inventors and philosophers of their age. The labourers who now lounge away the day in idleness and intoxication would be seen hurrying along, with cheerful faces and clean attire, not to the close and smoky atmosphere of the public-house, but to the fresh and airy fields. Fancy the pleasant scene. Throngs of people, pouring out from the lanes and alleys of the metropolis, to various places of common resort at some short distance from the town, to join in the refreshing sports and exercises of the day — the children gambolling in crowds upon the grass, the mothers looking on, and enjoying, themselves, the little game they seem only to direct ; other parties strolling along some pleasant walks, or reposing in the shade of the stately trees ; others, again, intent upon their different amusements. Nothing should be heard on all sides but the sharp stroke of the bat as it sent the ball skimming along the ground, the clear ring of the quoit, as it struck upon the iron peg ; the noisy murmur of many voices, and the loud shout of mirth and delight, which would awaken the echoes far and wide, till the fields rung with it. The day would pass away, in a series of enjoyments which would awaken no painful reflections when night arrived ; for they would be calculated to bring with them only health and contentment. The young would lose that dread of religion, which the sour austerity of its professors too often inculcates in youthful bosoms; and the old would find less difficulty in persuading them to respect its observances. The drunken and dissipated, deprived of any excuse for their misconduct, would no longer excite pity but disgust. Above all, the more ignorant and humble class of men, who now partake of many of the bitters of life, and taste but few of its sweets, would naturally feel attachment and respect for that code of morality which, regarding the many hardships of their station, strove to alleviate its rigours, and endeavoured to soften its asperity.

This is what Sunday might be made, and what it might be made without impiety or profanation. The wise and beneficent Creator, who places men upon earth, requires that they shall perform the duties of that station of life to which they are called, and He can never intend that the more a man strives to discharge those duties, the more he shall be debarred from happiness and enjoyment. Let those who have six days in the week for all the world's pleasures appropriate the seventh to fasting and gloom, either for their own sins or those of other people, if they like to bewail them; but let those who employ their six days in a worthier manner devote their seventh to a different purpose. Let divines set the example of true morality: preach it to their flocks in the morning, and dismiss them to enjoy true rest in the afternoon; and let them select for their text, and let Sunday legislators take for their motto, the words which fell from the lips of that Master, whose precepts they misconstrue, and whose lessons they pervert: "The Sabbath was made for man, and not man for the Sabbath."

THE MUDFOG PAPERS

I

ı PUBLIC LIFE OF MR. TULRUMBLE, ONCE MAYOR OF MUDFOG

MUDFOG is a pleasant town — a remarkably pleasant town
— situated in a charming hollow by the side of a river, from
which river, Mudfog derives an agreeable scent of pitch, tar,
coals, and rope-yarn, a roving population in oil-skin hats, a
pretty steady influx of drunken bargemen, and a great many
other maritime advantages. There is a good deal of water
about Mudfog, and yet it is not exactly the sort of town for a
watering-place, either.   Water is a perverse sort of element at
the best of times, and in Mudfog it is particularly so.   In
winter, it comes oozing down the streets and tumbling over the
fields, — ay, rushes into the very cellars and kitchens of the
houses, with a lavish prodigality that might well be dispensed
with ; but in the hot summer weather it *will* dry up, and turn
green : and, although green is a very good colour in its way,
especially in grass, still it certainly is not becoming to water ;
and it cannot be denied that the beauty of Mudfog is rather
impaired, even by this trifling circumstance.   Mudfog is a
healthy place — very healthy, — damp, perhaps, but none the
worse for that.   It's quite a mistake to suppose that damp is
unwholesome : plants thrive best in damp situations, and why
should n't men ?   The inhabitants of Mudfog are unanimous in
asserting that there exists not a finer race of people on the face
of the earth ; here we have an indisputable and veracious contradiction of the vulgar error at once.   So, admitting Mudfog
to be damp, we distinctly state that it is salubrious.

The town of Mudfog is extremely picturesque.   Limehouse
and Ratcliff Highway are both something like it, but they give
you a very faint idea of Mudfog.   There are a great many more
public-houses in Mudfog — more than in Ratcliff Highway and
Limehouse put together.   The public buildings, too, are very

imposing. We consider the town-hall one of the finest specimens of shed architecture extant: it is a combination of the
pig-sty and tea-garden-box orders ; and the simplicity of its
design is of surpassing beauty. The idea of placing a large
window on one side of the door, and a small one on the other,
is particularly happy. There is a fine bold Doric beauty, too,
about the padlock and scraper, which is strictly in keeping with
the general effect.

In this room do the mayor and corporation of Mudfog
assemble together in solemn council for the public weal.
Seated on the massive wooden benches, which, with the table
in the centre, form the only furniture of the whitewashed
apartment, the sage men of Mudfog spend hour after hour in
grave deliberation. Here they settle at what hour of the night
the public-houses shall be closed, at what hour of the morning
they shall be permitted to open, how soon it shall be lawful
for people to eat their dinner on church-days, and other great
political questions ; and some times, long after silence has
fallen on the town, and the distant lights from the shops and
houses have ceased to twinkle, like far-off stars, to the sight of
the boatmen on the river, the illumination in the two unequal-
sized windows of the town-hall warns the inhabitants of Mudfog
that its little body of legislators, like a larger and better-known
body of the same genus, a great deal more noisy, and not a whit
more profound, are patriotically dozing away in company, far
into the night, for their country's good.

Among this knot of sage and learned men, no one was
so eminently distinguished, during many years, for the quiet
modesty of his appearance and demeanour, as Nicholas Tulrumble, the well-known coal-dealer. However exciting the
subject of discussion, however animated the tone of the debate,
or however warm the personalities exchanged (and even in
Mudfog we get personal sometimes), Nicholas Tulrumble was
always the same. To say truth, Nicholas, being an industrious
man, and always up betimes, was apt to fall asleep when a
debate began, and to remain asleep till it was over, when he
would wake up very much refreshed, and give his vote with
the greatest complacency. The fact was, that Nicholas Tulrumble, knowing that everybody there had made up his mind
beforehand, considered the talking as just a long botheration
about nothing at all ; and to the present hour it remains a

question, whether, on this point at all events, Nicholas Tulrumble was not pretty near right.

Time, which strews a man's head with silver, sometimes fills
his pockets with gold. As he gradually performed one good
office for Nicholas Tulrumble, he was obliging enough not to
omit the other. Nicholas began life in a wooden tenement of
four feet square, with a capital of two and ninepence, and a
stock in trade of three bushels and a half of coals, exclusive
of the large lump which hung, by way of signboard, outside.
Then he enlarged the shed, and kept a truck; then he left
the shed, and the truck too, and started a donkey and a Mrs.
Tulrumble; then he moved again and set up a cart; the cart
was soon afterwards exchanged for a wagon; and so he went
on like his great predecessor Whittington — only without a cat
for a partner — increasing in wealth and fame, until at last he
gave up business altogether, and retired with Mrs. Tulrumble
and family to Mudfog Hall, which he had himself erected, on
something which he attempted to delude himself into the belief
was a hill, about a quarter of a mile distant from the town of
Mudfog.

About this time, it began to be murmured in Mudfog that
Nicholas Tulrumble was growing vain and haughty; that prosperity and success had corrupted the simplicity of his manners,
and tainted the natural goodness of his heart; in short, that he
was setting up for a public character, and a great gentleman,
and affected to look down upon his old companions with compassion and contempt. Whether these reports were at the time
well founded, or not, certain it is that Mrs. Tulrumble very
shortly afterwards started a four-wheel chaise, driven by a tall
postilion in a yellow cap, — that Mr. Tulrumble junior took to
smoking cigars, and calling the footman a " feller," — and that
Mr. Tulrumble, from that time forth, was no more seen in his
old seat in the chimney corner of the Lighterman's Arms at
night. This looked bad; but, more than this, it began to be
observed that Mr. Nicholas Tulrumble attended the corporation
meetings more frequently than heretofore; and he no longer
went to sleep as he had done for so many years, but propped
his eyelids open with his two forefingers; that he read the
newspapers by himself at home; and that he was in the habit
of indulging abroad in distant and mysterious allusions to
" masses of people," and " the property of the country," and

" productive power," and " the monied interest : " all of which
denoted and proved that Nicholas Tulrumble was either mad, or
worse ; and it puzzled the good people of Mudfog amazingly.
At length, about the middle of the month of October, Mr.
Tulrumble and family went up to London ; the middle of October being, as Mrs. Tulrumble informed her acquaintance in
Mudfog, the very height of the fashionable season.

Somehow or other, just about this time, despite the health-
preserving air of Mudfog, the mayor died. It was a most
extraordinary circumstance ; he had lived in Mudfog for eighty-
five years. The corporation did n't understand it at all ; indeed,
it was with great difficulty that one old gentleman, who was a
great stickler for forms, was dissuaded from proposing a vote of
censure on such unaccountable conduct. Strange as it was,
however, die he did, without taking the slightest notice of the
corporation ; and the corporation were imperatively called upon
to elect his successor. So they met for the purpose ; and being
very full of Nicholas Tulrumble just then, and Nicholas Tulrumble being a very important man, they elected him, and
wrote off to London by the very next post to acquaint Nicholas
Tulrumble with his new elevation.

Now, it being November time, and Mr. Nicholas Tulrumble
being in the capital, it fell out that he was present at the Lord
Mayor's show and dinner, at sight of the glory and splendour
whereof, he, Mr. Tulrumble, was greatly mortified, inasmuch as
the reflection would force itself on his mind that, had he been
in London instead of in Mudfog, he might have been a Lord
Mayor too, and have patronised the judges, and been affable to
the Lord Chancellor, and friendly with the Premier, and coldly
condescending to the Secretary to the Treasury, and have dined
with a flag behind his back, and done a great many other acts
and deeds which unto Lord Mayors of London peculiarly apper
tain. The more he thought of the Lord Mayor, the more envi
able a personage he seemed. To be a King was all very well ;
but what was the King to the Lord Mayor ! When the King
made a speech, everybody knew it was somebody else's writing ;
whereas here was the Lord Mayor, talking away for half an
hour — all out of his own head — amidst the enthusiastic applause of the whole company, while it was notorious that the
King might talk to his parliament till he was black in the face
without getting so much as a single cheer. As all these reflec

tions passed through the mind of Mr. Nicholas Tulrumble, the Lord Mayor of London appeared to him the greatest sovereign on the face of the earth, beating the Emperor of Russia all to nothing, and leaving the Great Mogul immeasurably behind.

Mr. Nicholas Tulrumble was pondering over these things, and inwardly cursing the fate which had pitched his coal-shed in Mudfog, when the letter of the corporation was put into his hand. A crimson flush mantled over his face as he read it, for visions of brightness were already dancing before his imagination.

"My dear," said Mr. Tulrumble to his wife, "they have elected me mayor of Mudfog."

"Lor'-a-mussy!" said Mrs. Tulrumble : "why what's become of old Sniggs?"

"The late Mr. Sniggs, Mrs. Tulrumble," said Mr. Tulrumble sharply, for he by no means approved of the notion of unceremoniously designating a gentleman who filled the high office of mayor, as "old Sniggs," — "the late Mr. Sniggs, Mrs. Tulrumble, is dead."

The communication was very unexpected; but Mrs. Tulrumble only ejaculated "Lor'-a-mussy!" once again, as if a mayor were a mere ordinary Christian, at which Mr. Tulrumble frowned gloomily.

"What a pity 't ain't in London, ain't it?" said Mrs. Tulrumble, after a short pause; "what a pity 't ain't in London, where you might have had a show."

"I *might* have a show in Mudfog, if I thought proper, I apprehend," said Mr. Tulrumble mysteriously.

"Lor'! so you might, I declare," replied Mrs. Tulrumble.

"And a good one too," said Mr. Tulrumble.

"Delightful!" exclaimed Mrs. Tulrumble.

"One which would rather astonish the ignorant people down there," said Mr. Tulrumble.

"It would kill them with envy," said Mrs. Tulrumble.

So it was agreed that his Majesty's lieges in Mudfog should be astonished with splendour, and slaughtered with envy, and that such a show should take place as had never been seen in that town, or in any other town before, — no, not even in London itself.

On the very next day after the receipt of the letter, down came the tall postilion in a post-chaise, — not upon one of the horses, but inside — actually inside the chaise, — and, driving up to the very door of the town hall, where the corporation were assembled, delivered a letter, written by the Lord knows who, and signed by Nicholas Tulrumble, in which Nicholas said, all through four sides of closely-written, gilt-edged, hot-pressed, Bath post letter paper, that he responded to the call of his fellow-townsmen with feelings of heartfelt delight; that he accepted the arduous office which their confidence had imposed upon him; that they would never find him shrinking from the discharge of his duty; that he would endeavour to execute his functions with all that dignity which their magnitude and importance demanded; and a great deal more to the same effect. But even this was not all. The tall postilion produced from his right-hand top-boot a damp copy of that afternoon's number of the county paper; and there, in large type, running the whole length of the very first column, was a long address from Nicholas Tulrumble to the inhabitants of Mudfog, in which he said that he cheerfully complied with their requisition, and, in short, as if to prevent any mistake about the matter, told them over again what a grand fellow he meant to be, in very much the same terms as those in which he had already told them all about the matter in his letter.

The corporation stared at one another very hard at all this, and then looked as if for explanation to the tall postilion, but as the tall postilion was intently contemplating the gold tassel on the top of his yellow cap, and could have afforded no explanation whatever, even if his thoughts had been entirely disengaged, they contented themselves with coughing very dubiously, and looking very grave. The tall postilion then delivered another letter, in which Nicholas Tulrumble informed the corporation that he intended repairing to the town hall, in grand state and gorgeous procession, on the Monday afternoon next ensuing. At this the corporation looked still more solemn; but as the epistle wound up with a formal invitation to the whole body to dine with the mayor on that day, at Mudfog Hall, Mudfog Hill, Mudfog, they began to see the fun of the thing directly, and sent back their compliments, and they'd be sure to come.

Now there happened to be in Mudfog, as somehow or other there does happen to be, in almost every town in the British dominions, and perhaps in foreign dominions too — we think it very likely, but, being no great traveller, cannot distinctly say

— there happened to be, in Mudfog, a merry-tempered, pleasant-faced, good-for-nothing sort of vagabond, with an invincible dislike to manual labour, and an unconquerable attachment to strong beer and spirits, whom everybody knew, and nobody, except his wife, took the trouble to quarrel with, who inherited from his ancestors the appellation of Edward Twigger, and rejoiced in the *sobriquet* of Bottle-nosed Ned. He was drunk upon the average once a day, and penitent upon an equally fair calculation once a month; and when he was penitent, he was invariably in the very last stage of maudlin intoxication. He was a ragged, roving, roaring kind of fellow, with a burly form, a sharp wit, and a ready head, and could turn his hand to anything when he chose to do it. He was by no means opposed to hard labour on principle, for he would work away at a cricket-match by the day together, — running, and catching, and batting, and bowling, and revelling in toil which would exhaust a galley-slave. He would have been invaluable to a fire-office; never was a man with such a natural taste for pumping engines, running up ladders, and throwing furniture out of two-pair-of-stairs windows; nor was this the only element in which he was at home : he was a humane society in himself, a portable drag, an animated life-preserver, and had saved more people, in his time, from drowning, than the Plymouth life-boat, or Captain Manby's apparatus. With all these qualifications, notwithstanding his dissipation, Bottle-nosed Ned was a general favourite; and the authorities of Mudfog, remembering his numerous services to the population, allowed him in return to get drunk in his own way, without the fear of stocks, fine, or imprisonment. He had a general licence, and he showed his sense of the compliment by making the most of it.

We have been thus particular in describing the character and avocations of Bottle-nosed Ned, because it enables us to introduce a fact politely, without hauling it into the reader's presence with indecent haste by the head and shoulders, and brings us very naturally to relate, that on the very same evening on which Mr. Nicholas Tulrumble and family returned to Mudfog, Mr. Tulrumble's new secretary, just imported from London, with a pale face and light whiskers, thrust his head down to the very bottom of his neckcloth-tie, in at the tap-room door of the Lighterman's Arms, and, inquiring whether one Ned Twigger was luxuriating within, announced himself as the bearer of a message from Nicholas Tulrumble, Esquire, requiring Mr. Twigger's immediate attendance at the hall, on private and particular business. It being by no means Mr. Twigger's interest to affront the mayor, he rose from the fireplace with a slight sigh, and followed the light-whiskered secretary through the dirt and wet of Mudfog streets, up to Mudfog Hall, without further ado.

Mr. Nicholas Tulrumble was seated in a small cavern with a skylight, which he called his library, sketching out a plan of the procession on a large sheet of paper; and into the cavern the secretary ushered Ned Twigger.

"Well, Twigger!" said Nicholas Tulrumble, condescendingly.

There was a time when Twigger would have replied, "Well, Nick!" but that was in the days of the truck, and a couple of years before the donkey; so he only bowed.

"I want you to go into training, Twigger," said Mr. Tulrumble.

"What for, sir?" inquired Ned, with a stare.

"Hush, hush, Twigger!" said the mayor. "Shut the door, Mr. Jennings. Look here, Twigger."

As the mayor said this, he unlocked a high closet, and disclosed a complete suit of brass armour, of gigantic dimensions.

"I want you to wear this next Monday, Twigger," said the mayor.

"Bless your heart and soul, sir!" replied Ned, "you might as well ask me to wear a seventy-four pounder, or a cast-iron boiler."

"Nonsense, Twigger, nonsense!" said the mayor.

"I could n't stand under it, sir," said Twigger; "it would make mashed potatoes of me, if I attempted it."

"Pooh, pooh, Twigger!" returned the mayor. "I tell you I have seen it done with my own eyes, in London, and the man was n't half such a man as you are, either."

"I should as soon have thought of a man's wearing the case of an eight-day clock to save his linen," said Twigger, casting a look of apprehension at the brass suit.

"It 's the easiest thing in the world," rejoined the mayor.

"It 's nothing," said Mr. Jennings.

"When you 're used to it," added Ned.

"You do it by degrees," said the mayor. "You would begin with one piece to-morrow, and two the next day, and so on, till you had got it all on. Mr. Jennings, give Twigger a glass of rum. Just try the breast-plate, Twigger. Stay ; take another glass of rum first. Help me to lift it, Mr. Jennings. Stand firm, Twigger! There! — it is n't half as heavy as it looks, is it ? "

Twigger was a good strong, stout fellow; so, after a great deal of staggering, he managed to keep himself up, under the breast-plate, and even contrived, with the aid of another glass of rum, to walk about in it, and the gauntlets into the bargain. He made a trial of the helmet, but was not equally successful, inasmuch as he tipped over instantly — an accident which Mr. Tulrumble clearly demonstrated to be occasioned by his not having a counteracting weight of brass on his legs.

" Now, wear that with grace and propriety on Monday next," said Tulrumble, " and I 'll make your fortune."

" I 'll try what I can do, sir," said Twigger.

" It must be kept a profound secret," said Tulrumble.

" Of course, sir," replied Twigger.

" And you must be sober," said Tulrumble; "perfectly sober."

Mr. Twigger at once solemnly pledged himself to be as sober as a judge, and Nicholas Tulrumble was satisfied, although, had we been Nicholas, we should certainly have exacted some promise of a more specific nature; inasmuch as, having attended the Mudfog assizes in the evening more than once, we can solemnly testify to having seen judges with very strong symptoms of dinner under their wigs. However, that 's neither here nor there.

The next day, and the day following, and the day after that, Ned Twigger was securely locked up in the small cavern with the skylight, hard at work at the armour. With every additional piece he could manage to stand upright in, he had an additional glass of rum ; and at last, after many partial suffocations, he contrived to get on the whole suit, and to stagger up and down the room in it, like an intoxicated effigy from Westminster Abbey.

Never was man so delighted as Nicholas Tulrumble; never was woman so charmed as Nicholas Tulrumble's wife. Here was a sight for the common people of Mudfog! A live man in brass armour! Why, they would go wild with wonder!

The day — the Monday — arrived.

If the morning had been made to order, it could n't have been better adapted to the purpose. They never showed a better fog in London on Lord Mayor's day than enwrapped the town of Mudfog on that eventful occasion. It had risen slowly and surely from the green and stagnant water with the first light of morning, until it reached a little above the lamp-post tops; and there it had stopped, with a sleepy, sluggish obstinacy, which bade defiance to the sun, who had got up very blood-shot about the eyes, as if he had been at a drinking-party over night, and was doing his day's work with the worst possible grace. The thick damp mist hung over the town like a huge gauze curtain. All was dim and dismal. The church steeples had bidden a temporary adieu to the world below; and every object of lesser importance — houses, barns, hedges, trees, and barges — had all taken the veil.

The church clock struck one. A cracked trumpet from the front garden of Mudfog Hall produced a feeble flourish, as if some asthmatic person had coughed into it accidentally; the gate flew open, and out came a gentleman, on a moist-sugar coloured charger, intended to represent a herald, but bearing a much stronger resemblance to a court-card on horseback. This was one of the Circus people, who always came down to Mudfog at that time of the year, and who had been engaged by Nicholas Tulrumble expressly for the occasion. There was the horse, whisking his tail about, balancing himself on his hind-legs, and flourishing away with his fore-feet, in a manner which would have gone to the hearts and souls of any reasonable crowd. But a Mudfog crowd never was a reasonable one, and in all probability never will be. Instead of scattering the very fog with their shouts, as they ought most indubitably to have done, and were fully intended to do, by Nicholas Tulrumble, they no sooner recognised the herald, than they began to growl forth the most unqualified disapprobation at the bare notion of his riding like any other man. If he had come out on his head indeed, or jumping through a hoop, or flying through a red-hot drum, or even standing on one leg with his other foot in his mouth, they might have had something to say to him; but for a professional gentleman to sit astride in the saddle, with his feet in the stirrups, was rather too good a joke. So the herald was a decided failure, and the crowd hooted with great energy, as he pranced ingloriously away.

On the procession came. We are afraid to say how many
supernumeraries there were, in striped shirts and black velvet
caps, to imitate the London watermen, or how many base imitations of running-footmen, or how many banners, which, owing
to the heaviness of the atmosphere, could by no means be prevailed on to display their inscriptions ; still less do we feel
disposed to relate how the men who played the wind instruments, looking up into the sky (we mean the fog) with musical
fervour, walked through pools of water and hillocks of mud,
till they covered the powdered heads of the running footmen
aforesaid with splashes, that looked curious, but not ornamental ;
or how the barrel-organ performer put on the wrong stop, and
played one tune while the band played another ; or how the
horses, being used to the arena, and not to the streets, would
stand still and dance, instead of going on and prancing, — all
of which are matters which might be dilated upon to great
advantage, but which we have not the least intention of dilating
upon, notwithstanding.

Oh ! it was a grand and beautiful sight to behold a corporation in glass coaches, provided at the sole cost and charge of
Nicholas Tulrumble, coming rolling along, like a funeral out of
mourning, and to watch the attempts the corporation made to
look great and solemn, when Nicholas Tulrumble himself, in the
four-wheel chaise, with the tall postilion, rolled out after them,
with Mr. Jennings on one side to look like a chaplain, and a supernumerary on the other, with an old life-guardsman's sabre, to
imitate the sword-bearer ; and to see the tears rolling down the
faces of the mob as they screamed with merriment.   This was
beautiful ! and so was the appearance of Mrs. Tulrumble and
son, as they bowed with grave dignity out of their coach
window to all the dirty faces that were laughing around them :
but it is not even with this that we have to do, but with the
sudden stopping of the procession at another blast of the
trumpet, whereat, and whereupon, a profound silence ensued,
and all eyes were turned towards Mudfog Hall, in the confident
anticipation of some new wonder.

"They won't laugh now, Mr. Jennings," said Nicholas Tulrumble.

"I think not, sir," said Mr. Jennings.

"See how eager they look," said Nicholas Tulrumble. "Aha !
the laugh will be on our side now ; eh, Mr. Jennings ? "

"No doubt of that, sir," replied Mr. Jennings; and Nicholas Tulrumble, in a state of pleasurable excitement, stood up in the four-wheel chaise, and telegraphed gratification to the mayoress behind.

While all this was going forward, Ned Twigger had descended into the kitchen of Mudfog Hall for the purpose of indulging the servants with a private view of the curiosity that was to burst upon the town; and, somehow or other, the footman was so companionable, and the housemaid so kind, and the cook so friendly, that he could not resist the offer of the firstmentioned to sit down and take something — just to drink success to master in.

So down Ned Twigger sat himself in his brass livery on the top of the kitchen table; and in a mug of something strong, paid for by the unconscious Nicholas Tulrumble, and provided by the companionable footman, drank success to the mayor and his procession; and as Ned laid by his helmet to imbibe 'the something strong, the companionable footman put it on his own head, to the immeasurable and unrecordable delight of the cook and housemaid. The companionable footman was very facetious to Ned, and Ned was very gallant to the cook and housemaid by turns. They were all very cosy and comfortable; and the something strong went briskly round.

At last Ned Twigger was loudly called for, by the procession people; and, having had his helmet fixed on, in a very complicated manner, by the companionable footman, and the kind housemaid, and the friendly cook, he walked gravely forth, and appeared before the multitude.

The crowd roared — it was not with wonder, it was not with surprise; it was most decidedly and unquestionably with laughter.

"What!" said Mr. Tulrumble, starting up in the four-wheel chaise. "Laughing? If they laugh at a man in real brass armour, they'd laugh when their own fathers were dying. Why does n't he go into his place, Mr. Jennings? What's he rolling down towards us for? he has no business here!"

"I am afraid, sir — " faltered Mr. Jennings.

"Afraid of what, sir?" said Nicholas Tulrumble, looking up into the secretary's face.

"I am afraid he's drunk, sir," replied Mr. Jennings.

Nicholas Tulrumble took one look at the extraordinary figure that was bearing down upon them; and then, clasping his secretary by the arm, uttered an audible groan in anguish of spirit.

It is a melancholy fact that Mr. Twigger, having full licence to demand a single glass of rum on the putting on of every piece of the armour, got, by some means or other, rather out of his calculation in the hurry and confusion of preparation, and drank about four glasses to a piece instead of one, not to mention the something strong which went on the top of it. Whether the brass armour checked the natural flow of perspiration, and thus prevented the spirit from evaporating, we are not scientific enough to know; but whatever the cause was, Mr. Twigger no sooner found himself outside the gate of Mudfog Hall, than he also found himself in a very considerable state of intoxication; and hence his extraordinary style of progressing. This was bad enough, but, as if fate and fortune had conspired against Nicholas Tulrumble, Mr. Twigger, not having been penitent for a good calendar month, took it into his head to be most especially and particularly sentimental, just when his repentance could have been most conveniently dispensed with. Immense tears were rolling down his cheeks, and he was vainly endeavouring to conceal his grief by applying to his eyes a blue cotton pocket-handkerchief with white spots, — an article not strictly in keeping with a suit of armour some three hundred years old, or thereabouts.

"Twigger, you villain!" said Nicholas Tulrumble, quite forgetting his dignity, "go back."

"Never," said Ned. "I'm a miserable wretch. I'll never leave you."

The bystanders of course received this declaration with acclamations of "That's right, Ned; don't!"

"I don't intend it," said Ned, with all the obstinacy of a very tipsy man. "I'm very unhappy. I'm the wretched father of an unfortunate family; but I am very faithful, sir. I'll never leave you." Having reiterated this obliging promise, Ned proceeded in broken words to harangue the crowd upon the number of years he had lived in Mudfog, the excessive respectability of his character, and other topics of the like nature.

"Here! will anybody lead him away?" said Nicholas; "if they'll call on me afterwards, I'll reward them well."

Two or three men stepped forward, with the view of bearing
Ned off, when the secretary interposed.
"Take care! take care!" said Mr. Jennings. "I beg your
pardon, sir; but they'd better not go too near him, because, if
he falls over, he'll certainly crush somebody."
At this hint the crowd retired on all sides to a very respectful distance, and left Ned, like the Duke of Devonshire, in a
little circle of his own.
"But, Mr. Jennings," said Nicholas Tulrumble, "he'll be
suffocated."
"I'm very sorry for it, sir," replied Mr. Jennings; "but
nobody can get that armour off, without his own assistance.
I'm quite certain of it from the way he put it on."
Here Ned wept dolefully, and shook his helmeted head, in a
manner that might have touched a heart of stone; but the
crowd had not hearts of stone, and they laughed heartily.
"Dear me, Mr. Jennings," said Nicholas, turning pale at
the possibility of Ned's being smothered in his antique costume,
— "dear me, Mr. Jennings, can nothing be done with him?"
"Nothing at all," replied Ned, "nothing at all. Gentlemen, I'm an unhappy wretch. I'm a body, gentlemen, in a
brass coffin." At this poetical idea of his own conjuring up,
Ned cried so much that the people began to get sympathetic,
and to ask what Nicholas Tulrumble meant by putting a man
into such a machine as that; and one individual in a hairy
waistcoat like the top of a trunk, who had previously expressed
his opinion that if Ned had n't been a poor man, Nicholas
would n't have dared to do it, hinted at the propriety of breaking the four-wheel chaise, or Nicholas's head, or both, which
last compound proposition the crowd seemed to consider a very
good notion.
It was not acted upon, however, for it had hardly been
broached, when Ned Twigger's wife made her appearance
abruptly in the little circle before noticed, and Ned no sooner
caught a glimpse of her face and form than from the mere force
of habit he set off towards his home just as fast as his legs
could carry him; and that was not very quick in the present
instance either, for, however ready they might have been to
carry *him*, they could n't get on very well under the brass
armour. So Mrs. Twigger had plenty of time to denounce
Nicholas Tulrumble to his face; to express her opinion that he

was a decided monster; and to intimate that, if her ill-used husband sustained any personal damage from the brass armour, she would have the law of Nicholas Tulrumble for manslaughter. When she had said all this with due vehemence, she posted after Ned, who was dragging himself along as best he could, and deploring his unhappiness in most dismal tones. What a wailing and screaming Ned's children raised when he got home at last ! Mrs. Twigger tried to undo the armour, first in one place, and then in another, but she could n't manage it ; so she tumbled Ned into bed, helmet, armour, gauntlets, and all. Such a creaking as the bedstead made, under Ned's weight in his new suit ! It did n't break down, though ; and there Ned lay, like the anonymous vessel in the Bay of Biscay, till next day, drinking barley water, and looking miserable ; and every time he groaned, his good lady said it served him right, which was all the consolation Ned Twigger got.

Nicholas Tulrumble and the gorgeous procession went on together to the town hall, amid the hisses and groans of all the spectators, who had suddenly taken it into their heads to consider poor Ned a martyr. Nicholas was formally installed in his new office, in acknowledgment of which ceremony he delivered himself of a speech, composed by the secretary, which was very long, and no doubt very good, only the noise of the people outside prevented anybody from hearing it but Nicholas Tulrumble himself. After which, the procession got back to Mudfog Hall anyhow it could ; and Nicholas and the corporation sat down to dinner.

But the dinner was flat, and Nicholas was disappointed. They were such dull sleepy old fellows, that corporation. Nicholas made quite as long speeches as the Lord Mayor of London had done, nay, he said the very same things that the Lord Mayor of London had said, and the deuce a cheer the corporation gave him. There was only one man in the party who was thoroughly awake ; and he was insolent, and called him Nick. Nick ! What would be the consequence, thought Nicholas, of anybody presuming to call the Lord Mayor of London "Nick" ! He should like to know what the sword-bearer would say to that ; or the recorder, or the toast-master, or any other of the great officers of the city. They 'd nick him.

But these were not the worst of Nicholas Tulrumble's doings. If they had been, he might have remained a mayor to this day, and have talked till he lost his voice. He contracted a relish for statistics, and got philosophical; and the statistics and the philosophy together, led him into an act which increased his unpopularity and hastened his downfall.

At the very end of the Mudfog High-street, and abutting on the river-side, stands the Jolly Boatmen, an old-fashioned low-roofed, bay-windowed house, with a bar, kitchen, and tap-room all in one, and a large fireplace with a kettle to correspond, round which the working-men have congregated time out of mind on a winter's night, refreshed by draughts of good strong beer, and cheered by the sounds of a fiddle and tambourine: the Jolly Boatmen having been duly licensed by the Mayor and corporation, to scrape the fiddle and thumb the tambourine from time whereof the memory of the oldest inhabitants goeth not to the contrary. Now Nicholas Tulrumble had been reading pamphlets on crime, and parliamentary reports, — or had made the secretary read them to him, which is the same thing in effect, — and he at once perceived that this fiddle and tambourine must have done more to demoralise Mudfog than any other operating causes that ingenuity could imagine. So he read up for the subject, and determined to come out on the corporation with a burst, the very next time the licence was applied for.

The licensing day came, and the red-faced landlord of the Jolly Boatmen walked into the town hall, looking as jolly as need be, having actually put on an extra fiddle for that night, to commemorate the anniversary of the Jolly Boatmen's music licence. It was applied for in due form, and was just about to be granted as a matter of course, when up rose Nicholas Tulrumble, and drowned the astonished corporation in a torrent of eloquence. He descanted in glowing terms upon the increasing depravity of his native town of Mudfog, and the excesses committed by its population. Then he related how shocked he had been, to see barrels of beer sliding down into the cellar of the Jolly Boatmen week after week; and how he had sat at a window opposite the Jolly Boatmen for two days together, to count the people who went in for beer between the hours of twelve and one o'clock alone — which, by the bye, was the time at which the great majority of the Mudfog people dined. Then he went on to state, how the number of people who came out with beer-jugs averaged twenty-one in five minutes, which,

being multiplied by twelve, gave two hundred and fifty-two
people with beer-jugs in an hour, and multiplied again by fifteen
(the number of hours during which the house was open daily)
yielded three thousand seven hundred and eighty people with
beer-jugs per day, or twenty-six thousand four hundred and
sixty people with beer-jugs, per week. Then he proceeded to
show that a tambourine and moral degradation were synony-
mous terms, and a fiddle and vicious propensities wholly
inseparable. All these arguments he strengthened and demonstrated by frequent references to a large book with a blue cover,
and sundry quotations from the Middlesex magistrates ; and in
the end, the corporation, who were posed with the figures, and
sleepy with the speech, and sadly in want of dinner into the
bargain, yielded the palm to Nicholas Tulrumble, and refused
the music licence to the Jolly Boatmen.

But although Nicholas triumphed, his triumph was short.
He carried on the war against beer-jugs and fiddles, forgetting
the time when he was glad to drink out of the one, and to dance to
the other, till the people hated, and his old friends shunned him.
He grew tired of the lonely magnificence of Mudfog Hall, and
his heart yearned towards the Lighterman's Arms. He wished
he had never set up as a public man, and sighed for the good
old times of the coal-shop, and the chimney corner.

At length old Nicholas, being thoroughly miserable, took
heart of grace, paid the secretary a quarter's wages in advance,
and packed him off to London by the next coach. Having
taken this step, he put his hat on his head, and his pride in his
pocket, and walked down to the old room at the Lighterman's
Arms. There were only two of the old fellows there, and they
looked coldly on Nicholas as he proffered his hand.

" Are you going to put down pipes, Mr. Tulrumble ? " said
one.

" Or trace the progress of crime to 'bacca ? " growled another.

" Neither," replied Nicholas Tulrumble, shaking hands with
them both, whether they would or not. " I 've come down to
say that I 'm very sorry for having made a fool of myself, and
that I hope you 'll give me up the old chair again."

The old fellows opened their eyes, and three or four more old
fellows opened the door, to whom Nicholas, with tears in his
eyes, thrust out his hand too, and told the same story. They
raised a shout of joy, that made the bells in the ancient church

tower vibrate again, and wheeling the old chair into the warm corner, thrust old Nicholas down into it, and ordered in the very largest-sized bowl of hot punch, with an unlimited number of pipes, directly.

The next day, the Jolly Boatmen got the licence, and the next night, old Nicholas and Ned Twigger's wife led off a dance to the music of the fiddle and tambourine, the tone of which seemed mightily improved by a little rest, for they never had played so merrily before. Ned Twigger was in the very height of his glory, and he danced hornpipes, and balanced chairs on his chin, and straws on his nose, till the whole company, including the corporation, were in raptures of admiration at the brilliancy of his acquirements.

Mr. Tulrumble junior could n't make up his mind to be anything but magnificent, so he went up to London and drew bills on his father; and when he had overdrawn, and got into debt, he grew penitent, and came home again.

As to old Nicholas, he kept his word, and having had six weeks of public life, never tried it any more. He went to sleep in the town hall at the very next meeting; and, in full proof of his sincerity, has requested us to write this faithful narrative. We wish it could have the effect of reminding the Tulrumbles of another sphere, that puffed-up conceit is not dignity, and that snarling at the little pleasures they were once glad to enjoy, because they would rather forget the times when they were of lower station, renders them objects of contempt and ridicule.

This is the first time we have published any of our gleanings from this particular source. Perhaps, at some future period, we may venture to open the chronicles of Mudfog.

II

FULL REPORT OF THE FIRST MEETING OF THE MUDFOG ASSOCIA-
TION FOR THE ADVANCEMENT OF EVERYTHING

WE have made the most unparalleled and extraordinary exertions to place before our readers a complete and accurate account of the proceedings at the late grand meeting of the Mudfog Association, holden in the town of Mudfog; it affords is great happiness to lay the result before them, in the shape óf variòus communications received from our able, talented, anⱡ graphic correspondent, expressly sent down for the purpose, who has immortalised us, himself, Mudfog, and the association, all at one and the same time. We have been, indeed, for somɛ days unable to determine who will transmit the greatest namɛ to posterity; ourselves, who sent our correspondent down; oui correspondent, who wrote an account of the matter; or the association, who gave our correspondent something to write about. We rather incline to the opinion that we are the greatest man of the party, inasmuch as the notion of an exclusive and authentic report originated with us; this may be prejudice: it may arise from a prepossession on our part in our own favour. Be it so. We have no doubt that every gentleman concerned in this mighty assemblage is troubled with the same complaint in a greater or less degree; and it is a consolation to us to know that we have at least this feeling in common with the great scientific stars, the brilliant and extraordinary luminaries, whose speculations we record.

We give our correspondent's letters in the order in which they reached us. Any attempt at amalgamating them into one beautiful whole would only destroy that glowing tone, that dash of wildness, and rich vein of picturesque interest, which pervade them throughout.

"MUDFOG, Monday night, seven o'clock.

"We are in a state of great excitement here. Nothing is spoken of but the approaching meeting of the association. The inn doors are thronged with waiters anxiously looking for the expected arrivals; and the numerous bills which are waferɛ up in the windows of private houses, intimating that there arɛ beds to let within, give the streets a very animated and cheerful appearance, the wafers being of a great variety of colours, and the monotony of printed inscriptions being relieved by every possible size and style of handwriting. It is confidently rumoured that Professors Snore, Doze, and Wheezy have engaged three beds and a sitting-room at the Pig and Tinder-Box. I give you the rumour as it has reached me; but I cannot, as yet, vouch for its accuracy. The moment I have been enabled to obtain any certain information upon this interesting point, you may depend upon receiving it."

"Half-past seven.

"I have just returned from a personal interview with the landlord of the Pig and Tinder-Box. He speaks confidently of the probability of Professors Snore, Doze, and Wheezy taking up their residence at his house during the sitting of the association, but denies that the beds have been yet engaged; in which representation he is confirmed by the chambermaid, — a girl of artless manners, and interesting appearance. The boots denies that it is at all likely that Professors Snore, Doze, and Wheezy will put up here; but I have reason to believe that this man has been suborned by the proprietor of the Original Pig, which is the opposition hotel. Amid such conflicting testimony it is difficult to arrive at the real truth; but you may depend upon receiving authentic information upon this point the moment the fact is ascertained. The excitement still continues. A boy fell through the window of the pastry-cook's shop at the corner of the High-street about half an hour ago, which has occasioned much confusion. The general impression is that it was an accident. Pray Heaven it may prove so!"

"Tuesday noon.

"At an early hour this morning the bells of all the churches struck seven o'clock; the effect of which, in the present lively state of the town, was extremely singular. While I was at breakfast, a yellow gig, drawn by a dark grey horse, with a patch of white over his right eyelid, proceeded at a rapid pace in the direction of the Original Pig stables; it is currently reported that this gentleman has arrived here for the purpose of attending the association, and, from what I have heard, I consider it extremely probable, although nothing decisive is yet known regarding him. You may conceive the anxiety with which we are all looking forward to the arrival of the four o'clock coach this afternoon.

"Notwithstanding the excited state of the populace, no outrage has yet been committed, owing to the admirable discipline and discretion of the police, who are nowhere to be seen. A barrel-organ is playing opposite my window, and groups of people, offering fish and vegetables for sale, parade the streets. With these exceptions everything is quiet, and I trust will continue so."

"Five o'clock.

"It is now ascertained, beyond all doubt, that Professors Snore, Doze, and Wheezy will *not* repair to the Pig and Tinder-Box, but have actually engaged apartments at the Original Pig. This intelligence is *exclusive ;* and I leave you and your readers to draw their own inferences from it. Why Professor Wheezy, of all people in the world, should repair to the Original Pig in preference to the Pig and Tinder-Box, it is not easy to conceive. The professor is a man who should be above all such petty feelings. Some people here openly impute treachery, and a distinct breach of faith to Professors Snore and Doze ; while others, again, are disposed to acquit them of any culpability in the transaction, and to insinuate that the blame rests solely with Professor Wheezy. I own that I incline to the latter opinion ; and although it gives me great pain to speak in terms of censure or disapprobation of a man of such transcendent genius and acquirements, still I am bound to say that, if my suspicions be well founded, and if all the reports which have reached my ears be true, I really do not well know what to make of the matter.

" Mr. Slug, so celebrated for his statistical researches, arrived this afternoon by the four o'clock stage. His complexion is a dark purple, and he has a habit of sighing constantly. He looked extremely well, and appeared in high health and spirits. Mr. Woodensconce also came down in the same conveyance. The distinguished gentleman was fast asleep on his arrival, and I am informed by the guard that he had been so the whole way. He was, no doubt, preparing for his approaching fatigues ; but what gigantic visions must those be that flit through the brain of such a man when his body is in a state of torpidity !

" The influx of visitors increases every moment. I am told (I know not how truly) that two post-chaises have arrived at the Original Pig within the last half hour, and I myself observed a wheelbarrow, containing three carpet bags and a bundle, entering the yard of the Pig and Tinder-Box no longer ago than five minutes since. The people are still quietly pursuing their ordinary occupations ; but there is a wildness in their eyes, and an unwonted rigidity in the muscles of their countenances, which shows to the observant spectator that their expectations are strained to the very utmost pitch. I fear, unless some very extraordinary arrivals take place to-night, that consequences may arise from this popular ferment, which every man of sense and feeling would deplore."

"Twenty minutes past six.

" I have just heard that the boy who fell through the pastry-cook's window last night has died of the fright. He was suddenly called upon to pay three and sixpence for the damage done, and his constitution, it seems, was not strong enough to bear up against the shock. The inquest, it is said, will be held to-morrow."

"Three-quarters past seven.

" Professors Muff and Nogo have just driven up to the hotel door; they at once ordered dinner with great condescension. We are all very much delighted with the urbanity of their manners, and the ease with which they adapt themselves to the forms and ceremonies of ordinary life. Immediately on their arrival they sent for the head waiter, and privately requested him to purchase a live dog, — as cheap a one as he could meet with, — and to send him up after dinner, with a pie-board, a knife and fork, and a clean plate. It is conjectured that some experiments will be tried upon the dog to-night; if any particulars should transpire, I will forward them by express."

"Half-past eight.

" The animal has been procured. He is a pug dog, of rather intelligent appearance, in good condition, and with very short legs. He has been tied to a curtain peg in a dark room, and is howling dreadfully."

"Ten minutes to nine.

" The dog has just been rung for. With an instinct which would appear almost the result of reason, the sagacious animal seized the waiter by the calf of the leg when he approached to take him, and made a desperate, though ineffectual resistance. I have not been able to procure admission to the apartment occupied by the scientific gentlemen; but judging from the sounds which reached my ears when I stood upon the landing-place outside the door, just now, I should be disposed to say that the dog had retreated growling beneath some article of furniture, and was keeping the professors at bay. This conjecture is confirmed by the testimony of the ostler, who, after peeping through the keyhole, assures me that he distinctly saw Professor Nogo on his knees, holding forth a

small bottle of prussic acid, to which the animal, who was
crouched beneath an arm-chair, obstinately declined to smell.
You cannot imagine the feverish state of irritation we are in,
lest the interests of science should be sacrificed to the prejudices of a brute creature, who is not endowed with sufficient sense to foresee the incalculable benefits which the
whole human race may derive from so very slight a concession on his part."

"Nine o'clock.

"The dog's tail and ears have been sent down stairs to be
washed; from which circumstance we infer that the animal is
no more. His forelegs have been delivered to the boots to be
brushed, which strengthens the supposition."

"Half after ten.

"My feelings are so overpowered by what has taken place in
the course of the last hour and a half, that I have scarcely
strength to detail the rapid succession of events which have
quite bewildered all those who are cognisant of their occurrence.
It appears that the pug dog mentioned in my last was surreptitiously obtained, — stolen, in fact, — by some person attached
to the stable department, from an unmarried lady resident in
this town. Frantic on discovering the loss of her favourite,
the lady rushed distractedly into the street, calling in the most
heart-rending and pathetic manner upon the passengers to
restore her, her Augustus, — for so the deceased was named, in
affectionate remembrance of a former lover of his mistress, to
whom he bore a striking personal resemblance, which renders
the circumstances additionally affecting. I am not yet in a condition to inform you what circumstance induced the bereaved
lady to direct her steps to the hotel which had witnessed the
last struggles of her *protégé*. I can only state that she arrived
there, at the very instant when his detached members were
passing through the passage on a small tray. Her shrieks still
reverberate in my ears! I grieve to say that the expressive
features of Professor Muff were much scratched and lacerated by
the injured lady; and that Professor Nogo, besides sustaining
several severe bites, has lost some handfuls of hair from the
same cause. It must be some consolation to these gentlemen to
know that their ardent attachment to scientific pursuits has
alone occasioned these unpleasant consequences; for which the

sympathy of a grateful country will sufficiently reward them. The unfortunate lady remains at the Pig and Tinder-Box, and up to this time is reported in a very precarious state.

"I need scarcely tell you that this unlooked-for catastrophe has cast a damp and gloom upon us in the midst of our exhilaration ; natural in any case, but greatly enhanced in this, by the amiable qualities of the deceased animal, who appears to have been much and deservedly respected by the whole of his acquaintance."

"Twelve o'clock.

"I take the last opportunity before sealing my parcel to inform you that the boy who fell through the pastry-cook's window is not dead, as was universally believed, but alive and well. The report appears to have had its origin in his mysterious disappearance. He was found half an hour since on the premises of a sweet-stuff maker, where a raffle had been announced for a second-hand sealskin cap and a tambourine ; and where — a sufficient number of members not having been obtained at first — he had patiently waited until the list was completed. This fortunate discovery has in some degree restored our gaiety and cheerfulness. It is proposed to get up a subscription for him without delay.

"Everybody is nervously anxious to see what to-morrow will bring forth. If any one should arrive in the course of the night, I have left strict directions to be called immediately. I should have sat up, indeed, but the agitating events of this day have been too much for me.

"No news yet of either of the Professors Snore, Doze, or Wheezy. It is very strange !"

"Wednesday afternoon.

"All is now over ; and upon one point at least I am at length enabled to set the minds of your readers at rest. The three professors arrived at ten minutes after two o'clock, and, instead of taking up their quarters at the Original Pig, as it was universally understood in the course of yesterday that they would assuredly have done, drove straight to the Pig and Tinder-Box, where they threw off the mask at once, and openly announced their intention of remaining. Professor Wheezy *may* reconcile this very extraordinary conduct with *his* notions of fair and equitable dealing, but I would recommend Professor Wheezy to be cautious how he presumes too far upon his well-earned reputation.

How such a man as Professor Snore, or, which is still more extraordinary, such an individual as Professor Doze, can quietly allow himself to be mixed up with such proceedings as these, you will naturally inquire. Upon this head, rumour is silent ; I have my speculations, but forbear to give utterance to them just now."

"Four >'clock.

" The town is filling fast ; eighteenpence has been offered for a bed and refused. Several gentlemen were under the necessity last night of sleeping in the brick-fields, and on the steps of doors, for which they were taken before the magistrates in a body this morning, and committed to prison as vagrants for various terms. One of these persons I understand to be a highly respectable tinker, of great practical skill, who had forwarded a paper to the President of Section D. Mechanical Science, on the construction of pipkins with copper bottoms and safety-valves, of which report speaks highly. The incarceration of this gentleman is greatly to be regretted, as his absence will preclude any discussion on the subject.

" The bills are being taken down in all directions, and lodgings are being secured on almost any terms. I have heard of fifteen shillings a week for two rooms, exclusive of coals and attendance, but I can scarcely believe it. The excitement is dreadful. I was informed this morning that the civil authorities, apprehensive of some outbreak of popular feeling, had commanded a recruiting sergeant and two corporals to be under arms ; and that, with the view of not irritating the people unnecessarily by their presence, they had been requested to take up their position before daybreak in a turnpike, distant about a quarter of a mile from the town. The vigour and promptness of these measures cannot be too highly extolled.

" Intelligence has just been brought me that an elderly female, in a state of inebriety, has declared in the open street her intention to ' do ' for Mr. Slug. Some statistical returns compiled by that gentleman, relative to the consumption of raw spirituous liquors in this place, are supposed to be the cause of the wretch's animosity. It is added that this declaration was loudly cheered by a crowd of persons who had assembled on the spot ; and that one man had the boldness to designate Mr. Slug aloud by the opprobrious epithet of " Stick-in-the-mud ! " It is earnestly to be hoped that now, when the moment

has arrived for their interference, the magistrates will not shrink
from the exercise of that power which is vested in them by the
constitution of our common country."

"Half-past ten.

" The disturbance, I am happy to inform you, has been completely quelled, and the ringleader taken into custody. She
had a pail of cold water thrown over her, previous to being
locked up, and expresses great contrition and uneasiness. We
are all in a fever of anticipation about to-morrow ; but, now
that we are within a few hours of the meeting of the association, and at last enjoy the proud consciousness of having its
illustrious members amongst us, I trust and hope everything
may go off peaceably. I shall send you a full report of to-morrow's proceedings by the night coach."

"Eleven o'clock.

" I open my letter to say that nothing whatever has occurred
since I folded it up."

"Thursday.

" The sun rose this morning at the usual hour. I did not
observe anything particular in the aspect of the glorious planet,
except that he appeared to me (it might have been a delusion
of my heightened fancy) to shine with more than common brilliancy, and to shed a refulgent lustre upon the town, such as I
had never observed before. This is the more extraordinary, as
the sky was perfectly cloudless, and the atmosphere peculiarly
fine. At half-past nine o'clock the general committee assembled, with the last year's president in the chair. The report of
the council was read ; and one passage, which stated that the
council had corresponded with no less than three thousand five
hundred and seventy-one persons (all of whom paid their own
postage), on no fewer than seven thousand two hundred and
forty-three topics, was received with a degree of enthusiasm
which no efforts could suppress. The various committees and
sections having been appointed, and the more formal business
transacted, the great proceedings of the meeting commenced at
eleven o'clock precisely. I had the happiness of occupying a
most eligible position at that time, in

" Section A. — Zoölogy and Botany.

" GREAT ROOM, PIG AND TINDER-BOX.

" *President* — Professor Snore.   *Vice-Presidents* — Professors
Doze and Wheezy.

" The scene at this moment was particularly striking.   The
sun streamed through the windows of the apartments, and tinted
the whole scene with its brilliant rays, bringing out in strong
relief the noble visages of the professors and scientific gentlemen, who, some with bald heads, some with red heads, some
with brown heads, some with grey heads, some with black
heads, some with block heads, presented a *coup d'œil* which no
eye-witness will readily forget.   In front of these gentlemen
were papers and inkstands; and round the room, on elevated
benches extending as far as the forms could reach, were assembled a brilliant concourse of those lovely and elegant women for
which Mudfog is justly acknowledged to be without a rival in
the whole world.   The contrast between their fair faces and
the dark coats and trousers of the scientific gentlemen I shall
never cease to remember while Memory holds her seat.

" Time having been allowed for a slight confusion, occasioned
by the falling down of the greater part of the platforms, to subside, the president called on one of the secretaries to read a
communication entitled, ' Some remarks on the industrious fleas,'
with considerations on the importance of establishing infant-
schools among that numerous class of society ; of directing
their industry to useful and practical ends ; and of applying the
surplus fruits thereof towards providing for them a comfortable
and respectable maintenance in their old age.'

" The author stated that, having long turned his attention
to the moral and social condition of these interesting animals,
he had been induced to visit an exhibition in Regent Street,
London, commonly known by the designation of ' The Industrious Fleas.'   He had there seen many fleas, occupied certainly
in various pursuits and avocations, but occupied, he was bound
to add, in a manner which no man of well-regulated mind could
fail to regard with sorrow and regret.   One flea, reduced to the
level of a beast of burden, was drawing about a miniature gig,
containing a particularly small effigy of his Grace the Duke of
Wellington ; while another was staggering beneath the weight

of a golden model of his great adversary Napoleon Bonaparte. Some, brought up as mountebanks and ballet-dancers, were performing a figure-dance (he regretted to observe that, of the fleas so employed, several were females) ; others were in training, in a small cardboard box, for pedestrians, — mere sporting characters, — and two were actually engaged in the cold-blooded and barbarous occupation of duelling; a pursuit from which human- ity recoiled with horror and disgust. He suggested that measures should be immediately taken to employ the labour of these fleas as part and parcel of the productive power of the country, which might easily be done by the establishment among them of infant-schools and houses of industry, in which a system of virtuous education, based upon sound principles, should be observed, and moral precepts strictly inculcated. He proposed that every flea who presumed to exhibit, for hire, music, or dancing, or any species of theatrical entertainment, without a licence, should be considered a vagabond, and treated accordingly ; in which respect he only placed him upon a level with the rest of mankind. He would further suggest that their labour should be placed under the control and regulation of the state, who should set apart from the profits a fund for the support of superannuated or disabled fleas, their widows and orphans. With this view, he proposed that liberal premiums should be offered for the three best designs for a general almshouse ; from which — as insect architecture was well known to be in a very advanced and perfect state — we might possibly derive many valuable hints for the improvement of our metropolitan universities, national galleries, and other public edifices.

"The President wished to be informed how the ingenious gentleman proposed to open a communication with fleas gener-. ally, in the first instance, so that they might be thoroughly imbued with a sense of the advantages they must necessarily derive from changing their mode of life and applying themselves to honest labour. This appeared to him the only difficulty.

"The author submitted that this difficulty was easily overcome, or rather that there was no difficulty at all in the case. Obviously the course to be pursued, if her Majesty's government could be prevailed upon to take up the plan, would be to secure at a remunerative salary the individual to whom he had alluded as presiding over the exhibition in Regent Street at the period of his visit. That gentleman would at once be able to put himself in communication with the mass of the fleas, and to instruct them in pursuance of some general plan of education, to be sanctioned by Parliament, until such time as the more intelligent among them were advanced enough to officiate as teachers to the rest.

" The President and several members of the section highly complimented the author of the paper last read, on his most ingenious and important treatise. It was determined that the subject should be recommended to the immediate consideration of the council.

" Mr. Wigsby produced a cauliflower somewhat larger than a chaise-umbrella, which had been raised by no other artificial means than the simple application of highly carbonated soda-water as manure. He explained that by scooping out the head, which would afford a new and delicious species of nourishment for the poor, a parachute, in principle something similar to that constructed by M. Garnerin, was at once obtained ; the stalk of course being kept downwards. He added that he was perfectly willing to make a descent from a height of not less than three miles and a quarter ; and had in fact already proposed the same to the proprietors of Vauxhall Gardens, who in the handsomest manner at once consented to his wishes, and appointed an early day next summer for the undertaking ; merely stipulating that the rim of the cauliflower should be previously broken in three or four places to insure the safety of the descent.

" The President congratulated the public on the grand gala in store for them, and warmly eulogised the proprietors of the establishment alluded to, for their love of science, and regard for the safety of human life, both of which did them the highest honour.

" A Member wished to know how many thousand additional lamps the royal property would be illuminated with, on the night after the descent.

" Mr. Wigsby replied that the point was not yet finally decided ; but he believed it was proposed, over and above the ordinary illuminations, to exhibit in various devices eight millions and a half of additional lamps.

" The Member expressed himself much gratified with this announcement.

" Mr. Blunderum delighted the section with a most interesting and valuable paper ' on the last moments of the learned pig,' which produced a very strong impression on the assembly, the account being compiled from the personal recollecticns of his favourite attendant. The account stated in the most emphatic terms that the animal's name was not Toby, but Solomon; and distinctly proved that he could have no near relatives in the profession, as many designing persons had falsely stated, inasmuch as his father, mother, brothers, and sisters, had all fallen victims to the butcher at different times. An unclo of his, indeed, had with very great labour been traced to a sty in Somers Town ; but as he was in a very infirm state at the time, being afflicted with measles, and shortly afterwards disappeared, there appeared too much reason to conjecture that he had been converted into sausages. The disorder of the learned pig was originally a severe cold, which, being aggravated by excessive trough indulgence, finally settled upon the lungs, and terminated in a general decay of the constitution. A melancholy instance of a presentiment entertained by the animal, of his approaching dissolution, was recorded. After gratifying a numerous and fashionable company with his performances, in which no falling off whatever was visible, he fixed his eyes on the biographer, and, turning to the watch which lay on the floor, and on which he was accustomed to point out the hour, deliberately passed his snout twice round the dial. In precisely four-and-twenty hours from that time he had ceased to exist !

" Professor Wheezy inquired whether, previous to his demise, the animal had expressed, by signs or otherwise, any wishes regarding the disposal of his little property.

" Mr. Blunderum replied that, when the biographer took up the pack of cards at the conclusion of the performance, the animal grunted several times in a significant manner, and nodded his head as he was accustomed to do, when gratified. From these gestures it was understood that he wished the attendant to keep the cards, which he had ever since done. He had not expressed any wish relative to his watch, which had accordingly been pawned by the same individual.

" The President wished to know whether any Member of the section had ever seen or conversed with the pig-faced lady, who was reported to have worn a black velvet mask, and to have taken her meals from a golden trough.

"After some hesitation a Member replied that the pig-faced

lady was his mother-in-law, and that he trusted the President would not violate the sanctity of private life.

"The President begged pardon. He had considered the pig-faced lady a public character. Would the honourable member object to state, with a view to the advancement of science, whether she was in any way connected with the learned pig?

"The Member replied in the same low tone that, as the question appeared to involve a suspicion that the learned pig might be his half-brother, he must decline answering it.

"SECTION B. — ANATOMY AND MEDICINE.

"COACH-HOUSE, PIG AND TINDER-BOX.

"*President* — Dr. TOORELL. *Vice - Presidents* — Professors MUFF and NOGO.

"Dr. Kutankumagen (of Moscow) read to the section a report of a case which had occurred within his own practice, strikingly illustrative of the power of medicine, as exemplified in his successful treatment of a virulent disorder. He had been called in to visit the patient on the 1st of April, 1837. He was then labouring under symptoms peculiarly alarming to any medical man. His frame was stout and muscular, his step firm and elastic, his cheeks plump and red, his voice loud, his appetite good, his pulse full and round. He was in the constant habit of eating three meals *per diem*, and of drinking at least one bottle of wine, and one glass of spirituous liquors diluted with water, in the course of the four-and-twenty hours. He laughed constantly, and in so hearty a manner that it was terrible to hear him. By dint of powerful medicine, low diet, and bleeding, the symptoms in the course of three days perceptibly decreased. A rigid perseverance in the same course of treatment for only one week, accompanied with small doses of water-gruel, weak broth, and barley-water, led to their entire disappearance. In the course of a month he was sufficiently recovered to be carried down stairs by two nurses, and to enjoy an airing in a close carriage, supported by soft pillows. At the present moment he was restored so far as to walk about, with the slight assistance of a crutch and a boy. It would perhaps be gratifying to the section to learn that he ate little, drank little, slept little, and was never heard to laugh by any accident whatever.

"Dr. W. R. Fee, in complimenting the honourable member upon the triumphant cure he had effected, begged to ask whether the patient still bled freely?

"Dr. Kutankumagen replied in the affirmative.

"Dr. W. R. Fee. — And you found that he bled freely during the whole course of the disorder?

"Dr. Kutankumagen. — Oh dear, yes; most freely.

"Dr. Neeshawts supposed that, if the patient had not submitted to be bled with great readiness and perseverance, so extraordinary a cure could never, in fact, have been accomplished. Dr. Kutankumagen rejoined, certainly not.

"Mr. Knight Bell (M. R. C. S.) exhibited a wax preparation of the interior of a gentleman who in early life had inadvertently swallowed a door-key. It was a curious fact that a medical student of dissipated habits, being present at the *post mortem* examination, found means to escape unobserved from the room, with that portion of the coats of the stomach upon which an exact model of the instrument was distinctly impressed, with which he hastened to a locksmith of doubtful character, who made a new key from the pattern so shown to him. With this key the medical student entered the house of the deceased gentleman, and committed a burglary to a large amount, for which he was subsequently tried and executed.

"The President wished to know what became of the original key after the lapse of years. Mr. Knight Bell replied that the gentleman was always much accustomed to punch, and it was supposed the acid had gradually devoured it.

"Dr. Neeshawts and several of the members were of opinion that the key must have lain very cold and heavy upon the gentleman's stomach.

"Mr. Knight Bell believed it did at first. It was worthy of remark, perhaps, that for some years the gentleman was troubled with a night-mare, under the influence of which he always imagined himself a wine-cellar door.

"Professor Muff related a very extraordinary and convincing proof of the wonderful efficacy of the system of infinitesimal doses, which the section were doubtless aware was based upon the theory that the very minutest amount of any given drug, properly dispersed through the human frame, would be productive of precisely the same result as a very large dose administered in the usual manner. Thus, the fortieth part of a grain of calomel was supposed to be equal to a five-grain calomel pill, and so on in proportion throughout the whole range of medicine. He had tried the experiment in a curious manner upon a publican who had been brought into the hospital with a broken head, and was cured upon the infinitesimal system in the incredibly short space of three months. This man was a hard drinker. He (Professor Muff) had dispersed three drops of rum through a bucket of water, and requested the man to drink the whole. What was the result? Before he had drunk a quart, he was in a state of beastly intoxication; and five other men were made dead drunk with the remainder.

"The President wished to know whether an infinitesimal dose of soda-water would have recovered them. Professor Muff replied that the twenty-fifth part of a teaspoonful, properly administered to each patient, would have sobered him immediately. The President remarked that this was a most important discovery, and he hoped the Lord Mayor and Court of Aldermen would patronise it immediately.

"A Member begged to be informed whether it would be possible to administer — say, the twentieth part of a grain of bread and cheese to all grown-up paupers, and the fortieth part to children, with the same satisfying effect as their present allowance.

"Professor Muff was willing to stake his professional reputation on the perfect adequacy of such a quantity of food to the support of human life — in workhouses; the addition of the fifteenth part of a grain of pudding twice a week would render it a high diet.

"Professor Nogo called the attention of the section to a very extraordinary case of animal magnetism. A private watchman, being merely looked at by the operator from the opposite side of a wide street, was at once observed to be in a very drowsy and languid state. He was followed to his box, and, being once slightly rubbed on the palms of the hands, fell into a sound sleep, in which he continued without intermission for ten hours.

" SECTION C. — STATISTICS.

" HAY-LOFT, ORIGINAL PIG.

"President — Mr. WOODENSCONCE. *Vice-Presidents* — Mr. LEDBRAIN and Mr. TIMBEBED.

" Mr. Slug stated to the section the result of some calculations he had made with great difficulty and labour, regarding the state of infant education among the middle classes of London. He found that, within a circle of three miles from the Elephant and Castle, the following were the names and numbers of children's books principally in circulation : —

" Jack the Giant-killer	7,943
Ditto and Bean-stalk	8,621
Ditto and Eleven Brothers	2,845
Ditto and Jill	1,998
Total	21,407

" He found that the proportion of Robinson Crusoes to Philip Quarlls was as four and a half to one ; and that the preponderance of Valentine and Orsons over Goody Two Shoeses was as three and an eighth of the former to half a one of the latter ; a comparison of Seven Champions with Simple Simons gave the same result. The ignorance that prevailed was lamentable. One child, on being asked whether he would rather be Saint George of England or a respectable tallow-chandler, instantly replied, 'Taint George of Ingling.' Another, a little boy of eight years old, was found to be firmly impressed with a belief in the existence of dragons, and openly stated that it was his intention when he grew up, to rush forth sword in hand for the deliverance of captive princesses, and the promiscuous slaughter of giants. Not one child among the number interrogated had ever heard of Mungo Park, — some inquiring whether he was at all connected with the black man that swept the crossing; and others whether he was in any way related to the Regent's Park. They had not the slightest conception of the commonest principles of mathematics, and considered Sinbad the Sailor the most enterprising voyager that the world had ever produced. " A Member, strongly deprecating the use of all the other books mentioned, suggested that Jack and Jill might perhaps be exempted from the general censure, inasmuch as the hero and heroine, in the very outset of the tale, were depicted as going *up* a hill to fetch a pail of water, which was a laborious and useful occupation, — supposing the family linen was being washed, for instance.

"Mr. Slug feared that the moral effect of this passage was more than counterbalanced by another in a subsequent part of the poem, in which very gross allusion was made to the mode in which the heroine was personally chastised by her mother

'For laughing at Jack's disaster ;'

besides, the whole work had this one great fault, *it was not true.*

"The President complimented the honourable member on the excellent distinction he had drawn. Several other Members, too, dwelt upon the immense and urgent necessity of storing the minds of children with nothing but facts and figures; which process, the President very forcibly remarked, had made them (the section) the men they were.

"Mr. Slug then stated some curious calculations respecting the dogs'-meat barrows of London. He found that the total number of small carts and barrows engaged in dispensing provision to the cats and dogs of the metropolis was one thousand seven hundred and forty-three. The average number of skewers delivered daily with the provender, by each dogs'-meat cart or barrow, was thirty-six. Now, multiplying the number of skewers so delivered by the number of barrows, a total of sixty-two thousand seven hundred and forty-eight skewers daily would be obtained. Allowing that, of these sixty-two thousand seven hundred and forty-eight skewers, the odd two thousand seven hundred and forty-eight were accidentally devoured with the meat, by the most voracious of the animals supplied, it followed that sixty thousand skewers per day, or the enormous number of twenty-one millions nine hundred thousand skewers annually, were wasted in the kennels and dustholes of London ; which, if collected and warehoused, would in ten years' time afford a mass of timber more than sufficient for the construction of a first-rate vessel of war for the use of her Majesty's navy, to be called 'The Royal Skewer,' and to become under that name the terror of all the enemies of this island.

"Mr. X. Ledbrain read a very ingenious communication, from which it appeared that the total number of legs belonging to the manufacturing population of one great town in Yorkshire was, in round numbers, forty thousand, while the total number of chair and stool legs in their houses was only thirty thousand, which, upon the very favourable average of three legs to a seat, yielded only ten thousand seats in all. From this calculation it would appear, — not taking wooden or cork legs into the account, but allowing two legs to every person, — that ten thousand individuals (one half of the whole population) were either destitute of any rest for their legs at all, or passed the whole of their leisure time in sitting upon boxes.

"SECTION D. — MECHANICAL SCIENCE.

"COACH-HOUSE, ORIGINAL PIG.

"*President* — Mr. CARTER. *Vice-Presidents* — Mr. TRUCK and Mr. WAGHORN.

"Professor Queerspeck exhibited an elegant model of a portable railway, neatly mounted in a green case, for the waistcoat pocket. By attaching this beautiful instrument to his boots, any bank or public-office clerk could transport himself from his place of residence to his place of business at the easy rate of sixty-five miles an hour, which, to gentlemen of sedentary pursuits, would be an incalculable advantage.

"The President was desirous of knowing whether it was necessary to have a level surface on which the gentleman was to run.

"Professor Queerspeck explained that City gentlemen would run in trains, being handcuffed together to prevent confusion or unpleasantness. For instance, trains would start every morning at eight, nine, and ten o'clock, from Camden Town, Islington, Camberwell, Hackney, and various other places in which City gentlemen are accustomed to reside. It would be necessary to have a level, but he had provided for this difficulty by proposing that the best line that the circumstances would admit of should be taken through the sewers which undermine the streets of the Metropolis, and which, well lighted by jets from the gas pipes which run immediately above them, would form a pleasant and commodious arcade, especially in winter-time, when the inconvenient custom of carrying umbrellas, now so general, could be wholly dispensed with. In reply to another question, Professor Queerspeck stated that no substitute for the purposes to

which these arcades were at present devoted had yet occurred
to him, but that he hoped no fanciful objection on this head
would be allowed to interfere with so great an undertaking.

"Mr. Jobba produced a forcing-machine on a novel plan, for
bringing joint-stock railway shares prematurely to a premium.
The instrument was in the form of an elegant gilt weather-glass,
of most dazzling appearance, and was worked behind, by strings,
after the manner of a pantomime trick, the strings being always
pulled by the directors of the company to which the machine
belonged. The quicksilver was so ingeniously placed, that
when the acting directors held shares in their pockets, figures
denoting very small expenses and very large returns appeared
upon the glass; but the moment the directors parted with these
pieces of paper, the estimate of needful expenditure suddenly
increased itself to an immense extent, while the statements of
certain profits became reduced in the same proportion. Mr.
Jobba stated that the machine had been in constant requisition
for some months past, and he had never once known it to fail.

"A Member expressed his opinion that it was extremely
neat and pretty. He wished to know whether it was not liable
to accidental derangement? Mr. Jobba said that the whole
machine was undoubtedly liable to be blown up, but that was
the only objection to it.

"Professor Nogo arrived from the anatomical section to
exhibit a model of a safety fire-escape, which could be fixed at
any time, in less than half an hour, and by means of which the
youngest or most infirm persons (successfully resisting the progress of the flames until it was quite ready) could be preserved
if they merely balanced themselves for a few minutes on the
sill of their bedroom window, and got into the escape without
falling into the street. The Professor stated that the number
of boys who had been rescued in the daytime by this machine,
from houses which were not on fire, was almost incredible.
Not a conflagration had occurred in the whole of London for
many months past to which the escape had not been carried on
the very next day, and put in action before a concourse of
persons.

"The President inquired whether there was not some difficulty in ascertaining which was the top of the machine, and
which the bottom, in cases of pressing emergency.

"Professor Nogo explained that of course it could not be

expected to act quite as well when there was a fire, as when there was not a fire; but in the former case he thought it would be of equal service whether the top were up or down."

With the last section our correspondent concludes his most able and faithful report, which will never cease to reflect credit upon him for his scientific attainments, and upon us for our enterprising spirit. It is needless to take a review of the subjects which have been discussed; of the mode in which they have been examined; of the great truths which they have elicited. They are now before the world, and we leave them to read, to consider, and to profit.

The place of meeting for next year has undergone discussion, and has at length been decided, regard being had to, and evidence being taken upon, the goodness of its wines, the supply of its markets, the hospitality of its inhabitants, and the quality of its hotels. We hope at this next meeting our correspondent may again be present, and that we may once more be the means of placing his communications before the world. Until that period we have been prevailed upon to allow this number of our Miscellany to be retailed to the public, or wholesaled to the trade, without any advance upon our usual price.

We have only to add, that the committees are now broken up, and that Mudfog is once again restored to its accustomed tranquillity, — that Professors and Members have had balls, and *soirées*, and suppers, and great mutual complimentations, and have at length dispersed to their several homes, — whither all good wishes and joys attend them, until next year!

[Signed]   Boz.

III

FULL REPORT OF THE SECOND MEETING OF THE MUDFOG ASSOCIA-
TION FOR THE ADVANCEMENT OF EVERYTHING

In October last, we did ourselves the immortal credit of recording, at an enormous expense, and by dint of exertions unparalleled in the history of periodical publication, the proceedings of the Mudfog Association for the Advancement of Everything, which in that month held its first great half-yearly meeting, to the wonder and delight of the whole empire. We announced at the conclusion of that extraordinary and most remarkable Report, that when the Second Meeting of the Society should take place, we should be found again at our post, renewing our gigantic and spirited endeavours, and once more making the world ring with the accuracy, authenticity, immeasurable superiority, and intense remarkability of our account of its proceedings. In redemption of this pledge, we caused to be despatched per steam to Oldcastle (at which place this second meeting of the Society was held on the 20th instant) the same superhumanly endowed gentleman who furnished the former report, and who — gifted by nature with transcendent abilities, and furnished by us with a body of assistants scarcely inferior to himself — has forwarded a series of letters, which, for faithfulness of description, power of language, fervour of thought, happiness of expression, and importance of subject matter, have no equal in the epistolary literature of any age or country. We give this gentleman's correspondence entire, and in the order in which it reached our office.

" Saloon of Steamer, Thursday night, half-past eight.

" When I left New Burlington Street this evening in the hackney cabriolet, number four thousand two hundred and eighty-five, I experienced sensations as novel as they were oppressive. A sense of the importance of the task I had undertaken, a consciousness that I was leaving London, and, stranger still, going somewhere else, a feeling of loneliness and a sensation of jolting, quite bewildered my thoughts, and for a time rendered me even insensible to the presence of my carpet bag and hat-box. I shall ever feel grateful to the driver of a Blackwell omnibus who, by thrusting the pole of his vehicle through the small door of the cabriolet, awakened me from a tumult of imaginings that are wholly indescribable. But of such materials is our imperfect nature composed !

" I am happy to say that I am the first passenger on board, and shall thus be enabled to give you an account of all that happens in the order of its occurrence. The chimney is smoking a good deal, and so are the crew ; and the captain, I am informed, is very drunk in a little house upon deck, something like a black turnpike. I should infer from all I hear that he has got the steam up.

" You will readily guess with what feelings I have just made the discovery that my berth is in the same closet with those engaged by Professor Woodensconce, Mr. Slug, and Professor Grime. Professor Woodensconce has taken the shelf above me, and Mr. Slug and Professor Grime the two shelves opposite. Their luggage has already arrived. On Mr. Slug's bed is a long tin tube of about three inches in diameter, carefully closed at both ends. What can this contain? Some powerful instrument of a new construction, doubtless."

"Ten minutes past nine.

"Nobody has yet arrived, nor has anything fresh come in my way except several joints of beef and mutton, from which I conclude that a good plain dinner has been provided for to-morrow. There is a singular smell below, which gave me some uneasiness at first; but as the steward says it is always there, and never goes away, I am quite comfortable again. I learn from this man that the different sections will be distributed at the Black Boy and Stomach-Ache, and the Boot-Jack and Countenance. If this intelligence be true (and I have no reason to doubt it), your readers will draw such conclusions as their different opinions may suggest.

"I write down these remarks as they occur to me, or as the facts come to my knowledge, in order that my first impressions may lose nothing of their original vividness. I shall despatch them in small packets as opportunities arise."

"Half-past nine.

"Some dark object has just appeared upon the wharf. I think it is a travelling carriage."

"A quarter to ten.

"No, it is n't."

"Half-past ten.

"The passengers are pouring in every instant. Four omnibuses-full have just arrived upon the wharf, and all is bustle and activity. The noise and confusion are very great. Cloths are laid in the cabins, and the steward is placing blue plates-full of knobs of cheese at equal distances down the centre of the tables. He drops a great many knobs; but, being used to it, picks them up again with great dexterity, and, after wiping them on his sleeve, throws them back into the plates. He is a young man of exceedingly prepossessing appearance — either dirty or a mulatto, but I think the former.

" An interesting old gentleman, who came to the wharf in an omnibus, has just quarrelled violently with the porters, and is staggering towards the vessel with a large trunk in his arms. I trust and hope that he may reach it in safety; but the board he has to cross is narrow and slippery. Was that a splash? Gracious powers!

" I have just returned from the deck. The trunk is standing upon the extreme brink of the wharf, but the old gentleman is nowhere to be seen. The watchman is not sure whether he went down or not, but promises to drag for him the first thing to-morrow morning. May his humane efforts prove successful!

" Professor Nogo has this moment arrived with his nightcap on under his hat. He has ordered a glass of cold brandy and water, with a hard biscuit and a basin, and has gone straight to bed. What can this mean?

" The three other scientific gentlemen to whom I have already alluded have come on board, and have all tried their beds, with the exception of Professor Woodensconce, who sleeps in one of the top ones, and can't get into it. Mr. Slug, who sleeps in the other top one, is unable to get out of his, and is to have his supper handed up by a boy. I have had the honour to introduce myself to these gentlemen, and we have amicably arranged the order in which we shall retire to rest; which it is necessary to agree upon, because, although the cabin is very comfortable, there is not room for more than one gentleman to be out of bed at a time, and even he must take his boots off in the passage.

" As I anticipated, the knobs of cheese were provided for the passengers' supper, and are now in course of consumption. Your readers will be surprised to hear that Professor Woodensconce has abstained from cheese for eight years, although he takes butter in considerable quantities. Professor Grime, having lost several teeth, is unable, I observe, to eat his crusts without previously soaking them in his bottled porter. How interesting are these peculiarities!"

" Half-past eleven.

" Professors Woodensconce and Grime, with a degree of good humour that delights us all, have just arranged to toss for a bottle of mulled port. There has been some discussion whether the payment should be decided by the first toss or the best out of three. Eventually the latter course has been determined on. Deeply do I wish that both gentlemen could win; but that being impossible, I own that my personal aspirations (I speak as an individual, and do not compromise either you or your readers by this expression of feeling) are with Professor Woodensconce. I have backed that gentleman to the amount of eighteenpence."

"Twenty minutes to twelve.

"Professor Grime has inadvertently tossed his half-crown out of one of the cabin windows, and it has been arranged that the steward shall toss for him. Bets are offered on any side to any amount, but there are no takers.

"Professor Woodensconce has just called 'woman;' but the coin having lodged in a beam is a long time coming down again. The interest and suspense of this one moment are beyond anything that can be imagined."

"Twelve o'clock.

"The mulled port is smoking on the table before me, and Professor Grime has won. Tossing is a game of chance; but on every ground, whether of public or private character, intellectual endowments, or scientific attainments, I cannot help expressing my opinion that Professor Woodensconce *ought* to have come off victorious. There is an exultation about Professor Grime incompatible, I fear, with true greatness."

"A quarter past twelve.

"Professor Grime continues to exult, and to boast of his victory in no very measured terms, observing that he always does win, and that he knew it would be a a 'head' beforehand, with many other remarks of a similar nature. Surely this gentleman is not so lost to every feeling of decency and propriety as not to feel and know the superiority of Professor Woodensconce? Is Professor Grime insane? or does he wish to be reminded in plain language of his true position in society, and the precise level of his acquirements and abilities? Professor Grime will do well to look to this."

"One o'clock.

"I am writing in bed. The small cabin is illuminated by the feeble light of a flickering lamp suspended from the ceiling; Professor Grime is lying on the opposite shelf on the broad of his back, with his mouth wide open. The scene is indescribably solemn. The rippling of the tide, the noise of the sailors' feet overhead, the gruff voices on the river, the dogs on the shore, the snoring of the passengers, and a constant creaking of every plank in the vessel, are the only sounds that meet the ear. With these exceptions, all is profound silence.

" My curiosity has been within the last moment very much excited. Mr. Slug, who lies above Professor Grime, has cautiously withdrawn the curtains of his berth, and, after looking anxiously out, as if to satisfy himself that his companions are asleep, has taken up the tin tube of which I have before spoken, and is regarding it with great interest. What rare mechanical combination can be contained in that mysterious case ? It is evidently a profound secret to all."

" A quarter-past one.

" The behaviour of Mr. Slug grows more and more mysterious. He has unscrewed the top of the tube, and now renews his observations upon his companions, evidently to make sure that he is wholly unobserved. He is clearly on the eve of some great experiment. Pray Heaven that it be not a dangerous one ; but the interests of science must be promoted, and I am prepared for the worst."

" Five minutes later.

" He has produced a large pair of scissors, and drawn a roll of some substance, not unlike parchment in appearance, from the tin case. The experiment is about to begin. I must strain my eyes to the utmost, in the attempt to follow its minutest operation."

" Twenty minutes before two.

" I have at length been enabled to ascertain that the tin tube contains a few yards of some celebrated plaster, recommended — as I discover on regarding the label attentively through my eye-glass — as a preservative against sea-sickness. Mr. Slug has cut it up into small portions, and is now sticking it over himself in every direction."

" Three o'clock.

" Precisely a quarter of an hour ago we weighed anchor, and the machinery was suddenly put in motion with a noise so appalling, that Professor Woodensconce (who had ascended to his berth by means of a platform of carpet bags arranged by himself on geometrical principles) darted from his shelf head foremost, and, gaining his feet with all the rapidity of extreme terror, ran wildly into the ladies' cabin, under the impression that we were sinking, and uttering loud cries for aid. I am assured that the scene which ensued baffles all description. There were one hundred and forty-seven ladies in their respective berths at the time.

"Mr. Slug has remarked, as an additional instance of the extreme ingenuity of the steam engine as applied to purposes of navigation, that in whatever part of the vessel a passenger's berth may be situated, the machinery always appears to be exactly under his pillow. He intends stating this very beautiful, though simple discovery, to the association."

"Half-past three.

"We are still in smooth water; that is to say, in as smooth water as a steam vessel ever can be, for, as Professor Woodensconce (who has just woke up) learnedly remarks, another great point of ingenuity about a steamer is, that it always carries a little storm with it. You can scarcely conceive how exciting the jerking pulsation of the ship becomes. It is a matter of positive difficulty to get to sleep."

"Friday afternoon, six o'clock.

"I regret to inform you that Mr. Slug's plaster has proved of no avail. He is in great agony, but has applied several large, additional pieces notwithstanding. How affecting is this extreme devotion to science and pursuit of knowledge under the most trying circumstances!

"We were extremely happy this morning, and the breakfast was one of the most animated description. Nothing unpleasant occurred until noon, with the exception of Doctor Foxey's brown silk umbrella and white hat becoming entangled in the machinery while he was explaining to a knot of ladies the construction of the steam engine. I fear the gravy soup for lunch was injudicious. We lost a great many passengers almost immediately afterwards."

"Half-past six.

"I am again in bed. Anything so heart-rending as Mr. Slug's sufferings it has never yet been my lot to witness."

"Seven o'clock.

"A messenger has just come down for a clean pocket-handkerchief from Professor Woodensconce's bag, that unfortunate gentleman being quite unable to leave the deck, and imploring constantly to be thrown overboard. From this man I under-

stand that Professor Nogo, though in a state of utter exhaustion,
clings feebly to the hard biscuit and cold brandy and water,
under the impression that they will yet restore him. Such is
the triumph of mind over matter.

"Professor Grime is in bed, to all appearance quite well;
but he *will* eat, and it is disagreeable to see him. Has this
gentleman no sympathy with the sufferings of his fellow-
creatures? If he has, on what principle can he call for mutton-
chops — and smile?"

"Black Boy and Stomach-Ache,
Oldcastle, Saturday noon.

"You will be happy to learn that I have at length arrived
here in safety. The town is excessively crowded, and all the
private lodgings and hotels are filled with *savans* of both sexes.
The tremendous assemblage of intellect that one encounters in
every street is in the last degree overwhelming.

"Notwithstanding the throng of people here, I have been
fortunate enough to meet with very comfortable accommodation
on very reasonable terms, having secured a sofa in the first-floor
passage at one guinea per night, which includes permission to
take my meals in the bar, on condition that I walk about the
streets at all other times, to make room for other gentlemen
similarly situated. I have been over the outhouses intended to
be devoted to the reception of the various sections, both here
and at the Boot-Jack and Countenance, and am much delighted
with the arrangements. Nothing can exceed the fresh appearance of the saw-dust with which the floors are sprinkled. The
forms are of unplaned deal, and the general effect, as you can
well imagine, is extremely beautiful."

"Half-past nine.

"The number and rapidity of the arrivals are quite bewilder-
ing. Within the last ten minutes a stage coach has driven up
to the door, filled inside and out with distinguished characters,
comprising Mr. Muddlebranes, Mr. Drawley, Professor Muff,
Mr. X. Misty, Mr. X. X. Misty, Mr. Purblind, Professor
Rummun, The Honourable and Reverend Mr. Long Eers,
Professor John Ketch, Sir William Joltered, Doctor Buffer, Mr.
Smith (of London), Mr. Brown (of Edinburgh), Sir Hookham
Snivey, and Professor Pumpkinskull. The ten last-named
gentlemen were wet through, and looked extremely intelligent."

"Sunday, two o'clock P. M.

" The Honourable and Reverend Mr. Long Eers, accompanied by Sir William Joltered, walked and drove this morning. They accomplished the former feat in boots, and the latter in a hired fly. This has naturally given rise to much discussion.

" I have just learnt that an interview has taken place at the Boot-Jack and Countenance between Sowster, the active and intelligent beadle of this place, and Professor Pumpkinskull, who, as your readers are doubtless aware, is an influential member of the council. I forbear to communicate any of the rumours to which this very extraordinary proceeding has given rise until I have seen Sowster, and endeavoured to ascertain the truth from him."

"Half-past six.

" I engaged a donkey chaise shortly after writing the above, and proceeded at a brisk trot in the direction of Sowster's residence, passing through a beautiful expanse of country, with red brick buildings on either side, and stopping in the market-place to observe the spot where Mr. Kwakley's hat was blown off yesterday. It is an uneven piece of paving, but has certainly no appearance which would lead one to suppose that any such event had recently occurred there. From this point 1 proceeded — passing the gas-works and tallow-melter's — to a lane which had been pointed out to me as the beadle's place of residence; and before I had driven a dozen yards further, I had the good fortune to meet Sowster himself advancing towards me.

" Sowster is a fat man, with a more enlarged development of that peculiar conformation of countenance which is vulgarly termed a double chin than I remember to have ever seen before. He has also a very red nose, which he attributes to a habit of early rising — so red, indeed, that but for this explanation I should have supposed it to proceed from occasional inebriety. He informed me that he did not feel himself at liberty to relate what had passed between himself and Professor Pumpkinskull, but had no objection to state that it was connected with a matter of police regulation, and added with peculiar significance, ' Never wos sitch times ! '

" You will easily believe that this intelligence gave me considerable surprise, not wholly unmixed with anxiety, and that I lost no time in waiting on Professor Pumpkinskull, and stating the object of my visit. After a few moments' reflection, the professor, who, I am bound to say, behaved with the utmost politeness, openly avowed (I mark the passage in italics) *that he had requested Sowster to attend on the Monday morning at the Boot-Jack and Countenance, to keep off the boys ; and that he had further desired that the under-beadle might be stationed, with the same object, at the Black Boy and Stomach-Ache!*

"Now I leave this unconstitutional proceeding to your comments and the consideration of your readers. I have yet to learn that a beadle, without the precincts of a church, churchyard, or workhouse, and acting otherwise than under the express orders of churchwardens and overseers in council assembled, to enforce the law against people who come upon the parish, and other offenders, has any lawful authority whatever over the rising youth of this country. I have yet to learn that a beadle can be called out by any civilian to exercise a domination and despotism over the boys of Britain. I have yet to learn that a beadle will be permitted by the commissioners of poor-law regulation to wear out the soles and heels of his boots in illegal interference with the liberties of people not proved poor or otherwise criminal. I have yet to learn that a beadle has power to stop up the Queen's highway at his will and pleasure, or that the whole width of the street is not free and open to any man, boy, or woman in existence, up to the very walls of the houses — ay, be they Black Boys and Stomach-Aches, or Boot-Jacks and Countenances, I care not."

"Nine o'clock.

"1 have procured a local artist to make a faithful sketch of the tyrant Sowster, which, as he has acquired this infamous celebrity, you will no doubt wish to have engraved for the purpose of presenting a copy with every copy of your next number. I inclose it. The under-beadle has consented to write his life, but it is to be strictly anonymous.

"The accompanying likeness is of course from the life, and complete in every respect. Even if I had been totally ignorant of the man's real character, and it had been placed before me without remark, I should have shuddered involuntarily. There is an intense malignity of expression in the features, and a baleful ferocity of purpose in the ruffian's eye, which appalls and sickens. His whole air is rampant with cruelty, nor is the stomach less characteristic of his demoniac propensities."

"Monday.

"The great day has at length arrived. I have neither eyes, nor ears, nor pens, nor ink, nor paper, for anything but the wonderful proceedings that have astounded my senses. Let me collect my energies and proceed to the account.

"SECTION A. — ZOÖLOGY AND BOTANY.

"FRONT PARLOUR, BLACK BOY AND STOMACH-ACHE.

"*President* — Sir WILLIAM JOLTERED. *Vice-Presidents* — Mr. MUD-DLEBRANES and Mr. DRAWLEY.

"Mr. X. X. Misty communicated some remarks on the disappearance of dancing bears from the streets of London, with observations on the exhibition of monkeys as connected with barrel-organs. The writer had observed, with feelings of the utmost pain and regret, that some years ago a sudden and unaccountable change in the public taste took place with reference to itinerant bears, who, being discountenanced by the populace, gradually fell off one by one from the streets of the metropolis, until not one remained to create a taste for natural history in the breasts of the poor and uninstructed. One bear, indeed, — a brown and ragged animal, — had lingered about the haunts of his former triumphs, with a worn and dejected visage and feeble limbs, and had essayed to wield his quarter-staff for the amusement of the multitude; but hunger, and an utter want of any due recompense for his abilities, had at length driven him from the field, and it was only too probable that he had fallen a sacrifice to the rising taste for grease. He regretted to add that a similar, and no less lamentable, change had taken place with reference to monkeys. These delightful animals had formerly been almost as plentiful as the organs on the tops of which they were accustomed to sit; the proportion in the year 1829 (it appeared by the parliamentary return) being as one monkey to three organs. Owing, however, to an altered taste in musical instruments, and the substitution, in a great measure, of narrow boxes of music for organs, which left the monkeys nothing to sit upon, this source of public amusement was wholly dried up. Considering it a matter of the

deepest importance, in connection with national education, that
the people should not lose such opportunities of making themselves acquainted with the manners and customs of two most
interesting species of animals, the author submitted that some
measures should be immediately taken for the restoration of
these pleasing and truly intellectual amusements.

"The President inquired by what means the honourable
member proposed to attain this most desirable end?

"The Author submitted that it could be most fully and
satisfactorily accomplished, if her Majesty's government would
cause to be brought over to England, and maintained at the
public expense, and for the public amusement, such a number
of bears as would enable every quarter of the town to be visited
— say at least by three bears a week. No difficulty whatever
need be experienced in providing a fitting place for the reception of these animals, as a commodious bear-garden could be
erected in the immediate neighbourhood of both Houses of
Parliament, — obviously the most proper and eligible spot for
such an establishment.

"Professor Mull doubted very much whether any correct
ideas of natural history were propagated by the means to which
the honourable member had so ably adverted. On the contrary,
he believed that they had been the means of diffusing very
incorrect and imperfect notions on the subject. He spoke
from personal observation and personal experience, when he
said that many children of great abilities had been induced to
believe, from what they had observed in the streets, at and
before the period to which the honourable gentleman had
referred, that all monkeys were born in red coats and spangles,
and that their hats and feathers also came by nature. He
wished to know distinctly whether the honourable gentleman
attributed the want of encouragement the bears had met with
to the decline of public taste in that respect, or to a want of
ability on the part of the bears themselves?

"Mr. X. X. Misty replied, that he could not bring himself
to believe but that there must be a great deal of floating talent
among the bears and monkeys generally; which, in the absence
of any proper encouragement, was dispersed in other directions.

"Professor Pumpkinskull wished to take that opportunity of
calling the attention of the section to a most important and
serious point. The author of the treatise just read had alluded

to the prevalent taste for bears'-grease as a means of promoting the growth of hair, which undoubtedly was diffused to a very great and (as it appeared to him) very alarming extent. No gentleman attending that section could fail to be aware of the fact that the youth of the present age evinced, by their behaviour in the streets, and at all places of public resort, a considerable lack of that gallantry and gentlemanly feeling which, in more ignorant times, had been thought becoming. He wished to know whether it were possible that a constant outward application of bears'-grease by the young gentlemen about town had imperceptibly infused into those unhappy persons something of the nature and quality of the bear. He shuddered as he threw out the remark; but if this theory, on inquiry, should prove to be well-founded, it would at once explain a great deal of unpleasant eccentricity of behaviour, which, without some such discovery, was wholly unaccountable.

"The President highly complimented the learned gentleman on his most valuable suggestion, which produced the greatest effect upon the assembly; and remarked that only a week previous he had seen some young gentlemen at a theatre eyeing a box of ladies with a fierce intensity, which nothing but the influence of some brutish appetite could possibly explain. It was dreadful to reflect that our youth were so rapidly verging into a generation of bears.

"After a scene of scientific enthusiasm it was resolved that this important question should be immediately submitted to the consideration of the council.

"The President wished to know whether any gentleman could inform the section what had become of the dancing dogs?

"A Member replied, after some hesitation, that on the day after three glee-singers had been committed to prison as criminals by a late most zealous police magistrate of the metropolis, the dogs had abandoned their professional duties, and dispersed themselves in different quarters of the town to gain a livelihood by less dangerous means. He was given to understand that since that period they had supported themselves by lying in wait for and robbing blind men's poodles.

"Mr. Flummery exhibited a twig, claiming to be a veritable branch of that noble tree known to naturalists as the SHAKE-SPEARE, which has taken root in every land and climate, and gathered under the shade of its broad green boughs the great family of mankind. The learned gentleman remarked that the twig had been undoubtedly called by other names in its time; but that it had been pointed out to him by an old lady in Warwickshire, where the great tree had grown, as a shoot of the genuine SHAKESPEARE, by which name he begged to introduce it to his countrymen.

"The President wished to know what botanical definition the honourable gentleman could afford of the curiosity.

"Mr. Flummery expressed his opinion that it was A DECIDED PLANT.

"SECTION B. — DISPLAY OF MODELS AND MECHANICAL SCIENCE.

"LARGE ROOM, BOOT-JACK AND COUNTENANCE.

"*President* — Mr. MALLETT.   *Vice-Presidents* — Messrs. LEAVER and SCROO.

"Mr. Crinkles exhibited a most beautiful and delicate machine, of little larger size than an ordinary snuff-box, manufactured entirely by himself, and composed exclusively of steel, by the aid of which more pockets could be picked in one hour than by the present slow and tedious process in four-and-twenty. The inventor remarked that it had been put into active operation in Fleet Street, the Strand, and other thoroughfares, and had never been once known to fail.

"After some slight delay, occasioned by the various members of the section buttoning their pockets,

"The President narrowly inspected the invention, and declared that he had never seen a machine of more beautiful or exquisite construction. Would the inventor be good enough to inform the section whether he had taken any and what means for bringing it into general operation?

"Mr. Crinkles stated that, after encountering some preliminary difficulties, he had succeeded in putting himself in communication with Mr. Fogle Hunter, and other gentlemen connected with the Swell Mob, who had awarded the invention the very highest and most unqualified approbation. He regretted to say, however, that these distinguished practitioners, in common with a gentleman of the name of Gimlet-eyed Tommy, and other members of a secondary grade of the profession whom he was understood to represent, entertained an

insuperable objection to its being brought into general use, on
the ground that it would have the inevitable effect of almost
entirely superseding manual labour, and throwing a great number of highly deserving persons out of employment.

" The President hoped that no such fanciful objections would
be allowed to stand in the way of such a great public improvement.

" Mr. Crinkles hoped so too; but he feared that if the
gentlemen of the Swell Mob persevered in their objection,
nothing could be done.

" Professor Grime suggested, that surely, in that case, her
Majesty's government might be prevailed upon to take it up.

" Mr. Crinkles said, that if the objection were found to be
insuperable he should apply to Parliament, which he thought
could not fail to recognise the utility of the invention.

" The President observed that, up to this time Parliament
had certainly got on very well without it; but as they did
their business on a very large scale, he had no doubt they
would gladly adopt the improvement. His only fear was that
the machine might be worn out by constant working.

" Mr. Coppernose called the attention of the section to a
proposition of great magnitude and interest, illustrated by a
vast number of models, and stated with much clearness and
perspicuity in a treatise entitled ' Practical Suggestions on the
necessity of providing some harmless and wholesome relaxation
for the young noblemen of England.' His proposition was,
that a space of ground of not less than ten miles in length and
four in breadth should be purchased by a new company, to be
incorporated by Act of Parliament, and inclosed by a brick wall
of not less than twelve feet in height. He proposed that it
should be laid out with highway roads, turnpikes, bridges,
miniature villages, and every object that could conduce to the
comfort and glory of Four-in-hand Clubs, so that they might be
fairly presumed to require no drive beyond it. This delightful
retreat would be fitted up with most commodious and extensive
stables, for the convenience of such of the nobility and gentry
as had a taste for ostlering, and with houses of entertainment
furnished in the most expensive and handsome style. It would
be further provided with whole streets of door-knockers and
bell-handles of extra size, so constructed that they could be
easily wrenched off at night, and regularly screwed on again, by

attendants provided for the purpose, every day. There would also be gas lamps of real glass, which could be broken at a comparatively small expense per dozen, and a broad and handsome foot pavement for gentlemen to drive their cabriolets upon when they were humorously disposed — for the full enjoyment of which feat live pedestrians would be procured from the workhouse at a very small charge per head. The place being inclosed, and carefully screened from the intrusion of the public, there would be no objection to gentlemen laying aside any article of their costume that was considered to interfere with a pleasant frolic, or, indeed, to their walking about without any costume at all, if they liked that better. In short, every facility of enjoyment would be afforded that the most gentlemanly person could possibly desire. But as even these advantages would be incomplete unless there were some means provided of enabling the nobility and gentry to display their prowess when they sallied forth after dinner, and as some inconvenience might be experienced in the event of their being reduced to the necessity of pummelling each other, the inventor had turned his attention to the construction of an entirely new police force, composed exclusively of automaton figures, which, with the assistance of the ingenious Signor Gagliardi, of Windmill Street, in the Haymarket, he had succeeded in making with such nicety that a policeman, cab-driver, or old woman, made upon the principle of the models exhibited, would walk about until knocked down like any real man; nay, more, if set upon and beaten by six or eight noblemen or gentlemen, after it was down, the figure would utter divers groans, mingled with entreaties for mercy, thus rendering the illusion complete, and the enjoyment perfect. But the invention did not stop even here; for station-houses would be built, containing good beds for noblemen and gentlemen during the night, and in the morning they would repair to a commodious police office, where a pantomimic investigation would take place before the automaton magistrates, — quite equal to life, — who would find them in so many counters, with which they would be previously provided for the purpose. This office would be furnished with an inclined plane, for the convenience of any nobleman or gentleman who might wish to bring in his horse as a witness; and the prisoners would be at perfect liberty, as they were now, to interrupt the complainants as much as they pleased, and to make any remarks that they thought proper. The charge for these amusements would amount to very little more than they already cost, and the inventor submitted that the public would be much benefited and comforted by the proposed arrangement.

"Professor Nogo wished to be informed what amount of automaton police force it was proposed to raise in the first instance.

" Mr. Coppernose replied, that it was proposed to begin with seven divisions of police of a score each, lettered from A to G inclusive. It was proposed that not more than half this number should be placed on active duty, and that the remainder should be kept on shelves in the police office ready to be called out at a moment's notice.

"The President, awarding the utmost merit to the ingenious gentleman who had originated the idea, doubted whether the automaton police would quite answer the purpose. He feared that noblemen and gentlemen would perhaps require the excitement of threshing living subjects.

" Mr. Coppernose submitted, that as the usual odds in such cases were ten noblemen or gentlemen to one policeman or cab-driver, it could make very little difference in point of excitement whether the policeman or cab-driver were a man or a block. The great advantage would be, that a policeman's limbs might be all knocked off, and yet he would be in a condition to do duty next day. He might even give his evidence next morning with his head in his hand, and give it equally well.

" PROFESSOR MUFF. — Will you allow me to ask you, sir, of what materials it is intended that the magistrates' heads shall be composed ?

" MR. COPPERNOSE. — The magistrates will have wooden heads of course, and they will be made of the toughest and thickest materials that can possibly be obtained.

" PROFESSOR MUFF. — I am quite satisfied. This is a great invention.

" PROFESSOR NOGO. — I see but one objection to it. It appears to me that the magistrates ought to talk.

" Mr. Coppernose no sooner heard this suggestion than he touched a small spring in each of the two models of magistrates which were placed upon the table ; one of the figures immediately began to exclaim with great volubility that he was sorry

to see gentlemen in such a situation, and the other to express a
fear that the policeman was intoxicated.

" The section, as with one accord, declared with a shout of
applause that the invention was complete; and the President,
much excited, retired with Mr. Coppernose to lay it before the
council. On his return,

" Mr. Tickle displayed his newly invented spectacles, which
enabled the wearer to discern, in very bright colours, objects at
a great distance, and rendered him wholly blind to those immediately before him. It was, he said, a most valuable and useful
invention, based strictly upon the principle of the human eye.

" The President required some information upon this point.
He had yet to learn that the human eye was remarkable for the
peculiarities of which the honourable gentleman had spoken.

" Mr. Tickle was rather astonished to hear this, when the
President could not fail to be aware that a large number of most
excellent persons and great statesmen could see, with the naked
eye, most marvellous horrors on West India plantations, while
they could discern nothing whatever in the interior of Manchester cotton mills. He must know, too, with what quickness of
perception most people could discover their neighbour's faults,
and how very blind they were to their own. If the President
differed from the great majority of men in this respect, his eye
was a defective one, and it was to assist his vision that these
glasses were made.

" Mr. Blank exhibited a model of a fashionable annual, composed of copper-plates, gold leaf, and silk boards, and worked
entirely by milk and water.

" Mr. Prosee, after examining the machine, declared it to be
so ingeniously composed, that he was wholly unable to discover
how it went on at all.

" MR. BLANK. — Nobody can, and that is the beauty of it.

" SECTION C. — ANATOMY AND MEDICINE.

" BAR-ROOM, BLACK BOY AND STOMACH-ACHE.

" *President* — Dr. SOEMUP.   *Vice-Presidents* — Messrs. PESSELL and
MORTAIR.

" Dr. Grummidge stated to the section a most interesting
case of monomania, and described the course of treatment he had
pursued with perfect success. The patient was a married lady

in the middle rank of life, who, having seen another lady at an evening party in a full suit of pearls, was suddenly seized with a desire to possess a similar equipment, although her husband's finances were by no means equal to the necessary outlay. Finding her wish ungratified, she fell sick, and the symptoms soon became so alarming that he (Dr. Grummidge) was called in. At this period the prominent tokens of the disorder were sullenness, a total indisposition to perform domestic duties, great peevishness, and extreme languor, except when pearls were mentioned, at which times the pulse quickened, the eyes grew brighter, the pupils dilated, and the patient, after various incoherent exclamations, burst into a passion of tears, and exclaimed that nobody cared for her, and that she wished herself dead. Finding that the patient's appetite was affected in the presence of company, he began by ordering a total abstinence from all stimulants, and forbidding any sustenance but weak gruel; he then took twenty ounces of blood, applied a blister under each ear, one upon the chest, and another on the back; having done which, and administered five grains of calomel, he left the patient to her repose. The next day she was somewhat low, but decidedly better, and all appearances of irritation were removed. The next day she improved still further, and on the next again. On the fourth there was some appearance of a return of the old symptoms, which no sooner developed themselves than he administered another dose of calomel, and left strict orders that, unless a decidedly favourable change occurred within two hours, the patient's head should be immediately shaved to the very last curl. From that moment she began to mend, and in less than four-and-twenty hours was perfectly restored. She did not now betray the least emotion at the sight or mention of pearls or any other ornaments. She was cheerful and good-humoured, and a most beneficial change had been effected in her whole temperament and condition.

" Mr. Pipkin (M. R. C. S.) read a short but most interesting communication in which he sought to prove the complete belief of Sir William Courtenay, otherwise Thom, recently shot at Canterbury, in the Homœopathic system. The section would bear in mind that one of the Homœopathic doctrines was, that infinitesimal doses of any medicine which would occasion the disease under which the patient laboured, supposing him to be in a healthy state, would cure it. Now, it was a remarkable circumstance — proved in the evidence — that the deceased Thom employed a woman to follow him about all day with a pail of water, assuring her that one drop (a purely homœopathic remedy, the section would observe), placed upon his tongue after death, would restore him. What was the obvious inference ? That Thom, who was marching and countermarching in osier beds, and other swampy places, was impressed with a presentiment that he should be drowned ; in which case, had his instructions been complied with, he could not fail to have been brought to life again instantly by his own prescription. As it was, if this woman, or any other person, had administered an infinitesimal dose of lead and gunpowder immediately after he fell, he would have recovered forthwith. But unhappily the woman concerned did not possess the power of reasoning by analogy, or carrying out a principle, and thus the unfortunate gentleman had been sacrificed; to the ignorance of the peasantry.

" Section D. — Statistics.

" out-house, black boy and stomach-ache.

" *President* — Mr. Slug.   *Vice-Presidents* — Messrs. Noakes and Styles.

" Mr. Kwakley stated the result of some most ingenious statistical inquiries relative to the difference between the value of the qualification of several members of Parliament as published to the world, and its real nature and amount. After reminding the section that every member of Parliament for a town or borough was supposed to possess a clear freehold estate of three hundred pounds per annum, the honourable gentleman excited great amusement and laughter by stating the exact amount of freehold property possessed by a column of legislators, in which he had included himself. It appeared from this table, that the amount of such income possessed by each was 0 pounds, 0 shillings, and 0 pence, yielding an average of the same. (Great laughter.) It was pretty well known that there were accommodating gentlemen in the habit of furnishing new members with temporary qualifications, to the ownership of which they swore solemnly — of course as a mere matter of form. He argued from these *data* that it was wholly unnecessary for members of Parliament to possess any property at all, especially as when they had none the public could get them so much cheaper.

"SUPPLEMENTARY SECTION, E. — UMBUGOLOGY AND
DITCHWATERISTICS.

"*President* — Mr. GRUB. *Vice-Presidents* — Messrs. DULL and
DUMMY.

" A paper was read by the secretary descriptive of a bay pony with one eye, which had been seen by the author standing in a butcher's cart at the corner of Newgate Market. The communication described the author of the paper as having, in the prosecution of a mercantile pursuit, betaken himself one Saturday morning last summer from Somers Town to Cheapside; in the course of which expedition he had beheld the extraordinary appearance above described. The pony had one distinct eye, and it had been pointed out to him by his friend Captain Blunderbore, of the Horse Marines, who assisted the author in his search, that whenever he winked this eye he whisked his tail (possibly to drive the flies off), but that he always winked and whisked at the same time. The animal was lean, spavined, and tottering; and the author proposed to constitute it of the family of *Fitfordogsmeataurious*. It certainly did occur to him that there was no case on record of a pony with one clearly defined and distinct organ of vision, winking and whisking at the same moment.

" Mr. Q. J. Snuffletoffle had heard of a pony winking his eye, and likewise of a pony whisking his tail, but whether they were two ponies or the same pony he could not undertake positively to say. At all events, he was acquainted with no authenticated instance of a simultaneous winking and whisking, and he really could not but doubt the existence of such a marvellous pony in opposition to all those natural laws by which ponies were governed. Referring, however, to the mere question of his one organ of vision, might he suggest the possibility of this pony having been literally half asleep at the time he was seen, and having closed only one eye.

" The President observed that, whether the pony was half asleep or fast asleep, there could be no doubt that the association was wide awake, and therefore that they had better get the business over, and go to dinner. He had certainly never seen

anything analogous to this pony, but he was not prepared to
doubt its existence; for he had seen many queerer ponies in his
time, though he did not pretend to have seen any more remarkable donkeys than the other gentlemen around him.

"Professor John Ketch was then called upon to exhibit the
skull of the late Mr. Greenacre, which he produced from a blue
bag, remarking, on being invited to make any observations that
occurred to him, 'that he'd pound it as that 'ere 'spectable
section had never seed a more gamerer cove nor he vos.'

"A most animated discussion upon this interesting relic ensued; and, some difference of opinion arising respecting the
real character of the deceased gentleman, Mr. Blubb delivered a
lecture upon the cranium before him, clearly showing that Mr.
Greenacre possessed the organ of destructiveness to a most unusual extent, with a most remarkable development of the organ
of carveativeness. Sir Hookham Snivey was proceeding to
combat this opinion, when Professor Ketch suddenly interrupted
the proceedings by exclaiming, with great excitement of manner, 'Walker!'

"The President begged to call the learned gentleman to
order.

"Professor Ketch. 'Order be blowed! you've got the
wrong un, I tell you. It ain't no ed at all; it's a coker-nut as
my brother-in-law has been a carvin', to hornament his new
baked-tatur stall wots a comin' down 'ere vile the 'sociation's in
the town. Hand over, vill you?'

"With these words, Professor Ketch hastily repossessed
himself of the cocoa-nut, and drew forth the skull, in mistake
for which he had exhibited it. A most interesting conversation
ensued; but as there appeared some doubt ultimately whether
the skull was Mr. Greenacre's, or a hospital patient's, or a
pauper's, or a man's, or a woman's, or a monkey's, no particular
result was obtained."

"I cannot," says our talented correspondent in conclusion,
"I cannot close my account of these gigantic researches and sublime and noble triumphs without repeating a *bon mot* of Professor Woodensconce's, which shows how the greatest minds
may occasionally unbend when truth can be presented to listening ears, clothed in an attractive and playful form. I was standing by, when, after a week of feasting and feeding, that learned

gentleman, accompanied by the whole body of wonderful men,
entered the hall yesterday, where a sumptuous dinner was prepared ; where the richest wines sparkled on the board, and fat
bucks — propitiatory sacrifices to learning — sent forth their
savoury odours. ' Ah ! ' said Professor Woodensconce, rubbing
his hands, ' This is what we meet for ; this is what inspires us ;
this is what keeps us together, and beckons us onward ; this is
the *spread* of science, and a glorious spread it is.' "

STRAY CHAPTERS BY BOZ

I

THE PANTOMIME OF LIFE

BEFORE we plunge headlong into this paper, let us at once confess to a fondness for pantomimes — to a gentle sympathy with
clowns and pantaloons — to an unqualified admiration of harlequins and columbines — to a chaste delight in every action of
their brief existence, varied and many-coloured as those actions
are, and inconsistent though they occasionally be with those
rigid and formal rules of propriety which regulate the proceedings of meaner and less comprehensive minds. We revel in
pantomimes — not because they dazzle one's eyes with tinsel
and gold leaf ; not because they present to us, once again, the
well-beloved chalked faces and goggle eyes of our childhood ;
not even because, like Christmas Day, and Twelfth Night, and
Shrove Tuesday, and one's own birthday, they come to us but
once a year, — our attachment is founded on a graver and a very
different reason. A pantomime is to us a mirror of life ; nay
more, we maintain that it is so to audiences generally, although
they are not aware of it, and that this very circumstance is the
secret cause of their amusement and delight.

Let us take a slight example. The scene is a street : an
elderly gentleman, with a large face and strongly marked
features, appears. His countenance beams with a sunny smile,
and a perpetual dimple is on his broad, red cheek. He is evidently an opulent elderly gentleman, comfortable in circumstances, and well to do in the world. He is not unmindful of
the adornment of his person, for he is richly, not to say gaudily,
dressed ; and that he indulges to a reasonable extent in the
pleasures of the table may be inferred from the joyous and oily
manner in which he rubs his stomach, by way of informing the
audience that he is going home to dinner. In the fulness of
his heart, in the fancied security of wealth, in the possession and

enjoyment of all the good things of life, the elderly gentleman
suddenly loses his footing, and stumbles. How the audience
roar! He is set upon by a noisy and officious crowd, who
buffet and cuff him unmercifully. They scream with delight!
Every time the elderly gentleman struggles to get up, his relent-
less persecutors knock him down again. The spectators are
convulsed with merriment! And when at last the elderly gentleman does get up, and staggers away, despoiled of hat, wig,
and clothing, himself battered to pieces, and his watch and
money gone, they are exhausted with laughter, and express their
merriment and admiration in rounds of applause.

Is this like life? Change the scene to any real street —
to the Stock Exchange, or the City banker's; the merchant's
counting-house, or even the tradesman's shop. See any one of
these men fall — the more suddenly, and the nearer the zenith of
his pride and riches, the better. What a wild hallo is raised
over his prostrate carcase by the shouting mob; how they
whoop and yell as he lies humbled beneath them! Mark how
eagerly they set upon him when he is down; and how they
mock and deride him as he slinks away! Why, it is the pantomime to the very letter.

Of all the pantomimic *dramatis personæ*, we consider the
pantaloon the most worthless and debauched. Independent of
the dislike one naturally feels at seeing a gentleman of his years
engaged in pursuits highly unbecoming his gravity and time of
life, we cannot conceal from ourselves the fact that he is a
treacherous, worldly-minded old villain, constantly enticing his
younger companion, the clown, into acts of fraud or petty
larceny, and generally standing aside to watch the result of the
enterprise. If it be successful, he never forgets to return for
his share of the spoil; but if it turn out a failure, he generally retires with remarkable caution and expedition, and keeps
carefully aloof until the affair has blown over. His amorous
propensities, too, are eminently disagreeable; and his mode of
addressing ladies in the open street at noon-day is downright
improper, being usually neither more nor less than a perceptible
tickling of the aforesaid ladies in the waist, after committing
which, he starts back, manifestly ashamed (as well he may be)
of his own indecorum and temerity; continuing, nevertheless,
to ogle and beckon to them from a distance in a very unpleasant and immoral manner.

Is there any man who cannot count a dozen pantaloons in his own social circle ? Is there any man who has not seen them swarming at the west end of the town on a sunshiny day or a summer's evening, going through the last-named pantomimic feats with as much liquorish energy, and as total an absence of reserve, as if they were on the very stage itself ? We can tell upon our fingers a dozen pantaloons of our acquaintance at this moment — capital pantaloons, who have been performing all kinds of strange freaks, to the great amusement of their friends and acquaintance, for years past; and who to this day are making such comical and ineffectual attempts to be young and dissolute, that all beholders are like to die with laughter.

Take that old gentleman who has just emerged from the *Café de l'Europe* in the Haymarket, where he has been dining at the expense of the young man upon town with whom he shakes hands as they part at the door of the tavern. The affected warmth of that shake of the hand, the courteous nod, the obvious recollection of the dinner, the savoury flavour of which still hangs upon his lips, are all characteristics of his great prototype. He hobbles away humming an opera tune, and twirling his cane to and fro, with affected carelessness. Suddenly he stops — 't is at the milliner's window. He peeps through one of the large panes of glass ; and, his view of the ladies within being obstructed by the India shawls, directs his attentions to the young girl with the bandbox in her hand, who is gazing in at the window also. See ! he draws beside her. He coughs; she turns away from him. He draws near her again ; she disregards him. He gleefully chucks her under the chin, and, retreating a few steps, nods and beckons with fantastic grimaces, while the girl bestows a contemptuous and supercilious look upon his wrinkled visage. She turns away with a flounce, and the old gentleman trots after her with a toothless chuckle. The pantaloon to the life !

But the close resemblance which the clowns of the stage bear to those of every-day life is perfectly extraordinary. Some people talk with a sigh of the decline of pantomime, and murmur in low and dismal tones the name of Grimaldi. We mean no disparagement to the worthy and excellent old man when we say that this is downright nonsense. Clowns that beat Grimaldi all to nothing turn up every day, and nobody patronises them — more 's the pity !

"I know what you mean," says some dirty-faced patron of Mr. Osbaldistone's, laying down the Miscellany when he has got thus far, and bestowing upon vacancy a most knowing glance; "you mean C. J. Smith as did Guy Fawkes, and George Barnwell at the Garden." The dirty-faced gentleman has hardly uttered the words, when he is interrupted by a young gentleman in no shirt-collar and a Petersham coat. "No, no," says the young gentleman; "he means Brown, King, and Gibson, at the 'Delphi.'" Now, with great deference, both to the first-named gentleman with the dirty face, and the last-named gentleman in the non-existing shirt-collar, we do *not* mean either the performer who so grotesquely burlesqued the Popish conspirator, or the three unchangeables who have been dancing the same dance under different imposing titles, and doing the same thing under various high-sounding names, for some five or six years last past. We have no sooner made this avowal than the public, who have hitherto been silent witnesses of the dispute, inquire what on earth it is we *do* mean; and with becoming respect, we proceed to tell them.

It is very well known to all playgoers and pantomime-seers, that the scenes in which a theatrical clown is at the very height of his glory are those which are described in the play-bills as "Cheesemonger's Shop and Crockery Warehouse," or "Tailor's Shop and Mrs. Queertable's Boarding-House," or places bearing some such title, where the great fun of the thing consists in the hero's taking lodgings which he has not the slightest intention of paying for, or obtaining goods under false pretences, or abstracting the stock in trade of the respectable shop-keeper next door, or robbing warehouse porters as they pass under his window; or, to shorten the catalogue, in his swindling everybody he possibly can, it only remaining to be observed that, the more extensive the swindling is, and the more barefaced the impudence of the swindler, the greater the rapture and ecstasy of the audience. Now it is a most remarkable fact that precisely this sort of thing occurs in real life day after day, and nobody sees the humour of it. Let us illustrate our position by detailing the plot of this portion of the pantomime — not of the theatre, but of life.

The Honourable Captain Fitz-Whisker Fiercy, attended by his livery servant Do'em — a most respectable servant to look at, who has grown grey in the service of the captain's family —

views, treats for, and ultimately obtains possession of, the unfur-
nished house, such a number, such a street. All the tradesmen
in the neighbourhood are in agonies of competition for the captain's custom; the captain is a good-natured, kind-hearted, easy
man, and, to avoid being the cause of disappointment to any,
he most handsomely gives orders to all. Hampers of wine,
baskets of provisions, cart-loads of furniture, boxes of jewellery,
supplies of luxuries of the costliest description, flock to the
house of the Honourable Captain Fitz-Whisker Fiercy, where
they are received with the utmost readiness by the highly
respectable Do'em; while the captain himself struts and swag-
gers about with that compound air of conscious superiority and
general bloodthirstiness which a military captain should always,
and does most times, wear, to the admiration and terror of
plebeian men. But the tradesmen's backs are no sooner turned
than the captain, with all the eccentricity of a mighty mind,
and assisted by the faithful Do'em, whose devoted fidelity is
not the least touching part of his character, disposes of everything to great advantage; for although the articles fetch small
sums, still they are sold considerably above cost price, the cost
to the captain having been nothing at all. After various manœuvres, the imposture is discovered, Fitz-Fiercy and Do'em
are recognised as confederates, and the police office to which
they are both taken is thronged with their dupes.

Who can fail to recognise in this the exact counterpart of
the best portion of a theatrical pantomime, — Fitz-Whisker
Fiercy by the clown; Do'em by the pantaloon; and supernumeraries by the tradesmen? The best of the joke, too, is,
that the very coal-merchant, who is loudest in his complaints
against the person who defrauded him, is the identical man who
sat in the centre of the very front row of the pit last night and
laughed the most boisterously at this very same thing, — and
not so well done either. Talk of Grimaldi, we say again! Did
Grimaldi, in his best days, ever do anything in this way equal
to Da Costa?

The mention of this latter justly celebrated clown reminds us
of his last piece of humour, the fraudulently obtaining certain
stamped acceptances from a young gentleman in the army. We
had scarcely laid down our pen to contemplate for a few moments
this admirable actor's performance of that exquisite practical
joke, than a new branch of our subject flashed suddenly upon
us. So we take it up again at once.

All people who have been behind the scenes, and most people who have been before them, know that, in the representation of a pantomime, a good many men are sent upon the stage for the express purpose of being cheated, or knocked down, or both. Now, down to a moment ago, we had never been able to understand for what possible purpose a great number of odd, lazy, large-headed men, whom one is in the habit of meeting here, and there, and everywhere, could ever have been created. We see it all, now. They are the supernumeraries in the pantomime of life; the men who have been thrust into it, with no other view than to be constantly tumbling over each other, and running their heads against all sorts of strange things. We sat opposite to one of these men at a supper-table, only last week. Now we think of it, he was exactly like the gentlemen with the pasteboard heads and faces, who do the corresponding business in the theatrical pantomimes; there was the same broad stolid simper — the same dull leaden eye — the same unmeaning, vacant stare; and whatever was said, or whatever was done, he always came in at precisely the wrong place, or jostled against something that he had not the slightest business with. We looked at the man across the table again and again; and could not satisfy ourselves what race of beings to class him with. How very odd that this never occurred to us before!

We will frankly own that we have been much troubled with the harlequin. We see harlequins of so many kinds in the real living pantomime that we hardly know which to select as the proper fellow of him of the theatres. At one time we were disposed to think that the harlequin was neither more nor less than a young man of family and independent property, who had run away with an opera dancer, and was fooling his life and his means away in light and trivial amusements. On reflection, however, we remembered that harlequins are occasionally guilty of witty, and even clever acts, and we are rather disposed to acquit our young men of family and independent property, generally speaking, of any such misdemeanours. On a more mature consideration of the subject, we have arrived at the conclusion that the harlequins of life are just ordinary men, to be found in no particular walk or degree, on whom a certain station, or particular conjunction of circumstances, confers the magic wand. And this brings us to a few words on the pantomime of public and political life, which we shall say at once, and then conclude — merely premising in this place that we decline any reference whatever to the columbine, being in no wise satisfied of the nature of her connection with her parti-coloured lover, and not feeling by any means clear that we should be justified in introducing her to the virtuous and respectable ladies who peruse our lucubrations.

We take it that the commencement of a Session of Parliament is neither more nor less than the drawing up of the curtain for a grand comic pantomime, and that his Majesty's most gracious speech on the opening thereof may be not inaptly compared to the clown's opening speech of "Here we are!" "My lords and gentlemen, here we are!" appears, to our mind at least, to be a very good abstract of the point and meaning of the propitiatory address of the ministry. When we remember how frequently this speech is made, immediately after *the change* too, the parallel is quite perfect, and still more singular.

Perhaps the cast of our political pantomime never was richer than at this day. We are particularly strong in clowns. At no former time, we should say, have we had such astonishing tumblers, or performers so ready to go through the whole of their feats for the amusement of an admiring throng. Their extreme readiness to exhibit, indeed, has given rise to some ill-natured reflections; it having been objected that by exhibiting gratuitously through the country when the theatre is closed, they reduce themselves to the level of mountebanks, and thereby tend to degrade the respectability of the profession. Certainly Grimaldi never did this sort of thing; and though Brown, King, and Gibson have gone to the Surrey in vacation time, and Mr. C. J. Smith has ruralised at Sadler's Wells, we find no theatrical precedent for a general tumbling through the country, except in the gentleman, name unknown, who threw summersets on behalf of the late Mr. Richardson, and who is no authority either, because he had never been on the regular boards.

But, laying aside this question, which after all is a mere matter of taste, we may reflect with pride and gratification of heart on the proficiency of our clowns as exhibited in the season. Night after night will they twist and tumble about, till two, three, and four o'clock in the morning; playing the strangest antics, and giving each other the funniest slaps on the face that can possibly be imagined, without evincing the smallest tokens of fatigue. The strange noises, the confusion, the shouting and roaring, amid which all this is done, too, would put to shame the most turbulent sixpenny gallery that ever yelled through a boxing-night.

It is especially curious to behold one of these clowns compelled to go through the most surprising contortions by the irresistible influence of the wand of office, which his leader or harlequin holds above his head. Acted upon by this wonderful charm he will become perfectly motionless, moving neither hand, foot, nor finger, and will even lose the faculty of speech at an instant's notice; or on the other hand, he will become all life and animation if required, pouring forth a torrent of words without sense or meaning, throwing himself into the wildest and most fantastic contortions, and even grovelling on the earth and licking up the dust. These exhibitions are more curious than pleasing; indeed, they are rather disgusting than otherwise, except to the admirers of such things, with whom we confess we have no fellow-feeling.

Strange tricks — very strange tricks — are also performed by the harlequin who holds for the time being the magic wand which we have just mentioned. The mere waving it before a man's eyes will dispossess his brains of all the notions previously stored there, and fill it with an entirely new set of ideas; one gentle tap on the back will alter the colour of a man's coat completely; and there are some expert performers, who, having this wand held first on one side and then on the other, will change from side to side, turning their coats at every evolution, with so much rapidity and dexterity, that the quickest eye can scarcely detect their motions. Occasionally, the genius who confers the wand wrests it from the hand of the temporary possessor, and consigns it to some new performer; on which occasions all the characters change sides, and then the race and the hard knocks begin anew.

We might have extended this chapter to a much greater length — we might have carried the comparison into the liberal professions — we might have shown, as was, in fact, our original purpose, that each is in itself a little pantomime with scenes and characters of its own, complete; but, as we fear we have been quite lengthy enough already, we shall leave this chapter just where it is. A gentleman, not altogether unknown as a dramatic poet, wrote thus a year or two ago : —

> " All the world 's a stage,
> And all the men and women merely players : "

and we, tracking out his footsteps at the scarcely-worth-mentioning little distance of a few millions of leagues behind, venture to add, by way of new reading, that he meant a Pantomime, and that we are all actors in The Pantomime of Life.

II

SOME PARTICULARS CONCERNING A LION

WE have a great respect for lions in the abstract. In common with most other people, we have heard and read of many instances of their bravery and generosity. We have duly admired that heroic self-denial and charming philanthropy which prompts them never to eat people except when they are hungry, and we have been deeply impressed with a becoming sense of the politeness they are said to display towards unmarried ladies of a certain state. All natural histories teem with anecdotes illustrative of their excellent qualities; and one old spelling book in particular recounts a touching instance of an old lion, of high moral dignity and stern principle, who felt it his imperative duty to devour a young man who had contracted a habit of swearing, as a striking example to the rising generation.

All this is extremely pleasant to reflect upon, and, indeed, says a very great deal in favour of lions as a mass. We are bound to state, however, that such individual lions as we ha· happened to fall in with have not put forth any very striki. characteristics, and have not acted up to the chivalrous character assigned them by their chroniclers. We never saw a lion in what is called his natural state, certainly; that is to say, we have never met a lion out walking in a forest, or crouching in his lair under a tropical sun, waiting till his dinner should happen to come by, hot from the baker's. But we have seen some under the influence of captivity, and the pressure of misfortune; and we must say that they appeared to us very apathetic, heavy-headed fellows.

The lion at the Zoölogical Gardens, for instance. He is all very well; he has an undeniable mane, and looks very fierce; but, Lord bless us! what of that? The lions of the fashionable world look just as ferocious, and are the most harmless creatures breathing. A box-lobby lion or a Regent Street animal will put on a most terrible aspect, and roar fearfully, if you affront him; but he will never bite, and if you offer to attack him manfully, will fairly turn tail and sneak off. Doubtless these creatures roam about sometimes in herds, and if they meet any especially meek-looking and peaceably disposed fellow, will endeavour to frighten him ; but the faintest show of a vigorous resistance is sufficient to scare them even then. These are pleasant characteristics, whereas we make it matter of distinct charge against the Zoölogical lion and his brethren at the fairs, that they are sleepy, dreamy, sluggish quadrupeds.

We do not remember to have ever seen one of them perfectly awake, except at feeding-time. In every respect we uphold the biped lions against their four-footed namesakes, and we boldly challenge controversy upon the subject.

With these opinions it may be easily imagined that our curiosity and interest were very much excited the other day, when a lady of our acquaintance called on us and resolutely declined to accept our refusal of her invitation to an evening party ; " for," said she, " I have got a lion coming." We at once retracted our plea of a prior engagement, and became as anxious to go, as we had previously been to stay away.

We went early, and posted ourselves in an eligible part of the drawing-room, from whence we could hope to obtain a full view of the interesting animal. Two or three hours passed, the quadrilles began, the room filled ; but no lion appeared. The lady of the house became inconsolable, — for it is one of the peculiar privileges of these lions to make solemn appointments and never keep them, — when all of a sudden there came a tremendous double rap at the street door, and the master of the house, after gliding out (unobserved as he flattered himself) to peep over the banisters, came into the room, rubbing his hands together with great glee, and cried out in a very important voice, " My dear, Mr. —— (naming the lion) has this moment arrived."

Upon this, all eyes were turned towards the door, and we observed several young ladies, who had been laughing and conversing previously with great gaiety and good humour, grow extremely quiet and sentimental ; while some young gentlemen, who had been cutting great figures in the facetious and small-talk way, suddenly sank very obviously in the estimation of the company, and were looked upon with great coldness and indifference. Even the young man who had been ordered from the music-shop to play the pianoforte was visibly affected, and struck several false notes in the excess of his excitement.

All this time there was a great talking outside, more than once accompanied by a loud laugh, and a cry of " Oh ! capital ! excellent ! " from which we inferred that the lion was jocose, and that these exclamations were occasioned by the transports of his keeper and our host. Nor were we deceived ; for when the lion at last appeared, we overheard his keeper, who was a little prim man, whisper to several gentlemen of his acquaintance, with uplifted hands, and every expression of half-suppressed admiration, that —— (naming the lion again) was in *such* cue to-night !

The lion was a literary one. Of course, there was a vast number of people present who had admired his roarings, and were anxious to be introduced to him ; and very pleasant it was to see them brought up for the purpose, and to observe the patient dignity with which he received all their patting and caressing. This brought forcibly to our mind what we had so often witnessed at country fairs, where the other lions are compelled to go through as many forms of courtesy as they chance to be acquainted with, just as often as admiring parties happen to drop in upon them.

While the lion was exhibiting in this way, his keeper was not idle, for he mingled among the crowd, and spread his praises most industriously. To one gentleman he whispered some very choice thing that the noble animal had said in the very act of coming up stairs, which, of course, rendered the mental effort still more astonishing ; to another he murmured a hasty account of a grand dinner that had taken place the day before, where twenty-seven gentlemen had got up all at once to demand an extra cheer for the lion ; and to the ladies he made sundry promises of interceding to procure the majestic brute's sign-manual for their albums. Then there were little private consultations in different corners, relative to the personal appearance and stature of the lion : whether he was shorter than they had expected to see him, or taller, or thinner, or fatter, or younger, or older ; whether he was like his portrait, or unlike it ; and whether the particular shade of his eyes was black, or blue, or hazel, or green, or yellow, or mixture. At all these consultations the keeper assisted ; and, in short, the lion was the sole and single subject of discussion till they sat him down to whist, and then the people relapsed into their old topics of conversation — themselves and each other.

We must confess that we looked forward with no slight impatience to the announcement of supper; for if you wish to see a tame lion under particularly favourable circumstances, feeding-time is the period of all others to pitch upon. We were therefore very much delighted to observe a sensation among the guests, which we well knew how to interpret, and immediately afterwards to behold the lion escorting the lady of the house down stairs. We offered our arm to an elderly female of our acquaintance, who — dear old soul! — is the very best person that ever lived, to lead down to any meal; for be the room ever so small, or the party ever so large, she is sure, by some intuitive perception of the eligible, to push and pull herself and conductor close to the best dishes on the table, — we say we offered our arm to this elderly female, and, descending the stairs shortly after the lion, were fortunate enough to obtain a seat nearly opposite him.

Of course the keeper was there already. He had planted himself at precisely that distance from his charge which afforded him a decent, pretext for raising his voice, when he addressed him, to so loud a key as could not fail to attract the attention of the whole company, and immediately began to apply himself seriously to the task of bringing the lion out, and putting him through the whole of his manœuvres. Such flashes of wit as he elicited from the lion! First of all, they began to make puns upon a salt-cellar, and then upon the breast of a fowl, and then upon the trifle; but the best jokes of all were decidedly on the lobster salad, upon which latter subject the lion came out most vigorously, and, in the opinion of the most competent authorities, quite outshone himself. This is a very excellent mode of shining in society, and is founded, we humbly conceive, upon the classic model of the dialogues between Mr. Punch and his friend the proprietor, wherein the latter takes all the uphill work, and is content to pioneer to the jokes and repartees of Mr. P. himself, who never fails to gain great credit and excite much laughter thereby. Whatever it be founded on, however, we recommend it to all lions, present and to come; for in this instance it succeeded to admiration, and perfectly dazzled the whole body of hearers.

When the salt-cellar, and the fowl's breast, and the trifle, and the lobster salad were all exhausted, and could not afford standing room for another solitary witticism, the keeper performed that very dangerous feat which is still done with some of the caravan lions, although in one instance it terminated fatally, of putting his head in the animal's mouth, and placing himself entirely at its mercy. Boswell frequently presents a melancholy instance of the lamentable results of this achievement, and other keepers and jackals have been terribly lacerated for their daring. It is due to our lion to state, that he condescended to be trifled with, in the most gentle manner, and finally went home with the showman in a hack cab, perfectly peaceable, but slightly fuddled.

Being in a contemplative mood, we were led to make some reflections upon the character and conduct of this genus of lions as we walked homewards, and we were not long in arriving at the conclusion that our former impression in their favour was very much strengthened and confirmed by what we had recently seen. While the other lions receive company and compliments in a sullen, moody, not to say snarling manner, these appear flattered by the attentions that are paid them; while those conceal themselves to the utmost of their power from the vulgar gaze, these court the popular eye, and, unlike their brethren, whom nothing short of compulsion will move to exertion, are ever ready to display their acquirements to the wondering throng. We have known bears of undoubted ability who, when the expectations of a large audience have been wound up to the utmost pitch, have peremptorily refused to dance; well-taught monkeys, who have unaccountably objected to exhibit on the slack wire; and elephants of unquestioned genius, who have suddenly declined to turn the barrel-organ; but we never once knew or heard of a biped lion, literary or otherwise, — and we state it as a fact which is highly creditable to the whole species, — who, occasion offering, did not seize with avidity on any opportunity which was afforded him, of performing to his heart's content on the first violin.

MR. ROBERT BOLTON

THE "GENTLEMAN CONNECTED WITH THE PRESS"

In the parlour of the Green Dragon, a public-house in the immediate neighbourhood of Westminster Bridge, everybody talks politics every evening, the great political authority being Mr. Robert Bolton, an individual who defines himself as "a gentleman connected with the press," which is a definition of peculiar indefiniteness. Mr. Robert Bolton's regular circle of admirers and listeners are an undertaker, a greengrocer, a hair-dresser, a baker, a large stomach surmounted by a man's head, and placed on the top of two particularly short legs, and a thin man in black, name, profession, and pursuit unknown, who always sits in the same position, always displays the same long, vacant face, and never opens his lips, surrounded as he is by most enthusiastic conversation, except to puff forth a volume of tobacco smoke, or give vent to a very snappy, loud, and shrill *hem !* The conversation sometimes turns upon literature, Mr. Bolton being a literary character, and always upon such news of the day as is exclusively possessed by that talented individual. I found myself (of course accidentally) in the Green Dragon the other evening, and, being somewhat amused by the following conversation, preserved it.

"Can you lend me a ten-pound note till Christmas ?" inquired the hair-dresser of the stomach.

"Where's your security, Mr. Clip ?"

"My stock in trade, — there's enough of it, I'm thinking, Mr. Thicknesse. Some fifty wigs, two poles, half a dozen head blocks, and a dead Bruin."

"No, I won't, then," growled out Thicknesse. "I lends nothing on the security of the whigs or the Poles either. As for whigs, they're cheats ; as for the Poles, they've got no cash. I never have nothing to do with blockheads, unless I can't awoid it (ironically), and a dead bear's about as much use to me as I could be to a dead bear."

" Well, then," urged the other, " there 's a book as belonged to Pope, Byron's Poems, valued at forty pounds, because it 's got Pope's identical scratch on the back ; what do you think of that for security ? "

" Well, to be sure ! " cried the baker. "·But how d' ye mean, Mr. Clip ? "

" Mean ! why, that it 's got the *hottergruff* of Pope.

' Steal not this book, for fear of hangman's rope ;
For it belongs to Alexander Pope.'

All that 's written on the inside of the binding of the book ; so, as my son says, we 're *bound* to believe it."

" Well, sir," observed the undertaker deferentially, and in a half whisper, leaning over the table, and knocking over the hairdresser's grog as he spoke, " that argument 's very easy upset."

" Perhaps, sir," said Clip, a little flurried, " you 'll pay for the first upset afore you thinks of another."

" Now," said the undertaker, bowing amicably to the hairdresser, " I *think*, I says I *think* — you 'll excuse me, Mr. Clip, I *think*, you see, that won't go down with the present company — unfortunately, my master had the honour of making the coffin of that 'ere Lord's housemaid, not no more nor twenty year ago. Don't think I 'm proud on it, gentlemen ; others might be ; but I hate rank of any sort. I 've no more respect for a Lord's footman than I have for any respectable tradesman in this room. I may say no more nor I have for Mr. Clip ! (bowing). Therefore, that ere Lord must have been born long after Pope died. And it 's a logical interference to defer that they neither of them lived at the same time. So what I mean is this here, that Pope never had no book, never seed, felt, never smelt no book (triumphantly) as belonged to that ere Lord. And, gentlemen, when I consider how patiently you have 'eared the ideas what I have expressed, I feel bound, as the best way to reward you for the kindness you have exhibited, to sit down without saying anything more — partickler as I perceive a worthier visitor nor myself is just entered. I am not in the habit of paying compliments, gentlemen ; when I do, therefore, I hope I strikes with double force."

" Ah, Mr. Murgatroyd ! what 's all this about striking with double force ? " said the object of the above remark, as he entered. " I never excuse a man 's getting into a rage during winter, even when he 's seated so close to the fire as you are. It is very injudicious to put yourself into such a perspiration. What is the cause of this extreme physical and mental excitement, sir ? "

Such was the very philosophical address of Mr. Robert Bolton, a shorthand-writer, as he termed himself — a bit of equivoque passing current among his fraternity, which must give the uninitiated a vast idea of the establishment of the ministerial organ, while to the initiated it signifies that no one paper can lay claim to the enjoyment of their services. Mr. Bolton was a young man, with a somewhat sickly and very dissipated expression of countenance. His habiliments were composed of an exquisite union of gentility, slovenliness, assumption, simplicity, *newness*, and old age. Half of him was dressed for the winter, the other half for the summer. His hat was of the newest cut, the D'Orsay ; his trousers had been white, but the inroads of mud and ink, etc., had given them a piebald appearance ; round his throat he wore a very high black cravat, of the most tyrannical stiffness ; while his *tout ensemble* was hidden beneath the enormous folds of an old brown poodle-collared great-coat, which was closely buttoned up to the aforesaid cravat. His fingers peeped through the ends of his black kid gloves, and two of the toes of each foot took a similar view of society through the extremities of his high-lows. Sacred to the bare walls of his garret be the mysteries of his interior dress! He was a short, spare man, of a somewhat inferior deportment. Everybody seemed influenced by his entry into the room, and his salutation of each member partook of the patronising. The hair-dresser made way for him between himself and the stomach. A minute afterwards he had taken possession of his pint and pipe. A pause in the conversation took place. Everybody was waiting, anxious for his first observation.

"Horrid murder in Westminster this morning," observed Mr. Bolton.

Everybody changed their positions. All eyes were fixed upon the man of paragraphs.

"A baker murdered his son by boiling him in a copper," said Mr. Bolton.

"Good heavens!" exclaimed everybody, in simultaneous horror.

"Boiled him, gentlemen!" added Mr. Bolton, with the most effective emphasis ; "*boiled* him!"

"And the particulars, Mr. B.," inquired the hair-dresser, — "the particulars ? "

Mr. Bolton took a very long draught of porter, and some two or three dozen whiffs of tobacco, doubtless to instil into the commercial capacities of the company the superiority of a gentleman connected with the press, and then said : —

"The man was a baker, gentlemen. (Every one looked at the baker present, who stared at Bolton.) His victim, being his son, also was necessarily the son of a baker. The wretched murderer had a wife, whom he was frequently in the habit, while in an intoxicated state, of kicking, pummelling, flinging mugs at, knocking down, and half killing while in bed, by inserting in her mouth a considerable portion of a sheet or blanket."

The speaker took another draught, everybody looked at everybody else, and exclaimed, " Horrid ! "

"It appeared in evidence, gentlemen," continued Mr. Bolton, "that, on the evening of yesterday, Sawyer the baker came home in a reprehensible state of beer. Mrs. S., connubially considerate, carried him in that condition up stairs into his chamber, and consigned him to their mutual couch. In a minute or two she lay sleeping beside the man whom the morrow's dawn beheld a murderer ! " (Entire silence informed the reporter that his picture had attained the awful effect he desired.) "The son came home about an hour afterwards, opened the door, and went up to bed. Scarcely (gentlemen, conceive his feelings of alarm), scarcely had he taken off his indescribables, when shrieks (to his experienced ear *maternal* shrieks) scared the silence of surrounding night. He put his indescribables on again, and ran down stairs. He opened the door of the parental bedchamber. His father was dancing upon his mother. What must have been his feelings ! In the agony of the minute he rushed at his male parent as he was about to plunge a knife into the side of his female. The mother shrieked. The father caught the son (who had wrested the knife from the paternal grasp) up in his arms, carried him down stairs, shoved him into a copper of boiling water among some linen, closed the lid, and jumped upon the top of it, in which position he was found with a ferocious countenance by the mother, who arrived in the melancholy wash-house just as he had so settled himself.

" ' Where 's my boy ? ' shrieked the mother.

"'In that copper, boiling,' coolly replied the benign father.

"Struck by the awful intelligence, the mother rushed from the house and alarmed the neighbourhood. The police entered a minute afterwards. The father, having bolted the wash-house door, had bolted himself. They dragged the lifeless body of the boiled baker from the cauldron, and, with a promptitude commendable in men of their station, they immediately carried it to the station-house. Subsequently, the baker was apprehended while seated on the top of a lamp-post in Parliament Street, lighting his pipe."

The whole horrible ideality of the Mysteries of Udolpho, condensed into the pithy effect of a ten-line paragraph, could not possibly have so affected the narrator's auditory. Silence, the purest and most noble of all kinds of applause, bore ample testimony to the barbarity of the baker, as well as to Bolton's knack of narration ; and it was only broken after some minutes had elapsed by interjectional expressions of the intense indignation of every man present. The baker wondered how a British baker could so disgrace himself and the highly honourable calling to which he belonged ; and the others indulged in a variety of wonderments connected with the subject ; among which not the least wonderment was that which was awakened by the genius and information of Mr. Robert Bolton, who, after a glowing eulogium on himself, and his unspeakable influence with the daily press, was proceeding, with a most solemn countenance, to hear the pros and cons of the Pope autograph question, when I took up my hat, and left.

FAMILIAR EPISTLE FROM A PARENT TO A CHILD

AGED TWO YEARS AND TWO MONTHS

My Child, — To recount with what trouble I have brought you up, — with what an anxious eye I have regarded your progress, — how late and how often I have sat up at night working for you, — and how many thousand letters I have received from, and written to, your various relations and friends, many of whom have been of a querulous and irritable turn, — to dwell on the anxiety and tenderness with which I have (as far as I possessed the power) inspected and chosen your food; rejecting the indigestible and heavy matter which some injudicious but well-meaning old ladies would have had you swallow, and retaining only those light and pleasant articles which I deemed calculated to keep you free from all gross humours, and to render you an agreeable child, and one who might be popular with society in general, — to dilate on the steadiness with which I have prevented your annoying any company by talking politics; always assuring you that you would thank me for it yourself some day when you grew older, — to expatiate, in short, upon my own assiduity as a parent, is beside my present purpose, though I cannot but contemplate your fair appearance, your robust health, and unimpeded circulation (which I take to be the great secret of your good looks) without the liveliest satisfaction and delight.

It is a trite observation, and one which, young as you are, I have no doubt you have often heard repeated, that we have fallen upon strange times, and live in days of constant shiftings and changes. I had a melancholy instance of this only a week or two since. I was returning from Manchester to London by the Mail Train, when I suddenly fell into another train — a mixed train — of reflection, occasioned by the dejected and disconsolate demeanour of the Post Office Guard. We were stopping at some station where they take in water, when he dismounted slowly from the little box in which he sits in ghastly mockery of his old condition with pistol and blunder-buss beside him, ready to shoot the first highwayman (or rail-wayman) who shall attempt to stop the horses, which now travel (when they travel at all) *inside* and in a portable stable invented for the purpose, — he dismounted, I say, slowly and sadly, from his post, and looking mournfully about him as if in dismal recollection of the old roadside public-house, the blazing fire, the glass of foaming ale, the buxom handmaid and admiring hangers-on of taproom and stable, all honoured by his notice; and, retiring a little apart, stood leaning against a signal-post, surveying the engine with a look of combined affliction and disgust which no words can describe. His scar-let coat and golden lace were tarnished with ignoble smoke; flakes of soot had fallen on his bright green shawl, his pride in days of yore; the steam condensed in the tunnel from which we had just emerged shone upon his hat like rain. His eye betokened that he was thinking of the coachman; and as it wandered to his own seat and his own fast-fading garb, it was plain to see that he felt his office and himself had alike no business there, and were nothing but an elaborate practical joke.

As we whirled away, I was led insensibly into an anticipa-tion of those days to come, when mail-coach guards shall no longer be judges of horse-flesh, when a mail-coach guard shall never even have seen a horse, when stations shall have super-seded stables, and corn shall have given place to coke. "In those dawning times," thought I, "exhibition-rooms shall teem with portraits of her Majesty's favourite engine, with boilers after Nature by future Landseers. Some Amburgh, yet unborn, shall break wild horses by his magic power; and in the dress of a mail-coach guard exhibit his trained animals in a mock mail-coach. Then shall wondering crowds observe how that, with the exception of his whip, it is all his eye; and crowned heads shall see them fed on oats, and stand alone unmoved and undismayed, while courtiers flee affrighted when the coursers neigh."

Such, my child, were the reflections from which I was only awakened then, as I am now, by the necessity of attending to matters of present though minor importance. I offer no apol-ogy to you for the digression, for it brings me very naturally to the subject of change, which is the very subject of which I desire to treat.

In fact, then, my child, you have changed hands. Henceforth, I resign you to the guardianship and protection of one of my most intimate and valued friends, Mr. Ainsworth, with whom, and with you, my best wishes and warmest feelings will ever remain. I reap no gain or profit by parting from you. Nor will any conveyance of your property be required, for, in this respect, you have always been literally "Bentley's" Miscellany, and never mine.

Unlike the driver of the old Manchester mail, I regard this altered state of things with feelings of unmingled pleasure and satisfaction. Unlike the guard of the new Manchester mail, *your* guard is at home in his new place, and has roystering highwaymen and gallant desperadoes ever within call. And if I might compare you, my child, to an engine (not a Tory engine, nor a Whig engine, but a brisk and rapid locomotive); your friends and patrons to passengers; and he who now stands towards you *in loco parentis* as the skilful engineer and supervisor of the whole, I would humbly crave leave to postpone the departure of the train on its new and auspicious course for one brief instant, while, with hat in hand, I approach side by side with the friend who travelled with me on the old road, and presume to solicit favour and kindness in behalf of him and his new charge, both for their sakes and that of the old coachman, **Boz.**

SKETCHES OF YOUNG GENTLEMEN

I

DEDICATION

To the Young Ladies of the United Kingdom of Great Britain and Ireland ; also the Young Ladies of the Principality of Wales; and likewise the Young Ladies resident in the Isles of Guernsey, Jersey, Alderney, and Sark, the humble Dedication of their devoted Admirer.

SHEWETH, — That your Dedicator has perused, with feelings of virtuous indignation, a work purporting to be "Sketches of Young Ladies;" written by Quiz, illustrated by Phiz, and published in one volume, square twelvemo.

That after an attentive and vigilant perusal of the said work, your Dedicator is humbly of opinion that so many libels, upon your Honourable sex, were never contained in any previously published work, in twelvemo or any other mo.

That in the title page and preface to the said work, your Honourable sex are described and classified as animals; and although your Dedicator is not at present prepared to deny that you *are* animals, still he humbly submits that it is not polite to call you so.

That in the aforesaid preface, your Honourable sex are also described as Troglodites, which, being a hard word, may, for aught your Honourable sex or your Dedicator can say to the contrary, be an injurious and disrespectful appellation.

That the author of the said work applied himself to his task in malice prepense and with wickedness aforethought; a fact which, your Dedicator contends, is sufficiently demonstrated, by his assuming the name of Quiz, which, your Dedicator submits, denotes a foregone conclusion, and implies an intention of quizzing.

That in the execution of his evil design, the said Quiz, or author of the said work, must have betrayed some trust or confidence reposed in him by some members of your Honourable

sex; otherwise he never could have acquired so much information relative to the manners and customs of your Honourable
sex in general.

That actuated by these considerations, and further moved
by various slanders and insinuations respecting your Honourable sex contained in the said work, square twelvemo, entitled
"Sketches of Young Ladies," your Dedicator ventures to produce another work, square twelvemo, entitled "Sketches of
Young Gentlemen," of which he now solicits your acceptance
and approval.

That as the Young Ladies are the best companions of the
Young Gentlemen, so the Young Gentlemen should be the best
companions of the Young Ladies; and extending the comparison from animals (to quote the disrespectful language of the
said Quiz) to inanimate objects, your Dedicator humbly suggests that such of your Honourable sex as purchased the bane
should possess themselves of the antidote, and that those of
your Honourable sex who were not rash enough to take the
first should lose no time in swallowing the last, — prevention
being in all cases better than cure, as we are informed upon
the authority, not only of general acknowledgment, but also of
traditionary wisdom.

That with reference to the said bane and antidote, your
Dedicator has no further remarks to make than are comprised
in the printed directions issued with Doctor Morison's pills;
namely, that whenever your Honourable sex take twenty-five
of Number 1, you will be pleased to take fifty of Number 2,
without delay.

And your Dedicator shall ever pray, etc.

II

THE BASHFUL YOUNG GENTLEMAN

WE found ourselves seated at a small dinner party the other
day, opposite a stranger of such singular appearance and manner that he irresistibly attracted our attention.

This was a fresh-coloured young gentleman, with as good a
promise of light whisker as one might wish to see, and possessed of a very velvet-like, soft-looking countenance. We do

not use the latter term invidiously, but merely to denote a pair of smooth, plump, highly coloured cheeks of capacious dimensions, and a mouth rather remarkable for the fresh hue of the lips than for any marked or striking expression it presented. His whole face was suffused with a crimson blush, and bore that downcast, timid, retiring look, which betokens a man ill at ease with himself.

There was nothing in these symptoms to attract more than a passing remark, but our attention had been originally drawn to the bashful young gentleman, on his first appearance in the drawing-room above stairs, into which he was no sooner introduced than, making his way towards us who were standing in a window, and wholly neglecting several persons who warmly accosted him, he seized our hand with visible emotion, and pressed it with a convulsive grasp for a good couple of minutes, after which he dived in a nervous manner across the room, oversetting in his way a fine little girl of six years and a quarter old — and, shrouding himself behind some hangings, was seen no more, until the eagle eye of the hostess detecting him in his concealment, on the announcement of dinner, he was requested to pair off with a lively single lady, of two or three and thirty.

This most flattering salutation from a perfect stranger would have gratified us not a little as a token of his having held us in high respect, and for that reason been desirous of our acquaintance, if we had not suspected from the first that the young gentleman, in making a desperate effort to get through the ceremony of introduction, had, in the bewilderment of his ideas, shaken hands with us at random. This impression was fully confirmed by the subsequent behaviour of the bashful young gentleman in question, which we noted particularly, with the view of ascertaining whether we were right in our conjecture.

The young gentleman seated himself at table with evident misgivings, and, turning sharp round to pay attention to some observation of his loquacious neighbour, overset his bread. There was nothing very bad in this, and if he had had the presence of mind to let it go, and say nothing about it, nobody but the man who had laid the cloth would have been a bit the wiser; but the young gentleman, in various semi-successful attempts to prevent its fall, played with it a little, as gentle-

men in the streets may be seen to do with their hats on a
windy day, and then giving the roll a smart rap in his anxiety
to catch it, knocked it with great adroitness into a tureen of
white soup at some distance, to the unspeakable terror and
disturbance of a very amiable bald gentleman, who was dispensing the contents. We thought the bashful young gentleman
would have gone off in an apoplectic fit, consequent upon the
violent rush of blood to his face at the occurrence of this catastrophe.

From this moment we perceived, in the phraseology of the
fancy, that it was "all up" with the bashful young gentleman,
and so indeed it was. Several benevolent persons endeavoured
to relieve his embarrassment by taking wine with him, but
finding that it only augmented his sufferings, and that after
mingling sherry, champagne, hock, and moselle together, he
applied the greater part of the mixture externally, instead of
internally, they gradually dropped off, and left him to the
exclusive care of the talkative lady, who, not noting the wildness of his eye, firmly believed she had secured a listener. He
broke a glass or two in the course of the meal, and disappeared
shortly afterwards; it is inferred that he went away in some
confusion, inasmuch as he left the house in another gentleman's
coat, and the footman's hat.

This little incident led us to reflect upon the most prominent
characteristics of bashful young gentlemen in the abstract; and
as this portable volume will be the great text-book of young
ladies in all future generations, we record them here for their
guidance and behoof.

If the bashful young gentleman, in turning a street corner,
chance to stumble suddenly upon two or three young ladies of
his acquaintance, nothing can exceed his confusion and agitation. His first impulse is to make a great variety of bows,
and dart past them, which he does, until, observing that they
wish to stop, but are uncertain whether to do so or not, he
makes several feints of returning, which causes them to do the
same; and at length, after a great quantity of unnecessary
dodging and falling up against the other passengers, he returns
and shakes hands most affectionately with all of them, in doing
which he knocks out of their grasp sundry little parcels, which
he hastily picks up, and returns very muddy and disordered.
The chances are that the bashful young gentleman then observes

it is very fine weather, and being reminded that it has only just left off raining for the first time these three days, he blushes very much, and smiles as if he had said a very good thing. The young lady who was most anxious to speak here inquires, with an air of great commiseration, how his dear sister Harriet is to-day; to which the young gentleman, without the slightest consideration, replies, with many thanks, that she is remarkably well. "Well, Mr. Hopkins!" cries the young lady; "why, we heard she was bled yesterday evening, and have been perfectly miserable about her." "Oh, ah," says the young gentleman, "so she was. Oh, she's very ill, very ill, indeed." The young gentleman then shakes his head, and looks very desponding (he has been smiling perpetually up to this time), and after a short pause gives his glove a great wrench at the wrist, and says, with a strong emphasis on the adjective, "*Good* morning, *good* morning." And making a great number of bows in acknowledgment of several little messages to his sister, walks backward a few paces, and comes with great violence against a lamp-post, knocking his hat off in the contact, which in his mental confusion and bodily pain he is going to walk away without, until a great roar from a carter attracts his attention, when he picks it up, and tries to smile cheerfully to the young ladies, who are looking back, and who, he has the satisfaction of seeing, are all laughing heartily.

At a quadrille party, the bashful young gentleman always remains as near the entrance of the room as possible, from which position he smiles at the people he knows as they come in, and sometimes steps forward to shake hands with more intimate friends: a process which on each repetition seems to turn him a deeper scarlet than before. He declines dancing the first set or two, observing, in a faint voice, that he would rather wait a little; but at length is absolutely compelled to allow himself to be introduced to a partner, when he is led, in a great heat and blushing furiously, across the room to a spot where half a dozen unknown ladies are congregated together.

"Miss Lambert, let me introduce Mr. Hopkins for the next quadrille." Miss Lambert inclines her head graciously. Mr. Hopkins bows, and his fair conductress disappears, leaving Mr. Hopkins, as he too well knows, to make himself agreeable. The young lady more than half expects that the bashful young gentleman will say something, and the bashful young gentleman, feeling this, seriously thinks whether he has got anything to say, which, upon mature reflection, he is rather disposed to conclude he has not, since nothing occurs to him. Meanwhile, the young lady, after several inspections of her bouquet, all made in the expectation that the bashful young gentleman is going to talk, whispers her mamma, who is sitting next her, which whisper the bashful young gentleman immediately suspects (and possibly with very good reason) must be about *him*. In this comfortable condition he remains until it is time to "stand up," when murmuring a "Will you allow me?" he gives the young lady his arm, and after inquiring where she will stand, and receiving a reply that she has no choice, conducts her to the remotest corner of the quadrille, and making one attempt at conversation, which turns out a desperate failure, preserves a profound silence until it is all over, when he walks her twice round the room, deposits her in her old seat, and retires in confusion.

A married bashful gentleman — for these bashful gentlemen *do* get married sometimes; how it is ever brought about is a mystery to us — a married bashful gentleman either causes his wife to appear bold by contrast, or merges her proper importance in his own insignificance. Bashful young gentlemen should be cured, or avoided. They are never hopeless, and never will be, while female beauty and attractions retain their influence, as any young lady will find who may think it worth while on this confident assurance to take a patient in hand.

III

THE OUT-AND-OUT YOUNG GENTLEMAN

Out-and-out young gentlemen may be divided into two classes — those who have something to do, and those who have nothing. I shall commence with the former, because that species come more frequently under the notice of young ladies, whom it is our province to warn and to instruct.

The out-and-out young gentleman is usually no great dresser, his instructions to his tailor being all comprehended in the one general direction to "make that what's-a-name a regular bang-up sort of thing." For some years past, the favourite costume of the out-and-out young gentleman has been a rough pilot coat, with two gilt hooks and eyes to the velvet collar; buttons somewhat larger than crown-pieces; a black or fancy neckerchief, loosely tied; a wide-brimmed hat, with a low crown; tightish inexpressibles, and iron-shod boots. Out of doors he sometimes carries a large ash stick, but only on special occasions, for he prefers keeping his hands in his coat pockets. He smokes at all hours, of course, and swears considerably.

The out-and-out young gentleman is employed in a city counting-house or solicitor's office, in which he does as little as he possibly can; his chief places of resort are the streets, the taverns, and the theatres.   In the streets at evening-time, out-and-out young gentlemen have a pleasant custom of walking six or eight abreast, thus driving females and other inoffensive persons into the road, which never fails to afford them the highest satisfaction, especially if there be any immediate danger of their being run over, which enhances the fun of the thing materially.   In all places of public resort, the out-and-outers are careful to select each a seat to himself, upon which he lies at full length, and (if the weather be very dirty, but not in any other case) he lies with his knees up, and the soles of his boots planted firmly on the cushion, so that if any low fellow should ask him to make room for a lady, he takes ample revenge upon her dress, without going at all out of his way to do it.   He always sits with his hat on, and flourishes his stick in the air while the play is proceeding, with a dignified contempt of the performance; if it be possible for one or two out-and-out young gentlemen to get up a little crowding in the passages, they are quite in their element, squeezing, pushing, whooping, and shouting in the most humorous manner possible. If they can only succeed in irritating the gentleman who has a family of daughters under his charge, they are like to die with laughing, and boast of it among their companions for a week afterwards, adding, that one or two of them were "devilish fine girls," and that they really thought the youngest would have fainted, which was the only thing wanted to render the joke complete.

If the out-and-out young gentleman have a mother and sisters, of course he treats them with becoming contempt, inasmuch as they (poor things!) having no notion of life or gaiety, are far too weak-spirited and moping for him. Sometimes however, on a birthday or at Christmas-time, he cannot very well help accompanying them to a party at some old friend's, with which view he comes home when they have been dressed an hour or two, smelling very strongly of tobacco and spirits, and, after exchanging his rough coat for some more suitable attire (in which, however, he loses nothing of the out-and-outer), gets into the coach and grumbles all the way at his own good-nature; his bitter reflections aggravated by the recollection that Tom Smith has taken the chair at a little impromptu dinner at a fighting-man's, and that a set-to was to take place on a dining-table, between the fighting-man and his brother-in-law, which is probably "coming off" at that very instant.

As the out-and-out young gentleman is by no means at his ease in ladies' society, he shrinks into a corner of the drawing-room when they reach the friend's, and, unless one of his sisters is kind enough to talk to him, remains there without being much troubled by the attentions of other people, until he espies, lingering outside the door, another gentleman, whom he at once knows, by his air and manner (for there is a kind of freemasonry in the craft), to be a brother out-and-outer, and towards whom he accordingly makes his way. Conversation being soon opened by some casual remark, the second out-and-outer confidentially informs the first that he is one of the rough sort and hates that kind of thing, only he could n't very well be off coming; to which the other replies that that 's just his case; — "and I 'll tell you what," continues the out-and-outer in a whisper, "I should like a glass of warm brandy and water just now." "Or a pint of stout and a pipe," suggests the other out-and-outer.

The discovery is at once made that they are sympathetic souls; each of them says at the same moment that he sees the other understands what 's what; and they become fast friends at once, more especially when it appears that the second out-and-outer is no other than a gentleman, long favourably known to his familiars as "Mr. Warmint Blake," who, upon divers occasions, has distinguished himself in a manner that would not have disgraced the fighting-man, and who — having been a pretty long time about town — had the honour of once shaking hands with the celebrated Mr. Thurtell himself.

At supper, these gentlemen greatly distinguish themselves, brightening up very much when the ladies leave the table, and

proclaiming aloud their intention of beginning to spend the
evening — a process which is generally understood to be satisfactorily performed, when a great deal of wine is drunk and a
great deal of noise made, both of which feats the out-and-out
young gentlemen execute to perfection. Having protracted
their sitting until long after the host and the other guests have
adjourned to the drawing-room, and finding that they have
drained the decanters empty, they follow them thither, with
complexions rather heightened, and faces rather bloated with
wine; and the agitated lady of the house whispers her friends
as they waltz together, to the great terror of the whole room,
that "both Mr. Blake and Mr. Dummins are very nice sort of
young men in their way, only they are eccentric persons, and
unfortunately *rather too wild !* "

The remaining class of out-and-out young gentlemen is composed of persons, who, having no money of their own and a
soul above earning any, enjoy similar pleasures, nobody knows
how. These respectable gentlemen, without aiming quite so
much at the out-and-out in external appearance, are distinguished by all the same amiable and attractive characteristics,
in an equal or perhaps greater degree, and now and then find
their way into society, through the medium of the other class
of out-and-out young gentlemen, who will sometimes carry
them home, and who usually pay their tavern bills. As they
are equally gentlemanly, clever, witty, intelligent, wise, and
well-bred, we need scarcely have recommended them to the
peculiar consideration of the young ladies, if it were not that
some of the gentle creatures whom we hold in such high
respect are perhaps a little too apt to confound a great many
heavier terms with the light word eccentricity, which we beg
them henceforth to take in a strictly Johnsonian sense, without any liberality or latitude of construction.

IV

THE VERY FRIENDLY YOUNG GENTLEMAN

WE know — and all people know — so many specimens of
this class that, in selecting the few heads our limits enable us
to take from a great number, we have been induced to give the

very friendly young gentleman the preference over many others, to whose claims upon a more cursory view of the question we had felt disposed to assign the priority.

The very friendly young gentleman is very friendly to everybody, but he attaches himself particularly to two, or at most to three families; regulating his choice by their dinners, their circle of acquaintance, or some other criterion in which he has an immediate interest. He is of any age between twenty and forty, unmarried of course, must be fond of children, and is expected to make himself generally useful if possible. Let us illustrate our meaning by an example, which is the shortest mode and the clearest.

We encountered one day, by chance, an old friend of whom we had lost sight for some years, and who — expressing a strong anxiety to renew our former intimacy — urged us to dine with him on an early day, that we might talk over old times. We readily assented, adding, that we hoped we should be alone. "Oh, certainly, certainly," said our friend; "not a soul with us but Mincin." "And who is Mincin?" was our natural inquiry. "Oh, don't mind him," replied our friend; "he's a most particular friend of mine, and a very friendly fellow you will find him;" and so he left us.

We thought no more about Mincin until we duly presented ourselves at the house next day, when, after a hearty welcome, our friend motioned towards a gentleman who had been previously showing his teeth by the fireplace, and gave us to understand that it was Mr. Mincin, of whom he had spoken. It required no great penetration on our part to discover at once that Mincin was in every respect a very friendly young gentleman.

"I am delighted," said Mincin, hastily advancing, and pressing our hand warmly between both of his; "I am delighted, I am sure, to make your acquaintance — (here he smiled) — very much delighted indeed — (here he exhibited a little emotion) — I assure you that I have looked forward to it anxiously for a very long time;" here he released our hands, and, rubbing his own, observed that the day was severe, but that he was delighted to perceive from our appearance that it agreed with us wonderfully; and then went on to observe that, notwithstanding the coldness of the weather, he had that morning seen in the paper an exceedingly curious paragraph, to the effect that there was now in the garden of Mr. Wilkins of Chichester a pumpkin, measuring four feet in height, and eleven feet seven inches in circumference, which he looked upon as a very extraordinary piece of intelligence. We ventured to remark that we had a dim recollection of having once or twice before observed a similar paragraph in the public prints, upon which Mr. Mincin took us confidentially by the button, and said, Exactly, exactly, to be sure, we were very right, and he wondered what the editors meant by putting in such things. Who the deuce, he should like to know, did they suppose cared about them? that struck him as being the best of it.

The lady of the house appeared shortly afterwards, and Mr. Mincin's friendliness, as will readily be supposed, suffered no diminution in consequence; he exerted much strength and skill in wheeling a large easy-chair up to the fire, and the lady being seated in it, carefully closed the door, stirred the fire, and looked to the windows to see that they admitted no air; having satisfied himself upon all these points, he expressed himself quite easy in his mind, and begged to know how she found herself to-day. Upon the lady's replying very well, Mr. Mincin (who it appeared was a medical gentleman) offered some general remarks upon the nature and treatment of colds in the head, which occupied us agreeably until dinner-time. During the meal, he devoted himself to complimenting everybody, not forgetting himself, so that we were an uncommonly agreeable quartette.

"I'll tell you what, Capper," said Mr. Mincin to our host, as he closed the room door after the lady had retired, "you have very great reason to be fond of your wife. Sweet woman, Mrs. Capper, sir!" "Nay, Mincin — I beg," interposed the host, as we were about to reply that Mrs. Capper unquestionably was particularly sweet. "Pray, Mincin, don't." "Why not?" exclaimed Mr. Mincin, "why not? Why should you feel any delicacy before your old friend — our old friend, if I may be allowed to call you so, sir; why should you, I ask?" We of course wished to know why he should also, upon which our friend admitted that Mrs. Capper *was* a very sweet woman, at which admission Mr. Mincin cried "Bravo!" and begged to propose Mrs. Capper with heartfelt enthusiasm, whereupon our host said, "Thank you, Mincin," with deep

feeling; and gave us, in a low voice, to understand that
Mincin had saved Mrs. Capper's cousin's life no less than fourteen times in a year and a half, which he considered no common circumstance — an opinion to which we most cordially
subscribed.

Now that we three were left to entertain ourselves with conversation, Mr. Mincin's extreme friendliness became every
moment more apparent; he was so amazingly friendly, indeed,
that it was impossible to talk about anything in which he had
not the chief concern. We happened to allude to some affairs
in which our friend and we had been mutually engaged nearly
fourteen years before, when Mr. Mincin was all at once reminded of a joke which our friend had made on that day four
years, which he positively must insist upon telling — and
which he did tell accordingly, with many pleasant recollections
of what he said, and what Mrs. Capper said, and how he well
remembered that they had been to the play with orders on the
very night previous, and had seen "Romeo and Juliet," and
the pantomime, and how Mrs. Capper being faint had been led
into the lobby, where she smiled, said it was nothing after all,
and went back again, — with many other interesting and absorbing particulars; after which the friendly young gentleman
went on to assure us that our friend had experienced a marvellously prophetic opinion of that same pantomime, which was
of such an admirable kind that two morning papers took the
same view next day: to this our friend replied, with a little
triumph, that in that instance he had some reason to think he
had been correct, which gave the friendly young gentleman
occasion to believe that our friend was always correct; and so
we went on, until our friend, filling a bumper, said he must
drink one glass to his dear friend Mincin, than whom he would
say no man saved the lives of his acquaintances more, or had
a more friendly heart. Finally, our friend having emptied his
glass, said, "God bless you, Mincin," — and Mr. Mincin and
he shook hands across the table with much affection and earnestness.

But great as the friendly young gentleman is, in a limited
scene like this, he plays the same part on a larger scale with
increased *éclat*. Mr. Mincin is invited to an evening party
with his dear friends the Martins, where he meets his dear
friends the Cappers, and his dear friends the Watsons, and a

hundred other dear friends too numerous to mention. He is
as much at home with the Martins as with the Cappers; but
how exquisitely he balances his attentions, and divides them
among his dear friends! If he flirts with one of the Miss
Watsons, he has one little Martin on the sofa pulling his hair,
and the other little Martin on the carpet riding on his foot.
He carries Mrs. Watson down to supper on one arm, and Miss
Martin on the other, and takes wine so judiciously, and in
such exact order, that it is impossible for the most punctilious
old lady to consider herself neglected. If any young lady,
being prevailed upon to sing, become nervous afterwards, Mr.
Mincin leads her tenderly into the next room, and restores her
with port wine, which she must take medicinally. If any
gentleman be standing by the piano during the progress of the
ballad, Mr. Mincin seizes him by the arm at one point of the
melody, and, softly beating time the while with his head,
expresses in dumb show his intense perception of the delicacy
of the passage. If anybody's self-love is to be flattered, Mr.
Mincin is at hand. If anybody's overweening vanity is to be
pampered, Mr. Mincin will surfeit it. What wonder that
people of all stations and ages recognise Mr. Mincin's friendliness; that he is universally allowed to be handsome as amiable;
that mothers think him an oracle, daughters a dear, brothers
a beau, and fathers a wonder! And who would not have the
reputation of the very friendly young gentleman?

V

THE MILITARY YOUNG GENTLEMAN

WE are rather at a loss to imagine how it has come to pass
that military young gentlemen have obtained so much favour
in the eyes of the young ladies of this kingdom. We cannot
think so lightly of them as to suppose that the mere circumstance of a man's wearing a red coat insures him a ready passport to their regard; and even if this were the case, it would
be no satisfactory explanation of the circumstance, because,
although the analogy may in some degree hold good in the case
of mail-coachmen and guards, still general postmen wear red
coats, and *they* are not to our knowledge better received than

other men; nor are firemen either, who wear (or used to wear)
not only red coats, but very resplendent and massive badges
besides — much larger than epaulettes. Neither do the twopenny post-office boys, if the result of our inquiries be correct,
find any peculiar favour in woman's eyes, although they wear
very bright red jackets, and have the additional advantage of
constantly appearing in public on horseback, which last circumstance may be naturally supposed to be greatly in their
favour.

We have sometimes thought that this phenomenon may take
its rise in the conventional behaviour of captains and colonels
and other gentlemen in red coats on the stage, where they are
invariably represented as fine, swaggering fellows, talking of
nothing but charming girls, their king and country, their
honour, and their debts, and crowing over the inferior classes
of the community, whom they occasionally treat with a little
gentlemanly swindling, no less to the improvement and pleasure of the audience than to the satisfaction and approval of
the choice spirits who consort with them. But we will not
devote these pages to our speculations upon the subject, inasmuch as our business at the present moment is not so much
with the young ladies who are bewitched by her Majesty's
livery as with the young gentlemen whose heads are turned by
it. For "heads" we had written "brains;" but upon consideration, we think the former the more appropriate word of
the two.

These young gentlemen may be divided into two classes —
young gentlemen who are actually in the army, and young
gentlemen who, having an intense and enthusiastic admiration
for all things appertaining to a military life, are compelled by
adverse fortune or adverse relations to wear out their existence
in some ignoble counting-house. We will take this latter description of military young gentlemen first.

The whole heart and soul of the military young gentleman
are concentrated in his favourite topic. There is nothing that
he is so learned upon as uniforms; he will tell you, without
faltering for an instant, what the habiliments of any one regiment are turned up with, what regiments wear stripes down
the outside and inside of the leg, and how many buttons the
Tenth had on their coats; he knows to a fraction how many
yards and odd inches of gold lace it takes to make an ensign

in the Guards; is deeply read in the comparative merits of different bands, and the apparelling of trumpeters; and is very luminous indeed in descanting upon "crack regiments," and the "crack" gentlemen who compose them, of whose mightiness and grandeur he is never tired of telling.

We were suggesting to a military young gentleman only the other day, after he had related to us several dazzling instances of the profusion of half a dozen honourable ensign somebodies or nobodies in the articles of kid gloves and polished boots, that possibly "cracked" regiments would be an improvement upon "crack," as being a more expressive and appropriate designation, when he suddenly interrupted us by pulling out his watch, and observing that he must hurry off to the Park in a cab, or he would be too late to hear the band play. Not wishing to interfere with so important an engagement, and being in fact already slightly overwhelmed by the anecdotes of the honourable ensigns aforementioned, we made no attempt to detain the military young gentleman, but parted company with ready good-will.

· Some three or four hours afterwards, we chanced to be walking down Whitehall, on the Admiralty side of the way, when, as we drew near to one of the little stone places in which a couple of horse-soldiers mount guard in the daytime, we were attracted by the motionless appearance and eager gaze of a young gentleman, who was devouring both man and horse with his eyes, so eagerly that he seemed deaf and blind to all that was passing around him. We were not much surprised at the discovery that it was our friend, the military young gentleman, but we *were* a little astonished when we returned from a walk to South Lambeth to find him still there, looking on with the same intensity as before. As it was a very windy day, we felt bound to awaken the young gentleman from his reverie, when he inquired of us with great enthusiasm, whether "that was not a glorious spectacle," and proceeded to give us a detailed account of the weight of every article of the spectacle's trappings, from the man's gloves to the horse's shoes.

We have made it a practice since, to take the Horse-Guards in our daily walk, and we find it is the custom of military young gentlemen to plant themselves opposite the sentries, and contemplate them at leisure, in periods varying from fifteen minutes to fifty, and averaging twenty-five. We were much

struck a day or two since by the behaviour of a very promising
young butcher who (evincing an interest in the service, which
cannot be too strongly commended or encouraged), after a prolonged inspection of the sentry, proceeded to handle his boots
with great curiosity, and as much composure and indifference
as if the man were wax-work.

But the really military young gentleman is waiting all this
time, and at the very moment that an apology rises to our lips,
he emerges from the barrack gate (he is quartered in a garrison
town), and takes the way towards the High-street.   He wears
his undress uniform, which somewhat mars the glory of his
outward man; but still how great, how grand, he is!   What
a happy mixture of ease and ferocity in his gait and carriage,
and how lightly he carries that dreadful sword under his arm,
making no more ado about it than if it were a silk umbrella!
The lion is sleeping; only think, if an enemy were in sight,
how soon he'd whip it out of the scabbard, and what a terrible fellow he would be!

But he walks on, thinking of nothing less than blood and
slaughter; and now he comes in sight of three other military
young gentlemen, arm in arm, who are bearing down towards
him, clanking their iron heels on the pavement, and clashing
their swords with a noise, which should cause all peaceful men
to quail at heart.   They stop to talk.   See how the flaxen-
haired young gentleman with the weak legs — he who has his
pocket-handkerchief thrust into the breast of his coat — glares
upon the faint-hearted civilians who linger to look upon his
glory; how the next young gentleman elevates his head in the
air, and majestically places his arms akimbo, while the third
stands with his legs very wide apart, and clasps his hands
behind him.   Well may we inquire — not in familiar jest, but
in respectful earnest — if you call that nothing.   Oh! if some
encroaching foreign power — the Emperor of Russia, for
instance, or any of those deep fellows — could only see those
military young gentlemen as they move on together towards
the billiard-room over the way, would n't he tremble a little!

And then, at the theatre at night, when the performances
are by command of Colonel Fitz-Sordust and the officers of the
garrison — what a splendid sight it is!   How sternly the
defenders of their country look round the house, as if in mute
assurance to the audience that they may make themselves

comfortable regarding any foreign invasion, for they (the military young gentlemen) are keeping a sharp lookout, and are ready for anything. And what a contrast between them and that stage-box full of grey-headed officers with tokens of many battles about them, who have nothing at all in common with the military young gentlemen, and who — but for an old-fashioned kind of manly dignity in their looks and bearing — might be common, hard-working soldiers for anything they take the pains to announce to the contrary!

Ah! here is a family just come in who recognise the flaxen-headed young gentleman; and the flaxen-headed young gentleman recognises them too, only he does n't care to show it just now. Very well done, indeed! He talks louder to the little group of military young gentlemen who are standing by him, and coughs to induce some ladies in the next box but one to look round, in order that their faces may undergo the same ordeal of criticism to which they have subjected, in not a wholly inaudible tone, the majority of the female portion of the audience. Oh! a gentleman in the same box looks round as if he were disposed to resent this as an impertinence; and the flaxen-headed young gentleman sees his friends at once, and hurries away to them with the most charming cordiality.

Three young ladies, one young man, and the mamma of the party receive the military young gentleman with great warmth and politeness, and in five minutes afterwards the military young gentleman, stimulated by the mamma, introduces the two other military young gentlemen with whom he was walking in the morning, who take their seats behind the young ladies and commence conversation; whereat the mamma bestows a triumphant bow upon a rival mamma, who has not succeeded in decoying any military young gentlemen, and prepares to consider her visitors from that moment three of the most elegant and superior young gentlemen in the whole world.

VI

THE POLITICAL YOUNG GENTLEMAN

ONCE upon a time — *not* in the days when pigs drank wine, but in a more recent period of our history — it was customary

to banish politics when ladies were present. If this usage
still prevailed, we should have had no chapter for political
young gentlemen, for ladies would have neither known nor
cared what kind of monster a political young gentleman was.
But as this good custom in common with many others has
"gone out," and left no word when it is likely to be home
again; as political young ladies are by no means rare, and
political young gentlemen the very reverse of scarce, we are
bound in the strict discharge of our most responsible duty not
to neglect this natural division of our subject.

If the political young gentleman be resident in a country
town (and there are political young gentlemen in country
towns sometimes), he is wholly absorbed in his politics; as a
pair of purple spectacles communicate the same uniform tint to
all objects near and remote, so the political glasses, with which
the young gentleman assists his mental vision, give to everything the hue and tinge of party feeling. The political young
gentleman would as soon think of being struck with the beauty
of a young lady in the opposite interest, as he would dream of
marrying his sister to the opposite member.

If the political young gentleman be a Conservative, he has
usually some vague ideas about Ireland and the Pope which he
cannot very clearly explain, but which he knows are the right
sort of thing, and not to be very easily got over by the other
side. He has also some choice sentences regarding church and
state, culled from the banners in use at the last election, with
which he intersperses his conversation at intervals with surprising effect. But his great topic is the constitution, upon which
he will declaim, by the hour together, with much heat and
fury; not that he has any particular information on the subject, but because he knows that the constitution is somehow
church and state, and church and state somehow the constitution, and that the fellows on the other side say it is n't, which
is quite a sufficient reason for him to say it is, and to stick to
it.

Perhaps his greatest topic of all, though, is the people. If
a fight takes place in a populous town, in which many noses
are broken, and a few windows, the young gentleman throws
down the newspaper with a triumphant air, and exclaims,
"Here 's your precious people!" if half a dozen boys run across
the course at race time, when it ought to be kept clear, the

young gentleman looks indignantly round, and begs you to
observe the conduct of the people; if the gallery demand a
hornpipe between the play and the after-piece, the same young
gentleman cries, "No" and "Shame," till he is hoarse, and
then inquires with a sneer what you think of popular modera-
tion *now ;* in short, the people form a never-failing theme for
him; and when the attorney, on the side of his candidate,
dwells upon it with great power of eloquence at election time,
as he never fails to do, the young gentleman and his friends,
and the body they head, cheer with great violence against *the
other people,* with whom, of course, they have no possible
connection. In much the same manner the audience at a
theatre never fail to be highly amused with any jokes at the
expense of the public — always laughing heartily at some other
people, and never at themselves.

If the political young gentleman be a Radical, he is usually
a very profound person indeed, having great store of theoretical
questions to put to you, with an infinite variety of possible
cases and logical deductions therefrom. If he be of the utilitarian school, too, which is more than probable, he is particularly pleasant company, having many ingenious remarks to
offer upon the voluntary principle and various cheerful disquisitions connected with the population of the country, the position of Great Britain in the scale of nations, and the balance of
power. Then he is exceedingly well versed in all doctrines of
political economy as laid down in the newspapers, and knows
a great many parliamentary speeches by heart; nay, he has a
small stock of aphorisms, none of them exceeding a couple of
lines in length, which will settle the toughest question and
leave you nothing to say. He gives all the young ladies to
understand, that Miss Martineau is the greatest woman that
ever lived; and when they praise the good looks of Mr. Haw-
kins the new member, says he's very well for a representative,
all things considered, but he wants a little calling to account,
and he is more than half afraid it will be necessary to bring
him down on his knees for that vote on the miscellaneous
estimates. At this, the young ladies express much wonderment, and say surely a Member of Parliament is not to be
brought upon his knees so easily ; in reply to which the political young gentleman smiles sternly, and throws out dark hints
regarding the speedy arrival of that day, when Members of

Parliament will be paid salaries, and required to render weekly accounts of their proceedings, at which the young ladies utter many expressions of astonishment and incredulity, while their lady-mothers regard the prophecy as little else than blasphemous.

It is extremely improving and interesting to hear two political young gentlemen, of diverse opinions, discuss some great question across a dinner-table; such as, whether, if the public were admitted to Westminster Abbey for nothing, they would or would not convey small chisels and hammers in their pockets, and immediately set about chipping all the noses off the statues; or whether, if they once got into the Tower for a shilling, they would not insist upon trying the crown on their own heads, and loading and firing off all the small arms in the armoury, to the great discomposure of Whitechapel and the Minories. Upon these, and many other momentous questions which agitate the public mind in these desperate days, they will discourse with great vehemence and irritation for a considerable time together, both leaving off precisely where they began, and each thoroughly persuaded that he has got the better of the other.

In society, at assemblies, balls, and playhouses, these political young gentlemen are perpetually on the watch for a political allusion, or anything which can be tortured or construed into being one; when, thrusting themselves into the very smallest openings for their favourite discourse, they fall upon the unhappy company tooth and nail. They have recently had many favourable opportunities of opening in churches, but as there the clergyman has it all his own way, and must not be contradicted, whatever politics he preaches, they are fain to hold their tongues until they reach the outer door, though at the imminent risk of bursting in the effort.

As such discussions can please nobody but the talkative parties concerned, we hope they will henceforth take the hint and discontinue them, otherwise we now give them warning, that the ladies have our advice to discountenance such talkers altogether.

VII

THE DOMESTIC YOUNG GENTLEMAN

LET us make a slight sketch of our amiable friend, Mr. Felix Nixon. We are strongly disposed to think, that if we put him in this place, he will answer our purpose without another word of comment.

Felix, then, is a young gentleman who lives at home with his mother, just within the twopenny post-office circle of three miles from St. Martin le Grand. He wears India-rubber goloshes when the weather is at all damp, and always has a silk handkerchief neatly folded up in the right-hand pocket of his great-coat, to tie over his mouth when he goes home at night; moreover, being rather near-sighted, he carries spectacles for particular occasions, and has a weakish tremulous voice, of which he makes great use, for he talks as much as any old lady breathing.

The two chief subjects of Felix's discourse are himself and his mother, both of whom would appear to be very wonderful and interesting persons. As Felix and his mother are seldom apart in body, so Felix and his mother are scarcely ever separate in spirit. If you ask Felix how he finds himself to-day, he prefaces his reply with a long and minute bulletin of his mother's state of health; and the good lady in her turn edifies her acquaintance with a circumstantial and alarming account, how he sneezed four times and coughed once after being out in the rain the other night, but having his feet promptly put into hot water and his head into a flannel-something, which we will not describe more particularly than by this delicate allusion, was happily brought round by the next morning, and enabled to go to business as usual.

Our friend is not a very adventurous or hot-headed person, but he has passed through many dangers, as his mother can testify. There is one great story in particular, concerning a hackney coachman who wanted to overcharge him one night for bringing them home from the play, upon which Felix gave the aforesaid coachman a look which his mother thought would have crushed him to the earth, but which did not crush him quite, for he continued to demand another sixpence, notwithstanding that Felix took out his pocket-book, and, with the aid of a flat candle, pointed out the fare in print, which the coachman obstinately disregarding, he shut the street door with a slam which his mother shudders to think of; and then, roused to the most appalling pitch of passion by the coachman knocking a double-knock to show that he was by no means convinced, he broke with uncontrollable force from his parent and the servant girl, and running into the street without his hat, actually shook his fist at the coachman, and came back again with a face as white, Mrs. Nixon says, looking about her for a simile, as white as that ceiling. She never will forget his fury that night, Never!

To this account Felix listens with a solemn face, occasionally looking at you to see how it affects you, and when his mother has made an end of it, adds that he looked at every coachman he met for three weeks afterwards, in hopes that he might see the scoundrel; whereupon Mrs. Nixon, with an exclamation of terror, requests to know what he would have done to him if he *had* seen him, at which Felix smiling darkly and clenching his right fist, she exclaims, "Goodness gracious!" with a distracted air, and insists upon extorting a promise that he never will on any account do anything so rash, which her dutiful son — it being something more than three years since the offence was committed — reluctantly concedes, and his mother, shaking her head prophetically, fears with a sigh that his spirit will lead him into something violent yet. The discourse then, by an easy transition, turns upon the spirit which glows within the bosom of Felix, upon which point Felix himself becomes eloquent, and relates a thrilling anecdote of the time when he used to sit up till two o'clock in the morning reading French, and how his mother used to say, "Felix, you will make yourself ill, I know you will;" and how *he* used to say, "Mother, I don't care — I will do it;" and how at last his mother privately procured a doctor to come and see him, who declared, the moment he felt his pulse, that if he had gone on reading one night more — only one night more — he must have put a blister on each temple, and another between his shoulders; and who, as it was, sat down upon the instant, and writing a prescription for a blue pill, said it must be taken immediately, or he wouldn't answer for the consequences. The recital of these and many other moving perils of the like nature constantly harrows up the feelings of Mr. Nixon's friends.

Mrs. Nixon has a tolerably extensive circle of female acquaintance, being a good-humoured, talkative, bustling little body, and to the unmarried girls among them she is constantly vaunting the virtues of her son, hinting that she will be a very happy person who wins him, but that they must mind their P's and Q's, for he is very particular, and terribly severe upon young ladies. At this last caution the young ladies resident in the same row, who happen to be spending the evening there, put their pocket-handkerchiefs before their mouths, and are troubled with a short cough; just then Felix knocks at the door, and his mother, drawing the tea-table nearer the fire, calls out to him as he takes off his boots in the back parlour that he need n't mind coming in in his slippers, for there are only the two Miss Greys and Miss Thompson, and she is quite sure they will excuse *him*, and nodding to the two Miss Greys, she adds, in a whisper, that Julia Thompson is a great favourite with Felix, at which intelligence the short cough comes again, and Miss Thompson in particular is greatly troubled with it, till Felix coming in, very faint for want of his tea, changes the subject of discourse, and enables her to laugh out boldly and tell Amelia Grey not to be so foolish. Here they all three laugh, and Mrs. Nixon says they are giddy girls; in which stage of the proceedings, Felix, who has by this time refreshened himself with the grateful herb that "cheers but not inebriates," removes his cup from his countenance and says with a knowing smile, that all girls are; whereat his admiring mamma pats him on the back and tells him not to be sly, which calls forth a general laugh from the young ladies, and another smile from Felix, who, thinking he looks very sly indeed, is perfectly satisfied.

Tea being over, the young ladies resume their work, and Felix insists upon holding a skein of silk while Miss Thompson winds it on a card. This process having been performed to the satisfaction of all parties, he brings down his flute in compliance with a request from the youngest Miss Grey, and plays divers tunes out of a very small music-book till supper-time, when he is very facetious and talkative indeed. Finally, after half a tumblerful of warm sherry and water, he gallantly puts on his goloshes over his slippers, and telling Miss Thompson's servant to run on first and get the door open, escorts that young lady to her house, five doors off; the Miss Greys who live in the next house but one stopping to peep with merry faces from their own door till he comes back again, when they call out "Very well, Mr. Felix," and trip into the passage with a laugh more musical than any flute that was ever played. Felix is rather prim in his appearance, and perhaps a little priggish about his books and flute, and so forth, which have all their peculiar corners of peculiar shelves in his bedroom; indeed, all his female acquaintance (and they are good judges) have long ago set him down as a thorough old bachelor. He is a favourite with them, however, in a certain way, as an honest, inoffensive, kind-hearted creature; and as his peculiarities harm nobody, not even himself, we are induced to hope that many who are not personally acquainted with him will take our good word in his behalf, and be content to leave him to a long continuance of his harmless existence.

VIII

THE CENSORIOUS YOUNG GENTLEMAN

THERE is an amiable kind of young gentleman going about in society, upon whom, after much experience of him, and considerable turning over of the subject in our mind, we feel it our duty to affix the above appellation. Young ladies mildly call him a "sarcastic" young gentleman, or a "severe" young gentleman. We, who know better, beg to acquaint them with the fact, that he is merely a censorious young gentleman, and nothing else.

The censorious young gentleman has the reputation among his familiars of a remarkably clever person, which he maintains by receiving all intelligence and expressing all opinions with a dubious sneer, accompanied with a half smile, expressive of anything you please but good-humour. This sets people about thinking what on earth the censorious young gentleman means, and they speedily arrive at the conclusion that he means something very deep indeed; for they reason in this way — "This young gentleman looks so very knowing that he must mean something, and as I am by no means a dull individual, what a very deep meaning he must have if *I* can't find it out!" It is extraordinary how soon a censorious young gentleman may make a reputation in his own small circle if he bear this in his mind, and regulate his proceedings accordingly.

As young ladies are generally, not curious, but laudably desirous to acquire information, the censorious young gentleman is much talked about among them, and many surmises are hazarded regarding him. "I wonder," exclaims the eldest Miss Greenwood, laying down her work to turn up the lamp, — "I wonder whether Mr. Fairfax will ever be married?" "Bless me, dear," cries Miss Marshall, "what ever made you think of him?" "Really I hardly know," replies Miss Greenwood; "he is such a very mysterious person, that I often wonder about him." "Well, to tell you the truth," replies Miss Marshall, "and so do I." Here two other young ladies profess that they are constantly doing the like, and all present appear in the same condition except one young lady, who, not scrupling to state that she considers Mr. Fairfax "a horror," draws down all the opposition of the others, which having been expressed in a great many ejaculatory passages, such as "Well, did I ever!" — and "Lor', Emily, dear!" ma takes up the subject, and gravely states that she must say she does not think Mr. Fairfax by any means a horror, but rather takes him to be a young man of very great ability; "and I am quite sure," adds the worthy lady, "he always means a great deal more than he says."

The door opens at this point of the discourse, and who of all people alive walks into the room, but the very Mr. Fairfax, who has been the subject of conversation! "Well, it really is curious," cries ma, "we were at that very moment talking about you." "You did me great honour," replies Mr. Fairfax; "may I venture to ask what you were saying?" "Why, if you must know," returns the eldest girl, "we were remarking what a very mysterious man you are." "Ay, ay!" observes Mr. Fairfax, "indeed!" Now Mr. Fairfax says this ay, ay, and indeed, which are slight words enough in themselves, with so very unfathomable an air, and accompanies them with such a very equivocal smile, that ma and the young ladies are more than ever convinced that he means an immensity, and so tell him he is a very dangerous man, and seems to be always thinking ill of somebody, which is precisely the sort of character the censorious young gentleman is most desirous to establish; wherefore he says, "Oh, dear, no," in a tone obviously intended to mean, "You have me there," and which gives them to understand that they have hit the right nail on the very centre of its head.

When the conversation ranges from the mystery overhanging the censorious young gentleman's behaviour to the general topics of the day, he sustains his character to admiration. He considers the new tragedy well enough *for* a new tragedy, but Lord bless us — well, no matter; he could say a great deal on that point, but he would rather not, lest he should be thought ill-natured, as he knows he would be. "But is not Mr. So and So's performance truly charming?" inquires a young lady. "Charming!" replies the censorious young gentleman. "Oh, dear, yes, certainly; very charming — oh, very charming indeed." After this, he stirs the fire, smiling contemptuously all the while; and a modest young gentleman, who has been a silent listener, thinks what a great thing it must be to have such a critical judgment. Of music, pictures, books, and poetry, the censorious young gentleman has an equally fine conception. As to men and women, he can tell all about them at a glance. "Now let us hear your opinion of young Mrs. Barker," says some great believer in the powers of Mr. Fairfax, "but don't be too severe." "I never am severe," replies the censorious young gentleman. "Well, never mind that now. She is very lady-like, is she not?" "Lady-like!" repeats the censorious young gentleman (for he always repeats when he is at a loss for anything to say); "did you observe her manner? Bless my heart and soul, Mrs. Thompson, did you observe her manner? — that's all I ask." "I thought I had done so," rejoins the poor lady, much perplexed; "I did not observe it very closely, perhaps." "Oh, not very closely," rejoins the censorious young gentleman triumphantly. "Very good; then *I* did. Let us talk no more about her." The censorious young gentleman purses up his lips, and nods his head sagely, as he says this; and it is forthwith whispered about, that Mr. Fairfax (who, though he is a little prejudiced, must be admitted to be a very excellent judge) has observed something exceedingly odd in Mrs. Barker's manner.

IX

THE FUNNY YOUNG GENTLEMAN

As one funny young gentleman will serve as a sample of all funny young gentlemen, we purpose merely to note down the conduct and behaviour of an individual specimen of this class, whom we happened to meet at an annual family Christmas party in the course of this very last Christmas that ever came.

We were all seated round a blazing fire which crackled pleasantly as the guests talked merrily and the urn steamed cheerily — for, being an old-fashioned party, there *was* an urn, and a teapot besides — when there came a postman's knock at the door, so violent and sudden, that it startled the whole circle, and actually caused two or three very interesting and most unaffected young ladies to scream aloud and to exhibit many afflicting symptoms of terror and distress, until they had been several times assured by their respective adorers that they were in no danger. We were about to remark that it was surely beyond post-time, and must have been a runaway knock, when our host, who had hitherto been paralysed with wonder, sank into a chair in a perfect ecstasy of laughter, and offered to lay twenty pounds that it was that droll dog Griggins. He had no sooner said this, than the majority of the company and all the children of the house burst into a roar of laughter too, as if some inimitable joke flashed upon them simultaneously, and gave vent to various exclamations of — To be sure it must be Griggins, and How like him that was, and What spirits he was always in! with many other commendatory remarks of the like nature.

Not having the happiness to know Griggins, we became extremely desirous to see so pleasant a fellow, the more especially as a stout gentleman with a powdered head, who was sitting with his breeches buckles almost touching the hob, whispered us he was a wit of the first water, when the door opened, and Mr. Griggins being announced, presented himself, amidst another shout of laughter and a loud clapping of hands from the younger branches. This welcome he acknowledged by sundry contortions of countenance, imitative of the clown in one of the new pantomimes, which were so extremely suc-

cessful, that one stout gentleman rolled upon an ottoman i ↲
paroxysm of delight, protesting, with many gasps, that if
somebody did n't make that fellow Griggins leave off, he would
be the death of him, he knew. At this the company only
laughed more boisterously than before, and as we always like
to accommodate our tone and spirit if possible to the humour
of any society in which we find ourself, we laughed with the
rest, and exclaimed, "Oh! capital, capital!" as loud as any of
them.

When he had quite exhausted all beholders, Mr. Griggins
received the welcomes and congratulations of the circle, and
went through. the needful introductions with much ease and
many puns. This ceremony over, he avowed his intention of
sitting in somebody's lap unless the young ladies made room
for him on the sofa, which being done, after a great deal of
tittering and pleasantry, he squeezed himself among them, and
likened his condition to that of love among the roses. At this
novel jest we all roared once more. "You should consider
yourself highly honoured, sir," said we. "Sir," replied Mr.
Griggins, "you do me proud." Here everybody laughed again;
and the stout gentleman by the fire whispered in our ear that
Griggins was making a dead set at us.

The tea things having been removed, we all sat down to
a round game, and here Mr. Griggins shone forth with peculiar
brilliancy, abstracting other people's fish, and looking over
their hands in the most comical manner. He made one most
excellent joke in snuffing a candle, which was neither more nor
less than setting fire to the hair of a pale young gentleman who
sat next him, and afterwards begging his pardon with considerable humour. As the young gentleman could not see the joke
however, possibly in consequence of its being on the top of his
own head, it did not go off quite as well as it might have
done; indeed, the young gentleman was heard to murmur some
general references to "impertinence," and a "rascal," and to
state the number of his lodgings in an angry tone — a turn of
the conversation which might have been productive of slaugh-
terous consequences, if a young lady, betrothed to the young
gentleman, had not used her immediate influence to bring about
a reconciliation; emphatically declaring in an agitated whisper,
intended for his peculiar edification but audible to the whole
table, that if he went on in that way, she never would think

of him otherwise than as a friend, though as that she must always regard him. At this terrible threat the young gentleman became calm, and the young lady, overcome by the revulsion of feeling, instantaneously fainted.

Mr. Griggins's spirits were slightly depressed for a short period by this unlooked-for result of such a harmless pleasantry, but being promptly elevated by the attentions of the host and several glasses of wine, he soon recovered, and became even more vivacious than before, insomuch that the stout gentleman previously referred to assured us that although he had known him since he was *that* high (something smaller than a nutmeg-grater), he had never beheld him in such excellent cue.

When the round game and several games at blind man's buff which followed it were all over, and we were going down to supper, the inexhaustible Mr. Griggins produced a small sprig of mistletoe from his waistcoat pocket, and commenced a general kissing of the assembled females, which occasioned great commotion and much excitement. We observed that several young gentlemen — including the young gentleman with the pale countenance — were greatly scandalised at this indecorous proceeding, and talked very big among themselves in corners; and we observed, too, that several young ladies when remonstrated with by the aforesaid young gentlemen, called each other to witness how they had struggled, and protested vehemently that it was very rude, and that they were surprised at Mrs. Brown's allowing it, and that they could n't bear it, and had no patience with such impertinence. But such is the gentle and forgiving nature of woman, that although we looked very narrowly for it, we could not detect the slightest harshness in the subsequent treatment of Mr. Griggins. Indeed, upon the whole, it struck us that among the ladies he seemed rather more popular than before!

To recount all the drollery of Mr. Griggins at supper would fill such a tiny volume as this, to the very bottom of the outside cover. How he drank out of other people's glasses, and ate of other people's bread; how he frightened into screaming convulsions a little boy who was sitting up to supper in a high chair, by sinking below the table and suddenly reappearing with a mask on; how the hostess was really surprised that anybody could find a pleasure in tormenting children, and how the host frowned at the hostess, and felt convinced that Mr.

Griggins had done it with the very best intentions; how Mr. Griggins explained, and how everybody's good-humour was restored but the child's; — to tell these and a hundred other things ever so briefly, would occupy more of our room and our readers' patience, than either they or we can conveniently spare. Therefore we change the subject, merely observing that we have offered no description of the funny young gentleman's personal appearance, believing that almost every society has a Griggins of its own, and leaving all readers to supply the deficiency, according to the particular circumstances of their particular case.

X

THE THEATRICAL YOUNG GENTLEMAN

ALL gentlemen who love the drama — and there are few gentlemen who are not attached to the most intellectual and rational of all our amusements — do not come within this definition. As we have no mean relish for theatrical entertainments ourself, we are disinterestedly anxious that this should be perfectly understood.

The theatrical young gentleman has early and important information on all theatrical topics. "Well," says he abruptly, when you meet him in the street, "here's a pretty to-do. Flimkins has thrown up his part in the melodrama at the Surrey." "And what's to be done?" you inquire with as much gravity as you can counterfeit. "Ah, that's the point," replies the theatrical young gentleman, looking very serious; "Boozle declines it; positively declines it. From all I am told, I should say it was decidedly in Boozle's line, and that he would be very likely to make a great hit in it; but he objects on the ground of Flimkins having been put up in the part first, and says no earthly power shall induce him to take the character. It's a fine part, too — excellent business, I'm told. He has to kill six people in the course of the piece, and to fight over a bridge in red fire, which is as safe a card, you know, as can be. Don't mention it; but I hear that the last scene, when he is first poisoned, and then stabbed, by Mrs. Flimkins as Vengedora, will be the greatest thing that has been done these many years." With this piece of news, and laying his finger on his lips as a caution for you not to excite the town with it, the theatrical young gentleman hurries away.

The theatrical young gentleman, from often frequenting the different theatrical establishments, has pet and familiar names for them all. Thus Covent Garden is the Garden, Drury Lane, the Lane; the Victoria, the Vic.; and the Olympic, the Pic. Actresses, too, are always designated by their surnames only, as Taylor, Nisbett, Faucit, Honey; that talented and lady-like girl Sheriff, that clever little creature Horton, and so on. In the same manner he prefixes Christian names when he mentions the actors; as, Charley Young, Jemmy Buckstone, Fred. Yates, Paul Bedford. When he is at a loss for a Christian name, the word "old" applied indiscriminately answers quite as well; as, old Charley Matthews at Vestris's, old Harley, and old Braham. He has a great knowledge of the private proceedings of actresses, especially of their getting married, and can tell you in a breath half a dozen who have changed their names without avowing it. Whenever an alteration of this kind is made in the play-bills, he will remind you that he let you into the secret six months ago.

The theatrical young gentleman has a great reverence for all that is connected with the stage department of the different theatres. He would, at any time, prefer going a street or two out of his way, to omitting to pass a stage entrance, into which he always looks with a curious and searching eye. If he can only identify a popular actor in the street, he is in a perfect transport of delight; and no sooner meets him than he hurries back, and walks a few paces in front of him so that he can turn round from time to time, and have a good stare at his features. He looks upon a theatrical-fund dinner as one of the most enchanting festivities ever known; and thinks that to be a member of the Garrick Club, and see so many actors in their plain clothes, must be one of the highest gratifications the world can bestow.

The theatrical young gentleman is a constant half-price visitor at one or other of the theatres, and has an infinite relish for all pieces which display the fullest resources of the establishment. He likes to place implicit reliance upon the play-bills when he goes to see a show-piece, and works himself up to such a pitch of enthusiasm as not only to believe (if the bills say so) that there are three hundred and seventy-five people on the stage at one time in the last scene, but is highly indignant with you unless you believe it also. He considers that if the stage be opened from the footlights to the back wall, in any new play, the piece is a triumph of dramatic writing, and applauds accordingly. He has a great notion of trapdoors, too; and thinks any character going down or coming up a trap (no matter whether he be an angel or a demon — they both do it occasionally) one of the most interesting feats in the whole range of scenic illusion.

Besides these acquirements, he has several veracious accounts to communicate of the private manners and customs of different actors, which, during the pauses of a quadrille, he usually communicates to his partner, or imparts to his neighbour at a supper-table. Thus he is advised that Mr. Liston always had a footman in gorgeous livery waiting at the side-scene with a brandy-bottle and tumbler, to administer half a pint or so of spirit to him every time he came off, without which assistance he must infallibly have fainted. He knows for a fact that, after an arduous part, Mr. George Bennett is put between two feather beds, to absorb the perspiration; and is credibly informed that Mr. Baker has, for many years, submitted to a course of lukewarm toast and water, to qualify him to sustain his favourite characters. He looks upon Mr. Fitz-Ball as the principal dramatic genius and poet of the day; but holds that there are great writers extant besides him, — in proof whereof he refers you to various dramas and melodramas recently produced, of which he takes in all the sixpenny and threepenny editions as fast as they appear.

The theatrical young gentleman is a great advocate for violence of emotion and redundancy of action. If a father has to curse a child upon the stage, he likes to see it done in the thorough-going style, with no mistake about it: to which end it is essential that the child should follow the father on her knees, and be knocked violently over on her face by the old gentleman as he goes into a small cottage, and shuts the door behind him. He likes to see a blessing invoked upon the young lady, when the old gentleman repents, with equal earnestness, and accompanied by the usual conventional forms, which consist of the old gentleman looking anxiously up into the clouds, as if to see whether it rains, and then spreading an imaginary tablecloth in the air over the young lady's head —

soft music playing all the while. Upon these, and other
points of a similar kind, the theatrical young gentleman is a
great critic indeed. He is likewise very acute in judging of
natural expressions of the passions, and knows precisely the
frown, wink, nod, or leer, which stands for any one of them,
or the means by which it may be converted into any other; as,
jealousy, with a good stamp of the right foot, becomes anger;
or wildness, with the hands clasped before the throat, instead
of tearing the wig, is passionate love. If you venture to
express a doubt of the accuracy of any of these portraitures,
the theatrical young gentleman assures you, with a haughty
smile, that it always has been done in that way, and he supposes they are not going to change it at this time of day to
pleaes you; to which, of course, you meekly reply that you
suppose not.

There are innumerable disquisitions of this nature, in which
the theatrical young gentleman is very profound, especially to
ladies whom he is most in the habit of entertaining with them;
but as we have no space to recapitulate them at greater length,
we must rest content with calling the attention of the young
ladies in general to the theatrical young gentlemen of their
own acquaintance.

XI

THE POETICAL YOUNG GENTLEMAN

Time was, and not very long ago either, when a singular
epidemic raged among the young gentlemen, vast numbers
of whom, under the influence of the malady, tore off their
neckerchiefs, turned down their shirt-collars, and exhibited
themselves in the open streets with bare throats and dejected
countenances, before the eyes of an astonished public. These
were poetical young gentlemen. The custom was gradually
found to be inconvenient, as involving the necessity of too
much clean linen and too large washing-bills, and these outward symptoms have consequently passed away; but we are
disposed to think, notwithstanding, that the number of poetical
young gentlemen is considerably on the increase.

We know a poetical young gentleman — a very poetical
young gentleman. We do not mean to say that he is troubled

with the gift of poesy in any remarkable degree, but his coun‑
tenance is of a plaintive and melancholy cast, his manner is
abstracted and bespeaks affliction of soul: he seldom has his
hair cut, and often talks about being an outcast and wanting
a kindred spirit; from which, as well as from many general
observations in which he is wont to indulge, concerning myste‑
rious impulses, and yearnings of the heart, and the supremacy
of intellect gilding all earthly things with the glowing magic
of immortal verse, it is clear to all his friends that he has been
stricken poetical.

The favourite attitude of the poetical young gentleman is
lounging on a sofa with his eyes fixed upon the ceiling, or sit‑
ting bolt upright in a high-backed chair, staring with very
round eyes at the opposite wall. When he is in one of these
positions, his mother, who is a worthy, affectionate old soul,
will give you a nudge to bespeak your attention without dis‑
turbing the abstracted one, and whisper, with a shake of the
head, that John's imagination is at some extraordinary work or
other, you may take her word for it. Hereupon John looks
more fiercely intent upon vacancy than before, and suddenly
snatching a pencil from his pocket puts down three words,
and a cross on the back of a card, sighs deeply, paces once or
twice across the room, inflicts a most unmerciful slap upon his
head, and walks moodily up to his dormitory.

The poetical young gentleman is apt to acquire peculiar
notions of things, too, which plain ordinary people, unblessed
with a poetical obliquity of vision, would suppose to be rather
distorted. For instance, when the sickening murder and
mangling of a wretched woman was affording delicious food
wherewithal to gorge the insatiable curiosity of the public, our
friend the poetical young gentleman was in ecstasies — not of
disgust, but admiration. "Heavens!" cried the poetical young
gentleman, "how grand; how great!" We ventured deferen‑
tially to inquire upon whom these epithets were bestowed; our
humble thoughts oscillating between the police officer who
found the criminal, and the lock-keeper who found the head.
"Upon whom!" exclaimed the poetical young gentleman in a
frenzy of poetry, "upon whom should they be bestowed but
upon the murderer!" — and thereupon it came out, in a fine
torrent of eloquence, that the murderer was a great spirit, a
bold creature, full of daring and nerve, a man of dauntless

heart and determined courage, and withal a great casuist and able reasoner, as was fully demonstrated in his philosophical colloquies with the great and noble of the land. We held our peace, and meekly signified our indisposition to controvert these opinions — firstly, because we were no match at quotation for the poetical young gentleman; and, secondly, because we felt it would be of little use our entering into any disputation if we were; being perfectly convinced that the respectable and immortal hero in question is not the first and will not be the last hanged gentleman upon whom false sympathy or diseased curiosity will be plentifully expended.

This was a stern mystic flight of the poetical young gentleman. In his milder and softer moments he occasionally lays down his neckcloth, and pens stanzas, which sometimes find their way into a Lady's Magazine, or the "Poet's Corner" of some country newspaper; or which, in default of either vent for his genius, adorn the rainbow leaves of a lady's album. These are generally written upon some such occasions as contemplating the Bank of England by midnight, or beholding St. Paul's in a snow-storm; and when these gloomy objects fail to afford him inspiration, he pours forth his soul in a touching address to a violet, or a plaintive lament that he is no longer a child, but has gradually grown up.

The poetical young gentleman is fond of quoting passages from his favourite authors, who are all of the gloomy and desponding school. He has a great deal to say, too, about the world, and is much given to opining, especially if he has taken anything strong to drink, that there is nothing in it worth living for. He gives you to understand, however, that, for the sake of society, he means to bear his part in the tiresome play, manfully resisting the gratification of his own strong desire to make a premature exit; and consoles himself with the reflection that immortality has some chosen nook for himself and the other great spirits whom earth has chafed and wearied.

When the poetical young gentleman makes use of adjectives, they are all superlatives. Everything is of the grandest, greatest, noblest, mightiest, loftiest; or the lowest, meanest, obscurest, vilest, and most pitiful. He knows no medium: for enthusiasm is the soul of poetry; and who so enthusiastic as a poetical young gentleman? "Mr. Milkwash," says a young lady as she unlocks her album to receive the young gentleman's

original impromptu contribution, "how very silent you are! I
think you must be in love." "Love!" cries the poetical
young gentleman, starting from his seat by the fire and terrify-
ing the cat who scampers off at full speed, "love! that burning consuming passion; that ardour of the soul, that fierce
glowing of the heart. Love! The withering blighting influence of hope misplaced and affection slighted. Love, did you
say! Ha, ha, ha!"

With this, the poetical young gentleman laughs a laugh
belonging only to poets and Mr. O. Smith of the Adelphi
Theatre, and sits down, pen in hand, to throw off a page or
two of verse in the biting, semi-atheistical, demoniac style,
which, like the poetical young gentleman himself, is full of
sound and fury, signifying nothing.

XII

THE "THROWING-OFF" YOUNG GENTLEMAN

THERE is a certain kind of impostor — a bragging, vaunting,
puffing young gentleman — against whom we are desirous to
warn that fairer part of the creation, to whom we more peculiarly devote these our labours. And we are particularly
induced to lay especial stress upon this division of our subject
by a little dialogue we held some short time ago with an
esteemed young lady of our acquaintance, touching a most
gross specimen of this class of men. We had been urging all
the absurdities of his conduct and conversation, and dwelling
upon the impossibilities he constantly recounted, — to which,
indeed, we had not scrupled to prefix a certain hard little word
of one syllable and three letters, — when our fair friend, unable
to maintain the contest any longer, reluctantly cried, "Well;
he certainly has a habit of throwing-off, but then — " What
then? Throw him off yourself, said we. And so she did;
but not at our instance, for other reasons appeared, and it
might have been better if she had done so at first.

The throwing-off young gentleman has so often a father possessed of vast property in some remote district of Ireland that
we look with some suspicion upon all young gentlemen who
volunteer this description of themselves. The deceased grand

father of the throwing-off young gentleman was a man of immense possessions, and untold wealth; the throwing-off young gentleman remembers, as well as if it were only yesterday, the deceased baronet's library, with its long rows of scarce and valuable books in superbly embossed bindings, arranged in cases, reaching from the lofty ceiling to the oaken floor; and the fine antique chairs and tables, and the noble old castle of Ballykillbabaloo, with its splendid prospect of hill and dale, and wood, and rich wild scenery, and the fine hunting stables and the spacious courtyards, "and — and — everything upon the same magnificent scale," says the throwing-off young gentleman, "princely; quite princely. Ah!" And he sighs as if mourning over the fallen fortunes of his noble house.

The throwing-off young gentleman is a universal genius; at walking, running, rowing, swimming, and skating, he is unrivalled; at all games of chance or skill, at hunting, shooting, fishing, riding, driving, or amateur theatricals, no one can touch him — that is, *could* not, because he gives you carefully to understand, lest there should be any opportunity of testing his skill, that he is quite out of practice just now, and has been for some years. If you mention any beautiful girl of your common acquaintance in his hearing, the throwing-off young gentleman starts, smiles, and begs you not to mind him, for it was quite involuntary; people do say indeed that they were once engaged, but no — although she is a very fine girl, he was so situated at that time that he could n't possibly encourage the — "but it's of no use talking about it!" he adds, interrupting himself, "she has got over it now, and I firmly hope and trust is happy." With this benevolent aspiration he nods his head in a mysterious manner, and whistling the first part of some popular air, thinks perhaps it will be better to change the subject.

There is another great characteristic of the throwing-off young gentleman, which is, that he "happens to be acquainted" with a most extraordinary variety of people in all parts of the world. Thus in all disputed questions, when the throwing-off young gentleman has no argument to bring forward, he invariably happens to be acquainted with some distant person, intimately connected with the subject, whose testimony decides the point against you, to the great — may we say it — to the great admiration of three young ladies out of every four, who consider the throwing-off young gentleman a very highly con-nected young man, and a most charming person.

Sometimes the throwing-off young gentleman happens to look in upon a little family circle of young ladies who are quietly spending the evening together, and then indeed is he at the very height and summit of his glory; for it is to be observed that he by no means shines to equal advantage in the presence of men as in the society of over-credulous young ladies, which is his proper element. It is delightful to hear the number of pretty things the throwing-off young gentleman gives utterance to, during tea, and still more so to observe the ease with which, from long practice and study, he delicately blends one compliment to a lady with two for himself. "Did you ever see a more lovely blue than this flower, Mr. Cave-ton?" asks a young lady who, truth to tell, is rather smitten with the throwing-off young gentleman. "Never," he replies, bending over the object of admiration, — "never but in your eyes." "Oh, Mr. Caveton," cries the young lady, blushing of course. "Indeed I speak the truth," replies the throwing-off young gentleman, "I never saw any approach to them. I used to think my cousin's blue eyes lovely, but they grow dim and colourless beside yours." "Oh! a beautiful cousin, Mr. Caveton!" replies the young lady, with that perfect artlessness which is the distinguishing characteristic of all young ladies; "an affair, of course." "No; indeed, indeed you wrong me," rejoins the throwing-off young gentleman with great energy. "I fervently hope that her attachment towards me may be nothing but the natural result of our close intimacy in child-hood, and that in change of scene and among new faces she may soon overcome it. *I* love her! Think not so meanly of me, Miss Lowfield, I beseech, as to suppose that title, lands, riches, and beauty, can influence *my* choice. The heart, the heart, Miss Lowfield." Here the throwing-off young gentle-man sinks his voice to a still lower whisper; and the young lady duly proclaims to all the other ladies when they go up stairs, to put their bonnets on, that Mr. Caveton's relations are all immensely rich, and that he is hopelessly beloved by title, lands, riches, and beauty.

We have seen a throwing-off young gentleman who, to our certain knowledge, was innocent of a note of music, and

scarcely able to recognise a tune by ear, volunteer a Spanish
air upon the guitar when he had previously satisfied himself
that there was not such an instrument within a mile of the
house.

We have heard another throwing-off young gentleman, after
striking a note or two upon the piano, and accompanying it
correctly (by dint of laborious practice) with his voice, assure
a circle of wondering listeners that so acute was his ear that
he was wholly unable to sing out of tune, let him try as he
would. We have lived to witness the unmasking of another
throwing-off young gentleman, who went out a visiting in a
military cap with a gold band and tassel, and who, after passing successfully for a captain and being lauded to the skies for
his red whiskers, his bravery, his soldierly bearing and his
pride, turned out to be the dishonest son of an honest linen-
draper in a small country town, and whom, if it were not for
this fortunate exposure, we should not yet despair of encountering as the fortunate husband of some rich heiress. Ladies,
ladies, the throwing-off young gentlemen are often swindlers,
and always fools. So pray you avoid them.

XIII

THE YOUNG LADIES' YOUNG GENTLEMAN

THIS young gentleman has several titles. Some young
ladies consider him "a nice young man," others "a fine young
man," others "quite a lady's man," others "a handsome man,"
others "a remarkably good-looking young man." With some
young ladies he is "a perfect angel," and with others "quite a
love." He is likewise a charming creature, a duck, and a
dear.

The young ladies' young gentleman has usually a fresh
colour and very white teeth, which latter articles, of course,
he displays on every possible opportunity. He has brown or
black hair, and whiskers of the same, if possible; but a slight
tinge of red, or the hue which is vulgarly known as *sandy*, is
not considered an objection. If his head and face be large,
his nose prominent, and his figure square, he is an uncommonly fine young man, and worshipped accordingly. Should

his whiskers meet beneath his chin, so much the better, though this is not absolutely insisted on; but he must wear an under-waistcoat, and smile constantly.

There was a great party got up by some party-loving friends of ours last summer, to go and dine in Epping Forest. As we hold that such wild expeditions should never be indulged in, save by people of the smallest means, who have no dinner at home, we should indubitably have excused ourself from attending, if we had not recollected that the projectors of the excursion were always accompanied on such occasions by a choice sample of the young ladies' young gentleman, whom we were very anxious to have an opportunity of meeting. This determined us, and we went.

We were to make for Chigwell in four glass coaches, each with a trifling company of six or eight inside, and a little boy belonging to the projectors on the box, and to start from the residence of the projectors, Woburn Place, Russell Square, at half-past ten precisely. We arrived at the place of rendezvous at the appointed time, and found the glass coaches and the little boys quite ready, and divers young ladies and young gentlemen looking anxiously over the breakfast-parlour blinds, who appeared by no means so much gratified by our approach as we might have expected, but evidently wished we had been somebody else. Observing that our arrival in lieu of the unknown occasioned some disappointment, we ventured to inquire who was yet to come, when we found from the hasty reply of a dozen voices, that it was no other than the young ladies' young gentleman.

"I cannot imagine," said the mamma, "what has become of Mr. Balim — always so punctual, always so pleasant and agreeable. I am sure I can-*not* think." As these last words were uttered in that measured, emphatic manner which painfully announces that the speaker has not quite made up his or her mind what to say, but is determined to talk on nevertheless, the eldest daughter took up the subject, and hoped no accident had happened to Mr. Balim, upon which there was a general chorus of "Dear Mr. Balim!" and one young lady, more adventurous than the rest, proposed that an express should be straightway sent to dear Mr. Balim's lodgings. This, however, the papa resolutely opposed, observing, in what a young lady behind us termed "quite a bearish way," that if Mr.

Balim did n't choose to come, he might stop at home. At this all the daughters raised a murmur of "Oh, pa!" except one sprightly little girl of eight or ten years old, who, taking advantage of a pause in the discourse, remarked, that perhaps Mr. Balim might have been married that morning — for which impertinent suggestion she was summarily ejected from the room by her eldest sister.

We were all in a state of great mortification and uneasiness, when one of the little boys, running into the room as airily as little boys usually run who have an unlimited allowance of animal food in the holidays, and keep their hands constantly forced down to the bottoms of very deep trouser-pockets when they take exercise, joyfully announced that Mr. Balim was at that moment coming up the street in a hackney-cab; and the intelligence was confirmed beyond all doubt a minute afterwards by the entry of Mr. Balim himself, who was received with repeated cries of "Where have you been, you naughty creature?" whereunto the naughty creature replied, that he had been in bed, in consequence of a late party the night before, and had only just risen. The acknowledgment awakened a variety of agonising fears that he had taken no breakfast; which appearing after a slight cross-examination to be the real state of the case, breakfast for one was immediately ordered, notwithstanding Mr. Balim's repeated protestations that he could n't think of it. He did think of it though, and thought better of it too, for he made a remarkably good meal when it came, and was assiduously served by a select knot of young ladies. It was quite delightful to see how he ate and drank, while one pair of fair hands poured out his coffee, and another put in the sugar, and another the milk; the rest of the company ever and anon casting angry glances at their watches and the glass coaches, — and the little boys looking on in an agony of apprehension lest it should begin to rain before we set out; it might have rained all day, after we were once too far to turn back again, and welcome for aught they cared.

However, the cavalcade moved at length, every coachman being accommodated with a hamper between his legs something larger than a wheelbarrow; and the company being packed as closely as they possibly could in the carriages, "according," as one married lady observed, "to the immemorial custom, which was half the diversion of gipsy parties." Thinking it very likely it might be (we have never been able to discover the other half), we submitted to be stowed away with a cheerful aspect, and were fortunate enough to occupy one corner of a coach in which were one old lady, four young ladies, and the renowned Mr. Balim, the young ladies' young gentleman.

We were no sooner fairly off, than the young ladies' young gentleman hummed a fragment of an air, which induced a young lady to inquire whether he had danced to that the night before. "By Heaven, then I did," replied the young gentleman, "and with a lovely heiress; a superb creature, with twenty thousand pounds." "You seem rather struck," observed another young lady. "'Gad, she was a sweet creature," returned the young gentleman, arranging his hair. "Of course *she* was struck too?" inquired the first young lady. "How can you ask, love?" interposed the second; "could she fail to be?" "Well, honestly, I think she was," observed the young gentleman. At this point of the dialogue, the young lady who had spoken first, and who sat on the young gentleman's right, struck him a severe blow on the arm with a rosebud, and said he was a vain man — whereupon the young gentleman insisted on having the rosebud, and the young lady appealing for help to the other young ladies, a charming struggle ensued, terminating in the victory of the young gentleman, and the capture of the rosebud. This little skirmish over, the married lady, who was the mother of the rosebud, smiled sweetly upon the young gentleman, and accused him of being a flirt; the young gentleman pleading not guilty, a most interesting discussion took place upon the important point whether the young gentleman was a flirt or not, which being an agreeable conversation of a light kind, lasted a considerable time. At length, a short silence occurring, the young ladies on either side of the young gentleman fell suddenly fast asleep; and the young gentleman, winking upon us to preserve silence, won a pair of gloves from each, thereby causing them to wake with equal suddenness and to scream very loud. The lively conversation to which this pleasantry gave rise lasted for the remainder of the ride, and would have eked out a much longer one.

We dined rather more comfortably than people usually do under such circumstances, nothing having been left behind but the corkscrew and the bread. The married gentlemen were unusually thirsty, which they attributed to the heat of the weather; the little boys ate to inconvenience; mammas were very jovial, and their daughters very fascinating; and the attendants, being well-behaved men, got exceedingly drunk at a respectful distance.

We had our eye on Mr. Balim at dinner-time, and perceived that he flourished wonderfully, being still surrounded by a little group of young ladies, who listened to him as an oracle while he ate from their plates and drank from their glasses in a manner truly captivating from its excessive playfulness. His conversation, too, was exceedingly brilliant. In fact, one elderly lady assured us, that in the course of a little lively *badinage* on the subject of ladies' dresses, he had evinced as much knowledge as if he had been born and bred a milliner.

As such of the fat people who did not happen to fall asleep after dinner entered upon a most vigorous game at ball, we slipped away alone into a thicker part of the wood, hoping to fall in with Mr. Balim, the greater part of the young people having dropped off in twos and threes, and the young ladies' young gentleman among them. Nor were we disappointed, for we had not walked far, when, peeping through the trees, we discovered him before us, and truly it was a pleasant thing to contemplate his greatness.

The young ladies' young gentleman was seated upon the ground, at the feet of a few young ladies who were reclining on a bank; he was so profusely decked with scarfs, ribbons, flowers, and other pretty spoils, that he looked like a lamb — or perhaps a calf would be a better simile — adorned for the sacrifice. One young lady supported a parasol over his interesting head, another held his hat, and a third his neckcloth, which in romantic fashion he had thrown off; the young gentleman himself, with his hand upon his breast, and his face moulded into an expression of the most honeyed sweetness, was warbling forth some choice specimens of vocal music in praise of female loveliness, in a style so exquisitely perfect, that we burst into an involuntary shout of laughter, and made a hasty retreat.

What charming fellows these young ladies' young gentlemen are! Ducks, dears, loves, angels, are all terms inadequate to express their merit. They are such amazingly, uncommonly, wonderfully, nice men.

XIV

CONCLUSION

As we have placed before the young ladies so many specimens of young gentlemen, and have also in the dedication of
this volume given them to understand how much we reverence
and admire their numerous virtues and perfections; as we have
given them such strong reasons to treat us with confidence, and
to banish, in our case, all that reserve and distrust of the male
sex which, as a point of general behaviour, they cannot do
better than preserve and maintain — we say, as we have done
all this, we feel that now, when we have arrived at the close
of our task, they may naturally press upon us the inquiry,
what particular description of young gentlemen we can conscientiously recommend.

Here we are at a loss. We look over our list, and can
neither recommend the bashful young gentleman, nor the out-
and-out young gentleman, nor the very friendly young gentleman, nor the military young gentleman, nor the political young
gentleman, nor the domestic young gentleman, nor the censorious young gentleman, nor the funny young gentleman, nor
the theatrical young gentleman, nor the poetical young gentleman, nor the throwing-off young gentleman, nor the young
ladies' young gentleman.

As there are some good points about many of them, which
still are not sufficiently numerous to render any one among
them eligible, as a whole, our respectful advice to the young
ladies is, to seek for a young gentleman who unites in himself
the best qualities of all, and the worst weaknesses of none, and
to lead him forthwith to the hymeneal altar, whether he will
or no. And to the young lady who secures him, we beg to
tender one short fragment of matrimonial advice, selected from
many sound passages of a similar tendency, to be found in a
letter written by Dean Swift to a young lady on her marriage.

"The grand affair of your life will be, to gain and preserve
the esteem of your husband. Neither good-nature nor virtue
will suffer him to *esteem* you against his judgment; and
although he is not capable of using you ill, yet you will in
time grow a thing indifferent and perhaps contemptible; unless

you can supply the loss of youth and beauty with more durable qualities. You have but a very few years to be young and
handsome in the eyes of the world; and as few months to be
so in the eyes of a husband who is not a fool; for I hope you
do not still dream of charms and raptures, which marriage ever
did, and ever will, put a sudden end to."

From the anxiety we express for the proper behaviour of the
fortunate lady after marriage, it may possibly be inferred that
the young gentleman to whom we have so delicately alluded
is no other than ourself. Without in any way committing
ourself upon this point, we have merely to observe, that we
are ready to receive sealed offers containing a full specification
of age, temper, appearance, and condition; but we beg it to be
distinctly understood that we do not pledge ourself to accept
the highest bidder.

These offers may be forwarded to the Publishers, Messrs.
Chapman and Hall, one hundred and eighty-six, Strand, London; to whom all pieces of plate and other testimonials of
approbation from the young ladies generally are respectfully
requested to be addressed.

SKETCHES OF YOUNG COUPLES;

WITH AN

URGENT REMONSTRANCE TO THE GENTLEMEN OF ENGLAND

(BEING BACHELORS AND WIDOWERS)

ON THE PRESENT ALARMING CRISIS

I

DEDICATION

To the Gentlemen of England (being bachelors or widowers), the remon-
strance of their faithful fellow-subject,

SHEWETH, — That Her Most Gracious Majesty, Victoria,
by the grace of God of the United Kingdom of Great Britain
and Ireland Queen, Defender of the Faith, did, on the 23d day
of November last past, declare and pronounce to Her Most
Honourable Privy Council, Her Majesty's Most Gracious intention of entering into the bonds of wedlock;

That Her Most Gracious Majesty, in so making known Her
Most Gracious intention to Her Most Honourable Privy Council as aforesaid, did use and employ the words, "It is my intention to ally myself in marriage with Prince Albert of Saxe-
Coburg and Gotha;"

That the present is Bissextile, or Leap Year, in which it is
held and considered lawful for any lady to offer and submit proposals of marriage to any gentleman, and to enforce and insist
upon acceptance of the same, under pain of a certain fine or penalty, — to wit, one silk or satin dress of the first quality, to be
chosen by the lady, and paid (or owed) for by the gentleman;

That these and other horrors and dangers with which the
said Bissextile, or Leap Year, threatens the gentlemen of England on every occasion of its periodical return, have been greatly
aggravated and augmented by the terms of Her Majesty's said
most gracious communication, which have filled the heads of
divers young ladies in this Realm with certain new ideas de-

structive to the peace of mankind, that never entered their imagination before;

That a case has occurred in Camberwell, in which a young lady informed her papa that "she intended to ally herself in marriage" with Mr. Smith of Stepney, and that another, and a very distressing case, has occurred at Tottenham, in which a young lady not only stated her intention of allying herself in marriage with her Cousin John, but, taking violent possession of her said cousin, actually married him;

That similar outrages are of constant occurrence, not only in the capital and its neighbourhood, but throughout the kingdom, and that unless the excited female populace be speedily checked and restrained in their lawless proceedings, most deplorable results must ensue therefrom, — among which may be anticipated a most alarming increase in the population of the country, with which no efforts of the agricultural or manufacturing interest can possibly keep pace;

That there is strong reason to suspect the existence of a most extensive plot, conspiracy, or design, secretly contrived by vast numbers of single ladies in the United Kingdom of Great Britain and Ireland, and now extending its ramifications in every quarter of the land, — the object and intent of which plainly appears to be the holding and solemnising of an enormous and unprecedented number of marriages, on the day on which the nuptials of Her said Most Gracious Majesty are performed;

That such plot, conspiracy, or design strongly savours of Popery, as tending to the discomfiture of the clergy of the Established Church, by entailing upon them great mental and physical exhaustion, and that such Popish plots are fomented and encouraged by Her Majesty's Ministers, which clearly appears, not only from Her Majesty's principal Secretary of State for Foreign Affairs traitorously getting married while holding office under the Crown, but from Mr. O'Connell having been heard to declare and avow, that, if he had a daughter to marry, she should be married on the same day as Her said Most Gracious Majesty;

That such arch plots, conspiracies, and designs, besides being fraught with danger to the Established Church, and (consequently) to the State, cannot fail to bring ruin and bankruptcy upon a large class of Her Majesty's subjects, as a great and sudden increase in the number of married men, occasioning the comparative desertion (for a time) of taverns, hotels, billiard-rooms, and gaming-houses, will deprive the proprietors of their accustomed profits and returns, — and in further proof of the depth and baseness of such designs, it may be here observed, that all proprietors of taverns, hotels, billiard-rooms, and gaming-houses are (especially the last) solemnly devoted to the Protestant religion:

For all these reasons, and many others of no less gravity and import, an urgent appeal is made to the gentlemen of England (being bachelors or widowers) to take immediate steps for convening a public meeting to consider of the best and surest means of averting the dangers with which they are threatened by the recurrence of Bissextile, or Leap Year, and the additional sensation created among single ladies by the terms of Her Majesty's most gracious declaration; to take measures, without delay, for resisting the said single Ladies, and counteracting their evil designs; and to pray Her Majesty to dismiss her present ministers, and to summon to her councils those distinguished gentlemen in various honourable professions, who, by insulting on all occasions the only lady in England who can be insulted with safety, have given a sufficient guaranty to Her Majesty's loving subjects that they, at least, are qualified to make war with women, and are already expert in the use of those weapons which are common to the lowest and most abandoned of the sex.

II

THE YOUNG COUPLE

THERE is to be a wedding this morning at the corner house in the terrace. The pastry-cook's people have been there half a dozen times already; all day yesterday there was a great stir and bustle, and they were up this morning as soon as it was light. Miss Emma Fielding is going to be married to young Mr. Harvey.

Heaven alone can tell in what bright colours this marriage is painted upon the mind of the little housemaid at number six, who has hardly slept a wink all night with thinking of it, and now stands on the unswept doorsteps leaning upon her broom, and looking wistfully towards the enchanted house. Nothing short of Omniscience can divine what visions of the baker, or the greengrocer, or the smart and most insinuating butterman, are flitting across her mind, — what thoughts of how she would look on such an occasion, if she were a lady; of how she would dress, if she were only a bride; of how cook would dress, being bridesmaid, conjointly with her sister "in place" at Fulham, and how the clergyman, deeming them so many ladies, would be quite humbled and respectful. What day-dreams of hope and happiness; of life being one perpetual holiday, with no master and no mistress to grant and withhold it; of every Sunday being a Sunday out; of pure freedom as to curls and ringlets, and no obligation to hide fine heads of hair in caps, — with pictures of happiness, vast and immense to her, but utterly ridiculous to us, — bewilder the brain of the little housemaid at number six, all called into existence by the wedding at the corner!

We smile at such things; and so we should, though perhaps for a better reason than commonly presents itself. It should be pleasant to us to know that there are notions of happiness so moderate and limited, since upon those who entertain them happiness and lightness of heart are very easily bestowed.

But the little housemaid is awakened from her revery; for forth from the door of the magical corner house there runs towards her, all fluttering in smart new dress and streaming ribbons, her friend, Jane Adams, who comes all out of breath to redeem a solemn promise of taking her in, under cover of the confusion, to see the breakfast-table spread forth in state, and — sight of sights! — her young mistress ready dressed for church.

And there, in good truth, when they have stolen up stairs on tiptoe, and edged themselves in at the chamber-door, — there is Miss Emma "looking like the sweetest picter," in a white chip-bonnet and orange-flower, and all other elegances becoming a bride (with the make, shape, and quality of every article of which the girl is perfectly familiar in one moment, and never forgets to her dying day); and there is Miss Emma's mamma in tears, and Miss Emma's papa comforting her, and saying how that of course she has been long looking forward to this, and how happy she ought to be; and there, too, is Miss Emma's sister with her arms around her neck, and the other bridesmaid, all smiles and tears, quieting the children, who would cry more but that they are so finely dressed, and yet sob for fear sister Emma should be taken away, — and it is all so affecting that the two servant-girls cry more than anybody; and Jane Adams, sitting down upon the stairs, when they have crept away, declares that her legs tremble so that she don't know what to do, and that she will say for Miss Emma, that she never had a hasty word from her, and that she does hope and pray she may be happy.

But Jane soon comes round again; and then surely there never was anything like the breakfast-table, glittering with plate and china, and set out with flowers and sweets, and long-necked bottles, in the most sumptuous and dazzling manner. In the centre, too, is the mighty charm, — the cake, glistening with frosted sugar, and garnished beautiful. They agree that there ought to be a little Cupid under one of the barley-sugar temples, or at least two hearts and an arrow; but with this exception, there is nothing to wish for, and a table could not be handsomer. As they arrive at this conclusion, who should come in but Mr. John, to whom Jane says that it's only Anne from number six; and John says he knows, for he's often winked his eye down the area, which causes Anne to blush and look confused. She is going away, indeed, when Mr. John will have it that she must drink a glass of wine; and he says, "Never mind it's being early in the morning, it won't hurt her;" so they shut the door, and pour out the wine; and Anne, drinking Jane's health, and adding, "And here's wishing you yours, Mr. John," drinks it in a great many sips, — Mr. John all the time making jokes appropriate to the occasion. At last Mr. John, who has waxed bolder by degrees, pleads the usage at weddings, and claims the privilege of a kiss, which he obtains after a great scuffle; and footsteps being now heard on the stairs, they disperse suddenly.

By this time a carriage had driven up to convey the bride to church; and Anne of number six, prolonging the process of "cleaning her door," has the satisfaction of beholding the bride and bridesmaids, and the papa and mamma, hurry into the same, and drive rapidly off. Nor is this all; for soon other carriages begin to arrive with a posse of company all beautifully dressed, at whom she could stand and gaze for ever; but having something else to do, is compelled to take one last long look, and shut the street door.

And now the company have gone down to breakfast, and tears have given place to smiles; for all the corks are out of the long-necked bottles, and their contents are disappearing rapidly. Miss Emma's papa is at the top of the table; Miss Emma's mamma at the bottom; and beside the latter are Miss Emma herself and her husband, — admitted on all hands to be the handsomest and most interesting young couple ever known. All down both sides of the table, too, are various young ladies, beautiful to see, and various young gentlemen who seem to think so; and there, in a post of honour, is an unmarried aunt of Miss Emma, reported to possess unheard-of riches, and to have expressed vast testamentary intentions respecting her favourite niece and new nephew. This lady has been very liberal and generous already, as the jewels worn by the bride abundantly testify; but that is nothing to what she means to do, or even to what she has done; for she put herself in close communication with the dressmaker three months ago, and prepared a wardrobe (with some articles worked by her own hands) fit for a princess. People may call her an old maid, and so she may be; but she is neither cross nor ugly for all that; on the contrary, she is very cheerful and pleasant-looking, and very kind and tender-hearted; which is no matter of surprise, except to those who yield to popular prejudices without thinking why, and will never grow wiser and never know better.

Of all the company, though, none are more pleasant to behold, or better pleased with themselves, than two young children, who, in honour of the day, have seats among the guests. Of these, one is a little fellow of six or eight years old, brother to the bride; and the other a girl of the same age, or something younger, whom he calls "his wife." The real bride and bridegroom are not more devoted than they; he all love and attention, and she all blushes and fondness, toying with a little bouquet which he gave her this morning, and placing the scattered rose-leaves in her bosom with Nature's own coquettishness. They have dreamt of each other in their quiet dreams, these children; and their little hearts have been nearly broken when the absent one has been dispraised in jest. When will there come in after life a passion so earnest, generous, and true as theirs? What, even in its gentlest realities, can have the grace and charm that hover round such fairy lovers?

By this time the merriment and happiness of the feast have gained their height. Certain ominous looks begin to be exchanged between the bridesmaids; and somehow it gets whispered about that the carriage which is to take the young couple has arrived. Such members of the party as are most disposed to prolong its enjoyments affect to consider this a false alarm; but it turns out too true, being speedily confirmed, first by the retirement of the bride and a select file of intimates who are to prepare her for the journey, and secondly by the withdrawal of the ladies generally. To this there ensues a particularly awkward pause, in which everybody essays to be facetious, and nobody succeeds; at length the bridegroom makes a mysterious disappearance in obedience to some equally mysterious signal, and the table is deserted.

Now, for at least six weeks last past, it has been solemnly devised and settled that the young people should go away in secret; but they no sooner appear without the door than the drawing-room windows are blocked up with ladies waving their handkerchiefs and kissing their hands, and the dining-room panes with gentlemen's faces beaming farewell in every queer variety of its expression. The hall and steps are crowded with servants in white favours, mixed up with particular friends and relations who have darted out to say good-bye; and foremost in the group are the tiny lovers, arm in arm, thinking, with fluttering hearts, what happiness it would be to dash away together in that gallant coach, and never part again.

The bride has barely time for one hurried glance at her old home, when the steps rattle, the door slams, the horses clatter on the pavement, and they have left it far away.

A knot of women-servants still remain clustered in the hall, whispering among themselves; and there, of course, is Anne from number six, who has made another escape on some plea or other, and been an admiring witness of the departure. There are two points on which Anne expatiates over and over again, without the smallest appearance of fatigue, or intending to leave off: one is, that she "never see in all her life such a — oh, such a angel of a gentleman as Mr. Harvey!" and the other, that she "can't tell how it is, but it don't seem a bit like a work-a-day, or a Sunday neither, — it's all so unsettled and unregular."

III

THE FORMAL COUPLE

THE formal couple are the most prim, cold, immovable, and unsatisfactory people on the face of the earth. Their faces, voices, dress, house, furniture, walk, and manner are all the essence of formality, unrelieved by one redeeming touch of frankness, heartiness, or nature.

Everything with the formal couple resolves itself into a matter of form. They don't call upon you on your account, but their own; not to see how you are, but to show how they are; it is not a ceremony to do honour to you, but to themselves; not due to your position, but to theirs. If one of a friend's children die, the formal couple are as sure and punctual in sending to the house as the undertaker; if a friend's family be increased, the monthly nurse is not more attentive than they. The formal couple, in fact, joyfully seize all occasions of testifying their good breeding and precise observance of the little usages of society; and for you, who are the means to this end, they care as much as a man does for the tailor who has enabled him to cut a figure, or a woman for the milliner who has assisted her to a conquest.

Having an extensive connection among that kind of people who make acquaintances and eschew friends, the formal gentleman attends from time to time a great many funerals, to which he is formally invited, and to which he formally goes, as returning a call for the last time. Here his deportment is of the most faultless description; he knows the exact pitch of voice it is proper to assume, the sombre look he ought to wear, the melancholy tread which should be his gait for the day. He is perfectly acquainted with all the dreary courtesies to be observed in a mourning-coach; knows when to sigh, and when to hide his nose in the white handkerchief; and looks into the grave and shakes his head when the ceremony is concluded, with the sad formality of a mute.

"What kind of a funeral was it?" says the formal lady, when he returns home. "Oh," replies the formal gentleman, "there never was such a gross and disgusting impropriety! there were no feathers." "No feathers!" cries the lady, as if on wings of black feathers dead people fly to heaven, and, lacking them, they must of necessity go elsewhere. Her husband shakes his head, and further adds, that they had seed-cake instead of plum-cake, and that it was all white wine. "All white wine!" exclaims his wife. "Nothing but sherry and Madeira," says the husband. "What! no port?" "Not a drop." No port, no plums, and no feathers! "You will recollect, my dear," says the formal lady, in a voice of stately reproof, "that when we first met this poor man who is now dead and gone, and he took that very strange course of address-ing me at dinner without being previously introduced, I ven-tured to express my opinion that the family were quite igno-rant of etiquette, and very imperfectly acquainted with the decencies of life. You have now had a good opportunity of judging for yourself; and all I have to say is, that I trust you will never go to a funeral *there* again." "My dear," replies the formal gentleman, "I never will." So the informal de-ceased is cut in his grave; and the formal couple, when they tell the story of the funeral, shake their heads, and wonder what some people's feelings *are* made of, and what their notions of propriety *can* be!

If the formal people have a family (which they sometimes have), they are not children, but little, pale, sour, sharp-nosed men and women; and so exquisitely brought up, that they might be very old dwarfs for anything that appeareth to the contrary. Indeed, they are so acquainted with forms and conventionalities, and conduct themselves with such strict decorum, that to see the little girl break a looking-glass in some wild outbreak, or the little boy kick his parents, would be to any visitor an unspeakable relief and consolation.

The formal couple are always sticklers for what is rigidly proper, and have a great readiness in detecting hidden impro-priety of speech or thought, which by less scrupulous people would be wholly unsuspected. Thus, if they pay a visit to the theatre, they sit all night in a perfect agony lest anything improper or immoral should proceed from the stage; and if anything should happen to be said which admits of a double construction, they never fail to take it up directly, and to express by their looks the great outrage which their feelings have sustained. Perhaps this is their chief reason for absent-ing themselves almost entirely from places of public amuse-

ment. They go sometimes to the exhibition of the Royal
Academy; but that is often more shocking than the stage
itself, and the formal lady thinks that it really is high time
Mr. Etty was prosecuted and made a public example of.

We made one at a christening party not long since, where
there was amongst the guests a formal couple, who suffered the
acutest torture from certain jokes, incidental to such an occasion, cut — and very likely dried also — by one of the god-
fathers, a red-faced, elderly gentleman, who, being highly
popular with the rest of the company, had it all his own way,
and was in great spirits. It was at supper-time that this gentleman came out in full force. We — being of a grave and quiet
demeanour — had been chosen to escort the formal lady down
stairs, and, sitting beside her, had a favourable opportunity of
observing her emotions.

We have a shrewd suspicion, that in the very beginning,
and in the first blush — literally the first blush — of the matter, the formal lady had not felt quite certain whether the
being present at such a ceremony, and encouraging, as it were,
the public exhibition of a baby, was not an act involving some
degree of indelicacy and impropriety; but certain we are, that
when that baby's health was drunk, and allusions were made,
by a grey-headed gentleman proposing it, to the time when he
had dandled in his arms the young Christian's mother, — certain we are, that then the formal lady took the alarm, and
recoiled from the old gentleman as from a hoary profligate.
Still she bore it; she fanned herself with an indignant air, but
still she bore it. A comic song was sung, involving a confession from some imaginary gentleman that he had kissed a
female, and yet the formal lady bore it. But when at last
the health of the godfather before mentioned being drunk, the
godfather rose to return thanks, and in the course of his observations darkly hinted at babies yet unborn, and even contemplated the possibility of the subject of that festival having
brothers and sisters, the formal lady could endure no more;
but bowing slightly round, and sweeping haughtily past the
offender, left the room in tears, under the protection of the
formal gentleman.

IV

THE LOVING COUPLE

THERE cannot be a better practical illustration of the wise saw and ancient incident, that there may be too much of a good thing, than is presented by a loving couple. Undoubtedly it is meet and proper, that two persons joined together in holy matrimony should be loving, and unquestionably it is pleasant to know and see that they are so; but there is a time for all things, and the couple who happen to be always in a loving state before company are wellnigh intolerable.

And in taking up this position we would have it distinctly understood, that we do not seek alone the sympathy of bachelors, in whose objection to loving couples we recognise interested motives and personal considerations. We grant that to that unfortunate class of society there may be something very irritating, tantalising, and provoking, in being compelled to witness those gentle endearments and chaste interchanges which to loving couples are quite the ordinary business of life. But while we recognise the natural character of the prejudice to which these unhappy men are subject, we can neither receive their biassed evidence, nor address ourself to their inflamed and angered minds. Dispassionate experience is our only guide; and in these moral essays we seek no less to reform hymeneal offenders than to hold out a timely warning to all rising couples, and even to those who have not yet set forth upon their pilgrimage towards the matrimonial altar.

Let all couples, present or to come, therefore, profit by the example of Mr. and Mrs. Leaver, themselves a loving couple in the first degree.

Mr. and Mrs. Leaver are pronounced by Mrs. Starling, a widow lady who lost her husband when she was young, and lost herself about the same time (for by her own count she has never since grown five years older), to be a perfect model of wedded felicity. "You would suppose," says the romantic lady, "that they were lovers only just now engaged. Never was such happiness! They are so tender, so affectionate, so attached to each other, so enamoured, that positively nothing can be more charming!"

"Augusta, my soul," says Mr. Leaver. "Augustus, my life," replies Mrs. Leaver. "Sing some little ballad, darling," quoth Mr. Leaver. "I could n't, indeed, dearest," returns Mrs. Leaver. "Do, my dove," says Mr. Leaver. "I could n't possibly, my love," replies Mrs. Leaver; "and it's very naughty of you to ask me." "Naughty, darling!" cries Mr. Leaver. "Yes, very naughty, and very cruel," returns Mrs. Leaver; "for you know I have a sore throat, and that to sing would give me great pain. You're a monster, and I hate you. Go away!" Mrs. Leaver has said, "Go away," because Mr. Leaver has tapped her under the chin; Mr. Leaver not doing as he is bid, but, on the contrary, sitting down beside her, Mrs. Leaver slaps Mr. Leaver, and Mr. Leaver in return slaps Mrs. Leaver; and, it being now time for all persons present to look the other way, they look the other way, and hear a still small sound as of kissing, at which Mrs. Starling is thoroughly enraptured, and whispers her neighbour that if all married couples were like that, what a heaven this earth would be!

The loving couple are at home when this occurs, and may be only three or four friends are present; but, unaccustomed to reserve upon this interesting point, they are pretty much the same abroad. Indeed, upon some occasions, such as a picnic or a water-party, their lovingness is even more developed, as we had an opportunity last summer of observing in person.

There was a great water-party made up to go to Twickenham and dine, and afterwards dance in an empty villa by the river-side, hired expressly for the purpose. Mr. and Mrs. Leaver were of the company; and it was our fortune to have a seat in the same boat, which was an eight-oared galley, manned by amateurs with a blue-striped awning of the same pattern as their Guernsey shirts, and a dingy red flag of the same shade as the whiskers of the stroke-oar. A coxswain being appointed, and all other matters adjusted, the eight gentlemen threw themselves into strong paroxysms, and pulled up with the tide, stimulated by the compassionate remarks of the ladies, who one and all exclaimed that it seemed an immense exertion, — as indeed it did. At first we raced the other boat, which came alongside in gallant style; but this being found an unpleasant amusement, as giving rise to a great quantity of splashing, and rendering the cold pies and other viands very moist, it was

unanimously voted down, and we were suffered to shoot ahead,
while the second boat followed ingloriously in our wake.

It was at this time that we first recognised Mr. Leaver.
There were two firemen-watermen in the boat, lying by until
somebody was exhausted; and one of them, who had taken
upon himself the direction of affairs, was heard to cry in a
gruff voice, "Pull away, number two; give it her, number
two; take a long reach, number two; now, number two, sir!
think you 're winning a boat." The greater part of the company had no doubt begun to wonder which of the striped
Guernseys it might be that stood in need of such encouragement, when a stifled shriek from Mrs. Leaver confirmed the
doubtful and informed the ignorant; and Mr. Leaver, still
further disguised in a straw hat and no neckcloth, was observed
to be in a fearful perspiration, and failing visibly. Nor was
the general consternation diminished at this instant by the
same gentleman (in the performance of an accidental aquatic
feat, termed "catching a crab") plunging suddenly backward,
and displaying nothing of himself to the company but two
violently struggling legs. Mrs. Leaver shrieked again several
times, and cried piteously, "Is he dead? Tell me the worst,
is he dead?"

Now, a moment's reflection might have convinced the loving
wife that, unless her husband were endowed with some most
surprising powers of muscular action, he never could be dead
while he kicked so hard; but still Mrs. Leaver cried, "Is he
dead? is he dead?" and still everybody else cried, "No, no,
no," — until such time as Mr. Leaver was replaced in a sitting
posture, and his oar (which had been going through all kinds
of wrong-headed performances on its own acccunt) was once
more put in his hand by the exertions of the two firemen-
watermen. Mrs. Leaver then exclaimed, "Augustus, my
child, come to me;" and Mr. Leaver said, "Augusta, my love,
compose yourself; I am not injured." But Mrs. Leaver cried
again more piteously than before, "Augustus, my child, come
to me;" and now the company generally, who seemed to be
apprehensive that if Mr. Leaver remained where he was he
might contribute more than his proper share towards the drowning of the party, disinterestedly took part with Mrs. Leaver,
and said he really ought to go, and that he was not strong
enough for such violent exercise, and ought never to have

undertaken it. Reluctantly Mr. Leaver went and laid himself down at Mrs. Leaver's feet; and Mrs. Leaver, stooping over him, said, "Oh, Augustus! how could you terrify me so?" and Mr. Leaver said, "Augusta, my sweet, I never meant to terrify you;" and Mrs. Leaver said, "You are faint, my dear;" and Mr. Leaver said, "I am rather so, my love;" and they were very loving indeed under Mrs. Leaver's veil, until at length Mr. Leaver came forth again, and pleasantly asked if he had not heard something said about bottled stout and sandwiches.

Mrs. Starling, who was one of the party, was perfectly delighted with this scene, and frequently murmured half aside, "What a loving couple you are!" or, "How delightful it is to see man and wife so happy together!" To us she was quite poetical (for we are a kind of cousins); observing that hearts beating in unison like that made life a paradise of sweets, and that, when kindred creatures were drawn together by sympa- thies so fine and delicate what more than mortal happiness did not our souls partake. To all this we answered, "Certainly," or "Very true," or merely sighed, as the case might be. At every new act of the loving couple, the widow's admiration broke out afresh; and when Mrs. Leaver would not permit Mr. Leaver to keep his hat off, lest the sun should strike to his head, and give him a brain-fever, Mrs. Starling actually shed tears, and said it reminded her of Adam and Eve.

The loving couple were thus loving all the way to Twicken- ham; but when we arrived there (by which time the amateur crew looked very thirsty and vicious) they were more playful than ever; for Mrs. Leaver threw stones at Mr. Leaver, and Mr. Leaver ran after Mrs. Leaver on the grass, in a most inno- cent and enchanting manner. At dinner, too, Mr. Leaver *would*. steal Mrs. Leaver's tongue, and Mrs. Leaver *would* retaliate upon Mr. Leaver's fowl; and when Mrs. Leaver was going to take some lobster-salad, Mr. Leaver would n't let her have any, saying that it made her ill, and she was always sorry for it afterwards, which afforded Mrs. Leaver an opportunity of pretending to be cross, and showing many other prettinesses. But this was merely the smiling surface of their loves, not the mighty depths of the stream, down to which the company, to say the truth, dived rather unexpectedly, from the following accident: It chanced that Mr. Leaver took upon himself to propose the bachelors who had first originated the notion of that entertainment; in doing which he affected to regret that he was no longer of their body himself, and pretended grievously to lament his fallen state. This Mrs. Leaver's feelings could not brook, even in jest; and consequently, exclaiming aloud, "He loves me not, he loves me not!" she fell in a very pitiable state into the arms of Mrs. Starling, and directly becoming insensible, was conveyed by that lady and her husband into another room. Presently Mr. Leaver came running back to know if there was a medical gentleman in company; and, as there was (in what company is there not?), both Mr. Leaver and the medical gentleman hurried away together.

The medical gentleman was the first who returned; and among his intimate friends he was observed to laugh and wink, and look as unmedical as might be; but when Mr. Leaver came back he was very solemn, and, in answer to all inquiries, shook his head, and remarked that Augusta was far too sensitive to be trifled with, — an opinion which the widow subsequently confirmed. Finding that she was in no imminent peril, however, the rest of the party betook themselves to dancing on the green; and very merry and happy they were, and a vast quantity of flirtation there was; the last circumstance being no doubt attributable partly to the fineness of the weather, and partly to the locality, which is well known to be favourable to all harmless recreations.

In the bustle of the scene, Mr. and Mrs. Leaver stole down to the boat, and disposed themselves under the awning; Mrs. Leaver reclining her head upon Mr. Leaver's shoulder, and Mr. Leaver grasping her hand with great fervour, and looking in her face from time to time with a melancholy and sympathetic aspect. The widow sat apart, feigning to be occupied with a book, but stealthily observing them from behind her fan; and the two firemen-watermen, smoking their pipes on the bank hard by, nudged each other, and grinned in enjoyment of the joke. Very few of the party missed the loving couple; and the few who did heartily congratulated each other on their disappearance.

V

THE CONTRADICTORY COUPLE

ONE would suppose that two people who are to pass their whole lives together, and must necessarily be very often alone with each other, could find little pleasure in mutual contradiction; and yet what is more common than a contradictory couple?

The contradictory couple agree in nothing but contradiction. They return home from Mrs. Bluebottle's dinner-party, each in an opposite corner of the coach, and do not exchange a syllable until they have been seated for at least twenty minutes by the fireside at home, when the gentleman, raising his eyes from the stove, all at once breaks silence.

"What a very extraordinary thing it is," says he, "that you *will* contradict, Charlotte?" "*I* contradict!" cries the lady; "but that's just like you." "What's like me?" says the gentleman sharply. "Saying that I contradict you," replies the lady. "Do you mean to say that you do *not* contradict me?" retorts the gentleman; "do you mean to say that you have not been contradicting me the whole of this day? Do you mean to tell me now, that you have not?" "I mean to tell you nothing of the kind," replies the lady quietly; "when you are wrong, of course I shall contradict you."

During this dialogue the gentleman has been taking his brandy and water on one side of the fire, and the lady, with her dressing-case on the table, has been curling her hair on the other. She now lets down her back hair, and proceeds to brush it; preserving at the same time an air of conscious rectitude and suffering virtue, which is intended to exasperate the gentleman, — and does so.

"I do believe," he says, taking the spoon out of his glass, and tossing it on the table, "that of all the obstinate, positive, wrong-headed creatures that were ever born, you are the most so, Charlotte." "Certainly, certainly, have it your own way, pray. You see how much *I* contradict you," rejoins the lady. "Of course, you didn't contradict me at dinner-time, — oh, no, not you!" says the gentleman. "Yes, I did," says the lady. "Oh! you did?" cries the gentleman; "you admit that?" "If you call that contradiction, I do," the lady answers; "and I say again, Edward, when I know you are wrong I will contradict you. I am not your slave." "Not my slave," repeats the gentleman bitterly; "and you still mean to say that in the Blackburns' new house there are not more than fourteen doors, including the door of the wine-cellar!" "I mean to say," retorts the lady, beating time with her hair-brush on the palm of her hand, "that in that house there are fourteen doors, and no more." "Well, then," cries the gentleman, rising in despair, and pacing the room with rapid strides. "By G—, this is enough to destroy a man's intellect, and drive him mad!"

By and by the gentleman comes to a little, and, passing his hand gloomily across his forehead, reseats himself in his former chair. There is a long silence, and this time the lady begins. "I appealed to Mr. Jenkins, who sat next to me on the sofa in the drawing-room during tea —" "Morgan, you mean," interrupts the gentleman. "I do not mean anything of the kind," answers the lady. "Now, by all that is aggravating and impossible to bear," cries the gentleman, clinching his hands, and looking upwards in agony, "she is going to insist upon it that Morgan is Jenkins." "Do you take me for a perfect fool?" exclaims the lady; "do you suppose I don't know the one from the other? Do you suppose I don't know that the man in the blue coat was Mr. Jenkins?" "Jenkins in a blue coat!" cries the gentleman with a groan; "Jenkins in a blue coat! a man who would suffer death rather than wear anything but brown!" "Do you dare to charge me with telling an untruth?" demands the lady, bursting into tears. "I charge you, ma'am," retorts the gentleman, starting up, "with being a monster of contradiction, a monster of aggravation, a — a — a — Jenkins in a blue coat! what have I done that I should be doomed to hear such statements?"

Expressing himself with great scorn and anguish, the gentleman takes up his candle, and stalks off to bed, where, feigning to be fast asleep when the lady comes up stairs, drowned in tears, murmuring lamentations over her hard fate, and indistinct intentions of consulting her brothers, he undergoes the secret torture of hearing her exclaim between whiles, "I know there are only fourteen doors in the house, I know it was Mr. Jenkins, I know he had a blue coat on, and I would say it as

positively as I now do if they were the last words I had to
speak!"

If the contradictory couple are blessed with children, they
are not the less contradictory on that account. Master James
and Miss Charlotte present themselves after dinner, and being
in perfect good-humour, and finding their parents in the same
amiable state, augur from these appearances half a glass of
wine apiece and other extraordinary indulgences. But unfortunately, Master James, growing talkative upon such prospects,
asks his mamma how tall Mrs. Parsons is, and whether she is
not six feet high; to which his mamma replies, "Yes, she
should think she was; for Mrs. Parsons is a very tall lady
indeed, quite a giantess." "For Heaven's sake, Charlotte,"
cries her husband, "do not tell the child such preposterous
nonsense. Six feet high!" "Well," replies the lady,
"surely I may be permitted to have an opinion; my opinion
is that she is six feet high, — at least six feet." "Now, you
know, Charlotte," retorts the gentleman sternly, "that that is
not your opinion, that you have no such idea, and that you
only say this for the sake of contradiction." "You are
exceedingly polite," his wife replies; "to be wrong about such
a paltry question as anybody's height would be no great crime;
but I say again, that I believe Mrs. Parsons to be six feet, —
more than six feet; nay, I believe you know her to be full six
feet, and only say she is not because I say she is." This taunt
disposes the gentleman to become violent; but he checks himself, and is content to mutter in a haughty tone, "Six feet; ha,
ha! Mrs. Parsons six feet!" And the lady answers, "Yes,
six feet. I am sure I am glad you are amused; and I'll say it
again, — six feet." Thus the subject gradually drops off, and
the contradiction begins to be forgotten, when Master James,
with some undefined notion of making himself agreeable, and
putting things to rights again, unfortunately asks his mamma
what the moon's made of; which gives her occasion to say that
he had better not ask her, for she is always wrong, and never
can be right; that he only exposes her to contradiction by asking questions of her; and that he had better ask his papa, who
is infallible, and never can be wrong. Papa, smarting under
this attack, gives a terrible pull at the bell, and says, that if
the conversation is to proceed in this way, the children had
better be removed. Removed they are, after a few tears and

many struggles; and pa, having looked at ma sideways for a minute or two, with a baleful eye, draws his pocket-handkerchief over his face, and composes himself for his after-dinner nap.

The friends of the contradictory couple often deplore their frequent disputes, though they rather make light of them at the same time; observing, that there is no doubt they are very much attached to each other, and that they never quarrel except about trifles. But neither the friends of the contradictory couple, nor the contradictory couple themselves, reflect, that as the most stupendous objects in nature are but vast collections of minute particles, so the slightest and least considered trifles make up the sum of human happiness or misery.

VI

THE COUPLE WHO DOTE UPON THEIR CHILDREN

THE couple who dote upon their children have usually a great many of them, — six or eight at least. The children are either the healthiest in all the world, or the most unfortunate in existence. In either case, they are equally the theme of their doting parents, and equally a source of mental anguish and irritation to their doting parents' friends.

The couple who dote upon their children recognise no dates but those connected with their births, accidents, illnesses, or remarkable deeds. They keep a mental almanac with a vast number of Innocents' days, all in red letters. They recollect the last coronation, because on that day little Tom fell down the kitchen stairs; the anniversary of the Gunpowder Plot, because it was on the 5th of November that Ned asked whether wooden legs were made in heaven, and cocked hats grew in gardens. Mrs. Whiffler will never cease to recollect the last day of the old year as long as she lives, for it was on that day that the baby had the four red spots on its nose which they took for measles; nor Christmas Day, for twenty-one days after Christmas Day the twins were born; nor Good Friday, for it was on a Good Friday that she was frightened by the donkey-cart when she was in the family way with Georgiana. The movable feasts have no motion for Mr. and Mrs. Whiffler, but remain pinned down tight and fast to the shoulders of some small child, from whom they can never be separated any more. Time was made, according to their creed, not for slaves but for girls and boys; the restless sands in his glass are but little children at play.

As we have already intimated, the children of this couple can know no medium. They are either prodigies of good health or prodigies of bad health; whatever they are, they must be prodigies. Mr. Whiffler must have to describe at his office such excruciating agonies constantly undergone by his eldest boy, as nobody else's eldest boy ever underwent; or he must be able to declare that there never was a child endowed with such amazing health, such an indomitable constitution, and such a cast-iron frame, as his child. His children must be, in some respect or other, above and beyond the children of all other people. To such an extent is this feeling pushed, that we were once slightly acquainted with a lady and gentleman who carried their heads so high and became so proud after their youngest child fell out of a two-pair-of-stairs window without hurting himself much, that the greater part of their friends were obliged to forego their acquaintance.

But perhaps this may be an extreme case, and one not justly entitled to be considered as a precedent of general application.

If a friend happen to dine in a friendly way with one of these couples who dote upon their children, it is nearly impossible for him to divert the conversation from their favourite topic. Everything reminds Mr. Whiffler of Ned, or Mrs. Whiffler of Mary Anne, or of the time before Ned was born, or the time before Mary Anne was thought of. The slightest remark, however harmless in itself, will awaken slumbering recollections of the twins. It is impossible to steer clear of them. They will come uppermost, let the poor man do what he may. Ned has been known to be lost sight of for half an hour, Dick has been forgotten, the name of Mary Anne has not been mentioned, but the twins will out. Nothing can keep down the twins.

"It's a very extraordinary thing, Saunders," says Mr. Whiffler to the visitor; "but — you have seen our little babies, the — the — twins?" The friend's heart sinks within him as he answers, "Oh, yes! often." "Your talking of the pyramids," says Mr. Whiffler, quite as a matter of course.

"reminds me of the twins. It's a very extraordinary thing about those babies, — what colour should you say their eyes were?" "Upon my word," the friend stammers, "I hardly know how to answer," — the fact being, that except as the friend does not remember to have heard of any departure from the ordinary course of Nature in the instance of these twins, they might have no eyes at all for aught he has observed to the contrary. "You would n't say they were red, I suppose?" says Mr. Whiffler. The friend hesitates, and rather thinks they are; but inferring from the expression of Mr. Whiffler's face that red is not the colour, smiles with some confidence, and says, "No, no! very different from that." "What should you say to blue?" says Mr. Whiffler. The friend glances at him, and, observing a different expression in his face, ventures to say, "I should say they *were* blue, — a decided blue." "To be sure!" cries Mr. Whiffler triumphantly; "I knew you would! But what should you say if I was to tell you that the boy's eyes are blue and the girl's hazel, eh?" "Impossible!" exclaims the friend, not at all knowing why it should be impossible. "A fact, notwithstanding," cries Mr. Whiffler; "and let me tell you, Saunders, *that*'s not a common thing in twins, or a circumstance that'll happen every day."

In this dialogue Mrs. Whiffler, as being deeply responsible for the twins, their charms and singularities, has taken no share; but she now relates, in broken English, a witticism of little Dick's bearing upon the subject just discussed, which delights Mr. Whiffler beyond measure, and causes him to declare that he would have sworn that was Dick's if he had heard it anywhere. Then he requests that Mrs. Whiffler will tell Saunders what Tom said about mad bulls; and Mrs. Whiffler relating the anecdote, a discussion ensues upon the different character of Tom's wit and Dick's wit, from which it appears that Dick's humour is of a lively turn, while Tom's style is the dry and caustic. This discussion, being enlivened by various illustrations, lasts a long time, and is only stopped by Mrs. Whiffler instructing the footman to ring the nursery-bell, as the children were promised that they should come down and taste the pudding.

The friend turns pale when this order is given, and paler still when it is followed up by a great pattering on the staircase (not unlike the sound of rain upon a skylight), a violent burst-

ing open of the dining-room door, and the tumultuous appearance of six small children, closely succeeded by a strong nur-
sery-maid with a twin in each arm. As the whole eight are
screaming, shouting, or kicking, — some influenced by a raven-
ous appetite, some by a horror of the stranger, and some by a
conflict of the two feelings, — a pretty long space elapses before
all their heads can be ranged round the table and anything like
order restored; in bringing about which happy state of things
both the nurse and footman are severely scratched.   At length
Mrs. Whiffler is heard to say, "Mr. Saunders, shall I give you
some pudding?" A breathless silence ensues, and sixteen
small eyes are fixed upon the guest in expectation of his reply.
A wild shout of joy proclaims that he has said, "No; thank
you." Spoons are waved in the air, legs appear above the
tablecloth in uncontrollable ecstasy, and eighty short fingers
dabble in damson sirup.

While the pudding is being disposed of, Mr. and Mrs.
Whiffler look on with beaming countenances; and Mr. Whiffler, nudging his friend Saunders, begs him take notice of
Tom's eyes, or Dick's chin, or Ned's nose, or Mary Anne's
hair, or Emily's figure, or little Bob's calves, or Fanny's
mouth, or Cary's head, as the case may be.   Whatever the
intention of Mr. Saunders is called to, Mr. Saunders admires
of course; though he is rather confused about the sex of the
youngest branches, and looks at the wrong children, turning to
a girl when Mr. Whiffler directs his attention to a boy, and
falling into raptures with a boy when he ought to be enchanted
with a girl.   Then the dessert comes; and there is a vast deal
of scrambling after fruit, and sudden spirting forth of juice out
of tight oranges into infant eyes, and much screeching and
wailing in consequence.   At length it becomes time for Mrs.
Whiffler to retire; and all the children are by force of arms
compelled to kiss and love Mr. Saunders before going up
stairs, except Tom, who, lying on his back in the hall, proclaims that Mr. Saunders "is a naughty beast;" and Dick,
who, having drunk his father's wine when he was looking
another way, is found to be intoxicated, and is carried out very
limp and helpless.

Mr. Whiffler and his friend are left alone together; but Mr.
Whiffler's thoughts are still with his family, if his family are
not with him.   "Saunders," says he, after a short silence, "if

you please, we'll drink Mrs. Whiffler and the children." Mr.
Saunders feels this to be a reproach against himself for not
proposing the same sentiment, and drinks it in some confusion.
"Ah!" Mr. Whiffler sighs, "these children, Saunders, make
one quite an old man." Mr. Saunders thinks that, if they
were his, they would make him a very old man; but he says
nothing. "And yet," pursues Mr. Whiffler, "what can equal
domestic happiness? what can equal the engaging ways of children? Saunders, why don't *you* get married?" Now, this is
an embarrassing question, because Mr. Saunders has been
thinking that, if he had at any time entertained matrimonial
designs, the revelation of that day would surely have routed
them for ever. "I am glad, however," says Mr. Whiffler,
"that you *are* a bachelor, — glad on one account, Saunders, —
a selfish one, I admit. Will you do Mrs. Whiffler and myself
a favour?" Mr. Saunders is surprised, — evidently surprised;
but he replies, "With the greatest pleasure." "Then, will
you, Saunders," says Mr. Whiffler, in an impressive manner,
"will you cement and consolidate our friendship by coming
into the family (so to speak) as a godfather?" "I shall be
proud and delighted," replies Mr. Saunders; "which of the
children is it? really, I thought they were all christened; or — "
"Saunders," Mr. Whiffler interposes, "they *are* all christened:
you are right. The fact is, that Mrs. Whiffler is — in short,
we expect another." "Not a ninth!" cries the friend, all
aghast at the idea. "Yes, Saunders," rejoins Mr. Whiffler
solemnly, "a ninth. Did we drink Mrs. Whiffler's health?
Let us drink it again, Saunders, and wish her well over it!"

Dr. Johnson used to tell a story of a man who had but one
idea, which was a wrong one. The couple who dote upon
their children are in the same predicament; at home or abroad,
at all times, and in all places, their thoughts are bound up in
this one subject, and have no sphere beyond. They relate the
clever things their offspring say or do, and weary every company with their prolixity and absurdity. Mr. Whiffler takes
a friend by the button at a street corner on a windy day to tell
him a *bon mot* of his youngest boy's; and Mrs. Whiffler, calling to see a sick acquaintance, entertains her with a cheerful
account of all her own past sufferings and present expectations.
In such cases the sins of the fathers indeed descend upon the
children; for people soon come to regard them as predestined

little bores. The couple who dote upon their children cannot be said to be actuated by a general love for these engaging little people (which would be a great excuse); for they are apt to underrate and entertain a jealousy of any children but their own. If they examined their own hearts, they would perhaps find at the bottom of all this more self-love and egotism than they think of. Self-love and egotism are bad qualities, of which the unrestrained exhibition, though it may be sometimes amusing, never fails to be wearisome and unpleasant. Couples who dote upon their children, therefore, are best avoided.

VII

THE COOL COUPLE

THERE is an old-fashioned weather-glass representing a house with two doorways, in one of which is the figure of a gentleman, in the other the figure of a lady. When the weather is to be fine the lady comes out, and the gentleman goes in; when wet, the gentleman comes out, and the lady goes in. They never seek each other's society, are never elevated and depressed by the same cause, and have nothing in common. They are the model of a cool couple, except that there is something of politeness and consideration about the behaviour of the gentleman in the weather-glass, in which neither of the cool couple can be said to participate.

The cool couple are seldom alone together, and, when they are, nothing can exceed their apathy and dulness; the gentleman being for the most part drowsy, and the lady silent. If they enter into conversation, it is usually of an ironical or recriminatory nature. Thus, when the gentleman has indulged in a very long yawn, and settled himself more snugly in his easy-chair, the lady will perhaps remark, "Well, I am sure, Charles! I hope you're comfortable." To which the gentleman replies, "Oh, yes! he's quite comfortable, — quite." "There are not many married men, I hope," returns the lady, "who seek comfort in such selfish gratifications as you do." "Nor many wives who seek comfort in such selfish gratifications as *you* do, I hope," retorts the gentleman. "Whose fault is that?" demands the lady. The gentleman becoming more sleepy returns no answer. "Whose fault is that?" the lady repeats. The gentleman still returning no answer, she goes on to say that she believes there never was in all this world anybody so attached to her home, so thoroughly domestic, so unwilling to seek a moment's gratification or pleasure beyond her own fireside, as she. God knows that before she was married she never thought or dreamt of such a thing; and she remembers that her poor papa used to say again and again, almost every day of his life, "Oh, my dear Louisa, if you only marry a man who understands you, and takes the trouble to consider your happiness and accommodate himself a very little to your disposition, what a treasure he will find in you!" She supposes her papa knew what her disposition was, — he had known her long enough, — he ought to have been acquainted with it; but what can she do? If her home is always dull and lonely, and her husband is always absent, and finds no pleasure in her society, she is naturally sometimes driven (seldom enough, she is sure) to seek a little recreation elsewhere; she is not expected to pine and mope to death, she hopes. "Then come, Louisa," says the gentleman, waking up as suddenly as he fell asleep, "stop at home this evening, and so will I." "I should be sorry to suppose, Charles, that you took a pleasure in aggravating me," replies the lady; "but you know as well as I do that I am particularly engaged to Mrs. Mortimer, and that it would be an act of the grossest rudeness and ill-breeding, after accepting a seat in her box and preventing her from inviting anybody else, not to go." "Ah, there it is!" says the gentleman, shrugging his shoulders; "I knew that perfectly well. I knew you couldn't devote an evening to your own home. Now, all I have to say, Louisa, is this: recollect that *I* was quite willing to stay at home, and that it's no fault of *mine* we are not oftener together."

With that the gentleman goes away to keep an old appointment at his club, and the lady hurries off to dress for Mrs. Mortimer's; and neither thinks of the other until by some odd chance they find themselves alone again.

But it must not be supposed that the cool couple are habitually a quarrelsome one. Quite the contrary. These differences are only occasions for a little self-excuse, — nothing more. In general they are as easy and careless, and dispute as seldom, as any common acquaintances may; for it is neither worth their while to put each other out of the way, nor to ruffle themselves.

When they meet in society, the cool couple are the best-bred people in existence. The lady is seated in a corner among a little knot of lady friends, one of whom exclaims, "Why, I vow and declare! there is your husband, my dear." "Whose?—mine?" she says carelessly. "Ay, yours; and coming this way too." "How very odd!" says the lady, in a languid tone: "I thought he had been in Dover." The gentleman coming up, and speaking to all the other ladies, and nodding slightly to his wife, it turns out that he has been at Dover, and has just now returned. "What a strange creature you are!" cries his wife; "and what on earth brought you here, I wonder?" "I came to look after you, *of course,*" rejoins her husband. This is so pleasant a jest that the lady is mightily amused, as are all the other ladies similarly situated who are within hearing; and, while they are enjoying it to the full, the gentleman nods again, turns upon his heel, and saunters away.

There are times, however, when his company is not so agreeable, though equally unexpected; such as when the lady has invited one or two particular friends to tea and scandal, and he happens to come home in the very midst of their diversion. It is a hundred chances to one that he remains in the house half an hour; but the lady is rather disturbed by the intrusion, notwithstanding, and reasons within herself, "I am sure I never interfere with him, and why should he interfere with me? It can scarcely be accidental: it never happens that I have a particular reason for not wishing him to come home, but he always comes. It's very provoking and tiresome; and I am sure when he leaves me so much alone for his own pleasure, the least he could do would be to do as much for mine." Observing what passes in her mind, the gentleman, who has come home for his own accommodation, makes a merit of it with himself; arrives at the conclusion that it is the very last place in which he can hope to be comfortable; and determines, as he takes up his hat and cane, never to be so virtuous again.

Thus a great many cool couples go on until they are cold couples, and the grave has closed over their folly and indifference. Loss of name, station, character, life itself, has ensued from causes as slight as these before now; and when gossips tell such tales, and aggravate their deformities, they elevate their hands and eyebrows, and call each other to witness what a cool couple Mr. and Mrs. So-and-so always were, even in the best of times.

VIII

THE PLAUSIBLE COUPLE

THE plausible couple have many titles. They are a "delightful couple," "an affectionate couple," "a most agreeable couple," "a good-hearted couple," and "the best-natured couple in existence." The truth is that the plausible couple are people of the world; and either the way of pleasing the world has grown much easier than it was in the days of the old man and his ass, or the old man was but a bad hand at it, and knew very little of the trade.

"But is it really possible to please the world?" says some doubting reader. It is, indeed. Nay, it is not only very possible, but very easy. The ways are crooked, and sometimes foul and low. What then? A man need but crawl upon his hands and knees, know when to close his eyes and when his ears, when to stoop and when to stand upright; and, if by the world is meant that atom of it in which he moves himself, he shall please it, never fear.

Now, it will be readily seen that, if a plausible man or woman have an easy means of pleasing the world by an adaptation of self to all its twistings and twinings, a plausible man *and* woman, or, in other words, a plausible couple, playing into each other's hands, and acting in concert, have a manifest advantage. Hence it is that plausible couples scarcely ever fail of success on a pretty large scale; and hence it is that if the reader, laying down this unwieldy volume at the next full-stop, will have the goodness to review his or her circle of acquaintance, and to search particularly for some man and wife with a large connection and a good name, not easily referable to their abilities or their wealth, he or she (that is, the male or female reader) will certainly find that gentleman and lady, on a very short reflection, to be a plausible couple.

The plausible couple are the most ecstatic people living; the most sensitive people — to merit — on the face of the earth.

Nothing clever or virtuous escapes them. They have microscopic eyes for such endowments, and can find them anywhere. The plausible couple never fawn, — oh, no! They don't even scruple to tell their friends of their faults. One is too generous, another too candid; a third has a tendency to think all people like himself, and to regard mankind as a company of angels; a fourth is kind-hearted to a fault. "We never flatter, my dear Mrs. Jackson," says the plausible couple: "we speak our minds. Neither you nor Mr. Jackson have faults enough. It may sound strangely, but it is true. You have not faults enough. You know our way, — we must speak out, and always do. Quarrel with us for saying so, if you will; but, we repeat it, you have not faults enough!"

The plausible couple are no less plausible to each other than to third parties. They are always loving and harmonious. The plausible gentleman calls his wife "darling," and the plausible lady addresses him as "dearest." If it be Mr. and Mrs. Bobtail Widger, Mrs. Widger is "Lavinia darling," and Mr. Widger is "Bobtail dearest." Speaking of each other, they observe the same tender form. Mrs. Widger relates what "Bobtail" said, and Mr. Widger recounts what "darling" thought and did.

If you sit next to the plausible lady at a dinner-table, she takes the earliest opportunity of expressing her belief that you are acquainted with the Clickits: she is sure she has heard the Clickits speak of you, — she must not tell you in what terms, or you will take her for a flatterer. You admit a knowledge of the Clickits; the plausible lady immediately launches out in their praise. She quite loves the Clickits. Were there ever such true-hearted, hospitable, excellent people? — such a gentle, interesting little woman as Mrs. Clickit, or such a frank, unaffected creature as Mr. Clickit? Were there ever two people, in short, so little spoiled by the world as they are? "As who, darling?" cries Mr. Widger from the opposite side of the table. "The Clickits, dearest," replies Mrs. Widger. "Indeed you are right, darling," Mr. Widger rejoins; "the Clickits are a very high-minded, worthy, estimable couple." Mrs. Widger remarking that Bobtail always grows quite eloquent upon this subject, Mr. Widger admits that he feels very strongly whenever such people as the Clickits and some other friends of his (here he glances at the host and

hostess) are mentioned; for they are an honour to human
nature, and do one good to think of. "*You* know the Clickits,
Mrs. Jackson?" he says, addressing the lady of the house.
"No, indeed; we have not that pleasure," she replies. "You
astonish me!" exclaims Mr. Widger: "not know the Clickits!
why, you are the very people of all others who ought to be
their bosom friends. You are kindred beings; you are one
and the same thing, — not know the Clickits! Now, *will* you
know the Clickits? Will you make a point of knowing them?
Will you meet them in a friendly way at our house one evening, and be acquainted with them?" Mrs. Jackson will be
quite delighted; nothing would give her more pleasure.
"Then, Lavinia, my darling," says Mr. Widger, "mind you
don't lose sight of that; now, pray take care that Mr. and
Mrs. Jackson know the Clickits without loss of time. Such
people ought not to be strangers to each other." Mrs. Widger
books both families as the centre of attraction for her next
party; and Mr. Widger, going on to expatiate upon the virtues
of the Clickits, adds to their other moral qualities that they
keep one of the neatest phaetons in town, and have two thousand a year.

As the plausible couple never laud the merits of any absent
person, without dexterously contriving that their praises shall
reflect upon somebody who is present, so they never depreciate
anything or anybody without turning their depreciation to
the same account. Their friend, Mr. Slummery, say they, is
unquestionably a clever painter, and would no doubt be very
popular, and sell his pictures at a very high price, if that cruel
Mr. Fithers had not forestalled him in his department of art,
and made it thoroughly and completely his own, — Fithers, it
is to be observed, being present and within hearing, and Slummery elsewhere. Is Mrs. Tabblewick really as beautiful as
people say? Why, there indeed you ask them a very puzzling
question, because there is no doubt that she is a very charming
woman, and they have long known her intimately. She is no
doubt beautiful, — very beautiful; they once thought her the
most beautiful woman ever seen: still, if you press them for
an honest answer, they are bound to say that this was before
they had ever seen our lovely friend on the sofa (the sofa is
hard by, and our lovely friend can't help hearing the whispers
in which this is said); since that time, perhaps, they have

been hardly fair judges. Mrs. Tabblewick is no doubt extremely handsome, — very like our friend, in fact, in the form of the features, — but, in point of expression and soul and figure, and air all together — oh, dear!

But, while the plausible couple depreciate, they are still careful to preserve their character for amiability and kind feeling; indeed, the depreciation itself is often made to grow out of their excessive sympathy and good-will. The plausible lady calls on a lady who dotes upon her children, and is sitting with a little girl upon her knee, enraptured by her artless replies, and protesting that there is nothing she delights in so much as conversing with these fairies; when the other lady inquires if she has seen young Mrs. Finching lately, and whether the baby has turned out a finer one than it promised to be. "Oh, dear!" cries the plausible lady, "you cannot think how often Bobtail and I have talked about poor Mrs. Finching, — she is such a dear soul, and was so anxious that the baby should be a fine child; and, very naturally, because she was very much here at one time, and there is, you know, a natural emulation among mothers, — that it is impossible to tell you how much we have felt for her." "Is it weak, or plain, or what?" inquires the other. "Weak, or plain, my love!" returns the plausible lady: "it's a fright, — a perfect little fright: you never saw such a miserable creature in all your days. Positively you must not let her see one of these beautiful dears again, or you'll break her heart, — you will indeed. Heaven bless this child! see how she is looking in my face! can you conceive anything prettier than that? If poor Mrs. Finching could only hope — but that's impossible, — and the gifts of Providence, you know — What *did* I do with my pocket-handkerchief!"

What prompts the mother, who dotes upon her children, to comment to her lord that evening on the plausible lady's engaging qualities and feeling heart? and what is it that procures Mr. and Mrs. Bobtail Widger an immediate invitation to dinner?

IX

A CUSTOM once prevailed, in old-fashioned circles, that when a lady or gentleman was unable to sing a song he or she should enliven the company with a story. As we find ourself in the predicament of not being able to describe (to our own satisfaction) nice little couples in the abstract, we purpose telling in this place a little story about a nice little couple of our acquaintance.

Mr. and Mrs. Chirrup are the nice little couple in question. Mr. Chirrup has the smartness, and something of the brisk, quick manner, of a small bird. Mrs. Chirrup is the prettiest of all little women, and has the prettiest little figure conceivable. She has the neatest little foot, and the softest little voice, and the pleasantest little smile, and the tidiest little curls, and the brightest little eyes, and the quietest little manner, and is, in short, altogether one of the most engaging of all little women, dead or alive. She is a condensation of all the domestic virtues; a pocket edition of "The Young Man's Best Companion;" a little woman at a very high pressure, with an amazing quantity of goodness and usefulness in an exceedingly small space. Little as she is, Mrs. Chirrup might furnish forth matter for the moral equipment of a score of housewives, six feet high in their stockings, — if, in the presence of ladies, we may be allowed the expression, — and of corresponding robustness.

Nobody knows all this better than Mr. Chirrup, though he rather takes on that he don't. Accordingly, he is very proud of his better half, and evidently considers himself, as all other people consider him, rather fortunate in having her to wife. We say evidently, because Mr. Chirrup is a warm-hearted little fellow; and if you catch his eye, when he has been slily glancing at Mrs. Chirrup in company, there is a certain complacent twinkle in it, accompanied, perhaps, by a half-expressed toss of the head, which as clearly indicates what has been passing in his mind as if he had put it into words, and shouted it out through a speaking-trumpet. Moreover, Mr. Chirrup has a particularly mild and bird-like manner of calling Mrs. Chir-

rup "my dear;" and — for he is of a jocose turn — of cutting
little witticisms upon her, and making her the subject of various harmless pleasantries which nobody enjoys more thoroughly
than Mrs. Chirrup herself.   Mr. Chirrup, too, now and then
affects to deplore his bachelor days, and to bemoan (with a
marvellously contented and smirking face) the loss of his freedom, and the sorrow of his heart at having been taken captive
by Mrs. Chirrup, — all of which circumstances combine to
show the secret triumph and satisfaction of Mr. Chirrup's soul.
    We have already had occasion to observe that Mrs. Chirrup
is an incomparable housewife.   In all the arts of domestic
arrangement and management, in all the mysteries of confec-
tionery-making, pickling, and preserving, never was such a
thorough adept as that nice little body.   She is, besides, a
cunning worker in muslin and fine linen, and a special hand at
marketing to the very best advantage.   But if there be one
branch of housekeeping in which she excels to an utterly
unparalleled and unprecedented extent, it is in the important
one of carving.   A roast goose is universally allowed to be the
great stumbling-block in the way of young aspirants to perfection in this department of science; many promising carvers,
beginning with legs of mutton, and preserving a good reputation through fillets of veal, sirloins of beef, quarters of lamb,
fowls, and even ducks, have sunk before a roast goose, and lost
caste and character for ever.   To Mrs. Chirrup the resolving a
goose into its smallest component parts is a pleasant pastime,
— a practical joke, — a thing to be done in a minute or so,
without the smallest interruption to the conversation of the
time.   No handing the dish over to an unfortunate man upon
her right or left, no wild sharpening of the knife, no hacking
and sawing at an unruly joint, no noise, no splash, no heat,
no leaving off in despair; all is confidence and cheerfulness.
The dish is set upon the table, the cover is removed: for an
instant, and only an instant, you observe that Mrs. Chirrup's
attention is distracted; she smiles, but heareth not.   You
proceed with your story; meanwhile the glittering knife is
slowly upraised, both Mrs. Chirrup's wrists are slightly but
not ungracefully agitated, she compresses her lips for an
instant, then breaks into a smile, and all is over.   The legs
of the bird slide gently down into a pool of gravy, the wings
seem to melt from the body, the breast separates into a row of

juicy slices, the smaller and more complicated parts of his anatomy are perfectly developed, a cavern of stuffing is revealed, and the goose is gone!

To dine with Mr. and Mrs. Chirrup is one of the pleasantest things in the world. Mr. Chirrup has a bachelor friend, who lived with him in his own days of single blessedness, and to whom he is mightily attached. Contrary to the usual custom, this bachelor friend is no less a friend of Mrs. Chirrup's, and, consequently, whenever you dine with Mr. and Mrs. Chirrup, you meet the bachelor friend. It would put any reasonably conditioned mortal into good-humour to observe the unanimity which subsists between these three; but there is a quiet welcome dimpling in Mrs. Chirrup's face, a bustling hospitality oozing as it were out of the waistcoat pockets of Mr. Chirrup, and a patronising enjoyment of their cordiality and satisfaction on the part of the bachelor friend, which is quite delightful. On these occasions Mr. Chirrup usually takes an opportunity of rallying the friend on being single, and the friend retorts upon Mr. Chirrup for being married, at which moments some single young ladies present are like to die of laughter; and we have more than once observed them bestow looks upon the friend, which convinces us that his position is by no means a safe one, as, indeed, we hold no bachelor's to be who visits married friends, and cracks jokes on wedlock; for certain it is that such men walk among traps and nets and pitfalls innumerable, and often find themselves down upon their knees at the altar-rails, taking M. or N. for their wedded wives before they know anything about the matter.

However, this is no business of Mr. Chirrup's, who talks and laughs, and drinks his wine, and laughs again, and talks more, until it is time to repair to the drawing-room, where, coffee served over and over, Mrs. Chirrup prepares for a round game, by sorting the nicest possible little fish into the nicest possible little pools, and calling Mr. Chirrup to assist her, which Mr. Chirrup does. As they stand side by side, you find that Mr. Chirrup is the least possible shadow of a shade taller than Mrs. Chirrup, and that they are the neatest and best-matched little couple that can be, which the chances are ten to one against your observing with such effect at any other time, unless you see them in the street arm in arm, or meet them some rainy day trotting along under a very small umbrella. The round game (at which Mr. Chirrup is the merriest of the party) being done and over, in course of time a nice little tray appears, on which is a nice little supper; and when that is finished likewise, and you have said, "Good-night," you find yourself repeating a dozen times as you ride home, that there never was such a nice little couple as Mr. and Mrs. Chirrup.

Whether it is that pleasant qualities, being packed more closely in small bodies than in large, come more readily to hand than when they are diffused over a wider space, and have to be gathered together for use, we don't know; but, as a general rule, — strengthened like all other rules by its exceptions, — we hold that little people are sprightly and good-natured. The more sprightly and good-natured people we have, the better; therefore let us wish well to all nice little couples, and hope that they may increase and multiply.

X

THE EGOTISTICAL COUPLE

EGOTISM in couples is of two kinds. It is our purpose to show this by two examples.

The egotistical couple may be young, old, middle-aged, well-to-do, or ill-to-do; they may have a small family, a large family, or no family at all. There is no outward sign by which an egotistical couple may be known and avoided. They come upon you unawares; there is no guarding against them. No man can of himself be forewarned or forearmed against an egotistical couple.

The egotistical couple have undergone every calamity, and experienced every pleasurable and painful sensation, of which our nature is susceptible. You cannot by possibility tell the egotistical couple anything they don't know, or describe to them anything they have not felt. They have been every-thing but dead. Sometimes we are tempted to wish they had been even that, but only in our uncharitable moments, which are few and far between.

We happened the other day, in the course of a morning call, to encounter an egotistical couple, nor were we suffered to remain long in ignorance of the fact; for our very first inquiry of the lady of the house brought them into active and vigorous operation. The inquiry was of course touching the lady's health; and the answer happened to be that she had not been very well. "Oh, my dear!" said the egotistical lady, "don't talk of not being well. We have been in *such* a state since we saw you last!" The lady of the house happening to remark that her lord had not been well either, the egotistical gentleman struck in, "Never let Briggs complain of not being well, — never let Briggs complain, my dear Mrs. Briggs, after what I have undergone within these six weeks. He does n't know what it is to be ill; he has n't the least idea of it, — not the faintest conception." "My dear," interposed his wife, smiling, "you talk as if it were almost a crime in Mr. Briggs not to have been as ill as we have been, instead of feeling thankful to Providence that both he and our dear Mrs. Briggs are in such blissful ignorance of real suffering." "My love," returned the egotistical gentleman, in a low and pious voice, "you mistake me; I feel grateful, — very grateful. I trust our friends may never purchase their experience as dearly as we have bought ours; I hope they never may!"

Having put down Mrs. Briggs upon this theme, and settled the question thus, the egotistical gentleman turned to us, and after a few preliminary remarks, all tending towards and leading up to the point he had in his mind, inquired if we happened to be acquainted with the Dowager Lady Snorflerer. On our replying in the negative, he presumed we had often met Lord Slang, or, beyond all doubt, that we were on intimate terms with Sir Chipkins Clogwog. Finding that we were equally unable to lay claim to either of these distinctions, he expressed great astonishment, and, turning to his wife with a retrospective smile, inquired who it was that had told that capital story about the mashed potatoes. "Who, my dear?" returned the egotistical lady; "why, Sir Chipkins, of course; how can you ask! Don't you remember his applying it to our cook, and saying that you and I were so like the prince and princess that he could almost have sworn we were they?" "To be sure, I remember that," said the egotistical gentleman; "but are you quite certain that did n't apply to the other anecdote about the Emperor of Austria and the pump?" "Upon my word, then, I think it did," replied his wife.

"To be sure it did," said the egotistical gentleman; "it was Slang's story, I remember now, perfectly." However, it turned out, a few seconds afterwards, that the egotistical gentleman's memory was rather treacherous, as he began to have a misgiving that the story had been told by the Dowager Lady Snorflerer the very last time they dined there; but there appearing, on further consideration, strong circumstantial evidence tending to show that this couldn't be, inasmuch as the Dowager Lady Snorflerer had been, on the occasion in question, wholly engrossed by the egotistical lady, the egotistical gentleman recanted this opinion; and after laying the story at the doors of a great many great people, happily left it last with the Duke of Scuttlewig, observing that it was not extraordinary he had forgotten his grace hitherto, as it often happened that the names of those with whom we were upon the most familiar footing were the very last to present themselves to our thoughts.

It not only appeared that the egotistical couple knew everybody, but that scarcely any event of importance or notoriety had occurred for many years with which they had not been in some way or other connected. Thus we learned that when the well-known attempt upon the life of George the Third was made by Hatfield, in Drury Lane Theatre, the egotistical gentleman's grandfather sat upon his right hand, and was the first man who collared him; and that the egotistical lady's aunt, sitting within a few boxes of the royal party, was the only person in the audience who heard his Majesty exclaim, "Charlotte, Charlotte, don't be frightened, don't be frightened; they're letting off squibs, they're letting off squibs." When the fire broke out which ended in the destruction of the two Houses of Parliament, the egotistical couple, being at the time at a drawing-room window on Blackheath, then and there simultaneously exclaimed, to the astonishment of a whole party, "It's the House of Lords!" Nor was this a solitary instance of their peculiar discernment; for, chancing to be (as by a comparison of dates and circumstances they afterwards found) in the same omnibus with Mr. Greenacre, when he carried his victim's head about town in a blue bag, they both remarked a singular twitching in the muscles of his countenance; and walking down Fish Street Hill, a few weeks since, the egotistical gentleman said to his lady, slightly casting up his eyes to the top of the Monument, "There's a boy up there, my dear, reading a Bible. It's very strange; I don't like it. In five seconds afterwards, sir," says the egotistical gentleman, bringing his hands together with one violent clap, "the lad was over!"

Diversifying these topics by the introduction of many others of the same kind, and entertaining us between whiles with a minute account of what weather and diet agreed with them, and what weather and diet disagreed with them, and at what time they usually got up, and at what time went to bed, with many other particulars of their domestic economy too numerous to mention, the egotistical couple at length took their leave, and afforded us an opportunity of doing the same.

Mr. and Mrs. Sliverstone are an egotistical couple of another class; for all the lady's egotism is about her husband, and all the gentleman's about his wife. For example: Mr. Sliverstone is a clerical gentleman, and occasionally writes sermons, as clerical gentlemen do. If you happen to obtain admission at the street door while he is so engaged, Mrs. Sliverstone appears on tiptoe, and speaking in a solemn whisper, as if there were at least three or four particular friends up stairs, all upon the point of death, implores you to be very silent; for Mr. Sliverstone is composing, and she need not say how very important it is that he should not be disturbed. Unwilling to interrupt anything so serious, you hasten to withdraw, with many apologies; but this Mrs. Sliverstone will by no means allow, observing that she knows you would like to see him, as it is very natural you should, and that she is determined to make a trial for you, as you are a great favourite. So you are led up stairs — still on tiptoe — to the door of a little back room, in which, as the lady informs you in a whisper, Mr. Sliverstone always writes. No answer being returned to a couple of soft taps, the lady opens the door; and there, sure enough, is Mr. Sliverstone, with dishevelled hair, powdering away, with pen, ink, and paper, at a rate which, if he has any power of sustaining it, would settle the longest sermon in no time. At first he is too much absorbed to be roused by this intrusion; but presently looking up, says faintly, "Ah!" and, pointing to his desk with a weary and languid smile, extends his hand and hopes you'll forgive him. Then Mrs. Sliverstone sits down beside him, and, taking his

hand in hers, tells you how that Mr. Sliverstone has been
shut up there ever since nine o'clock in the morning (it is by
this time twelve at noon), and how she knows it cannot be
good for his health, and is very uneasy about it. Unto this
Mr. Sliverstone replies firmly, that "it must be done;" which
agonises Mrs. Sliverstone still more, and she goes on to tell
you that such were Mr. Sliverstone's labours last week —
what with the buryings, marryings, churchings, christenings,
and all together — that, when he was going up the pulpit-
stairs on Sunday evening, he was obliged to hold on by the
rails, or he would certainly have fallen over into his own pew.
Mr. Sliverstone, who has been listening and smiling meekly,
says, "Not quite so bad as that, not quite so bad!" He
admits though, on cross-examination, that he *was* very near
falling upon the verger who was following him up to bolt the
door; but adds, that it was his duty as a Christian to fall upon
him, if need were, and that he, Mr. Sliverstone (and possibly
the verger too), ought to glory in it.

This sentiment communicates new impulse to Mrs. Sliverstone, who launches into new praises of Mr. Sliverstone's
worth and excellence; to which he listens in the same meek
silence, save when he puts in a word of self-denial relative to
some question of fact, as, "Not seventy-two christenings that
week, my dear; only seventy-one, only seventy-one." At
length his lady has quite concluded; and then he says, Why
should he repine, why should he give way, why should he
suffer his heart to sink within him? Is it he alone who toils
and suffers? What has she gone through, he should like to
know? What does she go through every day for him and for
society?

With such an exordium Mr. Sliverstone launches out into
glowing praises of the conduct of Mrs. Sliverstone in the production of eight young children, and the subsequent rearing
and fostering of the same; and thus the husband magnifies the
wife, and the wife the husband.

This would be well enough if Mr. and Mrs. Sliverstone kept
it to themselves, or even to themselves and a friend or two;
but they do not. The more hearers they have the more
egotistical the couple become, and the more anxious they are
to make believers in their merits. Perhaps this is the worst
kind of egotism. It has not even the poor excuse of being

spontaneous, but is the result of a deliberate system and malice aforethought. Mere empty-headed conceit excites our pity, but ostentatious hypocrisy awakens our disgust.

XI

THE COUPLE WHO CODDLE THEMSELVES

Mrs. Merrywinkle's maiden name was Chopper. She was the only child of Mr. and Mrs. Chopper. Her father died when she was, as the play-books express it, "yet an infant;" and so old Mrs. Chopper, when her daughter married, made the house of her son-in-law her home from that time henceforth, and set up her staff of rest with Mr. and Mrs. Merrywinkle.

Mr. and Mrs. Merrywinkle are a couple who coddle themselves; and the venerable Mrs. Chopper is an aider and abettor in the same.

Mr. Merrywinkle is a rather lean and long-necked gentleman, middle-aged and middle-sized, and usually troubled with a cold in the head. Mrs. Merrywinkle is a delicate-looking lady, with very light hair, and is exceedingly subject to the same unpleasant disorder. The venerable Mrs. Chopper — who is strictly entitled to the appellation, her daughter not being very young, otherwise than by courtesy, at the time of her marriage, which was some years ago — is a mysterious old lady who lurks behind a pair of spectacles, and is afflicted with a chronic disease respecting which she has taken a vast deal of medical advice, and referred to a vast number of medical books, without meeting any definition of symptoms that at all suits her, or enables her to say, "That's my complaint." Indeed, the absence of authentic information upon the subject of this complaint would seem to be Mrs. Chopper's greatest ill, as in all other respects she is an uncommonly hale and hearty gentlewoman.

Both Mr. and Mrs. Merrywinkle wear an extraordinary quantity of flannel, and have a habit of putting their feet in hot water to an unnatural extent. They likewise indulge in chamomile tea and such-like compounds, and rub themselves on the slightest provocation with camphorated spirits and other

lotions applicable to mumps, sore throat, rheumatism, or lum-
bago.

Mr. Merrywinkle's leaving home to go to business on a
damp or wet morning is a very elaborate affair. He puts on
wash-leather socks over his stockings, and India-rubber shoes
above his boots, and wears under his waistcoat a cuirass of
hair-skin. Besides these precautions, he winds a thick shawl
round his throat, and blocks up his mouth with a large silk
handkerchief. Thus accoutred, and furnished besides with a
great-coat and umbrella, he braves the dangers of the streets;
travelling in severe weather at a gentle trot, the better to preserve the circulation, and bringing his mouth to the surface to
take breath but very seldom, and with the utmost caution.
His office door opened, he shoots past his clerk at the same
pace, and, diving into his own private room, closes the door,
examines the window-fastenings, and gradually unrobes himself, — hanging his pocket-handkerchief on the fender to air,
and determining to write to the newspapers about the fog,
which, he says, "has really got to that pitch that it is quite
unbearable."

In this last opinion Mrs. Merrywinkle and her respected
mother fully concur; for though not present, their thoughts
and tongues are occupied with the same subject, which is their
constant theme all day. If anybody happens to call, Mrs.
Merrywinkle opines that they must assuredly be mad; and her
first salutation is, "Why, what in the name of goodness can
bring you out in such weather? You know you *must* catch
your death." This assurance is corroborated by Mrs. Chopper,
who adds, in further confirmation, a dismal legend concerning
an individual of her acquaintance, who, making a call under
precisely parallel circumstances, and being then in the best
health and spirits, expired in forty-eight hours afterwards, of
a complication of inflammatory disorders. The visitor, rendered not altogether comfortable perhaps by this and other
precedents, inquires very affectionately after Mr. Merrywinkle,
but by so doing brings about no change of the subject; for Mr.
Merrywinkle's name is inseparably connected with his complaints, and his complaints are inseparably connected with Mrs.
Merrywinkle's; and when these are done with, Mrs. Chopper,
who has been biding her time, cuts in with the chronic disorder, — a subject upon which the amiable old lady never

leaves off speaking until she is left alone, and very often not then.

But Mr. Merrywinkle comes home to dinner. He is received by Mrs. Merrywinkle and Mrs. Chopper, who, on his remarking that he thinks his feet are damp, turn pale as ashes, and drag him up stairs, imploring him to have them rubbed directly with a dry coarse towel. Rubbed they are, one by Mrs. Merrywinkle and one by Mrs. Chopper, until the friction causes Mr. Merrywinkle to make horrible faces, and look as if he had been smelling very powerful onions; when they desist, and the patient, provided for his better security with thick worsted stockings and list slippers, is borne down stairs to dinner. Now, the dinner is always a good one, the appetites of the diners being delicate, and requiring a little of what Mrs. Merrywinkle calls "tittivation;" the secret of which is understood to lie in good cookery and tasteful spices, and which process is so successfully performed in the present instance, that both Mr. and Mrs. Merrywinkle eat a remarkably good dinner, and even the afflicted Mrs. Chopper wields her knife and fork with much of the spirit and elasticity of youth. But Mr. Merrywinkle, in his desire to gratify his appetite, is not unmindful of his health; for he has a bottle of carbonate of soda with which to qualify his porter, and a little pair of scales in which to weigh it out. Neither in his anxiety to take care of his body is he unmindful of the welfare of his immortal part, as he always prays that for what he is going to receive he may be made truly thankful, and, in order that he may be as thankful as possible, eats and drinks to the utmost.

Either from eating and drinking so much, or from being the victim of this constitutional infirmity, among others, Mr. Merrywinkle, after two or three glasses of wine, falls fast asleep; and he has scarcely closed his eyes, when Mrs. Merrywinkle and Mrs. Chopper fall asleep likewise. It is on awakening at tea-time that their most alarming symptoms prevail; for then Mr. Merrywinkle feels as if his temples were tightly bound round with the chain of the street door, and Mrs. Merrywinkle as if she had made a hearty dinner of half-hundredweights, and Mrs. Chopper as if cold water were running down her back, and oyster-knives with sharp points were plunging of their own accord into her ribs. Symptoms like these are enough to make people peevish; and no wonder that they remain so until supper-time, doing little more than doze and complain, unless Mr. Merrywinkle calls out very loud to a servant "to keep that draught out," or rushes into the passage to flourish his fist in the countenance of the twopenny postman, for daring to give such a knock as he had just performed at the door of a private gentleman with nerves.

Supper, coming after dinner, should consist of some gentle provocative; and therefore the tittivating art is again in requisition, and again done honour to by Mr. and Mrs. Merrywinkle, still comforted and abetted by Mrs. Chopper. After supper, it is ten to one but the last-named old lady becomes worse, and is led off to bed with the chronic complaint in full vigour. Mr. and Mrs. Merrywinkle, having administered to her a warm cordial, which is something of the strongest, then repair to their own room, where Mr. Merrywinkle, with his legs and feet in hot water, superintends the mulling of some wine which he is to drink at the very moment he plunges into bed; while Mrs. Merrywinkle, in garments whose nature is unknown to and unimagined by all but married men, takes four small pills with a spasmodic look between each, and finally comes to something hot and fragrant out of another little saucepan, which serves as her composing-draught for the night.

There is another kind of couple who coddle themselves, and who do so at a cheaper rate and on more spare diet, because they are niggardly and parsimonious; for which reason they are kind enough to coddle their visitors too. It is unnecessary to describe them; for our readers may rest assured of the accuracy of these general principles: that all couples who coddle themselves are selfish and slothful; that they charge upon every wind that blows, every rain that falls, and every vapour that hangs in the air, the evils which arise from their own imprudence or the gloom which is engendered in their own tempers; and that all men and women, in couples or otherwise, who fall into exclusive habits of self-indulgence, and forget their natural sympathy and close connection with everybody and everything in the world around them, not only neglect the first duty of life, but, by a happy retributive justice, deprive themselves of its truest and best enjoyment.

XII

THE OLD COUPLE

THEY are grandfather and grandmother to a dozen grown people, and have great-grandchildren besides; their bodies are bent, their hair is grey, their step tottering and infirm. Is this the lightsome pair whose wedding was so merry? and have the young couple indeed grown old so soon?

It seems but yesterday; and yet what a host of cares and griefs are crowded into the intervening time, which, reckoned by them, lengthens out to a century! How many new associations have wreathed themselves about their hearts since then! The old time is gone; and a new time has come for others, — not for them. They are but the rusting link that feebly joins the two, and is silently loosening its hold and dropping asunder.

It seems but yesterday; and yet three of their children have sunk into the grave, and the tree that shades it has grown quite old. One was an infant; they wept for him. The next a girl, a slight young thing, too delicate for earth; her loss was hard indeed to bear. The third a man. That was the worst of all; but even that grief is softened now.

It seems but yesterday; and yet how the gay and laughing faces of that bright morning have changed, and vanished from above ground! Faint likenesses of some remain about them yet; but they are very faint, and scarcely to be traced. The rest are only seen in dreams; and even they are unlike what they were, in eyes so old and dim.

One or two dresses from the bridal wardrobe are yet preserved. They are of a quaint and antique fashion, and seldom seen except in pictures. White has turned yellow, and brighter hues have faded. Do you wonder, child? The wrinkled face was once as smooth as yours, the eyes as bright, the shrivelled skin as fair and delicate. It is the work of hands that have been dust these many years.

Where are the fairy lovers of that happy day, whose annual return comes upon the old man and his wife like the echo of some village-bell which has long been silent? Let yonder peevish bachelor, racked by rheumatic pains, and quarrelling

with the world, let him answer to the question. He recollects
something of a favourite playmate; her name was Lucy, — so
they tell him. He is not sure whether she was married, or
went abroad, or died. It is a long while ago, and he don't
remember.

Is nothing as it used to be? Does no one feel or think or
act as in days of yore? Yes; there is an aged woman who
once lived servant with the old lady's father, and is sheltered
in an almshouse not far off. She is still attached to the
family, and loves them all; she nursed the children in her lap,
and tended in their sickness those who are no more. Her old
mistress has still something of youth in her eyes; the young
ladies are like what she was, but not quite so handsome, nor
are the gentlemen as stately as Mr. Harvey used to be. She
has seen a great deal of trouble; her husband and her son died
long ago; but she has got over that, and is happy now, —
quite happy.

If ever her attachment to her old protectors was disturbed
by fresher cares and hopes, it has long since resumed its former
current. It has filled the void in the poor creature's heart,
and replaced the love of kindred. Death has not left her
alone; and this, with a roof above her head, and a warm hearth
to sit by, makes her cheerful and contented. Does she remember the marriage of great-grandmamma? Ay, that she does,
as well as if it was only yesterday. You would n't think it to
look at her now, and perhaps she ought not to say so of herself;
but she was as smart a young girl then as you 'd wish to see.
She recollects she took a friend of hers up stairs to see Miss
Emma dressed for church. Her name was — ah! she forgets
the name; but she remembers that she was a very pretty girl,
and that she married not long afterwards, and lived — it has
quite passed out of her mind where she lived; but she knows
she had a bad husband, who used her ill, and that she died in
Lambeth workhouse. Dear, dear, in Lambeth workhouse!

And the old couple, — have they no comfort or enjoyment
of existence? See them among their grandchildren and great-
grandchildren; how garrulous they are! how they compare one
with another, and insist on likenesses which no one else can
see! how gently the old lady lectures the girls on the points of
breeding and decorum, and points the moral by anecdotes of
herself in her young days! how the old gentleman chuckles

over boyish feats and roguish tricks, and tells long stories of a "barring-out" achieved at the school he went to, which was very wrong, he tells the boys, and never to be imitated of course, but which he cannot help letting them know was very pleasant too, — especially when he kissed the master's niece. This last, however, is a point on which the old lady is very tender; for she considers it a shocking and indelicate thing to talk about, and always says so whenever it is mentioned, never failing to observe that he ought to be very penitent for having been so sinful. So the old gentleman gets no further; and what the schoolmaster's niece said afterwards (which he is always going to tell) is lost to posterity.

The old gentleman is eighty years old to-day. "Eighty years old, Crofts, and never had a headache," he tells the barber who shaves him (the barber being a young fellow and very subject to that complaint). "That's a great age, Crofts," says the old gentleman. "I don't think it's sich a wery great age, sir," replies the barber. "Crofts," rejoins the old gentleman, "you're talking nonsense to me. Eighty not a great age?" "It's a wery great age, sir, for a gentleman to be as healthy and active as you are," returns the barber; "but my grandfather, sir, he was ninety-four." "You don't mean that, Crofts?" says the old gentleman. "I do, indeed, sir," retorts the barber, "and as wiggerous as Julius Cæsar, my grandfather was." The old gentleman muses a little time, and then says, "What did he die of, Crofts?" "He died accidentally, sir," returns the barber; "he didn't mean to do it. He always would go a running about the streets, — walking never satisfied *his* spirit; and he run against a post, and died of a hurt in his chest." The old gentleman says no more until the shaving is concluded, and then he gives Crofts half a crown to drink his health. He is a little doubtful of the barber's veracity afterwards; and, telling the anecdote to the old lady, affects to make very light of it, — though, to be sure (he adds), there was old Parr, and in some parts of England ninety-five or so is a common age, — quite a common age.

This morning the old couple are cheerful but serious; recalling old times as well as they can remember them, and dwelling upon many passages in their past lives which the day brings to mind. The old lady reads aloud, in a tremulous voice, out of a great Bible; and the old gentleman, with his hand to his ear, listens with profound respect. When the book is closed, they sit silent for a short space, and afterwards resume their conversation, with a reference perhaps to their dead children, as a subject not unsuited to that they have just left. By degrees they are led to consider which of those who survive are the most like those dearly remembered objects; and so they fall into a less solemn strain, and become cheerful again.

How many people in all, grandchildren, great-grandchildren, and one or two intimate friends of the family, dine together to-day at the eldest son's to congratulate the old couple, and wish them many happy returns, is a calculation beyond our powers; but this we know, that the old couple no sooner present themselves, very sprucely and carefully attired, than there is a violent shouting and rushing forward of the younger branches with all manner of presents, such as pocket-books, pencil-cases, pen-wipers, watch-papers, pin-cushions, sleeve-buckles, worked slippers, watch-guards, and even a nutmeg-grater, — the latter article being presented by a very chubby and very little boy, who exhibits it in great triumph as an extraordinary variety. The old couple's emotion at these tokens of remembrance occasions quite a pathetic scene, of which the chief ingredients are a vast quantity of kissing and hugging, and repeated wipings of small eyes and noses with small square pocket-handkerchiefs, which don't come at all easily out of small pockets. Even the peevish bachelor is moved; and he says, as he presents the old gentleman with a queer sort of antique ring from his own finger, that he 'll be de'ed if he does n't think he looks younger than he did ten years ago.

But the great time is after dinner, when the dessert and wine are on the table, which is pushed back to make plenty of room, and they are all gathered in a large circle round the fire; for it is then — the glasses being filled, and everybody ready to drink the toast — that two great-grandchildren rush out at a given signal, and presently return, dragging in old Jane Adams, leaning upon her crutched stick, and trembling with age and pleasure. Who so popular as poor old Jane, nurse and story-teller in ordinary to two generations! and who so happy as she, striving to bend her stiff limbs into a curtsey, while tears of pleasure steal down her withered cheeks!

The old couple sit side by side, and the old time seems like yesterday indeed. Looking back upon the path they have travelled, its dust and ashes disappear; the flowers that withered long ago show brightly again upon its borders, and they grow young once more in the youth of those about them.

XIII

CONCLUSION

WE have taken for the subjects of the foregoing moral essays twelve samples of married couples, carefully selected from a large stock on hand, open to the inspection of all comers. These samples are intended for the benefit of the rising generation of both sexes, and, for their more easy and pleasant information, have been separately ticketed and labelled in the manner they have seen.

We have purposely excluded from consideration the couple in which the lady reigns paramount and supreme, holding such cases to be of a very unnatural kind, and, like hideous births and other monstrous deformities, only to be discreetly and sparingly exhibited.

And here our self-imposed task would have ended, but that to those young ladies and gentlemen who are yet revolving singly round the church, awaiting the advent of that time when the mysterious laws of attraction shall draw them towards it in couples, we are desirous of addressing a few last words.

Before marriage, and afterwards, let them learn to centre all their hopes of real and lasting happiness in their own fireside; let them cherish the faith that in home, and all the English virtues which the love of home engenders, lies the only true source of domestic felicity; let them believe that round the household gods contentment and tranquillity cluster in their gentlest and most graceful forms, and that many weary hunters of happiness through the noisy world have learnt this truth too late, and found a cheerful spirit and a quiet mind only at home at last.

How much may depend on the education of daughters and the conduct of mothers; how much of the brightest part of our old national character may be perpetuated by their wisdom or frittered away by their folly; how much of it may have been lost already, and how much more in danger of vanishing every day, are questions too weighty for discussion here, but well deserving a little serious consideration from all young couples, nevertheless.

To that one young couple on whose bright destiny the thoughts of nations are fixed may the youth of England look, and not in vain, for an example. From that one couple, blest and favoured as they are, may they learn that even the glare and glitter of a court, the splendour of a palace, and the pomp and glory of a throne, yield in their power of conferring happiness to domestic worth and virtue! From that one young couple may they learn that the crown of a great empire, costly and jewelled though it be, gives place in the estimation of a queen to the plain gold ring that links her woman's nature to that of tens of thousands of her humble subjects, and guards in her woman's heart one secret store of tenderness, whose proudest boast shall be that it knows no royalty save Nature's own, and no pride of birth but being the child of Heaven!

So shall the highest young couple in the land for once hear the truth, when men throw up their caps, and cry, with loving shouts, —

GOD BLESS THEM!

PREFACE TO "MEMOIRS OF JOSEPH GRIMALDI"

IT is some years now since we first conceived a strong vener-
ation for clowns, and an intense anxiety to know what they
did with themselves out of pantomime time, and off the stage.
As a child, we were accustomed to pester our relations and
friends with questions out of number concerning these gentry:
whether their appetite for sausages and such like wares was
always the same, and if so, at whose expense they were maintained; whether they were ever taken up for pilfering other
people's goods, or were forgiven by everybody because it was
only done in fun; how it was they got such beautiful complexions, and where they lived; and whether they were born
clowns, or gradually turned into clowns as they grew up.   On
these and a thousand other points our curiosity was insatiable.   Nor were our speculations confined to clowns alone;
they extended to Harlequins, Pantaloons, and Columbines, all
of whom we believed to be real and veritable personages, exist-
ing in the same forms and characters all the year round.   How
often have we wished that the Pantaloon were our godfather!
and how often thought that to marry a Columbine would be to
attain the highest pitch of all human felicity!
    The delights, the ten thousand million delights of a panto-
mime, come streaming upon us now, even of the pantomime
which came lumbering down in Richardson's wagons at fair-
time to the dull little town in which we had the honour to be
brought up, and which a long row of small boys, with frills as
white as they could be washed, and hands as clean as they
would come, were taken to behold the glories of, in fair daylight.
    We feel again all the pride of standing in a body or the
platform, the observed of all observers in the crowd below,
while the junior usher pays away twenty-four ninepences to a
stout gentleman under a Gothic arch, with a hoop of variegated
lamps swinging over his head.   Again we catch a glimpse (too
brief, alas!) of the lady with a green parasol in her hand, on

the outside stage of the next show but one, who supports herself on one foot, on the back of a majestic horse, blotting-paper
coloured and white; and once again our eyes open wide with
wonder, and our hearts throb with emotion, as we deliver our
cardboard check into the very hands of the Harlequin himself,
who, all glittering with spangles, and dazzling with many colours, deigns to give us a word of encouragement and commen-
dation as we pass into the booth!

But what was this, even this, to the glories of the inside,
where, amid the smell of sawdust and orange-peel, sweeter far
than violets to youthful noses, the first play being over, the
lovers united, the ghost appeased, the baron killed, and everything made comfortable and pleasant, the pantomime itself
began! What words can describe the deep gloom of the opening scene, where a crafty magician holding a young lady in
bondage was discovered, studying an enchanted book to the
soft music of a gong! or in what terms can we express the thrill
of ecstasy with which, his magic power opposed by superior
art, we beheld the monster himself converted into clown!
What mattered it that the stage was three yards wide, and four
deep? we never saw it. We had no eyes, ears, or corporeal
senses, but for the pantomime. And when its short career was
run, and the baron previously slaughtered, coming forward
with his hand upon his heart, announced that for that favour
Mr. Richardson returned his most sincere thanks, and the performances would commence again in a quarter of an hour, wha¹
jest could equal the effects of the baron's indignation and sur·
prise when the clown, unexpectedly peeping from behind the
curtain, requested the audience "not to believe it, for it was
all gammon!" Who but a clown could have called forth the
roar of laughter that succeeded; and what witchery but a
clown's could have caused the junior usher himself to declare
aloud, as he shook his sides and smote his knee in a moment of
irrepressible joy, that that was the very best thing he had ever
heard said!

We have lost that clown now; he is still alive, though, for
we saw him only the day before last Bartholomew Fair, eating
a real saveloy, and we are sorry to say he had deserted to the
illegitimate drama, for he was seated on one of "Clark's
Circus" wagons; we have lost that clown and that pantomime,
but our relish for the entertainment still remains unimpaired.

Each successive boxing-day finds us in the same state of high excitement and expectation. On that eventful day, when new pantomimes are played for the first time at the two great theatres, and at twenty or thirty of the little ones, we still gloat as formerly upon the bills which set forth tempting descriptions of the scenery in staring red and black letters, and still fall down upon our knees, with other men and boys, upon the pavement by shop-doors, to read them down to the very last line. Nay, we still peruse with all eagerness and avidity the exclusive accounts of the coming wonders in the theatrical newspapers of the Sunday before, and still believe them as devoutly as we did before twenty years' experience had shown us that they are always wrong.

With these feelings upon the subject of pantomimes, it is no matter of surprise that when we first heard that Grimaldi had left some memoirs of his life behind him, we were in a perfect fever until we had perused the manuscript. It was no sooner placed in our hands by "the adventurous and spirited publisher" (if our recollection serve us, this is the customary style of the complimentary little paragraphs regarding new books which usually precede advertisements about Savory's clocks in the newspapers) than we sat down at once and read it every word.

See how pleasantly things come about, if you let them take their own course! This mention of the manuscript brings us at once to the very point we are anxious to reach, and which we should have gained long ago, if we had not travelled into those irrelevant remarks concerning pantomimic representations.

For about a year before his death Grimaldi was employed in writing a full account of his life and adventures. It was his chief occupation and amusement; and as people who write their own lives, even in the midst of very many occupations, often find time to extend them to a most inordinate length, it is no wonder that his account of himself was exceedingly voluminous.

This manuscript was confided to Mr. Thomas Egerton Wilks, to alter and revise with a view to its publication. Mr. Wilks, who was well acquainted with Grimaldi and his connections, applied himself to the task of condensing it throughout, and wholly expunging considerable portions, which, so far as the public were concerned, possessed neither interest nor amusement. He likewise interspersed here and there the substance of such personal anecdotes as he had gleaned from the writer in desultory conversation. While he was thus engaged, Grimaldi died.

Mr. Wilks, having by the commencement of September concluded his labours, offered the manuscript to the present publisher, by whom it was shortly afterwards purchased unconditionally, with the full consent and concurrence of Mr. Richard Hughes, Grimaldi's executor.

The present editor of these Memoirs has felt it necessary to say thus much in explanation of their origin, in order to establish beyond doubt the unquestionable authenticity of the memoirs they contain.

His own share of them is stated in a few words. Being much struck by several incidents in the manuscript, — such as the description of Grimaldi's infancy, the burglary, the brother's return from sea under the extraordinary circumstances detailed, the adventure of the man with the two fingers on his left hand, the account of Mackintosh and his friends, and many other passages, — and thinking that they might be related in a more attractive manner (they were at that time told in the first person, as if by Grimaldi himself, although they had necessarily lost any original manner which his recital might have imparted to them), he accepted a proposal from the publisher to edit the book, and *has* edited it to the best of his ability, altering its form throughout, and making such other alterations as he conceived would improve the narration of the facts, without any departure from the facts themselves.

He has merely to add, that there has been no *book-making* in this case. He has not swelled the quantity of matter, but materially abridged it. The account of Grimaldi's first courtship may appear lengthy in its present form; but it has undergone a double and most comprehensive process of abridgment. The old man was garrulous upon a subject on which the youth had felt so keenly; and as the feeling did him honour in both stages of life, the editor has not had the heart to reduce it further.

Here is the book, then, at last. After so much pains from so many hands, including the good right hand of George Cruikshank, which has seldom been better exercised, he humbly hopes it may find favour with the public.

. DOUGHTY STREET, February, 1838.

THREATENING LETTER TO THOMAS HOOD

FROM AN ANCIENT GENTLEMAN

BY FAVOUR OF CHARLES DICKENS

MR. HOOD:

Sir, — The Constitution is going at last! You need n't laugh, Mr. Hood. I am aware that it has been going, two or three times before — perhaps four times; but it is on the move now, sir, and no mistake.

I beg to say, that I use those last expressions advisedly, sir, and not in the sense in which they are now used by jackanapeses. There were no jackanapeses when I was a boy, Mr. Hood. England was Old England when I was young. I little thought it would ever come to be Young England when I was old. But everything is going backward.

Ah! governments were governments, and judges were judges, in my day, Mr. Hood. There was no nonsense then. Any of your seditious complainings, and we were ready with the military on the shortest notice. We should have charged Covent Garden Theatre, sir, on a Wednesday night, at the point of the bayonet. Then, the judges were full of dignity and firmness, and knew how to administer the law. There is only one judge who knows how to do his duty now. He tried that revolutionary female the other day, who, though she was in full work (making shirts at three halfpence apiece), had no pride in her country, but treasonably took it in her head, in the distraction of having been robbed of her easy earnings, to attempt to drown herself and her young child; and the glorious man went out of his way, sir, — out of his way, — to call her up for instant sentence of Death; and to tell her she had no hope of mercy in this world — as you may see yourself if you look in the papers of Wednesday, the 17th of April. He won't be supported, sir, I know he won't; but it is worth remembering that his words were carried into every manufacturing town of this kingdom, and read aloud to crowds in every political parlour, beer-shop, news-room, and secret or open place of assembly, frequented by the discontented working men; and that no milk-and-water weakness on the part of the executive can ever blot them out. Great things like that are caught up, and stored up, in these times, and are not forgotten, Mr. Hood. The public at large (especially those who wish for peace and conciliation) are universally obliged to him. If it is reserved for any man to set the Thames on fire, it is reserved for him; and indeed I am told he very nearly did it, once.

But even he won't save the Constitution, sir; it is mauled beyond his power of preservation. Do you know in what foul weather it will be sacrificed and shipwrecked, Mr. Hood? Do you know on what rock it will strike, sir? You don't, I am certain; for nobody does know, as yet, but myself. I will tell you.

The Constitution will go down, sir (nautically speaking), in the degeneration of the human species in England, and its reduction into a mingled race of savages and pigmies.

That is my proposition. That is my prediction. That is the event of which I give you warning. I am now going to prove it, sir.

You are a literary man, Mr. Hood, and have written, I am told, some things worth reading. I say I am told, because I never read what is written in these days. You'll excuse me; but my principle is, that no man ought to know anything about his own time, except that it is the worst time that ever was, or is ever likely to be. That is the only way, sir, to be truly wise and happy.

In your station, as a literary man, Mr. Hood, you are frequently at the court of Her Gracious Majesty the Queen. God bless her! You have reason to know that the three great keys to the royal palace (after rank and politics) are Science, Literature, Art. I don't approve of this myself. I think it ungenteel and barbarous, and quite un-English; the custom having been a foreign one, ever since the reigns of the uncivilised sultans in the Arabian Nights, who always called the wise men of their time about them. But so it is. And when you don't dine at the royal table, there is always a knife and fork for you at the equerries' table; where, I understand, all gifted men are made particularly welcome.

But all men can't be gifted, Mr. Hood. Neither scientific, literary, nor artistical powers are any more to be inherited than the property arising from scientific, literary, or artistic productions, which the law, with a beautiful imitation of nature, declines to protect in the second generation. Very good, sir. Then, people are naturally very prone to cast about in their minds for other means of getting at court favour; and, watching the signs of the times, to hew out for themselves, or their descendants, the likeliest roads to that distinguished goal.

Mr. Hood, it is pretty clear, from recent records in the Court Circular, that if a father wish to train up his son in the way he should go, to go to court, and cannot indenture him to be a scientific man, an author, or an artist, three courses are open to him. He must endeavour by artificial means to make him a dwarf, a wild man, or a Boy-Jones.

Now, sir, this is the shoal and quicksand on which the Constitution will go to pieces.

I have made inquiry, Mr. Hood, and find that in my neighbourhood two families and a fraction out of every four, in the lower and middle classes of society, are studying and practising all conceivable arts to keep their infant children down. Understand me. I do not mean down in their numbers, or down in their precocity, but down in their growth, sir. A destructive and subduing drink, compounded of gin and milk in equal quantities, such as is given to puppies to retard their growth, — not something short, but something shortening, — is administered to these young creatures many times a day. An unnatural and artificial thirst is first awakened in these infants by meals of salt beef, bacon, anchovies, sardines, red herrings, shrimps, olives, pea-soup, and that description of diet; and when they screech for drink, in accents that might melt a heart of stone, which they do constantly (I allude to screeching, not to melting), this liquid is introduced into their too confiding stomachs. At such an early age, and to so great an extent, is this custom of provoking thirst, then quenching it with a stunting drink, observed, that brine-pap has already superseded the use of tops-and-bottoms; and wet-nurses, previously free from any kind of reproach, have been seen to stagger in the streets; owing, sir, to the quantity of gin introduced into their systems, with a view to its gradual and natural conversion into the fluid I have already mentioned.

Upon the best calculation I can make, this is going on, as I have said, in the proportion of about two families and a fraction in four. In one more family and a fraction out of the same number, efforts are being made to reduce the children to a state of nature; and to inculcate, at a tender age, the love of raw flesh, train-oil, new rum, and the acquisition of scalps. Wild and outlandish dances are also in vogue (you will have observed the prevailing rage for the polka); and savage cries and whoops are much indulged in (as you may discover, if you doubt it, in the House of Commons any night). Nay, some persons, Mr. Hood (and persons of some figure and distinction too), have already succeeded in breeding wild sons; who have been publicly shown in the courts of bankruptcy, and in police-offices, and in other commodious exhibition-rooms, with great effect, but who have not yet found favour at court, in consequence, as I infer, of the impression made by Mr. Rankin's wild men being too fresh and recent. To say nothing of Mr. Rankin's wild men being foreigners.

I need not refer you, sir, to the late instance of the Ojibbeway Bride. But I am credibly informed that she is on the eve of retiring into a savage fastness, where she may bring forth and educate a wild family who shall in course of time, by the dextrous use of the popularity they are certain to acquire at Windsor and St. James's, divide with dwarfs the principal offices of state, of patronage, and power, in the United Kingdom.

Consider the deplorable consequences, Mr. Hood, which must result from these proceedings, and the encouragement they receive from the highest quarters.

The dwarf being the favourite, sir, it is certain that the public mind will run in a great and eminent degree upon the production of dwarfs. Perhaps the failures only will be brought up, wild. The imagination goes a long way in these cases; and all that the imagination *can* do, will be done, and is doing. You may convince yourself of this, by observing the condition of those ladies who take particular notice of General Tom Thumb at the Egyptian Hall, during his hours of performance.

The rapid increase of dwarfs will be first felt in Her Majesty's recruiting department. The standard will, of necessity, be lowered; the dwarfs will grow smaller and smaller; the vulgar expression "a man of his inches" will become a figure of fact, instead of a figure of speech; crack regiments, household troops especially, will pick the smallest men from all parts of the country; and in the two little porticoes at the Horse Guards, two Tom Thumbs will be daily seen doing duty, mounted on a pair of Shetland ponies. Each of them will be relieved (as Tom Thumb is, at this moment, in the intervals of his performance), by a wild man; and a British grenadier will either go into a quart pot, or be an Old Boy, a Blue Gull, a Flying Bull, or some other savage chief of that nature.

I will not expatiate upon the number of dwarfs who will be found representing Grecian statues in all parts of the metropolis, because I am inclined to think that this will be a change for the better, and that the engagement of two or three in Trafalgar Square will tend to the improvement of the public taste.

The various genteel employments at court being held by dwarfs, sir, it will be necessary to alter, in some respects, the present regulations. It is quite clear that not even General Tom Thumb himself could preserve a becoming dignity on state occasions, if required to walk about with a scaffolding-pole under his arm; therefore the gold and silver sticks at present used must be cut down into skewers of those precious metals; a twig of the black rod will be quite as much as can be conveniently preserved; the coral and bells of his Royal Highness the Prince of Wales will be used in lieu of the mace at present in existence; and that bauble (as Oliver Cromwell called it, Mr. Hood), its value being first calculated by Mr. Finlayson, the government actuary, will be placed to the credit of the National Debt.

All this, sir, will be the death of the Constitution. But this is not all. The Constitution dies hard, perhaps; but there is enough disease impending, Mr. Hood, to kill it three times over.

Wild men will get into the House of Commons. Imagine that, sir! Imagine Strong Wind in the House of Commons! It is not an easy matter to get through a debate now; but, I say, imagine Strong Wind speaking for the benefit of his constituents, upon the floor of the House of Commons! or imagine (which is pregnant with more awful consequences still) the ministry having an interpreter in the House of Commons, to tell the country, in English, what it really means!

Why, sir, that in itself would be blowing the Constitution out of the mortar in St. James's Park, and leaving nothing of it to be seen but smoke.

But this, I repeat it, is the state of things to which we are fast tending, Mr. Hood; and I inclose my card for your private eye, that you may be quite certain of it. What the condition of this country will be, when its standing army is composed of dwarfs, with here and there a wild man to throw its ranks into confusion, like the elephants employed in war in former times, I leave you to imagine, sir. It may be objected by some hopeful jackanapeses that the number of impressments in the navy, consequent upon the seizure of the Boy-Joneses, or remaining portion of the population ambitious of court favour, will be in itself sufficient to defend our island from foreign invasion. But I tell those jackanapeses, sir, that, while I admit the wis-, dom of the Boy-Jones precedent, of kidnapping such youths after the expiration of their several terms of imprisonment as vagabonds, hurrying them on board ship, and packing them off to sea again whenever they venture to take the air on shore, I deny the justice of the inference, inasmuch as it appears to me that the inquiring minds of those young outlaws must naturally lead to their being hanged by the enemy as spies, early in their career; and before they shall have been rated on the books of our fleet as able seamen.

Such, Mr. Hood, sir, is the prospect before us! And unless you, and some of your friends who have influence at court, can get up a giant as a forlorn hope, it is all over with this ill-fated land.

In reference to your own affairs, sir, you will take whatever course may seem to you most prudent and advisable after this warning. It is not a warning to be slighted; that I happen to know. I am informed by the gentleman who favours this, that you have recently been making some changes and improvements in your Magazine, and are, in point of fact, starting afresh. If I be well informed, and this be really so, rely upon it that you cannot start too small, sir. Come down to the duodecimo size instantly, Mr. Hood. Take time by the forelock; and, reducing the stature of your Magazine every month, bring it at last to the dimensions of the little almanac no longer issued, I regret to say, by the ingenious Mr. Schloss; which was invisible to the naked eye until examined through a little eye-glass. You project, I am told, the publication of a new novel, by yourself, in the pages of your Magazine. A word in your ear. I am not a young man, sir, and have had some experience. Don't put your own name on the title-page; it would be suicide and madness. Treat with General Tom Thumb, Mr. Hood, for the use of his name on any terms. If the gallant general should decline to treat with you, get Mr. Barnum's name, which is the next best in the market. And when, through this politic course, you shall have received, in presents, a richly jewelled set of tablets from Buckingham Palace, and a gold watch and appendages from Marlborough House; and when those valuable trinkets shall be left under a glass case at your publisher's for inspection by your friends and the public in general, — then, sir, you will do me the justice of remembering this communication.

It is unnecessary for me to add, after what I have observed in the course of this letter, that I am not,

Sir,
Ever
Your
CONSTANT READER.

Tuesday, 23d April, 1844.

P. S. — Impress it upon your contributors that they cannot be too short; and that if not dwarfish, they must be wild — or at all events not tame.

PREFACE TO JOHN OVERS'S "EVENINGS OF A WORKING MAN"

THE indulgent reader of this little book — not called indulgent, I may hope, by courtesy alone, but with some reference also to its title and pretensions — may very naturally inquire how it comes to have a preface to which my name is attached; nor is the reader's right or inclination to be satisfied on this head likely to be much diminished, when I state, in the outset, that I do not recommend it as a book of surpassing originality or transcendent merit. That I do not claim to have discovered, in humble life, an extraordinary and brilliant genius. That I cannot charge mankind in general with having entered into a conspiracy to neglect the author of this volume, or to leave him pining in obscurity. That I have not the smallest intention of comparing him with Burns, the exciseman; or with Bloomfield, the shoemaker; or with Ebenezer Elliott, the worker in iron; or with James Hogg, the shepherd. That I see no reason to be hot, or bitter, or lowering, or sarcastic, or indignant, or fierce, or sour, or sharp, in his behalf. That I have nothing to rail at; nothing to exalt; nothing to flourish in the face of a stony-hearted world; and have but a very short and simple tale to tell.

But, such as it is, it has interested me; and I hope it may interest the reader too, if I state it unaffectedly and plainly.

JOHN OVERS, the writer of the following pages, is, as is set forth on the title-page, a working man. A man who earns his weekly wages (or who did when he was strong enough) by plying of the hammer, plane, and chisel. He became known to me, to the best of my recollection, nearly six years ago, when he sent me some songs, appropriate to the different months of the year, with a letter, stating under what circumstances they had been composed, and in what manner he was occupied from morning until night. I was, just then, relin-

quishing the conduct of a monthly periodical,[1] or I would
gladly have published them. As it was, I returned them to
him, with a private expression of the interest I felt in such
productions. They were afterwards accepted, with much readiness and consideration, by Mr. Tait, of Edinburgh; and were
printed in his Magazine.

Finding, after some further correspondence with my new
friend, that his authorship had not ceased with these verses,
but that he still occupied his leisure moments in writing, I
took occasion to remonstrate with him seriously against his
pursuing that course. I pointed out to him a few of the
uncertainties, anxieties, and difficulties of such a life, at the
best. I entreated him to remember the position of heavy disadvantage in which he stood, by reason of his self-education
and imperfect attainments; and I besought him to consider
whether, having one or two of his pieces accepted occasionally,
here and there, after long suspense and many refusals, it was
probable that he would find himself, in the end, a happier or
a more contented man. On all these grounds, I told him, his
persistence in his new calling made me uneasy; and I advised
him to abandon it, as strongly as I could.

In answer to this dissuasion of mine, he wrote me as manly
and straightforward, but withal as modest a letter, as ever I
read in my life. He explained to me how limited his ambition
was; soaring no higher than the establishment of his wife in
some light business and the better education of his children.
He set before me the difference between his evening and holiday studies, such as they were, and the having no better
resource than an alehouse or a skittle-ground. He told me
how every small addition to his stock of knowledge made his
Sunday walks the pleasanter; the hedge-flowers sweeter;
everything more full of interest and meaning to him. He
assured me that his daily work was not neglected for his self-
imposed pursuits, but was faithfully and honestly performed;
and so, indeed, it was. He hinted to me that his greater self-
respect was some inducement and reward, supposing every
other to elude his grasp; and showed me how the fancy that
he would turn this or that acquisition from his books to
account, by and by, in writing, made him more fresh and eager

[1] *Bentley's Miscellany.*

to peruse and profit by them when his long day's work was done.

I would not, if I could, have offered one solitary objection more to arguments so unpretending and so true.

From that time to the present, I have seen him frequently. It has been a pleasure to me to put a few books in his way; to give him a word or two of counsel in his little projects and difficulties; and to read his compositions with him, when he has had an hour, or so, to spare. I have never altered them, otherwise than by recommending condensation now and then; nor have I, in looking over these sheets, made any emendation in them beyond the ordinary corrections of the press; desiring them to be his genuine work, as they have been his sober and rational amusement.

The latter observation brings me to the origin of the present volume, and of this my slight share in it. The reader will soon comprehend why I touch the subject lightly, and with a sorrowful and faltering hand.

In all the knowledge I have had of John Overs, and in all the many conversations I have held with him, I have invariably found him, in every essential particular but one, the same. I have found him from first to last a simple, frugal, steady, upright, honourable man; especially to be noted for the unobtrusive independence of his character, the instinctive propriety of his manner, and the perfect neatness of his appearance. The extent of his information — regard being had to his opportunities of acquiring it — is very remarkable; and the discrimination with which he has risen superior to the mere prejudices of the class with which he is associated, without losing his sympathy for all their real wrongs and grievances, — they have a few, — impressed me, in the beginning of our acquaintance, strongly in his favour.

The one respect in which he is not what he was, is in his hold on life.

He is very ill; the faintest shadow of the man who came into my little study for the first time half a dozen years ago, after the correspondence I have mentioned. He has been very ill for a long, long period; his disease is a severe and wasting affection of the lungs, which has incapacitated him, these many months, for every kind of occupation. "If I could only do a hard day's work," he said to me the other day, "how happy I should be!"

Having these papers by him, amongst others, he bethought himself that if he could get a bookseller to purchase them for publication in a volume, they would enable him to make some temporary provision for his sick wife and very young family. We talked the matter over together; and that it might be easier of accomplishment, I promised him that I would write an introduction to his book.

I would to Heaven that I could do him better service! I would to Heaven it were an introduction to a long, and vigorous, and useful life! But Hope will not trim her lamp the less brightly for him and his, because of this impulse to their struggling fortunes; and trust me, reader, they deserve her light, and need it sorely.

He has inscribed this book to one [1] whose skill will help him, under Providence, in all that human skill can do. To one who never could have recognised in any potentate on earth a higher claim to constant kindness and attention than he has recognised in him.

I have little more to say of it. While I do not commend it, on the one hand, as a prodigy, I do sincerely believe it, on the other, to possess some points of real interest, however considered; but which, if considered with reference to its title and origin, are of great interest.

If any delicate readers should approach the perusal of these "Evenings of a Working Man" with a genteel distaste to the principle of a working man turning author at all, I may perhaps be permitted to suggest that the best protection against such an offence will be found in the Universal Education of the people; for the enlightenment of the many will effectually swamp any interest that may now attach in vulgar minds to the few among them who are enabled, in any degree, to overcome the great difficulties of their position.

And if such readers should deny the immense importance of communicating to this class, at this time, every possible means of knowledge, refinement, and recreation, or the cause we have to hail with delight the least token that may arise among them of a desire to be wiser, better, and more gentle, I earnestly entreat them to educate themselves in this neglected branch of

[1] Doctor Elliotson.

their own learning without delay; promising them that it is the easiest in its acquisition of any; requiring only open eyes and ears, and six easy lessons of an hour each in a working town. Which will render them perfect for the rest of their lives.

PUBLIC EXECUTIONS

TWO LETTERS TO THE EDITOR OF THE LONDON "TIMES"

I

DEVONSHIRE TERRACE, Tuesday, 13th November, 1849.

SIR, — I was a witness of the execution at Horsemonger Lane this morning. I went there with the intention of observing the crowd gathered to behold it, and I had excellent opportunities of doing so, at intervals all through the night, and continuously from daybreak until after the spectacle was over. I do not address you on the subject with any intention of discussing the abstract question of capital punishment, or any of the arguments of its opponents or advocates. I simply wish to turn this dreadful experience to some account for the general good, by taking the readiest and most public means of adverting to an intimation given by Sir G. Grey in the last session of Parliament, that the government might be induced to give its support to a measure making the infliction of capital punishment a private solemnity within the prison walls (with such guarantees for the last sentence of the law being inexorably and surely administered as should be satisfactory to the public at large), and of most earnestly beseeching Sir G. Grey, as a solemn duty which he owes to society, and a responsibility which he cannot for ever put away, to originate such a legislative change himself. I believe that a sight so inconceivably awful as the wickedness and levity of the immense crowd collected at that execution this morning could be imagined by no man, and could be presented in no heathen land under the sun. The horrors of the gibbet and of the crime which brought the wretched murderers to it faded in my mind before the atrocious bearing, looks, and language of the assembled spectators. When I came upon the scene at midnight, the *shrillness* of the cries and howls that were raised from time to time, denoting that they came from a concourse of boys and girls already assembled in the best places, made my blood run cold. As the night went on, screeching, and laughing, and yelling in strong chorus of parodies on negro melodies, with substitutions of "Mrs. Manning" for "Susannah," and the like, were added to these. When the day dawned, thieves, low prostitutes, ruffians, and vagabonds of every kind, flocked on to the ground, with every variety of offensive and foul behaviour. Fightings, faintings, whistlings, imitations of Punch, brutal jokes, tumultuous demonstrations of indecent delight when swooning women were dragged out of the crowd by the police, with their dresses disordered, gave a new zest to the general entertainment. When the sun rose brightly — as it did — it gilded thousands upon thousands of upturned faces, so inexpressibly odious in their brutal mirth or callousness, that a man had cause to feel ashamed of the shape he wore, and to shrink from himself, as fashioned in the image of the Devil. When the two miserable creatures who attracted all this ghastly sight about them were turned quivering into the air, there was no more emotion, no more pity, no more thought that two immortal souls had gone to judgment, no more restraint in any of the previous obscenities, than if the name of Christ had never been heard in this world, and there were no belief among men but that they perished like the beasts.

I have seen, habitually, some of the worst sources of general contamination and corruption in this country, and I think there are not many phases of London life that could surprise me. I am solemnly convinced that nothing that ingenuity could devise to be done in this city, in the same compass of time, could work such ruin as one public execution, and I stand astounded and appalled by the wickedness it exhibits. I do not believe that any community can prosper where such a scene of horror and demoralisation as was enacted this morning outside Horsemonger Lane Jail is presented at the very doors of good citizens, and is passed by unknown or forgotten. And when in our prayers and thanksgivings for the season we are humbly expressing before God our desire to remove the moral evils of the land, I would ask your readers to consider whether it is not a time to think of this one, and to root it out.

I am, sir, your faithful servant.

II

SIR, — When I wrote to you on Tuesday last I had no intention of troubling you again; but as one of your correspondents has to-day expressed a reasonable desire that I would explain myself more clearly, and as I hope I may do no injury to the cause I would serve by stating my views upon it a little more in detail, I shall be glad to do so if you will allow me the opportunity.

My positions in reference to the demoralising nature of public executions are: —

First, that they chiefly attract as spectators the lowest, the most depraved, the most abandoned of mankind, in whom they inspire no wholesome emotions whatever.

Second, that the public infliction of a violent death is not a salutary spectacle for any class of people; but that it is in the nature of things that on the class by whom it is generally witnessed it should have a debasing and hardening influence.

On the first head I must appeal again to my own experience of the execution of last Tuesday morning; to all the evidence that has ever been taken upon the subject, showing that executions have been the favourite sight of convicts of all descriptions; to the knowledge possessed by the magistracy and police of the general character of such crowds; to the police reports that are sure to follow their assemblage; to the unvarying description of them given in the newspapers; to the indisputable fact that no decent father is willing that his son, and no decent master is willing that his apprentices or servants, should mingle in them; to the indisputable fact that all society, its dregs excepted, recoil from them as masses of abomination and brutality. That there were not more robberies committed at this last execution was not the fault of the assembled thieves, whose numbers on the occasion the Home Secretary may easily learn from the commissioners in Scotland Yard, but the merit of the police, whose vigilance was beyond all praise.

On the second head, after a passing allusion to the hardening influence which familiarity, even with natural death, produces on coarse minds, I must again refer to my own experience. Nothing would have been a greater comfort to me, nothing would have so much relieved in my mind the unspeakable terrors of the scene, as to have been enabled to believe that any portion of the immense crowd — that any grains of sand in the vast moral desert stretching away on every side — were moved to any sentiments of fear, repentance, pity, or natural horror by what they saw upon the drop. It was impossible to look around and rest in any such belief. With every consideration and respect for your suggestion that the concourse may have been belying their mental struggles by frantic exaggerations, I am confident that if you had been there beside me, seeing what I saw, and hearing what I heard, you could never have admitted the thought. Such a state of mind has its signs and tokens equally with any other, and no such signs and tokens were there. The mirth was not hysterical, the shoutings and fightings were not the efforts of a strained excitement seeking to vent itself in any relief. The whole was unmistakably callous and bad, as the ferocious woman who was charged on the same day with threatening to murder another in the midst of the multitude, proclaiming that she had a knife about her, and would have her heart's blood, and be hanged on the same gibbet with her namesake, Mrs. Manning, whose death she had come to see — as she had her evil passions excited to the utmost by the scene, so had all the crowd. I believe this was the whole and sole effect of what they had come to see, and I hold that no human being, not being the better for such a sight, could go away without being the worse for it.

To prevent such frightful spectacles in a Christian country, and all the incalculable evils they engender, I would have the last sentence of the law executed with comparative privacy within the prison walls. Before I state how, let me strengthen this proposal with some words of Fielding on this subject, to whose profound knowledge of human nature you, I know, will render full justice: —

"The execution should be in some degree private. And here the poets will again assist us. Foreigners have found fault with the cruelty of the English drama, in representing frequent murders upon the stage. In fact, this is not only cruel, but highly injudicious; a murder behind the scenes, if the poet knows how to manage it, will affect the audience with greater terror than if it was acted before their eyes. Of this we have an instance in the murder of the king in " Macbeth." Terror hath, I believe, been carried higher by this single instance than by all the blood which hath been spilt upon the stage. To the poets I may add the priests, whose politics have never been doubted. Those of Egypt in particular, where the sacred mysteries were first devised, well knew the use of hiding from the eyes of the vulgar what they intended should inspire them with the greatest awe and dread. The mind of man is so much more capable of magnifying than his eye, that I question whether every object is not lessened by being looked upon; and this more especially when the passions are concerned; for those are ever apt to fancy much more satisfaction in those objects which they affect, and much more of mischief in those which they abhor, than are really to be found in either. If executions, therefore, were so contrived that few could be present at them, they would be much more shocking and terrible to the crowd without doors than at present, as well as much more dreadful to the criminals themselves."

From the moment of a murderer's being sentenced to death, I would dismiss him to the dread obscurity to which the wisest judge upon the bench consigned the murderer Rush. I would allow no curious visitors to hold any communication with him; I would place every obstacle in the way of his sayings and doings being served up in print on Sunday mornings for the perusal of families. His execution within the walls of the prison should be conducted with every terrible solemnity that careful consideration could devise. Mr. Calcraft, the hangman (of whom I have some information in reference to this last occasion), should be restrained in his unseemly briskness, in his jokes, his oaths, and his brandy. To attend the execution I would summon a jury of twenty-four, to be called the witness jury, eight to be summoned on a low qualification, eight on a higher, eight on a higher still! so that it might fairly represent all classes of society. There should be present, likewise, the governor of the jail, the chaplain, the surgeon, and other officers, the sheriff of the county or city, and two inspectors of prisons. All these should sign a grave and solemn form of certificate (the same in every case) that on such a day, at such an hour, in such a jail, for such a crime, such a murderer was hanged in their sight. There should be another certificate from the officers of the prison that the person hanged was that person, and no other; a third, that that person was buried. These should be posted on the prison gate for twenty-one days, printed in "The Gazette," and exhibited in other public places; and during the hour of the body's hanging I would have the bells of all the churches in that town or city tolled, and all the shops shut up, that all might be reminded of what was being done.

I submit to you that, with the law so changed, the public would (as is right) know much more of the infliction of this tremendous punishment than they know of the infliction of any other. There are not many common subjects, I think, of which they know less than transportation; and yet they never doubt that when a man is ordered to be sent abroad he goes abroad. The details of the commonest prison in London are unknown to the public at large, but they are quite satisfied that prisoners said to be in this or that jail are really there and really undergo its discipline. The "mystery" of private execution is objected to; but has not mystery been the character of every improvement in convict treatment and prison discipline effected within the last twenty years? From the police van to Norfolk Island, are not all the changes, changes that make the treatment of the prisoner mysterious? His seclusion in his conveyance hither and thither from the public sight, instead of his being walked through the streets, strung with twenty more to a chain, like the galley slaves in "Don Quixote" (as I remember to have seen in my school days), makes a mystery of him. His being known by a number instead of by a name, and his being under the rigorous discipline of the associated silent system, — to say nothing of the solitary, which I regard as a mistake, — is all mysterious. I cannot understand that the mystery of such an execution as I propose would be other than a fitting climax to all these wise regulations, or why, if there be anything in this objection, we should not return to the days when ladies paid visits to highwaymen, drinking their punch in the condemned cells of Newgate; or Ned Ward, the London spy, went upon a certain regular day of the week to Bridewell to see the women whipped.

Another class of objectors I know there are, who, desiring the total abolition of capital punishment, will have nothing less, and who, not doubting the fearful influence of public executions, would have it protracted for an indefinite term, rather than spare the demoralisation they do not dispute, at the risk of losing sight for a while of their final end.   But of these I say nothing, considering them, however good and pure in intention, unreasonable, and not to be argued with.

With many thanks to you for your courtesy, and begging most earnestly to assure you that I write in a deep conviction that I incurred a duty when I became a witness of the execution on Tuesday last, from which nothing ought to move me, and which every hour's reflection strengthens,

I am, sir, your faithful servant.

CONTRIBUTIONS TO "HOUSEHOLD WORDS"

I

THE BEGGING-LETTER WRITER

THE amount of money he annually diverts from wholesome and useful purposes in the United Kingdom would be a set-off against the Window Tax. He is one of the most shameless frauds and impositions of this time. In his idleness, his mendacity, and the immeasurable harm he does to the deserving, — dirtying the stream of true benevolence, and muddling the brains of foolish justices, with inability to distinguish between the base coin of distress and the true currency we have always among us, — he is more worthy of Norfolk Island than three fourths of the worst characters who are sent there. Under any rational system he would have been sent there long ago.

I, the writer of this paper, have been, for some time, a chosen receiver of Begging Letters. For fourteen years, my house has been made as regular a Receiving House for such communications as any one of the great branch Post-Offices is for general correspondence. I ought to know something of the Begging-Letter Writer. He has besieged my door, at all hours of the day and night; he has fought my servant; he has lain in ambush for me, going out and coming in; he has followed me out of town into the country; he has appeared at provincial hotels, where I have been staying for only a few hours; he has written to me from immense distances, when I have been out of England. He has fallen sick; he has died, and been buried; he has come to life again, and again departed from this transitory scene; he has been his own son, his own mother, his own baby, his idiot brother, his uncle, his aunt, his aged grandfather. He has wanted a great-coat, to go to India in; a pound to set him up in life for ever; a pair of boots, to take him to the coast of China; a hat, to get him into a permanent situation under Government. He has fre-

quently been exactly seven-and-sixpence short of independence.
He has had such openings at Liverpool — posts of great trust
and confidence in merchants' houses, which nothing but seven-
and-sixpence was wanting to him to secure — that I wonder he
is not Mayor of that flourishing town at the present moment.

The natural phenomena of which he has been the victim
are of a most astounding nature. He has had two children,
who have never grown up; who have never had anything to
cover them at night; who have been continually driving him
mad, by asking in vain for food; who have never come out of
fevers and measles (which, I suppose, has accounted for his
fuming his letters with tobacco smoke, as a disinfectant); who
have never changed in the least degree, through fourteen long
revolving years. As to his wife, what that suffering woman
has undergone, nobody knows. She has always been in an
interesting situation through the same long period, and has
never been confined yet. His devotion to her has been unceas-
ing. He has never cared for himself; *he* could have perished,
— he would rather, in short, — but was it not his Christian
duty as a man, a husband, and a father, to write begging letters when he looked at her? (He has usually remarked that
he would call in the evening for an answer to this question.)

He has been the sport of the strangest misfortunes. What
his brother has done to him would have broken anybody else's
heart. His brother went into business with him, and ran
away with the money; his brother got him to be security for
an immense sum, and left him to pay it; his brother would
have given him employment to the tune of hundreds a year, if
he would have consented to write letters on a Sunday; his
brother enunciated principles incompatible with his religious
views, and he could not (in consequence) permit his brother
to provide for him. His landlord has never shown a spark
of human feeling. When he put in that execution I don't
know, but he has never taken it out. The broker's man has
grown grey in possession. They will have to bury him some
day.

He has been attached to every conceivable pursuit. He has
been in the army, in the navy, in the church, in the law; connected with the press, the fine arts, public institutions, every
description and grade of business. He has been brought up
as a gentleman; he has been at every college in Oxford and

Cambridge; he can quote Latin in his letters (but generally misspells some minor English word); he can tell you what Shakespeare says about begging better than you know it. It is to be observed, that in the midst of his afflictions he always reads the newspapers, and rounds off his appeals with some allusion, that may be supposed to be in my way, to the popular subject of the hour.

His life presents a series of inconsistencies. Sometimes he has never written such a letter before. He blushes with shame. That is the first time; that shall be the last. Don't answer it, and let it be understood that, then, he will kill himself quietly. Sometimes (and more frequently) he *has* written a few such letters. Then he incloses the answers, with an intimation that they are of inestimable value to him, and a request that they may be carefully returned. He is fond of inclosing something — verses, letters, pawnbrokers' duplicates, anything to necessitate an answer. He is very severe upon "the pampered minion of fortune," who refused him the half-sovereign referred to in the inclosure number two — but he knows me better.

He writes in a variety of styles; sometimes in low spirits; sometimes quite jocosely. When he is in low spirits, he writes down hill, and repeats words — these little indications being expressive of the perturbation of his mind. When he is more vivacious, he is frank with me; he is quite the agreeable rattle. I know what human nature is, — who better? Well! He had a little money once, and he ran through it — as many men have done before him. He finds his old friends turn away from him now — many men have done that before him, too! Shall he tell me why he writes to me? Because he has no kind of claim upon me. He puts it on that ground, plainly; and begs to ask for the loan (as I know human nature) of two sovereigns, to be repaid next Tuesday six weeks, before twelve at noon.

Sometimes, when he is sure that I have found him out, and that there is no chance of money, he writes to inform me that I have got rid of him at last. He has enlisted into the Company's service, and is off directly — but he wants a cheese. He is informed by the sergeant that it is essential to his prospects in the regiment that he should take out a single-Gloucester cheese, weighing from twelve to fifteen pounds. Eight or nine shillings would buy it. He does not ask for money, after what has passed; but if he calls at nine to-morrow morning, may he hope to find a cheese? And is there anything he can do to show his gratitude in Bengal?

Once, he wrote me rather a special letter proposing relief in kind. He had got into a little trouble by leaving parcels of mud done up in brown paper, at people's houses, on pretence of being a Railway Porter, in which character he received carriage money. This sportive fancy he expiated in the House of Correction. Not long after his release, and on a Sunday morning, he called with a letter (having first dusted himself all over), in which he gave me to understand that, being resolved to earn an honest livelihood, he had been travelling about the country with a cart of crockery. That he had been doing pretty well, until the day before, when his horse had dropped down dead near Chatham, in Kent. That this had reduced him to the unpleasant necessity of getting into the shafts himself, and drawing the cart of crockery to London — a somewhat exhausting pull of thirty miles. That he did not venture to ask again for money; but that if I would have the goodness *to leave him out a donkey*, he would call for the animal before breakfast!

At another time, my friend (I am describing actual experiences) introduced himself as a literary gentleman in the last extremity of distress. He had had a play accepted at a certain Theatre — which was really open; its representation was delayed by the indisposition of a leading actor — who was really ill; and he and his were in a state of absolute starvation. If he made his necessities known to the Manager of the Theatre, he put it to me to say what kind of treatment he might expect? Well! we got over that difficulty to our mutual satisfaction. A little while afterwards he was in some other strait, — I think Mrs. Southcote, his wife, was in extremity, — and we adjusted that point too. A little while afterwards, he had taken a new house, and was going headlong to ruin for want of a water-butt. I had my misgivings about the water-butt, and did not reply to that epistle. But a little while afterwards, I had reason to feel penitent for my neglect. He wrote me a few broken-hearted lines, informing me that the dear partner of his sorrows died in his arms last night at nine o'clock!

I despatched a trusty messenger to comfort the bereaved mourner and his poor children; but the messenger went so soon that the play was not ready to be played out; my friend was not at home, and his wife was in a most delightful state of health. He was taken up by the Mendicity Society (informally it afterwards appeared), and I presented myself at a London Police-Office with my testimony against him. The Magistrate was wonderfully struck by his educational acquirements, deeply impressed by the excellence of his letters, exceedingly sorry to see a man of his attainments there, complimented him highly on his powers of composition, and was quite charmed to have the agreeable duty of discharging him. A collection was made for the "poor fellow," as he was called in the reports, and I left the court with a comfortable sense of being universally regarded as a sort of monster. Next day, comes to me a friend of mine, the governor of a large prison. "Why did you ever go to the Police-Office against that man," says he, "without coming to me first? I know all about him and his frauds. He lodged in the house of one of my warders, at the very time when he first wrote to you; and then he was eating spring-lamb at eighteenpence a pound, and early asparagus at I don't know how much a bundle!" On that very same day, and in that very same hour, my injured gentleman wrote a solemn address to me, demanding to know what compensation I proposed to make him for his having passed the night "in a loathsome dungeon." And next morning, an Irish gentleman, a member of the same fraternity, who had read the case, and was very well persuaded I should be chary of going to that Police-Office again, positively refused to leave my door for less than a sovereign, and, resolved to besiege me into compliance, literally "sat down" before it for ten mortal hours. The garrison being well provisioned, I remained within the walls; and he raised the siege at midnight, with a prodigious alarum on the bell.

The Begging-Letter Writer often has an extensive circle of acquaintance. Whole pages of the Court Guide are ready to be references for him. Noblemen and gentlemen write to say there never was such a man for probity and virtue. They have known him time out of mind, and there is nothing they would n't do for him. Somehow, they don't give him that one pound ten he stands in need of; but perhaps it is not enough — they want to do more, and his modesty will not allow it. It is to be remarked of his trade that it is a very fascinating one. He never leaves it; and those who are near to him become smitten with a love of it, too, and sooner or later set up for themselves. He employs a messenger — man, woman, or child. That messenger is certain ultimately to become an independent Begging-Letter Writer. His sons and daughters succeed to his calling, and write begging-letters when he is no more. He throws off the infection of begging-letter writing, like the contagion of disease. What Sydney Smith so happily called "the dangerous luxury of dishonesty" is more tempting, and more catching, it would seem, in this instance than in any other.

He always belongs to a Corresponding Society of Begging-Letter Writers. Any one who will may ascertain this fact. Give money to-day, in recognition of a begging-letter, — no matter how unlike a common begging-letter, — and for the next fortnight you will have a rush of such communications. Steadily refuse to give, and the begging-letters become Angels' visits, until the Society is from some cause or other in a dull way of business, and may as well try you as anybody else. It is of little use inquiring into the Begging-Letter Writer's circumstances. He may be sometimes accidentally found out, as in the case already mentioned (though that was not the first inquiry made); but apparent misery is always a part of his trade, and real misery very often is, in the intervals of spring-lamb and early asparagus. It is naturally an incident of his dissipated and dishonest life.

That the calling is a successful one, and that large sums of money are gained by it, must be evident to anybody who reads the Police Reports of such cases. But prosecutions are of rare occurrence, relatively to the extent to which the trade is carried on. The cause of this is to be found (as no one knows better than the Begging-Letter Writer, for it is a part of his speculation) in the aversion people feel to exhibit themselves as having been imposed upon, or as having weakly gratified their consciences with a lazy, flimsy substitute for the noblest of all virtues. There is a man at large, at the moment when this paper is preparing for the press (on the 29th of April, 1850), and never once taken up yet, who, within these twelve-months, has been probably the most audacious and the most successful swindler that even this trade has ever known. There has been something singularly base in this fellow's proceedings; it has been his business to write to all sorts and conditions of people, in the names of persons of high reputation and unblemished honour, professing to be in distress — the general admiration and respect for whom has insured a ready and generous reply.

Now, in the hope that the results of the real experience of a real person may do something more to induce reflection on this subject than any abstract treatise — and with a personal knowledge of the extent to which the Begging-Letter Trade has been carried on for some time, and has been for some time constantly increasing — the writer of this paper entreats the attention of his readers to a few concluding words. His experience is a type of the experience of many; some on a smaller, some on an infinitely larger scale. All may judge of the soundness or unsoundness of his conclusions from it.

Long doubtful of the efficacy of such assistance in any case whatever, and able to recall but one, within his whole individual knowledge, in which he had the least after-reason to suppose that any good was done by it, he was led, last autumn, into some serious considerations. The begging-letters flying about by every post made it perfectly manifest, That a set of lazy vagabonds were interposed between the general desire to do something to relieve the sickness and misery under which the poor were suffering, and the suffering poor themselves. That many who sought to do some little to repair the social wrongs, inflicted in the way of preventible sickness and death upon the poor, were strengthening those wrongs, however innocently, by wasting money on pestilent knaves cumbering society. That imagination — soberly following one of these knaves into his life of punishment in jail, and comparing it with the life of one of these poor in a cholera-stricken alley, or one of the children of one of these poor, soothed in its dying hour by the late lamented Mr. Drouet — contemplated a grim farce, impossible to be presented very much longer before God or man. That the crowning miracle of all the miracles summed up in the New Testament, after the miracle of the blind seeing, and the lame walking, and the restoration of the dead to life, was the miracle that the poor had the gospel preached to them. That while the poor were unnaturally and unnecessarily cut off by the thousand, in the prematurity of their age, or in the rottenness of their youth, — for of flower or blossom such youth has none, — the gospel was NOT preached to them, saving in hollow and unmeaning voices. That of all wrongs, this was the first mighty wrong the Pestilence warned us to set right. And that no Post-Office Order to any amount, given to a Begging-Letter Writer for the quieting of an uneasy breast, would be presentable on the Last Great Day as anything towards it.

The poor never write these letters. Nothing could be more unlike their habits. The writers are public robbers; and we who support them are parties to their depredations. They trade upon every circumstance within their knowledge that affects us, public or private, joyful or sorrowful; they pervert the lessons of our lives; they change what ought to be our strength and virtue into weakness and encouragement of vice. There is a plain remedy, and it is in our own hands. We must resolve, at any sacrifice of feeling, to be deaf to such appeals, and crush the trade.

There are degrees in murder. Life must be held sacred among us in more ways than one — sacred, not merely from the murderous weapon, or the subtle poison, or the cruel blow, but sacred from preventible diseases, distortions, and pains. That is the first great end we have to set against this miserable imposition. Physical life respected, moral life comes next. What will not content a Begging-Letter Writer for a week would educate a score of children for a year. Let us give all we can; let us give more than ever. Let us do all we can; let us do more than ever. But let us give, and do, with a high purpose; not to endow the scum of the earth, to its own greater corruption, with the offals of our duty.

II

A WALK IN A WORKHOUSE

ON a certain Sunday, I formed one of the congregation assembled in the chapel of a large metropolitan workhouse. With the exception of the clergyman and clerk, and a very few officials, there were none but paupers present. The children sat in the galleries; the women in the body of the chapel, and in one of the side aisles; the men in the remaining aisle. The service was decorously performed, though the sermon might have been much better adapted to the comprehension and to the circumstances of the hearers. The usual supplications were offered, with more than the usual significancy in such a place, for the fatherless children and widows, for all sick persons and young children, for all that were desolate and oppressed, for the comforting and helping of the weak-hearted, for the raising-up of them that had fallen; for all that were in danger, necessity, and tribulation. The prayers of the congregation were desired "for several persons in the various wards dangerously ill;" and others who were recovering returned their thanks to Heaven.

Among this congregation were some evil-looking young women, and beetle-browed young men; but not many — perhaps that kind of characters kept away. Generally, the faces (those of the children excepted) were depressed and subdued, and wanted colour. Aged people were there, in every variety. Mumbling, blear-eyed, spectacled, stupid, deaf, lame; vacantly winking in the gleams of sun that now and then crept in through the open doors, from the paved yard; shading their listening ears or blinking eyes with their withered hands; poring over their books, leering at nothing, going to sleep, crouching and drooping in corners. There were weird old women, all skeleton within, all bonnet and cloak without, continually wiping their eyes with dirty dusters of pocket-handkerchiefs; and there were ugly old crones, both male and female, with a ghastly kind of contentment upon them which was not at all comforting to see. Upon the whole, it was the dragon, Pauperism, in a very weak and impotent condition; toothless, fangless, drawing his breath heavily enough, and hardly worth chaining up.

When the service was over, I walked with the humane and conscientious gentleman whose duty it was to take that walk, that Sunday morning, through the little world of poverty inclosed within the workhouse walls. It was inhabited by a population of some fifteen hundred or two thousand paupers, ranging from the infant newly born or not yet come into the pauper world to the old man dying on his bed.

In a room opening from a squalid yard, where a number of listless women were lounging to and fro, trying to get warm in the ineffectual sunshine of the tardy May morning, — in the "itch-ward," not to compromise the truth, — a woman, such as Hogarth has often drawn, was hurriedly getting on her gown before a dusty fire. She was the nurse, or wardswoman, of that insalubrious department — herself a pauper — flabby, raw-boned, untidy — unpromising and coarse of aspect as need be. But on being spoken to about the patients whom she had in charge, she turned round, with her shabby gown half on, half off, and fell a crying with all her might. Not for show, not querulously, not in any mawkish sentiment, but in the deep grief and affliction of her heart; turning away her dishevelled head; sobbing most bitterly, wringing her hands, and letting fall abundance of great tears, that choked her utterance. What was the matter with the nurse of the itch-ward? Oh, "the dropped child" was dead! Oh, the child that was found in the street, and she had brought up ever since, had died an hour ago, and see where the little creature lay, beneath this cloth! The dear, the pretty dear!

The dropped child seemed too small and poor a thing for Death to be in earnest with, but Death had taken it; and already its diminutive form was neatly washed, composed, and stretched as if in sleep upon a box. I thought I heard a voice from Heaven saying, It shall be well for thee, O nurse of the itch-ward, when some less gentle pauper does those offices to thy cold form, that such as the dropped child are the angels who behold my Father's face!

In another room were several ugly old women crouching, witch-like, round a hearth, and chattering and nodding, after the manner of the monkeys. "All well here? And enough to eat?" A general chattering and chuckling; at last an answer from a volunteer. "Oh, yes, gentleman! Bless you gentleman! Lord bless the parish of St. So-and-So! It feed

the hungry, sir, and give drink to the thusty, and it warm them which is cold, so it do, and good luck to the parish of St. So-and-So, and thankee gentleman!" Elsewhere, a party of pauper nurses were at dinner. "How do *you* get on?" "Oh, pretty well, sir! We works hard, and we lives hard — like the sodgers!"

In another room, a kind of purgatory or place of transition, six or eight noisy madwomen were gathered together, under the superintendence of one sane attendant. Among them was a girl of two or three and twenty, very prettily dressed, of most respectable appearance, and good manners, who had been brought in from the house where she had lived as domestic servant (having, I suppose, no friends), on account of being subject to epileptic fits, and requiring to be removed under the influence of a very bad one. She was by no means of the same stuff, or the same breeding, or the same experience, or in the same state of mind, as those by whom she was surrounded; and she pathetically complained that the daily association and the nightly noise made her worse, and was driving her mad — which was perfectly evident. The case was noted for inquiry and redress, but she said she had already been there for some weeks.

If this girl had stolen her mistress's watch, I do not hesitate to say she would have been infinitely better off. We have come to this absurd, this dangerous, this monstrous pass, that the dishonest felon is, in respect of cleanliness, order, diet, and accommodation, better provided for, and taken care of, than the honest pauper.

And this conveys no special imputation on the workhouse of the parish of St. So-and-So, where, on the contrary, I saw many things to commend. It was very agreeable, recollecting that most infamous and atrocious enormity committed at Tooting, — an enormity which, a hundred years hence, will still be vividly remembered in the byways of English life, and which has done more to engender a gloomy discontent and suspicion among many thousands of the people than all the Chartist leaders could have done in all their lives, — to find the pauper children in this workhouse looking robust and well, and apparently the objects of very great care. In the Infant School — a large, light, airy room at the top of the building — the little creatures, being at dinner, and eating their potatoes heartily, were not cowed by the presence of strange visitors, but stretched out their small hands to be shaken, with a very pleasant confidence. And it was comfortable to see two mangy pauper rocking-horses rampant in a corner. In the girls' school, where the dinner was also in progress, everything bore a cheerful and healthy aspect. The meal was over, in the boys' school, by the time of our arrival there, and the room was not yet quite rearranged; but the boys were roaming unrestrained about a large and airy yard, as any other school-boys might have done. Some of them had been drawing large ships upon the schoolroom wall; and if they had a mast with shrouds and stays set up for practice (as they have in the Middlesex House of Correction), it would be so much the better. At present, if a boy should feel a strong impulse upon him to learn the art of going aloft, he could only gratify it, I presume, as the men and women paupers gratify their aspirations after better board and lodging, by smashing as many workhouse windows as possible, and being promoted to prison.

In one place, the Newgate of the Workhouse, a company of boys and youths were locked up in a yard alone; their day-room being a kind of kennel where the casual poor used for-merly to be littered down at night. Divers of them had been there some long time. "Are they never going away?" was the natural inquiry. "Most of them are crippled, in some form or other," said the wardsman, "and not fit for any-thing." They slunk about, like dispirited wolves or hyenas; and made a pounce at their food when it was served out, much as those animals do. The big-headed idiot shuffling his feet along the pavement, in the sunlight outside, was a more agree-able object every way.

Groves of babies in arms; groves of mothers and other sick women in bed; groves of lunatics; jungles of men in stone-paved down-stairs day-rooms, waiting for their dinners; longer and longer groves of old people, in up-stairs infirmary wards, wearing out life, God knows how — this was the scenery through which the walk lay, for two hours. In some of these latter chambers there were pictures stuck against the wall, and a neat display of crockery and pewter on a kind of sideboard; now and then it was a treat to see a plant or two; in almost every ward there was a cat.

In all of these Long Walks of aged and infirm, some old
people were bedridden, and had been for a long time; some
were sitting on their beds half naked; some dying in their
beds; some out of bed, and sitting at a table near the fire. A
sullen or lethargic indifference to what was asked, a blunted
sensibility to everything but warmth and food, a moody absence
of complaint as being of no use, a dogged silence and resentful
desire to be left alone again, I thought were generally apparent. On our walking into the midst of one of these dreary
perspectives of old men, nearly the following little dialogue
took place, the nurse not being immediately at hand: —
"All well here ?"
‘ No answer. An old man in a Scotch cap sitting among
others on a form at the table, eating out of a tin porringer,
pushes back his cap a little to look at us, claps it down on his
forehead again with the palm of his hand, and goes on eating.
"All well here ?" (repeated.)
No answer. Another old man sitting on his bed, paralyti-
cally peeling a boiled potato, lifts his head and stares.
"Enough to eat ?"
No answer. Another old man, in bed, turns himself and
coughs.
"How are *you* to-day ?" To the last old man.
That old man says nothing; but another old man, a tall old
man of very good address, speaking with perfect correctness,
comes forward from somewhere, and volunteers an answer.
The reply almost always proceeds from a volunteer, and not
from the person looked at or spoken to.
"We are very old, sir," in a mild, distinct voice. "We
can't expect to be well, most of us."
"Are you comfortable ?"
"I have no complaint to make, sir." With a half shake of
his head, a half shrug of his shoulders, and a kind of apologetic
smile.
"Enough to eat ?"
"Why, sir, I have but a poor appetite," with the same air
as before; "and yet I get through my allowance very easily."
"But," showing a porringer with a Sunday dinner in it,
"here is a portion of mutton and three potatoes. You can't
starve on that ?"
"Oh, dear, no, sir," with the same apologetic air. "Not
starve."

"What do you want?"

"We have very little bread, sir. It's an exceedingly small quantity of bread."

The nurse, who is now rubbing her hands at the questioner's elbow, interferes with, "It ain't much raly, sir. You see they've only six ounces a day, and when they've took their breakfast, there *can* only be a little left for night, sir."

Another old man, hitherto invisible, rises out of his bed-clothes, as out of a grave, and looks on.

"You have tea at night?" The questioner is still addressing the well-spoken old man.

"Yes, sir, we have tea at night."

"And you save what bread you can from the morning, to eat with it?"

"Yes, sir — if we can save any."

"And you want more to eat with it?"

"Yes, sir." With a very anxious face.

The questioner, in the kindness of his heart, appears a little discomposed, and changes the subject.

"What has become of the old man who used to lie in that bed in the corner?"

The nurse don't remember what old man is referred to. There has been such a many old men. The well-spoken old man is doubtful. The spectral old man who has come to life in bed says, "Billy Stevens." Another old man who has previously had his head in the fireplace pipes out: —

"Charley Walters."

Something like a feeble interest is awakened. I suppose Charley Walters had conversation in him.

"He's dead," says the piping old man.

Another old man, with one eye screwed up, hastily displaces the piping old man, and says: —

"Yes! Charley Walters died in that bed, and — and — "

"Billy Stevens," persists the spectral old man.

"No, no! and Johnny Rogers died in that bed, and — and — they're both on 'em dead — and Sam'l Bowyer" (this seems very extraordinary to him), "he went out!"

With this he subsides, and all the old men (having had quite enough of it) subside, and the spectral old man goes into his grave again, and takes the shade of Billy Stevens with him.

As we turn to go out at the door, another previously invisible old man, a hoarse old man in a flannel gown, is standing there, as if he had just come up through the floor.

"I beg your pardon, sir, could I take the liberty of saying a word?"

"Yes; what is it?"

"I am greatly better in my health, sir; but what I want, to get me quite round," with his hand on his throat, "is a little fresh air, sir. It has always done my complaint so much good, sir. The regular leave for going out comes round so seldom, that if the gentlemen, next Friday, would give me leave to go out walking, now and then — for only an hour or so, sir — "

Who could wonder, looking through those weary vistas of bed and infirmity, that it should do him good to meet with some other scenes, and assure himself that there was something else on earth? Who could help wondering why the old men lived on as they did; what grasp they had on life; what crumbs of interest or occupation they could pick up from its bare board; whether Charley Walters had ever described to them the days when he kept company with some old pauper woman in the bud, or Billy Stevens ever told them of the time when he was a dweller in the far-off foreign land called Home!

The morsel of burnt child, lying in another room, so patiently, in bed, wrapped in lint, and looking steadfastly at us with his bright quiet eyes when we spoke to him kindly, looked as if the knowledge of these things, and of all the tender things there are to think about, might have been in his mind — as if he thought, with us, that there was a fellow-feeling in the pauper nurses which appeared to make them more kind to their charges than the race of common nurses in the hospitals — as if he mused upon the Future of some older children lying around him in the same place, and thought it best, perhaps, all things considered, that he should die — as if he knew, without fear, of those many coffins, made and unmade, piled up in the store below, and of his unknown friend, "the dropped child," calm upon the box-lid covered with a cloth. But there was something wistful and appealing, too, in his tiny face, as if, in the midst of all the hard necessities and incongruities he pondered on, he pleaded, in behalf of the helpless and the aged poor, for a little more liberty — and a little more bread.

III

A MONUMENT OF FRENCH FOLLY

It was profoundly observed by a witty member of the Court of Common Council, in Council assembled in the City of London, in the year of our Lord one thousand eight hundred and fifty, that the French are a frog-eating people, who wear wooden shoes.

We are credibly informed, in reference to the nation whom this choice spirit so happily disposed of, that the caricatures and stage representations which were current in England some half a century ago exactly depict their present condition. For example, we understand that every Frenchman, without exception, wears a pigtail and curl-papers; that he is extremely sallow, thin, long-faced, and lantern-jawed; that the calves of his legs are invariably undeveloped; that his legs fail at the knees, and that his shoulders are always higher than his ears. We are likewise assured that he rarely tastes any food but soup maigre, and an onion; that he always says, "By Gar! Aha! Vat you tell me, Sare?" at the end of every sentence he utters; and that the true generic name of his race is the Mounseers, or the Parly-voos. If he be not a dancing-master, or a barber, he must be a cook; since no other trades but those three are congenial to the tastes of the people, or permitted by the Institutions of the country. He is a slave, of course. The ladies of France (who are also slaves) invariably have their heads tied up in Belcher handkerchiefs, wear long earrings, carry tambourines, and beguile the weariness of their yoke by singing in head voices through their noses — principally to barrel-organs.

It may be generally summed up, of this inferior people, that they have no idea of anything.

Of a great Institution like Smithfield, they are unable to form the least conception. A Beast Market in the heart of Paris would be regarded an impossible nuisance. Nor have they any notion of slaughter-houses in the midst of a city. One of these benighted frog-eaters would scarcely understand your meaning, if you told him of the existence of such a British bulwark.

It is agreeable, and perhaps pardonable, to indulge in a little self-complacency when our right to it is thoroughly established.   At the present time, to be rendered memorable by a final attack on that good old market which is the (rotten) apple of the Corporation's eye, let us compare ourselves, to our national delight and pride as to these two subjects of slaughter-house and beast-market, with the outlandish foreigner.

The blessings of Smithfield are too well understood to need recapitulation; all who run (away from mad bulls and pursuing oxen) may read.   Any market-day they may be beheld in glorious action.   Possibly the merits of our slaughter-houses are not yet quite so generally appreciated.

Slaughter-houses, in the large towns of England, are always (with the exception of one or two enterprising towns) most numerous in the most densely crowded places, where there is the least circulation of air.   They are often underground, in cellars; they are sometimes in close back yards; sometimes (as in Spitalfields) in the very shops where the meat is sold. Occasionally, under good private management, they are ventilated and clean.   For the most part, they are unventilated and dirty; and to the reeking walls, putrid fat and other offensive animal matter cling with a tenacious hold.   The busiest slaughter-houses in London are in the neighbourhood of Smithfield, in Newgate Market, in Whitechapel, in Newport Market, in Leadenhall Market, in Clare Market.   All these places are surrounded by houses of a poor description, swarming with inhabitants.   Some of them are close to the worst burial-grounds in London.   When the slaughter-house is below the ground, it is a common practice to throw the sheep down areas, neck and crop — which is exciting, but not at all cruel.   When it is on the level surface, it is often extremely difficult of approach.   Then, the beasts have to be worried, and goaded, and pronged, and tail-twisted, for a long time before they can be got in — which is entirely owing to their natural obstinacy. When it is not difficult of approach, but is in a foul condition, what they see and scent makes them still more reluctant to enter — which is their natural obstinacy again.   When they do get in at last, after no trouble and suffering to speak of (for there is nothing in the previous journey into the heart of London, the night's endurance in Smithfield, the struggle out again, among the crowded multitude, the coaches, carts, wagons, omnibuses, gigs, chaises, phaetons, cabs, trucks, dogs, boys, whoopings, roarings, and ten thousand other distractions), they are represented to be in a most unfit state to be killed, according to microscopic examinations made of their fevered blood by one of the most distinguished physiologists in the world, Professor Owen — but that's humbug. When they *are* killed, at last, their reeking carcasses are hung in impure air, to become, as the same professor will explain to you, less nutritious and more unwholesome — but he is only an *un*common counsellor, so don't mind *him*. In half a quarter of a mile's length of Whitechapel, at one time, there shall be six hundred newly slaughtered oxen hanging up, and seven hundred sheep — but the more the merrier — proof of prosperity. Hard by Snow Hill and Warwick Lane, you shall see the little children, inured to sights of brutality from their birth, trotting along the alleys, mingled with troops of horribly busy pigs, up to their ankles in blood — but it makes the young rascals hardy. Into the imperfect sewers of this overgrown city, you shall have the immense mass of corruption, engendered by these practices, lazily thrown out of sight, to rise, in poisonous gases, into your house at night, when your sleeping children will most readily absorb them, and to find its languid way, at last, into the river that you drink — but the French are a frog-eating people who wear wooden shoes, and it's O the roast beef of England, my boy, the jolly old English roast beef.

It is quite a mistake — a new-fangled notion altogether — to suppose that there is any natural antagonism between putrefaction and health. They know better than that, in the Common Council. You may talk about Nature, in her wisdom, always warning man through his sense of smell, when he draws near to something dangerous; but that won't go down in the city. Nature very often don't mean anything. Mrs. Quickly says that prunes are ill for a green wound; but whosoever says that putrid animal substances are ill for a green wound, or for robust vigour, or for anything or for anybody, is a humanity-monger and a humbug. Britons never, never, never, etc., therefore. And prosperity to cattle-driving, cattle-slaughtering, bone-crushing, blood-boiling, trotter-scraping, tripe-dressing, paunch-cleaning, gut-spinning, hide-preparing, tallow-melting, and other salubrious proceedings, in the midst of hospitals, churchyards, workhouses, schools, infirmaries, refuges, dwellings, provision-shops, nurseries, sick-beds, every stage and baiting-place in the journey from birth to death!

These *un*common counsellors, your Professor Owens and fellows, will contend that to tolerate these things in a civilised city is to reduce it to a worse condition than Bruce found to prevail in Abyssinia. For there (say they) the jackals and wild dogs came at night to devour the offal; whereas here there are no such natural scavengers, and quite as savage customs. Further, they will demonstrate that nothing in nature is intended to be wasted, and that, besides the waste which such abuses occasion in the articles of health and life, — main sources of the riches of any community, — they lead to a prodigious waste of changing matters, which might, with proper preparation, and under scientific direction, be safely applied to the increase of the fertility of the land. Thus (they argue) does Nature ever avenge infractions of her beneficent laws, and so surely as Man is determined to warp any of her blessings into curses shall they become curses, and shall he suffer heavily. But this is cant. Just as it is cant of the worst description to say to the London Corporation, "How can you exhibit to the people so plain a spectacle of dishonest equivocation, as to claim the right of holding a market in the midst of the great city, for one of your vested privileges, when you know that when your last market-holding charter was granted to you by King Charles the First, Smithfield stood in the Suburbs of London, and is in that very charter so described in those five words?" — which is certainly true, but has nothing to do with the question.

Now to the comparison, in these particulars of civilisation, between the capital of England and the capital of that frogeating and wooden-shoe wearing country, which the illustrious Common Councilman so sarcastically settled.

In Paris there is no Cattle Market. Cows and calves are sold within the city, but the Cattle Markets are at Poissy, about thirteen miles off, on a line of railway; and at Sceaux, about five miles off. The Poissy market is held every Thursday; the Sceaux market, every Monday. In Paris there are no slaughter-houses, in our acceptation of the term. There **are** five public Abattoirs, — within the walls, though in the suburbs, — and in these all the slaughtering for the city must be performed. They are managed by a Syndicat or Guild of Butchers, who confer with the Minister of the Interior on all matters affecting the trade, and who are consulted when any new regulations are contemplated for its government. They are, likewise, under the vigilant superintendence of the police. Every butcher must be licensed, — which proves him at once to be a slave, for we don't license butchers in England — we only license apothecaries, attorneys, postmasters, publicans, hawkers, retailers of tobacco, snuff, pepper, and vinegar — and one or two other little trades not worth mentioning. Every arrangement in connection with the slaughtering and sale of meat is matter of strict police regulation. (Slavery again, though we certainly have a general sort of a Police Act here.)

But in order that the reader may understand what a monument of folly these frog-eaters have raised in their abattoirs and cattle markets, and may compare it with what common counselling has done for us all these years, and would still do but for the innovating spirit of the times, here follows a short account of a recent visit to these places: —

It was as sharp a February morning as you would desire to feel at your fingers' ends when I turned out — tumbling over a chiffonier with his little basket and rake, who was picking up the bits of coloured paper that had been swept out, over night, from a Bon-Bon shop — to take the Butchers' Train to Poissy. A cold dim light just touched the high roofs of the Tuileries, which have seen such changes, such distracted crowds, such riot and bloodshed; and they looked as calm, and as old, all covered with white frost, as the very Pyramids. There was not light enough, yet, to strike upon the towers of Notre Dame across the water; but I thought of the dark pavement of the old Cathedral as just beginning to be streaked with grey; and of the lamps in the "House of God," the Hospital close to it, burning low and being quenched; and of the keeper of the Morgue going about with a fading lantern, busy in the arrangement of his terrible waxwork for another sunny day.

The sun was up, and shining merrily when the butchers and I, announcing our departure with an engine-shriek to sleepy Paris, rattled away for the Cattle Market. Across the country, over the Seine, among a forest of scrubby trees, — the hoarfrost lying cold in shady places, and glittering in the light, — and here we are at Poissy! Out leap the butchers who have been chattering all the way like madmen, and off they straggle for the Cattle Market (still chattering, of course, incessantly), in hats and caps of all shapes, in coats and blouses, in calf-skins, cow-skins, horse-skins, furs, shaggy mantles, hairy coats, sacking, baize, oil-skin, anything you please that will keep a man and a butcher warm upon a frosty morning.

Many a French town have I seen, between this spot of ground and Strasburg or Marseilles, that might sit for your picture, little Poissy! Barring the details of your old church, I know you well, albeit we make acquaintance, now, for the first time. I know your narrow, straggling, winding streets, with a kennel in the midst, and lamps slung across. I know your picturesque street corners, winding up hill Heaven knows why or where! I know your tradesmen's inscriptions, in letters not quite fat enough; your barber's brazen basins dangling over little shops; your Cafés and Estaminets, with cloudy bottles of stale syrup in the windows, and pictures of crossed billiard-cues outside. I know this identical grey horse with his tail rolled up in a knot like the "back hair" of an untidy woman, who won't be shod, and who makes himself heraldic by clattering across the street on his hind-legs, while twenty voices shriek and growl at him as a Brigand, an accursed Robber, and an everlastingly doomed Pig. I know your sparkling town-fountain too, my Poissy, and am glad to see it near a cattle market, gushing so freshly, under the auspices of a gallant little sublimated Frenchman wrought in metal, perched upon the top. Through all the land of France I know this unswept room at The Glory, with its peculiar smell of beans and coffee, where the butchers crowd about the stove, drinking the thinnest of wine from the smallest of tumblers; where the thickest of coffee-cups mingle with the longest of loaves, and the weakest of lump sugar; where Madame at the counter easily acknowledges the homage of all entering and departing butchers; where the billiard-table is covered up in the midst like a great bird-cage — but the bird may sing by and by!

A bell! The Calf Market! Polite departure of butchers. Hasty payment and departure on the part of amateur Visitor. Madame reproaches Ma'amselle for too fine a susceptibility in reference to the devotion of a butcher in a bear-skin. Monsieur, the landlord of The Glory, counts a double handful of sous, without an unobliterated inscription, or an undamaged crowned head, among them.

There is little noise without, abundant space, and no confusion. The open area devoted to the market is divided into three portions: the Calf Market, the Cattle Market, the Sheep Market. Calves at eight, cattle at ten, sheep at mid-day. All is very clean.

The Calf Market is a raised platform of stone, some three or four feet high, open on all sides, with a lofty over-spreading roof, supported on stone columns, which give it the appearance of a sort of vineyard from Northern Italy. Here, on the raised pavement, lie innumerable calves, all bound hind-legs and fore-legs together, and all trembling violently — perhaps with cold, perhaps with fear, perhaps with pain; for this mode of tying, which seems to be an absolute superstition with the peasantry, can hardly fail to cause great suffering. Here they lie, patiently, in rows, among the straw, with their stolid faces and inexpressive eyes, superintended by men and women, boys and girls; here they are inspected by our friends, the butchers, bargained for, and bought. Plenty of time; plenty of room; plenty of good-humour. "Monsieur François in the bear-skin, how do you do, my friend? You come from Paris by the train? The fresh air does you good. If you are in want of three or four fine calves this market-morning, my angel, I, Madame Doche, shall be happy to deal with you. Behold these calves, Monsieur François! Great Heaven, you are doubtful! Well, sir, walk round and look about you. If you find better for the money, buy them. If not, come to me!" Monsieur François goes his way leisurely, and keeps a wary eye upon the stock. No other butcher jostles Monsieur François; Monsieur François jostles no other butcher. Nobody is flustered and aggravated. Nobody is savage. In the midst of the country blue frocks and red handkerchiefs, and the butchers' coats, shaggy, furry, and hairy — of calf-skin, cow-skin, horse-skin, and bear-skin — towers a cocked hat and a blue cloak. Slavery! For *our* Police wear great-coats and glazed hats.

But now the bartering is over, and the calves are sold. "Ho! Gregorie, Antoine, Jean, Louis! Bring up the carts, my children! Quick, brave infants! Hola! Hi!"

The carts, well littered with straw, are backed up to the edge of the raised pavement, and various hot infants carry calves upon their heads, and dexterously pitch them in, while other hot infants, standing in the carts, arrange the calves, and pack them carefully in straw. Here is a promising young calf, not sold, whom Madame Doche unbinds. Pardon me, Madame Doche, but I fear this mode of tying the four legs of a quadruped together, though strictly à la mode, is not quite right. You observe, Madame Doche, that the cord leaves deep indentations in the skin, and that the animal is so cramped at first as not to know, or even remotely suspect, that he *is* unbound, until you are so obliging as to kick him, in your delicate little way, and pull his tail like a bell-rope. Then, he staggers to his knees, not being able to stand, and stumbles about like a drunken calf, or the horse at Franconi's, whom you may have seen, Madame Doche, who is supposed to have been mortally wounded in battle. But, what is this rubbing against me, as I apostrophise Madame Doche? It is another heated infant with a calf upon his head. "Pardon, Monsieur, but will you have the politeness to allow me to pass?" "Ah, sir, willingly. I am vexed to obstruct the way." On he staggers, calf and all, and makes no allusion whatever either to my eyes or limbs.

Now, the carts are all full. More straw, my Antoine, to shake over these top rows; then, off we will clatter, rumble, jolt, and rattle, a long row of us, out of the first town-gate, and out at the second town-gate, and past the empty sentry-box, and the little thin square bandbox of a guard-house, where nobody seems to live; and away for Paris, by the paved road, lying, a straight straight line, in the long long avenue of trees. We can neither choose our road, nor our pace, for that is all prescribed to us. The public convenience demands that our carts should get to Paris by such a route, and no other (Napoleon had leisure to find that out, while he had a little war with the world upon his hands), and woe betide us if we infringe orders.

Droves of oxen stand in the Cattle Market, tied to iron bars fixed into posts of granite. Other droves advance slowly down the long avenue, past the second town-gate, and the first town-gate, and the sentry-box, and the bandbox, thawing the morning with their smoky breath as they come along. Plenty of room; plenty of time. Neither man nor beast is driven out of his wits by coaches, carts, wagons, omnibuses, gigs, chaises, phaetons, cabs, trucks, boys, whoopings, roarings, and multitudes. No tail-twisting is necessary — no iron pronging is necessary. There are no iron prongs here. The market for cattle is held as quietly as the market for calves. In due time, off the cattle go to Paris; the drovers can no more choose their road, nor their time, nor the numbers they shall drive, than they can choose their hour for dying in the course of nature.

Sheep next. The Sheep-pens are up here, past the Branch Bank of Paris established for the convenience of the butchers, and behind the two pretty fountains they are making in the Market. My name is Bull; yet I think I should like to see as good twin fountains — not to say in Smithfield, but in England anywhere. Plenty of room; plenty of time. And here are sheep-dogs, sensible as ever, but with a certain French air about them — not without a suspicion of dominoes — with a kind of flavour of mustache and beard; demonstrative dogs, shaggy and loose where an English dog would be tight and close — not so troubled with business calculations as our English drovers' dogs, who have always got their sheep upon their minds, and think about their work, even resting, as you may see by their faces, but dashing, showy, rather unreliable dogs, who might worry me instead of their legitimate charges if they saw occasion — and might see it somewhat suddenly. The market for sheep passes off like the other two; and away they go, by *their* allotted road to Paris. My way being the Railway, I make the best of it at twenty miles an hour; whirling through the now high-lighted landscape; thinking that the inexperienced green buds will be wishing before long they had not been tempted to come out so soon; and wondering who lives in this or that château, all window and lattice, and what the family may have for breakfast this sharp morning.

After the Market comes the Abattoir. What abattoir shall I visit first? Montmartre is the largest. So I will go there.

The abattoirs are all within the walls of Paris, with an eye to the receipt of the octroi duty; but they stand in open places in the suburbs, removed from the press and bustle of the city. They are managed by the Syndicat or Guild of Butchers, under the inspection of the Police. Certain smaller items of the revenue derived from them are in part retained by the Guild for the payment of their expenses, and in part devoted by it to charitable purposes in connection with the trade. They cost six hundred and eighty thousand pounds; and they return to the city of Paris an interest on that outlay, amounting to nearly six and a half per cent.

Here, in a sufficiently dismantled space, is the Abattoir of Montmartre, covering nearly nine acres of ground, surrounded by a high wall, and looking from the outside like a cavalry barrack. At the iron gates is a small functionary in a large cocked hat. "Monsieur desires to see the abattoir? Most certainly." State being inconvenient in private transactions, and Monsieur being already aware of the cocked hat, the functionary puts it into a little official bureau which it almost fills, and accompanies me in the modest attire — as to his head — of ordinary life.

Many of the animals from Poissy have come here. On the arrival of each drove, it was turned into yonder ample space, where each butcher who had bought selected his own purchases. Some, we see now, in these long perspectives of stalls with a high overhanging roof of wood and open tiles rising above the walls. While they rest here, before being slaughtered, they are required to be fed and watered, and the stalls must be kept clean. A stated amount of fodder must always be ready in the loft above; and the supervision is of the strictest kind. The same regulations apply to sheep and calves, for which portions of these perspectives are strongly railed off. All the buildings are of the strongest and most solid description.

After traversing these lairs, through which, besides the upper provision for ventilation just mentioned, there may be a thorough current of air from opposite windows in the side walls, and from doors at either end, we traverse the broad, paved courtyard until we come to the slaughter-houses. They are all exactly alike, and adjoin each other, to the number of eight or nine together, in blocks of solid building. Let us walk into the first.

It is firmly built and paved with stone. It is well lighted, thoroughly aired, and lavishly provided with fresh water. It has two doors opposite each other; the first, the door by which I entered from the main yard; the second, which is opposite, opening on another smaller yard, where the sheep and calves are killed on benches. The pavement of that yard, I see, slopes downward to a gutter, for its being more easily cleansed. The slaughter-house is fifteen feet high, sixteen feet and a half wide, and thirty-three feet long. It is fitted with a powerful windlass, by which one man at the handle can bring the head or an ox down to the ground to receive the blow from the pole-axe that is to fell him, — with the means of raising the carcass and keeping it suspended during the after-operation of dressing, — and with hooks on which carcasses can hang, when completely prepared, without touching the walls. Upon the pavement of this first stone chamber lies an ox scarcely dead. If I except the blood draining from him, into a little stone well in a corner of the pavement, the place is free from offence as the Place de la Concorde. It is infinitely purer and cleaner, I know, my friend the functionary, than the Cathedral of Notre Dame. Ha, ha! Monsieur is pleasant, but, truly, there is reason, too, in what he says.

I look into another of these slaughter-houses. "Pray enter," says a gentleman in bloody boots. "This is a calf I have killed this morning. Having a little time upon my hands, I have cut and punctured this lace pattern in the coats of his stomach. It is pretty enough. I did it to divert myself." "It is beautiful, Monsieur the slaughterer!" He tells me I have the gentility to say so.

I look into rows of slaughter-houses. In many, retail dealers, who have come here for the purpose, are making bargains for meat. There is killing enough, certainly, to satiate an unused eye; and there are steaming carcasses enough to suggest the expediency of a fowl and salad for dinner; but, everywhere, there is an orderly, clean, well-systematised routine of work in progress — horrible work at the best, if you please; but so much the greater reason why it should be made the best of. I don't know (I think I have observed my name is Bull) that a Parisian of the lowest order is particularly delicate, or that his nature is remarkable for an infinitesimal infusion of ferocity, but I do know, my potent, grave, and common counselling Signors, that he is forced, when at this work, to submit himself to a thoroughly good system, and to make an Englishman very heartily ashamed of you.

Here, within the walls of the same abattoir, in other roomy and commodious buildings, are a place for converting the fat

into tallow and packing it for market — a place for cleansing
and scalding calves' heads and sheep's feet — a place for preparing tripe — stables and coach-houses for the butchers —
innumerable conveniences, aiding in the diminution of offen-
siveness to its lowest possible point, and the raising of cleanliness and supervision to their highest.   Hence, all the meat
that goes out of the gate is sent away in clean covered carts.
And if every trade connected with the slaughtering of animals
were obliged by law to be carried on in the same place, I
doubt, my friend, now reinstated in the cocked hat (whose
civility these two francs imperfectly acknowledge, but appear
munificently to repay), whether there could be better regulations than those which are carried out at the Abattoir of Montmartre.   Adieu, my friend, for I am away to the other side
of Paris, to the Abattoir of Grenelle!   And there, I find
exactly the same thing on a smaller scale, with the addition of
a magnificent Artesian well, and a different sort of conductor,
in the person of a neat little woman with neat little eyes, and
a neat little voice, who picks her neat little way among the
bullocks in a very neat little pair of shoes and stockings.

Such is the Monument of French Folly which a foreigneer-
ing people have erected, in a national hatred and antipathy for
common counselling wisdom.   That wisdom, assembled in the
City of London, having distinctly refused, after a debate three
days long, and by a majority of nearly seven to one, to associate itself with any Metropolitan Cattle Market unless it be
held in the midst of the City, it follows that we shall lose the
inestimable advantages of common counselling protection, and
be thrown, for a market, on our own wretched resources.   In
all human probability we shall thus come, at last, to erect a
monument of folly very like this French monument.   If that
be done, the consequences are obvious.   The leather trade
will be ruined by the introduction of American timber, to be
manufactured into shoes for the fallen English; the Lord
Mayor will be required, by the popular voice to live entirely
on frogs; and both these changes will (how, is not at present
quite clear, but certainly somehow or other) fall on that
unhappy landed interest which is always being killed, yet is
always found to be alive — and kicking.

IV

BILL-STICKING

IF I had an enemy whom I hated, — which Heaven forbid, — and if I knew of something that sat heavy on his conscience, I think I would introduce that something into a Posting-Bill, and place a large impression in the hands of an active sticker. I can scarcely imagine a more terrible revenge. I should haunt him, by this means, night and day. I do not mean to say that I would publish his secret, in red letters two feet high, for all the town to read; I would darkly refer to it. It should be between him, and me, and the Posting-Bill. Say, for example, that, at a certain period of his life, my enemy had surreptitiously possessed himself of a key. I would then embark my capital in the lock business, and conduct that business on the advertising principle. In all my placards and advertisements, I would throw up the line Secret Keys. Thus, if my enemy passed an uninhabited house, he would see his conscience glaring down on him from the parapets, and peeping up at him from the cellars. If he took a dead wall in his walk, it would be alive with reproaches. If he sought refuge in an omnibus, the panels thereof would become Belshazzar's palace to him. If he took boat, in a wild endeavour to escape, he would see the fatal words lurking under the arches of the bridges over the Thames. If he walked the streets with downcast eyes, he would recoil from the very stones of the pavement, made eloquent by lamp-black lithograph. If he drove or rode, his way would be blocked up, by enormous vans, each proclaiming the same words over and over again from its whole extent of surface. Until, having gradually grown thinner and paler, and having at last totally rejected food, he would miserably perish, and I should be revenged. This conclusion I should, no doubt, celebrate by laughing a hoarse laugh in three syllables, and folding my arms tight upon my chest agreeably to most of the examples of glutted animosity that I have had an opportunity of observing in connection with the Drama — which, by the bye, as involving a good deal of noise, appears to me to be occasionally confounded with the Drummer.

The foregoing reflections presented themselves to my mind, the other day, as I contemplated (being newly come to London from the East Riding of Yorkshire, on a house-hunting expedition for next May) an old warehouse which rotting paste and rotting paper had brought down to the condition of an old cheese. It would have been impossible to say, on the most conscientious survey, how much of its front was brick and mortar, and how much decaying and decayed plaster. It was so thickly encrusted with fragments of bills, that no ship's keel after a long voyage could be half so foul. All traces of the broken windows were billed out, the doors were billed across, the water-spout was billed over. The building was shored up to prevent its tumbling into the street; and the very beams erected against it were less wood than paste and paper, they had been so continually posted and reposted. The forlorn dregs of old posters so encumbered this wreck, that there was no hold for new posters, and the stickers had abandoned the place in despair, except one enterprising man who had hoisted the last masquerade to a clear spot near the level of the stack of chimneys where it waved and drooped like a shattered flag. Below the rusty cellar-grating, crumpled remnants of old bills torn down rotted away in wasting heaps of fallen leaves. Here and there, some of the thick rind of the house had peeled off in strips, and fluttered heavily down, littering the street; but, still, below these rents and gashes, layers of decomposing posters showed themselves, as if they were interminable. I thought the building could never even be pulled down, but in one adhesive heap of rottenness and poster. As to getting in — I don't believe that if the Sleeping Beauty and her Court had been so billed up the young Prince could have done it.

Knowing all the posters that were yet legible, intimately, and pondering on their ubiquitous nature, I was led into the reflections with which I began this paper, by considering what an awful thing it would be ever to have wronged — say M. Jullien, for example, and to have his avenging name in char acters of fire incessantly before my eyes. Or to have injured Madame Tussaud, and undergo a similar retribution. Has any man a self-reproachful thought associated with pills or ointment? What an avenging spirit to that man is Professor Holloway! Have I sinned in oil? Cabburn pursues me. Have I a dark remembrance associated with any gentlemanly garments, bespoke or ready made? Moses and Son are on my track. Did I ever aim a blow at a defenceless fellow-creature's head? That head eternally being measured for a wig, or that worse head which was bald before it used the balsam and hirsute afterwards, — enforcing the benevolent moral, "Better to be bald as a Dutch cheese than come to this," — undoes me. Have I no sore places in my mind which Mechi touches — which Nicoll probes — which no registered article whatever lacerates? Does no discordant note within me thrill responsive to mysterious watchwords, as "Revalenta Arabica," or "Number One St. Paul's Churchyard"? Then may I enjoy life, and be happy.

Lifting up my eyes, as I was musing to this effect, I beheld advancing towards me (I was then on Cornhill near to the Royal Exchange) a solemn procession of three advertising vans, of first-class dimensions, each drawn by a very little horse. As the cavalcade approached, I was at a loss to reconcile the careless deportment of the drivers of these vehicles with the terrific announcements they conducted through the city, which, being a summary of the contents of a Sunday newspaper, were of the most thrilling kind. Robbery, fire, murder, and the ruin of the united kingdom — each discharged in a line by itself, like a separate broadside of red-hot shot — were among the least of the warnings addressed to an unthinking people. Yet, the Ministers of Fate who drove the awful cars leaned forward with their arms upon their knees in a state of extreme lassitude, for want of any subject of interest. The first man, whose hair I might naturally have expected to see standing on end, scratched his head — one of the smoothest I ever beheld — with profound indifference. The second whistled. The third yawned.

Pausing to dwell upon this apathy, it appeared to me, as the fatal cars came by me, that I descried in the second car, through the portal in which the charioteer was seated, a figure stretched upon the floor. At the same time, I thought I smelt tobacco. The latter impression passed quickly from me; the former remained. Curious to know whether this prostrate figure was the one impressible man of the whole capital who had been stricken insensible by the terrors revealed to him, and whose form had been placed in the car by the charioteer, from motives of humanity, I followed the procession. It turned into Leadenhall Market, and halted at a public-house. Each driver dismounted. I then distinctly heard, proceeding from the second car, where I had dimly seen the prostrate form, the words: —

"And a pipe!"

The driver entering the public-house with his fellows, apparently for purposes of refreshment, I could not refrain from mounting on the shaft of the second vehicle, and looking in at the portal. I then beheld, reclining on his back upon the floor, on a kind of mattress or divan, a little man in a shooting-coat. The exclamation "Dear me!" which irresistibly escaped my lips, caused him to sit upright, and survey me. I found him to be a good-looking little man of about fifty, with a shining face, a tight head, a bright eye, a moist wink, a quick speech, and a ready air. He had something of a sporting way with him.

He looked at me, and I looked at him, until the driver displaced me by handing in a pint of beer, a pipe, and what I understand is called "a screw" of tobacco — an object which has the appearance of a curl-paper taken off the barmaid's head, with the curl in it.

"I beg your pardon," said I, when the removed person of the driver again admitted of my presenting my face at the portal. "But — excuse my curiosity, which I inherit from my mother — do you live here?"

"That's good, too!" returned the little man, composedly laying aside a pipe he had smoked out, and filling the pipe just brought to him.

"Oh, you *don't* live here then?" said I.

He shook his head, as he calmly lighted his pipe by means of a German tinder-box, and replied, "This is my carriage. When things are flat, I take a ride sometimes, and enjoy myself. I am the inventor of these wans."

His pipe was now alight. He drank his beer all at once, and he smoked and he smiled at me.

"It was a great idea!" said I.

"Not so bad," returned the little man, with the modesty of merit.

"Might I be permitted to inscribe your name upon the tablets of my memory?" I asked.

"There's not much odds in the name," returned the little

man, — " no name particular — I am the King of the Bill-
Stickers."

"Good gracious!" said I.

The monarch informed me, with a smile, that he had never
been crowned or installed with any public ceremonies, but
that he was peaceably acknowledged as King of the Bill-Stickers in right of being the oldest and most respected member of
"the old school of bill-sticking." He likewise gave me to
understand that there was a Lord Mayor of the Bill-Stickers,
whose genius was chiefly exercised within the limits of the
city. He made some allusion, also, to an inferior potentate,
called "Turkey-legs;" but I did not understand that this gentleman was invested with much power. I rather inferred that
he derived his title from some peculiarity of gait, and that it
was of an honorary character.

"My father," pursued the King of the Bill-Stickers, "was
Engineer, Beadle, and Bill-Sticker to the parish of St.
Andrew's, Holborn, in the year one thousand seven hundred
and eighty. My father stuck bills at the time of the riots of
London."

"You must be acquainted with the whole subject of bill-
sticking, from that time to the present!" said I.

"Pretty well so," was the answer.

"Excuse me," said I, "but I am a sort of collector — "

"Not Income-tax?" cried His Majesty, hastily removing
his pipe from his lips.

"No, no," said I.

"Water-rate?" said His Majesty.

"No, no," I returned.

"Gas? Assessed? Sewers?" said His Majesty.

"You misunderstand me," I replied soothingly. "Not that
sort of collector at all — a collector of facts."

"Oh! if it's only facts," cried the King of the Bill-Stickers,
recovering his good-humour, and banishing the great mistrust
that had suddenly fallen upon him, "come in and welcome.
If it had been income, or winders, I think I should have
pitched you out of the wan, upon my soul!"

Readily complying with the invitation, I squeezed myself
in at the small aperture. His Majesty, graciously handing me
a little three-legged stool on which I took my seat in a corner,
inquired if I smoked.

"I do, — that is, I can," I answered.

"Pipe and a screw!" said His Majesty to the attendant charioteer. "Do you prefer a dry smoke, or do you moisten it?"

As unmitigated tobacco produces most disturbing effects upon my system (indeed, if I had perfect moral courage, I doubt if I should smoke at all, under any circumstances), I advocated moisture, and begged the Sovereign of the Bill-Stickers to name his usual liquor, and to concede to me the privilege of paying for it. After some delicate reluctance on his part, we were provided, through the instrumentality of the attendant charioteer, with a can of cold rum and water, flavoured with sugar and lemon. We were also furnished with a tumbler, and I was provided with a pipe. His Majesty, then, observing that we might combine business with conversation, gave the word for the car to proceed; and, to my great delight, we jogged away at a foot-pace.

I say to my great delight, because I am very fond of novelty, and it was a new sensation to be jolting through the tumult of the city, in that secluded Temple, partly open to the sky, surrounded by the roar without, and seeing nothing but the clouds. Occasionally, blows from whips fell heavily on the Temple's walls, when by stopping up the road longer than usual we irritated carters and coachmen to madness; but they fell harmless upon us within and disturbed not the serenity of our peaceful retreat. As I looked upward, I felt, I should imagine, like the Astronomer Royal. I was enchanted by the contrast between the freezing nature of our external mission on the blood of the populace and the perfect composure reigning within those sacred precincts; where His Majesty, reclining easily on his left arm, smoked his pipe and drank his rum and water from his own side of the tumbler, which stood impartially between us. As I looked down from the clouds and caught his royal eye, he understood my reflections. "I have an idea," he observed, with an upward glance, "of training scarlet runners across in the season, — making an arbour of it, — and sometimes taking tea in the same, according to the song."

I nodded approval.

"And here you repose and think?" said I.

"And think," said he, "of posters — walls — and hoardings."

We were both silent, contemplating the vastness of the subject. I remembered a surprising fancy of dear Thomas Hood's, and wondered whether this monarch ever sighed to repair to the great wall of China, and stick bills all over it.

"And so," said he, rousing himself, "it's facts as you collect?"

"Facts," said I.

"The facts of bill-sticking," pursued His Majesty, in a benignant manner, "as known to myself, air as following. When my father was Engineer, Beadle, and Bill-Sticker to the parish of St. Andrew's, Holborn, he employed women to post bills for him. He employed women to post bills at the time of the riots of London. He died at the age of seventy-five year, and was buried by the murdered Eliza Grimwood, over in the Waterloo Road."

As this was somewhat in the nature of a royal speech, I listened with deference and silently. His Majesty, taking a scroll from his pocket, proceeded, with great distinctness, to pour out the following flood of information: —

"'The bills being at that period mostly proclamations and declarations, and which were only a demy size, the manner of posting the bills (as they did not use brushes) was by means of a piece of wood which they called a "dabber." Thus things continued till such time as the State Lottery was passed, and then the printers began to print larger bills, and men were employed instead of women, as the State Lottery Commissioners then began to send men all over England to post bills, and would keep them out for six or eight months at a time, and they were called by the London bill-stickers "*trampers*," their wages at the time being ten shillings per day, besides expenses. They used sometimes to be stationed in large towns for five or six months together, distributing the schemes to all the houses in the town. And then there were more caricature wood-block engravings for posting-bills than there are at the present time, the principal printers, at that time, of posting-bills being Messrs. Evans and Ruffy, of Budge Row; Thoroughgood and Whiting, of the present day; and Messrs. Gye and Balne, Gracechurch Street, City. The largest bills printed at that period were a two-sheet double crown; and when they commenced printing four-sheet bills, two bill-stickers would work together. They had no settled wages per week, but had a fixed price for their work, and the London bill-stickers, during a lottery week, have been known to earn each eight or nine pounds per week, till the day of drawing; likewise the men who carried boards in the street used to have one pound per week, and the bill-stickers at that time would not allow any one to wilfully cover or destroy their bills, as they had a society amongst themselves, and very frequently dined together at some public-house where they used to go of an evening to have their work delivered out untoe 'em.' "

All this His Majesty delivered in a gallant manner; posting it, as it were, before me, in a great proclamation. I took advantage of the pause he now made to inquire what a "two-sheet double crown " might express.

"A two-sheet double crown," replied the King, "is a bill thirty-nine inches wide by thirty inches high."

"Is it possible," said I, my mind reverting to the gigantic admonitions we were then displaying to the multitude, — which were as infants to some of the posting-bills on the rotten old warehouse, — "that some few years ago the largest bill was no larger than that ? "

"The fact," returned the King, "is undoubtedly so." Here he instantly rushed again into the scroll.

" ' Since the abolishing of the State Lottery all that good feeling has gone, and nothing but jealousy exists, through the rivalry of each other. Several bill-sticking companies have started, but have failed. The first party that started a company was twelve year ago; but what was left of the old school and their dependants joined together and opposed them. And for some time we were quiet again, till a printer of Hatton Garden formed a company by hiring the sides of houses; but he was not supported by the public, and he left his wooden frames fixed up for rent. The last company that started took advantage of the New Police Act, and hired of Messrs. Grisell and Peto the hoarding of Trafalgar Square, and established a bill-sticking office in Cursitor Street, Chancery Lane, and engaged some of the new bill-stickers to do their work, and for a time got the half of all our work, and with such spirit did they carry on their opposition towards us, that they used to give us in charge before the magistrate, and get us fined; but they found it so expensive, that they could not keep it up, for they were always employing a lot of ruffians from the Seven

Dials to come and fight us; and on one occasion the old bill-
stickers went to Trafalgar Square to attempt to post bills,
when they were given in custody by the watchman in their
employ, and fined at Queen Square five pounds, as they would
not allow any of us to speak in the office; but when they were
gone, we had an interview with the magistrate, who mitigated
the fine to fifteen shillings. During the time the men were
waiting for the fine, this company started off to a public-house
that we were in the habit of using, and waited for us coming
back, where a fighting scene took place that beggars description. Shortly after this, the principal one day came and
shook hands with us, and acknowledged that he had broken up
the company, and that he himself had lost five hundred pound
in trying to overthrow us. We then took possession of the
hoarding in Trafalgar Square; but Messrs. Grisell and Peto
would not allow us to post our bills on the said hoarding without paying them — and from first to last we paid upwards of
two hundred pounds for that hoarding, and likewise the hoarding of the Reform Club-house, Pall Mall.' "

His Majesty, being now completely out of breath, laid down
his scroll (which he appeared to have finished), puffed at his
pipe, and took some rum and water. I embraced the opportunity of asking how many divisions the art and mystery of
bill-sticking comprised? He replied, three — auctioneers' bill-
sticking, theatrical bill-sticking, general bill-sticking.

"The auctioneers' porters," said the King, "who do their
bill-sticking, are mostly respectable and intelligent, and generally well paid for their work, whether in town or country.
The price paid by the principal auctioneers for country work is
nine shillings per day; that is, seven shillings for day's work,
one shilling for lodging, and one for paste. Town work is
five shillings a day, including paste."

"Town work must be rather hot work," said I, "if there
be many of those fighting scenes that beggar description among
the bill-stickers?"

"Well," replied the King, "I ain't a stranger, I assure
you, to black eyes; a bill-sticker ought to know how to handle
his fists a bit. As to that row I have mentioned, that grew
out of competition, conducted in an uncompromising spirit. Besides a man in a horse-and-shay continually following us about,
the company had a watchman on duty, night and day, to pre-

vent us sticking bills upon the hoarding in Trafalgar Square. We went there, early one morning, to stick bills and to black-wash their bills if we were interfered with. We *were* interfered with, and I gave the word for laying on the wash. It *was* laid on, — pretty brisk, — and we were all taken to Queen Square; but they could n't fine *me*. *I* knew that," — with a bright smile, — "I 'd only given directions — I was only the General."

Charmed with this monarch's affability, I inquired if he had ever hired a hoarding himself.

"Hired a large one," he replied, "opposite the Lyceum Theatre, when the buildings was there. Paid thirty pound for it; let out places on it, and called it ' The External Paper-Hanging Station.' But it did n't answer. Ah!" said His Majesty thoughtfully, as he filled the glass, "bill-stickers have a deal to contend with. The bill-sticking clause was got into the Police Act by a Member of Parliament that employed me at his election. The clause is pretty stiff respecting where bills go; but *he* did n't mind where *his* bills went. It was all right enough so long as they was *his* bills!"

Fearful that I observed a shadow of misanthropy on the King's cheerful face, I asked whose ingenious invention that was, which I greatly admired, of sticking bills under the arches of the bridges.

"Mine!" said His Majesty; "I was the first that ever stuck a bill under a bridge! Imitators soon rose up, of course. When don't they? But they stuck 'em at low-water, and the tide came and swept the bills clean away. *I* knew that!" The King laughed.

"What may be the name of that instrument, like an immense fishing-rod," I inquired, "with which bills are posted on high places?"

"The joints," returned His Majesty. "Now, we use the joints where formerly we used ladders — as they do still in country places. Once, when Madame" (Vestris, understood) "was playing in Liverpool, another bill-sticker and me were at it together on the wall outside the Clarence Dock — me with the joints — him on a ladder. Lord! I had my bill up, right over his head, yards above him, ladder and all, while he was crawling to his work. The people going in and out of the docks stood and laughed! — It 's about thirty years since the joints come in."

"Are there any bill-stickers who can't read?" I took the liberty of inquiring.

"Some," said the King. "But they know which is the right side up'ards of their work. They keep it as it's given out to 'em. I have seen a bill or so stuck wrong side up'ards. But it's very rare."

Our discourse sustained some interruption at this point by the procession of cars occasioning a stoppage of about three quarters of a mile in length, as nearly as I could judge. His Majesty, however, entreating me not to be discomposed by the contingent uproar, smoked with great placidity, and surveyed the firmament.

When we were again in motion, I begged to be informed what was the largest poster His Majesty had ever seen. The King replied, "A thirty-six sheet poster." I gathered, also, that there were about a hundred and fifty bill-stickers in London, and that His Majesty considered an average hand equal to the posting of one hundred bills (single sheets) in a day. The King was of opinion that, although posters had much increased in size, they had not increased in number, as the abolition of the State Lotteries had occasioned a great falling off, especially in the country. Over and above which change, I bethought myself that the custom of advertising in newspapers had greatly increased. The completion of many London improvements, as Trafalgar Square (I particularly observed the singularity of His Majesty's calling *that* an improvement), the Royal Exchange, etc., had of late years reduced the number of advantageous posting-places. Bill-stickers at present rather confine themselves to districts, than to particular descriptions of work. One man would strike over Whitechapel; another would take round Houndsditch, Shoreditch, and the City Road; one (the King said) would stick to the Surrey side; another would make a beat of the West End.

His Majesty remarked, with some approach to severity, on the neglect of delicacy and taste, gradually introduced into the trade by the new school: a profligate and inferior race of impostors who took jobs at almost any price, to the detriment of the old school, and the confusion of their own misguided employers. He considered that the trade was overdone with competition, and observed, speaking of his subjects, "There are too many of 'em." He believed, still, that things were a

little better than they had been; adducing, as a proof, the fact
that particular posting-places were now reserved, by common
consent, for particular posters; those places, however, must be
regularly occupied by those posters, or they lapsed and fell
into other hands. It was of no use giving a man a Drury
Lane bill this week and not next. Where was it to go?
He was of opinion that going to the expense of putting up
your own board, on which your sticker could display your own
bills, was the only complete way of posting yourself at the
present time; but even to effect this, on payment of a shilling
a week to the keepers of steamboat piers and other such places,
you must be able, besides, to give orders for theatres and public exhibitions, or you would be sure to be cut out by somebody. His Majesty regarded the passion for orders as one of
the most inappeasable appetites of human nature. If there
were a building, or if there were repairs, going on, anywhere,
you could generally stand something and make it right with
the foreman of the works; but orders would be expected from
you, and the man who could give the most orders was the man
who would come off best. There was this other objectionable
point, in orders, that workmen sold them for drink, and often
sold them to persons who were likewise troubled with the
weakness of thirst; which led (His Majesty said) to the presentation of your orders at Theatre doors, by individuals who
were "too shakery" to derive intellectual profit from the entertainments, and who brought a scandal on you. Finally, His
Majesty said that you could hardly put too little in a poster;
what you wanted was, two or three good catch-lines for the
eye to rest on — then, leave it alone — and there you were!

These are the minutes of my conversation with His Majesty,
as I noted them down shortly afterwards. I am not aware
that I have been betrayed into any alteration or suppression.
The manner of the King was frank in the extreme; and he
seemed to me to avoid, at once that slight tendency to repetition which may have been observed in the conversation of His
Majesty King George the Third, and that slight undercurrent
of egotism which the curious observer may perhaps detect in
the conversation of Napoleon Bonaparte.

I must do the King the justice to say that it was I, and not
he, who closed the dialogue. At this juncture, I became the
subject of a remarkable optical delusion; the legs of my stool

appeared to me to double up; the car to spin round and round with great violence; and a mist to arise between myself and His Majesty. In addition to these sensations, I felt extremely unwell. I refer these unpleasant effects either to the paste with which the posters were affixed to the van, which may have contained some small portion of arsenic, or to the printer's ink, which may have contained some equally deleterious ingredient. Of this, I cannot be sure. I am only sure that I was not affected either by the smoke or the rum and water. I was assisted out of the vehicle, in a state of mind which I have only experienced in two other places, — I allude to the Pier at Dover, and to the corresponding portion of the town of Calais, — and sat upon a door-step until I recovered. The procession had then disappeared. I have since looked anxiously for the King in several other cars, but I have not yet had the happiness of seeing His Majesty.

V

· ON DUTY WITH INSPECTOR FIELD

How goes the night? St. Giles's clock is striking nine. The weather is dull and wet, and the long lines of street lamps are blurred, as if we saw them through tears. A damp wind blows and rakes the pieman's fire out, when he opens the door of his little furnace, carrying away an eddy of sparks. St. Giles's clock strikes nine. We are punctual. Where is Inspector Field? Assistant Commissioner of Police is already here, enwrapped in oil-skin cloak, and standing in the shadow of St. Giles's steeple. Detective Sergeant, weary of speaking French all day to foreigners unpacking at the Great Exhibition, is already here. Where is Inspector Field?

Inspector Field is, to-night, the guardian genius of the British Museum. He is bringing his shrewd eye to bear on every corner of its solitary galleries, before he reports "all right." Suspicious of the Elgin marbles, and not to be done by cat-faced Egyptian giants with their hands upon their knees, Inspector Field, sagacious, vigilant, lamp in hand, throwing monstrous shadows on the walls and ceilings, passes through the spacious rooms. If a mummy trembled in an atom of its dusty covering, Inspector Field would say, "Come out of that, Tom Green. I know you!" If the smallest "Gonoph" about town were crouching at the bottom of a classic bath, Inspector Field would nose him with a finer scent than the ogre's, when adventurous Jack lay trembling in his kitchen copper. But all is quiet, and Inspector Field goes warily on, making little outward show of attending to anything in particular, just recognising the Ichthyosaurus as a familiar acquaintance, and wondering, perhaps, how the detectives did it in the days before the Flood.

Will Inspector Field be long about this work? He may be half an hour longer. He sends his compliments by Police Constable, and proposes that we meet at St. Giles's Station House, across the road. Good. It were as well to stand by the fire, there, as in the shadow of St. Giles's steeple.

Anything doing here to-night? Not much. We are very quiet. A lost boy, extremely calm and small, sitting by the fire, whom we now confide to a constable to take home, for the child says that if you show him Newgate Street he can show you where he lives — a raving drunken woman in the cells, who has screeched her voice away, and has hardly power enough left to declare, even with the passionate help of her feet and arms, that she is the daughter of a British officer, and strike her blind and dead, but she'll write a letter to the Queen! but who is soothed with a drink of water — in another cell, a quiet woman with a child at her breast, for begging — in another, her husband in a smock-frock, with a basket of watercresses — in another a pickpocket — in another, a meek tremulous old pauper man who has been out for a holiday, "and has took but a little drop, but it has overcome him arter so many months in the house" — and that's all as yet. Presently, a sensation at the Station House door. Mr. Field, gentlemen!

Inspector Field comes in, wiping his forehead, for he is of a burly figure, and has come fast from the ores and metals of the deep mines of the earth, and from the Parrot Gods of the South Sea Islands, and from the birds and beetles of the tropics, and from the Arts of Greece and Rome, and from the Sculptures of Nineveh, and from the traces of an elder world, when these were not. Is Rogers ready? Rogers is ready, strapped and great-coated, with a flaming eye in the middle of his waist, like a deformed Cyclops. Lead on, Rogers, to Rats' Castle!

How many people may there be in London who, if we had brought them deviously and blindfold, to this street, fifty paces from the Station House, and within call of St. Giles's church, would know it for a not remote part of the city in which their lives are passed? How many, who amidst this compound of sickening smells, these heaps of filth, these tumbling houses, with all their vile contents, animate and inanimate, slimily overflowing into the black road, would believe that they breathe *this* air? How much Red Tape may there be that could look round on the faces which now hem us in — for our appearance here has caused a rush from all points to a common centre — the lowering foreheads, the sallow cheeks, the brutal eyes, the matted hair, the infected, vermin-haunted heaps of rags — and say, "I have thought of this. I have not dismissed the thing. I have neither blustered it away, nor frozen it away, nor tied it up and put it away, nor smoothly said Pooh, pooh! to it, when it has been shown to me?"

This is not what Rogers wants to know, however. What Rogers wants to know is, whether you *will* clear the way here, some of you, or whether you won't; because if you don't do it right on end, he'll lock you up! What! *You* are there, are you, Bob Miles? You haven't had enough of it yet, haven't you? You want three months more, do you? Come away from that gentleman! What are you creeping round there for?

"What am I a doing, thinn, Mr. Rogers?" says Bob Miles, appearing, villanous, at the end of a lane of light, made by the lantern.

"I'll let you know pretty quick, if you don't hook it. WILL you hook it?"

A sycophantic murmur rises from the crowd. "Hook it, Bob, when Mr. Rogers and Mr. Field tells you! Why don't you hook it when you are told to?"

The most importunate of the voices strikes familiarly on Mr. Rogers's ear. He suddenly turns his lantern on the owner.

"What! *You* are there, are you, Mister Click? You hook it too — come?"

"What for?" says Mr. Click discomfited.

"You hook it, will you!" says Mr. Rogers, with stern emphasis.

Both Click and Miles *do* "hook it" without another word, or, in plainer English, sneak away.

"Close up there, my men!" says Inspector Field to two constables on duty who have followed. "Keep together, gentlemen; we are going down here. Heads!"

St. Giles's church strikes half-past ten. We stoop low, and creep down a precipitous flight of steps into a dark close cellar. There is a fire. There is a long deal table. There are benches. The cellar is full of company, chiefly very young men in various conditions of dirt and raggedness. Some are eating supper. There are no girls or women present. Welcome to Rats' Castle, gentlemen, and to this company of noted thieves!

"Well, my lads! How are you, my lads? What have you been doing to-day? Here's some company come to see you, my lads! *There's* a plate of beefsteak, sir, for the supper of a fine young man! And there's a mouth for a steak, sir! Why, I should be too proud of such a mouth as that, if I had it myself! Stand up and show it, sir! Take off your cap. There's a fine young man for a nice little party, sir! Ain't he?"

Inspector Field is the bustling speaker. Inspector Field's eye is the roving eye that searches every corner of the cellar as he talks. Inspector Field's hand is the well-known hand that has collared half the people here, and motioned their brothers, sisters, fathers, mothers, male and female friends, inexorably to New South Wales. Yet Inspector Field stands in this den, the Sultan of the place. Every thief here cowers before him, like a schoolboy before his schoolmaster. All watch him, all answer when addressed, all laugh at his jokes, all seek to propitiate him. This cellar-company alone — to say nothing of the crowd surrounding the entrance from the street above, and making the steps shine with eyes — is strong enough to murder us all, and willing enough to do it; but let Inspector Field have a mind to pick out one thief here, and take him; let him produce that ghostly truncheon from his pocket, and say, with his business-air, "My lad, I want you!" and all Rats' Castle shall be stricken with paralysis, and not a finger move against him, as he fits the handcuffs on!

Where's the Earl of Warwick? — Here he is, Mr. Field! Here's the Earl of Warwick, Mr. Field! — Oh, there you are, my Lord. Come for'ard. There's a chest, sir, not to have a clean shirt on. Ain't it. Take your hat off, my Lord. Why, I should be ashamed if I was you — and an Earl, too — to show myself to a gentleman with my hat on! — The Earl of Warwick laughs and uncovers. All the company laugh. One pickpocket, especially, laughs with great enthusiasm. Oh, what a jolly game it is when Mr. Field comes down — and don't want nobody!

So, *you* are here, too, are you, you tall, grey, soldierly looking, grave man, standing by the fire? — Yes, sir. Good evening, Mr. Field! — Let us see. You lived servant to a nobleman once? — Yes, Mr. Field. — And what is it you do now; I forget? — Well, Mr. Field, I job about as well as I

can. I left my employment on account of delicate health.
The family is still kind to me. Mr. Wix of Piccadilly is also
very kind to me when I am hard up. Likewise Mr. Nix of
Oxford Street. I get a trifle from them occasionally, and rub
on as well as I can, Mr. Field. Mr. Field's eye rolls enjoy-
ingly, for this man is a notorious begging-letter writer. — Good
night, my lads! — Good night, Mr. Field, and thank'ee sir!
Clear the street here, half a thousand of you! Cut it, Mrs.
Stalker — none of that — we don't want you! Rogers of the
flaming eye, lead on to the tramps' lodging-house!

A dream of baleful faces attends to the door. Now, stand
back all of you! In the rear Detective Sergeant plants himself, composedly whistling, with his strong right arm across the
narrow passage. Mrs. Stalker, I am something'd that need
not be written here, if you won't get yourself into trouble,
in about half a minute, if I see that face of yours again!

St. Giles's church clock, striking eleven, hums through
our hand from the dilapidated door of a dark outhouse as we
open it, and are stricken back by the pestilent breath that
issues from within. Rogers to the front with the light, and
let us look!

Ten, twenty, thirty — who can count them! Men, women,
children, for the most part naked, heaped upon the floor like
maggots in a cheese! Ho! In that dark corner yonder!
Does anybody lie there? Me, sir, Irish me, a widder, with six
children. And yonder? Me, sir, Irish me, with me wife and
eight poor babes. And to the left there? Me, sir, Irish me,
along with two more Irish boys as is me friends. And to the
right there? Me, sir, and the Murphy fam'ly, numbering five
blessed souls. And what's this, coiling, now, about my foot?
Another Irish me, pitifully in want of shaving, whom I have
awakened from sleep — and across my other foot lies his wife
— and by the shoes of Inspector Field lie their three eldest —
and their three youngest are at present squeezed between the
open door and the wall. And why is there no one on that
little mat before the sullen fire? Because O'Donovan, with
his wife and daughter, is not come in from selling Lucifers!
Nor on the bit of sacking in the nearest corner? Bad luck!
Because that Irish family is late to-night, a cadging in the
streets!

They are all awake now, the children excepted, and most of

them sit up, to stare. Wheresoever Mr. Rogers turns the
flaming eye, there is a spectral figure rising, unshrouded, from
a grave of rags. Who is the landlord here? — I am, Mr.
Field! says a bundle of ribs and parchment against the wall,
scratching itself. — Will you spend this money fairly, in the
morning, to buy coffee for 'em all? — Yes, sir, I will! — Oh,
he'll do it, sir, he'll do it fair. He's honest! cry the spec-
tres. And with thanks and Good Night sink into their graves
again.

Thus, we make our New Oxford Streets, and our other new
streets, never heeding, never asking, where the wretches whom
we clear out crowd. With such scenes at our doors, with all
the plagues of Egypt tied up with bits of cobweb in kennels
so near our homes, we timorously make our Nuisance Bills and
Boards of Health nonentities, and think to keep away the
Wolves of Crime and Filth by our electioneering ducking to
little vestrymen and our gentlemanly handling of Red Tape!

Intelligence of the coffee money has got abroad. The yard
is full, and Rogers of the flaming eye is beleaguered with
entreaties to show other Lodging-Houses. Mine next! Mine!
Mine! Rogers, military, obdurate, stiff-necked, immovable,
replies not, but leads away; all falling back before him.
Inspector Field follows. Detective Sergeant, with his barrier
of arm across the little passage, deliberately waits to close the
procession. He sees behind him, without any effort, and
exceedingly disturbs one individual far in the rear by coolly
calling out, "It won't do, Mr. Michael! Don't try it!"

After council holden in the street, we enter other lodging-
houses, public-houses, many lairs and holes; all noisome and
offensive; none so filthy and so crowded as where Irish are.
In one, The Ethiopian party are expected home presently —
were in Oxford Street when last heard of — shall be fetched,
for our delight, within ten minutes. In another, one of the
two or three Professors who draw Napoleon Bonaparte and a
couple of mackerel, on the pavement, and then let the work of
art out to a speculator, is refreshing after his labours. In
another, the vested interest of the profitable nuisance has been
in one family for a hundred years, and the landlord drives in
comfortably from the country to his snug little stew in town.
In all, Inspector Field is received with warmth. Coiners and
smashers droop before him; pickpockets defer to him; the

gentle sex (not very gentle here) smile upon him. Half-drunken hags check themselves in the midst of pots of beer, or pints of gin, to drink to Mr. Field, and pressingly to ask the honour of his finishing the draught. One beldame in rusty black has such admiration for him, that she runs a whole street's length to shake him by the hand; tumbling into a heap of mud by the way, and still pressing her attentions when her very form has ceased to be distinguishable through it. Before the power of the law, the power of superior sense, — for common thieves are fools beside these men, — and the power of a perfect mastery of their character, the garrison of Rats' Castle and the adjacent Fortresses make but a skulking show indeed when reviewed by Inspector Field.

St. Giles's clock says it will be midnight in half an hour, and Inspector Field says we must hurry to the Old Mint in the Borough. The cab-driver is low-spirited, and has a solemn sense of his responsibility. Now, what's your fare, my lad? — Oh, *you* know, Inspector Field, what's the good of asking *me!*

Say, Parker, strapped and great-coated, and waiting in dim Borough doorway by appointment, to replace the trusty Rogers whom we left deep in St. Giles's, are you ready? Ready, Inspector Field, and at a motion of my wrist behold my flaming eye.

This narrow street, sir, is the chief part of the Old Mint, full of low lodging-houses, as you see by the transparent canvas-lamps and blinds, announcing beds for travellers! But it is greatly changed, friend Field, from my former knowledge of it; it is infinitely quieter and more subdued than when I was here last, some seven years ago? Oh, yes! Inspector Haynes, a first-rate man, is on this station now and plays the Devil with them!

Well, my lads! How are you to-night, my lads! Playing cards here, eh? Who wins? — Why, Mr. Field, I, the sulky gentleman with the damp flat side-curls, rubbing my bleared eye with the end of my neckerchief which is like a dirty eel-skin, am losing just at present, but I suppose I must take my pipe out of my mouth, and be submissive to *you* — I hope I see you well, Mr. Field? — Aye, all right, my lad. Deputy, who have you got up stairs? Be pleased to show the rooms!

Why Deputy, Inspector Field can't say. He only knows

that the man who takes care of the beds and lodgers is always called so. Steady, O Deputy, with the flaring candle in the blacking-bottle, for this is a slushy back-yard, and the wooden staircase outside the house creaks and has holes in it.

Again, in these confined intolerable rooms, burrowed out like the holes of rats or the nests of insect-vermin, but fuller of intolerable smells, are crowds of sleepers, each on his foul truckle-bed coiled up beneath a rug. Halloa here! Come! Let us see you! Show your face! Pilot Parker goes from bed to bed and turns their slumbering heads towards us, as a salesman might turn sheep. Some wake up with an execration and a threat. — What! who spoke? Oh! If it's the accursed glaring eye that fixes me, go where I will, I am helpless. Here! I sit up to be looked at. Is it me you want? — Not you, lie down again! — and I lie down, with a woeful growl.

Wherever the turning lane of light becomes stationary for a moment, some sleeper appears at the end of it, submits himself to be scrutinised, and fades away into the darkness.

There should be strange dreams here, Deputy. They sleep sound enough, says Deputy, taking the candle out of the black-ing-bottle, snuffing it with his fingers, throwing the snuff into the bottle, and corking it up with the candle; that's all *I* know. What is the inscription, Deputy, on all the discoloured sheets? A precaution against loss of linen. Deputy turns down the rug of an unoccupied bed and discloses it. STOP THIEF!

To lie at night, wrapped in the legend of my slinking life: to take the cry that pursues me, waking, to my breast in sleep; to have it staring at me, and clamouring for me, as soon as consciousness returns; to have it for my first-foot on New Year's Day, my Valentine, my Birthday salute, my Christmas greeting, my parting with the old year. STOP THIEF!

And to know that I *must* be stopped, come what will. To know that I am no match for this individual energy and keen-ness, or this organised and steady system! Come across the street, here, and entering by a little shop, and yard, examine these intricate passages and doors, contrived for escape, flap-ping and counter-flapping, like the lids of the conjurer's boxes. But what avail they? Who gets in by a nod, and shows their secret working to us? Inspector Field.

Don't forget the old Farm House, Parker! Parker is not

the man to forget it. We are going there, now. It is the old
Manor House of these parts, and stood in the country once.
Then, perhaps, there was something, which was not the beastly
street, to see from the shattered low fronts of the overhanging
wooden houses we are passing under — shut up now, pasted
over with bills about the literature and drama of the Mint, and
mouldering away. This long paved yard was a paddock or a
garden once, or a court in front of the Farm House. Per-
chance, with a dovecot in the centre, and fowls pecking about
— with fair elm-trees, then, where discoloured chimney-stacks
and gables are now — noisy, then, with rooks which have
yielded to a different sort of rookery. It's likelier than not,
Inspector Field thinks, as we turn into the common kitchen,
which is in the yard, and many paces from the house.

Well, my lads and lasses, how are you all! Where 's Blackey,
who has stood near London Bridge these five-and-twenty years,
with a painted skin to represent disease? — Here he is, Mr.
Field! — How are you, Blackey? — Jolly, sa! — Not playing
the fiddle to-night, Blackey? — Not a night, sa! — A sharp,
smiling youth, the wit of the kitchen, interposes. He ain't
musical to-night, sir. I've been giving him a moral lecture;
I've been a talking to him about his latter end, you see. A
good many of these are my pupils, sir. This here young man
(smoothing down the hair of one near him, reading a Sunday
paper) is a pupil of mine. I'm a teaching of him to read, sir.
He's a promising cove, sir. He's a smith, he is, and gets
his living by the sweat of the brow, sir. So do I, myself,
sir. This young woman is my sister, Mr. Field. *She's* getting on very well too. I've a deal of trouble with 'em, sir,
but I'm richly rewarded, now I see 'em all a doing so well,
and growing up so creditable. That 's a great comfort, that
is, ain't it, sir? — In the midst of the kitchen (the whole
kitchen is in ecstasies with this impromptu "chaff") sits a
young, modest, gentle-looking creature, with a beautiful child
in her lap. She seems to belong to the company, but is so
strangely unlike it. She has such a pretty, quiet face and
voice, and is so proud to hear the child admired — thinks you
would hardly believe that he is only nine months old! Is she
as bad as the rest, I wonder? Inspectorial experience does
not engender a belief contrariwise, but prompts the answer,
Not a ha'porth of difference!

There is a piano going in the old Farm House as we approach. It stops. Landlady appears. Has no objections, Mr. Field, to gentlemen being brought, but wishes it were at earlier hours, the lodgers complaining of ill-conwenience. Inspector Field is polite and soothing — knows his woman and the sex. Deputy (a girl in this case) shows the way up a heavy broad old staircase, kept very clean, into clean rooms where many sleepers are, and where painted panels of an older time look strangely on the truckle-beds. The sight of whitewash and the smell of soap — two things we seem by this time to have parted from in infancy — make the old Farm House a phenomenon, and connect themselves with the so curiously misplaced picture of the pretty mother and child long after we have left it, — long after we have left, besides, the neighbouring nook with something of a rustic flavour in it yet, where once, beneath a low wooden colonnade still standing as of yore, the eminent Jack Sheppard condescended to regale himself, and where, now, two old bachelor brothers in broad hats (who are whispered in the Mint to have made a compact long ago that if either should ever marry, he must forfeit his share of the joint property) still keep a sequestered tavern, and sit o' nights smoking pipes in the bar, among ancient bottles and glasses, as our eyes behold them.

How goes the night now? St. George of Southwark answers with twelve blows upon his bell. Parker, good night, for Williams is already waiting over in the region of Ratcliffe Highway, to show the houses where the sailors dance.

I should like to know where Inspector Field was born. In Ratcliffe Highway, I would have answered with confidence, but for his being equally at home wherever we go. *He* does not trouble his head as I do, about the river at night. *He* does not care for its creeping, black and silent, on our right there, rushing through sluice gates, lapping at piles and posts and iron rings, hiding strange things in its mud, running away with suicides and accidentally drowned bodies faster than midnight funeral should, and acquiring such various experience between its cradle and its grave. It has no mystery for *him*. Is there not the Thames Police!

Accordingly, Williams leads the way. We are a little late, for some of the houses are already closing. No matter. You show us plenty. All the landlords know Inspector Field.

All pass him, freely and good-humouredly, wheresoever he wants to go. So thoroughly are all these houses open to him and our local guide, that, granting that sailors must be entertained in their own way, — as I suppose they must, and have a right to be, — I hardly know how such places could be better regulated. Not that I call the company very select, or the dancing very graceful, — even so graceful as that of the German Sugar Bakers, whose assembly, by the Minories, we stopped to visit, — but there is watchful maintenance of order in every house, and swift expulsion where need is. Even in the midst of drunkenness, both of the lethargic kind and the lively, there is sharp landlord supervision, and pockets are in less peril than out of doors. These houses show, singularly, how much of the picturesque and romantic there truly is in the sailor, requiring to be especially addressed. All the songs (sung in a hailstorm of halfpence, which are pitched at the singer without the least tenderness for the time or tune, — mostly from great rolls of copper carried for the purpose, — and which he occasionally dodges like shot as they fly near his head) are of the sentimental sea sort. All the rooms are decorated with nautical subjects. Wrecks, engagements, ships on fire, ships passing lighthouses on iron-bound coasts, ships blowing up, ships going down, ships running ashore, men lying out upon the main yard in a gale of wind, sailors and ships in every variety of peril, constitute the illustrations of fact. Nothing can be done in the fanciful way without a thumping boy upon a scaly dolphin.

How goes the night now? Past one. Black and Green are waiting in Whitechapel to unveil the mysteries of Wentworth Street. Williams, the best of friends must part. Adieu!

Are not Black and Green ready at the appointed place? Oh, yes! They glide out of shadow as we stop. Imperturbable Black opens the cab-door; Imperturbable Green takes a mental note of the driver. Both Green and Black then open, each his flaming eye, and marshal us the way that we are going.

The lodging-house we want is hidden in a maze of streets and courts. It is fast shut. We knock at the door, and stand hushed looking up for a light at one or other of the begrimed old lattice windows in its ugly front, when another constable comes up — supposes that we want "to see the school." Detective Sergeant meanwhile has got over a rail, opened a gate, dropped down an area, overcome some other little obstacles, and tapped at a window. Now returns. The landlord will send a deputy immediately. Deputy is heard to stumble out of bed. Deputy lights a candle, draws back a bolt or two, and appears at the door. Deputy is a shivering shirt and trousers by no means clean, a yawning face, a shock head much confused externally and internally. We want to look for some one. You may go up with the light, and take 'em all, if you like, says Deputy, resigning it, and sitting down upon a bench in the kitchen with his ten fingers sleepily twisting in his hair. Halloa here! Now then! Show yourselves. That 'll do. It 's not you. Don't disturb yourself any more! So on, through a labyrinth of airless rooms, each man responding, like a wild beast, to the keeper who has tamed him, and who goes into his cage. What, you have n't found him, then? says Deputy, when we come down. A woman, mysteriously sitting up all night in the dark by the smouldering ashes of the kitchen fire, says it 's only tramps and cadgers here; it 's gonophs over the way. A man, mysteriously walking about the kitchen all night in the dark, bids her hold her tongue. We come out. Deputy fastens the door and goes to bed again.

Black and Green, you know Bark, lodging-house keeper and receiver of stolen goods? — Oh, yes, Inspector Field. — Go to Bark's next.

Bark sleeps in an inner wooden hutch, near his street door. As we parley on the step with Bark's Deputy, Bark growls in his bed. We enter, and Bark flies out of bed. Bark is a red villain and a wrathful, with a sanguine throat that looks very much as if it were expressly made for hanging, as he stretches it out, in pale defiance, over the half-door of his hutch. Bark's parts of speech are of an awful sort — principally adjectives. I won't, says Bark, have no adjective police and adjective strangers in my adjective premises! I won't, by adjective and substantive! Give me my trousers, and I 'll send the whole adjective police to adjective and substantive! Give me, says Bark, my adjective trousers! I 'll put an adjective knife in the whole bileing of 'em. I 'll punch their adjective heads. I 'll rip up their adjective substantives. Give me my adjective trousers! says Bark, and I 'll spile the bileing of 'em!

Now, Bark, what's the use of this? Here's Black and
Green, Detective Sergeant, and Inspector Field. You know
we will come in. — I know you won't! says Bark. Somebody
give me my adjective trousers! Bark's trousers seem difficult
to find. He calls for them, as Hercules might for his club.
Give me my adjective trousers! says Bark, and I'll spile the
bileing of 'em!

Inspector Field holds that it's all one whether Bark likes
the visit or don't like it. He, Inspector Field, is an Inspector
of the Detective Police, Detective Sergeant *is* Detective Sergeant, Black and Green are constables in uniform. Don't you
be a fool, Bark, or you know it will be the worse for you. —
I don't care, says Bark. Give me my adjective trousers!

At two o'clock in the morning, we descend into Bark's low
kitchen, leaving Bark to foam at the mouth above, and Imperturbable Black and Green to look at him. Bark's kitchen is
crammed full of thieves, holding a *conversazione* there by lamp-
light. It is by far the most dangerous assembly we have seen
yet. Stimulated by the ravings of Bark, above, their looks
are sullen, but not a man speaks. We ascend again. Bark
has got his trousers, and is in a state of madness in the passage
with his back against a door that shuts off the upper staircase.
We observe, in other respects, a ferocious individuality in Bark.
Instead of "STOP THIEF!" on his linen, he prints, "STOLEN
FROM BARKS'!"

Now Bark, we are going up stairs! — No, you ain't! — You
refuse admission to the Police, do you, Bark? — Yes, I do!
I refuse it to all the adjective police and to all the adjective
substantives. If the adjective coves in the kitchen was men,
they'd come up now, and do for you! Shut me that there
door! says Bark, and suddenly we are inclosed in the passage.
They'd come up and do for you! cries Bark, and waits. Not
a sound in the kitchen! They'd come up and do for you!
cries Bark again, and waits. Not a sound in the kitchen!
We are shut up, half a dozen of us, in Bark's house in the
innermost recesses of the worst part of London, in the dead of
the night, — the house is crammed with notorious robbers and
ruffians, — and not a man stirs. No, Bark. They know the
weight of the law, and they know Inspector Field and Co. too
well.

We leave bully Bark to subside at leisure out of his passion and his trousers, and, I dare say, to be inconveniently reminded of this little brush before long. Black and Green do ordinary duty here, and look serious.

As to White, who waits on Holborn Hill to show the courts that are eaten out of Rotten Gray's Inn Lane, where other lodging-houses are, and where (in one blind alley) the Thieves' Kitchen and Seminary for the teaching of the art to children, is, the night has so worn away, being now

Almost at odds with morning, which is which,

that they are quiet, and no light shines through the chinks in the shutters. As undistinctive Death will come here, one day, sleep comes now. The wicked cease from troubling sometimes, even in this life.

VI

OUR ENGLISH WATERING-PLACE

In the Autumn-time of the year, when the great metropolis is so much hotter, so much noisier, so much more dusty or so much more water-carted, so much more crowded, so much more disturbing and distracting in all respects, than it usually is, a quiet sea-beach becomes indeed a blessed spot. Half awake and half asleep, this idle morning in our sunny window on the edge of a chalk cliff in the old-fashioned watering-place to which we are a faithful resorter, we feel a lazy inclination to sketch its picture.

The place seems to respond. Sky, sea, beach, and village lie as still before us as if they were sitting for the picture. It is dead low-water. A ripple plays among the ripening corn upon the cliff, as if it were faintly trying from recollection to imitate the sea; and the world of butterflies hovering over the crop of radish-seed are as restless in their little way as the gulls are in their larger manner when the wind blows. But the ocean lies winking in the sunlight like a drowsy lion — its glassy waters scarcely curve upon the shore — the fishing-boats in the tiny harbour are all stranded in the mud — our two colliers (our watering-place has a maritime trade employing that amount of shipping) have not an inch of water within a quarter of a mile of them, and turn, exhausted, on their sides, like faint fish of an antediluvian species. Rusty cables and chains, ropes and rings, undermost parts of posts and piles and confused timber-defences against the waves, lie strewn about, in a brown litter of tangled sea-weed and fallen cliff which looks as if a family of giants had been making tea here for ages, and had observed an untidy custom of throwing their tea-leaves on the shore.

In truth our watering-place itself has been left somewhat high and dry by the tide of years. Concerned as we are for its honour, we must reluctantly admit that the time when this pretty little semicircular sweep of houses tapering off at the end of the wooden pier into a point in the sea was a gay place, and when the lighthouse overlooking it shone at day-break on company dispersing from public balls, is but dimly traditional now. There is a bleak chamber in our watering-place which is yet called the Assembly "Rooms," and under-stood to be available on hire for balls or concerts; and, some few seasons since, an ancient little gentleman came down and stayed at the hotel, who said he had danced there, in bygone ages, with the Honourable Miss Peepy, well known to have been the Beauty of her day and the cruel occasion of innumer-able duels. But he was so old and shrivelled, and so very rheumatic in the legs, that it demanded more imagination than our watering-place can usually muster, to believe him; there-fore, except the Master of the "Rooms" (who to this hour wears knee-breeches, and who confirmed the statement with tears in his eyes), nobody did believe in the little lame old gentleman, or even in the Honourable Miss Peepy, long deceased.

As to subscription balls in the Assembly Rooms of our watering-place now red-hot cannon-balls are less improbable. Sometimes, a misguided wanderer of a Ventriloquist, or an Infant Phenomenon, or a Juggler, or somebody with an Orrery that is several stars behind the time, takes the place for a night, and issues bills with the name of his last town lined out, and the name of ours ignominiously written in, but you may be sure this never happens twice to the same unfortunate person. On such occasions the discoloured old Billiard Table that is seldom played at (unless the ghost of the Honourable Miss Peepy plays at pool with other ghosts) is pushed into a corner, and benches are solemnly constituted into front seats, back seats, and reserved seats — which are much the same after you have paid — and a few dull candles are lighted — wind permitting — and the performer and the scanty audience play out a short match which shall make the other most low-spir-ited — which is usually a drawn game. After that, the per-former instantly departs with maledictory expressions, and is never heard of more.

But the most wonderful feature of our Assembly Rooms is, that an annual sale of "Fancy and other China" is announced here with mysterious constancy and perseverance. Where the china comes from, where it goes to, why it is annually put up to auction when nobody ever thinks of bidding for it, how it comes to pass that it is always the same china, whether it would not have been cheaper, with the sea at hand, to have thrown it away, say in eighteen hundred and thirty, are standing enigmas. Every year the bills come out; every year the Master of the Rooms gets into a little pulpit on a table, and offers it for sale; every year nobody buys it; every year it is put away somewhere until next year, when it appears again as if the whole thing were a new idea. We have a faint remembrance of an unearthly collection of clocks, purporting to be the work of Parisian and Genevese artists, — chiefly bilious-faced clocks, supported on sickly white crutches, with their pendulums dangling like lame legs, — to which a similar course of events occurred for several years, until they seemed to lapse away of mere imbecility.

Attached to our Assembly Rooms is a library. There is a wheel of fortune in it, but it is rusty and dusty, and never turns. A large doll, with movable eyes, was put up to be raffled for, by five-and-twenty members at two shillings, seven years ago this autumn, and the list is not full yet. We are rather sanguine, now, that the raffle will come off next year. We think so, because we only want nine members, and should only want eight, but for number two having grown up since her name was entered, and withdrawn it when she was married. Down the street there is a toy-ship of considerable burden, in the same condition. Two of the boys who were entered for that raffle have gone to India in real ships, since; and one was shot, and died in the arms of his sister's lover, by whom he sent his last words home.

This is the library for the Minerva Press. If you want that kind of reading, come to our watering-place. The leaves of the romances, reduced to a condition very like curl-paper, are thickly studded with notes in pencil — sometimes complimentary, sometimes jocose. Some of these commentators, like commentators in a more extensive way, quarrel with one another. One young gentleman who sarcastically writes "O!!!" after every sentimental passage is pursued through his literary career by another, who writes "Insulting Beast!" Miss Julia Mills has read the whole collection of these books. She has left marginal notes on the pages, as "Is not this truly touching? J. M." "How thrilling! J. M." "Entranced here by the Magician's potent spell. J. M." She has also italicised her favourite traits in the description of the hero, as "his hair, which was *dark* and *wavy*, clustered in *rich profusion* around a *marble brow*, whose lofty paleness bespoke the intellect within." It reminds her of another hero. She adds, "How like B. L.! Can this be mere coincidence? J. M."

You would hardly guess which is the main street of our watering-place, but you may know it by its being always stopped up with donkey-chaises. Whenever you come here, and see harnessed donkeys eating clover out of barrows drawn completely across a narrow thoroughfare, you may be quite sure you are in our High Street. Our Police you may know by his uniform, likewise by his never on any account interfering with anybody — especially the tramps and vagabonds. In our fancy shops we have a capital collection of damaged goods, among which the flies of countless summers "have been roaming." We are great in obsolete seals, and in faded pin-cushions, and in rickety camp-stools, and in exploded cutlery, and in miniature vessels, and in stunted little telescopes, and in objects made of shells that pretend not to be shells. Diminutive spades, barrows, and baskets, are our principal articles of commerce; but even they don't look quite new somehow. They always seem to have been offered and refused somewhere else, before they came down to our watering-place.

Yet, it must not be supposed that our watering-place is an empty place, deserted by all visitors except a few stanch persons of approved fidelity. On the contrary, the chances are that if you came down here in August or September, you would n't find a house to lay your head in. As to finding either house or lodging of which you could reduce the terms, you could scarcely engage in a more hopeless pursuit. For all this, you are to observe that every season is the worst season ever known, and that the householding population of our watering-place are ruined regularly every autumn. They are like the farmers, in regard that it is surprising how much ruin they will bear. We have an excellent hotel — capital baths, warm, cold, and shower — first-rate bathing-machines — and as good butchers, bakers, and grocers, as heart could desire. They all do business, it is to be presumed, from motives of philanthropy; but it is quite certain that they are all being ruined. Their interest in strangers and their politeness under ruin bespeak their amiable nature. You would say so, if you only saw the baker helping a new-comer to find suitable apartments.

So far from being at a discount as to company, we are in fact what would be popularly called rather a nobby place. Some tip-top "Nobbs" come down occasionally — even Dukes and Duchesses. We have known such carriages to blaze among the donkey-chaises as made beholders wink. Attendant on these equipages come resplendent creatures in plush and powder, who are sure to be stricken disgusted with the indifferent accommodation of our watering-place, and who, of an evening (particularly when it rains), may be seen very much out of drawing, in rooms far too small for their fine figures, looking discontentedly out of little back windows into by-streets. The lords and ladies get on well enough and quite good-humouredly; but if you want to see the gorgeous phenomena who wait upon them, at a perfect nonplus, you should come and look at the resplendent creatures with little back parlours for servants' halls, and turn-up bedsteads to sleep in, at our watering-place. You have no idea how they take it to heart.

We have a pier — a queer old wooden pier, fortunately without the slightest pretensions to architecture, and very picturesque in consequence. Boats are hauled up upon it, ropes are coiled all over it; lobster-pots, nets, masts, oars, spars, sails, ballast, and rickety capstans, make a perfect labyrinth of it. For ever hovering about this pier, with their hands in their pockets, or leaning over the rough bulwark it opposes to the sea, gazing through telescopes which they carry about in the same profound receptacles, are the Boatmen of our watering-place. Looking at them, you would say that surely these must be the laziest boatmen in the world. They lounge about, in obstinate and inflexible pantaloons that are apparently made of wood, the whole season through. Whether talking together about the shipping in the Channel, or gruffly unbending over mugs of beer at the public-house, you would consider them the slowest of men. The chances are a thousand to one that you might stay here for ten seasons, and never see a boatman in a hurry. A certain expression about his loose hands, when they are not in his pockets, as if he were carrying a considerable lump of iron in each, without any inconvenience, suggests

strength, but he never seems to use it. He has the appearance of perpetually strolling — running is too inappropriate a
word to be thought of — to seed. The only subject on which
he seems to feel any approach to enthusiasm is pitch. He
pitches everything he can lay hold of, — the pier, the palings,
his boat, his house; when there is nothing else left he turns
to and even pitches his hat, or his rough-weather clothing.
Do not judge him by deceitful appearances. These are among
the bravest and most skilful mariners that exist. Let a gale
arise and swell into a storm, let a sea run that might appal
the stoutest heart that ever beat, let the light-boat on these
dangerous sands throw up a rocket in the night, or let them
hear through the angry roar the signal-guns of a ship in distress, and these men spring up into activity so dauntless, so
valiant, and heroic, that the world cannot surpass it. Cavillers
may object that they chiefly live upon the salvage of valuable
cargoes. So they do, and God knows it is no great living
that they get out of the deadly risks they run. But put that
hope of gain aside. Let these rough fellows be asked, in any
storm, who volunteers for the life-boat to save some perishing
souls, as poor and empty-handed as themselves, whose lives
the perfection of human reason does not rate at the value of a
farthing each, and that boat will be manned, as surely and as
cheerfully, as if a thousand pounds were told down on the
weather-beaten pier. For this, and for the recollection of
their comrades whom we have known, whom the raging sea
has engulfed before their children's eyes in such brave efforts,
whom the secret sand has buried, we hold the boatmen of our
watering-place in our love and honour, and are tender of the
fame they well deserve.

So many children are brought down to our watering-place
that, when they are not out of doors, as they usually are in
fine weather, it is wonderful where they are put; the whole
village seeming much too small to hold them under cover. In
the afternoons, you see no end of salt and sandy little boots
drying on upper window-sills. At bathing-time in the morning, the little bay re-echoes with every shrill variety of shriek
and splash; after which, if the weather be at all fresh, the
sands teem with small blue mottled legs. The sands are the
children's great resort. They cluster there, like ants; so busy
burying their particular friends, and making castles with infi-

nite labour which the next tide overthrows, that it is curious
to consider how their play, to the music of the sea, foreshadows
the realities of their after lives.

It is curious, too, to observe a natural ease of approach th
there seems to be between the children and the boatmer:
They mutually make acquaintance, and take individual likings,
without any help. You will come upon one of those slow
heavy fellows sitting down patiently mending a little ship for
a mite of a boy, whom he could crush to death by throwing
his lightest pair of trousers on him. You will be sensible of
the oddest contrast between the smooth little creature and the
rough man who seems to be carved out of hard-grained wood
— between the delicate hand expectantly held out and the
immense thumb and finger that can hardly feel the rigging of
thread they mend — between the small voice and the gruff
growl, — and yet there is a natural propriety in the companionship, always to be noted in confidence between a child and a
person who has any merit of reality and genuineness, which is
admirably pleasant.

We have a preventive station at our watering-place, and
much the same thing may be observed — in a lesser degree,
because of their official character — of the coast blockade; a
steady, trusty, well-conditioned, well-conducted set of men,
with no misgiving about looking you full in the face, and with
a quiet, thoroughgoing way of passing along to their duty at
night, carrying huge sou'-wester clothing in reserve, that is
fraught with all good prepossession. They are handy fellows
— neat about their houses — industrious at gardening — would
get on with their wives, one thinks, in a desert island — and
people it, too, soon.

As to the naval officer of the station, with his hearty, fresh
face, and his blue eye that has pierced all kinds of weather, it
warms our hearts when he comes into church on a Sunday,
with that bright mixture of blue coat, buff waistcoat, black
neckerchief, and gold epaulette, that is associated in the minds
of all Englishmen with brave, unpretending, cordial, national
service. We like to look at him in his Sunday state; and if
we were First Lord (really possessing the indispensable qualification for the office of knowing nothing whatever about the
sea), we would give him a ship to-morrow.

We have a church, by the bye, of course — a hideous temple

of flint, like a great petrified haystack. Our chief clerical dignitary, who, to his honour, has done much for education both in time and money, and has established excellent schools, is a sound, shrewd, healthy gentleman, who has got into little occasional difficulties with the neighbouring farmers, but has had a pestilent trick of being right. Under a new regulation, he has yielded the church of our watering-place to another clergyman. Upon the whole we get on in church well. We are a little bilious, sometimes, about these days of fraternisation, and about nations arriving at a new and more unprejudiced knowledge of each other (which our Christianity don't quite approve), but it soon goes off, and then we get on very well.

There are two dissenting chapels, besides, in our small watering-place; being in about the proportion of a hundred and twenty guns to a yacht. But the dissension that has torn us lately has not been a religious one. It has arisen on the novel question of Gas. Our watering-place has been convulsed by the agitation, Gas or No Gas. It was never reasoned why No Gas, but there was a great No Gas party. Broadsides were printed and stuck about — a startling circumstance in our watering-place. The No Gas party rested content with chalking "No Gas!" and "Down with Gas!" and other such angry war-whoops, on the few back gates and scraps of wall which the limits of our watering-place afford; but the Gas party printed and posted bills, wherein they took the high ground of proclaiming against the No Gas party, that it was said, Let there be light and there was light; and that not to have light (that is, gas light) in our watering-place was to contravene the great decree. Whether by these thunderbolts or not, the No Gas party were defeated; and in this present season we have had our handful of shops illuminated for the first time. Such of the No Gas party, however, as have got shops remain in opposition and burn tallow — exhibiting in their windows the very picture of the sulkiness that punishes itself, and a new illustration of the old adage about cutting off your nose to be revenged on your face, in cutting off their gas to be revenged on their business.

Other population than we have indicated, our watering-place has none. There are a few old, used-up boatmen who creep about in the sunlight with the help of sticks, and there is a poor imbecile shoemaker who wanders his lonely life away among the rocks, as if he were looking for his reason — which he will never find. Sojourners in neighbouring watering-places come occasionally in flys to stare at us, and drive away again as if they thought us very dull; Italian boys come, Punch comes, the Fantoccini come, the Tumblers come, the Ethiopians come; Glee-singers come at night, and hum and vibrate (not always melodiously) under our windows. But they all go soon, and leave us to ourselves again. We once had a travelling Circus and Wombwell's Menagerie at the same time. They both know better than ever to try it again; and the Menagerie had nearly razed us from the face of the earth in getting the elephant away — his caravan was so large, and the watering-place so small. We have a fine sea, wholesome for all people; profitable for the body, profitable for the mind. The poet's words are sometimes on its awful lips: —

> "And the stately ships go on
> To their haven under the hill ;
> But O for the touch of a vanish'd hand,
> And the sound of a voice that is still!

> "Break, break, break,
> At the foot of thy crags, O Sea!
> But the tender grace of a day that is dead!
> Will never come back to me."

Yet it is not always so, for the speech of the sea is various, and wants not abundant resource of cheerfulness, hope, and lusty encouragement. And since I have been idling at the window here, the tide has risen. The boats are dancing on the bubbling water; the colliers are afloat again; the white-bordered waves rush in; the children

> "Do chase the ebbing Neptune, and do fly him
> When he comes back ;"

the radiant sails are gliding past the shore, and shining on the far horizon; all the sea is sparkling, heaving, swelling up with life and beauty, this bright morning.

VII

A FLIGHT

WHEN Don Diego de — I forget his name — the inventor of
the last new Flying Machines, price so many francs for ladies,
so many more for gentlemen — when Don Diego, by permission
of Deputy Chaff Wax and his noble band, shall have taken
out a Patent for the Queen's dominions, and shall have opened
a commodious Warehouse in an airy situation, and when all
persons of any gentility will keep at least a pair of wings, and
be seen skimming about in every direction, I shall take a
flight to Paris (as I soar round the world) in a cheap and independent manner. At present, my reliance is on the South
Eastern Railway Company, in whose Express Train here I sit,
at eight of the clock on a very hot morning, under the very
hot roof of the Terminus at London Bridge, in danger of being
"forced" like a cucumber, or a melon, or a pine-apple. And
talking of pine-apples, I suppose there never were so many
pine-apples in a train as there appear to be in this Train.
Whew! The hot-house air is faint with pine-apples. Every
French citizen or citizeness is carrying pine-apples home. The
compact little Enchantress in the corner of my carriage (French
actress, to whom I yielded up my heart under the auspices of
that brave child, "MEAT-CHELL," at the St. James's Theatre,
the night before last) has a pine-apple in her lap. Compact
Enchantress's friend, confidante, mother, mystery, Heaven
knows what, has two pine-apples in her lap, and a bundle of
them under the seat. Tobacco-smoky Frenchman in Algerine
wrapper, with peaked hood behind, who might be Abd-el-
Kader dyed rifle-green, and who seems to be dressed entirely
in dirt and braid, carries pine-apples in a covered basket.
Tall, grave, melancholy Frenchman, with black Vandyke beard,
and hair close cropped, with expansive chest to waistcoat, and
compressive waist to coat; saturnine as to his pantaloons, calm
as to his feminine boots, precious as to his jewellery, smooth
and white as to his linen; dark-eyed, high-foreheaded, hawk-
nosed, — got up, one thinks, like Lucifer or Mephistopheles,

or Zamiel, transformed into a highly genteel Parisian, — has the green end of a pine-apple sticking out of his neat valise.

Whew! If I were to be kept here long, under this forcing-frame, I wonder what would become of me, — whether I should be forced into a giant, or should sprout or blow into some other phenomenon! Compact Enchantress is not ruffled by the heat — she is always composed, always compact. Oh, look at her little ribbons, frills, and edges, at her shawl, at her gloves, at her hair, at her bracelets, at her bonnet, at everything about her! How is it accomplished? What does she do to be so neat? How is it that every trifle she wears belongs to her, and cannot choose but be a part of her? And even Mystery, look at *her!* A model. Mystery is not young, not pretty, though still of an average candle-light passability; but she does such miracles in her own behalf, that, one of these days, when she dies, they'll be amazed to find an old woman in her bed, distantly like her. She was an actress once, I shouldn't wonder, and had a Mystery attendant on herself. Perhaps, Compact Enchantress will live to be a Mystery, and to wait with a shawl at the side-scenes, and to sit opposite to Mademoiselle in railway carriages, and smile and talk subserviently, as Mystery does now. That's hard to believe!

Two Englishmen, and now our carriage is full. First Englishman, in the moneyed interest — flushed, highly respectable — Stock Exchange, perhaps — City, certainly. Faculties of second Englishman entirely absorbed in hurry. Plunges into the carriage, blind. Calls out of window concerning his luggage, deaf. Suffocates himself under pillows of great-coats, for no reason, and in a demented manner. Will receive no assurance from any porter whatsoever. Is stout and hot, and wipes his head, and makes himself hotter by breathing so hard. Is totally incredulous respecting assurance of Collected Guard that "there's no hurry." No hurry! And a flight to Paris in eleven hours!

It is all one to me in this drowsy corner, hurry or no hurry. Until Don Diego shall send home my wings, my flight is with the South Eastern Company. I can fly with the South Eastern more lazily, at all events, than in the upper air. I have but to sit here thinking as idly as I please and be whisked away. I am not accountable to anybody for the idleness of my thoughts in such an idle summer flight; my flight is provided for by the South Eastern, and is no business of mine.

The bell! With all my heart. It does not require *me* to do so much as even to flap my wings. Something snorts for me, something shrieks for me, something proclaims to everything else that it had better keep out of my way, — and away I go.

Ah! The fresh air is pleasant after the forcing-frame, though it does blow over these interminable streets, and scatter the smoke of this vast wilderness of chimneys. Here we are — no, I mean there we were, for it has darted far into the rear — in Bermondsey where the tanners live. Flash! The distant shipping in the Thames is gone. Whir! The little streets of new brick and red tile, with here and there a flag-staff growing like a tall weed out of the scarlet beans, and, everywhere, plenty of open sewer and ditch for the promotion of the public health, have been fired off in a volley. Whiz! Dust-heaps, market-gardens, and waste grounds. Rattle! New Cross Station. Shock! There we were at Croydon. Bur-r-r-r! The tunnel.

I wonder why it is that when I shut my eyes in a tunnel I begin to feel as if I were going at an Express pace the other way. I am clearly going back to London now. Compact Enchantress must have forgotten something, and reversed the engine. No! After long darkness, pale fitful streaks of light appear. I am still flying on for Folkestone. The streaks grow stronger — become continuous — become the ghost of day — become the living day — became I mean — the tunnel is miles and miles away, and here I fly through sunlight, all among the harvest and the Kentish hops.

There is a dreamy pleasure in this flying. I wonder where it was, and when it was, that we exploded, blew into space somehow, a Parliamentary Train, with a crowd of heads and faces looking at us out of cages, and some hats waving. Moneyed Interest says it was at Reigate Station. Expounds to Mystery how Reigate Station is so many miles from London, which Mystery again develops to Compact Enchantress. There might be neither a Reigate nor a London for me, as I fly away among the Kentish hops and harvest. What do *I* care!

Bang! We have let another Station off, and fly away regardless. Everything is flying. The hop-gardens turn gracefully towards me, presenting regular avenues of hops in rapid flight, then whirl away. So do the pools and rushes, haystacks, sheep, clover in full bloom delicious to the sight and smell, corn-sheaves, cherry-orchards, apple-orchards, reapers, gleaners, hedges, gates, fields that taper off into little angular corners, cottages, gardens, now and then a church. Bang, bang! A double-barrelled Station! Now a wood, now a bridge, now a landscape, now a cutting, now a— Bang! a single-barrelled Station — there was a cricket match somewhere with two white tents, and then four flying cows, then turnips — now the wires of the electric telegraph are all alive, and spin, and blur their edges, and go up and down, and make the intervals between each other most irregular; contracting and expanding in the strangest manner. Now we slacken. With a screwing, and a grinding, and a smell of water thrown on ashes, now we stop!

Demented Traveller, who has been for two or three minutes watchful, clutches his great-coats, plunges at the door, rattles it, cries "Hi!" eager to embark on board of impossible packets, far inland. Collected. Guard appears. "Are you for Tunbridge, sir?" "Tunbridge? No. Paris." "Plenty of time, sir. No hurry. Five minutes here, sir, for refreshment." I am so blest (anticipating Zamiel by half a second) as to procure a glass of water for Compact Enchantress.

Who would suppose we had been flying at such a rate, and shall take wing again directly? Refreshment-room full, platform full, porter with watering-pot deliberately cooling a hot wheel, another porter with equal deliberation helping the rest of the wheels bountifully to ice cream. Moneyed Interest and I re-entering the carriage first, and being there alone, he intimates to me that the French are "no go" as a Nation. I ask why? He says, that Reign of Terror of theirs was quite enough. I ventured to inquire whether he remembers anything that preceded said Reign of Terror? He says not particularly. "Because," I remark, "the harvest that is reaped has sometimes been sown." Moneyed Interest repeats, as quite enough for him, that the French are revolutionary, — "and always at it."

Bell. Compact Enchantress, helped in by Zamiel (whom the stars confound!), gives us her charming little side-box look, and smites me to the core. Mystery eating sponge-cake. Pine-apple atmosphere faintly tinged with suspicions of sherry.

Demented Traveller flits past the carriage, looking for it. Is blind with agitation, and can't see it. Seems singled out by Destiny to be the only unhappy creature in the flight who has any cause to hurry himself. Is nearly left behind. Is seized by Collected Guard after the Train is in motion, and bundled in. Still has lingering suspicions that there must be a boat in the neighbourhood, and *will* look wildly out of window for it.

Flight resumed. Corn-sheaves, hop-gardens, reapers, gleaners, apple-orchards, cherry-orchards, Stations single and double barrelled, Ashford. Compact Enchantress (constantly talking to Mystery, in an exquisite manner) gives a little scream; a sound that seems to come from high up in her precious little head; from behind her bright little eyebrows. "Great Heaven, my pine-apple! My Angel! It is lost!" Mystery is desolated. A search made. It is not lost. Zamiel finds it. I curse him (flying) in the Persian manner. May his face be turned upside down, and jackasses sit upon his uncle's grave!

Now fresher air, now glimpses of uninclosed Down-land with flapping crows flying over it whom we soon outfly, now the Sea, now Folkestone at a quarter after ten. "Tickets ready, gentlemen!" Demented dashes at the door. "For Paris, sir? No hurry."

Not the least. We are dropped slowly down to the Port, and sidle to and fro (the whole Train) before the insensible Royal George Hotel for some ten minutes. The Royal George takes no more heed of us than its namesake under water at Spithead or under earth at Windsor does. The Royal George's dog lies winking and blinking at us, without taking the trouble to sit up; and the Royal George's "wedding party" at the open window (who seem, I must say, rather tired of bliss) don't bestow a solitary glance upon us, flying thus to Paris in eleven hours. The first gentleman in Folkestone is evidently used up, on this subject.

Meanwhile, Demented chafes. Conceives that every man's hand is against him, and exerting itself to prevent his getting to Paris. Refuses consolation. Rattles door. Sees smoke on the horizon, and "knows" it's the boat gone without him. Moneyed Interest resentfully explains that *he* is going to Paris too. Demented signifies that if Moneyed Interest chooses to be left behind, *he* don't.

"Refreshments in the Waiting-Room, ladies and gentlemen.

No hurry, ladies and gentlemen, for Paris. No hurry whatever!"

Twenty minutes' pause, by Folkestone clock, for looking at Enchantress while she eats a sandwich, and at Mystery while she eats of everything there that is eatable, from pork-pie, sausage, jam, and gooseberries, to lumps of sugar. All this time there is a very waterfall of luggage, with a spray of dust, tumbling slantwise from the pier into the steamboat. All this time Demented (who has no business with it) watches it with starting eyes, fiercely requiring to be shown *his* luggage. When it at last concludes the cataract, he rushes hotly to refresh — is shouted after, pursued, jostled, brought back, pitched into the departing steamer upside down, and caught by mariners disgracefully.

A lovely harvest day, a cloudless sky, a tranquil sea. The piston-rods of the engines so regularly coming up from below, to look (as well they may) at the bright weather, and so regularly almost knocking their iron heads against the cross beam of the skylight and never doing it! Another Parisian actress is on board, attended by another Mystery. Compact Enchantress greets her sister artist, — oh, the Compact One's pretty teeth! — and Mystery greets Mystery. *My* Mystery soon ceases to be conversational — is taken poorly, in a word, having lunched too miscellaneously — and goes below. The remaining Mystery then smiles upon the sister artists (who, I am afraid, would n't greatly mind stabbing each other), and is upon the whole ravished.

And now I find that all the French people on board begin to grow, and all the English people to shrink. The French are nearing home, and shaking off a disadvantage, whereas we are shaking it on. Zamiel is the same man, and Abd-el-Kader is the same man, but each seems to come into possession of an indescribable confidence that departs from us — from Moneyed Interest, for instance, and from me. Just what they gain, we lose. Certain British "Gents" about the steersman, intellectually nurtured at home on parody of everything and truth of nothing, become subdued, and in a manner forlorn; and when the steersman tells them (not unexultingly) how he has "been upon this station now eight year, and never see the old town of Bullum yet," one of them, with an imbecile reliance on a reed, asks him what he considers to be the best hotel in Paris.

Now I tread upon French ground, and am greeted by the three charming words, Liberty, Equality, Fraternity, painted up (in letters a little too thin for their height) on the Custom-House wall ; also by the sight of large cocked hats, without which demonstrative head-gear nothing of a public nature can be done upon this soil. All the rabid Hotel population of Boulogne howl and shriek outside a distant barrier, frantic to get at us. Demented, by some unlucky means peculiar to himself, is delivered over to their fury, and is presently seen struggling in a whirlpool of Touters — is somehow understood to be going to Paris — is, with infinite noise, rescued by two cocked hats, and brought into Custom-House bondage with the rest of us.

Here I resign the active duties of life to an eager being, of preternatural sharpness, with a shelving forehead and a shabby snuff-coloured coat, who (from the wharf) brought me down with his eye before the boat came into port. He darts upon my luggage, on the floor where all the luggage is strewn like a wreck at the bottom of the great deep; gets it proclaimed and weighed as the property of "Monsieur a traveller unknown;" pays certain francs for it to a certain functionary behind a Pigeon Hole, like a pay-box at a theatre (the arrangements in general are on a wholesale scale, half military and half theatrical); and I suppose I shall find it when I come to Paris — he says I shall. I know nothing about it, except that I pay him his small fee, and pocket the ticket he gives me, and sit upon a counter, involved in the general distraction.

Railway station. "Lunch or dinner, ladies and gentlemen. Plenty of time for Paris. Plenty of time!" Large hall, long counter, long strips of dining-table, bottles of wine, plates of meat, roast chickens, little loaves of bread, basins of soup, little caraffes of brandy, cakes, and fruit. Comfortably restored from these resources, I begin to fly again.

I saw Zamiel (before I took wing) presented to Compact Enchantress and Sister Artist by an officer in uniform, with a waist like a wasp's, and pantaloons like two balloons. They all got into the next carriage together, accompanied by the two Mysteries. They laughed. I am alone in the carriage (for I don't consider Demented anybody) and alone in the world.

Fields, windmills, low grounds, pollard-trees, windmills, fields, fortifications, Abbeville, soldiering and drumming. I

wonder where England is, and when I was there last — about
two years ago I should say.   Flying in and out among these
trenches and batteries, skimming the clattering drawbridges,
looking down into the stagnant ditches, I become a prisoner of
state, escaping.   I am confined with a comrade in a fortress.
Our room is in an upper story.   We have tried to get up the
chimney, but there's an iron grating across it, embedded in
the masonry.   After months of labour, we have worked the
grating loose with the poker, and can lift it up.   We have
also made a hook, and twisted our rugs and blankets into
ropes.   Our plan is, to go up the chimney, hook our ropes to
the top, descend hand over hand upon the roof of the guard-
house far below, shake the hook loose, watch the opportunity
of the sentinel's pacing away, hook again, drop into the ditch,
swim across it, creep into the shelter of the wood.   The time
is come — a wild and stormy night.   We are up the chimney,
we are on the guard-house roof, we are swimming in the murky
ditch, when lo!   "Qui v'là?"   a bugle, the alarm, a crash!
What is it?   Death?   No, Amiens.

More fortifications, more soldiering and drumming, more
basins of soup, more little loaves of bread, more bottles of
wine, more caraffes of brandy, more time for refreshment.
Everything good, and everything ready.   Bright, unsubstan-
tial-looking, scenic sort of station.   People waiting.   Houses,
uniforms, beards, mustaches, some sabots, plenty of neat women,
and a few old-visaged children.   Unless it be a delusion born
of my giddy flight, the grown-up people and the children seem
to change places in France.   In general, the boys and girls are
little old men and women, and the men and women lively
boys and girls.

Bugle, shriek, flight resumed.   Moneyed Interest has come
into my carriage.   Says the manner of refreshing is "not
bad," but considers it French.   Admits great dexterity and
politeness in the attendants.   Thinks a decimal currency may
have something to do with their despatch in settling accounts,
and don't know but what it's sensible and convenient.   Adds,
however, as a general protest, that they're a revolutionary
people — and always at it.

Ramparts, canals, cathedral, river, soldiering and drumming,
open country, river, earthenware manufactures, Creil.   Again
ten minutes.   Not even Demented in a hurry.   Station, a

drawing-room with a veranda, like a planter's house. Moneyed
Interest considers it a band box, and not made to last. Little
round tables in it, at one of which the Sister Artists and attend
ant Mysteries are established with Wasp and Zamiel, as if they
were going to stay a week.

Anon, with no more trouble than before, I am flying again,
and lazily wondering as I fly. What has the South Eastern
done with all the horrible little villages we used to pass
through, in the *Diligence?* What have they done with all
the summer dust, with all the winter mud, with all the dreary
avenues of little trees, with all the ramshackle postyards, with
all the beggars (who used to turn out at night with bits of
lighted candle, to look in at the coach windows), with all the
long-tailed horses who were always biting one another, with
all the big postilions in jack-boots, with all the mouldy cafés
that we used to stop at, where a long mildewed tablecloth, set
forth with jovial bottles of vinegar and oil, and with a Siamese
arrangement of pepper and salt, was never wanting? Where
are the grass-grown little towns, the wonderful little market-
places all unconscious of markets, the shops that nobody kept,
the streets that nobody trod, the churches that nobody went
to, the bells that nobody rang, the tumble-down old buildings
plastered with many-coloured bills that nobody read? Where
are the two-and-twenty weary hours of long, long day and
night journey, sure to be either insupportably hot or insupportably cold? Where are the pains in my bones, where are the
fidgets in my legs, where is the Frenchman with the nightcap
who never *would* have the little coupé window down, and who
always fell upon me when he went to sleep, and always slept
all night snoring onions?

A voice breaks in with "Paris! Here we are!"

I have overflown myself, perhaps, but I can't believe it. I
feel as if I were enchanted or bewitched. It is barely eight
o'clock yet — it is nothing like half past — when I have had
my luggage examined at that briskest of Custom - Houses
attached to the Station, and am rattling over the pavement in
a hackney cabriolet.

Surely not the pavement of Paris? Yes, I think it is, too.
I don't know any other place where there are all these high
houses, all these haggard-looking wine-shops, all these billiard
tables, all these stocking-makers with flat red or yellow legs of

wood for signboard, all these fuel shops with stacks of billets
painted outside and real billets sawing in the gutter, all these
dirty corners of streets, all these cabinet pictures over dark
doorways representing discreet matrons nursing babies. And
yet this morning — I'll think of it in a warm bath.

Very like a small room that I remember in the Chinese
Baths upon the Boulevard, certainly; and, though I see it
through the steam, I think that I might swear to that peculiar
hot-linen basket, like a large wicker hour-glass. When can it
have been that I left home? When was it that I paid "through
to Paris" at London Bridge, and discharged myself of all responsibility, except the preservation of a voucher ruled into
three divisions, of which the first was snipped off at Folkestone,
the second aboard the boat, and the third taken at my journey's
end? It seems to have been ages ago. Calculation is useless.
I will go out for a walk.

The crowds in the streets, the lights in the shops and balconies, the elegance, variety, and beauty of their decorations,
the number of the theatres, the brilliant cafés with their windows thrown up high and their vivacious groups at little tables
on the pavement, the light and glitter of the houses turned as
it were inside out, soon convince me that it is no dream; that
I am in Paris, howsoever I got here. I stroll down to the
sparkling Palais Royal, up the Rue de Rivoli, to the Place
Vendôme. As I glance into a print-shop window, Moneyed
Interest, my late travelling companion, comes upon me, laughing with the highest relish of disdain. "Here's a people!"
he says, pointing to Napoleon in the window and Napoleon on
the column. "Only one idea all over Paris! A monomania!"
Humph! I THINK I have seen Napoleon's match? There WAS
a statue, when I came away, at Hyde Park Corner, and another
in the City, and a print or two in the shops.

I walk up to the Barrière de l'Etoile, sufficiently dazed by
my flight to have a pleasant doubt of the reality of everything
about me; of the lively crowd, the overhanging trees, the performing dogs, the hobby-horses, the beautiful perspectives of
shining lamps, the hundred and one inclosures, where the
singing is, in gleaming orchestras of azure and gold, and where
a star-eyed Houri comes round with a box for voluntary offer-
ings. So I pass to my hotel, enchanted; sup, enchanted; go
to bed, enchanted; pushing back this morning (if it really were

this morning) into the remoteness of time, blessing the South Eastern Company for realising the Arabian Nights in these prose days, murmuring, as I wing my idle flight into the land of dreams, "No hurry, ladies and gentlemen, going to Paris in eleven hours. It is so well done that there really is no hurry!"

VIII

OUR SCHOOL

WE went to look at it only this last Midsummer, and found that the Railway had cut it up root and branch. A great trunk-line had swallowed the playground, sliced away the schoolroom, and pared off the corner of the house, which, thus curtailed of its proportions, presented itself, in a green stage of stucco, profilewise towards the road, like a forlorn flat-iron without a handle, standing on end.

It seems as if our schools were doomed to be the sport of change. We have faint recollections of a Preparatory Day School, which we have sought in vain, and which must have been pulled down to make a new street ages ago. We have dim impressions, scarcely amounting to a belief, that it was over a dyer's shop. We know that you went up steps to it; that you frequently grazed your knees in doing so; that you generally got your leg over the scraper in trying to scrape the mud off a very unsteady little shoe. The mistress of the Establishment holds no place in our memory; but, rampant on one eternal door-mat, in an eternal entry long and narrow, is a puffy pug-dog, with a personal animosity towards us, who triumphs over Time. The bark of that baleful pug, a certain radiating way he had of snapping at our undefended legs, the ghastly grinning of his moist black muzzle and white teeth, and the insolence of his crisp tail curled like a pastoral crook, all live and flourish. From an otherwise unaccountable association of him with a fiddle, we conclude that he was of French extraction, and his name *Fidèle*. He belonged to some female, chiefly inhabiting a back parlour, whose life appears to us to have been consumed in sniffing and in wearing a brown beaver bonnet. For her, he would sit up and balance cake upon his nose, and not eat it until twenty had been counted. To the best of our belief we were once called in to witness this performance; when, unable, even in his milder moments, to endure our presence, he instantly made at us, cake and all.

Why a something in mourning, called "Miss Frost," should

still connect itself with our preparatory school, we are unable to say. We retain no impression of the beauty of Miss Frost — if she were beautiful; or of the mental fascinations of Miss Frost — if she were accomplished; yet her name and her black dress hold an enduring place in our remembrance. An equally impersonal boy, whose name has long since shaped itself unalterably into "Master Mawls," is not to be dislodged from our brain. Retaining no vindictive feeling towards Mawls, — no feeling whatever, indeed, — we infer that neither he nor we can have loved Miss Frost. Our first impression of Death and Burial is associated with this formless pair. We all three nestled awfully in a corner one wintry day, when the wind was blowing shrill, with Miss Frost's pinafore over our heads; and Miss Frost told us in a whisper about somebody being "screwed down." It is the only distinct recollection we preserve of these impalpable creatures, except a suspicion that the manners of Master Mawls were susceptible of much improvement. Generally speaking, we may observe that whenever we see a child intently occupied with its nose, to the exclusion of all other subjects of interest, our mind reverts in a flash to Master Mawls.

But the School that was Our School before the Railroad came and overthrew it was quite another sort of place. We were old enough to be put into Virgil when we went there, and to get Prizes for a variety of polishing on which the rust has long accumulated. It was a school of some celebrity in its neighbourhood, — nobody could have said why, — and we had the honour to attain and hold the eminent position of first boy. The master was supposed among us to know nothing, and one of the ushers was supposed to know everything. We are still inclined to think the first-named supposition perfectly correct.

We have a general idea that its subject had been in the leather trade, and had bought us — meaning Our School — of another proprietor, who was immensely learned. Whether this belief had any real foundation we are not likely ever to know now. The only branches of education with which he showed the least acquaintance were, ruling and corporally punishing. He was always ruling ciphering-books with a bloated mahogany ruler, or smiting the palms of offenders with the same diabolical instrument, or viciously drawing a pair of pantaloons tight with one of his large hands, and caning the wearer with the other. We have no doubt whatever that this occupation was the principal solace of his existence.

A profound respect for money pervaded Our School, which was, of course, derived from its Chief. We remember an idiotic, goggle-eyed boy, with a big head and half - crowns without end, who suddenly appeared as a parlour boarder, and was rumoured to have come by sea from some mysterious part of the earth where his parents rolled in gold. He was usually called "Mr." by the Chief, and was said to feed in the parlour on steaks and gravy; likewise to drink currant wine. And he openly stated that if rolls and coffee were ever denied him at breakfast, he would write home to that unknown part of the globe from which he had come, and cause himself to be recalled to the regions of gold. He was put into no form or class, but learnt alone, as little as he liked, — and he liked very little, — and there was a belief among us that this was because he was too wealthy to be "taken down." His special treatment, and our vague association of him with the sea, and with storms, and sharks, and coral reefs, occasioned the wildest legends to be circulated as his history. A tragedy in blank verse was written on the subject, — if our memory does not deceive us by the hand that now chronicles these recollections, — in which his father figured as a Pirate, and was shot for a voluminous catalogue of atrocities; first imparting to his wife the secret of the cave in which his wealth was stored, and from which his only son's half-crowns now issued. Dumbledon (the boy's name) was represented as "yet unborn" when his brave father met his fate; and the despair and grief of Mrs. Dumbledon at that calamity was movingly shadowed forth as having weakened the parlour boarder's mind. This production was received with great favour, and was twice performed with closed doors in the dining-room. But it got wind, and was seized as libellous, and brought the unlucky poet into severe affliction. Some two years afterwards, all of a sudden one day, Dumbledon vanished. It was whispered that the Chief himself had taken him down to the Docks, and re-shipped him for the Spanish main; but nothing certain was ever known about his disappearance. At this hour we cannot thoroughly disconnect him from California.

Our School was rather famous for mysterious pupils. There was another, — a heavy young man, with a large double-cased silver watch, and a fat knife, the handle of which was a perfect tool-box,—who unaccountably appeared one day at a special desk of his own, erected close to that of the Chief, with whom he held familiar converse. He lived in the parlour, and went out for walks, and never took the least notice of us—even of us, the first boy—unless to give us a depreciatory kick, or grimly to take our hat off and throw it away, when he encountered us out of doors, which unpleasant ceremony he always performed as he passed—not even condescending to stop for the purpose. Some of us believed that the classical attainments of this phenomenon were terrific, but that his penmanship and arithmetic were defective, and he had come there to mend them; others, that he was going to set up a school, and had paid the Chief "twenty-five pound down" for leave to see Our School at work. The gloomier spirits even said that he was going to buy us; against which contingency conspiracies were set on foot for a general defection and running away. However, he never did that. After staying for a quarter, during which period, though closely observed, he was never seen to do anything but make pens out of quills, write small-hand in a secret portfolio, and punch the point of the sharpest blade in his knife into his desk all over it, he too disappeared, and his place knew him no more.

There was another boy, a fair, meek boy, with a delicate complexion and rich curling hair, who, we found out, or thought we found out (we have no idea now, and probably had none then, on what grounds, but it was confidentially revealed from mouth to mouth), was the son of a viscount who had deserted his lovely mother. It was understood that if he had his rights he would be worth twenty thousand a year. And that if his mother ever met his father, she would shoot him with a silver pistol, which she carried, always loaded to the muzzle, for that purpose. He was a very suggestive topic. So was a young mulatto, who was always believed (though very amiable) to have a dagger about him somewhere. But we think they were both outshone, upon the whole, by another boy who claimed to have been born on the 29th of February, and to have only one birthday in five years. We suspect this to have been a fiction, but he lived upon it all the time he was at Our School.

The principal currency of Our School was slate-pencil. It

had some inexplicable value, that was never ascertained, never reduced to a standard. To have a great hoard of it was somehow to be rich. We used to bestow it in charity, and confer it as a precious boon upon our chosen friends. When the holidays were coming, contributions were solicited for certain boys whose relatives were in India, and who were appealed for under the generic name of "Holiday-stoppers," — appropriate marks of remembrance that should enliven and cheer them in their homeless state. Personally, we always contributed these tokens of sympathy in the form of slate-pencil, and always felt that it would be a comfort and a treasure to them.

Our School was remarkable for white mice. Red-polls, linnets, and even canaries, were kept in desks, drawers, hat-boxes, and other strange refuges for birds; but white mice were the favourite stock. The boys trained the mice much better than the masters trained the boys. We recall one white mouse, who lived in the cover of a Latin dictionary, who ran up ladders, drew Roman chariots, shouldered muskets, turned wheels, and even made a very creditable appearance on the stage as the Dog of Montargis. He might have achieved greater things but for having the misfortune to mistake his way in a triumphal procession to the Capitol, when he fell into a deep inkstand, and was dyed black and drowned. The mice were the occasion of some most ingenious engineering in the construction of their houses and instruments of performance. The famous one belonged to a company of proprietors, some of whom have since made railroads, engines, and telegraphs; the chairman has erected mills and bridges in New Zealand.

The usher at Our School, who was considered to know everything as opposed to the Chief, who was considered to know nothing, was a bony, gentlé-faced, clerical-looking young man in rusty black. It was whispered that he was sweet upon one of Maxby's sisters (Maxby lived close by, and was a day pupil), and further, that he "favoured Maxby." As we remember, he taught Italian to Maxby's sisters on half-holidays. He once went to the play with them, and wore a white waistcoat and a rose, which was considered among us equivalent to a declaration. We were of opinion on that occasion, that to the last moment he expected Maxby's father to ask him to dinner at five o'clock, and therefore neglected his own dinner at half-past one, and finally got none. We exaggerated in our imaginations the extent to which he punished Maxby's father's cold meat at supper; and we agreed to believe that he was elevated with wine and water when he came home. But we all liked him, for he had a good knowledge of boys, and would have made it a much better school if he had had more power. He was writing-master, mathematical master, English master, made out the bills, mended the pens, and did all sorts of things. He divided the little boys with the Latin master (they were smuggled through their rudimentary books at odd times when there was nothing else to do), and he always called at parents' houses to inquire after sick boys, because he had gentlemanly manners. He was rather musical, and on some remote quarter-day had bought an old trombone; but a bit of it was lost, and it made the most extraordinary sounds when he sometimes tried to play it of an evening. His holidays never began (on account of the bills) until long after ours; but in the summer vacations he used to take pedestrian excursions with a knapsack; and at Christmas-time, he went to see his father at Chipping Norton, who we all said (on no authority) was a dairy-fed-pork-butcher. Poor fellow! He was very low all day on Maxby's sister's wedding-day, and afterwards was thought to favour Maxby more than ever, though he had been expected to spite him. He has been dead these twenty years. Poor fellow!

Our remembrance of Our School presents the Latin master as a colourless, doubled-up, near-sighted man with a crutch, who was always cold, and always putting onions into his ears for deafness, and always disclosing ends of flannel under all his garments, and almost always applying a ball of pocket-handkerchief to some part of his face with a screwing action round and round. He was a very good scholar, and took great pains where he saw intelligence and a desire to learn; otherwise, perhaps not. Our memory presents him (unless teased into a passion) with as little energy as colour — as having been worried and tormented into monotonous feebleness — as having had the best part of his life ground out of him in a mill of boys. We remember with terror how he fell asleep one sultry afternoon with the little smuggled class before him, and awoke not when the footstep of the Chief fell heavy on the floor; how the Chief aroused him, in the midst of a dread silence, and said, " Mr. Blinkins, are you ill, sir? " how he blushingly replied, "Sir, rather so;" how the Chief retorted with severity, "Mr. Blinkins, this is no place to be ill in " (which was very, very true), and walked back, solemn as the ghost in "Hamlet," until, catching a wandering eye, he caned that boy for inattention, and happily expressed his feelings towards the Latin master through the medium of a substitute.

There was a fat little dancing-master who used to come in a gig, and taught the more advanced among us hornpipes (as an accomplishment in great social demand in after-life); and there was a brisk little French master who used to come in the sunniest weather with a handleless umbrella, and to whom the Chief was always polite, because (as we believed), if the Chief offended him, he would instantly address the Chief in French, and for ever confound him before the boys with his inability to understand or reply.

There was besides a serving-man, whose name was Phil. Our retrospective glance presents Phil as a shipwrecked carpenter, cast away upon the desert island of a school, and carrying into practice an ingenious inkling of many trades. He mended whatever was broken, and made whatever was wanted. He was general glazier, among other things, and mended all the broken windows — at the prime cost (as was darkly rumoured among us) of ninepence for every square charged three and six to parents. We had a high opinion of his mechanical genius, and generally held that the Chief "knew something bad of him," and on pain of divulgence enforced Phil to be his bondsman. We particularly remember that Phil had a sovereign contempt for learning, which engenders in us a respect for his sagacity, as it implies his accurate observation of the relative positions of the Chief and the ushers. He was an impenetrable man, who waited at table between whiles, and throughout "the half" kept the boxes in severe custody. He was morose, even to the Chief, and never smiled, except at breaking-up, when, in acknowledgment of the toast, "Success to Phil! Hooray!" he would slowly carve a grin out of his wooden face, where it would remain until we were all gone. Nevertheless, one time when we had the scarlet fever in the school, Phil nursed all the sick boys of his own accord, and was like a mother to them.

There was another school not far off, and of course Our School could have nothing to say to that school. It is mostly the way with schools, whether of boys or men.   Well! the Railway has swallowed up ours, and the locomotives now run smoothly over its ashes.

> "So fades and languishes, grows dim and dies,
>   All that this world is proud of,"

— and is not proud of, too.   It had little reason to be proud of Our School, and has done much better since in that way, and will do far better yet.

IX

A PLATED ARTICLE

PUTTING up for the night in one of the chiefest towns of Staffordshire, I find it to be by no means a lively town. In fact, it is as dull and dead a town as any one could desire not to see. It seems as if its whole population might be imprisoned in its Railway Station. The Refreshment-Room at that Station is a vortex of dissipation compared with the extinct town-inn, the Dodo, in the dull High Street.

Why High Street? Why not rather Low Street, Flat Street, Low-Spirited Street, Used-Up Street? Where are the people who belong to the High Street? Can they all be dispersed over the face of the country, seeking the unfortunate Strolling Manager who decamped from the mouldy little theatre last week, in the beginning of his season (as his play-bills testify), repentantly resolved to bring him back, and feed him, and be entertained? Or can they all be gathered to their fathers in the two old churchyards near to the High Street? — retirement into which churchyards appears to be a mere ceremony, there is so very little life outside their confines, and such small discernible difference between being buried alive in the town and buried dead in the town tombs. Over the way, opposite to the staring blank bow-window of the Dodo, are a little ironmonger's shop, a little tailor's shop (with a picture of the fashions in the small window and a bandy-legged baby on the pavement staring at it), a watch-maker's shop, where all the clocks and watches must be stopped, I am sure, for they could never have the courage to go, with the town in general, and the Dodo in particular, looking at them. Shade of Miss Linwood, erst of Leicester Square, London, thou art welcome here, and thy retreat is fitly chosen! I myself was one of the last visitors to that awful storehouse of thy life's work, where an anchorite old man and woman took my shilling with a solemn wonder, and conducting me to a gloomy sepulchre of needle-work dropping to pieces with dust and age and shrouded in twilight at high noon, left me there, chilled, frightened, and alone. And now, in ghostly letters on all the dead walls of this dead town, I read thy honoured name, and find that thy Last Supper, worked in Berlin wool, invites inspection as a powerful excitement!

Where are the people who are bidden with so much cry to this feast of little wool? Where are they? Who are they? They are not the bandy-legged baby studying the fashions in the tailor's window. They are not the two earthy ploughmen lounging outside the saddler's shop, in the stiff square where the Town Hall stands, like a brick-and-mortar private on parade. They are not the landlady of the Dodo in the empty bar, whose eye had trouble in it and no welcome when I asked for dinner. They are not the turnkeys of the town jail, looking out of the gateway in their uniforms, as if they had locked up all the balance (as my American friends would say) of the inhabitants, and could now rest a little. They are not the two dusty millers in the white mill down by the river, where the great water-wheel goes heavily round and round, like the monotonous days and nights in this forgotten place. Then who are they, for there is no one else? No; this deponent maketh oath and saith that there is no one else save and except the waiter at the Dodo, now laying the cloth. I have paced the streets, and stared at the houses, and am come back to the blank bow-window of the Dodo; and the town clocks strike seven, and the reluctant echoes seem to cry, "Don't wake us!" and the bandy-legged baby has gone home to bed.

If the Dodo were only a gregarious bird — if it had only some confused idea of making a comfortable nest — I could hope to get through the hours between this and bed-time without being consumed by devouring melancholy. But the Dodo's habits are all wrong. It provides me with a trackless desert of sitting-room, with a chair for every day in the year, a table for every month, and a waste of sideboard where ¹ lonely china vase pines in a corner for its mate long departe⸲. and will never make a match with the candlestick in the oppo- site corner if it live till Doomsday. The Dodo has nothing in the larder. Even now, I behold the Boots returning with my sole in a piece of paper; and with that portion of my dinner, the Boots, perceiving me at the blank bow-window, slaps his leg as he comes across the road, pretending it is something else. The Dodo excludes the outer air. When I mount up to my bedroom, a smell of closeness and flue gets lazily up my nose like sleepy snuff. The loose little bits of carpet writhe under my tread, and take wormy shapes. I don't know the ridiculous man in the looking-glass, beyond having met him once or twice in a dish-cover, and I can never shave *him* to-morrow morning! The Dodo is narrow-minded as to towels; expects me to wash on a Freemason's apron without the trimming; when I ask for soap, gives me a stony-hearted something white, with no more lather in it than the Elgin marbles. The Dodo has seen better days, and possesses interminable stables at the back — silent, grass-grown, broken-windowed, horseless.

This mournful bird can fry a sole, however, which is much. Can cook a steak, too, which is more. I wonder where it gets its sherry! If I were to send my pint of wine to some famous chemist to be analysed, what would it turn out to be made of? It tastes of pepper, sugar, bitter almonds, vinegar, warm knives, any flat drink, and a little brandy. Would it unman a Spanish exile by reminding him of his native land at all? I think not. If there really be any townspeople out of the churchyards, and if a caravan of them ever do dine, with a bottle of wine per man, in this desert of the Dodo, it must make good for the doctor next day!

Where was the waiter born? How did he come here? Has he any hope of getting away from here? Does he ever receive a letter, or take a ride upon the railway, or see anything but the Dodo? Perhaps he has seen the Berlin wool. He appears to have a silent sorrow on him, and it may be that. He clears the table; draws the dingy curtains of the great bow-window, which so unwillingly consent to meet that they must be pinned together; leaves me by the fire with my pint decanter, and a little thin funnel-shaped wine-glass, and a plate of pale biscuits — in themselves engendering desperation.

No book, no newspaper! I left the Arabian Nights in the railway carriage, and have nothing to read but Bradshaw, and "that way madness lies." Remembering what prisoners and shipwrecked mariners have done to exercise their minds in solitude, I repeat the multiplication table, the pence table, and the shilling table, which are all the tables I happen to know. What if I write something? The Dodo keeps no pens but steel pens; and those I always stick through the paper, and can turn to no other account.

What am I to do? Even if I could have the bandy-legged baby knocked up and brought here, I could offer him nothing but sherry, and that would be the death of him. He would never hold up his head again if he touched it. I can't go to bed, because I have conceived a mortal hatred for my bedroom; and I can't go away, because there is no train for my place of destination until morning. To burn the biscuits will be but a fleeting joy; still it is a temporary relief, and here they go on the fire! Shall I break the plate? First let me look at the back, and see who made it. COPELAND.

Copeland! Stop a moment. Was it yesterday I visited Copeland's works, and saw them making plates? In the confusion of travelling about, it might be yesterday or it might be yesterday month; but I think it was yesterday. I appeal to the plate. The plate says, decidedly, yesterday. I find the plate, as I look at it, growing into a companion.

Don't you remember (says the plate) how you steamed away, yesterday morning, in the bright sun and the east wind, along the valley of the sparkling Trent? Don't you recollect how many kilns you flew past, looking like the bowls of gigantic tobacco pipes, cut short off from the stem and turned upside down? And the fires — and the smoke — and the roads made with bits of crockery, as if all the plates and dishes in the civilised world had been macadamised expressly for the laming of all the horses? Of course I do!

And don't you remember (says the plate) how you alighted at Stoke, — a picturesque heap of houses, kilns, smoke, wharfs, canals, and river, lying (as was most appropriate) in a basin, — and how, after climbing up the sides of the basin to look at the prospect, you trundled down again at a walking-match pace, and straight proceeded to my father's, Copeland's, where the whole of my family, high and low, rich and poor, are turned out upon the world from our nursery and seminary, covering some fourteen acres of ground? And don't you remember what we spring from, — heaps of lumps of clay, partially prepared and cleaned in Devonshire and Dorsetshire, whence said clay principally comes, and hills of flint, without which we should want our ringing sound and should never be musical? And as to the flint, don't you recollect that it is first burnt in kilns, and is then laid under the four iron feet of a demon slave, subject to violent stamping fits, who, when

they come on, stamps away insanely with his four iron legs,
and would crush all the flint in the Isle of Thanet to powder,
without leaving off? And as to the clay, don't you recollect
how it is put into mills or teazers, and is sliced, and dug, and
cut at, by endless knives, clogged and sticky, but persistent —
and is pressed out of that machine through a square trough,
whose form it takes — and is cut off in square lumps and
thrown into a vat, and there mixed with water, and beaten to
a pulp by paddle-wheels — and is then run into a rough house,
all rugged beams and ladders splashed with white, — superintended by Grindoff the Miller in his working clothes, all
splashed with white, — where it passes through no end of
machinery-moved sieves all splashed with white, arranged in
an ascending scale of fineness (some so fine that three hundred
silk threads cross each other in a single square inch of their
surface), and all in a violent state of ague with their teeth
for ever chattering, and their bodies for ever shivering? And
as to the flint again, isn't it mashed and mollified and troubled
and soothed, exactly as rags are in a paper-mill, until it is
reduced to a pap so fine that it contains no atom of "grit"
perceptible to the nicest taste? And as to the flint and the
clay together, are they not, after all this, mixed in the proportion of five of clay to one of flint, and isn't the compound —
known as "slip" — run into oblong troughs, where its superfluous moisture may evaporate; and finally, isn't it slapped
and banged and beaten and patted and kneaded and wedged
and knocked about like butter, until it becomes a beautiful
grey dough, ready for the potter's use?

In regard of the potter, popularly so called (says the plate),
you don't mean to say you have forgotten that a workman
called a Thrower is the man under whose hand this grey dough
takes the shapes of the simpler household vessels as quickly as
the eye can follow? You don't mean to say you cannot call
him up before you, sitting, with his attendant woman, at his
potter's wheel — a disc about the size of a dinner plate, revolving on two drums slowly or quickly as he wills — who made
you a complete breakfast set for a bachelor, as a good-humoured
little off-hand joke? You remember how he took up as much
dough as he wanted, and, throwing it on his wheel, in a
moment fashioned it into a teacup — caught up more clay and
made a saucer — a larger dab and whirled it into a teapot —

winked at a smaller dab and converted it into the lid of the teapot, accurately fitting by the measurement of his eye alone — coaxed a middle-sized dab for two seconds, broke it, turned it over at the rim, and made a milkpot — laughed, and turned out a slop-basin — coughed, and provided for the sugar? Neither, I think, are you oblivious of the newer mode of making various articles, but especially basins, according to which improvement a mould revolves instead of a disc? For you *must* remember (says the plate) how you saw the mould of a little basin spinning round and round, and how the workman smoothed and pressed a handful of dough upon it, and how with an instrument called a profile (a piece of wood, representing the profile of a basin's foot) he cleverly scraped and carved the ring which makes the base of any such basin, and then took the basin off the lathe like a doughy skull-cap to be dried, and afterwards (in what is called a green state) to be put into a second lathe, there to be finished and burnished with a steel burnisher. And as to moulding in general (says the plate), it can't be necessary for me to remind you that all ornamental articles, and indeed all articles not quite circular, are made in moulds. For you must remember how you saw the vegetable dishes, for example, being made in moulds; and how the handles of teacups, and the spouts of teapots, and the feet of tureens, and so forth, are all made in little separate moulds, and are each stuck on to the body corporate, of which it is destined to form a part, with a stuff called "slag," as quickly as you can recollect it. Further, you learnt — you know you did — in the same visit, how the beautiful sculptures in the delicate new material called Parian are all constructed in moulds; how into that material animal bones are ground up, because the phosphate of lime contained in bones makes it translucent; how everything is moulded, before going into the fire, one fourth larger than it is intended to come out of the fire, because it shrinks in that proportion in the intense heat; how, when a figure shrinks unequally, it is spoiled, emerging from the furnace a misshapen birth — a big head and a little body, or a little head and a big body, or a Quasimodo with long arms and short legs, or a Miss Biffin with neither legs nor arms worth mentioning.

And as to the kilns, in which the firing takes place, and in which some of the more precious articles are burnt repeatedly, in various stages of their process towards completion, — as to the kilns (says the plate, warming with the recollection), if you don't remember THEM with a horrible interest, what did you ever go to Copeland's for? When you stood inside of one of those inverted bowls of a pre-Adamite tobacco-pipe, looking up at the blue sky through the open top far off, as you might have looked up from a well, sunk under the centre of the pavement of the Pantheon at Rome, had you the least idea where you were? And when you found yourself surrounded, in that dome-shaped cavern, by innumerable columns of an unearthly order of architecture, supporting nothing, and squeezed close together as if a pre-Adamite Samson had taken a vast hall in his arms and crushed it into the smallest possible space, had you the least idea what they were? No (says the plate), of course not! And when you found that each of those pillars was a pile of ingeniously made vessels of coarse clay, — called saggers, — looking, when separate, like raised-pies for the table of the mighty Giant Blunderbore, and now all full of various articles of pottery ranged in them in baking order, the bottom of each vessel serving for the cover of the one below, and the whole kiln rapidly filling with these, tier upon tier, until the last workman should have barely room to crawl out, before the closing of the jagged aperture in the wall and the kindling of the gradual fire, did you not stand amazed to think that all the year round these dread chambers are heating, white-hot — and cooling — and filling — and emptying — and being bricked up — and broken open — humanly speaking, for ever and ever? To be sure you did! And standing in one of those kilns nearly full, and seeing a free crow shoot across the aperture atop, and learning how the fire would wax hotter and hotter by slow degrees, and would cool similarly through a space of from forty to sixty hours, did no remembrance of the days when human clay was burnt oppress you? Yes, I think so! I suspect that some fancy of a fiery haze and a shortening breath, and a growing heat, and a gasping prayer, and a figure in black interposing between you and the sky (as figures in black are very apt to do), and looking down, before it grew too hot to look and live, upon the heretic in his edifying agony — I say I suspect (says the plate) that some such fancy was pretty strong upon you when you went out into the air, and blessed God for the bright spring day and the degenerate times!

After that I need n't remind you what a relief it was to see
the simplest process of ornamenting this "biscuit" (as it is
called when baked) with brown circles and blue trees — converting it into the common crockery ware that is exported to
Africa, and used in cottages at home. For (says the plate) I
am well persuaded that you bear in mind how those particular
jugs and mugs were once more set upon a lathe and put in
motion; and how a man blew the brown color (having a strong
natural affinity with the material in that condition) on them
from a blow-pipe as they twirled; and how his daughter, with
a common brush, dropped blotches of blue upon them in the
right places; and how, tilting the blotches upside down, she
made them run into rude images of trees, and there an end.

And did n't you see (says the plate) planted upon my own
brother that astounding blue willow, with knobbed and gnarled
trunk, and foliage of blue ostrich feathers, which gives our
family the title of "willow pattern"? And did n't you
observe, transferred upon him at the same time, that blue
bridge which spans nothing, growing out from the roots of the
willow; and the three blue Chinese going over it into a blue
temple, which has a fine crop of blue bushes sprouting out of
the roof; and a blue boat sailing above them, the mast of
which is burglariously sticking itself into the foundations of a
blue villa, suspended sky-high, surmounted by a lump of blue
rock sky-higher, and a couple of billing bluebirds sky-highest
— together with the rest of that amusing blue landscape, which
has, in deference to our revered ancestors of the Cerulean
Empire, and in defiance of every known law of perspective
adorned millions of our family ever since the days of platters
Did n't you inspect the copper-plate on which my pattern wat
deeply engraved? Did n't you perceive an impression of it
taken in cobalt colour at a cylindrical press, upon a leaf of
thin paper, streaming from a plunge-bath of soap and water?
Was n't the paper impression daintily spread, by a light-fin-
gered damsel (you *know* you admired her!), over the surface
of the plate, and the back of the paper rubbed prodigiously
hard — with a long tight roll of flannel, tied up like a round
of hung beef — without so much as ruffling the paper, wet as
it was? Then (says the plate), was not the paper washed
away with a sponge, and did n't there appear, set off upon the
plate, *this* identical piece of pre-Raphaelite blue distemper

which you now behold? Not to be denied! I had seen all this — and more. I had been shown, at Copeland's, patterns of beautiful design, in faultless perspective, which are causing the ugly old willow to wither out of public favour; and which, being quite as cheap, insinuate good wholesome natural art into the humblest households. When Mr. and Mrs. Sprat have satisfied their material tastes by that equal division of fat and lean which has made their *ménage* immortal, and have, after the elegant tradition, "licked the platter clean," they can — thanks to modern artists in clay — feast their intellectual tastes upon excellent delineations of natural objects.

This reflection prompts me to transfer my attention from the blue plate to the forlorn but cheerfully painted vase on the sideboard. And surely (says the plate) you have not forgotten how the outlines of such groups of flowers as you see there are printed just as I was printed, and are afterwards shaded and filled in with metallic colours by women and girls? As to the aristocracy of our order, made of the finer clay — porcelain peers and peeresses; — the slabs, and panels, and table tops, and tazze; the endless nobility and gentry of dessert, breakfast, and tea services; the gemmed perfume bottles, and scarlet-and-gold salvers — you saw that they were painted by artists, with metallic colours laid on with camel-hair pencils, and afterwards burnt in.

And talking of burning in (says the plate), did n't you find that every subject, from the willow pattern to the landscape after Turner, — having been framed upon clay or porcelain biscuit, — has to be glazed? Of course you saw the glaze — composed of various vitreous materials — laid over every article; and of course you witnessed the close imprisonment of each piece in saggers, upon the separate system, rigidly enforced by means of fine-pointed earthenware stilts placed between the articles to prevent the slightest communication or contact. We had in my time — and I suppose it is the same now — fourteen hours firing to fix the glaze and to make it "run" all over us equally, so as to put a good shiny and unscratchable surface upon us. Doubtless you observed that one sort of glaze — called printing-body — is burnt into the better sort of ware *before* it is printed. Upon this you saw some of the finest steel engravings transferred, to be fixed by an after-glazing — did n't you? Why, of course you did!

Of course I did. I had seen and enjoyed everything that the plate recalled to me, and had beheld with admiration how the rotatory motion which keeps this ball of ours in its place in the great scheme, with all its busy mites upon it, was necessary throughout the process, and could only be dispensed with in the fire. So, listening to the plate's reminders, and musing upon them, I got through the evening after all, and went to bed. I made but one sleep of it, — for which I have no doubt I am also indebted to the plate, — and left the lonely Dodo in the morning, quite at peace with it, before the bandy-legged baby was up.

X

OUR HONOURABLE FRIEND

WE are delighted to find that he has got in! Our honour-able friend is triumphantly returned to serve in the next Par-liament. He is the honourable member for Verbosity — the best represented place in England.

Our honourable friend has issued an address of congratula-tion to the Electors, which is worthy of that noble constit-uency, and is a very pretty piece of composition. In electing him, he says, they have covered themselves with glory, and England has been true to herself. (In his preliminary address he had remarked, in a poetical quotation of great rarity, that nought could make us rue, if England to herself did prove but true.)

Our honourable friend delivers a prediction, in the same document, that the feeble minions of a faction will never hold up their heads any more; and that the finger of scorn will point at them in their dejected state, through countless ages of time. Further, that the hireling tools that would destroy the sacred bulwarks of our nationality are unworthy of the name of Englishmen; and that so long as the sea shall roll around our ocean-girded isle, so long his motto shall be, No Surrender. Certain dogged persons of low principles and no intellect have disputed whether anybody knows who the minions are, or what the faction is, or which are the hireling tools and which the sacred bulwarks, or what it is that is never to be surrendered, and if not, why not? But our honourable friend, the member for Verbosity, knows all about it.

Our honourable friend has sat in several Parliaments, and given bushels of votes. He is a man of that profundity in the matter of vote-giving that you never know what he means. When he seems to be voting pure white, he may be in reality voting jet black. When he says Yes, it is just as likely as not — or rather more so — that he means No. This is the statesmanship of our honourable friend. It is in this that he differs from mere unparliamentary men. *You* may not know what he meant then, or what he means now; but our honourable friend knows, and did from the first know, both what he meant then and what he means now; and when he said he did n't mean it then, he did in fact say that he means it now. And if you mean to say that you did not then, and do not now, know what he did mean then, or does mean now, our honourable friend will be glad to receive an explicit declaration from you whether you are prepared to destroy the sacred bulwarks of our nationality.

Our honourable friend, the member for Verbosity, has this great attribute, that he always means something, and always means the same thing. When he came down to that House and mournfully boasted in his place, as an individual member of the assembled Commons of this great and happy country, that he could lay his hand upon his heart and solemnly declare that no consideration on earth should induce him, at any time or under any circumstances, to go as far north as Berwick-upon-Tweed; and when he nevertheless, next year, did go to Berwick-upon-Tweed, and even beyond it, to Edinburgh, he had one single meaning, one and indivisible. And God forbid (our honourable friend says) that he should waste another argument upon the man who professes that he cannot understand it! "I do NOT, gentlemen," said our honourable friend, with indignant emphasis and amid great cheering, on one such public occasion, — "I do NOT, gentlemen, I am free to confess, envy the feelings of that man whose mind is so constituted as that he can hold such language to me, and yet lay his head upon his pillow, claiming to be a native of that land,

"Whose march is o'er the mountain waves,
Whose home is on the deep!"

(Vehement cheering, and man expelled.)

When our honourable friend issued his preliminary address to the constituent body of Verbosity on the occasion of one particular glorious triumph, it was supposed by some of his enemies that even he would be placed in a situation of difficulty by the following comparatively trifling conjunction of circumstances. The dozen noblemen and gentlemen whom our honourable friend supported had "come in," expressly to do a certain thing. Now, four of the dozen said, at a certain place, that they did n't mean to do that thing, and had never meant to do it; another four of the dozen said, at another certain place, that they did mean to do that thing, and had always meant to do it; two of the remaining four said, at two other certain places, that they meant to do half of that thing (but differed about which half), and to do a variety of nameless wonders instead of the other half; and one of the remaining two declared that the thing itself was dead and buried, while the other as strenuously protested that it was alive and kicking. It was admitted that the parliamentary genius of our honourable friend would be quite able to reconcile such small discrepancies as these, but there remained the additional difficulty that each of the twelve made entirely different statements at different places, and that all the twelve called everything visible and invisible, sacred and profane, to witness that they were a perfectly impregnable phalanx of unanimity. This, it was apprehended, would be a stumbling-block to our honourable friend.

The difficulty came before our honourable friend in this way. He went down to Verbosity to meet his free and independent constituents, and to render an account (as he informed them in the local papers) of the trust they had confided to his hands — that trust which it was one of the proudest privileges of an Englishman to possess — that trust which it was the proudest privilege of an Englishman to hold. It may be mentioned as a proof of the great general interest attaching to the contest, that a lunatic whom nobody employed or knew went down to Verbosity with several thousand pounds in gold, determined to give the whole away, which he actually did, and that all the publicans opened their houses for nothing. Likewise, several fighting men, and a patriotic group of burglars sportively armed with life-preservers, proceeded (in barouches and very drunk) to the scene of action at their own expense; these children of nature having conceived a warm attachment to our honourable friend, and intending, in their artless manner, to testify it by knocking the voters in the opposite interest on the head.

Our honourable friend being come into the presence of his constituents, and having professed with great suavity that he was delighted to see his good friend Tipkisson there, in his working dress, — his good friend Tipkisson being an inveterate saddler, who always opposes him, and for whom he has a mortal hatred, — made them a brisk, ginger-beery sort of speech, in which he showed them how the dozen noblemen and gentlemen

had (in exactly ten days from their coming in) exercised a
surprisingly beneficial effect on the whole financial condition of
Europe, had altered the state of the exports and imports for
the current half year, had prevented the drain of gold, had
made all that matter right about the glut of the raw material,
and had restored all sorts of balances with which the superseded
noblemen and gentlemen had played the deuce — and all this,
with wheat at so much a quarter, gold at so much an ounce,
and the Bank of England discounting good bills at so much
per cent.! He might be asked, he observed in a peroration of
great power, what were his principles? His principles were
what they always had been. His principles were written in
the countenances of the lion and unicorn; were stamped indeli-
bly upon the royal shield which those grand animals supported,
and upon the free words of fire which that shield bore. His
principles were, Britannia and her sea-king trident! His principles were, commercial prosperity co-existently with perfect
and profound agricultural contentment; but short of this he
would never stop. His principles were these, — with the addition of his colours nailed to the mast, — every man's heart in
the right place, every man's eye open, every man's hand ready,
every man's mind on the alert. His principles were these,
concurrently with a general revision of something — speaking
generally — and a possible re-adjustment of something else, not
to be mentioned more particularly. His principles, to sum up
all in a word, were, Hearths and Altars, Labour and Capital,
Crown and Sceptre, Elephant and Castle. And now, if his
good friend Tipkisson required any further explanation from
him he (our honourable friend) was there, willing and ready to
give it.

Tipkisson, who all this time had stood conspicuous in the
crowd, with his arms folded and his eyes intently fastened on
our honourable friend, — Tipkisson, who throughout our honourable friend's address had not relaxed a muscle of his visage,
but had stood there, wholly unaffected by the torrent of eloquence, an object of contempt and scorn to mankind (by which
we mean, of course, to the supporters of our honourable friend),
— Tipkisson now said that he was a plain man (cries of "You
are indeed!"), and that what he wanted to know was, what
our honourable friend and the dozen noblemen and gentlemen
were driving at.

Our honourable friend immediately replied, "At the illimi-table perspective."

It was considered by the whole assembly that this happy statement of our honourable friend's political views ought, immediately, to have settled Tipkisson's business and covered him with confusion; but that implacable person, regardless of the execrations that were heaped upon him from all sides (by which we mean, of course, from our honourable friend's side), persisted in retaining an unmoved countenance, and obstinately retorted that if our honourable friend meant that, he wished to know what *that* meant?

It was in repelling this most objectionable and indecent opposition that our honourable friend displayed his highest qualifications for the representation of Verbosity. His warmest supporters present, and those who were best acquainted with his generalship, supposed that the moment was come when he would fall back upon the sacred bulwarks of our nationality. No such thing. He replied thus: "My good friend Tipkisson, gentlemen, wishes to know what I mean when he asks me what we are driving at, and when I candidly tell him at the illimitable perspective. He wishes (if I understand him) to know what I mean?" "I do!" says Tipkisson, amid cries of "Shame" and "Down with him." "Gentlemen," says our honourable friend, "I will indulge my good friend Tipkisson, by telling him both what I mean and what I don't mean." (Cheers, and cries of "Give it him!") "Be it known to him then, and to all whom it may concern, that I do mean altars, hearths, and homes, and that I don't mean mosques and Mahommedanism!" The effect of this home-thrust was terrific. Tipkisson (who is a Baptist) was hooted down and hustled out, and has ever since been regarded as a Turkish Renegade who contemplates an early pilgrimage to Mecca. Nor was he the only discomfited man. The charge, while it stuck to him, was magically transferred to our honourable friend's opponent, who was represented in an immense variety of placards as a firm believer in Mahomet; and the men of Verbosity were asked to choose between our honourable friend and the Bible and our honourable friend's opponent and the Koran. They decided for our honourable friend, and rallied round the illimitable perspective.

It has been claimed for our honourable friend, with much

appearance of reason, that he was the first to bend sacred matters to electioneering tactics.   However this may be, the fine precedent was undoubtedly set in a Verbosity election; and it is certain that our honourable friend (who was a disciple of Brahma in his youth, and was a Buddhist when he had the honour of travelling with him a few years ago) always professes in public more anxiety than the whole Bench of Bishops, regarding the theological and doxological opinions of every man, woman, and child in the United Kingdom.

As we began by saying that our honourable friend has got in again at this last election, and that we are delighted to find that he has got in, so we will conclude.   Our honourable friend cannot come in for Verbosity too often.   It is a good sign; it is a great example.   It is to men like our honourable friend, and to contests like those from which he comes triumphant, that we are mainly indebted for that ready interest in politics, that fresh enthusiasm in the discharge of the duties of citizenship, that ardent desire to rush to the poll, at present so manifest throughout England.   When the contest lies (as it sometimes does) between two such men as our honourable friend, it stimulates the finest emotions of our nature, and awakens the highest admiration of which our heads and hearts are capable.

It is not too much to predict that our honourable friend will be always at his post in the ensuing session.   Whatever the question be, or whatever the form of its discussion, — address to the crown, election petition, expenditure of the public money, extension of the public suffrage, education, crime, in the whole house, in committee of the whole house, in select committee, in every parliamentary discussion of every subject, everywhere, — the Honourable Member for Verbosity will most certainly be found.

XI

OUR VESTRY

WE have the glorious privilege of being always in hot water if we like. We are a shareholder in a Great Parochial British Joint Stock Bank of Balderdash. We have a Vestry in our borough, and can vote for a Vestryman; might even *be* a Vestryman, mayhap, if we were inspired by a lofty and noble ambition — which we are not.

Our Vestry is a deliberate assembly of the utmost dignity and importance. Like the Senate of ancient Rome, its awful gravity overpowers (or ought to overpower) barbarian visitors. It sits in the Capitol (we mean in the capital building erected for it) chiefly on Saturdays, and shakes the earth to its centre with the echoes of its thundering eloquence, in a Sunday paper.

To get into this Vestry in the eminent capacity of Vestryman, gigantic efforts are made and herculean exertions used. It is made manifest to the dullest capacity at every election, that if we reject Snozzle we are done for, and that if we fail to bring in Blunderbooze at the top of the poll we are unworthy of the dearest rights of Britons. Flaming placards are rife on all the dead walls in the borough, public-houses hang out banners, hackney-cabs burst into full-grown flowers of type, and everybody is, or should be, in a paroxysm of anxiety.

At these momentous crises of the national fate we are much assisted in our deliberations by two eminent volunteers, one of whom subscribes himself A Fellow-Parishioner, the other, A Rate-Payer. Who they are, or what they are, or where they are, nobody knows; but whatever one asserts the other contradicts. They are both voluminous writers, inditing more epistles than Lord Chesterfield in a single week; and the greater part of their feelings are too big for utterance in anything less than capital letters. They require the additional aid of whole rows of notes of admiration, like balloons, to point their generous indignation; and they sometimes communicate a crushing severity to stars. As thus: —

MEN OF MOONEYMOUNT

Is it, or is it not, a * * * to saddle the parish with a debt
of £2,745 6s. 9d., yet claim to be a RIGID ECONOMIST?

Is it, or is it not, a * * * to state as a fact what is proved
to be *both a moral and a* PHYSICAL IMPOSSIBILITY?

Is it, or is it not, a * * * to call £2,745 6s. 9d. nothing;
and nothing, something?

Do you, or do you *not*, want a * * * * TO REPRESENT YOU
IN THE VESTRY?

Your consideration of these questions is recommended to
you by

A FELLOW-PARISHIONER.

It was to this important public document that one of our
first orators, Mr. Magg (of Little Winkling Street), adverted,
when he opened the great debate of the 14th of November
by saying, "Sir, I hold in my hand an anonymous slander" —
and when the interruption, with which he was at that point
assailed by the opposite faction, gave rise to that memorable
discussion on a point of order which will ever be remembered
with interest by constitutional assemblies. In the animated
debate to which we refer, no fewer than thirty-seven gentlemen, many of them of great eminence, including Mr. Wigsby
(of Chumbledon Square), were seen upon their legs at one time;
and it was on the same great occasion that Dogginson, regarded in our Vestry as "a regular John Bull" — we believe,
in consequence of his having always made up his mind on
every subject without knowing anything about it — informed
another gentleman of similar principles on the opposite side,
that if he "cheek'd him," he would resort to the extreme
measure of knocking his blessed head off.

This was a great occasion. But our Vestry shines habitually. In asserting its own pre-eminence, for instance, it is
very strong. On the least provocation, or on none, it will be
clamorous to know whether it is to be "dictated to," or "tram-
pled on," or "ridden over rough-shod." Its great watchword
is Self-Government. That is to say, supposing our Vestry to
favour any little harmless disorder like Typhus Fever, and
supposing the Government of the country to be by any accident in such ridiculous hands as that any of its authorities

should consider it a duty to object to Typhus Fever, — obviously an unconstitutional objection, — then, our Vestry cuts in with a terrible manifesto about Self-Government, and claims its independent right to have as much Typhus Fever as pleases itself. Some absurd and dangerous persons have represented, on the other hand, that though our Vestry may be able to "beat the bounds" of its own parish, it may not be able to beat the bounds of its own diseases; which (say they) spread over the whole land in an ever-expanding circle of waste, and misery, and death, and widowhood, and orphanage, and desolation. But our Vestry makes short work of any such fellows as these.

It was our Vestry — pink of Vestries as it is — that in support of its favourite principle took the celebrated ground of denying the existence of the last pestilence that raged in England, when the pestilence was raging at the Vestry doors. Dogginson said it was plums; Mr. Wigsby (of Chumbledon Square) said it was oysters; Mr. Magg (of Little Winkling Street) said, amid great cheering, it was the newspapers. The noble indignation of our Vestry with that un-English institution the Board of Health, under those circumstances, yields one of the finest passages in its history. It would n't hear of rescue. Like Mr. Joseph Miller's Frenchman, it would be drowned and nobody should save it. Transported beyond grammar by its kindled ire, it spoke in unknown tongues, and vented unintelligible bellowings, more like an ancient oracle than the modern oracle it is admitted on all hands to be. Rare exigencies produce rare things; and even our Vestry, new hatched to the woeful time, came forth a greater goose than ever.

But this, again, was a special occasion. Our Vestry, at more ordinary periods, demands its meed of praise.

Our Vestry is eminently parliamentary. Playing at Parliament is its favourite game. It is even regarded by some of its members as a chapel of ease to the House of Commons, a Little Go to be passed first. It has its strangers' gallery and its reported debates (see the Sunday paper before mentioned), and our Vestrymen are in and out of order, and on and off their legs, and above all are transcendently quarrelsome, after the pattern of the real original.

Our Vestry being assembled, Mr. Magg never begs to trouble Mr. Wigsby with a simple inquiry. He knows better than that. Seeing the honourable gentleman, associated in their minds with Chumbledon Square, in his place, he wishes to ask that honourable gentleman what the intentions of himself, and those with whom he acts, may be on the subject of the paving of the district known as Piggleum Buildings? Mr. Wigsby replies (with his eye on next Sunday's paper), that in reference to the question which has been put to him by the honourable gentleman opposite, he must take leave to say, that if that honourable gentleman had had the courtesy to give him notice of that question, he (Mr. Wigsby) would have consulted with his colleagues in reference to the advisability, in the present state of the discussions on the new paving-rate, of answering that question. But as the honourable gentleman has NOT had the courtesy to give him notice of that question (great cheering from the Wigsby interest), he must decline to give the honourable gentleman the satisfaction he requires. Mr. Magg, instantly rising to retort, is received with loud cries of "Spoke!" from the Wigsby interest, and with cheers from the Magg side of the house. Moreover, five gentlemen rise to order, and one of them, in revenge for being taken no notice of, petrifies the assembly by moving that this Vestry do now adjourn; but is persuaded to withdraw that awful proposal, in consideration of its tremendous consequences if persevered in. Mr. Magg, for the purpose of being heard, then begs to move, that you, sir, do now pass to the order of the day; and takes that opportunity of saying, that if an honourable gentleman whom he has in his eye, and will not demean himself by more particularly naming (oh, oh, and cheers), supposes that he is to be put down by clamour, that honourable gentleman — however supported he may be, through thick and thin, by a Fellow-Parishioner, with whom he is well acquainted (cheers and counter-cheers, Mr. Magg being invariably backed by the Rate-Payer) — will find himself mistaken. Upon this, twenty members of our Vestry speak in succession concerning what the two great men have meant, until it appears, after an hour and twenty minutes, that neither of them meant anything. Then our Vestry begins business.

We have said that, after the pattern of the real original, our Vestry in playing at Parliament is transcendently quarrelsome. It enjoys a personal altercation above all things. Perhaps the most redoubtable case of this kind we have ever had — though we have had so many that it is difficult to decide —

was that on which the last extreme solemnities passed between
Mr. Tiddypot (of Gumtion House) and Captain Banger (of
Wilderness Walk).

In an adjourned debate on the question whether water could
be regarded in the light of a necessary of life, respecting
which there were great differences of opinion, and many shades
of sentiment, Mr. Tiddypot, in a powerful burst of eloquence
against that hypothesis, frequently made use of the expression
that such and such a rumour had "reached his ears." Captain
Banger, following him, and holding that for purposes of ablu-
tion and refreshment a pint of water per diem was necessary
for every adult of the lower classes, and half a pint for every
child, cast ridicule upon his address in a sparkling speech, and
concluded by saying that instead of those rumours having
reached the ears of the honourable gentleman, he rather
thought the honourable gentleman's ears must have reached
the rumours, in consequence of their well-known length. Mr.
Tiddypot immediately rose, looked the honourable and gallant
gentleman full in the face, and left the Vestry.

The excitement, at this moment painfully intense, was
heightened to an acute degree when Captain Banger rose, and
also left the Vestry. After a few moments of profound silence
— one of these breathless pauses never to be forgotten — Mr.
Chib (of Tucket's Terrace, and the father of the Vestry) rose.
He said that words and looks had passed in that assembly
replete with consequences which every feeling mind must
deplore. Time pressed. The sword was drawn, and while
he spoke the scabbard might be thrown away. He moved
that those honourable gentlemen who had left the Vestry be
recalled, and required to pledge themselves upon their honour
that this affair should go no farther. The motion being by a
general union of parties unanimously agreed to (for everybody
wanted to have the belligerents there instead of out of sight,
which was no fun at all), Mr. Magg was deputed to recover
Captain Banger, and Mr. Chib himself to go in search of Mr.
Tiddypot. The captain was found in a conspicuous position,
surveying the passing omnibuses from the top step of the front
door immediately adjoining the beadle's box; Mr. Tiddypot
made a desperate attempt at resistance, but was overpowered
by Mr. Chib (a remarkably hale old gentleman of eighty-two),
and brought back in safety.

Mr. Tiddypot and the captain being restored to their places, and glaring on each other, were called upon by the chair to abandon all homicidal intentions, and give the Vestry an assurance that they did so. Mr. Tiddypot remained profoundly silent. The captain likewise remained profoundly silent, saving that he was observed by those around him to fold his arms like Napoleon Bonaparte, and to snort in his breathing — actions but too expressive of gunpowder.

The most intense emotion now prevailed. Several members clustered in remonstrance round the captain, and several round Mr. Tiddypot; but both were obdurate. Mr. Chib then presented himself amid tremendous cheering, and said, that not to shrink from the discharge of his painful duty, he must now move that both honourable gentlemen be taken into custody by the beadle, and conveyed to the nearest police-office, there to be held to bail. The union of parties still continuing, the motion was seconded by Mr. Wigsby, — on all usual occasions Mr. Chib's opponent, — and rapturously carried with only one dissentient voice. This was Dogginson's, who said from his place, "Let 'em fight it out with fistes," but whose coarse remark was received as it merited.

The beadle now advanced along the floor of the Vestry, and beckoned with his cocked hat to both members. Every breath was suspended. To say that a pin might have been heard to fall would be feebly to express the all-absorbing interest and silence. Suddenly, enthusiastic cheering broke out from every side of the Vestry. Captain Banger had risen — being, in fact, pulled up by a friend on either side, and poked up by a friend behind.

The captain said, in a deep determined voice, that he had every respect for that Vestry and every respect for that chair; that he also respected the honourable gentleman of Gumtion House; but that he respected his honour more. Hereupon the captain sat down, leaving the whole Vestry much affected. Mr. Tiddypot instantly rose, and was received with the same encouragement. He likewise said — and the exquisite art of this orator communicated to the observation an air of freshness and novelty — that he too had every respect for that Vestry; that he too had every respect for that chair; that he too respected the honourable and gallant gentleman of Wilderness Walk; but that he too respected his honour more. "Hows'-

ever," added the distinguished Vestryman, "if the honourable
or gallant gentleman's honour is never more doubted and dam
aged than it is by me, he's all right." Captain Banger immediately started up again, and said that after those observations,
involving as they did ample concession to his honour without
compromising the honour of the honourable gentleman, he
would be wanting in honour as well as in generosity if he did
not at once repudiate all intention of wounding the honour of
the honourable gentleman, or saying anything dishonourable to
his honourable feelings. These observations were repeatedly
interrupted by bursts of cheers. Mr. Tiddypot retorted that
he well knew the spirit of honour by which the honourable
and gallant gentleman was so honourably animated, and that
he accepted an honourable explanation, offered in a way that
did him honour; but he trusted that the Vestry would consider
that his (Mr. Tiddypot's) honour had imperatively demanded
of him that painful course which he had felt it due to his
honour to adopt. The captain and Mr. Tiddypot then touched
their hats to one another across the Vestry a great many times,
and it is thought that these proceedings (reported to the extent
of several columns in next Sunday's paper) will bring them in
as churchwardens next year.

All this was strictly after the pattern of the real original,
and so are the whole of our Vestry's proceedings. In all their
debates they are laudably imitative of the windy and wordy
slang of the real original, and of nothing that is better in it.
They have headstrong party animosities, without any reference
to the merits of questions; they tack a surprising amount of
debate to a very little business; they set more store by forms
than they do by substances, — all very like the real original!
It has been doubted in our borough whether our Vestry is of
any utility; but our own conclusion is, that it is of the use
to the borough that a diminishing mirror is to a painter, as
enabling it to perceive in a small focus of absurdity all the
surface defects of the real original.

XII

OUR BORE

IT is unnecessary to say that we keep a bore. Everybody
does. But the bore whom we have the pleasure and honour
of enumerating among our particular friends is such a generic
bore, and has so many traits (as it appears to us) in common with the great bore family, that we are tempted to make
him the subject of the present notes. May he be generally
accepted!

Our bore is admitted on all hands to be a good-hearted man.
He may put fifty people out of temper, but he keeps his own.
He preserves a sickly solid smile upon his face when other
faces are ruffled by the perfection he has attained in his art,
and has an equable voice which never travels out of one key
or rises above one pitch. His manner is a manner of tranquil
interest. None of his opinions are startling. Among his
deepest-rooted convictions, it may be mentioned that he considers the air of England damp, and holds that our lively
neighbours — he always calls the French our lively neighbours
— have the advantage of us in that particular. Nevertheless,
he is unable to forget that John Bull is John Bull all the
world over, and that England with all her faults is England
still.

Our bore has travelled. He could not possibly be a complete bore without having travelled. He rarely speaks of his
travels without introducing, sometimes on his own plan of construction, morsels of the language of the country, which he
always translates. You cannot name to him any little remote
town in France, Italy, Germany, or Switzerland, but he knows
it well; stayed there a fortnight under peculiar circumstances.
And talking of that little place, perhaps you know a statue
over an old fountain, up a little court, which is the second —
no, the third — stay — yes, the third turning on the right,
after you come out of the post-house, going up the hill towards
the market? You *don't* know that statue? Nor that fountain? You surprise him! They are not usually seen by trav-

ellers (most extraordinary, he has never yet met with a single
traveller who knew them, except one German, the most intelligent man he ever met in his life!), but he thought that YOU
would have been the man to find them out. And then he
describes them, in a circumstantial lecture half an hour long,
generally delivered behind a door which is constantly being
opened from the other side; and implores you, if you ever
revisit that place, now do go and look at that statue and fountain!

Our bore, in a similar manner, being in Italy, made a discovery of a dreadful picture, which has been the terror of a
large portion of the civilised world ever since. We have seen
the liveliest men paralysed by it, across a broad dining-table.
He was lounging among the mountains, sir, basking in the
mellow influences of the climate, when he came to *una piccola
chiesa* — a little church — or perhaps it would be more correct
to say *una piccolissima cappella* — the smallest chapel you
can possibly imagine — and walked in. There was nobody
inside but a *cieco* — a blind man — saying his prayers, and a
vecchio padre — old friar — rattling a money-box. But above
the head of that friar, and immediately to the right of the altar
as you enter — to the right of the altar? No. To the left of
the altar as you enter — or say near the centre — there hung a
painting (subject, Virgin and Child) so divine in its expression,
so pure and yet so warm and rich in its tone, so fresh in its
touch, at once so glowing in its colour and so statuesque in its
repose, that our bore cried out in an ecstasy, "That's the
finest picture in Italy!" And so it is, sir. There is no doubt
of it. It is astonishing that that picture is so little known.
Even the painter is uncertain. He afterwards took Blumb, of
the Royal Academy (it is to be observed that our bore takes
none but eminent people to see sights, and that none but eminent people take our bore), and you never saw a man so affected
in your life as Blumb was. He cried like a child! And then
our bore begins his description in detail, — for all this is intro-
ductory — and strangles his hearers with the folds of the purple
drapery.

By an equally fortunate conjunction of accidental circumstances, it happened that when our bore was in Switzerland
he discovered a valley, of that superb character that Chamouni
is not to be mentioned in the same breath with it. This is

how it was, sir. He was travelling on a mule — had been in the saddle some days — when, as he and the guide, Pierre Blanquo, whom you may know, perhaps? — our bore is sorry you don't, because he is the only guide deserving of the name — as he and Pierre were descending, towards evening, among those everlasting snows, to the little village of La Croix, our bore observed a mountain track turning off sharply to the right. At first he was uncertain whether it *was* a track at all, and, in fact, he said to Pierre, "*Qu'est que c'est donc, mon ami?* — What is that, my friend?" "*Où, monsieur?*" said Pierre — "Where, sir?" "*Là!* — There!" said our bore. "*Monsieur, ce n'est rien de tout* — Sir, it's nothing at all," said Pierre. "*Allons!* — Make haste. *Il va neiger* — It's going to snow!" But our bore was not to be done in that way, and he firmly replied, "I wish to go in that direction — *Je veux y aller.* I am bent upon it — *Je suis déterminé. En avant!* — Go ahead!" In consequence of which firmness on our bore's part, they proceeded, sir, during two hours of evening, and three of moonlight (they waited in a cavern till the moon was up), along the slenderest track, overhanging perpendicularly the most awful gulfs, until they arrived, by a winding descent, in a valley that possibly, and he may say probably, was never visited by any stranger before. What a valley! Mountains piled on mountains, avalanches stemmed by pine forests; waterfalls, châlets, mountain torrents, wooden bridges, every conceivable picture of Swiss scenery! The whole village turned out to receive our bore. The peasant girls kissed him, the men shook hands with him, one old lady of benevolent appearance wept upon his breast. He was conducted, in a primitive triumph, to the little inn; where he was taken ill next morning, and lay for six weeks, attended by the amiable hostess (the same benevolent old lady who had wept over night) and her charming daughter, Fanchette. It is nothing to say that they were attentive to him; they doted on him. They called him in their simple way, *l'Ange Anglais* — the English Angel. When our bore left the valley, there was not a dry eye in the place; some of the people attended him for miles. He begs and entreats of you as a personal favour, that if you ever go to Switzerland again (you have mentioned that your last visit was your twenty-third), you will go to that valley, and see Swiss scenery for the first time. And if you want really to know

the pastoral people of Switzerland, and to understand them,
mention, in that valley, our bore's name!

Our bore has a crushing brother in the East, who, somehow
or other, was admitted to smoke pipes with Mehemet Ali, and
instantly became an authority on the whole range of Eastern
matters, from Haroun Alraschid to the present Sultan. He
is in the habit of expressing mysterious opinions on this wide
range of subjects, but on questions of foreign policy more particularly, to our bore, in letters; and our bore is continually
sending bits of these letters to the newspapers (which they
never insert), and carrying other bits about in his pocket-book.
It is even whispered that he has been seen at the Foreign
Office, receiving great consideration from the messengers, and
having his card promptly borne into the sanctuary of the temple. The havoc committed in society by this Eastern brother
is beyond belief. Our bore is always ready with him. We
have known our bore to fall upon an intelligent young sojourner
in the wilderness, in the first sentence of a narrative, and beat
all confidence out of him with one blow of his brother. He
became omniscient, as to foreign policy, in the smoking of
those pipes with Mehemet Ali. The balance of power in
Europe, the machinations of the Jesuits, the gentle and human-
ising influence of Austria, the position and prospects of that
hero of the noble soul who is worshipped by happy France, are
all easy reading to our bore's brother. And our bore is so
provokingly self-denying about him! "I don't pretend to more
than a very general knowledge of these subjects myself," says
he, after enervating the intellects of several strong men, "but
these are my brother's opinions, and I believe he is known to
be well-informed."

The commonest incidents and places would appear to have
been made special, expressly for our bore. Ask him whether
he ever chanced to walk, between seven and eight in the morning, down St. James's Street, London, and he will tell you,
never in his life but once. But it's curious that that once
was in 1830; and that as our bore was walking down the street
you have just mentioned, at the hour you have just mentioned
— half-past seven — or twenty minutes to eight. No! Let
him be correct! — exactly a quarter before eight by the Palace
clock — he met a fresh-coloured, grey-haired, good-humoured
looking gentleman, with a brown umbrella, who, as he passed

him, touched his hat and said, "Fine morning, sir fine morning!"—William the Fourth!

Ask our bore whether he has seen Mr. Barry's new Houses of Parliament, and he will reply that he has not yet inspected them minutely, but that you remind him that it was his singular fortune to be the last man to see the old Houses of Parliament before the fire broke out. It happened in this way. Poor John Spine, the celebrated novelist, had taken him over to South Lambeth to read to him the last few chapters of what was certainly his best book,—as our bore told him at the time, adding, "Now, my dear John, touch it, and you'll spoil it!"—and our bore was going back to the club by way of Millbank and Parliament Street, when he stopped to think of Canning, and look at the Houses of Parliament. Now you know far more of the philosophy of Mind than our bore does, and are much better able to explain to him than he is to explain to you why or wherefore, at that particular time, the thought of fire should come into his head. But it did. It did. He thought, What a national calamity if an edifice connected with so many associations should be consumed by fire! At that time there was not a single soul in the street but himself. All was quiet, dark, and solitary. After contemplating the building for a minute—or say a minute and a half, not more—our bore proceeded on his way, mechanically repeating, What a national calamity if such an edifice connected with such associations should be destroyed by—A man coming towards him in a violent state of agitation completed the sentence with the exclamation, Fire! Our bore looked round, and the whole structure was in a blaze.

In harmony and union with these experiences, our bore never went anywhere in a steamboat but he made either the best or the worst voyage ever known on that station. Either he overheard the captain say to himself, with his hands clasped, "We are all lost!" or the captain openly declared to him that he had never made such a run before, and never should be able to do it again. Our bore was in that express train on that railway when they made (unknown to the passengers) the experiment of going at the rate of a hundred miles an hour. Our bore remarked on that occasion to the other people in the carriage, "This is too fast, but sit still!" He was at the Norwich musical festival when the extraordinary echo, for

which science has been wholly unable to account, was heard
for the first and last time. He and the bishop heard it at the
same moment, and caught each other's eye. He was present
at that illumination of St. Peter's, of which the Pope is known
to have remarked, as he looked at it out of his window in
the Vatican, " *O Cielo!* *Questa cosa non sara fatta, mai
ancora, come questa* — O Heaven! this thing will never be
done again, like this!" He has seen every lion he ever saw
under some remarkably propitious circumstances. He knows
there is no fancy in it, because in every case the showman
mentioned the fact at the time, and congratulated him upon it.

At one period of his life our bore had an illness. It was
an illness of a dangerous character for society at large. Innocently remark that you are very well, or that somebody else
is very well, and our bore, with a preface that one never
knows what a blessing health is until one has lost it, is
reminded of that illness, and drags you through the whole of
its symptoms, progress, and treatment. Innocently remark
that you are not well, or that somebody else is not well, and
the same inevitable result ensues. You will learn how our
bore felt a tightness about here, sir, for which he could n't
account, accompanied with a constant sensation as if he were
being stabbed — or, rather, jobbed — that expresses it more
correctly — jobbed — with a blunt knife. Well, sir! This
went on, until sparks began to flit before his eyes, water-
wheels to turn round in his head, and hammers to beat incessantly thump, thump, thump, all down his back — along the
whole of the spinal vertebræ. Our bore, when his sensations
had come to this, thought it a duty he owed to himself to take
advice, and he said, Now, whom shall I consult? He naturally thought of Callow, at that time one of the most eminent
physicians in London, and he went to Callow. Callow said,
"Liver!" and prescribed rhubarb and calomel, low diet, and
moderate exercise. Our bore went on with this treatment,
getting worse every day, until he lost confidence in Callow,
and went to Moon, whom half the town was then mad about.
Moon was interested in the case; to do him justice he was
very much interested in the case; and he said, "Kidneys!"
He altered the whole treatment, sir — gave strong acids,
cupped, and blistered. This went on, our bore still getting
worse every day, until he openly told Moon it would be a

satisfaction to him if he would have a consultation with Clatter. The moment Clatter saw our bore, he said, "Accumula-
tion of fat about the heart!" Snugglewood, who was called
in with him, differed, and said, "Brain!" But what they all
agreed upon was, to lay our bore upon his back, to shave his
head, to leech him, to administer enormous quantities of medicine, and to keep him low; so that he was reduced to a mere
shadow, you wouldn't have known him, and nobody considered it possible that he could ever recover. This was his condition, sir, when he heard of Jilkins — at that period in a very
small practice, and living in the upper part of a house in Great
Portland Street; but still, you understand, with a rising reputation among the few people to whom he was known. Being
in that condition in which a drowning man catches at a straw,
our bore sent for Jilkins. Jilkins came. Our bore liked his
eye, and said, "Mr. Jilkins, I have a presentiment that you
will do me good." Jilkins's reply was characteristic of the
man. It was, "Sir, I mean to do you good." This confirmed
our bore's opinion of his eye, and they went into the case
together — went completely into it. Jilkins then got up,
walked across the room, came back, and sat down. His words
were these. "You have been humbugged. This is a case of
indigestion, occasioned by deficiency of power in the Stomach.
Take a mutton chop in half an hour, with a glass of the finest
old sherry that can be got for money. Take two mutton chops
to-morrow, and two glasses of the finest old sherry. Next
day, I'll come again." In a week our bore was on his legs,
and Jilkins's success dates from that period!

Our bore is great in secret information. He happens to
know many things that nobody else knows. He can generally
tell you where the split is in the Ministry; he knows a deal
about the Queen; and has little anecdotes to relate of the royal
nursery. He gives you the judge's private opinion of Sludge
the murderer, and his thoughts when he tried him. He happens to know what such a man got by such a transaction, and
it was fifteen thousand five hundred pounds, and his income is
twelve thousand a year. Our bore is also great in mystery.
He believes, with an exasperating appearance of profound
meaning, that you saw Parkins last Sunday? — Yes, you did.
— Did he say anything particular? — No, nothing particular.
— Our bore is surprised at that. — Why? — Nothing. Only

he understood that Parkins had come to tell you something. — What about? — Well! our bore is not at liberty to mention what about. But he believes you will hear that from Parkins himself soor., and he hopes it may not surprise you as it did him. Perhaps, however, you never heard about Parkins's wife's sister? — No. — Ah! says our bore, that explains it!

Our bore is also great in argument. He infinitely enjoys a long, humdrum, drowsy interchange of words of dispute about nothing. He considers that it strengthens the mind, consequently, he "don't see that" very often. Or, he would be glad to know what you mean by that. Or, he doubts that. Or, he has always understood exactly the reverse of that. Or, he can't admit that. Or, he begs to deny that. Or, surely you don't mean that. And so on. He once advised us; offered us a piece of advice, after the fact, totally impracticable and wholly impossible of acceptance, because it supposed the fact, then eternally disposed of, to be yet in abeyance. It was a dozen years ago, and to this hour our bore benevolently wishes, in a mild voice, on certain regular occasions, that we had thought better of his opinion.

The instinct with which our bore finds out another bore, and closes with him, is amazing. We have seen him pick his man out of fifty men, in a couple of minutes. They love to go (which they do naturally) into a slow argument on a previously exhausted subject, and to contradict each other, and to wear the hearers out, without impairing their own perennial freshness as bores. It improves the good understanding between them, and they get together afterwards, and bore each other amicably. Whenever we see our bore behind a door with another bore, we know that when he comes forth he will praise the other bore as one of the most intelligent men he ever met. And this bringing us to the close of what we had to say about our bore, we are anxious to have it understood that he never bestowed this praise on us.

XIII

LYING AWAKE

"My uncle lay with his eyes half closed, and his nightcap drawn almost down to his nose. His fancy was already wandering, and began to mingle up the present scene with the crater of Vesuvius, the French Opera, the Coliseum at Rome, Dolly's Chop-House in London, and all the farrago of noted places with which the brain of a traveller is crammed; in a word, he was just falling asleep."

Thus, that delightful writer, Washington Irving, in his "Tales of a Traveller." But it happened to me the other night to be lying, not with my eyes half closed, but with my eyes wide open; not with my nightcap drawn almost down to my nose, for on sanitary principles I never wear a nightcap, but with my hair pitchforked and tousled all over the pillow; not just falling asleep by any means, but glaringly, persistently, and obstinately, broad awake. Perhaps, with no scientific intention or invention, I was illustrating the theory of the Duality of the Brain; perhaps one part of my brain, being wakeful, sat up to watch the other part which was sleepy. Be that as it may, something in me was as desirous to go to sleep as it possibly could be, but something else in me *would not* go to sleep, and was as obstinate as George the Third.

Thinking of George the Third — for I devote this paper to my train of thoughts as I lay awake, most people lying awake sometimes, and having some interest in the subject — put me in mind of Benjamin Franklin, and so Benjamin Franklin's paper on the art of procuring pleasant dreams, which would seem necessarily to include the art of going to sleep, came into my head. Now, as I often used to read that paper when I was a very small boy, and as I recollect everything I read then as perfectly as I forget everything I read now, I quoted, "Get out of bed, beat up and turn your pillow, shake the bed-clothes well with at least twenty shakes, then throw the bed open and leave it to cool; in the mean while, continuing undrest, walk about your chamber. When you begin to feel the cold air unpleasant, then return to your bed, and you will soon fall asleep, and your sleep will be sweet and pleasant." Not a bit of it! I performed the whole ceremony, and if it were possible for me to be more saucer-eyed than I was before, that was the only result that came of it.

Except Niagara. The two quotations from Washington Irving and Benjamin Franklin may have put it in my head by an American association of ideas; but there I was, and the Horse-Shoe Fall was thundering and tumbling in my eyes and ears, and the very rainbows that I left upon the spray when I really did last look upon it were beautiful to see. The night-light being quite as plain, however, and sleep seeming to be many thousand miles further off than Niagara, I made up my mind to think a little about Sleep; which I no sooner did than I whirled off in spite of myself to Drury Lane Theatre, and there saw a great actor and dear friend of mine (whom I had been thinking of in the day) playing Macbeth, and heard him apostrophising "the death of each day's life," as I have heard him many a time, in the days that are gone.

But Sleep. I *will* think about Sleep. I am determined to think (this is the way I went on) about Sleep. I must hold the word Sleep tight and fast, or I shall be off at a tangent in half a second. I feel myself unaccountably straying, already, into Clare Market. Sleep. It would be curious, as illustrating the equality of sleep, to inquire how many of its phenomena are common to all classes, to all degrees of wealth and poverty, to every grade of education and ignorance. Here, for example, is her Majesty Queen Victoria in her palace, this present blessed night, and here is Winking Charley, a sturdy vagrant, in one of her Majesty's jails. Her Majesty has fallen, many thousands of times, from that same Tower, which *I* claim a right to tumble off now and then. So has Winking Charley. Her Majesty in her sleep has opened or prorogued Parliament, or has held a Drawing-Room, attired in some very scanty dress, the deficiencies and improprieties of which have caused her great uneasiness I, in my degree, have suffered unspeakable agitation of mind from taking the chair at a public dinner at the London Tavern in my night-clothes, which not all the courtesy of my kind friend and host Mr. Bathe could persuade me were quite adapted to the occasion. Winking Charley has been repeatedly tried in a worse condition. Her

Majesty is no stranger to a vault or firmament, of a sort of floor-cloth, with an indistinct pattern distantly resembling eyes, which occasionally obtrudes itself on her repose. Neither am I. Neither is Winking Charley. It is quite common to all three of us to skim along with airy strides a little above the ground; also to hold, with the deepest interest dialogues with various people, all represented by ourselves; and to be at our wits' end to know what they are going to tell us; and to be indescribably astonished by the secrets they disclose. It is probable that we have all three committed murders and hidden bodies. It is pretty certain that we have all desperately wanted to cry out, and have had no voice; that we have all gone to the play and not been able to get in; that we have all dreamed much more of our youth than of our later lives; that — I have lost it! The thread's broken.

And up I go. I, lying here with the night-light before me, up I go, for no reason on earth that I can find out, and drawn by no links that are visible to me, up the Great St. Bernard! I have lived in Switzerland, and rambled among the mountains; but why I should go there now, and why up the Great St. Bernard in preference to any other mountain, I have no idea. As I lie here broad awake, and with every sense so sharpened that I can distinctly hear distant noises inaudible to me at another time, I make that journey, as I really did, on the same summer day, with the same happy party, — ah! two since dead, I grieve to think, — and there is the same track, with the same black wooden arms to point the way, and there are the same storm-refuges here and there, and there is the same snow falling at the top, and there are the same frosty mists, and there is the same intensely cold convent with its menagerie smell, and the same breed of dogs fast dying out, and the same breed of jolly young monks whom I mourn to know as humbugs, and the same convent parlour with its piano and the sitting round the fire, and the same supper, and the same lone night in a cell, and the same bright fresh morning when going out into the highly rarefied air was like a plunge into an icy bath. Now see here what comes along; and why does this thing stalk into my mind on the top of a Swiss mountain!

It is a figure that I once saw, just after dark, chalked upon a door in a little back lane near a country church — my first church. How young a child I may have been at the time I don't know, but it horrified me so intensely — in connection with the churchyard, I suppose, for it smokes a pipe, and has a big hat with each of its ears sticking out in a horizontal line under the brim, and is not in itself more oppressive than a mouth from ear to ear, a pair of goggle eyes, and hands like two bunches of carrots, five in each, can make it — that it is still vaguely alarming to me to recall (as I have often done before, lying awake) the running home, the looking behind, the horror of its following me; though whether disconnected from the door, or door and all, I can't say, and perhaps never could. It lays a disagreeable train. I must resolve to think of something on the voluntary principle.

The balloon ascents of this last season. They will do to think about, while I lie awake, as well as anything else. I must hold them tight though, for I feel them sliding away, and in their stead are the Mannings, husband and wife, hanging on the top of Horsemonger Lane Jail. In connection with which dismal spectacle, I recall this curious fantasy of the mind. That, having beheld that execution, and having left those two forms dangling on the top of the entrance gateway, — the man's, a limp, loose suit of clothes as if the man had gone out of them; the woman's, a fine shape, so elaborately corseted and artfully dressed, that it was quite unchanged in its trim appearance as it slowly swung from side to side, — I never could, by my utmost efforts, for some weeks, present the outside of that prison to myself (which the terrible impression I had received continually obliged me to do) without presenting it with the two figures still hanging in the morning air. Until, strolling past the gloomy place one night, when the street was deserted and quiet, and actually seeing that the bodies were not there, my fancy was persuaded, as it were, to take them down and bury them within the precincts of the jail, where they have lain ever since.

The balloon ascents of last season. Let me reckon them up. There were the horse, the bull, the parachute, and the tumbler hanging on — chiefly by his toes, I believe — below the car. Very wrong, indeed, and decidedly to be stopped. But in connection with these and similar dangerous exhibitions, it strikes me that that portion of the public whom they entertain is unjustly reproached. Their pleasure is in the difficulty overcome. They are a public of great faith, and are quite confident that the gentleman will not fall off the horse, or the lady off the bull or out of the parachute, and that the tumbler has a firm hold with his toes. They do not go to see the adventurer vanquished, but triumphant. There is no parallel in public combats between men and beasts, because nobody can answer for the particular beast — unless it were always the same beast, in which case it would be a mere stage-show, which the same public would go in the same state of mind to see, entirely believing in the brute being beforehand safely subdued by the man. That they are not accustomed to calculate hazards and dangers with any nicety we may know from their rash exposure of themselves in overcrowded steamboats, and unsafe conveyances and places of all kinds. And I cannot help thinking that instead of railing, and attributing savage motives to a people naturally well disposed and humane, it is better to teach them, and lead them argumentatively and reasonably — for they are very reasonable, if you will discuss a matter with them — to more considerate and wise conclusions.

This is a disagreeable intrusion! Here is a man with his throat cut, dashing towards me as I lie awake! A recollection of an old story of a kinsman of mine, who, going home one foggy winter night to Hampstead, when London was much smaller and the road lonesome, suddenly encountered such a figure rushing past him, and presently two keepers from a madhouse in pursuit. A very unpleasant creature indeed to come into my mind unbidden, as I lie awake.

The balloon ascents of last season. I must return to the balloons. Why did the bleeding man start out of them? Never mind; if I inquire, he will be back again. The balloons. This particular public have inherently a great pleasure in the contemplation of physical difficulties overcome; mainly, as I take it, because the lives of a large majority of them are exceedingly monotonous and real, and, further, are a struggle against continual difficulties, and further still, because anything in the form of accidental injury, or any kind of illness or disability, is so very serious in their own sphere. I will explain this seeming paradox of mine. Take the case of a Christmas pantomime. Surely nobody supposes that the young mother in the pit who falls into fits of laughter when the baby is boiled or sat upon would be at all diverted by such an occurrence off the stage. Nor is the decent workman in the gallery, who is transported beyond the ignorant present by the delight with which he sees a stout gentleman pushed out of a two-pair-of-stairs window, to be slandered by the suspicion that he would be in the least entertained by such a spectacle in any street in London, Paris, or New York. It always appears to me that the secret of this enjoyment lies in the temporary superiority to the common hazards and mischances of life; in seeing casualties, attended when they really occur with bodily and mental suffering, tears, and poverty, happen through a very rough sort of poetry without the least harm being done to any one — the pretence of distress in a pantomime being so broadly humorous as to be no pretence at all. Much as in the comic fiction I can understand the mother with a very vulnerable baby at home greatly relishing the invulnerable baby on the stage, so in the Cremorne reality I can understand the mason who is always liable to fall off a scaffold in his working jacket and to be carried to the hospital having an infinite admiration of the radiant personage in spangles who goes into the clouds upon a bull, or upside down, and who, he takes it for granted, — not reflecting upon the thing, — has, by uncommon skill and dexterity, conquered such mischances as those to which he and his acquaintance are continually exposed.

I wish the Morgue in Paris would not come here as I lie awake, with its ghastly beds, and the swollen saturated clothes hanging up, and the water dripping, dripping all day long, upon that other swollen saturated something in the corner, like a heap of crushed over-ripe figs that I have seen in Italy! And this detestable Morgue comes back again at the head of a procession of forgotten ghost stories. This will never do. I must think of something else as I lie awake; or, like that sagacious animal in the United States who recognised the colonel who was such a dead shot, I am a gone 'coon. What shall I think of? The late brutal assaults. Very good subject. The late brutal assaults.

(Though whether, supposing I should see, here before me as I lie awake, the awful phantom described in one of those ghost stories, who, with a head-dress of shroud, was always seen looking in through a certain glass door at a certain dead hour — whether in such a case it would be the least consolation to me to know on philosophical grounds that it was merely my imagination is a question I can't help asking myself by the way.)

The late brutal assaults. I strongly question the expediency of advocating the revival of whipping for those crimes. It is a natural and generous impulse to be indignant at the perpetration of inconceivable brutality, but I doubt the whipping panacea gravely. Not in the least regard or pity for the criminal, whom I hold in far lower estimation than a mad wolf, but in consideration for the general tone and feeling, which is very much improved since the whipping times. It is bad for a people to be familiarised with such punishments. When the whip went out of Bridewell, and ceased to be flourished at the cart's tail and at the whipping-post, it began to fade out of madhouses, and workhouses, and schools, and families, and to give place to a better system everywhere than cruel driving. It would be hasty, because a few brutes may be inadequately punished, to revive, in any aspect, what, in so many aspects, society is hardly yet happily rid of. The whip is a very contagious kind of thing, and difficult to confine within one set of bounds. Utterly abolish punishment by fine — a barbarous device, quite as much out of date as wager by battle, but particularly connected in the vulgar mind with this class of offence, — at least quadruple the term of imprisonment for aggravated assaults, — and above all let us, in such cases, have no Pet Prisoning, vain-glorifying, strong soup, and roasted meats, but hard work, and one unchanging and uncompromising dietary of bread and water, well or ill; and we shall do much better than by going down into the dark to grope for the whip among the rusty fragments of the rack, and the branding-iron, and the chains and gibbet from the public roads, and the weights that pressed men to death in the cells of Newgate.

I had proceeded thus far, when I found I had been lying awake so long that the very dead began to wake too, and to crowd into my thoughts most sorrowfully. Therefore, I resolved to lie awake no more, but to get up and go out for a night walk — which resolution was an acceptable relief to me, as I dare say it may prove now to a great many more.

XIV

TRADING IN DEATH

SEVERAL years have now elapsed since it began to be clear
to the comprehension of most rational men that the English
people had fallen into a condition much to be regretted, in
respect of their funeral customs. A system of barbarous show
and expense was found to have gradually erected itself above
the grave, which, while it could possibly do no honour to the
memory of the dead, did great dishonour to the living, as
inducing them to associate the most solemn of human occasions
with unmeaning mummeries, dishonest debt, profuse waste,
and bad example in an utter oblivion of responsibility. The
more the subject was examined, and the lower the investigation
was carried, the more monstrous (as was natural) these usages
appeared to be, both in themselves and in their consequences.
No class of society escaped. The competition among the middle classes for superior gentility in funerals — the gentility
being estimated by the amount of ghastly folly in which the
undertaker was permitted to run riot — descended even to the
very poor; to whom the cost of funeral customs was so ruinous
and so disproportionate to their means that they formed clubs
among themselves to defray such charges. Many of these
clubs, conducted by designing villains who preyed upon the
general infirmity, cheated and wronged the poor most cruelly;
others, by presenting a new class of temptations to the wick-
edest natures among them, led to a new class of mercenary
murders, so abominable in their iniquity that language cannot
stigmatise them with sufficient severity. That nothing might
be wanting to complete the general depravity, hollowness, and
falsehood, of this state of things, the absurd fact came to light,
that innumerable harpies assumed the titles of furnishers of
funerals, who possessed no funeral furniture whatever, but who
formed a long file of middlemen between the chief mourner
and the real tradesman, and who hired out the trappings from
one to another, — passing them on like water-buckets at a fire.
— every one of them charging his enormous percentage on his

share of the "black job." Add to all this, the demonstration, by the simplest and plainest practical science, of the terrible consequences to the living, inevitably resulting from the practice of burying the dead in the midst of crowded towns; and the exposition of a system of indecent horror, revolting to our nature and disgraceful to our age and nation, arising out of the confined limits of such burial-grounds and the avarice of their proprietors; and the culminating point of this gigantic mockery is at last arrived at.

Out of such almost incredible degradation, saving that the proof of it is too easy, we are still very slowly and feebly emerging. There are now, we confidently hope, among the middle classes, many who, having made themselves acquainted with these evils through the parliamentary papers in which they are described, would be moved by no human consideration to perpetuate the old bad example; but who will leave it as their solemn injunction on their nearest and dearest survivors, that they shall not, in their death, be made the instruments of infecting either the minds or the bodies of their fellow-creatures. Among persons of note, such examples have not been wanting. The late Duke of Sussex did a national service when he desired to be laid, in the equality of death, in the cemetery of Kensal Green, and not with the pageantry of a state funeral in the royal vault at Windsor. Sir Robert Peel requested to be buried at Drayton. The late Queen Dowager left a pattern to every rank in these touching and admirable words: "I die in all humility, knowing well that we are all alike before the Throne of God; and I request, therefore, that my mortal remains be conveyed to the grave without any pomp or state. They are to be removed to St. George's Chapel, Windsor, where I request to have as private and quiet a funeral as possible. I particularly desire not to be laid out in state. I die in peace and wish to be carried to the tomb in peace, and free from the vanities and pomp of this world. I request not to be dissected or embalmed, and desire to give as little trouble as possible."

With such precedents and such facts fresh in the general knowledge, and at this transition time in so serious a chapter of our social history, the obsolete custom of a state funeral has been revived, in miscalled "honour" of the late Duke of Wellington. To whose glorious memory be all true honour while England lasts!

We earnestly submit to our readers that there is, and that there can be, no kind of honour in such a revival; that the more truly great the man, the more truly little the ceremony; and that it has been, from first to last, a pernicious instance and encouragement of the demoralising practice of trading in Death.

It is within the knowledge of the whole public, of all diversities of political opinion, whether or no any of the Powers that be have traded in this Death — have saved it up, and petted it, and made the most of it, and reluctantly let it go. On that aspect of the question we offer no further remark.

But of the general trading spirit which, in its inherent emptiness and want of consistency and reality, the long-deferred state funeral has appropriately awakened, we will proceed to furnish a few instances all faithfully copied from the advertising columns of "The Times."

First, of seats and refreshments. Passing over that desirable first floor where a party could be accommodated with "the use of a piano," and merely glancing at the decorous daily announcement of "The Duke of Wellington Funeral Wine," which was in such high demand that immediate orders were necessary; and also "The Duke of Wellington Funeral Cake," which "delicious article" could only be had of such a baker; and likewise "The Funeral Life Preserver," which could only be had of such a tailor; and further, "the celebrated lemon biscuits," at one and fourpence per pound, which were considered by the manufacturer as the only infallible assuagers of the national grief; let us pass in review some dozen of the more eligible opportunities the public had of profiting by the occasion.

LUDGATE HILL. — The fittings and arrangements for viewing this grand and solemnly imposing procession are now completed at this establishment, and those who are desirous of obtaining a fine and extensive view, combined with every personal convenience and comfort, will do well to make immediate inspection of the SEATS now remaining on hand.

FUNERAL, including Beds the night previous. — To be LET, a SECOND FLOOR, of three rooms, two windows, having a good view of the procession. Terms, including refreshment, 10 guineas. Single places, including bed and breakfast, from 15s.

THE DUKE'S FUNERAL. — A first-rate VIEW for 15 persons, also good clean beds and a sitting-room on reasonable terms.

SEATS and WINDOWS to be LET, in the best part of the Strand, a few doors from Coutts's banking-house. First floor windows, £8 each; second floor, £5 10s. each; third floor, £3 10s. each; two plate-glass shop windows, £7 each.

SEATS to VIEW the DUKE of WELLINGTON'S FUNERAL. Best position of all the route, no obstruction to the view. Apply Old Bailey. N. B. From the above position you can nearly see to St. Paul's and to Temple-bar.

FUNERAL of the late DUKE of WELLINGTON.— To be LET, a SECOND FLOOR, two windows, firing and every convenience. Terms moderate for a party. Also a few seats in front, one guinea each. Commanding a view from Piccadilly to Pall-mall.

FUNERAL of the DUKE of WELLINGTON.— The FIRST and SECOND FLOORS to be LET, either by the room or window, suited to gentlemen's families, for whom every comfort and accommodation will be provided, and commanding the very best view of this imposing spectacle. The ground floor is also fitted up with commodious seats, ranging in price from one guinea. Apply on the premises.

THE DUKE'S FUNERAL.— Terms very moderate.— TWO FIRST FLOOR ROOMS, with balcony and private entrance out of the Strand. The larger room capable of holding 15 persons. The small room to be let for eight guineas.

THE DUKE'S FUNERAL.— To be LET, a SHOP WINDOW, with seats erected for about 30, for 25 guineas. Also a Furnished First Floor, with two large windows. One of the best views in the whole range from Temple-bar to St. Paul's. Price 35 guineas. A few single seats one guinea each.

THE FUNERAL PROCESSION of the DUKE of WELLING– TON.— Cockspur-street, Charing-cross, decidedly the best position in the whole route, a few SEATS still DISENGAGED, which will be offered at reasonable prices. An early application is requisite, as they are fast filling up. Also a few places on the roof. A most excellent view.

FUNERAL of the Late DUKE of WELLINGTON.— To be LET, in the best part of the Strand, a SECOND FLOOR, for £10; a Third Floor, £7 10s., containing two windows in each; front seats in shop, at one guinea.

THE DUKE'S FUNERAL.— To be LET, for 25 guineas to a genteel family, in one of the most commanding situations in the line of route, a FIRST FLOOR, with safe balcony, and ante-room. Will accommodate 20 persons, with an uninterrupted and extensive view for all. For a family of less number a reduction will be made. Every accommodation will be afforded.

But above all let us not forget the

NOTICE TO CLERGYMEN.— T. C., Fleet-street, has reserved for clergymen exclusively, *upon condition only that they appear in their surplices,* FOUR FRONT SEATS, at £1 each; four second tier, at 15*s.* each; four third tier, at 12*s.* 6*d.*; four fourth tier, at 10*s.*; four fifth tier, at 7*s.* 6*d.*; and four sixth tier, at 5*s.* All the other seats are respectively 40*s.*, 30*s.*, 20*s.*, 15*s.*, 10*s.*

The anxiety of this enterprising tradesman to get up a reverend tableau in his shop window of four-and-twenty clergymen all on six rows is particularly commendable, and appears to us to shed a remarkable grace on the solemnity.

These few specimens are collected at random from scores upon scores of such advertisements, mingled with descriptions of non-existent ranges of view, and with invitations to a few agreeable gentlemen who are wanted to complete a little assembly of kindred souls, who have laid in abundance of "refreshments, wines, spirits, provisions, fruit, plate, glass, china," and other light matters too numerous to mention, and who keep "good fires." On looking over them we are constantly startled by the words in large capitals, "WOULD TO GOD NIGHT OR BLUCHER WERE COME!" which, referring to a work of art, are relieved by a legend setting forth how the lamented hero observed of it, "in his characteristic manner, 'Very good; very good indeed.'" O Art! *You* too trading in Death!

Then autographs fall into their place in the state funeral train. The sanctity of a seal, or the confidence of a letter, is a meaningless phrase that has no place in the vocabulary of the Traders in Death. Stop, trumpets, in the Dead March, and blow to the world how characteristic we autographs are!

WELLINGTON AUTOGRAPHS.—TWO consecutive LETTERS of the DUKE'S (1843) highly characteristic and authentic, with the Correspondence, &c., that elicited them, the whole forming quite a literary curiosity, for £15.

WELLINGTON AUTOGRAPHS.—To be DISPOSED OF, TWO AUTOGRAPH LETTERS of the DUKE of WELLINGTON, one dated Walmer Castle, 9th October, 1834, the other London, 17th May, 1843, with their post-marks and seals.

WELLINGTON.—THREE original NOTES, averaging 2¼ pages each (not lithographs), seal, and envelopes, to be SOLD. Supposed to be the most characteristic of his Grace yet published. The highest sum above £30 for the two, or £20 for the one, which is distinct, will be accepted.

TO BE DISPOSED OF, by a retired officer, FIVE LETTERS and NOTES of the late HERO—three when Sir A. Wellesley. Also a large Envelope. All with seals. Apply personally, or by letter.

THE DUKE'S LETTERS. — TWO highly interesting LETTERS, authentic, and relating to a most amusing and characteristic circumstance, to be SOLD.

THE DUKE of WELLINGTON. — AUTOGRAPH LETTER to a lady, with seal and envelope. This is quite in the Duke's peculiar style, and will be parted with for the highest offer. Apply — where the letter can be seen.

F. M. the DUKE of WELLINGTON. — To be SOLD, by a member of the family, to whom it was written, an ORIGINAL AUTOGRAPH LETTER of the late Duke of Wellington, on military affairs, six pages long, in the best preservation. Price £30.

FIELD-MARSHAL the DUKE of WELLINGTON'S AUTOGRAPH. — A highly characteristic LETTER of the DUKE'S for DISPOSAL, wherein he alludes to his living 100 years, date 1847, with envelope. Seal, with crest perfect. £10 will be taken.

DUKE of WELLINGTON. — An AUTOGRAPH LETTER of the DUKE, written immediately after the death of the Duchess in 1831, is for SALE; also Two Autograph Envelopes franked and sealed.

DUKE of WELLINGTON. — AUTOGRAPH BUSINESS LETTER, envelope, seal, post-mark, &c., complete. Style courteous and highly characteristic. Will be shown by the party and at the place addressed. Price £15.

FIELD-MARSHAL the DUKE of WELLINGTON. — TWO AUTOGRAPH LETTERS of his Grace, one written in his 61st, the other in his 72d year, both first-rate specimens of his characteristic graphic style, and on an important subject, to be SOLD. Their genuineness can be fully proved.

THE DUKE of WELLINGTON. — A very curious DOCUMENT, partly printed, and the rest written by his Grace to a lady. This is well worthy of a place in the cabinet of the curious. There is nothing like it. Highest offer will be taken.

TO be SOLD, SIX AUTOGRAPH LETTERS from F. M. the DUKE of WELLINGTON, with envelopes and seals, which have been most generously given to aid a lady in distressed circumstances.

THE DUKE of WELLINGTON. — A lady has in her possession a LETTER, written by his Grace on the 18th of June, in the present year (1852), and will be happy to DISPOSE OF the same. The letter is rendered more valuable by its being written on the last anniversary which his Grace was spared to celebrate. The letter bears date from Apsley House, with perfect envelope and seal.

A CLERGYMAN has TWO LETTERS, with Envelopes, addressed to him by the late DUKE, and bearing striking testimony to the extent of his Grace's private charities, to be DIS-

POSED OF at the highest offer (for one or both), received by the 18th instant (Nov. 1852). The offers may be contingent on further particulars being satisfactory.

THE DUKE of WELLINGTON. — A widow, in deep distress, has in her possession an AUTOGRAPH LETTER of his Grace the DUKE of WELLINGTON, written in 1830, enclosed and directed in an envelope, and sealed with his ducal coronet, which she would be happy to PART WITH for a trifle.

VALUABLE AUTOGRAPH NOTE of the late DUKE of WEL-LINGTON, dated March 27, 1850, to be SOLD, for £20, by the gentleman to whom it was addressed, together with envelope, perfect impression of Ducal seal, and Knightsbridge post-mark distinct. The whole in excellent preservation. A better specimen of the noble Duke's handwriting and highly characteristic style cannot be seen.

ONE of the last LETTERS of the DUKE of WELLINGTON for DISPOSAL, dated from Walmer Castle within a day or two of his death, highly characteristic, with seal and post-marks distinct. This being probably the last letter written by the late Duke its interest as a relic must be greatly enhanced. The highest offer accepted. May be seen on application.

THE GREAT DUKE. — A LETTER of the GREAT HERO, dated March 27, 1851, to be SOLD. Also a beautiful Letter from Jenny Lind, dated June 20, 1852. The highest offer will be accepted. Address with offers of price.

Miss Lind's autograph would appear to have lingered in the shade until the funeral train came by, when it modestly stepped into the procession and took a conspicuous place. We are in doubt which to admire most: the ingenuity of this little stroke of business; or the affecting delicacy that sells "probably the last letter written by the late Duke" before the aged hand that wrote it under some manly sense of duty is yet withered in its grave; or the piety of that excellent clergyman — did he appear in his surplice in the front row of T. C.'s shop window? — who is so anxious to sell "striking testimony to the extent of his Grace's private charities;" or the generosity of that Good Samaritan who poured "six letters with envelopes and seals" into the wounds of the lady in distressed circumstances.

Lastly come the relics — precious remembrances worn next to the bereaved heart, like Hardy's miniature of Nelson, and never to be wrested from the advertisers but with ready money.

MEMENTO of the late DUKE of WELLINGTON. — To be DISPOSED OF, a LOCK of the late illustrious DUKE'S

HAIR. Can be guaranteed. The highest offer will be accepted. Apply by letter prepaid.

THE DUKE of WELLINGTON. — A LOCK of HAIR of the late DUKE of WELLINGTON to be DISPOSED OF, now in the possession of a widow lady. Cut off the morning the Queen was crowned. Apply by letter, post-paid.

VALUABLE RELIC of the late DUKE of WELLINGTON. — A lady, having in her possession a quantity of the late illustrious DUKE'S HAIR, cut in 1841, is willing to PART WITH a portion of the same for £25. Satisfactory proof will be given of its identity, and of how it came into the owner's possession, on application by letter, prepaid.

RELIC of the DUKE of WELLINGTON for SALE. — The son of the late well-known hair-cutter to his Grace the late DUKE of WELLINGTON, at Strathfieldsaye, has a small quantity of HAIR, that his father cut from the Duke's head, which he is willing to DISPOSE OF. Any one desirous of possessing such a relic of England's hero are requested to make their offer for the same, by letter.

RELICS of the late DUKE of WELLINGTON. — For SALE, a WAISTCOAT, in good preservation, worn by his Grace some years back, which can be well authenticated as such.

Next, a very choice article — quite unique — the value of which may be presumed to be considerably enhanced by the conclusive impossibility of its being doubted in the least degree by the most suspicious mind.

A MEMENTO of the DUKE of WELLINGTON. — La Mort de Napoleon, Ode d'Alexandre Manzoni, avec la Traduction en Français, par Edmond Angelini, de Venise. — A book, of which the above is the title, was torn up by the Duke and thrown by him from the carriage, in which he was riding, as he was passing through Kent: the pieces of the book were collected and put together by a person who saw the Duke tear it and throw the same away. Any person desirous of obtaining the above memento will be communicated with.

Finally, a literary production of astonishing brilliancy and spirit; without which, we are authorised to state, no nobleman's or gentleman's library can be considered complete.

DUKE of WELLINGTON and SIR R. PEEL. — A talented, interesting, and valuable WORK, on Political Economy and Free Trade, was published in 1830, and immediately bought up by the above statesmen, except one copy, which is now for DISPOSAL. Apply by letter only.

Here, for the reader's sake, we terminate our quotations. They might easily have been much more extended.

We believe that a state funeral at this time of day — apart from the mischievously confusing effect it has on the general mind, as to the necessary union of funeral expense and pomp with funeral respect, and the consequent injury it may do to the cause of a great reform most necessary for the benefit of all classes of society — is, in itself, so plainly a pretence of being what it is not; is so unreal, such a substitution of the form for the substance; is so cut and dried, and stale; is such a palpably got up theatrical trick; that it puts the dread solemnity of death to flight, and encourages these shameless traders in their dealings on the very coffin-lid of departed greatness. That private letters and other memorials of the great Duke of Wellington would still have been advertised and sold, though he had been laid in his grave amid the silent respect of the whole country with the simple honours of a military commander, we do not doubt; but that, in that case, the traders would have been discouraged from holding anything like this Public Fair and Great Undertakers' Jubilee over his remains we doubt as little. It is idle to attempt to connect the frippery of the Lord Chamberlain's Office and the Herald's College with the awful passing away of that vain shadow in which man walketh and disquieteth himself in vain. There is a great gulf set between the two which is set there by no mortal hands, and cannot by mortal hands be bridged across. Does any one believe that, otherwise, "the Senate" would have been "mourning its hero" (in the likeness of a French Field-Marshal) on Tuesday evening, and that the same Senate would have been in fits of laughter with Mr. Hume on Wednesday afternoon when the same hero was still in question and unburied?

The mechanical exigencies of this journal render it necessary for these remarks to be written on the evening of the state funeral. We have already indicated in these pages that we consider the state funeral a mistake, and we hope temperately to leave the question here for temperate consideration. It is easy to imagine how it may have done much harm, and it is hard to imagine how it can have done any good. It is only harder to suppose that it can have afforded a grain of satisfaction to the immediate descendants of the great Duke of Wellington, or that it can reflect the faintest ray of lustre on so bright a name. If it were assumed that such a ceremonial was the general desire of the English people, we would reply that

that assumption was founded on a misconception of the popular character, and on a low estimate of the general sense; and that the sooner both were better appreciated in high places, the better it could not fail to be for us all. Taking for granted at this writing, what we hope may be assumed without any violence to the truth, namely, that the ceremonial was in all respects well conducted, and that the English people sustained throughout the high character they have nobly earned, to the shame of their silly detractors among their own countrymen, we must yet express our hope that state funerals in this land went down to their tomb, most fitly, in the tasteless and tawdry Car that nodded and shook through the streets of London on the eighteenth of November, eighteen hundred and fifty-two. And sure we are, with large consideration for opposite opinions, that when History shall rescue that very ugly machine — worthy to pass under decorated Temple Bar, as decorated Temple Bar was worthy to receive it — from the merciful shadows of obscurity, she will reflect with amazement — remembering his true, manly, modest, self-contained, and genuine character — that the man who, in making it the last monster of its race, rendered his last enduring service to the country he had loved and served so faithfully was Arthur, Duke of Wellington.

XV

DOWN WITH THE TIDE

A VERY dark night it was, and bitter cold; the east wind blowing bleak, and bringing with it stinging particles from marsh, and moor, and fen — from the Great Desert and Old Egypt, may be. Some of the component parts of the sharp-edged vapour that came flying up the Thames at London might be mummy-dust, dry atoms from the Temple at Jerusalem, camels' foot-prints, crocodiles' hatching-places, loosened grains of expression from the visages of blunt-nosed sphinxes, waifs and strays from caravans of turbaned merchants, vegetation from jungles, frozen snow from the Himalayas. Oh! It was very, very dark upon the Thames, and it was bitter, bitter cold.

"And yet," said the voice within the great peacoat at my side, "you 'll have seen a good many rivers too, I dare say ? "

"Truly," said I, "when I come to think of it, not a few. From the Niagara, downward to the mountain rivers of Italy, which are like the national spirit — very tame, or chafing suddenly and bursting bounds, only to dwindle away again. The Moselle, and the Rhine, and the Rhone; and the Seine, and the Saône; and the St. Lawrence, Mississippi, and Ohio; and the Tiber, the Po, and the Arno; and the — "

Peacoat coughing, as if he had had enough of that, I said no more. I could have carried the catalogue on to a teasing length, though, if I had been in the cruel mind.

"And after all," said he, "this looks so dismal ? "

"So awful," I returned, "at night. The Seine at Paris is very gloomy, too, at such a time, and is probably the scene of far more crime and greater wickedness; but this river looks so broad and vast, so murky and silent, seems such an image of death in the midst of the great city's life, that — "

That Peacoat coughed again. He *could not* stand my holding forth.

We were in a four-oared Thames Police Galley, lying on our oars in the deep shadow of Southwark Bridge, — under the corner arch on the Surrey side, — having come down with the tide from Vauxhall. We were fain to hold on pretty tight, though close inshore, for the river was swollen and the tide running down very strong. We were watching certain water-rats of human growth, and lay in the deep shade as quiet as mice, our light hidden and our scraps of conversation carried on in whispers. Above us, the massive iron girders of the arch were faintly visible, and below us its ponderous shadow seemed to sink down to the bottom of the stream.

We had been lying here some half an hour. With our backs to the wind, it is true; but the wind being in a determined temper blew straight through us, and would not take the trouble to go round. I would have boarded a fireship to get into action, and mildly suggested as much to my friend Pea.

"No doubt," says he, as patiently as possible; "but shore-going tactics would n't do with us. River thieves can always get rid of stolen property in a moment by dropping it overboard. We want to take them *with* the property, so we lurk about and come out upon 'em sharp. If they see us or hear us, over it goes."

Pea's wisdom being indisputable, there was nothing for it but to sit there and be blown through, for another half hour. The water-rats thinking it wise to abscond at the end of that time without commission of felony, we shot out, disappointed, with the tide.

"Grim they look, don't they?" said Pea, seeing me glance over my shoulder at the lights upon the bridge, and downward at their long crooked reflections in the river.

"Very," said I, "and make one think with a shudder of Suicides. What a night for a dreadful leap from that parapet!"

"Aye, but Waterloo 's the favourite bridge for making holes in the water from," returned Pea. "By the bye — avast pulling, lads! — would you like to speak to Waterloo on the subject?"

My face confessing a surprised desire to have some friendly conversation with Waterloo Bridge, and my friend Pea being the most obliging of men, we put about, pulled out of the force of the stream, and in place of going at great speed with the tide, began to strive against it, close inshore again. Every colour but black seemed to have departed from the world. The air was black, the water was black, the barges and hulks were black, the piles were black, the buildings were black, the shadows were only a deeper shade of black upon a black ground. Here and there, a coal fire in an iron crescent blazed upon a wharf; but one knew that it too had been black a little while ago, and would be black again soon. Uncomfortable rushes of water suggestive of gurgling and drowning, ghostly rattlings of iron chains, dismal clankings of discordant engines, formed the music that accompanied the dip of our oars and their rattling in the rullocks. Even the noises had a black sound to me — as the trumpet sounded red to the blind man.

Our dexterous boat's crew made nothing of the tide, and pulled us gallantly up to Waterloo Bridge. Here Pea and I disembarked, passed under the black stone archway, and climbed the steep stone steps. Within a few feet of their summit, Pea presented me to Waterloo (or an eminent toll-taker representing that structure), muffled up to the eyes in a thick shawl, and amply great-coated and fur-capped.

Waterloo received us with cordiality, and observed of the night that it was "a Searcher." He had been originally called the Strand Bridge, he informed us, but had received his present name at the suggestion of the proprietors, when Parliament had resolved to vote three hundred thousand pound for the erection of a monument in honour of the victory. Parliament took the hint (said Waterloo, with the least flavour of misanthropy) and saved the money. Of course the late Duke of Wellington was the first passenger, and of course he paid his penny, and of course a noble lord preserved it evermore. The treadle and index at the toll-house (a most ingenious contrivance for rendering fraud impossible) were invented by Mr. Lethbridge, then property-man at Drury Lane Theatre.

Was it suicide we wanted to know about? said Waterloo. Ha! Well, he had seen a good deal of that work, he did assure us. He had prevented some. Why, one day a woman, poorish looking, came in between the hatch, slapped down a penny, and wanted to go on without the change! Waterloo suspected this, and says to his mate, "Give an eye to the gate," and bolted after her. She had got to the third seat between the piers, and was on the parapet just a going over, when he caught her and gave her in charge. At the police office next morning, she said it was along of trouble and a bad husband.

"Likely enough," observed Waterloo to Pea and myself, as he adjusted his chin in his shawl. "There's a deal of trouble about, you see — and bad husbands too!"

Another time, a young woman, at twelve o'clock in the open day, got through, darted along, and before Waterloo could come near her, jumped upon the parapet, and shot herself over sideways. Alarm given, watermen put off, lucky escape. — Clothes buoyed her up.

"This is where it is," said Waterloo. "If people jump off straight forwards from the middle of the parapet of the bays of the bridge, they are seldom killed by drowning, but are smashed, poor things; that's what *they* are; they dash themselves upon the buttress of the bridge. But you jump off,". said Waterloo to me, putting his forefinger in a button-hole of my great-coat, — "you jump off from the side of the bay, and you'll tumble, true, into the stream under the arch. What you have got to do is to mind how you jump in! There was poor Tom Steele from Dublin. Did n't dive! Bless you, did n't dive at all! Fell down so flat into the water that he broke his breast-bone, and lived two days!"

I asked Waterloo if there were a favourite side of his bridge for this dreadful purpose? He reflected, and thought yes, there was. He should say the Surrey side.

Three decent looking men went through one day, soberly and quietly, and went on abreast for about a dozen yards, when the middle one, he sung out, all of a sudden, "Here goes, Jack!" and was over in a minute.

Body found? Well. Waterloo did n't rightly recollect about that. They were compositors, *they* were.

He considered it astonishing how quick people were! Why, there was a cab came up one Boxing-night, with a young woman in it, who looked, according to Waterloo's opinion of her, a little the worse for liquor; very handsome she was too — very handsome. She stopped the cab at the gate, and said she'd pay the cabman then; which she did, though there was a little hankering about the fare, because at first she did n't seem quite to know where she wanted to be drove to. However she paid the man, and the toll too, and looking Waterloo in the face (he thought she knew him, don't you see!) said, "I'll finish it somehow!" Well, the cab went off, leaving Waterloo a little doubtful in his mind, and while it was going on at full speed the young woman jumped out, never fell, hardly staggered, ran along the bridge pavement a little way, passing several people, and jumped over from the second opening. At the inquest it was giv' in evidence that she had been quarrelling at the Hero of Waterloo, and it was brought in jealousy. (One of the results of Waterloo's experience was that there was a deal of jealousy about.)

"Do we ever get madmen?" said Waterloo, in answer to an inquiry of mine. "Well, we *do* get madmen. Yes, we have had one or two; escaped from 'Sylums, I suppose. One had n't a halfpenny; and because I would n't let him through, he went back a little way, stooped down, took a run, and butted at the hatch like a ram. He smashed his hat rarely, but his head did n't seem no worse — in my opinion on account of his being wrong in it afore. Sometimes people have n't got a halfpenny. If they are really tired and poor we give 'em one and let 'em through. Other people will leave things — pocket-handkerchiefs mostly. I *have* taken cravats and gloves, pocket-knives, toothpicks, studs, shirt pins, rings (generally from young gents, early in the morning), but handkerchiefs is the general thing."

"Regular customers?" said Waterloo. "Lord, yes! We have regular customers. One, such a worn-out, used-up old file as you can scarcely picter, comes from the Surrey side as regular as ten o'clock at night comes; and goes over, *I* think, to some flash house on the Middlesex side. He comes back, he does, as reg'lar as the clock strikes three in the morning, and then can hardly drag one of his old legs after the other. He always turns down the water-stairs, comes up again, and then goes on down the Waterloo Road. He always does the same thing, and never varies a minute. Does it every night — even Sundays."

I asked Waterloo if he had given his mind to the possibility of this particular customer going down the water-stairs at three o'clock some morning, and never coming up again? He did n't think *that* of him, he replied. In fact, it was Waterloo's opinion, founded on his observation of that file, that he knowed a trick worth two of it.

"There 's another queer old customer," said Waterloo, "comes over, as punctual as the almanac, at eleven o'clock on the sixth of January, at eleven o'clock on the fifth of

April, at eleven o'clock on the sixth of July, at eleven o'clock on the tenth of October. Drives a shaggy, little rough pony, in a sort of a rattle-trap arm-chair sort of a thing. White hair he has, and white whiskers, and muffles himself up with all manner of shawls. He comes back again the same afternoon, and we never see more of him for three months. He is a captain in the navy — retired — wery old — wery odd — and served with Lord Nelson. He is particular about drawing his pension at Somerset House afore the clock strikes twelve every quarter. I *have* heerd say that he thinks it would n't be according to the Act of Parliament, if he did n't draw it afore twelve."

Having related these anecdotes in a natural manner, which was the best warranty in the world for their genuine nature, our friend Waterloo was sinking deep into his shawl again, as having exhausted his communicative powers and taken in enough east wind, when my other friend Pea in a moment brought him to the surface by asking whether he had not been occasionally the subject of assault and battery in the execution of his duty? Waterloo, recovering his spirits, instantly dashed into a new branch of his subject. We learnt how "both these teeth " — here he pointed to the places where two front teeth were not — were knocked out by an ugly customer who one night made a dash at him (Waterloo) while his (the ugly customer's) pal and coadjutor made a dash at the toll-taking apron where the money-pockets were; how Waterloo, letting the teeth go (to Blazes, he observed indefinitely), grappled with the apron-seizer, permitting the ugly one to run away; and how he saved the bank, and captured his man, and consigned him to fine and imprisonment. Also how, on another night, "a Cove " laid hold of Waterloo, then presiding at the horse gate of his bridge, and threw him unceremoniously over his knee, having first cut his head open with his whip. How Waterloo "got right," and started after the Cove all down the Waterloo Road, through Stamford Street, and round to the foot of Blackfriars Bridge, where the Cove "cut into " a public-house. How Waterloo cut in too; but how an aider and abettor of the Cove's, who happened to be taking a promiscuous drain at the bar, stopped Waterloo; and the Cove cut out again, ran across the road down Holland Street, and where not, and into a beer-shop. How Waterloo breaking away from

his detainer was close upon the Cove's heels, attended by no
end of people who, seeing him running with the blood streaming down his face, thought something worse was "up," and
roared Fire! and Murder! on the hopeful chance of the matter
in hand being one or both. How the Cove was ignominiously
taken, in a shed where he had run to hide, and how at the
Police Court they at first wanted to make a sessions job of it;
but eventually Waterloo was allowed to be "spoke to," and
the Cove made it square with Waterloo by paying his doctor's
bill (W. was laid up for a week) and giving him "Three, ten."
Likewise we learnt what we had faintly suspected before, that
your sporting amateur on the Derby day, albeit a captain, can
be — "if he be," as Captain Bobadil observes, "so generously
minded" — anything but a man of honour and a gentleman;
not sufficiently gratifying his nice sense of humour by the
witty scattering of flour and rotten eggs on obtuse civilians,
but requiring the further excitement of "bilking the toll," and
"pitching into" Waterloo, and "cutting him about the head
with his whip;" finally being, when called upon to answer for
the assault, what Waterloo described as "Minus," or, as I
humbly conceived it, not to be found. Likewise did Waterloo
inform us, in reply to my inquiries, admiringly and deferentially preferred through my friend Pea, that the takings at the
Bridge had more than doubled in amount since the reduction
of the toll one half. And being asked if the aforesaid takings
included much bad money, Waterloo responded, with a look
far deeper than the deepest part of the river, *he* should think
not! — and so retired into his shawl for the rest of the night.

Then did Pea and I once more embark in our four-oared
galley, and glide swiftly down the river with the tide. And
while the shrewd East rasped and notched us, as with jagged
razors, did my friend Pea impart to me confidences of interest relating to the Thames Police; we between whiles finding
"duty boats" hanging in dark corners under banks, like weeds,
— our own was a "supervision boat," — and they, as they
reported "All right!" flashing their hidden light on us, and we
flashing ours on them. These duty boats had one sitter in
each, an Inspector, and were rowed "Ran-dan," which — for
the information of those who never graduated, as I was once
proud to do, under a fireman-waterman and winner of Kean's
Prize Wherry, who, in the course of his tuition, took hun-

dreds of gallons of rum and egg (at my expense) at the various houses of note above and below bridge, not by any means because he liked it, but to cure a weakness in his liver, for which the faculty had particularly recommended it—may be explained as rowed by three men, two pulling an oar each, and one a pair of sculls.

Thus, floating down our black highway, sullenly frowned upon by the knitted brows of Blackfriars, Southwark, and London, each in his lowering turn, I was shown by my friend Pea that there are in the Thames Police Force, whose district extends from Battersea to Barking Creek, ninety-eight men, eight duty boats, and two supervision boats; and that these go about so silently, and lie in wait in such dark places, and so seem to be nowhere, and so may be anywhere, that they have gradually become a police of prevention, keeping the river almost clear of any great crimes, even while the increased vigilance on shore has made it much harder than of yore to live by "thieving" in the streets. And as to the various kinds of water thieves, said my friend Pea, there were the Tier-rangers, who silently dropped alongside the tiers of shipping in the Pool, by night, and who, going to the companion-head, listened for two snores—snore number one, the skipper's; snore number two, the mate's—mates and skippers always snoring great guns, and being dead sure to be hard at it if they had turned in and were asleep. Hearing the double fire, down went the Rangers into the skippers' cabins; groped for the skippers' inexpressibles, which it was the custom of those gentlemen to shake off, watch, money, braces, boots, and all together, on the floor; and therewith made off as silently as might be. Then there were the Lumpers, or labourers employed to unload vessels. They wore loose canvas jackets with a broad hem in the bottom, turned inside, so as to form a large circular pocket in which they could conceal, like clowns in pantomimes, packages of surprising sizes. A great deal of property was stolen in this manner (Pea confided to me) from steamers; first, because steamers carry a larger number of small packages than other ships; next, because of the extreme rapidity with which they are obliged to be unladen for their return voyages. The Lumpers dispose of their booty easily to marine store dealers, and the only remedy to be suggested is that marine store shops should be licensed, and thus brought under the eye of the police as rigidly as public-houses. Lumpers also smuggle goods ashore for the crews of vessels. The smuggling of tobacco is so considerable, that it is well worth the while of the sellers of smuggled tobacco to use hydraulic presses, to squeeze a single pound into a package small enough to be contained in an ordinary pocket. Next, said my friend Pea, there were the Truckers — less thieves than smugglers, whose business it was to land more considerable parcels of goods than the Lumpers could manage. They sometimes sold articles of grocery, and so forth, to the crews, in order to cloak their real calling, and get aboard without suspicion. Many of them had boats of their own, and made money. Besides these, there were the Dredgermen, who, under pretence of dredging up coals and such like from the bottom of the river, hung about barges and other undecked craft, and when they saw an opportunity, threw any property they could lay their hands on overboard, in order slyly to dredge it up when the vessel was gone. Sometimes, they dexterously used their dredges to whip away anything that might lie within reach. Some of them were mighty neat at this, and the accomplishment was called dry dredging. Then, there was a vast deal of property, such as copper nails, sheathing, hard-wood, etc., habitually brought away by shipwrights and other workmen from their employers' yards, and disposed of to marine store dealers, many of whom escaped detection through hard swearing, and their extraordinary artful ways of accounting for the possession of stolen property. Likewise, there were special-pleading practitioners, for whom barges "drifted away of their own selves," they having no hand in it, except first cutting them loose, and afterwards plundering them — innocents, meaning no harm, who had the misfortune to observe those foundlings wandering about the Thames.

We were now going in and out, with little noise and great nicety, among the tiers of shipping, whose many hulls, lying close together, rose out of the water like black streets. Here and there, a Scotch, an Irish, or a foreign steamer, getting up her steam as the tide made, looked, with her great chimney and high sides, like a quiet factory among the common buildings. Now the streets opened into clearer spaces, now contracted into alleys; but the tiers were so like houses, in the dark, that I could almost have believed myself in the narrower

by-ways of Venice. Everything was wonderfully still; for it
wanted full three hours of flood, and nothing seemed awake
but a dog here and there.

So we took no Tier-rangers captive, nor any Lumpers, nor
Truckers, nor Dredgermen, nor other evil-disposed person or
persons; but went ashore at Wapping, where the old Thames
Police Office is now a station-house, and where the old Court,
with its cabin windows looking on the river, is a quaint charge
room; with nothing worse in it usually than a stuffed cat in a
glass case, and a portrait, pleasant to behold, of a rare old
Thames Police officer, Mr. Superintendent Evans, now succeeded by his son. We looked over the charge books, admirably kept, and found the prevention so good, that there were
not five hundred entries (including drunken and disorderly) in
a whole year. Then we looked into the store-room; where
there was an oakum smell, and a nautical seasoning of dread-
naught clothing, rope yarn, boat hooks, sculls and oars, spare
stretchers, rudders, pistols, cutlasses, and the like. Then,
into the cell, aired high up in the wooden wall through an
opening like a kitchen plate-rack; wherein there was a drunken
man, not at all warm, and very wishful to know if it were
morning yet. Then into a better sort of watch and ward
room, where there was a squadron of stone bottles drawn up,
ready to be filled with hot water and applied to any unfortunate creature who might be brought in apparently drowned.
Finally, we shook hands with our worthy friend Pea, and ran
all the way to Tower Hill, under strong Police suspicion occasionally, before we got warm.

XVI

THE NOBLE SAVAGE

To come to the point at once, I beg to say that I have not
the least belief in the Noble Savage. I consider him a prodigious nuisance, and an enormous superstition. His calling
rum fire-water and me a pale-face wholly fail to reconcile me to
him. I don't care what he calls me. I call him a savage,
and I call a savage a something highly desirable to be civilised
off the face of the earth. I think a mere gent (which I take
to be the lowest form of civilisation) better than a howling,
whistling, clucking, stamping, jumping, tearing savage. It is
all one to me, whether he sticks a fish-bone through his visage,
or bits of trees through the lobes of his ears, or birds' feathers
in his head; whether he flattens his hair between two boards,
or spreads his nose over the breadth of his face, or drags his
lower lip down by great weights, or blackens his teeth, or
knocks them out, or paints one cheek red and the other blue,
or tattoos himself, or oils himself, or rubs his body with fat,
or crimps it with knives. Yielding to whichsoever of these
agreeable eccentricities, he is a savage — cruel, false, thievish,
murderous; addicted more or less to grease, entrails, and
beastly customs; a wild animal with the questionable gift of
boasting; a conceited, tiresome, bloodthirsty, monotonous humbug.

Yet it is extraordinary to observe how some people will
talk about him, as they talk about the good old times; how
they will regret his disappearance, in the course of this world's
development, from such and such lands where his absence is a
blessed relief and an indispensable preparation for the sowing
of the very first seeds of any influence that can exalt humanity;
how, even with the evidence of himself before them, they will
either be determined to believe, or will suffer themselves to be
persuaded into believing, that he is something which their five
senses tell them he is not.

There was Mr. Catlin, some few years ago, with his Ojibbeway Indians. Mr. Catlin was an energetic, earnest man, who

had lived among more tribes of Indians than I need reckon up here, and who had written a picturesque and glowing book about them. With his party of Indians squatting and spitting on the table before him, or dancing their miserable jigs after their own dreary manner, he called, in all good faith, upon his civilised audience to take notice of their symmetry and grace, their perfect limbs, and the exquisite expression of their pantomime; and his civilised audience, in all good faith, complied and admired. Whereas, as mere animals, they were wretched creatures, very low in the scale and very poorly formed; and as men and women possessing any power of truthful dramatic expression by means of action, they were no better than the chorus at an Italian Opera in England — and would have been worse if such a thing were possible.

Mine are no new views of the noble savage. The greatest writers on natural history found him out long ago. Buffon knew what he was, and showed why he is the sulky tyrant that he is to his women, and how it happens (Heaven be praised!) that his race is spare in numbers. For evidence of the quality of his moral nature, pass himself for a moment and refer to his "faithful dog." Has he ever improved a dog, or attached a dog, since his nobility first ran wild in woods, and was brought down (at a very long shot) by Pope? Or does the animal that is the friend of man always degenerate in his low society?

It is not the miserable nature of the noble savage that is the new thing; it is the whimpering over him with maudlin admiration, and the affecting to regret him, and the drawing of any comparison of advantage between the blemishes of civilisation and the tenor of his swinish life. There may have been a change now and then in those diseased absurdities, but there is none in him.

Think of the Bushmen. Think of the two men and the two women who have been exhibited about England for some years. Are the majority of persons — who remember the horrid little leader of that party in his festering bundle of hides, with his filth and his antipathy to water, and his straddled legs, and his odious eyes shaded by his brutal hand, and his cry of "Qu-u-u-u-aaa!" (Bosjesman for something desperately insulting I have no doubt) — conscious of an affectionate yearning towards that noble savage, or is it idiosyncratic in me to abhor, detest, abominate, and abjure him? I have no reserve on this subject, and will frankly state that, setting aside that stage of the entertainment when he counterfeited the death of some creature he had shot, by laying his head on his hand and shaking his left leg, — at which time I think it would have been justifiable homicide to slay him, — I have never seen that group sleeping, smoking, and expectorating round their brazier, but I have sincerely desired that something might happen to the charcoal smouldering therein, which would cause the immediate suffocation of the whole of the noble strangers.

There is at present a party of Zulu Kaffirs exhibiting at the St. George's Gallery, Hyde Park Corner, London. These noble savages are represented in a most agreeable manner; they are seen in an elegant theatre, fitted with appropriate scenery of great beauty, and they are described in a very sensible and unpretending lecture, delivered with a modesty which is quite a pattern to all similar exponents. Though extremely ugly, they are much better shaped than such of their predecessors as I have referred to; and they are rather picturesque to the eye, though far from odoriferous to the nose. What a visitor left to his own interpretings and imaginings might suppose these noblemen to be about, when they give vent to that pantomimic expression which is quite settled to be the natural gift of the noble savage, I cannot possibly conceive; for it is so much too luminous for my personal civilisation that it conveys no idea to my mind beyond a general stamping, ramping, and raving, remarkable (as everything in savage life is) for its dire uniformity. But let us — with the interpreter's assistance, of which I for one stand so much in need — see what the noble savage does in Zulu Kaffirland.

The noble savage sets a king to reign over him, to whom he submits his life and limbs without a murmur or question, and whose whole life is passed chin deep in a lake of blood; but who, after killing incessantly, is in his turn killed by his relations and friends the moment a grey hair appears on his head. All the noble savage's wars with his fellow-savages (and he takes no pleasure in anything else) are wars of extermination — which is the best thing I know of him, and the most comfortable to my mind when I look at him. He has no moral feelings of any kind, sort, or description; and his "mission" may be summed up as simply diabolical.

The ceremonies with which he faintly diversifies his life are, of course, of a kindred nature. If he wants a wife he appears before the kennel of the gentleman whom he has selected for his father-in-law, attended by a party of male friends of a very strong flavour, who screech and whistle and stamp an offer of so many cows for the young lady's hand. The chosen father-in-law — also supported by a high-flavoured party of male friends — screeches, whistles, and yells (being seated on the ground he can't stamp) that there never was such a daughter in the market as his daughter, and that he must have six more cows. The son-in-law and his select circle of backers screech, whistle, stamp, and yell in reply, that they will give three more cows. The father-in-law (an old deluder, overpaid at the beginning) accepts four, and rises to bind the bargain. The whole party, the young lady included, then falling into epileptic convulsions, and screeching, whistling, stamping, and yelling together — and nobody taking any notice of the young lady (whose charms are not to be thought of without a shudder) — the noble savage is considered married, and his friends make demoniacal leaps at him by way of congratulation.

When the noble savage finds himself a little unwell, and mentions the circumstance to his friends, it is immediately perceived that he is under the influence of witchcraft. A learned personage, called an Imyanger or Witch Doctor, is immediately sent for to Nooker the Umtargartie, or smell out the witch. The male inhabitants of the kraal being seated on the ground, the learned doctor, got up like a grizzly bear, appears, and administers a dance of a most terrific nature, during the exhibition of which remedy he incessantly gnashes his teeth, and howls: "I am the original physician to Nooker the Umtargartie. Yow yow yow! No connection with any other establishment. Till till till! All other Umtargarties are feigned Umtargarties, Boroo Boroo! but I perceive here a genuine and real Umtargartie, Hoosh Hoosh Hoosh! in whose blood I, the original Imyanger and Nookerer, Blizzerum Boo! will wash these bear's claws of mine. O yow yow yow!" All this time the learned physician is looking out among the attentive faces for some unfortunate man who owes him a cow, or who has given him any small offence, or against whom, without offence, he has conceived a spite. Him he never fails to Nooker as the Umtargartie, and he is instantly killed. In the absence of such an individual, the usual practice is to Nooker the quietest and most gentlemanly person in company. But the Nookering is invariably followed on the spot by the butchering.

Some of the noble savages in whom Mr. Catlin was so strongly interested, and the diminution of whose numbers, by rum and small-pox, greatly affected him, had a custom not unlike this, though much more appalling and disgusting in its odious details.

The women being at work in the fields, hoeing the Indian corn, and the noble savage being asleep in the shade, the chief has sometimes the condescension to come forth, and lighten the labour by looking at it. On these occasions he seats himself in his own savage chair, and is attended by his shield-bearer; who holds over his head a shield of cowhide — in shape like an immense mussel shell — fearfully and wonderfully, after the manner of a theatrical supernumerary. But lest the great man should forget his greatness in the contemplation of the humble works of agriculture, there suddenly rushes in a poet, retained for the purpose, called a Praiser. This literary gentleman wears a leopard's head over his own, and a dress of tiger's tails; he has the appearance of having come express on his hind legs from the Zoölogical Gardens; and he incontinently strikes up the chief's praises, plunging and tearing all the while. There is a frantic wickedness in this brute's manner of worrying the air, and gnashing out, "Oh, what a delightful chief he is! Oh, what a delicious quantity of blood he sheds! Oh, how majestically he laps it up! Oh, how charmingly cruel he is! Oh, how he tears the flesh of his enemies and crunches the bones! Oh, how like the tiger and the leopard and the wolf and the bear he is! Oh, row row row row, how fond I am of him!" — which might tempt the Society of Friends to charge at a hand-gallop into the Swartz-Kop location and exterminate the whole kraal.

When war is afoot among the noble savages — which is always — the chief holds a council to ascertain whether it is the opinion of his brothers and friends in general that the enemy shall be exterminated. On this occasion, after the performance of an Umsebeuza, or war song, — which is exactly like all the other songs, — the chief makes a speech to his brothers and friends, arranged in single file. No particular order is observed during the delivery of this address, but every gentleman who finds himself excited by the subject, instead of crying "Hear, hear!" as is the custom with us, darts from the rank and tramples out the life, or crushes the skull, or mashes the face, or scoops out the eyes, or breaks the limbs, or performs a whirlwind of atrocities on the body, of an imaginary enemy. Several gentlemen becoming thus excited at once, and pounding away without the least regard to the orator, that illustrious person is rather in the position of an orator in an Irish House of Commons. But several of these scenes of savage life bear a strong generic resemblance to an Irish election, and I think would be extremely well received and understood at Cork.

In all these ceremonies the noble savage holds forth to the utmost possible extent about himself; from which (to turn him to some civilised account) we may learn, I think, that as egotism is one of the most offensive and contemptible littlenesses a civilised man can exhibit, so it is really incompatible with the interchange of ideas; inasmuch as if we all talked about ourselves we should soon have no listeners, and must be all yelling and screeching at once on our own separate accounts, making society hideous. It is my opinion that if we retained in us anything of the noble savage, we could not get rid of it too soon. But the fact is clearly otherwise. Upon the wife and dowry question, substituting coin for cows, we have assuredly nothing of the Zulu Kaffir left. The endurance of despotism is one great distinguishing mark of a savage always. The improving world has quite got the better of that too. In like manner, Paris is a civilised city, and the Théâtre Français a highly civilised theatre; and we shall never hear and never have heard in these later days (of course) of the Praiser *there*. No, no, civilised poets have better work to do. As to Nookering Umtargarties, there are no pretended Umtargarties in Europe, and no European powers to Nooker them; that would be mere spydom, subornation, small malice, superstition, and false pretence. And as to private Umtargarties, are we not in the year eighteen hundred and fifty-three, with spirits rapping at our doors?

To conclude as I began. My position is, that if we have anything to learn from the noble savage, it is what to avoid. His virtues are a fable; his happiness is a delusion; his nobility, nonsense. We have no greater justification for being cruel to the miserable object than for being cruel to a William Shakespeare or an Isaac Newton; but he passes away before an immeasurably better and higher power than ever ran wild in any earthly woods, and the world will be all the better when his place knows him no more.

XVII

FRAUDS ON THE FAIRIES

WE may assume that we are not singular in entertaining a
very great tenderness for the fairy literature of our childhood.
What enchanted us then, and is captivating a million of young
fancies now, has, at the same blessed time of life, enchanted
vast hosts of men and women who have done their long day's
work, and laid their grey heads down to rest. It would be
hard to estimate the amount of gentleness and mercy that has
made its way among us through these slight channels. Forbearance, courtesy, consideration for the poor and aged, kind
treatment of animals, the love of nature, abhorrence of tyranny
and brute force — many such good things have been first nour-
ished in the child's heart by this powerful aid. It has greatly
helped to keep us, in some sense, ever young, by preserving
through our worldly ways one slender track not overgrown
with weeds, where we may walk with children, sharing their
delights.

In an utilitarian age, of all other times, it is a matter of
grave importance that fairy tales should be respected. Our
English red tape is too magnificently red ever to be employed
in the tying up of such trifles, but every one who has considered the subject knows full well that a nation without fancy,
without some romance, never did, never can, never will, hold
a great place under the sun. The theatre having done its
worst to destroy these admirable fictions, and having in a
most exemplary manner destroyed itself, its artists, and its
audiences, in that perversion of its duty, it becomes doubly
important that the little books themselves, nurseries of fancy
as they are, should be preserved. To preserve them in their
usefulness, they must be as much preserved in their simplicity,
and purity, and innocent extravagance, as if they were actual
fact. Whosoever alters them to suit his own opinions, whatever they are, is guilty, to our thinking, of an act of presumption, and appropriates to himself what does not belong to him.

We have lately observed, with pain, the intrusion of a

Whole Hog of unwieldy dimensions into the fairy flower garden.   The rooting of the animal among the roses would in
itself have awakened in us nothing but indignation; our pain
arises from his being violently driven in by a man of genius,
our own beloved friend, Mr. George Cruikshank.   That incomparable artist is, of all men, the last who should lay his exquisite hand on fairy text.   In his own art he understands it so
perfectly, and illustrates it so beautifully, so humorously, so
wisely, that he should never lay down his etching-needle to
"edit" the Ogre, to whom with that little instrument he can
render such extraordinary justice.   But to "editing" Ogres,
and Hop-o'-my-thumbs, and their families, our dear moralist
has in a rash moment taken, as a means of propagating the
doctrines of Total Abstinence, Prohibition of the sale of spirituous liquors, Free Trade, and Popular Education.   For the
introduction of these topics, he has altered the text of a fairy
story; and against his right to do any such thing we protest
with all our might and main.   Of his likewise altering it to
advertise that excellent series of plates, "The Bottle," we say
nothing more than that we foresee a new and improved edition
of Goody Two Shoes, edited by E. Moses and Son; of the
Dervish with the box of ointment, edited by Professor Holloway; and of Jack and the Beanstalk, edited by Mary Wedlake,
the popular authoress of Do you bruise your oats yet?
   Now it makes not the least difference to our objection
whether we agree or disagree with our worthy friend, Mr.
Cruikshank, in the opinions he interpolates upon an old fairy
story.   Whether good or bad in themselves, they are, in that
relation, like the famous definition of a weed; a thing growing
up in a wrong place.   He has no greater moral justification in
altering the harmless little books than we should have in altering his best etchings.   If such a precedent were followed we
must soon become disgusted with the old stories into which
modern personages so obtruded themselves, and the stories
themselves must soon be lost.   With seven Blue Beards in the
field, each coming at a gallop from his own platform mounted
on a foaming hobby, a generation or two hence would not
know which was which, and the great original Blue Beard
would be confounded with the counterfeits.   Imagine a Total
Abstinence edition of Robinson Crusoe, with the rum left out.
Imagine a Peace edition, with the gunpowder left out, and the

rum left in. Imagine a Vegetarian edition, with the goat's flesh left out. Imagine a Kentucky edition, to introduce a flogging of that 'tarnal old nigger Friday twice a week. Imagine an Aborigines Protection Society edition, to deny the cannibalism and make Robinson embrace the amiable savages whenever they landed. Robinson Crusoe would be "edited" out of his island in a hundred years, and the island would be swallowed up in the editorial ocean.

Among the other learned professions we have now the Platform profession, chiefly exercised by a new and meritorious class of commercial travellers who go about to take the sense of meetings on various articles: some, of a very superior description; some, not quite so good. Let us write the story of Cinderella, "edited" by one of these gentlemen, doing a good stroke of business, and having a rather extensive mission.

Once upon a time, a rich man and his wife were the parents of a lovely daughter. She was a beautiful child, and became, at her own desire, a member of the Juvenile Bands of Hope when she was only four years of age. When this child was only nine years of age her mother died, and all the Juvenile Bands of Hope in her district — the Central district, number five hundred and twenty-seven — formed in a procession of two and two, amounting to fifteen hundred, and followed her to the grave, singing chorus Number forty-two, "O come," etc. This grave was outside the town, and under the direction of the Local Board of Health, which reported at certain stated intervals to the General Board of Health, Whitehall.

The motherless little girl was very sorrowful for the loss of her mother, and so was her father too, at first; but, after a year was over, he married again — a very cross widow lady, with two proud tyrannical daughters as cross as herself. He was aware that he could have made his marriage with this lady a civil process by simply making a declaration before a Registrar; but he was averse to this course on religious grounds, and, being a member of the Montgolfian persuasion, was married according to the ceremonies of that respectable church by the Reverend Jared Jocks, who improved the occasion.

He did not live long with his disagreeable wife. Having been shamefully accustomed to shave with warm water instead

of cold, which he ought to have used (see Medical Appendix
B. and C.), his undermined constitution could not bear up
against her temper, and he soon died. Then this orphan was
cruelly treated by her stepmother and the two daughters, and
was forced to do the dirtiest of the kitchen work; to scour the
saucepans, wash the dishes, and light the fires — which did not
consume their own smoke, but emitted a dark vapour preju-
dicial to the bronchial tubes. The only warm place in the
house where she was free from ill-treatment was the kitchen
chimney corner; and as she used to sit down there, among the
cinders, when her work was done, the proud fine sisters gave
her the name of Cinderella.

About this time, the King of the land, who never made war
against anybody, and allowed everybody to make war against
him, — which was the reason why his subjects were the greatest
manufacturers on earth, and always lived in security and peace,
— gave a great feast, which was to last two days. This splendid banquet was to consist entirely of artichokes and gruel; and
from among those who were invited to it, and to hear the
delightful speeches after dinner, the King's son was to choose
a bride for himself. The proud fine sisters were invited, but
nobody knew anything about poor Cinderella, and she was to
stay at home.

She was so sweet-tempered, however, that she assisted the
haughty creatures to dress, and bestowed her admirable taste
upon them as freely as if they had been kind to her. Neither
did she laugh when they broke seventeen stay-laces in dressing; for, although she wore no stays herself, being sufficiently
acquainted with the anatomy of the human figure to be aware
of the destructive effects of tight-lacing, she always reserved
her opinions on that subject for the Regenerative Record (price
three halfpence in a neat wrapper), which all good people take
in, and to which she was a Contributor.

At length the wished-for moment arrived, and the proud
fine sisters swept away to the feast and speeches, leaving Cinderella in the chimney corner. But she could always occupy
her mind with the general question of the Ocean Penny Postage, and she had in her pocket an unread Oration on that subject, made by the well-known Orator, Nehemiah Nicks. She
was lost in the fervid eloquence of that talented Apostle when
she became aware of the presence of one of those female rela-

tives which (it may not be generally known) it is not lawful for a man to marry. I allude to her grandmother.

"Why so solitary, my child?" said the old lady to Cinderella.

"Alas, grandmother," returned the poor girl, "my sisters have gone to the feast and speeches, and here sit I in the ashes, Cinderella!"

"Never," cried the old lady with animation, "shall one of the Band of Hope despair! Run into the garden, my dear, and fetch me an American Pumpkin! American, because in some parts of that independent country there are prohibitory laws against the sale of alcoholic drinks in any form. Also, because America produced (among many great pumpkins) the glory of her sex, Mrs. Colonel Bloomer. None but an American Pumpkin will do, my child."

Cinderella ran into the garden, and brought the largest American Pumpkin she could find. This virtuously democratic vegetable her grandmother immediately changed into a splendid coach. Then she sent her for six mice from the mouse-trap, which she changed into prancing horses, free from the obnoxious and oppressive post-horse duty. Then to the rat-trap in the stable for a rat, which she changed to a state-coachman, not amenable to the iniquitous assessed taxes. Then to look behind a watering-pot for six lizards, which she changed into six footmen, each with a petition in his hand ready to present to the Prince, signed by fifty thousand persons, in favour of the early closing movement.

"But, grandmother," said Cinderella, stopping in the midst of her delight, and looking at her clothes, "how can I go to the palace in these miserable rags?"

"Be not uneasy about that, my dear," returned her grandmother.

Upon which the old lady touched her with her wand, her rags disappeared, and she was beautifully dressed. Not in the present costume of the female sex, which has been proved to be at once grossly immodest and absurdly inconvenient, but in rich sky-blue satin pantaloons gathered at the ankle, a puce-coloured satin pelisse sprinkled with silver flowers, and a very broad Leghorn hat. The hat was chastely ornamented with a rainbow-coloured ribbon hanging in two bell-pulls down the back; the pantaloons were ornamented with a golden stripe;

and the effect of the whole was unspeakably sensible, feminine, and retiring. Lastly, the old lady put on Cinderella's feet a pair of shoes made of glass; observing that but for the abolition of the duty on that article it never could have been devoted to such a purpose, the effect of all such taxes being to cramp invention, and embarrass the producer, to the manifest injury of the consumer. When the old lady had made these wise remarks, she dismissed Cinderella to the feast and speeches, charging her by no means to remain after twelve o'clock at night.

The arrival of Cinderella at the Monster Gathering produced a great excitement. As a delegate from the United States had just moved that the King do take the chair, and as the motion had been seconded and carried unanimously, the King himself could not go forth to receive her. But His Royal Highness the Prince (who was to move the second resolution) went to the door to hand her from her carriage. This virtuous Prince, being completely covered from head to foot with Total Abstinence Medals, shone as if he were attired in complete armour; while the inspiring strains of the Peace Brass Band in the gallery (composed of the Lambkin family, eighteen in number, who cannot be too much encouraged) awakened additional enthusiasm.

The King's son handed Cinderella to one of the reserved seats for pink tickets, on the platform, and fell in love with her immediately. His appetite deserted him; he scarcely tasted his artichokes, and merely trifled with his gruel. When the speeches began, and Cinderella, wrapped in the eloquence of the two inspired delegates who occupied the entire evening in speaking to the first Resolution, occasionally cried, "Hear, hear!" the sweetness of her voice completed her conquest of the Prince's heart. But indeed the whole male portion of the assembly loved her — and doubtless would have done so, even if she had been less beautiful, in consequence of the contrast which her dress presented to the bold and ridiculous garments of the other ladies.

At a quarter before twelve the second inspired delegate having drunk all the water in the decanter, and fainted away, the King put the question, "That this Meeting do now adjourn until to-morrow." Those who were of that opinion holding up their hands, and then those who were of the contrary

,theirs, there appeared an immense majority in favour of the resolution, which was consequently carried. Cinderella got home in safety, and heard nothing all that night, or all next day, but the praises of the unknown lady with the sky-blue satin pantaloons.

When the time for the feast and speeches came round again the cross stepmother and the proud fine daughters went out in good time to secure their places. As soon as they were gone, Cinderella's grandmother returned and changed her as before. Amid a blast of welcome from the Lambkin-family, she was again handed to the pink seat on the platform by His Royal Highness.

This gifted Prince was a powerful speaker, and had had the evening before him. He rose at precisely ten minutes before eight, and was greeted with tumultuous cheers and waving of handkerchiefs. When the excitement had in some degree subsided, he proceeded to address the meeting, who were never tired of listening to speeches, as no good people ever are. He held them enthralled for four hours and a quarter. Cinderella forgot the time, and hurried away so when she heard the first stroke of twelve that her beautiful dress changed back to her old rags at the door, and she left one of her glass shoes behind. The Prince took it up, and vowed — that is, made a declaration before a magistrate, for he objected on principle to the multiplying of oaths — that he would only marry the charming creature to whom that shoe belonged.

He accordingly caused an advertisement to that effect to be inserted in all the newspapers; for the advertisement duty, an impost most unjust in principle and most unfair in operation, did not exist in that country; neither was the stamp on newspapers known in that land — which had as many newspapers as the United States, and got as much good out of them. Innumerable ladies answered the advertisement and pretended that the shoe was theirs; but every one of them was unable to get her foot into it. The proud fine sisters answered it, and tried their feet with no greater success. Then Cinderella, who had answered it too, came forward amidst their scornful jeers, and the shoe slipped on in a moment. It is a remarkable tribute to the improved and sensible fashion of the dress her grandmother had given her, that if she had not worn it the Prince would probably never have seen her feet.

The marriage was solemnised with great rejoicing. When the honeymoon was over, the King retired from public life, and was succeeded by the Prince. Cinderella, being now a queen, applied herself to the government of the country on enlightened, liberal, and free principles. All the people who ate anything she did not eat, or who drank anything she did not drink, were imprisoned for life. All the newspaper offices from which any doctrine proceeded that was not her doctrine were burnt down. All the public speakers proved to demonstration that if there were any individual on the face of the earth who differed from them in anything, that individual was a designing ruffian and an abandoned monster. She also threw open the right of voting, and of being elected to public offices, and of making the laws, to the whole of her sex; who thus came to be always gloriously occupied with public life, and whom nobody dared to love. And they all lived happily ever afterwards.

Frauds on the Fairies once permitted, we see little reason why they may not come to this, and great reason why they may. The Vicar of Wakefield was wisest when he was tired of being always wise. The world is too much with us, early and late. Leave this precious old escape from it alone.

XVIII

THE LONG VOYAGE

WHEN the wind is blowing and the sleet or rain is driving against the dark windows, I love to sit by the fire, thinking of what I have read in books of voyage and travel. Such books have had a strong fascination for my mind from my earliest childhood; and I wonder it should have come to pass that I never have been round the world, never have been shipwrecked, ice-environed, tomahawked, or eaten.

Sitting on my ruddy hearth in the twilight of New Year's Eve, I find incidents of travel rise around me from all the latitudes and longitudes of the globe. They observe no order or sequence, but appear and vanish as they will — "come like shadows, so depart." Columbus, alone upon the sea with his disaffected crew, looks over the waste of waters from his high station on the poop of his ship, and sees the first uncertain glimmer of the light, "rising and falling with the waves, like a torch in the bark of some fisherman," which is the shining star of a new world. Bruce is caged in Abyssinia, surrounded by the gory horrors which shall often startle him out of his sleep at home when years have passed away. Franklin, come to the end of his unhappy overland journey, — would that it had been his last! — lies perishing of hunger with his brave companions: each emaciated figure stretched upon its miserable bed without the power to rise; all, dividing the weary days between their prayers, their remembrances of the dear ones at home, and conversation on the pleasures of eating; the last-named topic being ever present to them, likewise, in their dreams. All the African travellers, wayworn, solitary, and sad, submit themselves again to drunken, murderous, man-selling despots, of the lowest order of humanity; and Mungo Park, fainting under a tree and succoured by a woman, gratefully remembers how his Good Samaritan has always come to him in woman's shape, the wide world over.

A shadow on the wall, in which my mind's eye can discern some traces of a rocky seacoast, recalls to me a fearful story of travel derived from that unpromising narrator of such stories, a parliamentary blue-book. A convict is its chief figure, and this man escapes with other prisoners from a penal settlement. It is an island, and they seize a boat, and get to the main-land. Their way is by a rugged and precipitous seashore, and they have no earthly hope of ultimate escape, for the party of soldiers, despatched by an easier course to cut them off, must inevitably arrive at their distant bourne long before them, and retake them if by any hazard they survive the horrors of the way. Famine, as they all must have foreseen, besets them early in their course. Some of the party die and are eaten; some are murdered by the rest and eaten. This one awful creature eats his fill, and sustains his strength, and lives on to be recaptured and taken back. The unrelateable experiences through which he has passed have been so tremendous, that he is not hanged as he might be, but goes back to his old chained gang-work. A little time, and he tempts one other prisoner away, seizes another boat, and flies once more — necessarily in the old hopeless direction, for he can take no other. He is soon cut off, and met by the pursuing party, face to face, upon the beach. He is alone. In his former journey he acquired an inappeasable relish for his dreadful food. He urged the new man away, expressly to kill him and eat him. In the pockets on one side of his coarse convict-dress are portions of the man's body, on which he is regaling; in the pockets on the other side is an untouched store of salted pork (stolen before he left the island) for which he has no appetite. He is taken back and he is hanged. But I shall never see that sea-beach on the wall or in the fire without him, solitary monster, eating as he prowls along, while the sea rages and rises at him.

Captain Bligh (a worse man to be intrusted with arbitrary power there could scarcely be) is handed over the side of the Bounty, and turned adrift on the wide ocean in an open boat, by order of Fletcher Christian, one of his officers, at this very minute. Another flash of my fire, and "Thursday October Christian," five-and-twenty years of age, son of the dead and gone Fletcher by a savage mother, leaps aboard his Majesty's ship Briton, hove to off Pitcairn's Island; says his simple grace before eating, in good English; and knows that a pretty little animal on board is called a dog, because in his childhood he had heard of such strange creatures from his father and the other mutineers, grown grey under the shade of the bread-fruit trees, speaking of their lost country far away.

See the Halsewell, East Indiaman outward bound, driving madly on a January night towards the rocks near Seacombe, on the island of Purbeck! The captain's two dear daughters are aboard, and five other ladies. The ship has been driving many hours, has seven feet water in her hold, and her main-mast has been cut away. The description of her loss, familiar to me from my early boyhood, seems to be read aloud as she rushes to her destiny.

"About two in the morning of Friday the sixth of January, the ship still driving, and approaching very fast to the shore, Mr. Henry Meriton, the second mate, went again into the cuddy, where the captain then was. Another conversation taking place, Captain Pierce expressed extreme anxiety for the preservation of his beloved daughters, and earnestly asked the officer if he could devise any method of saving them. On his answering with great concern that he feared it would be impossible, but that their only chance would be to wait for morning, the captain lifted up his hands in silent and distress-ful ejaculation.

"At this dreadful moment the ship struck, with such vio-lence as to dash the heads of those standing in the cuddy against the deck above them, and the shock was accompanied by a shriek of horror that burst at one instant from every quarter of the ship.

"Many of the seamen, who had been remarkably inattentive and remiss in their duty during great part of the storm, now poured upon deck, where no exertions of the officers could keep them while their assistance might have been useful. They had actually skulked in their hammocks, leaving the working of the pumps and other necessary labours to the officers of the ship, and the soldiers, who had made uncommon exer-tions. Roused by a sense of their danger the same seamen, at this moment, in frantic exclamations, demanded of heaven and their fellow-sufferers that succour which their own efforts timely made might possibly have procured.

"The ship continued to beat on the rocks; and soon bilging, fell with her broadside towards the shore. When she struck, a number of the men climbed up the ensign-staff, under an apprehension of her immediately going to pieces.

"Mr. Meriton, at this crisis, offered to these unhappy beings the best advice which could be given; he recommended that all should come to the side of the ship lying lowest on the rocks, and singly to take the opportunities which might then offer of escaping to the shore.

"Having thus provided, to the utmost of his power, for the safety of the desponding crew, he returned to the round-house, where, by this time, all the passengers and most of the officers had assembled. The latter were employed in offering consolation to the unfortunate ladies, and, with unparalleled magnanimity, suffering their compassion for the fair and amiable companions of their misfortunes to prevail over the sense of their own danger.

"In this charitable work of comfort Mr. Meriton now joined, by assurances of his opinion, that the ship would hold together till the morning, when all would be safe. Captain Pierce observing one of the young gentlemen loud in his exclamations of terror, and frequently cry that the ship was parting, cheerfully bid him be quiet, remarking that though the ship should go to pieces, he would not, but would be safe enough.

"It is difficult to convey a correct idea of the scene of this deplorable catastrophe without describing the place where it happened. The Halsewell struck on the rocks at a part of the shore where the cliff is of vast height, and rises almost perpendicular from its base. But at this particular spot the foot of the cliff is excavated into a cavern of ten or twelve yards in depth, and of breadth equal to the length of a large ship. The sides of the cavern are so nearly upright as to be of extremely difficult access, and the bottom is strewed with sharp and uneven rocks, which seem, by some convulsion of the earth, to have been detached from its roof.

"The ship lay with her broadside opposite to the mouth of this cavern, with her whole length stretched almost from side to side of it. But when she struck, it was too dark for the unfortunate persons on board to discover the real magnitude of their danger and the extreme horror of such a situation.

"In addition to the company already in the round-house, they had admitted three black women and two soldiers' wives; who, with the husband of one of them, had been allowed to come in, though the seamen, who had tumultuously demanded entrance to get the lights, had been opposed and kept out by Mr. Rogers and Mr. Brimer, the third and fifth mates. The numbers there were, therefore, now increased to near fifty. Captain Pierce sat on a chair, a cot, or some other movable, with a daughter on each side, whom he alternately pressed to his affectionate breast. The rest of the melancholy assembly were seated on the deck, which was strewed with musical instruments and the wreck of furniture and other articles.

"Here also Mr. Meriton, after having cut several wax-candles in pieces, and stuck them up in various parts of the round-house, and lighted up all the glass lanthorns he could find, took his seat, intending to wait the approach of dawn, and then assist the partners of his dangers to escape. But observing that the poor ladies appeared parched and exhausted, he brought a basket of oranges and prevailed on some of them to refresh themselves by sucking a little of the juice. At this time they were all tolerably composed, except Miss Mansel, who was in hysteric fits on the floor of the deck of the round-house.

"But on Mr. Meriton's return to the company, he perceived a considerable alteration in the appearance of the ship; the sides were visibly giving way; the deck seemed to be lifting, and he discovered other strong indications that she could not hold much longer together. On this account, he attempted to go forward to look out, but immediately saw that the ship had separated in the middle, and that the forepart having changed its position, lay rather further out towards the sea. In such an emergency, when the next moment might plunge him into eternity, he determined to seize the present opportunity, and follow the example of the crew and the soldiers, who were now quitting the ship in numbers, and making their way to the shore, though quite ignorant of its nature and description.

"Among other expedients, the ensign-staff had been un-shipped, and attempted to be laid between the ship's side and some of the rocks, but without success, for it snapped asunder before it reached them. However, by the light of a lanthorn, which a seaman handed through the skylight of the round-house to the deck, Mr. Meriton discovered a spar which appeared to be laid from the ship's side to the rocks, and on this spar he resolved to attempt his escape.

"Accordingly, lying down upon it, he thrust himself forward; however, he soon found that it had no communication with the rock; he reached the end of it and then slipped off, receiving a very violent bruise in his fall, and before he could recover his legs he was washed off by the surge. He now supported himself by swimming, until a returning wave dashed him against the back part of the cavern. Here he laid hold of a small projection in the rock, but was so much benumbed that he was on the point of quitting it, when a seaman, who had already gained a footing, extended his hand, and assisted him until he could secure himself a little on the rock; from which he clambered on a shelf still higher, and out of the reach of the surf.

"Mr. Rogers, the third mate, remained with the captain and the unfortunate ladies and their companions nearly twenty minutes after Mr. Meriton had quitted the ship. Soon after the latter left the round-house, the captain asked what was become of him, to which Mr. Rogers replied, that he was gone on deck to see what could be done. After this, a heavy sea breaking over the ship, the ladies exclaimed, 'Oh, poor Meriton! he is drowned! had he stayed with us he would have been safe!' and they all, particularly Miss Mary Pierce, expressed great concern at the apprehension of his loss.

"The sea was now breaking in at the forepart of the ship, and reached as far as the mainmast. Captain Pierce gave Mr. Rogers a nod, and they took a lamp and went together into the stern-gallery, where, after viewing the rocks for some time, Captain Pierce asked Mr. Rogers if he thought there was any possibility of saving the girls; to which he replied, he feared there was none; for they could only discover the black face of the perpendicular rock, and not the cavern which afforded shelter to those who escaped. They then returned to the round-house, where Mr. Rogers hung up the lamp, and Captain Pierce sat down between his two daughters.

"The sea continuing to break in very fast, Mr. Macmanus, a midshipman, and Mr. Schutz, a passenger, asked Mr. Rogers what they could do to escape. 'Follow me,' he replied, and they all went into the stern-gallery, and from thence to the upper-quarter-gallery on the poop. While there, a very heavy sea fell on board, and the round-house gave way; Mr. Rogers heard the ladies shriek at intervals, as if the water reached them; the noise of the sea at other times drowning their voices.

"Mr. Brimer had followed him to the poop, where they remained together about five minutes, when on the breaking of this heavy sea they jointly seized a hen-coop. The same wave which proved fatal to some of those below carried him and his companion to the rock, on which they were violently dashed and miserably bruised.

"Here on the rock were twenty-seven men; but it now being low water, and as they were convinced that on the flowing of the tide all must be washed off, many attempted to get to the back or the sides of the cavern, beyond the reach of the returning sea. Scarcely more than six, besides Mr. Rogers and Mr. Brimer, succeeded.

"Mr. Rogers, on gaining this station, was so nearly exhausted that had his exertions been protracted only a few minutes longer, he must have sunk under them. He was now prevented from joining Mr. Meriton by at least twenty men between them, none of whom could move without the imminent peril of his life.

"They found that a very considerable number of the crew, seamen, and soldiers, and some petty officers, were in the same situation as themselves, though many who had reached the rocks below perished in attempting to ascend. They could yet discern some part of the ship, and in their dreary station solaced themselves with the hopes of its remaining entire until daybreak; for, in the midst of their own distress, the sufferings of the females on board affected them with the most poignant anguish, and every sea that broke inspired them with terror for their safety.

"But, alas, their apprehensions were too soon realised! Within a very few minutes of the time that Mr. Rogers gained the rock an universal shriek, which long vibrated in their ears, in which the voice of female distress was lamentably distinguished, announced the dreadful catastrophe. In a few moments all was hushed, except the roaring of the winds and the dashing of the waves; the wreck was buried in the deep, and not an atom of it was ever afterwards seen."

The most beautiful and affecting incident I know, associated with a shipwreck, succeeds this dismal story for a winter night.

The Grosvenor, East Indiaman homeward bound, goes ashore
on the coast of Caffraria. It is resolved that the officers, passengers, and crew, in number one hundred and thirty-five
souls, shall endeavour to penetrate on foot, across trackless
deserts, infested by wild beasts and cruel savages, to the Dutch
settlements at the Cape of Good Hope. With this forlorn
object before them, they finally separate into two parties —
never more to meet on earth.

There is a solitary child among the passengers — a little boy
of seven years old who has no relation there; and when the
first party is moving away he cries after some member of it
who has been kind to him. The crying of a child might be
supposed to be a little thing to men in such great extremity,
but it touches them, and he is immediately taken into that
detachment.

From which time forth this child is sublimely made a sacred
charge. He is pushed, on a little raft, across broad rivers, by
the swimming sailors; they carry him by turns through the
deep sand and long grass (he patiently walking at all other
times); they share with him such putrid fish as they find to
eat; they lie down and wait for him when the rough carpenter,
who becomes his especial friend, lags behind. Beset by lions
and tigers, by savages, by thirst, by hunger, by death in a
crowd of ghastly shapes, they never — O Father of all mankind, thy name be blessed for it! — forget this child. The
captain stops exhausted, and his faithful coxswain goes back
and is seen to sit down by his side, and neither of the two
shall be any more beheld until the great last day; but, as the
rest go on for their lives, they take the child with them. The
carpenter dies of poisonous berries eaten in starvation; and
the steward, succeeding to the command of the party, succeeds
to the sacred guardianship of the child.

God knows all he does for the poor baby; how he cheerfully carries him in his arms when he himself is weak and ill;
how he feeds him when he himself is griped with want; how
he folds his ragged jacket round him, lays his little worn face
with a woman's tenderness upon his sunburnt breast, soothes
him in his sufferings, sings to him as he limps along, unmindful of his own parched and bleeding feet. Divided for a few
days from the rest, they dig a grave in the sand and bury their
good friend the cooper, — these two companions alone in the

wilderness, — and then the time comes when they both are ill and beg their wretched partners in despair, reduced and few in number now, to wait by them one day. They wait by them one day, they wait by them two days. On the morning of the third, they move very softly about, in making their preparations for the resumption of their journey; for the child is sleeping by the fire, and it is agreed with one consent that he shall not be disturbed until the last moment. The moment comes, the fire is dying — and the child is dead.

His faithful friend, the steward, lingers but a little while behind him. His grief is great, he staggers on for a few days, lies down in the desert, and dies. But he shall be reunited in his immortal spirit — who can doubt it! — with the child, where he and the poor carpenter shall be raised up with the words, "Inasmuch as ye have done it unto the least of these, ye have done it unto Me."

As I recall the dispersal and disappearance of nearly all the participators in this once famous shipwreck (a mere handful being recovered at last), and the legends that were long afterwards revived from time to time among the English officers at the Cape of a white woman with an infant, said to have been seen weeping outside a savage hut far in the interior, who was whisperingly associated with the remembrance of the missing ladies saved from the wrecked vessel, and who was often sought but never found, thoughts of another kind of travel come into my mind.

Thoughts of a voyager unexpectedly summoned from home, who travelled a vast distance, and could never return. Thoughts of this unhappy wayfarer in the depths of his sorrow, in the bitterness of his anguish, in the helplessness of his self-reproach, in the desperation of his desire to set right what he had left wrong, and do what he had left undone.

For there were many, many things he had neglected. Little matters while he was at home and surrounded by them, but things of mighty moment when he was at an immeasurable distance. There were many, many blessings that he had inadequately felt; there were many trivial injuries that he had not forgiven; there was love that he had but poorly returned; there was friendship that he had too lightly prized; there were a million kind words that he might have spoken, a million kind looks that he might have given, uncountable slight, easy deeds in which he might have been most truly great and good. Oh, for a day (he would exclaim), for but one day to make amends! But the sun never shone upon that happy day, and out of his remote captivity he never came.

Why does this traveller's fate obscure, on New Year's Eve, the other histories of travellers with which my mind was filled but now, and cast a solemn shadow over me! Must I one day make his journey? Even so. Who shall say that I may not then be tortured by such late regrets; that I may not then look from my exile on my empty place and undone work? I stand upon a seashore, where the waves are years. They break and fall, and I may little heed them; but with every wave the sea is rising, and I know that it will float me on this traveller's voyage at last.

XIX

THE LATE MR. JUSTICE TALFOURD

THE readers of these pages will have known, many days
before the present number can come into their hands, that on
Monday, the thirteenth of March, this upright judge and good
man died suddenly at Stafford in the discharge of his duties.
Mercifully spared protracted pain and mental decay, he passed
away in a moment, with words of Christian eloquence, of
brotherly tenderness and kindness towards all men, yet unfinished on his lips.

As he died he had always lived. So amiable a man, so
gentle, so sweet-tempered, of such a noble simplicity, so perfectly unspoiled by his labours and their rewards, is very rare
indeed upon this earth. These lines are traced by the faltering hand of a friend; but none can so fully know how true
they are as those who knew him under all circumstances, and
found him ever the same.

In his public aspects, in his poems, in his speeches, on the
bench, at the bar, in Parliament, he was widely appreciated,
honoured, and beloved. Inseparable as his great and varied
abilities were from himself in life, it is yet to himself, and not
to them, that affection in its first grief naturally turns. They
remain, but he is lost.

The chief delight of his life was to give delight to others.
His nature was so exquisitely kind that to be kind was its
highest happiness. Those who had the privilege of seeing
him in his own home when his public successes were greatest,
so modest, so contented with little things, so interested in
humble persons and humble efforts, so surrounded by children
and young people, so adored in remembrance of a domestic
generosity and greatness of heart too sacred to be unveiled
here, can never forget the pleasure of that sight.

If ever there were a house in England, justly celebrated for
the reverse of the picture, where every art was honoured for
its own sake, and where every visitor was received for his own
claims and merits, that house was his. It was in this respect

a great example, as sorely needed as it will be sorely missed. Rendering all legitimate deference to rank and riches, there never was a man more composedly, unaffectedly, quietly, immovable by such considerations than the subject of this sorrowing remembrance. On the other hand, nothing would have astonished him so much as the suggestion that he was any·body's patron or protector. His dignity was ever of that highest and purest sort which has no occasion to proclaim itself, and which is not in the least afraid of losing itself.

In the first joy of his appointment to the judicial bench he made a summer visit to the seashore, "to share his exultation in the gratification of his long-cherished ambition with the friend " — now among the many friends who mourn his death and lovingly recall his virtues. Lingering in the bright moonlight at the close of a happy day, he spoke of his new functions, of his sense of the great responsibility he undertook, and of his placid belief that the habits of his professional life rendered him equal to their efficient discharge; but, above all, he spoke with an earnestness, never more to be separated in his friend's mind from the murmur of the sea upon a moonlight night, of his reliance on the strength of his desire to do right before God and man. He spoke with his own singleness of heart, and his solitary hearer knew how deep and true his purpose was. They passed, before parting for the night, into a playful dispute at what age he should retire, and what he would do at threescore years and ten. And ah! within five short years it is all ended like a dream!

But by the strength of his desire to do right he was animated to the last moment of his existence. Who, knowing England at this time, would wish to utter with his last breath a more righteous warning than that its curse is ignorance, or a miscalled education which is as bad or worse, and a want of the exchange of innumerable graces and sympathies among the various orders of society, each hardened unto each and holding itself aloof? Well will it be for us and for our children, if those dying words be never henceforth forgotten on the Judgment Seat.

An example in his social intercourse to those who are born to station, an example equally to those who win it for themselves, — teaching the one class to abate its stupid pride, the other to stand upon its eminence, not forgetting the road by

which it got there, and fawning upon no one, — the conscien
tious judge, the charming writer and accomplished speakeʳ
the gentle-hearted, guileless, affectionate man, has entered o
a brighter world. Very, very many have lost a friend; nothinᵦ
in Creation has lost an enemy.

The hand that lays this poor flower on his grave was a
mere boy's when he first clasped it, newly come from the worᴸ
in which he himself began life, little used to the plough it haᵉ
followed since, obscure enough, with much to correct and learn.
Each of its successive tasks through many intervening years
has been cheered by his warmest interest, and the friendship
then begun has ripened to maturity in the passage of time;
but there was no more self-assertion or condescension in his
winning goodness at first than at last. The success of other
men made as little change in him as his own.

XX

OUR FRENCH WATERING-PLACE

HAVING earned, by many years of fidelity, the right to be sometimes inconstant to our English watering-place, we have dallied for two or three seasons with a French watering-place, — once solely known to us as a town with a very long street, beginning with an abattoir and ending with a steamboat, which it seemed our fate to behold only at daybreak on winter morn-- ings, when (in the days before Continental railroads), just suffi- ciently awake to know that we were most uncomfortably asleep, it was our destiny always to clatter through it, in the coupé of the diligence from Paris, with a sea of mud behind us and a sea of tumbling waves before. In relation to which latter monster, our mind's eye now recalls a worthy Frenchman in a seal-skin cap with a braided hood over it, once our travelling companion in the coupé aforesaid, who waking up with a pale and crumpled visage, and looking ruefully out at the grim row of breakers enjoying themselves fanatically on an instrument of torture called "the Bar," inquired of us whether we were ever sick at sea? Both to prepare his mind for the abject creature we were presently to become, and also to afford him consolation, we replied, "Sir, your servant is always sick when it is possible to be so." He returned, altogether uncheered by the bright example, "Ah, Heaven, but I am always sick, even when it is *im*possible to be so."

The means of communication between the French capital and our French watering-place are wholly changed since those days; but the Channel remains unbridged as yet, and the old floundering and knocking about go on there. It must be con- fessed that saving in reasonable (and therefore rare) sea- weather, the act of arrival at our French watering-place from England is difficult to be achieved with dignity. Several little circumstances combine to render the visitor an object of humili- ation. In the first place, the steamer no sooner touches the port than all the passengers fall into captivity; being boarded by an overpowering force of Custom-House officers, and marched

into a gloomy dungeon. In the second place, the road to this
dungeon is fenced off with ropes breast-high, and outside those
ropes all the English in the place, who have lately been sea-sick
and are now well, assemble in their best clothes to enjoy the
degradation of their dilapidated fellow-creatures. "Oh, my
gracious! how ill this one has been!" "Here's a damp one
coming next!" "*Here's* a pale one!" "Oh! Ain't he
green in the face, this next one!" Even we ourself (not defi-
cient in natural dignity) have a lively remembrance of staggering up this detested lane one September day in a gale of wind,
when we were received like an irresistible comic actor, with a
burst of laughter and applause, occasioned by the extreme
imbecility of our legs.

We were coming to the third place. In the third place the
captives, being shut up in the gloomy dungeon, are strained,
two or three at a time, into an inner cell, to be examined as
to passports; and across the doorway of communication stands
a military creature making a bar of his arm. Two ideas are
generally present to the British mind during these ceremonies:
first, that it is necessary to make for the cell with violent
struggles, as if it were a life-boat and the dungeon a ship going
down; secondly, that the military creature's arm is a national
affront, which the government at home ought instantly to "take
up." The British mind and body becoming heated by these
fantasies, delirious answers are made to inquiries, and extravagant
actions performed. Thus, Johnson persists in giving Johnson
as his baptismal name, and substituting for his ancestral designation the national "Dam!" Neither can he by any means
be brought to recognise the distinction between a portmanteau
key and a passport, but will obstinately persevere in tendering
the one when asked for the other. This brings him to the
fourth place, in a state of mere idiotcy; and when he is, in
the fourth place, cast out at a little door into a howling wilderness of touters, he becomes a lunatic with wild eyes and floating hair until rescued and soothed. If friendless and unres-
cued, he is generally put into a railway omnibus and taken to
Paris.

But our French watering-place, when it is once got into, is
a very enjoyable place. It has a varied and beautiful country
around it, and many characteristic and agreeable things within
it. To be sure, it might have fewer bad smells and less decay-

ing refuse, and it might be better drained, and much cleaner in many parts, and therefore infinitely more healthy. Still, it is a bright, airy, pleasant, cheerful town; and if you were to walk down either of its three well-paved main streets, towards five o'clock in the afternoon, when delicate odours of cookery fill the air, and its hotel windows (it is full of hotels) give glimpses of long tables set out for dinner, and made to look sumptuous by the aid of napkins folded fan-wise, you would rightly judge it to be an uncommonly good town to eat and drink in.

We have an old walled town, rich in cool public wells of water, on the top of a hill within and above the present business town; and if it were some hundreds of miles further from England, instead of being, on a clear day, within sight of the grass growing in the crevices of the chalk cliffs of Dover, you would long ago have been bored to death about that town. It is more picturesque and quaint than half the innocent places which tourists, following their leader like sheep, have made impostors of. To say nothing of its houses with grave court-yards, its queer by-corners, and its many-windowed streets white and quiet in the sunlight, there is an ancient belfry in it that would have been in all the Annuals and Albums, going and gone, these hundred years, if it had but been more expensive to get at. Happily it has escaped so well, being only in our French watering-place, that you may like it of your own accord in a natural manner, without being required to go into convulsions about it. We regard it as one of the later blessings of our life that Bilkins, the only authority on Taste, never took any notice that we can find out of our French watering-place. Bilkins never wrote about it, never pointed out anything to be seen in it, never measured anything in it, always left it alone. For which relief, Heaven bless the town and the memory of the immortal Bilkins likewise!

There is a charming walk, arched and shaded by trees, on the old walls that form the four sides of this High Town, whence you get glimpses of the streets below, and changing views of the other town and of the river, and of the hills and of the sea. It is made more agreeable and peculiar by some of the solemn houses that are rooted in the deep streets below, bursting into a fresher existence atop, and having doors and windows, and even gardens, on these ramparts. A child going in at the courtyard gate of one of these houses, climbing up the many stairs, and coming out at the fourth-floor window, might conceive himself another Jack, alighting on enchanted ground from another beanstalk. It is a place wonderfully populous in children: English children, with governesses reading novels as they walk down the shady lanes of trees, or nursemaids interchanging gossip on the seats; French children with their smiling *bonnes* in snow-white caps, and themselves — if little boys — in straw head-gear like beehives, workbaskets, and church hassocks. Three years ago there were three weazen old men, one bearing a frayed red ribbon in his threadbare button-hole, always to be found walking together among these children, before dinner-time. If they walked for an appetite, they doubtless lived *en pension* — were contracted for — otherwise their poverty would have made it a rash action. They were stooping, blear-eyed, dull old men, slip-shod and shabby, in long-skirted, short-waisted coats and meagre trousers, and yet with a ghost of gentility hovering in their company. They spoke little to each other, and looked as if they might have been politically discontented if they had had vitality enough. Once, we overheard red-ribbon feebly complain to the other two that somebody, or something, was "a Robber;" and then they all three set their mouths so that they would have ground their teeth if they had had any. The ensuing winter gathered red-ribbon unto the great company of faded ribbons, and next year the remaining two were there — getting themselves entangled with hoops and dolls — familiar mysteries to the children — probably in the eyes of most of them harmless creatures who had never been like children, and whom children could never be like. Another winter came, and another old man went, and so, this present year, the last of the triumvirate left off walking, — it was no good, now, — and sat by himself on a little solitary bench, with the hoops and the dolls as lively as ever all about him.

In the Place d'Armes of this town a little decayed market is held, which seems to slip through the old gateway, like water, and go rippling down the hill, to mingle with the murmuring market in the lower town, and get lost in its movement and bustle. It is very agreeable on an idle summer morning to pursue this market-stream from the hill-top. It begins dozingly and dully, with a few sacks of corn; starts into a

surprising collection of boots and shoes; goes brawling down
the hill in, a diversified channel of old cordage, old iron, old
crockery, old clothes civil and military, old rags, new cotton
goods, flaming prints of saints, little looking-glasses, and incalculable lengths of tape; dives into a back way, keeping out of
sight for a little while, as streams will, or only sparkling for
a moment in the shape of a market drinking-shop; and suddenly reappears behind the great church, shooting itself into
a bright confusion of white-capped women and blue-bloused
men, poultry, vegetables, fruits, flowers, pots, pans, praying-
chairs, soldiers, country butter, umbrellas and other sun-
shades, girl-porters waiting to be hired with baskets at their
backs, and one weazen little old man in a cocked hat, wearing
a cuirass of drinking-glasses and carrying on his shoulder a
crimson temple fluttering with flags, like a glorified pavior's
rammer without the handle, who rings a little bell in all parts
of the scene, and cries his cooling drink Hola, Hola, Ho-o-o!
in a shrill cracked voice that somehow makes itself heard,
above all the chaffering and vending hum. Early in the afternoon the whole course of the stream is dry. The praying-
chairs are put back in the church, the umbrellas are folded up,
the unsold goods are carried away, the stalls and stands disappear, the square is swept, the hackney-coaches lounge there to
be hired, and on all the country roads (if you walk about as
much as we do) you will see the peasant women, always neatly
and comfortably dressed, riding home, with the pleasantest
saddle-furniture of clean milk-pails, bright butter-kegs, and
the like, on the jolliest little donkeys in the world.

We have another market in our French watering-place —
that is to say, a few wooden hutches in the open street, down
by the port — devoted to fish. Our fishing-boats are famous
everywhere; and our fishing people, though they love lively
colours and taste is neutral (see Bilkins), are among the most
picturesque people we ever encountered. They have not only
a Quarter of their own in the town itself, but they occupy
whole villages of their own on the neighbouring cliffs. Their
churches and chapels are their own; they consort with one
another, they intermarry among themselves, their customs are
their own, and their costume is their own and never changes.
As soon as one of their boys can walk, he is provided with a
long, bright red nightcap; and one of their men would as soon

think of going afloat without his head as without that indispensable appendage to it. Then they wear the noblest boots,
with the hugest tops — flapping and bulging over anyhow;
above which, they encase themselves in such wonderful overalls
and petticoat trousers, made to all appearance of tarry old sails,
so additionally stiffened with pitch and salt, that the wearers
have a walk of their own, and go straddling and swinging
about, among the boats and barrels and nets and rigging, a
sight to see. Then, their younger women, by dint of going
down to the sea barefoot, to fling their baskets into the boats
as they come in with the tide, and bespeak the first fruits of
the haul with propitiatory promises to love and marry that
dear fisherman who shall fill that basket like an Angel, have
the finest legs ever carved by Nature in the brightest mahogany, and they walk like Juno. Their eyes, too, are so lus-
trous that their long gold ear-rings turn dull beside those brilliant neighbours; and when they are dressed, what with these
beauties, and their fine fresh faces, and their many petticoats
— striped petticoats, red petticoats, blue petticoats, always
clean and smart, and never too long — and their home-made
stockings, mulberry-coloured, blue, brown, purple, lilac —
which the older women, taking care of the Dutch-looking children, sit in all sorts of places knitting, knitting, knitting, from
morning to night — and what with their little saucy bright
blue jackets, knitted too, and fitting close to their handsome
figures — and what with the natural grace with which they wear
the commonest cap, or fold the commonest handkerchief round
their luxuriant hair — we say, in a word and out of breath,
that taking all these premises into our consideration, it has
never been a matter of the least surprise to us that we have
never once met, in the cornfields, on the dusty roads, by the
breezy windmills, on the plots of short sweet grass overhanging
the sea — anywhere — a young fisherman and fisherwoman of
our French watering-place together, but the arm of that fisherman has invariably been, as a matter of course and without
any absurd attempt to disguise so plain a necessity, round the
neck or waist of that fisherwoman. And we have had no
doubt whatever, standing looking at their uphill streets, house
rising above house, and terrace above terrace, and bright garments here and there lying sunning on rough stone parapets,
that the pleasant mist on all such objects, caused by their being

seen through the brown nets hung across on poles to dry, is, in the eyes of every true young fisherman, a mist of love and beauty, setting off the goddess of his heart.

Moreover, it is to be observed that these are an industrious people, and a domestic people, and an honest people. And though we are aware that at the bidding of Bilkins it is our duty to fall down and worship the Neapolitans, we make bold very much to prefer the fishing people of our French watering-place — especially since our last visit to Naples within these twelvemonths, when we found only four conditions of men remaining in the whole city: to wit, lazzaroni, priests, spies, and soldiers, and all of them beggars; the paternal government having banished all its subjects except the rascals.

But we can never henceforth separate our French watering-place from our own landlord of two summers, M. Loyal Devasseur, citizen and town-councillor. Permit us to have the pleasure of presenting M. Loyal Devasseur.

His own family name is simply Loyal; but as he is married, and as in that part of France a husband always adds to his own name the family name of his wife, he writes himself Loyal Devasseur. He owns a compact little estate of some twenty or thirty acres on a lofty hillside, and on it he has built two country houses which he lets furnished. They are by many degrees the best houses that are so let near our French watering-place; we have had the honour of living in both, and can testify. The entrance-hall of the first we inhabited was ornamented with a plan of the estate, representing it as about twice the size of Ireland; insomuch that when we were yet new to the Property (M. Loyal always speaks of it as "la propriété") we went three miles straight on end, in search of the bridge of Austerlitz — which we afterwards found to be immediately outside the window. The Château of the Old Guard, in another part of the grounds, and, according to the plan, about two leagues from the little dining-room, we sought in vain for a week, until, happening one evening to sit upon a bench in the forest (forest in the plan), a few yards from the house door, we observed at our feet, in the ignominious circumstances of being upside down and greenly rotten, the Old Guard himself; that is to say, the painted effigy of a member of that distinguished corps, seven feet high, and in the act of carrying arms, who had had the misfortune to be blown down

in the previous winter. It will be perceived that M. Loyal
is a stanch admirer of the great Napoleon. He is an old
soldier himself, — captain of the National Guard, with a handsome gold vase on his chimney-piece, presented to him by his
company, — and his respect for the memory of the illustrious
general is enthusiastic. Medallions of him, portraits of him,
busts of him, pictures of him, are thickly sprinkled all over
the Property. During the first month of our occupation, it
was our affliction to be constantly knocking down Napoleon,
if we touched a shelf in a dark corner, he toppled over with a
crash; and every door we opened shook him to the soul. Yet
M. Loyal is not a man of mere castles in the air, or, as he
would say, in Spain. He has a specially practical, contriving,
clever, skilful eye and hand. His houses are delightful. He
unites French elegance and English comfort in a happy manner quite his own. He has an extraordinary genius for making
tasteful little bedrooms in angles of his roofs, which an Englishman would as soon think of turning to any account as
he would think of cultivating the Desert. We have ourself
reposed deliciously in an elegant chamber of M. Loyal's construction, with our head as nearly in the kitchen chimney-pot
as we can conceive it likely for the head of any gentleman, not
by profession a Sweep, to be. And into whatsoever strange
nook M. Loyal's genius penetrates, it, in that nook, infallibly
constructs a cupboard and a row of pegs. In either of our
houses, we could have put away the knapsacks and hung up
the hats of the whole regiment of Guides.

Aforetime, M. Loyal was a tradesman in the town. You
can transact business with no present tradesman in the town,
and give your card "chez M. Loyal," but a brighter face
shines upon you directly. We doubt if there is, ever was, or
ever will be, a man so universally pleasant in the minds of
people as M. Loyal is in the minds of the citizens of our
French watering-place. They rub their hands and laugh when
they speak of him. Ah, but he is such a good child, such a
brave boy, such a generous spirit, that Monsieur Loyal! It
is the honest truth. M. Loyal's nature is the nature of a
gentleman. He cultivates his ground with his own hands
(assisted by one little labourer, who falls into a fit now and
then); and he digs and delves from morn to eve in prodigious
perspirations, — "works always," as he says, — but cover him

with dust, mud, weeds, water, any stains you will, you never can cover the gentleman in M. Loyal. A portly, upright, broad-shouldered, brown-faced man, whose soldierly bearing gives him the appearance of being taller than he is, look into the bright eye of M. Loyal, standing before you in his working blouse and cap, not particularly well shaved, and, it may be, very earthy, and you shall discern in M. Loyal a gentleman whose true politeness is in grain, and confirmation of whose word by his bond you would blush to think of. Not without reason is M. Loyal when he tells that story, in his own vivacious way, of his travelling to Fulham, near London, to buy all these hundreds and hundreds of trees you now see upon the Property, then a bare, bleak hill; and of his sojourning in Fulham three months; and of his jovial evenings with the market-gardeners; and of the crowning banquet before his departure, when the market-gardeners rose as one man, clinked their glasses all together (as the custom at Fulham is), and cried, "Vive Loyal!"

M. Loyal has an agreeable wife, but no family; and he loves to drill the children of his tenants, or run races with them, or do anything with them, or for them, that is good-natured. He is of a highly convivial temperament, and his hospitality is unbounded. Billet a soldier on him, and he is delighted. Five-and-thirty soldiers had M. Loyal billeted on him this present summer, and they all got fat and red-faced in two days. It became a legend among the troops that whosoever got billeted on M. Loyal rolled in clover; and so it fell out that the fortunate man who drew the billet "M. Loyal Devasseur" always leaped into the air, though in heavy marching order. M. Loyal cannot bear to admit anything that might seem by any implication to disparage the military profession. We hinted to him once, that we were conscious of a remote doubt arising in our mind, whether a sou a day for pocket-money, tobacco, stockings, drink, washing, and social pleasures in general, left a very large margin for a soldier's enjoyment. Pardon! said Monsieur Loyal, rather wincing. It was not a fortune, but — à la bonne heure — it was better than it used to be! What, we asked him on another occasion, were all those neighbouring peasants, each living with his family in one room, and each having a soldier (perhaps two) billeted on him every other night, required to provide for those

soldiers? "Faith!" said M. Loyal reluctantly, "a bed, monsieur, and fire to cook with, and a candle. And they share
their supper with those soldiers. It is not possible that they
could eat alone." "And what allowance do they get for
this?" said we. Monsieur Loyal drew himself up taller, took
a step back, laid his hand upon his breast, and said, with
majesty, as speaking for himself and all France, "Monsieur, it
is a contribution to the State!"

It is never going to rain, according to M. Loyal. When it
is impossible to deny that it is now raining in torrents, he says
it will be fine — charming — magnificent — to-morrow. It is
never hot on the Property, he contends. Likewise it is never
cold. The flowers, he says, come out, delighting to grow
there; it is like Paradise this morning; it is like the Garden
of Eden. He is a little fanciful in his language: smilingly
observing of Madame Loyal, when she is absent at vespers,
that she is "gone to her salvation" — *allée à son salut*. He
has a great enjoyment of tobacco, but nothing would induce
him to continue smoking face to face with a lady. His short
black pipe immediately goes into his breast pocket, scorches
his blouse, and nearly sets him on fire. In the Town Council
and on occasions of ceremony, he appears in a full suit of
black, with a waistcoat of magnificent breadth across the chest,
and a shirt-collar of fabulous proportions. Good M. Loyal!
Under blouse or waistcoat, he carries one of the gentlest hearts
that beat in a nation teeming with gentle people. He has had
losses, and has been at his best under them. Not only the
loss of his way by night in the Fulham times, — when a bad
subject of an Englishman, under pretence of seeing him home,
took him into all the night public-houses, drank "arfanarf" in
every one at his expense, and finally fled, leaving him shipwrecked at Cleefeeway, which we apprehend to be Ratcliffe
Highway, — but heavier losses than that. Long ago, a family
of children and a mother were left in one of his houses, without money, a whole year. M. Loyal — anything but as rich
as we wish he had been — had not the heart to say, "You must
go;" so they stayed on and stayed on, and paying tenants who
would have come in could n't come in, and at last they managed to get helped home across the water, and M. Loyal kissed
the whole group, and said, "Adieu, my poor infants!" and sat
down in their deserted salon and smoked his pipe of peace.

"The rent, M. Loyal?" "Eh! well! The rent!" M. Loyal shakes his head. "Le bon Dieu," says M. Loyal presently, "will recompense me," and he laughs and smokes his pipe of peace. May he smoke it on the Property, and not be recom pensed, these fifty years! There are public amusements in our French watering-place, or it would not be French. They are very popular, and very cheap. The sea-bathing — which may rank as the most favoured daylight entertainment, inasmuch as the French visitors bathe all day long, and seldom appear to think of remaining less than an hour at a time in the water — is astoundingly cheap. Omnibuses convey you, if you please, from a convenient part of the town to the beach and back again; you have a clean and comfortable bathing-machine, dress, linen, and all appliances; and the charge for the whole is half a franc, or fivepence. On the pier, there is usually a guitar, which seems presumptuously enough to set its tinkling against the deep hoarseness of the sea, and there is always some boy or woman who sings, without any voice, little songs without any tune: the strain we have most frequently heard being an appeal to "the sportsman" not to bag that choicest of game, the swallow. For bathing purposes, we have also a subscription establishment with an esplanade, where people lounge about with telescopes, and seem to get a good deal of weariness for their money; and we have also an association of individual machine-proprietors combined against this formidable rival. M. Féroce, our own particular friend in the bathing line, is one of these. How he ever came by his name we cannot imagine. He is as gentle and polite a man as M. Loyal Devasseur himself; immensely stout withal, and of a beaming aspect. M. Féroce has saved so many people from drowning, and has been decorated with so many medals in consequence, that his stoutness seems a special dispensation of Providence to enable him to wear them; if his girth were the girth of an ordinary man, he could never hang them on, all at once. It is only on very great occasions that M. Féroce displays his shining honours. At other times they lie by, with rolls of manuscript testifying to the causes of their presentation, in a huge glass case in the red-sofa'd salon of his private residence on the beach, where M. Féroce also keeps his family pictures, his portraits of himself as he appears both in bathing life and in private life, his little

boats that rock by clock-work, and his other ornamental possessions.

Then we have a commodious and gay theatre — or had, for
it is burned down now — where the opera was always preceded
by a vaudeville, in which (as usual) everybody, down to the
little old man with the large hat and the little cane and tassel,
who always played either my Uncle or my Papa, suddenly,
broke out of the dialogue into the mildest vocal snatches, to
the great perplexity of unaccustomed strangers from Great
Britain, who never could make out when they were singing
and when they were talking; and indeed it was pretty much
the same. But the caterers in the way of entertainment to
whom we are most beholden are the Society of Welldoing,
who are active all the summer, and give the proceeds of their
good works to the poor. Some of the most agreeable fêtes
they contrive are announced as "Dedicated to the Children;"
and the taste with which they turn a small public inclosure
into an elegant garden beautifully illuminated, and the thorough-going heartiness and energy with which they personally
direct the childish pleasures, are supremely delightful. For
fivepence a head, we have on these occasions donkey races with
English "Jokeis," and other rustic sports; lotteries for toys;
roundabouts, dancing on the grass to the music of an admirable band, fire-balloons, and fireworks. Further, almost every
week all through the summer — never mind, now, on what day
of the week — there is a fête in some adjoining village (called
in that part of the country a Ducasse), where the people —
really *the people* — dance on the green turf in the open air,
round a little orchestra, that seems itself to dance, there is
such an airy motion of flags and streamers all about it. And
we do not suppose that between the Torrid Zone and the North
Pole there are to be found male dancers with such astonish-
ingly loose legs, furnished with so many joints in wrong places,
utterly unknown to Professor Owen, as those who here disport
themselves. Sometimes the fête appertains to a particular
trade; you will see among the cheerful young women at the
joint Ducasse of the milliners and tailors, a wholesome knowledge of the art of making common and cheap things uncommon
and pretty, by good sense and good taste, that is a practical
lesson to any rank of society in a whole island we could mention. The oddest feature of these agreeable scenes is the ever-

lasting roundabout (we preserve an English word wherever we can, as we are writing the English language), on the wooden horses of which machine grown-up people of all ages are wound round and round with the utmost solemnity, while the proprietor's wife grinds an organ, capable of only one tune, in the centre.

As to the boarding-houses of our French watering-place, they are Legion, and would require a distinct treatise. It is not without a sentiment of national pride that we believe them to contain more bores from the shores of Albion than all the clubs in London. As you walk timidly in their neighbourhood, the very neckcloths and hats of your elderly compatriots cry to you from the stones of the streets, "We are Bores— avoid us!" We have never overheard at street corners such lunatic scraps of political and social discussion as among these dear countrymen of ours. They believe everything that is impossible and nothing that is true. They carry rumours, and ask questions, and make corrections and improvements on one another, staggering to the human intellect. And they are for ever rushing into the English library, propounding such incomprehensible paradoxes to the fair mistress of that establishment, that we beg to recommend her to her Majesty's gracious consideration as a fit object for a pension.

The English form a considerable part of the population of our French watering-place, and are deservedly addressed and respected in many ways. Some of the surface-addresses to them are odd enough, as when a laundress puts a placard outside her house announcing her possession of that curious British instrument, a "Mingle;" or when a tavern-keeper provides accommodation for the celebrated English game of "Nokemdon." But, to us, it is not the least pleasant feature of our French watering-place that a long and constant fusion of the two great nations there has taught each to like the other, and to learn from the other, and to rise superior to the absurd prejudices that have lingered among the weak and ignorant in both countries equally.

Drumming and trumpeting of course go on for ever in our French watering-place. Flag-flying is at a premium, too; but we cheerfully avow that we consider a flag a very pretty object, and that we take such outward signs of innocent liveliness to our heart of hearts. The people, in the town and in the country, are a busy people who work hard; they are sober, temperate, good-humoured, light-hearted, and generally remarkable for their engaging manners. Few just men, not immoderately bilious, could see them in their recreations without very much respecting the character that is so easily, so harmlessly, and so simply pleased.

XXI

BY RAIL TO PARNASSUS

I AM a poor clerk, who, being out of employment, was on that morning travelling to Southampton to present myself to the firm of Heavahoy Brothers, in some little hope of procuring occupation in their counting-house. To my eyes things were dreary down below, for I am thirty-five years old, and do not see my way yet to a marriage with poor Lucy Jane whose first love-letter to me was dated in the year one thousand eight hundred and thirty-nine. I have been earning my own living for seventeen years, and have saved up to this date eighty-one pounds two shillings and ninepence. Nevertheless, Lucy Jane's friends, who are exceedingly respectable, consider me unable to keep myself, and still less able to keep a wife. What does the great world care about that? Nothing at all, to be sure, and yet it is to my purpose to say so much, for I desire it to be seen whether I had not full reason to be dismal on that morning of which I speak. Hopes and fears as to the success of my application to the Heavahoys had kept me awake all night. There are foreign agencies connected with their house for which my ambition was, if I once entered the service of the firm, to become qualified. With a view to some such opening I had been learning Spanish. My hope had come to be that I might some day carry Lucy Jane to Buenos Ayres, or some other distant place. No matter. I lay awake all night and rose, unrefreshed, at an uncomfortable hour. I left a half eaten breakfast to hurry to the Waterloo Road, running through rain in close May weather, with a great-coat on my back, a carpet-bag in one hand, and an umbrella in the other. I arrived at the station hot, damp, weary, wretched, and took my place in a third-class carriage with a discontented man close at my elbow and a crowd of noisy market people round about. I looked forward to the journey with dread. I was eager to be at the other end, and we were bound to lag on the road, stopping at every station.

The first bell had rung. Suddenly it occurred to me that

I would have a book. It was long since I had added one to
the small stock from which I got. solace of evenings in my
lodgings.   I had saved two shillings in cab-hire, and I was
saving more than five shillings by travelling third-class. For
my run through the wet and my discomfort on the road I
would repay myself by spending on a book half of what I had
saved in travelling expense. That would be three shillings
and sixpence. I had only time to jump upon the platform,
hurry to the railway-stall and take — partly for the name's
sake of its author, partly because the price was fitted to my
notion — a volume of Leigh Hunt's "Stories in Verse." With
that in my hand I regained my seat; the door was beaten in
after me; the second bell rang, and the engine heaved us out
into the misty weather.

For a time my sad thoughts were my only company. I
paid no attention to the chimneys among which we passed, or
to the meaning of the noise made by my companions, or the
talisman against dulness that reposed upon my lap. A stench
aroused me suddenly. The train was passing near the Thames
at Lambeth, and getting among the pest manufactories. I
looked out of window, and saw them through the rain. Close
by the line of rail were miserable garret windows; back yards
choked with enormous dust-heaps; tumble-down sheds and
despondent poultry.

"Call this May, sir?" cried my neighbour, shivering uncomfortably.   "I hope you don't object to tobacco?"

I smiled faintly. Nothing disgusts me more than the addition of the smoke of bad tobacco to an atmosphere already
loaded with the smoke out of the damp bodies and clothes of
dirty men.   But I am bound to love my fellow-creatures, and
be courteous to them.   I smiled faintly and opened my book,
to begin Leigh Hunt's "Story of Rimini: " —

"The sun is up, and 't is a morn of May round old Ravenna's clear-shown towers and bay — a morn the loveliest which
the year has seen, last of the spring, yet fresh with all its
green.   For a warm eve and gentle rains at night have left a
sparkling welcome for the light.   And there 's a crystal clearness all about — the leaves are sharp, the distant hills look out.
A balmy briskness comes upon the breeze, the smoke goes
dancing from the cottage trees; and when you listen you may
hear a coil of bubbling springs about the grassier soil; and all

the scene, in short — earth, sky, and sea, breathes like a
bright-eyed face, that laughs out openly."

Thereat I was myself almost ready to laugh out openly with
ease and pleasure; for my heavens and my earth were changed.
I did not raise my eye from the page of the poet to look freely
out upon the broad horizon whence my heart was gladly stirred
to see "the far ships, lifting their sails of white like joyful
hands, come up with scattered light — come gleaming up, true
to the wished-for day, and chase the whistling brine and swirl
into the bay."

Those words stand in the book line under line because they
are poetry; but they speak quite as well to the heart written
like prose, straight on together — also because they are poetry.
Never mind that. What do the ships bring? — why are the
people who make holiday all crowding to Ravenna? It is
because there "peace returning and processions rare, princes
and donatives and faces fair, and, to crown all, a marriage in
May weather, are summonses to bring blithe souls together.
For on this great glad day, Ravenna's pride, the daughter of
their prince, becomes a bride, a bride to ransom an exhausted
land; and he whose victories have obtained her hand has taken
with the dawn — so flies report — his promised journey to the
expecting court, with hasting pomp and squires of high degree,
the bold Giovanni, lord of Rimini." And having told me
this, the poet took me down into the streets of the gay city,
filled my ears with the stir of feet, the hum, the talk, the
laugh, callings, and clapping doors; filled my eyes with the
spectacle of armed bands making important way, gallant and
grave, the lords of holiday; caused me to note the greetings of
the neighbours; to pass through the crowds of pilgrims chant-
ing in the morning sun; to see the tapestry spread in the
windows, and the fair dames who took their seats with upward
gaze admired — some looking down, some forwards or aside;
some readjusting tresses newly tied; some turning a trim waist,
or o'er the flow of crimson cloths hanging a hand of snow;
but all with smiles prepared and garlands green, and all in fluttering talk impatient for the scene. Glorious fortune for a poor
fellow like me to chance to be at Ravenna on a day like that!
The train stopped. "Clapham! Clapham!" shouted a far
distant voice. Strange that I should have been able to hear
at Ravenna the voice of a man shouting at Clapham!

I paid not much heed to the marvel; for there was Duke Guido seated with his fair daughter over the marble gate of his palace; there was the square before them kept with guards; there were knights and ladies on a grass plot sitting under boughs of rose and laurel, and in the midst, fresh whistling through the scene, a lightsome fountain starts from out the green, clear and compact, till at its height o'errun, it shakes its loosening silver in the sun. The courtly knights are bending down in talk over the ladies, and the people are all looking up with love and wonder at the princely maid, the daughter of Duke Guido, the bride sought with so much pomp by a bridegroom whom she never saw, the sad and fair Francesca.

Now the procession comes with noise of cavalry and trumpets clear, a princely music unbedinned with drums; the mighty brass seems opening as it comes; and now it fills and now it shakes the air, and now it bursts into the sounding square. I saw the whole of it. In magic verse the storyteller caused trumpeter and heralds, squires and knights, to prance before me. Mine was a front place for looking at the show. I noted the dresses and the jewels, and the ladies' favours of the knights; the action of the horses and the faces of the riders; the life, the carelessness, the sudden heed; the body curving to the rearing steed; the patting hand, that best persuades the check, makes the quarrel up with a proud neck — the thigh broad-pressed, the spanning palm upon it, and the jerk'd feather flowing on the bonnet. Then came, after an interval of stately length, a troop of steeds, milk-white and unattired, Arabian bred, each by a blooming boy lightsomely led. What next? The pages of the court, in rows of three — of white and crimson is their livery. Space after space, and still the trains appear — a fervid whisper fills the general ear. Ah! yes — no — 'tis not he, but 'tis the squires who go before him when his pomp requires. And now his huntsman shows the lessening train — now the squire carver and the chamberlain. And now his banner comes, and now his shield, borne by the squire that waits him to the field. And then an interval — a lordly space — a pin-drop's silence strikes o'er all the place. The princess from a distance scarcely knows which way to look; her colour comes and goes, and with an impulse and affection free, she lays her hand upon her father's knee, who looks upon her with a labour'd smile, gathering it up into

his own the while. When some one's voice, as if it knew not
how to check itself, exclaims, "The Prince! Now — now!"
And on a milk-white courser, like the air, a glorious figure
springs into the square. Up with a burst of thunder goes the
shout — ["Wimbledon and Malden! Wimbledon and Malden!
Passengers for Wimbledon and Malden!"] — and rolls the
echoing walls and peopled roofs about.

The noble youth, at sight of whom surprise, relief, a joy
scarce understood, something, perhaps, of very gratitude, and
fifty feelings, undefined and new, danced through the bride
and flushed her faded hue, was Paulo. And, alas for a fair
maiden's love, he was to be no more to her than the brother
of the bridegroom, by whom he had been sent as proxy to be
wedded in his name and to convey the bride to Rimini. To
Paulo poor Francesca gave her hand in mockery, her heart in
truth. And as I read more of her tale the rainy weather
found its way into my eyes, so that I even murmured to
myself after Giovanni when he stood over the dead youth,
"And, Paulo, thou wert the completest knight that ever rode
with banner to the fight; and thou wert the most beautiful to
see that ever came in press of chivalry; and of a sinful man
thou wert the best that ever for his friend put spear in rest;
and thou wert the most meek and cordial that ever among
ladies ate in hall; and thou wert still, for all that bosom gor'd,
the kindest man that ever struck with sword."

"I could walk faster than this train is going," said my discontented neighbour; "we shall never see our journey's end
— it's shameful!"

I had the end to see of Francesca, and I did not answer
him. How could I? I knew nothing about the journey — it
was his journey, not mine — why should he talk to me about
it? But I had not remained much longer absorbed in my
book before my discontented neighbour put his head, pipe and
all, into my face to say: —

"Esher, sir! We have been twenty minutes coming from
Kingston Junction — twen-ty minutes! I ask you, sir, is it
not shameful?"

"Doubtless; I have not noticed."

"Not noticed, sir! Perhaps you've an objection to fast
travelling?"

"I — I don't think we've been sitting in the same train.

I was just thinking how agreeable it was to be carried in one minute from Rimini to the Hellespont, only to see Hero and Leander."

"Oh, where next ? "

"Why, sir," I said, turning a leaf or two, "my next station, I see, is in Sherwood Forest; I am to stop there to make friends with Robin Hood."

"The writer of that book drives a long excursion-train. I wouldn't mind a word with Robin Hood myself, God bless him! but, as for your poets, I hate them all; they tie their English into knots, and want a mile of it — knots and all — to say 'Fine weather for the ducks,' as, truly, it is this morning — Ugh!"

"I say nothing of that, sir; I have nothing just now in my mind except this book of stories — which is just a book of stories, all of them good ones, written in such verse as may be read by rich and poor with almost equal pleasure. They are only told in verse in order that the music may give force and beauty to the sense; read them or print them how you will, you cannot destroy their music or convict them of being by a syllable too wordy; they discharge their burden in plain sentences, without even going out of their way to avoid expressions common in the mouths of the people. Every picture in them is poetical in its conception, and in its expression musical. There is nothing far-fetched — there is no mystification; these are just stories in verse which may be enjoyed by the entire mass of the people. There is even as little as possible of simple meditation in them, though that would have been welcome from the mind of a pure-hearted man, beloved of poets in his youth and in his prime, now worthy to be loved of all mankind. Of him there are fewer to speak ill than even of Robin Hood, when not a soul in Locksley town would speak him an ill word; the friars raged; but no man's tongue nor even feature stirred; except among a very few, who dined in the abbey halls; and then with a sigh bold Robin knew his true friends from his false." I was not talking or reading to my neighbour with the pipe. I do not know at what stage of my discourse or meditation I had left my hold upon his ear. I had been thinking about Leigh Hunt to myself, and went on reading to myself of those unfaithful comrades, Roger the monk, and Midge, on whom Robin had never turned his face

but tenderly; with one or two, they say, besides — Lord! that
in this life's dream men should abandon one true thing, that
would abide with them.

> "We cannot bid our strength remain,
>   Our cheeks continue round ;
> We cannot say to an aged back,
>   Stoop not towards the ground:

> "We cannot bid our dim eyes see
>   Things as bright as ever,
> Nor tell our friends, though friends from youth,
>   That they 'll forsake us never:

> "But we can say, I never will,
>   False world, be false for thee:
> And oh, Sound Truth and Old Regard,
>   Nothing shall part us three."

"Woking Junction! Woking! Passengers for Guildford,
Godalming, and Alton, change here!"

I did not change there, but sat reading the brave legend of
the knight who cured a lady of disdain by doing battle in a
shift against three warriors in steel — a story with a pure and
tender moral for the innocent, the noble, and the wise.   And
when the train was off again I was not travelling by train at
all, but humming to myself — "The palfrey goes, the palfrey
goes, merrily well the palfrey goes; he carrieth laughter, he
carrieth woes, yet merrily ever the palfrey goes."   For I was
reading then of Sir Grey and Sir Guy, the proper old boys,
who met with a world of coughing and noise, to mar young
love like mine and Lucy Jane's.   Oh, if we had but a horse
that could in our behalf take, like the palfrey, vigorous
courses!   Well, but never mind that.   The palfrey carried me
merrily well to Farnborough, where there was a great tourna-
ment with lions in the presence of King Francis, and a knight
taught vanity a lesson.   The rest of the journey was a feast of
little stories.   I was shown what passed between Abou-ben-
Adhem and the Angel, told how the brave Mondeer, in spite
of the Sultan's order that no man should praise the dead Jaffàr,
stood forth in Bagdad daily in the square where once had stood
a happy house, and there harangued the tremblers at the
scimitar on all they owed to the divine Jaffàr.   "Bring me
this man," the caliph cried.   The man was brought — was
gazed upon — the mutes began to bind his arms.   "Welcome,

brave cords!" cried he; "from bonds far worse Jaffàr delivered
me; from wants, from shames, from loveless household fears;
made a man's eyes friends with delicious tears; restored me —
loved me — put me on a par with his great self. How can I
pay Jaffàr?" Haroun, who felt that on a soul like this the
mightiest vengeance could but fall amiss, now deigned to smile,
as one great lord of fate might smile upon another half as
great. He said, "Let worth grow frenzied if it will; the
caliph's judgment shall be master still. Go: and since gifts
thus move thee, take this gem, the richest in the Tartar's
diadem, and hold the giver as thou deemest fit." "Gifts!"
cried the friend. He took; and holding it high tow'rds the
heavens, as though to meet his star, exclaimed, "This, too, I
owe to thee, Jaffàr!"

More stories, as full of pleasant wit and noble feeling, were
told me after this; and when we got to Basingstoke, where
my neighbour swore a good deal at a crowd of market people
who had blocked him (and I suppose me) up with huge baskets and wet umbrellas, I had been introduced to Chaucer, and
was riding on the brazen horse of Cambus Khan. The brazen
horse which in a day and night, through the dark half as safely
as the light, o'er sea and land, and with your perfect ease, can
bear your body wheresoe'er you please. (It matters not if
skies be foul or fair; the thing is like a thought, and cuts the
air so smoothly, and so well observes the track, the man that
will may sleep upon his back.) This brazen horse, I say, suddenly dropped me at Southampton. There were some stories
told by the Italian poets told again in English waiting to be
heard, Dante's own Paulo and Francesca; his story of Ugolino;
Ariosto's Medora and Cloridano. I was vexed that I had
reached my journey's end, and must in that day read no more;
began to observe with surprise that it was raining; to look for
the first time at some of my departing fellow-passengers; to
resent the smell of my neighbour's bad tobacco, that impreg-
nated my clothes; to think about my carpet-bag, and all my
troubles; not resenting them, because my book had turned me
to a brave endurance of the troubles of this world, with, I
believe, the sole exception of the smell of stale tobacco. I
had made two journeys at one time, by packing off my body
as a parcel to Southampton, while all the rest of me, having
paid a trifling sum for a perpetual ticket (which I shall take

heed to keep by me), set out in company with a right genial and noble story-teller to Parnassus. Nevertheless, there was the whole of me at Heavahoy's when wanted; and I am happy to say that from the counting-house of that substantial firm I date the present communication. I have told a plain traveller's tale about traveller's tales, which, as the teller of them hopes, will be read and shown to one another by travellers who are descendants of those travellers about whom Chaucer discoursed: men who beguiled each other's way with tales as they rode side by side on horseback, while yet all horses in existence were of flesh and blood.

XXII

OUT OF TOWN

SITTING, on a bright September morning, among my books and papers at my open window on the cliff overhanging the sea-beach, I have the sky and ocean framed before me like a beautiful picture. A beautiful picture, but with such movement in it, such changes of light upon the sails of ships and wake of steamboats, such dazzling gleams of silver far out at sea, such fresh touches on the crisp wave-tops as they break and roll towards me — a picture with such music in the billowy rush upon the shingle, the blowing of the morning wind through the corn-sheaves where the farmers' wagons are busy, the singing of the larks, and the distant voices of children at play — such charms of sight and sound as all the galleries on earth can but poorly suggest.

So dreamy is the murmur of the sea below my window, that I may have been here, for anything I know, one hundred years. Not that I have grown old, for, daily on the neighbouring downs and grassy hillsides, I find that I can still in reason walk any distance, jump over anything, and climb up anywhere; but that the sound of the ocean seems to have become so customary to my musings, and other realities seem so to have gone aboard ship and floated away over the horizon, that, for aught I will undertake to the contrary, I am the enchanted son of the king my father, shut up in a tower on the seashore, for protection against an old she-goblin who insisted on being my godmother, and who foresaw at the font — wonderful creature! — that I should get into a scrape before I was twenty-one. I remember to have been in a city (my royal parent's dominions, I suppose), and apparently not long ago either, that was in the dreariest condition. The principal inhabitants had all been changed into old newspapers, and in that form were preserving their window-blinds from dust, and wrapping all their smaller household gods in curl-papers. I walked through gloomy streets where every house was shut up and newspapered, and where my solitary footsteps echoed on the deserted pavements. In the public rides there were no carriages, no horses, no animated existence, but a few sleepy policemen, and a few adventurous boys taking advantage of the devastation to swarm up the lamp-post. In the westward streets there was no traffic; in the westward shops, no business. The water-patterns which the 'prentices had trickled out on the pavements early in the morning remained uneffaced by human feet. At the corners of mews, Cochin-China fowls stalked gaunt and savage; nobody being left in the deserted city (as it appeared to me) to feed them. Public-houses, where splendid footmen swinging their legs over gorgeous hammer-cloths beside wigged coachmen were wont to regale, were silent, and the unused pewter pots shone, too bright for business, on the shelves. I beheld a Punch's Show leaning against a wall near Park Lane, as if it had fainted. It was deserted, and there were none to heed its desolation. In Belgrave Square I met the last man — an ostler — sitting on a post in a ragged red waistcoat, eating straw, and mildewing away.

If I recollect the name of the little town on whose shore this sea is murmuring, — but I am not just now, as I have premised, to be relied upon for anything, — it is Pavilionstone. Within a quarter of a century it was a little fishing town, and they do say that the time was when it was a little smuggling town. I have heard that it was rather famous in the hollands and brandy way, and that coevally with that reputation the lamplighter's was considered a bad life at the assurance offices. It was observed that if he were not particular about lighting up, he lived in peace; but that if he made the best of the oil-lamps in the steep and narrow streets, he usually fell over the cliff at an early age. Now, gas and electricity run to the very water's edge, and the South Eastern Railway Company screech at us in the dead of night.

But the old little fishing and smuggling town remains, and is so tempting a place for the latter purpose, that I think of going out some night next week, in a fur cap and a pair of petticoat trousers, and running an empty tub, as a kind of archæological pursuit. Let nobody with corns come to Pavilionstone, for there are breakneck flights of ragged steps, connecting the principal streets by back ways, which will cripple that visitor in half an hour. These are the ways by which, when I run that tub, I shall escape. I shall make a Ther·

mopylæ of the corner of one of them, defend it with my cutlass against the coast-guard until my brave companions have sheered off, then dive into the darkness, and regain my Susan's arms. In connection with these breakneck steps I observe some wooden cottages, with tumble-down out-houses, and back-yards three feet square, adorned with garlands of dried fish, in which (though the General Board of Health might object) my Susan dwells.

The South Eastern Company have brought Pavilionstone into such vogue, with their tidal trains and splendid steam-packets, that a new Pavilionstone is rising up. I am, myself, of New Pavilionstone. We are a little mortary and limy at present, but we are getting on capitally. Indeed, we were getting on so fast, at one time, that we rather overdid it, and built a street of shops, the business of which may be expected to arrive in about ten years. We are sensibly laid out in general; and with a little care and pains (by no means wanting, so far) shall become a very pretty place. We ought to be, for our situation is delightful, our air is delicious, and our breezy hills and downs, carpeted with wild thyme, and decorated with millions of wild flowers, are, on the faith of a pedestrian, perfect. In New Pavilionstone we are a little too much addicted to small windows with more bricks in them than glass, and we are not over-fanciful in the way of decorative architecture, and we get unexpected sea-views through cracks in the street doors; on the whole, however, we are very snug and comfortable, and well accommodated. But the Home Secretary (if there be such an officer) cannot too soon shut up the burial-ground of the old parish church. It is in the midst of us, and Pavilionstone will get no good of it if it be too long left alone.

The lion of Pavilionstone is its Great Hotel. A dozen years ago, going over to Paris by South Eastern Tidal Steamer, you used to be dropped upon the platform of the main line Pavilionstone Station (not a junction then), at eleven o'clock on a dark winter's night, in a roaring wind; and in the howling wilderness outside the station was a short omnibus which brought you up by the forehead the instant you got in at the door; and nobody cared about you, and you were alone in the world. You bumped over infinite chalk until you were turned out at a strange building which had just left off being a barn

without having quite begun to be a house, where nobody
expected your coming, or knew what to do with you when
you were come, and where you were usually blown about, until
you happened to be blown against the cold beef, and finally
into bed. At five in the morning you were blown out of bed,
and after a dreary breakfast, with crumpled company, in the
midst of confusion, were hustled on board a steamboat and lay
wretched on deck until you saw France lunging and surging at
you with great vehemence over the bowsprit.

Now you come down to Pavilionstone in a free-and-easy
manner, an irresponsible agent, made over in trust to the
South Eastern Company, until you get out of the railway-car-
riage at high-water mark. If you are crossing by the boat at
once, you have nothing to do but walk on board and be happy
there if you can — I can't. If you are going to our Great
Pavilionstone Hotel, the sprightliest porters under the sun,
whose cheerful looks are a pleasant welcome, shoulder your
luggage, drive it off in vans, bowl it away in trucks, and enjoy
themselves in playing athletic games with it. If you are for
public life at our Great Pavilionstone Hotel, you walk into
that establishment as if it were your club; and find ready
for you your news-room, dining-room, smoking-room, billiard-
room, music-room, public breakfast, public dinner twice a day
(one plain, one gorgeous), hot baths and cold baths. If you
want to be bored, there are plenty of bores always ready for
you, and from Saturday to Monday in particular, you can be
bored (if you like it) through and through. Should you want
to be private at our Great Pavilionstone Hotel, say but the
word, look at the list of charges, choose your floor, name your
figure — there you are, established in your castle, by the day,
week, month, or year, innocent of all comers or goers, unless
you have my fancy for walking early in the morning down the
groves of boots and shoes, which so regularly flourish at all the
chamber doors before breakfast, that it seems to me as if
nobody ever got up or took them in. Are you going across
the Alps, and would you like to air your Italian at our Great
Pavilionstone Hotel? Talk to the Manager — always conversational, accomplished, and polite. Do you want to be aided,
abetted, comforted, or advised, at our Great Pavilionstone
Hotel? Send for the good landlord, and he is your friend.
Should you or any one belonging to you ever be taken ill at

our Great Pavilionstone Hotel you will not soon forget him or
his kind wife. And when you pay your bill at our Great
Pavilionstone Hotel, you will not be put out of humour by
anything you find in it. A thoroughly good inn, in the days of coaching and posting,
was a noble place. But no such inn would have been equal
to the reception of four or five hundred people, all of them
wet through, and half of them dead sick, every day in the
year. This is where we shine, in our Pavilionstone Hotel.
Again — who, coming and going, pitching and tossing, boating
and training, hurrying in, and flying out, could ever have
calculated the fees to be paid at an old-fashioned house? In
our Pavilionstone Hotel vocabulary, there is no such word as
fee. Everything is done for you; every service is provided
at a fixed and reasonable charge; all the prices are hung up in
all the rooms; and you can make out your own bill beforehand as well as the book-keeper.

In the case of your being a pictorial artist, desirous of studying at small expense the physiognomies and beards of different
nations, come, on receipt of this, to Pavilionstone. You shall
find all the nations of the earth, and all the styles of shaving
and not shaving, hair-cutting and hair letting alone, for ever
flowing through our hotel. Couriers you shall see by hundreds; fat leathern bags for five-franc pieces, closing with
violent snaps, like discharges of fire-arms, by thousands; more
luggage in a morning than, fifty years ago, all Europe saw in
a week. Looking at trains, steamboats, sick travellers, and
luggage, is our great Pavilionstone recreation. We are not
strong in other public amusements. We have a Literary and
Scientific Institution, and we have a Working Men's Institution, — may it hold many gipsy holidays in summer fields, with
the kettle boiling, the band of music playing, and the people
dancing; and may I be on the hillside, looking on with pleasure at a wholesome sight too rare in England! — and we have
two or three churches, and more chapels than I have yet added
up. But public amusements are scarce with us. If a poor
theatrical manager comes with his company to give us, in a
loft, Mary Bax, or the Murder on the Sand Hills, we don't
care much for him — starve him out, in fact. We take more
kindly to wax-work, especially if it moves; in which case it
keeps much clearer of the second commandment than when it

is still. Cooke's Circus (Mr. Cooke is my friend, and always leaves a good name behind him) gives us only a night in passing through. Nor does the travelling menagerie think us worth a longer visit. It gave us a look-in the other day, bringing with it the residentiary van with the stained glass windows, which her Majesty kept ready-made at Windsor Castle until she found a suitable opportunity of submitting it for the proprietor's acceptance. I brought away five wonderments from this exhibition. I have wondered ever since, Whether the beasts ever do get used to those small places of confinement; Whether the monkeys have that very horrible flavour in their free state; Whether wild animals have a natural ear for time and tune, and therefore every four-footed creature began to howl in despair when the band began to play; What the giraffe does with his neck when his cart is shut up; and, Whether the elephant feels ashamed of himself when he is brought out of his den to stand on his head in the presence of the whole Collection.

We are a tidal harbour at Pavilionstone, as indeed I have implied already in my mention of tidal trains. At low water, we are a heap of mud, with an empty channel in it where a couple of men in big boots always shovel and scoop; with what exact object, I am unable to say. At that time, all the stranded fishing-boats turn over on their sides, as if they were dead marine monsters; the colliers and other shipping stick disconsolate in the mud; the steamers look as if their white chimneys would never smoke more, and their red paddles never turn again; the green sea-slime and weed upon the rough stones at the entrance seem records of obsolete high tides never more to flow; the flagstaff-halyards droop; the very little wooden lighthouse shrinks in the idle glare of the sun. And here I may observe of the very little wooden lighthouse, that when it is lighted at night — red and green — it looks so like a medical man's, that several distracted husbands have at various times been found, on occasions of premature domestic anxiety, going round and round it, trying to find the nightbell.

But the moment the tide begins to make, the Pavilionstone Harbour begins to revive. It feels the breeze of the rising water before the water comes, and begins to flutter and stir. When the little shallow waves creep in, barely over-lapping one another, the vanes at the mast-heads wake, and become agitated. As the tide rises, the fishing-boats get into good spirits and dance, the flagstaff hoists a bright red flag, the steamboat smokes, cranes creak, horses and carriages dangle in the air, stray passengers and luggage appear. Now the shipping is afloat, and comes up buoyantly, to look at the wharf. Now the carts that have come down for coals load away as hard as they can load. Now the steamer smokes immensely, and occasionally blows at the paddle-boxes like a vaporous whale — greatly disturbing nervous loungers. Now both the tide and the breeze have risen, and you are holding your hat on (if you want to see how the ladies hold *their* hats on, with a stay, passing over the broad brim and down the nose, come to Pavilionstone). Now everything in the harbour splashes, dashes, and bobs. Now the Down Tidal Train is telegraphed, and you know (without knowing how you know) that two hundred and eighty-seven people are coming. Now the fishing-boats that have been out sail in at the top of the tide. Now the bell goes, and the locomotive hisses and shrieks, and the train comes gliding in, and the two hundred and eighty-seven come scuffling out. Now there is not only a tide of water, but a tide of people, and a tide of luggage — all tumbling and flowing and bouncing about together. Now after infinite bustle, the steamer steams out, and we (on the pier) are all delighted when she rolls as if she would roll her funnel out, and are all disappointed when she don't. Now the other steamer is coming in, and the Custom-House prepares, and the wharf-labourers assemble, and the hawsers are made ready, and the hotel porters come rattling down with van and truck, eager to begin more Olympic games with more luggage. And this is the way in which we go on, down at Pavilionstone, every tide. And if you want to live a life of luggage, or to see it lived, or to breathe sweet air which will send you to sleep at a moment's notice at any period of the day or night, or to disport yourself upon or in the sea, or to scamper about Kent, or to come out of town for the enjoyment of all or any of these pleasures, come to Pavilionstone.

XXIII

A NIGHTLY SCENE IN LONDON

On the fifth of last November, I, the Conductor of this journal, accompanied by a friend well known to the public, accidentally strayed into Whitechapel. It was a miserable evening; very dark, very muddy, and raining hard.

There are many woeful sights in that part of London, and it has been well known to me in most of its aspects for many years. We had forgotten the mud and rain in slowly walking along and looking about us, when we found ourselves, at eight o'clock, before the Workhouse.

Crouched against the wall of the Workhouse, in the dark street, on the muddy pavement-stones, with the rain raining upon them, were five bundles of rags. They were motionless, and had no resemblance to the human form. Five great bee-hives, covered with rags, — five dead bodies taken out of graves, tied neck and heels, and covered with rags, — would have looked like those five bundles upon which the rain rained down in the public street.

"What is this!" said my companion. "What *is* this!"

"Some miserable people shut out of the Casual Ward, I think," said I.

We had stopped before the five ragged mounds, and were quite rooted to the spot by their horrible appearance. Five awful Sphinxes by the wayside, crying to every passer-by, "Stop and guess! What is to be the end of a state of society that leaves us here!"

As we stood looking at them, a decent working man, having the appearance of a stone-mason, touched me on the shoulder.

"This is an awful sight, sir," said he, "in a Christian country!"

"God knows it is, my friend," said I.

"I have often seen it much worse than this, as I have been going home from my work. I have counted fifteen, twenty, five and twenty, many a time. It's a shocking thing to see."

"A shocking thing, indeed," said I and my companion

together. The man lingered near us a little while, wished us good night, and went on.

We should have felt it brutal in us who had a better chance of being heard than the working man to leave the thing as it was, so we knocked at the Workhouse Gate. I undertook to be spokesman. The moment the gate was opened by an old pauper I went in, followed close by my companion. I lost no time in passing the old porter, for I saw in his watery eye a disposition to shut us out.

"Be so good as to give that card to the master of the Workhouse, and say I shall be glad to speak to him for a moment."

We were in a kind of covered gateway, and the old porter went across it with the card. Before he had got to a door on our left, a man in a cloak and hat bounced out of it very sharply, as if he were in the nightly habit of being bullied and of returning the compliment.

"Now, gentlemen," said he, in a loud voice, "what do you want here?"

"First," said I, "will you do me the favour to look at that card in your hand. Perhaps you may know my name."

"Yes," says he, looking at it. "I know this name."

"Good. I only want to ask you a plain question in a civil manner, and there is not the least occasion for either of us to be angry. It would be very foolish in me to blame you, and I don't blame you. I may find fault with the system you administer, but pray understand that I know you are here to do a duty pointed out to you, and that I have no doubt you do it. Now, I hope you won't object to tell me what I wan to know."

"No," said he, quite mollified, and very reasonable, "not at all. What is it?"

"Do you know that there are five wretched creatures outside?"

"I haven't seen them, but I dare say there are."

"Do you doubt that there are?"

"No, not at all. There might be many more."

"Are they men? Or women?"

"Women, I suppose. Very likely one or two of them were there last night, and the night before last."

"There all night, do you mean?"

"Very likely."

My companion and I looked at one another, and the master of the Workhouse added quickly, "Why, Lord bless my soul, what am I to do? What can I do? The place is full. The place is always full — every night. I must give the preference to women with children, must n't I? You would n't have me not do that?"

"Surely not," said I. "It is a very humane principle, and quite right; and I am glad to hear of it. Don't forget that I don't blame *you.*"

"Well!" said he. And subdued himself again.

"What I want to ask you," I went on, "is whether you know anything against those five miserable beings outside?"

"Don't know anything about them," said he, with a wave of his arm.

"I ask, for this reason: that we mean to give them a trifle to get a lodging — if they are not shelterless because they are thieves for instance. — You don't know them to be thieves?"

"I don't know anything about them," he repeated emphatically.

"That is to say, they are shut out, solely because the Ward is full?"

"Because the Ward is full."

"And if they got in, they would only have a roof for the night and a bit of bread in the morning, I suppose?"

"That's all. You 'll use your own discretion about what you give them. Only understand that I don't know anything about them beyond what I have told you."

"Just so. I wanted to know no more. You have answered my question civilly and readily, and I am much obliged to you. I have nothing to say against you, but quite the contrary. Good night!"

"Good night, gentlemen!" And out we came again.

We went to the ragged bundle nearest to the Workhouse door, and I touched it. No movement replying, I gently shook it. The rags began to be slowly stirred within, and by little and little a head was unshrouded. The head of a young woman of three or four and twenty, as I should judge; gaunt with want, and foul with dirt, but not naturally ugly.

"Tell us," said I, stooping down. "Why are you lying here?"

"Because I can't get into the Workhouse."

She spoke in a faint dull way, and had no curiosity or interest left. She looked dreamily at the black sky and the falling
rain, but never looked at me or my companion.

"Were you here last night?"

"Yes. All last night. And the night afore too."

"Do you know any of these others?"

"I know her next but one. She was here last night, and
she told me she come out of Essex. I don't know no more
of her."

"You were here all last night, but you have not been here
all day?"

"No. Not all day."

"Where have you been all day?"

"About the streets."

"What have you had to eat?"

"Nothing."

"Come!" said I. "Think a little. You are tired and
have been asleep, and don't quite consider what you are saying
to us. You have had something to eat to-day. Come! Think
of it!"

"No, I haven't. Nothing but such bits as I could pick
up about the market. *Why, look at me!*"

She bared her neck, and I covered it up again.

"If you had a shilling to get some supper and a lodging,
should you know where to get it?"

"Yes. I could do that."

"For God's sake get it, then!"

I put the money into her hand, and she feebly rose up and
went away. She never thanked me, never looked at me —
melted away into the miserable night, in the strangest manner
I ever saw. I have seen many strange things, but not one
that has left a deeper impression on my memory than the dull
impassive way in which that worn-out heap of misery took that
piece of money, and was lost.

One by one I spoke to all the five. In every one, interest
and curiosity were as extinct as in the first. They were all
dull and languid. No one made any sort of profession or
complaint; no one cared to look at me; no one thanked me.
When I came to the third, I suppose she saw that my companion and I glanced, with a new horror upon us, at the two
last, who had dropped against each other in their sleep, and

were lying like broken images. She said she believed they were young sisters. These were the only words that were originated among the five.

And now let me close this terrible account with a redeeming and beautiful trait of the poorest of the poor. When we came out of the Workhouse, we had gone across the road to a public-house, finding ourselves without silver, to get change for a sovereign. I held the money in my hand while I was speaking to the five apparitions. Our being so engaged attracted the attention of many people of the very poor sort usual to that place; as we leaned over the mounds of rags, they eagerly leaned over us to see and hear; what I had in my hand, and what I said, and what I did, must have been plain to nearly all the concourse. When the last of the five had got up and faded away, the spectators opened to let us pass; and not one of them, by word, or look, or gesture, begged of us. Many of the observant faces were quick enough to know that it would have been a relief to us to have got rid of the rest of the money with any hope of doing good with it. But there was a feeling among them all, that their necessities were not to be placed by the side of such a spectacle; and they opened a way for us in profound silence, and let us go.

My companion wrote to me, next day, that the five ragged bundles had been upon his bed all night. I debated how to add our testimony to that of many other persons who from time to time are impelled to write to the newspapers, by having come upon some shameful and shocking sight of this description. I resolved to write in these pages an exact account of what we had seen, but to wait until after Christ-mas, in order that there might be no heat or haste. I know that the unreasonable disciples of a reasonable school, demented disciples who push arithmetic and political economy beyond all bounds of sense (not to speak of such a weakness as human-ity), and hold them to be all-sufficient for every case, can easily prove that such things ought to be, and that no man has any business to mind them. Without disparaging those indispen-sable sciences in their sanity, I utterly renounce and abomi-nate them in their insanity; and I address people with a respect for the spirit of the New Testament, who do mind such things, and who think them infamous in our streets.

XXIV

PROPOSALS FOR A NATIONAL JEST-BOOK

IT has been ascertained, within the last two years, that Britannia is in want of nothing but an official joker. Having such exalted officer to poke her in the ribs when she considers her condition serious, and to put her off with a wink when she utters a groan, she must certainly be flourishing, and it shall be heresy to doubt the fact. By this sign ye shall know it.

My patriotism and my national pride have been so warmed by the discovery, that, following out the great idea, I have reduced to writing a scheme for the re-establishment of the obsolete office of Court Joker. It would be less expensive to maintain than a First Lord of the Jokery, and might lead to the discovery of better jokes than issue from that Department. My scheme is an adaptation of a plan I matured some years ago, for the revival of the office of Lord Mayor's Fool; a design which, I am authorised to mention, would have been adopted by the City of London, but for that eminent body, the Common Council, agreeing to hold the office in Commission, and to satisfy the public, in all their Addresses to great personages, that they are never unmindful of its comic duties.

It is not, however, of either of these ingenious proposals (if I may be permitted to call them so) that I now desire to treat. It is of another, and far more comprehensive project for the compilation of a National Jest-Book.

Few people, I submit, can fail to have observed what rich materials for such a collection are constantly being strewn about. The parliamentary debates, the audiences given to deputations at the public offices, the proceedings of Courts of Inquiry, the published correspondence of distinguished personages, teem with the richest humour. Is it not a reproach to us, as a humorous nation, that we have no recognised Encyclopædia of these facetious treasures, which may be preserved, and (in course of time) catalogued, by Signor Panizzi in the British Museum?

What I propose is, that a learned body of not fewer than

forty members, each to receive two thousand five hundred pounds per annum, free of Income Tax, and the whole to be chosen from the younger sons, nephews, cousins, and cousin-germans, of the aristocracy, be immediately appointed in perpetuity for the compilation of a National Jest-Book. That in these appointments, the preference shall be given to those young noblemen and gentlemen who know the least of the subject, and that every care shall be taken to exclude qualified persons. That the First Lord of the Jokery be, in right of his office, the president of this Board, and that in his patronage the appointments shall rest. That it shall meet as seldom as it thinks proper. That no one shall be a quorum. That on the first of April in every year, this learned society shall publish an annual volume, in imperial quarto, of the "National Jest-Book," price ten pounds.

I foresee that I shall be met at this point by the objection that the proposed price is high, and that the sale of the "National Jest-Book" will not remunerate the country for the cost of its production. But this objection will instantly vanish when I proceed to state that it is one of my leading ideas to make this gem of books the source of an immense addition to the public revenue, by passing an act of Parliament to render it compulsory on all householders, rated to the relief of the poor in the annual value of twenty-five pounds, to take a copy. The care of this measure I would entrust to Mr. Frederick Peel, the distinguished Under-Secretary for War, whose modest talents, conciliatory demeanour, and remarkable success in quartering soldiers on all the private families of Scotland, particularly point him out as the statesman for the purpose.

As the living languages are not much esteemed in the public schools frequented by the superior classes, and as it might be on the whole expedient to publish a national collection in the national tongue (though too common and accessible), it is probable that some revision of the labours of the learned Board would be necessary before any volume should be finally committed to the press. Such revision I would entrust to the Royal Literary Fund, finding it to have one professor of literature a member of its managing committee. It might not be amiss to embellish the first volume of the "National Jest-Book," with a view of that wealthy institution and with explanatory letter-press descriptive of its spending forty pounds in giving away a hundred; of its being governed by a council which can never meet nor be by any earthly power called together; of its boasted secrets touching the distresses of authors being officially accessible at all times, to more than one publisher; and of its being a neat example of a practical joke.

The style of the "National Jest-Book," in narrating those choice pieces of wit and humour of which it will be the storehouse, to be strictly limited (as everything in the United Kingdom of Great Britain and Ireland ought to be), by precedent. No departure from the established Jest-Book method to be sanctioned on any account. If the good old style were sufficient for our forefathers, it is sufficient for the present and all future generations. In my desire to render these proposals plain, complete, and practical, I proceed to offer some specimens of the manner in which the "National Jest-Book" will require to be conducted.

As in the precedents there is a supposititious personage, by name Tom Brown, upon whom witty observations are fathered which there is a difficulty in fastening on any one else, so, in the National Collection, it will be indispensable to introduce a similar fiction. I propose that a certain imaginary Mr. Bull be established as the Tom Brown of the National Collection.

Let us suppose, for example, that the learned Board, in pursuing their labours for the present year one thousand eight hundred and fifty-six, were reducing to writing the National Jests of the month of April. They would proceed according to the following example.

BULL AND THE M. P.

A waggish Member of Parliament, when vaccination had been introduced by Dr. Jenner upwards of half a century, and had saved innumerable thousands of people from premature death, from suffering, and from disfigurement, — as, down to that time, had been equally well known to wise men and fools, — rose in his place in the House of Commons and denounced it forsooth. "For," says he, "it is a failure, and the cause of death." One meeting Mr. Bull and telling him of this pretty speech, and further of its eliciting from that astonishing assembly no demonstration, "Ay," cries Bull, looking mighty grave, "but if the Member for Nineveh had mistaken, in that same place, the Christian name of a Cornet in the Guards, you should have had howling enough!"

Again, another example.

BULL AND THE BISHOP

A certain Bishop who was officially a learned priest and a devout, but who was individually either imbecile or an abusive and indecent common fellow, printed four letters wherein he called folks by bad names, as devils, liars, and the like. A Cambridge man, meeting Bull, asked him of what family this Bishop was and to whom he was related. "Nay, I know not," cries Bull, "but I take my oath he is neither of the line of the Apostles, nor descends from their Master." — "How, now," quoth the Cambridge man, "hath he no connection with the fishermen?" — "He hath the connection that Billingsgate hath with fishermen, and no other," says Bull. "But," quoth the Cambridge man again, "I understand him to be great in the dead tongues." — "He may be that too," says Bull, "and yet be small in the living ones, for he can neither write his own tongue nor yet hold it."

Sometimes it would be necessary, as in the Tom Brown precedents, to represent Bull in the light of being innocently victimised, and as not possessing that readiness which characterises him in the foregoing models. The learned body forming the National Collection would then adopt the following plan.

BULL GOT THE BETTER OF

Bull, riding once from market on a stout Galloway nag, was met upon the Tiverton highway by a footpad in a soldier's coat (an old hand), who rifled him of all he carried and jeered him besides, saying, "A fig for you. I can wind you round my finger, I can pull your nose any day" — and doing it, too, contemptuously, while he spoke, so that he brought the blood mounting into Bull's cheeks. "Prithee tell me," says Bull pacifically, "why do you want my money?" — "For the vigorous prosecution of your war against the birds of prey," replies the fellow, with his tongue in his cheek, who indeed had been hired by Bull to scare those vermin, just when the farm-traps and blunderbusses had been found to be horribly out of order,

and were beginning to be put right. For which he now took
all the credit. "But what have you done?" asks Bull.
"Never *you* mind," says the fellow, tweaking him by the nose
again. "You have not made one good shot in any direction
that I know of," cries Bull; "is *that* vigorous prosecution?"
— "Yes," cries the fellow, tweaking him by the nose again.
"You have discomfited me the best and bravest boys I sent
into the field," says Bull; "is *that* vigorous prosecution?"
— "Yes," cries the fellow, tweaking him by the nose again.
"You have brought down upon my head the heaviest and
shamefullest book with a blue cover (called the Fall of Kars)
in all my library," says Bull; "is *that* vigorous prosecution?"
— "Yes," says the fellow, tweaking him by the nose again.
"Then," whispers Bull to his Galloway nag, as he gave him
the rein, "you and I had better jog along feebly, for it should
seem to be the only true way of prospering." And so sneaked
off.

Occasionally, the learned body would resort to the dialogue
form, for variety's sake. As thus: throughout these instances,
I suppose them engaged with the compilation for the month
of April in the present year.

DIALOGUE BETWEEN BULL AND A PERSON OF QUALITY

PERSON OF Q. So, Bull, how dost?

BULL. My humble duty and service to your lordship, with
your lordship's gracious leave, — I am tolerable.

PERSON OF Q. The better for a firm, and durable, and
glorious peace; eh, Bull?

BULL. Humph!

PERSON OF Q. Why, what a curmudgeon art thou, Bull!
Dost thou begrudge the peace?

BULL. The Lord forbid! my humble duty and service to
your noble lordship. But I was thinking (by your lordship's
favour) how best to keep it.

PERSON OF Q. Be easy on that point. There shall be a
great standing army, and a great navy, and your relations and
friends shall have more than their share of the bad, doubtful,
and indifferent posts in both.

BULL. How as to the good posts, your honourable lord·
ship?

PERSON OF Q. Humph! (Laughing.)

BULL. Will your noble honour vouchsafe me a word?

PERSON OF Q. Quickly then, Bull, and don't be prosy. I can't abide being bored.

BULL. I humbly thank your noble honourable lordship for your noble honour's kind permission. Army and navy, I know, will both be necessary; but I was thinking (saving your noble lordship's gracious presence) that my good friends and allies, the people of France, can move in concert in large bodies, and are accustomed to the use of arms.

PERSON OF Q. (frowning). A military nation. None of that here, Bull, none of that here!

BULL. With your noble lordship's magnificent toleration, I would respectfully crave leave to scatter a few deferential syllables in the radiancy of your noble countenance. I find that this characteristic is not peculiar to my friends the French, but belongs, more or less, to all the peoples of Europe: whereof the English are the only people possessing the peculiarity of being quite untrained in the power of associating to defend themselves, their children, their women, and their native land. Will your noble honour's magnanimity bear with me if I represent that your noble lordship has, for some years now, discouraged the old British spirit, and disarmed the British hand? Your noble honour's game preserves and political sentiments have been the cause of —

PERSON OF Q. (interrupting). S'death, Bull, I am bored. Make an end of this.

BULL. With your honour's gracious attention, I will finish this minute. I was about to represent, with my humblest duty to your noble lordship, that if your honourable grace could find it in your benignity to take the occasion of this Peace to trust your countrymen a little — to show some greater confidence in their love of their country and their loyalty to their sovereign — to think more of the peasants and less of the pheasants, and if your worship's loftiness could deign to encourage the common English clay to become moulded into so much of a soldierly shape as would make it a rampart for the whole empire, and place the Englishman on an equality with the Frenchman, the Piedmontese, the German, the American, the Swiss, your noble honour would therein do a great right, timely, which you will otherwise, as certain as Death (if your

noble lordship will excuse that levelling word), at last conde-
scend to try to do in a hurry when it shall be too late.

PERSON OF Q. (yawning). Prithee get out, Bull. This
is revolutionary, and what not; and I am bored.

BULL. I humbly thank your noble lordship for your gracious attention. (And so, bowing low, retires, expressing his
high sense of the courtesy and patience with which he had had
the distinguished honour of being received.)

I shall conclude by offering one other example for the guidance of the learned Commission of forty compilers, which I
have no doubt will be appointed within a short time after the
publication of these suggestions. It is important, as introducing Mrs. Bull, and showing how she may be discreetly admitted
into the "National Jest-Book," on occasions, with the conjugal
object of eliciting Mr. Bull's best points.

MRS. BULL'S CURL-PAPERS

Bull, in this same month of April, takes it into his head
that he will make a trip to France. So away he goes, after
first repairing to the warehouse of honest Murray in Albemarle
Street, Piccadilly, to buy a guide-book, and travels with all
diligence both to Paris and Bordeaux. Suddenly, and while
Mrs. Bull supposeth him to be sojourning in the wine-growing
countries, not drinking water there you may be sure, lo, he
reappeareth at his own house in London, attended by a great
wagon filled with newspapers! Mrs. Bull, admiring to see so
many newspapers and those foreign, asks him why he hath
returned so soon and with that cargo? Saith Bull, "They are
French curl-papers for thy head, my dear." Mrs. Bull pro-
tests that in all her life she never can have need of a hundredth
part of that store. "Anyhow," saith Bull, "put them away
in the dark, housewife, for I am heartily ashamed of them." —
"Ashamed of them!" says she. "Yes," retorts Bull, "and
thus it is. While I was in France, sweetheart, a deputation
waited on the government in England, touching the duties on
foreign wines. And the French newspapers were so astounded
by the jokery with which the deputation was received, and by
the ignorance of the government, which was wrong in all its
statements (one of the best informed among them computes to
the extent, in one calculation, of seventeen hundred and fifty

pei cent.), that I was ashamed to see those journals lying about and bought up all I could find."

My project for a National Jest-Book is now before the public. I would merely remark, in conclusion, that if the revenue arising from the compulsory purchase of the collection should enable our enlightened government to dispense with the Income Tax, the public will be the gainers; inasmuch as the new impost will provide them with something tangible to show for their money.

XXV

OUT OF THE SEASON

IT fell to my lot, this last bleak spring, to find myself in a watering-place out of the season. A vicious northeast squall blew me into it from foreign parts, and I tarried in it alone for three days, resolved to be exceedingly busy.

On the first day I began business by looking for two hours at the sea, and staring the foreign militia out of countenance. Having disposed of these important engagements, I sat down at one of the two windows of my room, intent on doing something desperate in the way of literary composition, and writing a chapter of unheard-of excellence — with which the present essay has no connection.

It is a remarkable quality in a watering-place out of the season, that everything in it will and must be looked at. I had no previous suspicion of this fatal truth; but the moment I sat down to write, I began to perceive it. I had scarcely fallen into my most promising attitude, and dipped my pen in the ink, when I found the clock upon the pier — a red-faced clock with a white rim — importuning me in a highly vexatious manner to consult my watch, and see how I was off for Greenwich time. Having no intention of making a voyage or taking an observation, I had not the least need of Greenwich time, and could have put up with watering-place time as a sufficiently accurate article. The pier clock, however, persisting, I felt it necessary to lay down my pen, compare my watch with him, and fall into a grave solicitude about half seconds. I had taken up my pen again, and was about to commence that valuable chapter, when a Custom-House cutter under the window requested that I would hold a naval review of her immediately.

It was impossible, under the circumstances, for any mental resolution, merely human, to dismiss the Custom-House Cutter, because the shadow of her topmast fell upon my paper, and the vane played on the masterly blank chapter. I was therefore under the necessity of going to the other window; sitting astride of the chair there, like Napoleon bivouacking in the print, and inspecting the cutter as she lay, all that day, in the way of my chapter, O! She was rigged to carry a quantity of canvas, but her hull was so very small that four giants aboard of her (three men and a boy) who were vigilantly scraping at her, all together, inspired me with a terror lest they should scrape her away. A fifth giant, who appeared to consider himself "below," — as indeed he was, from the waist downwards, — meditated, in such close proximity with the little gusty chimney-pipe that he seemed to be smoking it. Several boys looked on from the wharf, and when the gigantic attention appeared to be fully occupied, one or other of these would furtively swing himself in mid-air over the Custom-House cutter, by means of a line pendent from her rigging, like a young spirit of the storm. Presently, a sixth hand brought down two little water-casks; presently afterwards, a truck came, and delivered a hamper. I was now under an obligation to consider that the cutter was going on a cruise, and to wonder where she was going, and when she was going, and why she was going, and at what date she might be expected back, and who commanded her? With these pressing questions I was fully occupied when the Packet, making ready to go across, and blowing off her spare steam, roared, "Look at me!"

It became a positive duty to look at the Packet preparing to go across; aboard of which, the people newly come down by the railroad were hurrying in a great fluster. The crew had got their tarry overalls on, — and one knew what *that* meant, — not to mention the white basins, ranged in neat little piles of a dozen each, behind the door of the after-cabin. One lady as I looked, one resigning and far-seeing woman, took her basin from the store of crockery as she might have taken a refreshment ticket, laid herself down on deck with that utensil at her ear, muffled her feet in one shawl, solemnly covered her countenance after the antique manner with another, and on the completion of these preparations appeared by the strength of her volition to become insensible. The mail-bags (O that I myself had the sea-legs of a mail-bag!) were tumbled aboard; the Packet left off roaring, warped out, and made at the white line upon the bar. One dip, one roll, one break of the sea over her bows, and Moore's Almanack or the sage Raphael could not have told me more of the state of things aboard than I knew.

The famous chapter was all but begun now, and would have been quite begun but for the wind. It was blowing stiffly from the east, and it rumbled in the chimney and shook the house. That was not much; but, looking out into the wind's grey eye for inspiration, I laid down my pen again to make the remark to myself, how emphatically everything by the sea declares that it has a great concern in the state of the wind. The trees blown all one way; the defences of the harbour reared highest and strongest against the raging point; the shingle flung up on the beach from the same direction; the number of arrows pointed at the common enemy; the sea tumbling in and rushing towards them as if it were inflamed by the sight. This put it in my head that I really ought to go out and take a walk in the wind; so I gave up the magnificent chapter for that day, entirely persuading myself that I was under a moral obligation to have a blow.

I had a good one, and that on the high road, — the very high road, — on the top of the cliffs, where I met the stage-coach with all the outsides holding their hats on and themselves too, and overtook a flock of sheep with the wool about their necks blown into such great ruffs that they looked like fleecy owls. The wind played upon the lighthouse as if it were a great whistle, the spray was driven over the sea in a cloud of haze, the ships rolled and pitched heavily, and at intervals long slants and flaws of light made mountain-steeps of communication between the ocean and the sky. A walk of ten miles brought me to a seaside town without a cliff, which, like the town I had come from, was out of the season too. Half of the houses were shut up; half of the other half were to let; the town might have done as much business as it was doing then if it had been at the bottom of the sea. Nobody seemed to flourish save the attorney; his clerk's pen was going in the bow-window of his wooden house; his brass door-plate alone was free from salt, and had been polished up that morning. On the beach, among the rough luggers and capstans, groups of storm-beaten boatmen, like a sort of marine monsters, watched under the lee of those objects, or stood leaning forward against the wind, looking out through battered spy-glasses. The parlour bell in the Admiral Benbow had grown so flat with being out of the season, that neither could I hear it ring when I pulled the handle for lunch, nor could the young woman in black stockings and strong shoes, who acted as waiter out of the season, until it had been tinkled three times. Admiral Benbow's cheese was out of the season, but his home-made bread was good, and his beer was perfect. Deluded by some earlier spring day which had been warm and sunny, the Admiral had cleared the firing out of his parlour stove, and had put some flower-pots in — which was amiable and hopeful in the Admiral, but not judicious; the room being, at that present visiting, transcendently cold. I therefore took the liberty of peeping out across a little stone passage into the Admiral's kitchen, and seeing a high settle with its back towards me drawn out in front of the Admiral's kitchen fire, I strolled in, bread and cheese in hand, munching and looking about. One landsman and two boatmen were seated on the settle, smoking pipes and drinking beer out of thick pint crockery mugs — mugs peculiar to such places, with parti-coloured rings round them, and ornaments between the rings like frayed-out roots. The landsman was relating his experience, as yet only three nights old, of a fearful running-down case in the Channel, and therein presented to my imagination a sound of music that it will not soon forget.

"At that identical moment of time," said he (he was a prosy man by nature, who rose with his subject), "the night being light and calm, but with a grey mist upon the water that did n't seem to spread for more than two or three mile, I was walking up and down the wooden causeway next the pier, off where it happened, along with a friend of mine, which his name is Mr. Clocker. Mr. Clocker is a grocer over yonder." (From the direction in which he pointed the bowl of his pipe, I might have judged Mr. Clocker to be a Merman, established in the grocery trade in five-and-twenty fathoms of water.) "We were smoking our pipes, and walking up and down the causeway, talking of one thing and talking of another. We were quite alone there, except that a few hovellers" (the Kentish name for 'longshore boatmen like his companions) "were hanging about their lugs, waiting while the tide made, as hovellers will." (One of the two boatmen, thoughtfully regarding me, shut up one eye; this I understood to mean: first, that he took me into the conversation; secondly, that he confirmed the proposition; thirdly, that he announced himself as a hoveller.) "All of a sudden Mr. Clocker and me stood:

rooted to the spot, by hearing a sound come through the still-ness, right over the sea, *like a great sorrowful flute or Æolian harp.* We did n't in the least know what it was, and judge of our surprise when we saw the hovellers, to a man, leap into the boats and tear about to hoist sail and get off, as if they had every one of 'em gone, in a moment, raving mad! But *they* knew it was the cry of distress from the sinking emigrant ship."

When I got back to my watering-place out of the season, and had done my twenty miles in good style, I found that the celebrated Black Mesmerist intended favouring the public that evening in the Hall of the Muses, which he had engaged for the purpose. After a good dinner, seated by the fire in an easy-chair, I began to waver in a design I had formed of wait-ing on the Black Mesmerist, and to incline towards the expe-diency of remaining where I was. Indeed, a point of gallantry was involved in my doing so, inasmuch as I had not left France alone, but had come from the prisons of St. Pélagie with my distinguished and unfortunate friend Madame Roland (in two volumes which I bought for two francs each, at the book-stall in the Place de la Concorde, Paris, at the corner of the Rue Royale). Deciding to pass the evening *tête-à-tête* with Madame Roland, I derived, as I always do, great pleasure from that spiritual woman's society, and the charms of her brave soul and engaging conversation. I must confess that if she had only some more faults, only a few more passionate fail-ings of any kind, I might love her better; but I am content to believe that the deficiency is in me, and not in her. We spent some sadly interesting hours together on this occasion, and she told me again of her cruel discharge from the Abbaye, and of her being re-arrested before her free feet had sprung lightly up half a dozen steps of her own staircase, and carried off to the prison which she only left for the guillotine.

Madame Roland and I took leave of one another before mid-night, and I went to bed full of vast intentions for next day, in connection with the unparalleled chapter. To hear the foreign mail-steamers coming in at dawn of day, and to know that I was not aboard or obliged to get up, was very comfort-able; so I rose for the chapter in great force.

I had advanced so far as to sit down at my window again on my second morning, and to write the first half line of the

chapter and strike it out, not liking it, when my conscience
reproached me with not having surveyed the watering-place out
of the season, after all, yesterday, but with having gone
straight out of it at the rate of four miles and a half an hour.
Obviously the best amends that I could make for this remiss-
ness was to go and look at it without another moment's delay.
So — altogether as a matter of duty — I gave up the magnificent chapter for another day, and sauntered out with my hands
in my pockets.

All the houses and lodgings ever let to visitors were to let
that morning. It seemed to have snowed bills with To Let
upon them. This put me upon thinking what the owners of
all those apartments did, out of the season; how they employed
their time, and occupied their minds. They could not be
always going to the Methodist chapels, of which I passed one
every other minute. They must have some other recreation.
Whether they pretended to take one another's lodgings, and
opened one another's tea-caddies in fun? Whether they cut
slices off their own beef and mutton, and made believe that
it belonged to somebody else? Whether they played little
dramas of life, as children do, and said, "I ought to come and
look at your apartments, and you ought to ask two guineas a
week too much, and then I ought to say I must have the rest
of the day to think of it, and then you ought to say that
another lady and gentleman with no children in family had
made an offer very close to your own terms, and you had
passed your word to give them a positive answer in half an
hour, and indeed were just going to take the bill down when
you heard the knock, and then I ought to take them you
know "? Twenty such speculations engaged my thoughts.
Then, after passing, still clinging to the walls, defaced rags of
the bills of last year's Circus, I came to a back field near a
timber-yard where the Circus itself had been, and where there
was yet a sort of monkish tonsure on the grass, indicating the
spot where the young lady had gone round upon her pet steed
Firefly in her daring flight. Turning into the town again, I
came among the shops, and they were emphatically out of the
season. The chemist had no boxes of ginger-beer powders,
no beautifying seaside soaps and washes, no attractive scents;
nothing but his great goggle-eyed red bottles, looking as if the
winds of winter and the drift of the salt sea had inflamed them.

The grocers' hot pickles, Harvey's Sauce, Doctor Kitchener's Zest, Anchovy Paste, Dundee Marmalade, and the whole stock of luxurious helps to appetite, were hibernating somewhere underground. The china-shop had no trifles from anywhere. The Bazaar had given in altogether, and presented a notice on the shutters that this establishment would re-open at Whitsuntide, and that the proprietor in the mean time might be heard of at Wild Lodge, East Cliff. At the Sea-Bathing Establishment, a row of neat little wooden houses seven or eight feet high, I *saw* the proprietor in bed in the shower-bath. As to the bathing-machines, they were (how they got there is not for me to say) at the top of a hill at least a mile and a half off. The library, which I had never seen otherwise than wide open, was tight shut; and two peevish bald old gentlemen seemed to be hermetically sealed up inside, eternally reading the paper. That wonderful mystery, the music-shop, carried it off as usual (except that it had more cabinet pianos in stock), as if season or no season were all one to it. It made the same prodigious display of bright brazen wind-instruments, horribly twisted, worth, as I should conceive, some thousands of pounds, and which it is utterly impossible that anybody in any season can ever play or want to play. It had five triangles in the window, six pairs of castanets, and three harps; likewise every polka with a coloured frontispiece that ever was published; from the original one where a smooth male and female Pole of high rank are coming at the observer with their arms akimbo to the Ratcatcher's Daughter. Astonishing establishment, amazing enigma! Three other shops were pretty much out of the season what they were used to be in it. First, the shop where they sell the sailors' watches, which had still the old collection of enormous timekeepers, apparently designed to break a fall from the mast-head; with places to wind them up, like fire-plugs. Secondly, the shop where they sell the sailors' clothing, which displayed the old sou'-westers, and the old oily suits, and the old pea-jackets, and the old one sea-chest, with its handles like a pair of rope ear-rings. Thirdly, the unchangeable shop for the sale of literature that has been left behind. Here, Dr. Faustus was still going down to very red and yellow perdition, under the superintendence of three green personages of a scaly humour, with excrescential serpents growing out of their blade-bones. Here, the Golden Dreamer and the Nor-

wood Fortune-Teller were still on sale at sixpence each, with
instructions for making the dumb cake, and reading destinies
in tea-cups, and with a picture of a young woman with a high
waist lying on a sofa in an attitude so uncomfortable as almost
to account for her dreaming at one and the same time of a conflagration, a shipwreck, an earthquake, a skeleton, a church-
porch, lightning, funerals performed, and a young man in a
bright blue coat and canary pantaloons. Here were Little
Warblers and Fairburn's Comic Songsters. Here, too, were
ballads on the old ballad paper and in the old confusion of
types; with an old man in a cocked hat, and an arm-chair, for
the illustration to Will Watch the bold Smuggler; and the
Friar of Orders Grey, represented by a little girl in a hoop,
with a ship in the distance. All these as of yore, when they
were infinite delights to me!

It took me so long fully to relish these many enjoyments,
that I had not more than an hour before bedtime to devote to
Madame Roland. We got on admirably together on the subject of her convent education, and I rose next morning with
the full conviction that the day for the great chapter was at
last arrived.

It had fallen calm, however, in the night, and as I sat at
breakfast I blushed to remember that I had not yet been on
the Downs. I a walker, and not yet on the Downs! Really,
on so quiet and bright a morning this must be set right. As
an essential part of the Whole Duty of Man, therefore, I left
the chapter to itself — for the present — and went on the
Downs. They were wonderfully green and beautiful, and gave
me a good deal to do. When I had done with the free air
and the view, I had to go down into the valley and look after
the hops (which I know nothing about), and to be equally
solicitous as to the cherry orchards. Then I took it on myself
to cross-examine a tramping family in black (mother alleged,
I have no doubt by herself in person, to have died last week),
and to accompany eighteenpence, which produced a great effect,
with moral admonitions which produced none at all. Finally,
it was late in the afternoon before I got back to the unprecedented chapter, and then I determined that it was out of the
season, as the place was, and put it away.

I went at night to the benefit of Mrs. B. Wedgington at the
theatre, who had placarded the town with the admonition,

"DON'T FORGET IT!" I made the house, according to my calculation, four and ninepence to begin with, and it may have warmed up, in the course of the evening, to half a sovereign. There was nothing to offend any one, — the good Mr. Baines of Leeds excepted. Mrs. B. Wedgington sang to a grand piano. Mr. B. Wedgington did the like, and also took off his coat, tucked up his trousers, and danced in clogs. Master B. Wedgington, aged ten months, was nursed by a shivering young person in the boxes, and the eye of Mrs. B. Wedgington wandered that way more than once. Peace be with all the Wedgingtons from A to Z. May they find themselves in the season somewhere!

CONTRIBUTIONS TO "ALL THE YEAR ROUND"

I

THE POOR MAN AND HIS BEER

MY friend Philosewers and I contemplating a farm-labourer the other day, who was drinking his mug of beer on a settle at a roadside alehouse door, we fell to humming the fag-end of an old ditty, of which the poor man and his beer, and the sin of parting them, form the doleful burden. Philosewers then mentioned to me that a friend of his in an agricultural county — say a Hertfordshire friend — had, for two years last past, endeavoured to reconcile the poor man and his beer to public morality, by making it a point of honour between himself and the poor man that the latter should use his beer and not abuse it. Interested in an effort of so unobtrusive and unspeechifying a nature, "O Philosewers," said I, after the manner of the dreary sages in Eastern apologues, "show me, I pray, the man who deems that temperance can be attained without a medal, an oration, a banner, and a denunciation of half the world, and who has at once the head and heart to set about it!"

Philosewers expressing, in reply, his willingness to gratify the Dreary sage, an appointment was made for the purpose. And on the day fixed, I, the Dreary one, accompanied by Philosewers, went down Nor'-West per railway, in search of temperate temperance. It was a thunderous day; and the clouds were so immoderately watery, and so very much disposed to sour all the beer in Hertfordshire, that they seemed to have taken the pledge.

But the sun burst forth gaily in the afternoon, and gilded the old gables, and old mullioned windows, and old weather-cock, and old clock face, of the quaint old house which is the dwelling of the man we sought. How shall I describe him? As one of the most famous practical chemists of the age? That designation will do as well as another — better, perhaps, than most others. And his name? Friar Bacon.

"Though, take notice, Philosewers," said I, behind my hand, "that the first Friar Bacon had not that handsome lady-wife beside him. Wherein, O Philosewers, he was a chemist, wretched and forlorn, compared with his successor. Young Romeo bade the holy father Lawrence hang a philosophy, unless philosophy could make a Juliet. Chemistry would infallibly be hanged if its life were staked on making anything half so pleasant as this Juliet." The gentle Philosewers smiled assent.

The foregoing whisper from myself, the Dreary one, tickled the ear of Philosewers, as we walked on the trim garden terrace before dinner, among the early leaves and blossoms; two peacocks, apparently in very tight new boots, occasionally crossing the gravel at a distance. The sun, shining through the old house-windows, now and then flashed out some brilliant piece of colour from bright hangings within, or upon the old oak panelling; similarly, Friar Bacon, as we paced to and fro, revealed little glimpses of his good work.

"It is not much," said he. "It is no wonderful thing. There used to be a great deal of drunkenness here, and I wanted to make it better if I could. The people are very ignorant, and have been much neglected, and I wanted to make *that* better, if I could. My utmost object was, to help them to a little self-government and a little homely pleasure. I only show the way to better things, and advise them. I never act for them; I never interfere; above all, I never patronise."

I had said to Philosewers as we came along Nor'-West that patronage was one of the curses of England. I appeared to rise in the estimation of Philosewers when thus confirmed.

"And so," said Friar Bacon, "I established my Allotment-club, and my Pig-clubs, and those little concerts by the ladies of my own family, of which we have the last of the season this evening. They are a great success, for the people here are amazingly fond of music. But there is the early dinner bell, and I have no need to talk of my endeavours when you will soon see them in their working-dress."

Dinner done, behold the Friar, Philosewers, and myself, the Dreary one, walking, at six o'clock, across the fields, to the "Club-house."

As we swung open the last field gate and entered the Allotment-grounds, many members were already on their way to the club, which stands in the midst of the allotments. Who could

help thinking of the wonderful contrast between these club-
men and the club-men of St. James's Street, or Pall Mall, in
London! Look at yonder prematurely old man, doubled up
with work, and leaning on a rude stick more crooked than
himself, slowly trudging to the club-house, in a shapeless hat
like an Italian harlequin's, or an old brown paper bag, leathern
leggings, and dull green smock-frock, looking as though duck-
weed had accumulated on it, — the result of its stagnant life,
— or as if it were a vegetable production, originally meant to
blow into something better, but stopped somehow. Compare
him with Old Cousin Feenix, ambling along St. James's
Street, got up in the style of a couple of generations ago, and
with a head of hair, a complexion, and a set of teeth, profoundly impossible to be believed in by the widest stretch of
human credulity. Can they both be men and brothers?
Verily they are. And although Cousin Feenix has lived so
fast that he will die at Baden-Baden, and although this club-
man in the frock has lived, ever since he came to man's estate,
on nine shillings a week, and is sure to die in the Union if he
die in bed, yet he brought as much into the world as Cousin
Feenix, and will take as much out — more, for more of him is
real.

A pretty, simple building, the club-house, with a rustic colonnade outside, under which the members can sit on wet evenings, looking at the patches of ground they cultivate for themselves; within, a well-ventilated room, large and lofty, cheerful
pavement of coloured tiles, a bar for serving out the beer,
good supply of forms and chairs, and a brave, big chimney
corner, where the fire burns cheerfully. Adjoining this room,
another.

"Built for a reading-room," said Friar Bacon; "but not
much used — yet."

The Dreary sage, looking in through the window, perceiving
a fixed reading-desk within, and inquiring its use —

"I have service there," said Friar Bacon. "They never
went anywhere to hear prayers, and of course it would be hopeless to help them to be happier and better if they had no
religious feeling at all."

"The whole place is very pretty." Thus the sage.

: "I am glad you think so. I built it for the holders of the
Allotment-grounds, and gave it them; only requiring them to

manage it by a committee of their own appointing, and never to get drunk there. They never have got drunk there."

"Yet they have their beer freely."

"Oh, yes. As much as they choose to buy. The club gets its beer direct from the brewer, by the barrel. So they get it good; at once much cheaper, and much better, than at the public-house. The members take it in turns to be steward, and serve out the beer; if a man would decline to serve when his turn came, he would pay a fine of twopence. The steward lasts, as long as the barrel lasts. When there is a new barrel, there is a new steward."

"What a noble fire is roaring up that chimney!"

"Yes, a capital fire. Every member pays a halfpenny a week."

"Every member must be a holder of an Allotment-garden?"

"Yes; for which he pays five shillings a year. The Allotments you see about us occupy some sixteen or eighteen acres, and each garden is as large as experience shows one man to be able to manage. You see how admirably they are tilled, and how much they get off them. They are always working in them in their spare hours; and when a man wants a mug of beer, instead of going off to the village and the public-house he gets it at the club, and goes back to his work. When he has done work, he likes to have his beer at the club, still, and to sit and look at his little crops as they thrive."

"They seem to manage the club very well."

"Perfectly well. Here are their own rules. They made them. I never interfere with them, except to advise them when they ask me."

RULES AND REGULATIONS

MADE BY THE COMMITTEE

From the 21st of September, 1857.

One half-penny per week to be paid to the club by each member.

1. Each member to draw the beer in order, according to the number of his allotment; on failing, a forfeit of twopence to be paid to the club.

2. The member that draws the beer to pay for the same, and bring his ticket up receipted when the subscriptions are paid; on failing to do so, a penalty of sixpence to be forfeited and paid to the club.

3. The subscriptions and forfeits to be paid at the club-room on the last Saturday night of each month.

4. The subscriptions and forfeits to be cleared up every quarter; if not, a penalty of sixpence to be paid to the club.

5. The member that draws the beer to be at the club-room by six o'clock every evening, and stay till ten; but in the event of no member being there, he may leave at nine; on failing so to attend, a penalty of sixpence to be paid to the club.

6. Any member giving beer to a stranger in this club-room, excepting to his wife or family, shall be liable to the penalty of one shilling.

7. Any member lifting his hand to strike another in this club-room shall be liable to the penalty of sixpence.

8. Any member swearing in this club-room shall be liable to a penalty of twopence each time.

9. Any member selling beer shall be expelled from the club.

10. Any member wishing to give up his allotment may apply to the committee, and they shall value the crop and the condition of the ground. The amount of the valuation shall be paid by the succeeding tenant, who shall be allowed to enter upon any part of the allotment which is uncropped at the time of notice of the leaving tenant.

11. Any member not keeping his Allotment-garden clear from seed-weeds, or otherwise injuring his neighbours, may be turned out of his garden by the votes of two thirds of the committee, one month's notice being given to him.

12. Any member carelessly breaking a mug is to pay the cost of replacing the same.

I was soliciting the attention of Philosewers to some old, old bonnets hanging in the Allotment-gardens to frighten the birds, and the fashion of which I should think would terrify a French bird to death at any distance, when Philosewers solicited my attention to the scrapers at the club-house door. The amount of the soil of England which every member brought there on his feet was indeed surprising; and even I, who am professedly a salad-eater, could have grown a salad for my dinner in the earth on any member's frock or hat.

"Now," said Friar Bacon, looking at his watch, "for the Pig-clubs!"

The Dreary sage entreated explanation.

"Why, a pig is so very valuable to a poor labouring man, and it is so very difficult for him at this time of the year to get money enough to buy one, that I lend him a pound for the purpose. But I do it in this way. I leave such of the club members as choose it and desire it to form themselves into parties of five. To every man in each company of five I lend ɛ pound, to buy a pig. But each man of the five becomes bound for every other man, as to the repayment of his money. Consequently, they look after one another, and pick out their partners with care; selecting men in whom they have confidence."

"They repay the money, I suppose, when the pig is fattened, killed, and sold?"

"Yes. Then they repay the money. And they do repay it. I had one man, last year, who was a little tardy (he was in the habit of going to the public-house); but even he did pay. It is an immense advantage to one of these poor fellows to have a pig. The pig consumes the refuse from the man's cottage and Allotment-garden, and the pig's refuse enriches the man's garden besides. The pig is the poor man's friend. Come into the club-house again."

The poor man's friend. Yes. I have often wondered who really was the poor man's friend among a great number of competitors, and I now clearly perceive him to be the pig. *He* never makes any flourishes about the poor man. *He* never gammons the poor man — except to his manifest advantage in the article of bacon. *He* never comes down to this house, or goes down to his constituents. He openly declares to the poor man, "I want my sty, because I am a pig; I desire to have as much to eat as you can by any means stuff me with, because I am a pig." *He* never gives the poor man a sovereign for bringing up a family. *He* never grunts the poor man's name in vain. And when he dies in the odour of porkity, he cuts up, a highly useful creature and a blessing to the poor man, from the ring in his snout to the curl in his tail. Which of the poor man's other friends can say as much. Where is the M. P. who means mere pork?

The Dreary sage had glided into these reflections, when he found himself sitting by the club-house fire, surrounded by green smock-frocks and shapeless hats: with Friar Bacon lively, busy, and expert, at a little table near him.

"Now, then, come. The first five!" said Friar Bacon. "Where are you?"

"Order!" cried a merry-faced little man, who had brought his young daughter with him to see life, and who always modestly hid his face in his beer-mug after he had thus assisted the business.

"John Nightingale, William Thrush, Joseph Blackbird, Cecil Robin, and Thomas Linnet!" cried Friar Bacon.

"Here, sir!" and "Here, sir!" And Linnet, Robin, Blackbird, Thrush, and Nightingale, stood confessed.

We, the undersigned, declare, in effect, by this written paper, that each of us is responsible for the repayment of this pig-money by each of the other. "Sure you understand, Nightingale?"

"Ees, sur."

"Can you write your name, Nightingale?"

"Na, sur."

Nightingale's eye upon his name, as Friar Bacon wrote it, was a sight to consider in after years. Rather incredulous was Nightingale, with a hand at the corner of his mouth, and his head on one side, as to those drawings really meaning him. Doubtful was Nightingale whether any virtue had gone out of him in that committal to paper. Meditative was Nightingale as to what would come of young Nightingale's growing up to the acquisition of that art. Suspended was the interest of Nightingale, when his name was done, as if he thought the letters were only sown, to come up presently in some other form. Prodigious and wrong-handed was the cross made by Nightingale on much encouragement, the strokes directed from him instead of towards him; and most patient and sweet-humoured was the smile of Nightingale as he stepped back into a general laugh.

"*Or*-der!" cried the little man, immediately disappearing into his mug.

"Ralph Mangel, Woger Wurzel, Edward Vetches, Matthew Carrot, and Charles Taters!" said Friar Bacon.

"All here, sir."

"You understand it, Mangel?"

"Iss, sir, I unnerstaans it."

"Can you write your name, Mangel?"

"Iss, sir."

Breathless interest. A dense background of smock-frocks accumulated behind Mangel, and many eyes in it looked doubtfully at Friar Bacon, as who should say, "Can he really though?" Mangel put down his hat, retired a little to get a good look at the paper, wetted his right hand thoroughly by drawing it slowly across his mouth, approached the paper with

great determination, flattened it, sat down at it, and got well
to his work. Circuitous and sea-serpent-like were the move-
ments of the tongue of Mangel while he formed the letters;
elevated were the eyebrows of Mangel and sidelong the eyes,
as, with his left whisker reposing on his left arm, they followed
his performance; many were the misgivings of Mangel, and
slow was his retrospective meditation touching the junction of
the letter p with h; something too active was the big forefinger
of Mangel in its propensity to rub out without proved cause.
At last, long and deep was the breath drawn by Mangel when
he laid down the pen; long and deep the wondering breath
drawn by the background, as if they had watched his walking
across the rapids of Niagara, on stilts, and now cried, "He has
done it!"

But Mangel was an honest man, if ever honest man lived.
"'Towt to be a hell, sir," said he, contemplating his work,
"and I ha' made a t on 't."

The over-fraught bosoms of the background found relief in
a roar of laughter.

"ORDER!" cried the little man, "CHEER!" And after that
second word, came forth from his mug no more.

Several other clubs signed, and received their money. Very
few could write their names; all who could not, pleaded that
they could not, more or less sorrowfully, and always with a
shake of the head, and in a lower voice than their natural
speaking voice. Crosses could be made standing; signatures
must be sat down to. There was no exception to this rule
Meantime, the various club-members smoked, drank their beer
and talked together quite unrestrained. They all wore their
hats, except when they went up to Friar Bacon's table. The
merry-faced little man offered his beer, with a natural good
fellowship, both to the Dreary one and Philosewers. Both
partook of it with thanks.

"Seven o'clock!" said Friar Bacon. "And now we had
better get across to the concert, men, for the music will be
beginning."

The concert was in Friar Bacon's laboratory; a large building near at hand, in an open field. The bettermost people of
the village and neighbourhood were in a gallery on one side,
and in a gallery opposite, the orchestra. The whole space
below was filled with the labouring people and their families,

to the number of five or six hundred. We had been obliged
to turn away two hundred to-night, Friar Bacon said, for want
of room, and that, not counting the boys, of whom we had
taken in only a few picked ones, by reason of the boys, as a
class, being given to too fervent a custom of applauding with
their boot heels.

The performers were the ladies of Friar Bacon's family, and
two gentlemen; one of them, who presided, a doctor of music.
A piano was the only instrument. Among the vocal pieces we
had a negro melody (rapturously encored), the Indian Drum
and the Village Blacksmith; neither did we want for fashionable Italian, having *Ah! non giunge*, and *Mi manca la voce*.
Our success was splendid; our good-humoured, unaffected, and
modest bearing, a pattern. As to the audience, they were far
more polite and far more pleased than at the opera; they were
faultless. Thus for barely an hour the concert lasted, with
thousands of great bottles looking on from the walls, containing the results of Friar Bacon's million and one experiments
in agricultural chemistry; and containing too, no doubt, a
variety of materials with which the Friar could have blown us
all through the roof at five minutes' notice.

God save the Queen being done, the good Friar stepped
forward and said a few words, more particularly concerning two
points: firstly, that Saturday half-holiday, which it would be
kind in farmers to grant; secondly, the additional Allotment-
grounds we were going to establish, in consequence of the
happy success of the system, but which we could not guarantee
should entitle the holders to be members of the club, because
the present members must consider and settle that question for
themselves; a bargain between man and man being always a
bargain, and we having made over the club to them as the
original Allotment-men. This was loudly applauded, and so,
with contented and affectionate cheering, it was all over.

As Philosewers and I the Dreary posted back to London,
looking up at the moon and discussing it as a world preparing
for the habitation of responsible creatures, we expatiated on
the honour due to men in this world of ours who try to prepare
it for a higher course, and to leave the race who live and die
upon it better than they found them.

Iī

PINCHER ASTRAY

HE was not handsome — at least in the common acceptation of the term. He had a speckly muzzle, and a hanging jowl, and rather watery eyes, and short crop ears. His legs were horribly bowed, and his tail curled over his back, like the end of a figure nine. He was a morose beast, and of most uncertain temper. He would rush out to a stranger at the gate with every demonstration of welcome, would leap up and bark round him, and then would run behind and bite him in the calves. He was the terror of the tradespeople; he loathed the butcher; he had a deadly hatred for the fishmonger's boy; and when I complained to the post-office of the non-receipt in due course of a letter from my aunt's legal adviser advising me to repair at once to the old lady's death-bed (owing to which non-receipt I was cut out of my aunt's will), I was answered that "the savage character of my dog — a circumstance with which the department could not interfere — prevented the letter-carrier from the due performance of his functions after night-fall." Still I loved Pincher, still I love him! What though my trousers-ends were frayed into hanging strips by his teeth; what though my slippers are a mass of chewed pulp; what though he has tousled all the corners of the manuscript of my work on Logarithms, — shall I reproach him now that he is lost to me? Never!

I saw him last, three mornings ago, leisurely straying round the garden with the strap of the baby's shoe hanging out of his mouth, and with a knowing wag of his tail, as much as to show me how he was enjoying himself. I remonstrated with him on the shoe question, and he seemed somewhat touched for a moment; but suddenly catching sight of a predatory cat on the wall, he galloped off without further parley. I watched the cat scuttle up a tree; I heard Pincher growling angrily at its base. The noise of the milkman's boots scrunching the gravel attracted his attention; he darted off, and was lost to me for ever. There was a fiendish grin on the housemaid's face

when she announced to me that Pincher was n't nowhere to
be found. Visions of henceforth unworried stocking-heels,
unsnapped-at ankles, rose before that damsel's mind as she
broke the news; and she smiled as she said they'd looked
everywheres they had, and nothin' was n't to be seen. I was
not crushed by the intelligence. I knew my dog's extensive
visiting-list, and thought that finding he had overstayed his
time, he had probably accepted the friendly hospitality of half
a kennel, and was then engaged in baying the moon, and con-
ducing to the sleeplessness of a neighbourhood unaccustomed
to his vocal powers. But, as I lay in bed in the morning, I
missed the various little dramas, the principal characters played
by Pincher and the tradespeople, of which I had long been the
silent audience. The butcher's boy, a fierce and beefy youth,
who openly defied the dog, and waved him off with hurlings
of his basket and threatenings of his feet, accompanied by
growls of "Git out, yer beast!" now entered silently; the
baker's apprentice, a mild and farinaceous lad, who proffered
to Pincher the raspings of black loaves, and usually endeavoured to propitiate his enemy by addressing him as "Poor fellow!" now entered silently; the fishmonger, who generally
made one wild scuttle from the garden gate to the kitchen-
entrance, and upon whose track Pincher usually hung as the
wolves hung upon Mazeppa's, now walked slowly up the path,
and whistled. Then I knew that Pincher was gone indeed!

I engaged the services of an unintelligible crier, and had a
description of my dog bellowed round the neighbourhood. I
brought the printing art into play, to portray Pincher's various
attributes, and all the palings and posts within the circle of
two miles burst out with an eruption of placards, of which the
words "Lost" and "Dog" were, without the aid of a powerful
microscope, the only legible portion. I concocted an advertisement for the "Times" newspaper. I patiently waited the
result of these various schemes. They had results, I allow.
I received at least twenty letters from sympathising persons,
who stated that in the event of not recovering my lost favourite,
they were in a position to provide another in his place. I
suppose that on the evening of the day on which the "Times"
issued the advertisement, at least five-and-twenty pairs of boots
had printed themselves off on my dining-room drugget, which,
being red in colour and fluffy in texture, is singularly capable

of retaining a clear impression. The boots, in every instance, belonged to short-haired stably gentlemen in large white over-coats, from the inner pockets of which they produced specimens of dogs, ugly and morose indeed, but none of them my Pincher. I need not say that my intimate friends came out ncbly under these circumstances. Jephson, who wore check trousers of a vivid pattern which had always aroused Pincher's ire, thanked fortune that "the infernal beast was got rid of some-how." Pooley, who, labouring under a belief that all dogs were intended for swimmers, had once tried to throw Pincher into the Hampstead ponds, and had had his hand bitten to the bone for his pains, hoped that "the brute had been made into sausages." Blinkhorn, who was of a facetious turn, was sure that Pincher had been sewn up in the skin of some deceased dog of fabulous beauty, and sold by a man in Regent Street to some old dowager. Hallmarke was the only one who gave me the least consolation. "Perhaps he's been picked up by some benevolent person," he said, "and sent to the Home. Go to the Home and see." — "The Home? what Home?" I asked. "For lost dogs, at Holloway. Go and see if he's there."

On further sifting this somewhat vague information, I found that there was a place where lost and starving dogs found in the street were temporarily received and cared for; and that this place was open to the visits of the public. I determined to repair thither at once. It is a good thing for the dogs that they are sent to the Home, for assuredly they would never find their own intricate way there. On being landed from the Favourite omnibus, I made several inquiries, and at last found myself in Hollinsworth Street; a pleasant locality, which would have been pleasanter had there been less mud and more pavement.

I looked around, but saw no sign of dogginess. At last I succeeded in fixing a red-faced matron who was cuffing her offspring, and of her I inquired, as civilly as might be, if she knew where the Dog's Home was situated? Following this lady's directions, I crossed the road, and soon found myself at the gates, when a sharp little lad, so soon as he heard my business, ushered me into the Home.

A big yard, at the opposite end of which I see a block of kennels with a wirework fenced show-place outside, very like that appropriated to the monkeys at the Zoölogical Gardens.

In this, a crowd of dogs, who no sooner see the boy accompanying me than they set up a tremendous howling. Not a painful yelping, nothing suggestive of hunger or physical suffering, but simply that under-toned howl which means, "Take me out and give me a run." Dogs of all kinds here, but nothing very valuable. "Mongrel, puppy, and whelp, and curs of low degree." Big dogs, half mastiff, half sheepdog, bastard Scotch and English terriers, in all instances with a cross of wrong blood in them; one or two that ought to have been beagles, but seemed to have gone to the bad; several lurchers looking as if they ought to have had a poacher's heels to follow, and a grand gathering of the genuine English cur: that cheery, dissipated, dishonest scoundrel, who betrays his villainy in the shiftiness of his eye, and the limpness of his tail; who is so often lame, and so perpetually taking furtive snatches of sleep in doorways; a citizen of the world, and yet a single-hearted brute, who will follow any one for miles on the strength of a kind word, and who, when kicked off, turns round philosophically and awaits some better fortune.

Comfortably housed are all these dogs, with plenty to eat and drink, and a large open space where they are periodically turned out for exercise. I asked whether the neighbours did not raise strong objections to the proximity of the Home. I was told that at first all kinds of legal persecutions were threatened, but that, as time passed, the ill feeling died away, and now no complaints were made. The dogs, who are invariably rescued from starvation, are so worn out on first reaching their new abode that they invariably sleep for many hours as soon as they have taken food, and, on recovering, seem already accustomed to their quarters, and consequently indisposed to whine. All the dogs of any standing look plump and well fed; but there are two or three new-comers with lack-lustre eyes and very painful anatomical developments. I carefully scrutinised them all. There were about eighty. Alas, Pincher was not among them. He might come in, the boy said; there was many pleacemen bringin' in what they 'd found in the night; my dog might come in yet; had n't I better see the lady and talk to her? I found "the lady" was the originator of the Home, living closely adjacent; and from her I obtained all the particulars of her amiable hobby.

The Home for lost and starving dogs has now been in existence more than three years. The establishment was started by the present honorary secretary: a lady who had for some time been in the habit of collecting such starving animals as she found in her own neighbourhood, and paying a person a weekly sum for their keep. After explaining her plan in the columns of one of the daily newspapers, she received warm assistance, and the co-operation of the Society for the Prevention of Cruelty to Animals having been obtained, the Home entered upon its present extended sphere of usefulness, and boasts a large number of annual subscribers. Its object will be gathered from the following

RULES AND REGULATIONS

1. Any dog found and brought to the Home, if applied for by the owner, will be given up to its master upon payment of the expenses of its keep.

2. Any dog lost by Subscribers and brought to the Home will be given up free of all expense.

3. Any dog brought to the Home, not identified and claimed within fourteen days from the time of its admission, will, by order of the Committee, be sold to pay expenses, or be otherwise disposed of.

4. To prevent dog-stealing, no reward will be given to persons bringing dogs to the Home. The Committee would hope that, to persons of ordinary humanity, the consciousness of having performed a merciful action would be sufficient recompense.

5. Accommodation is now made for the reception of dogs belonging to Ladies or Gentlemen who may wish to have care taken of them during their absence from home.

6. Ladies and Gentlemen finding lost or starving dogs in the street, at a distance from their own residences, are recommended to arrange with some poor person, for a specified remuneration, to convey them either to the "Home" itself, or to a receiving house. The money should on no account be given to the bearer of the dog beforehand, or only on production of a certificate in this form:

TEMPORARY HOME FOR LOST AND STARVING DOGS

The Bearer has brought   *dog to the Home.*

Date   . . . . . *Keeper.*

It is scarcely necessary to say that when the scheme was first mooted it shared the fate of many other good schemes, and received violent opposition. People who would have left the wounded traveller and passed by on the other side declaimed loudly against showing humanity to dogs while human creatures were starving; and some humorists pleasantly asked whether there was to be a home for lost and starving elephants. The Home has survived even these sarcasms, and unpretendingly does good; it is not very important in its benevolence, but as no sparrow falls to the ground without an all-wise supervision, it may be granted that the charity which provides food and shelter for a starving dog is worthy of approbation. The place does good in its sphere. To do some good in any sphere is much better than to do none.

Pincher returned: not from the Home for Lost Dogs, he knew better than so far to jeopardise his social standing. He returned with a ruffled coat, a torn ear, a fierceness of eye which bespoke recent trouble. I afterwards learned that he had been a principal in a combat held in the adjoining parish, where he acquitted himself with a certain amount of honour, and was pinning his adversary, when a rustic person from a farm broke in upon the ring and kicked both the combatants out of it. This ignominy was more than Pincher could bear; he flung himself upon the rustic's leg, and brought him to the ground: then fled and remained hidden in a wood until hunger compelled him to come home. We have interchanged no communication since, but regard each other with sulky dignity. I perceive that he intends to remain obdurate until I make the first advances.

III

EVERY artist, be he writer, painter, musician, or actor, must bear his private sorrows as he best can, and must separate them from the exercise of his public pursuit. But it sometimes happens, in compensation, that his private loss of a dear friend represents a loss on the part of the whole community. Then he may, without obtrusion of his individuality, step forth to lay his little wreath upon that dear friend's grave.

On Saturday, the eighteenth of May, 1867, Clarkson Stanfield died. On the afternoon of that day, England lost the great marine painter of whom she will be boastful ages hence; the national historian of her specialty, the sea; the man famous in all countries for his marvellous rendering of the waves that break upon her shores, of her ships and seamen, of her coasts and skies, of her storms and sunshine, of the many marvels of the deep. He who holds the oceans in the hollow of His hand had given, associated with them, wonderful gifts into his keeping; he had used them well through threescore and fourteen years; and on the afternoon of that spring day, relinquished them for ever.

It is superfluous to record that the painter of "The Battle of Trafalgar," of "The Victory being towed into Gibraltar with the Body of Nelson on Board," of "The Morning after the Wreck," of "The Abandoned," of fifty more such works, died in his seventy-fourth year, "Mr." Stanfield. He was an Englishman.

Those grand pictures will proclaim his powers while paint and canvas last. But the writer of these words had been his friend for thirty years; and when, a short week or two before his death, he laid that once so skilful hand upon the writer's breast and told him they would meet again, "but not here," the thoughts of the latter turned, for the time, so little to his noble genius, and so much to his noble nature!

He was the soul of frankness, generosity, and simplicity. The most genial, the most affectionate, the most loving, and the most lovable of men. Success had never for an instant

spoiled him. His interest in the theatre as an institution —
the best picturesqueness of which may be said to be wholly
due to him — was faithful to the last. His belief in a play,
his delight in one, the ease with which it moved him to tears
or to laughter were most remarkable evidences of the heart he
must have put into his old theatrical work, and of the thorough
purpose and sincerity with which it must have been done.
The writer was very intimately associated with him in some
amateur plays; and day after day, and night after night, there
were the same unquenchable freshness, enthusiasm, and impressibility in him, though broken in health, even then.

No artist can ever have stood by his art with a quieter dignity than he always did. Nothing would have induced him to
lay it at the feet of any human creature. To fawn, or to toady,
or to do undeserved homage to any one, was an absolute impossibility with him. And yet his character was so nicely balanced
that he was the last man in the world to be suspected of self-assertion, and his modesty was one of his most special qualities.

He. was a charitable, religious, gentle, truly good man. A
genuine man, incapable of pretence or of concealment. He
had been a sailor once; and all the best characteristics that are
popularly attributed to sailors being his, and being in him
refined by the influences of his art, formed a whole not likely
to be often seen. There is no smile that the writer can recall
like his; no manner so naturally confiding and so cheerfully
engaging. When the writer saw him for the last time on
earth, the smile and the manner shone out once through the
weakness, still: the bright unchanging soul within the altered
face and form.

No man was ever held in higher respect by his friends, and
yet his intimate friends invariably addressed him and spoke of
him by a pet name. It may need, perhaps, the writer's memory and associations to find in this a touching expression of
his winning character, his playful smile, and pleasant ways.
"You know Mrs. Inchbald's story, 'Nature and Art'?" wrote
Thomas Hood, once, in a letter: "What a fine edition of
'Nature and Art' is Stanfield!"

Gone! And many and many a dear old day gone with him!
But their memories remain. And his memory will not soon
fade out, for he has set his mark upon the restless waters, and
his fame will long be sounded in the roar of the sea.

IN MEMORIAM

WILLIAM MAKEPEACE THACKERAY

It has been desired by some of the personal friends of the great English writer who established this magazine, that its brief record of his having been stricken from among men should be written by the old comrade and brother-in-arms who pens these lines, and of whom he often wrote himself, and always with the warmest generosity.

I saw him first, nearly twenty-eight years ago, when he proposed to become the illustrator of my earliest book. I saw him last, shortly before Christmas, at the Athenæum Club, when he told me that he had been in bed three days, that, after these attacks, he was troubled with cold shiverings, "which quite took the power of work out of him," and that he had it in his mind to try a new remedy which he laughingly described. He was very cheerful, and looked very bright. In the night of that day week he died.

The long interval between those two periods is marked in my remembrance of him by many occasions when he was supremely humorous, when he was irresistibly extravagant, when he was softened and serious, when he was charming with children. But by none do I recall him more tenderly than by two or three that start out of the crowd, when he unexpectedly presented himself in my room, announcing how that some passage in a certain book had made him cry yesterday, and how that he had come to dinner, "because he could n't help it," and must talk such passage over. No one can ever have seen him more genial, natural, cordial, fresh, and honestly impulsive, than I have seen him at those times. No one can be surer than I of the greatness and the goodness of the heart that then disclosed itself.

We had our differences of opinion. I thought that he too much feigned a want of earnestness, and that he made a pretence of undervaluing his art, which was not good for the art that he held in trust. But, when we fell upon these topics, it was never very gravely, and I have a lively image of him in my mind, twisting both his hands in his hair, and stamping about, laughing, to make an end of the discussion.

When we were associated in remembrance of the late Mr. Douglas Jerrold, he delivered a public lecture in London, in the course of which he read his very best contribution to "Punch," describing the grown-up cares of a poor family of young children. No one hearing him could have doubted his natural gentleness, or his thoroughly unaffected manly sympathy with the weak and lowly. He read the paper most pathetically, and with a simplicity of tenderness that certainly moved one of his audience to tears. This was presently after his standing for Oxford, from which place he had despatched his agent to me, with a droll note (to which he afterwards added a verbal postscript), urging me to "come down and make a speech, and tell them who he was, for he doubted whether more than two of the electors had ever heard of him, and he thought there might be as many as six or eight who had heard of me." He introduced the lecture just mentioned with a reference to his late electioneering failure, which was full of good sense, good spirits, and good-humour.

He had a particular delight in boys, and an excellent way with them. I remember his once asking me with fantastic gravity, when he had been to Eton where my eldest son then was, whether I felt as he did in regard of never seeing a boy without wanting instantly to give him a sovereign? I thought of this when I looked down into his grave, after he was laid there, for I looked down into it over the shoulder of a boy to whom he had been kind.

These are slight remembrances; but it is to little familiar things suggestive of the voice, look, manner, never, never more to be encountered on this earth, that the mind first turns in a bereavement. And greater things that are known of him, in the way of his warm affections, his quiet endurance, his unselfish thoughtfulness for others, and his munificent hand, may not be told.

If, in the reckless vivacity of his youth, his satirical pen had ever gone astray or done amiss, he had caused it to prefer its own petition for forgiveness long before: —

"I 've writ the foolish fancy of his brain;
The aimless jest that, striking, hath caused pain;
The idle word that he 'd wish back again."

In no pages should I take it upon myself at this time to discourse of his books, of his refined knowledge of character, of his subtle acquaintance with the weaknesses of human nature, of his delightful playfulness as an essayist, of his quaint and touching ballads, of his mastery over the English language. Least of all, in these pages, enriched by his brilliant qualities from the first of the series, and beforehand accepted by the Public through the strength of his great name.

But on the table before me there lies all that he had written of his latest and last story. That it would be very sad to any one — that it is inexpressibly so to a writer — in its evidences of matured designs never to be accomplished, of intentions begun to be executed and destined never to be completed, of careful preparation for long roads of thought that he was never to traverse, and for shining goals that he was never to reach, will be readily believed. The pain, however, that I have felt in perusing it has not been deeper than the conviction that he was in the healthiest vigour of his powers when he wrought on this last labour. In respect of earnest feeling, far-seeing purpose, character, incident, and a certain loving picturesqueness blending the whole, I believe it to be much the best of all his works. That he fully meant it to be so, that he had become strongly attached to it, and that he bestowed great pains upon it, I trace in almost every page. It contains one picture which must have cost him extreme distress, and which is a masterpiece. There are two children in it, touched with a hand as loving and tender as ever a father caressed his little child with. There is some young love, as pure and innocent and pretty as the truth. And it is very remarkable that, by reason of the singular construction of the story, more than one main incident usually belonging to the end of such a fiction is anticipated in the beginning, and thus there is an approach to completeness in the fragment, as to the satisfaction of the reader's mind concerning the most interesting persons, which could hardly have been better attained if the writer's breaking-off had been foreseen.

The last line he wrote and the last proof he corrected are among these papers through which I have so sorrowfully made my way. The condition of the little pages of manuscript where Death stopped his hand shows that he had carried them about, and often taken them out of his pocket here and there, for patient revision and interlineation. The last words he corrected in print were, "And my heart throbbed with an exquisite bliss." God grant that on that Christmas Eve when he laid his head back on his pillow and threw up his arms as he had been wont to do when very weary, some consciousness of duty done and Christian hope throughout life humbly cherished may have caused his own heart so to throb, when he passed away to his Redeemer's rest!

He was found peacefully lying as above described, composed, undisturbed, and to all appearance asleep, on the twenty-fourth of December, 1863. He was only in his fifty-third year; so young a man, that the mother who blessed him in his first sleep blessed him in his last. Twenty years before he had written, after being in a white squall: —

> "And when, its force expended,
> The harmless storm was ended,
> And, as the sunrise splendid,
>   Came blushing o'er the sea;
> I thought, as day was breaking,
> My little girls were waking,
> And smiling, and making
>   A prayer at home for me."

Those little girls had grown to be women when the mournful day broke that saw their father lying dead. In those twenty years of companionship with him, they had learned much from him; and one of them has a literary course before her worthy of her famous name.

On the bright wintry day, the last but one of the old year, he was laid in his grave at Kensal Green, there to mingle the dust to which the mortal part of him had returned with that of a third child, lost in her infancy, years ago. The heads of a great concourse of his fellow-workers in the arts were bowed around his tomb.

INTRODUCTION

IN the spring of the year 1853, I observed, as conductor of the weekly journal, "Household Words," a short poem among the proffered contributions, very different, as I thought, from the shoal of verses perpetually setting through the office of such a periodical, and possessing much more merit. Its authoress was quite unknown to me. She was one Miss Mary Berwick, whom I had never heard of; and she was to be addressed by letter, if addressed at all, at a circulating library in the western district of London. Through this channel, Miss Berwick was informed that her poem was accepted, and was invited to send another. She complied, and became a regular and frequent contributor. Many letters passed between the journal and Miss Berwick, but Miss Berwick herself was never seen.

How we came gradually to establish, at the office of "Household Words," that we knew all about Miss Berwick, I have never discovered. But we settled somehow, to our complete satisfaction, that she was governess in a family; that she went to Italy in that capacity, and returned; and that she had long been in the same family. We really knew nothing whatever of her, except that she was remarkably business-like, punctual, self-reliant, and reliable; so I suppose we insensibly invented the rest. For myself, my mother was not a more real personage to me than Miss Berwick the governess became.

This went on until December, 1854, when the Christmas number, entitled "The Seven Poor Travellers," was sent to press. Happening to be going to dine that day with an old and dear friend, distinguished in literature as Barry Cornwall, 1 took with me an early proof of that number, and remarked, as I laid it on the drawing-room table, that it contained a very pretty poem, written by a certain Miss Berwick. Next day brought me the disclosure that I had so spoken of the poem to the mother of its writer, in its writer's presence; that I had no such correspondent in existence as Miss Berwick; and that the name had been assumed by Barry Cornwall's eldest daughter, Miss Adelaide Anne Procter.

The anecdote I have here noted down, besides serving to explain why the parents of the late Miss Procter have looked to me for these poor words of remembrance of their lamented child, strikingly illustrates the honesty, independence, and quiet dignity of the lady's character. I had known her when she was very young; I had been honoured with her father's friendship when I was myself a young aspirant; and she had said at home, "If I send him, in my own name, verses that he does not honestly like, either it will be very painful to him to return them, or he will print them for papa's sake, and not for their own. So I have made up my mind to take my chance fairly with the unknown volunteers."

Perhaps it requires an editor's experience of the profoundly unreasonable grounds on which he is often urged to accept unsuitable articles — such as having been to school with the writer's husband's brother-in-law, or having lent an alpenstock in Switzerland to the writer's wife's nephew, when that interesting stranger had broken his own — fully to appreciate the delicacy and the self-respect of this resolution.

Some verses by Miss Procter had been published in the "Book of Beauty," ten years before she became Miss Berwick. With the exception of two poems in the "Cornhill Magazine," two in "Good Words," and others in a little book called "A Chaplet of Verses" (issued in 1862 for the benefit of a Night Refuge), her published writings first appeared in "Household Words," or "All the Year Round." The present edition contains the whole of her Legends and Lyrics, and originates in the great favour with which they have been received by the public.

Miss Procter was born in Bedford Square, London, on the 30th of October, 1825. Her love of poetry was conspicuous at so early an age, that I have before me a tiny album made of small note-paper, into which her favourite passages were copied for her by her mother's hand before she herself could write. It looks as if she had carried it about as another little girl might have carried a doll. She soon displayed a remarkable memory, and great quickness of apprehension. When she was quite a young child, she learnt with facility several of the problems of Euclid. As she grew older, she acquired the French, Italian, and German languages, became a clever pianoforte player, and showed a true taste and sentiment in drawing. But as soon as she had completely vanquished the difficulties of any one branch of study, it was her way to lose interest in it, and pass to another. While her mental resources were being trained, it was not at all suspected in her family that she had any gift of authorship, or any ambition to become a writer. Her father had no idea of her having ever attempted to turn a rhyme, until her first little poem saw the light in print.

When she attained to womanhood, she had read an extraordinary number of books, and throughout her life she was always largely adding to the number. In 1853 she went to Turin and its neighbourhood, on a visit to her aunt, a Roman Catholic lady. As Miss Procter had herself professed the Roman Catholic faith two years before, she entered with the greater ardour on the study of the Piedmontese dialect, and the observation of the habits and manners of the peasantry. . . .

Those readers of Miss Procter's poems who should suppose from their tone that her mind was of a gloomy or despondent cast would be curiously mistaken. She was exceedingly humorous, and had a great delight in humour. Cheerfulness was habitual with her, she was very ready at a sally or a reply, and in her laugh (as I remember well) there was an unusual vivacity, enjoyment, and sense of drollery. She was perfectly unconstrained and unaffected: as modestly silent about her productions as she was generous with their pecuniary results. She was a friend who inspired the strongest attachments; she was a finely sympathetic woman, with a great accordant heart and a sterling noble nature. No claim can be set up for her, thank God! to the possession of any of the conventional poetical qualities. She never by any means held the opinion that she was among the greatest of human beings; she never suspected the existence of a conspiracy on the part of mankind against her; she never recognised in her best friends her worst enemies; she never cultivated the luxury of being misunderstood and unappreciated; she would far rather have died without seeing a line of her composition in print, than that I should have maundered about her, here, as "the Poet," or "the Poetess."

With the recollection of Miss Procter as a mere child and as a woman fresh upon me, it is natural that I should linger on my way to the close of this brief record, avoiding its end. But, even as the close came upon her, so must it come here.

Always impelled by an intense conviction that her life must not be dreamed away, and that her indulgence in her favourite pursuits must be balanced by action in the real world around her, she was indefatigable in her endeavours to do some good. Naturally enthusiastic, and conscientiously impressed with a deep sense of her Christian duty to her neighbour, she devoted herself to a variety of benevolent objects. Now, it was the visitation of the sick that had possession of her; now, it was the sheltering of the houseless; now, it was the elementary teaching of the densely ignorant; now, it was the raising up of those who had wandered and got trodden under foot; now, it was the wider employment of her own sex in the general business of life; now, it was all these things at once. Perfectly unselfish, swift to sympathise and eager to relieve, she wrought at such designs with a flushed earnestness that disregarded season, weather, time of day or night, food, rest. Under such a hurry of the spirits, and such incessant occupation, the strongest constitution will commonly go down. Hers, neither of the strongest nor the weakest, yielded to the burden, and began to sink.

To have saved her life, then, by taking action on the warning that shone in her eyes and sounded in her voice, would have been impossible without changing her nature. As long as the power of moving about in the old way was left to her, she must exercise it, or be killed by the restraint. And so the time came when she could move about no longer, and took to her bed.

All the restlessness gone then, and all the sweet patience of her natural disposition purified by the resignation of her soul, she lay upon her bed through the whole round of changes of the seasons. She lay upon her bed through fifteen months. In all that time, her old cheerfulness never quitted her. In all that time, not an impatient or a querulous minute can be remembered.

At length, at midnight on the 2d of February, 1864, she turned down a leaf of a little book she was reading, and shut it up.

The ministering hand that had copied the verses into the tiny album was soon around her neck, and she quietly asked, as the clock was on the stroke of one: "Do you think I am dying, mamma?"

"I think you are véry, very ill to-night, my dear."

"Send for my sister. My feet are so cold. Lift me up!"

Her sister entering as they raised her, she said: "It has come at last!" And with a bright and happy smile looked upward, and departed.

Well had she written: —

> "Why shouldst thou fear the beautiful angel, Death,
> Who waits thee at the portals of the skies,
> Ready to kiss away thy struggling breath,
> Ready with gentle hand to close thine eyes?
>
> "Oh, what were life, if life were all? Thine eyes
> Are blinded by their tears, or thou wouldst see
> Thy treasures wait thee in the far-off skies,
> And Death, thy friend, will give them all to thee."

ON MR. FECHTER'S ACTING

THE distinguished artist whose name is prefixed to these remarks purposes to leave England for a professional tour in the United States. A few words from me, in reference to his merits as an actor, I hope may not be uninteresting to some readers, in advance of his publicly proving them before an American audience, and I know will not be unacceptable to my intimate friend. I state at once that Mr. Fechter holds that relation towards me; not only because it is the fact, but also because our friendship originated in my public appreciation of him. I had studied his acting closely, and had admired it highly, both in Paris and in London, years before we exchanged a word. Consequently, my appreciation is not the result of personal regard, but personal regard has sprung out of my appreciation.

The first quality observable in Mr. Fechter's acting is, that it is in the highest degree romantic. However elaborated in minute details, there is always a peculiar dash and vigour in it, like the fresh atmosphere of the story whereof it is a part. When he is on the stage, it seems to me as though the story were transpiring before me for the first and last time. Thus there is a fervour in his love-making — a suffusion of his whole being with the rapture of his passion — that sheds a glory on its object, and raises her, before the eyes of the audience, into the light in which he sees her. It was this remarkable power that took Paris by storm when he became famous in the lover's part in the "Dame aux Camélias." It is a short part, really comprised in two scenes, but, as he acted it (he was its original representative), it left its poetic and exalting influence on the heroine throughout the play. A woman who could be so loved — who could be so devotedly and romantically adored — had a hold upon the general sympathy with which nothing less absorbing and complete could have invested her. When I first saw this play and this actor, I could not, in forming my lenient judgment of the heroine, forget that she had been the inspiration of a passion of which I had beheld such profound and affecting marks. I said to myself, as a child might have said: "A bad woman could not have been the object of that wonderful tenderness, could not have so subdued that worshipping heart, could not have drawn such tears from such a lover." I am persuaded that the same effect was wrought upon the Parisian audiences, both consciously and unconsciously, to a very great extent, and that what was morally disagreeable in the "Dame aux Camélias" first got lost in this brilliant halo of romance. I have seen the same play with the same part otherwise acted, and in exact degree as the love became dull and earthy, the heroine descended from her pedestal.

In "Ruy Blas," in "The Master of Ravenswood," and in "The Lady of Lyons," — three dramas in which Mr. Fechter especially shines as a lover, but notably in the first, — this remarkable power of surrounding the beloved creature, in the eyes of the audience, with the fascination that she has for him, is strikingly displayed. That observer must be cold indeed who does not feel, when Ruy Blas stands in the presence of the young unwedded Queen of Spain, that the air is enchanted; or, when she bends over him, laying her tender touch upon his bloody breast, that it is better so to die than to live apart from her, and that she is worthy to be so died for. When the Master of Ravenswood declares his love to Lucy Ashton, and she hers to him, and when, in a burst of rapture, he kisses the skirt of her dress, we feel as though we touched it with our lips to stay our goddess from soaring away into the very heavens. And when they plight their troth and break the piece of gold, it is we — not Edgar — who quickly exchange our half for the half she was about to hang about her neck, solely because the latter has for an instant touched the bosom we so dearly love. Again, in "The Lady of Lyons;" the picture on the easel in the poor cottage studio is not the unfinished portrait of a vain and arrogant girl, but becomes the sketch of a soul's high ambition and aspiration here and hereafter.

Picturesqueness is a quality above all others pervading Mr. Fechter's assumptions. Himself a skilled painter and sculptor, learned in the history of costume, and informing those accomplishments and that knowledge with a similar infusion of romance (for romance is inseparable from the man), he is always a picture, — always a picture in its right place in the group, always in true composition with the background of the scene. For picturesqueness of manner, note so trivial a thing as the turn of his hand in beckoning from a window, in "Ruy Blas," to a personage down in an outer courtyard to come up: or his assumption of the Duke's livery in the same scene; or his writing a letter from dictation. In the last scene of Victor Hugo's noble drama, his bearing becomes positively inspired; and his sudden assumption of the attitude of the headsman, in his denunciation of the Duke and threat to be his executioner, is, so far as I know, one of the most ferociously picturesque things conceivable on the stage.

The foregoing use of the word "ferociously" reminds me to remark that this artist is a master of passionate vehemence; in which aspect he appears to me to represent, perhaps more than in any other, an interesting union of characteristics of two great nations, — the French and the Anglo-Saxon. Born in London of a French mother, by a German father, but reared entirely in England and in France, there is, in his fury, a combination of French suddenness and impressibility with our more slowly demonstrative Anglo-Saxon way when we get, as we say, "our blood up," that produces an intensely fiery result. The fusion of two races is in it, and one cannot decidedly say that it belongs to either; but one can most decidedly say that it belongs to a powerful concentration of human passion and emotion, and to human nature.

Mr. Fechter has been in the main more accustomed to speak French than to speak English, and therefore he speaks our language with a French accent. But whosoever should suppose that he does not speak English fluently, plainly, distinctly, and with a perfect understanding of the meaning, weight, and value of every word, would be greatly mistaken. Not only is his knowledge of English — extending to the most subtle idiom, or the most recondite cant phrase — more extensive than that of many of us who have English for our mother tongue, but his delivery of Shakespeare's blank verse is remarkably facile, musical, and intelligent. To be in a sort of pain for him, as one sometimes is for a foreigner speaking English, or to be in any doubt of his having twenty synonymes at his tongue's end if he should want one, is out of the question after having been of his audience.

A few words on two of his Shakespearean impersonations, and I shall have indicated enough, in advance of Mr. Fechter's presentation of himself. That quality of picturesqueness, on which I have already laid stress, is strikingly developed in his Iago, and yet it is so judiciously governed that his Iago is not in the least picturesque according to the conventional ways of frowning, sneering, diabolically grinning, and elaborately doing everything else that would induce Othello to run him through the body very early in the play. Mr. Fechter's is the Iago who could, and did, make friends; who could dissect his master's soul, without flourishing his scalpel as if it were a walking-stick; who could overpower Emilia by other arts than a sign-of-the-Saracen's-Head grimness; who could be a boon companion without *ipso facto* warning all beholders off by the portentous phenomenon; who could sing a song and clink a can naturally enough, and stab men really in the dark, — not in a transparent notification of himself as going about seeking whom to stab. Mr. Fechter's Iago is no more in the conventional psychological mode than in the conventional hussar pantaloons and boots; and you shall see the picturesqueness of his wearing borne out in his bearing all through the tragedy down to the moment when he becomes invincibly and consistently dumb.

Perhaps no innovation in art was ever accepted with so much favour by so many intellectual persons pre-committed to, and pre-occupied by, another system, as Mr. Fechter's Hamlet. I take this to have been the case (as it unquestionably was in London), not because of its picturesqueness, not because of its novelty, not because of its many scattered beauties, but because of its perfect consistency with itself. As the animal-painter said of his favourite picture of rabbits, that there was more nature about those rabbits than you usually found in rabbits, so it may be said of Mr. Fechter's Hamlet, that there was more consistency about that Hamlet than you usually found in Hamlets. Its great and satisfying originality was in its possessing the merit of a distinctly conceived and executed idea. From the first appearance of the broken glass of fashion and mould of form, pale and worn with weeping for his father's death, and remotely suspicious of its cause, to his final struggle with Horatio for the fatal cup, there were cohesion and coherence in Mr. Fechter's view of the character. Devrient, the

German actor, had, some years before in London, fluttered the
theatrical doves considerably, by such changes as being seated
when instructing the players, and like mild departures from
established usage; but he had worn, in the main, the old non-
descript dress, and had held forth, in the main, in the old way,
hovering between sanity and madness.   I do not remember
whether he wore his hair crisply curled short, as if he were
going to an everlasting dancing-master's party at the Danish
Court; but I do remember that most other Hamlets since the
great Kemble had been bound to do so.   Mr. Fechter's Hamlet, a pale, woe-begone Norseman, with long flaxen hair, wearing a strange garb never associated with the part upon the
English stage (if ever seen there at all), and making a piratical
swoop upon the whole fleet of little theatrical prescriptions
without meaning, or, like Dr. Johnson's celebrated friend,
with only one idea in them, and that a wrong one, never could
have achieved its extraordinary success but for its animation
by one pervading purpose, to which all changes were made
intelligently subservient.   The bearing of this purpose on the
treatment of Ophelia, on the death of Polonius, and on the old
student fellowship between Hamlet and Horatio, was exceedingly striking; and the difference between picturesqueness of
stage arrangement for mere stage effect, and for the elucidation
of a meaning, was well displayed in there having been a gallery
of musicians at the play, and in one of them passing on his
way out, with his instrument in his hand, when Hamlet, seeing
it, took it from him to point his talk with Rosencrantz and
Guildenstern.

This leads me to the observation with which I have all along
desired to conclude: that Mr. Fechter's romance and picturesqueness are always united to a true artist's intelligence,
and a true artist's training in a true artist's spirit.   He became
one of the Théâtre Français when he was a very young man,
and he has cultivated his natural gifts in the best schools.
I cannot wish my friend a better audience than he will have in
the American people, and I cannot wish them a better actor
than they will have in my friend.

Lightning Source UK Ltd.
Milton Keynes UK
UKOW02f2159210915

259000UK00001B/60/P